Curcumin-Based Nanomedicines as Cancer Therapeutics

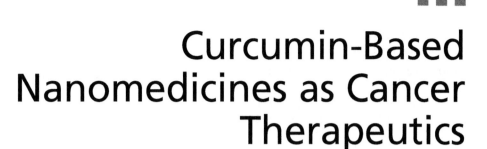

Curcumin-Based Nanomedicines as Cancer Therapeutics

Edited by

Prashant Kesharwani

Department of Pharmaceutics, School of Pharmaceutical Education and
Research, Jamia Hamdard, New Delhi, India

Amirhossein Sahebkar

Biotechnology Research Center, Pharmaceutical Technology Institute, Mashhad
University of Medical Sciences, Mashhad, Iran

ELSEVIER

ACADEMIC PRESS
An imprint of Elsevier

Academic Press is an imprint of Elsevier
125 London Wall, London EC2Y 5AS, United Kingdom
525 B Street, Suite 1650, San Diego, CA 92101, United States
50 Hampshire Street, 5th Floor, Cambridge, MA 02139, United States

Notices

Knowledge and best practice in this field are constantly changing. As new research and experience broaden our understanding, changes in research methods, professional practices, or medical treatment may become necessary.

Practitioners and researchers must always rely on their own experience and knowledge in evaluating and using any information, methods, compounds, or experiments described herein. In using such information or methods they should be mindful of their own safety and the safety of others, including parties for whom they have a professional responsibility.

To the fullest extent of the law, neither the Publisher nor the authors, contributors, or editors, assume any liability for any injury and/or damage to persons or property as a matter of products liability, negligence or otherwise, or from any use or operation of any methods, products, instructions, or ideas contained in the material herein.

ISBN: 978-0-443-15412-6

For Information on all Academic Press publications
visit our website at https://www.elsevier.com/books-and-journals

Publisher: Stacy Masucci
Acquisitions Editor: Linda Buschman
Editorial Project Manager: Deepak Vohra
Production Project Manager: Sajana Devasi P. K.
Cover Designer: Christian Bilbow

Typeset by MPS Limited, Chennai, India

Working together
to grow libraries in
developing countries

www.elsevier.com • www.bookaid.org

Contents

Part C   Recent advances and regulatory aspects of gold nanoparticles

9. Micelle-based curcumin delivery systems as cancer therapeutics

NILOUFAR RAHIMAN, SEYEDEH HODA ALAVIZADEH,
LUIS E. SIMENTAL-MENDÍA AND AMIRHOSSEIN SAHEBKAR

10. Liposome-based curcumin delivery systems as cancer therapeutics

NEDA MOSTAJERAN, SEYEDEH HODA ALAVIZADEH,
FATEMEH GHEYBI AND AMIRHOSSEIN SAHEBKAR

Part D   Recent advances in nanocurcumin delivery in cancer therapy

List of contributors

Priyanka Adhikari   Centre for GMP Extraction Facility, National Institute of Pharmaceutical Education and Research, Guwahati, Assam, India

Amir R. Afshari   Department of Physiology and Pharmacology, Faculty of Medicine, North Khorasan University of Medical Sciences, Bojnurd, Iran

Seyedeh Hoda Alavizadeh   Nanotechnology Research Center, Pharmaceutical Technology Institute, Mashhad University of Medical Sciences, Mashhad, Iran; Department of Pharmaceutical Nanotechnology, School of Pharmacy, Mashhad University of Medical Sciences, Mashhad, Iran

Éverton do Nascimento Alencar   Dispersed Systems Laboratory (LaSiD), Federal University of Rio Grande do Norte (UFRN), Rua Gen. Gustavo Cordeiro de Faria, SN, Natal, RN, Brazil; College of Pharmaceutical Sciences, Food and Nutrition (FACFAN), Federal University of Mato Grosso do Sul (UFMS), Av. Costa e Silva, SN, Campo Grande, MS, Brazil

Atefeh Amiri   Department of Medical Biotechnology and Nanotechnology, School of Medicine, Mashhad University of Medical Sciences, Mashhad, Iran

Talita Azevedo Amorim   Dispersed Systems Laboratory (LaSiD), Federal University of Rio Grande do Norte (UFRN), Rua Gen. Gustavo Cordeiro de Faria, SN, Natal, RN, Brazil

Gholamreza Askari   Nutrition and Food Security Research Center and Department of Community Nutrition, School of Nutrition and Food Science, Isfahan University of Medical Sciences, Isfahan, Iran; Anesthesia and Critical Care Research Center, Isfahan University of Medical Sciences, Isfahan, Iran

Anis Askarizadeh   Marine Pharmaceutical Science Research Center, Ahvaz Jundishapur University of Medical Sciences, Ahvaz, Iran

Mohammad Bagherniya   Nutrition and Food Security Research Center and Department of Community Nutrition, School of Nutrition and Food Science, Isfahan University of Medical Sciences, Isfahan, Iran; Anesthesia and Critical Care Research Center, Isfahan University of Medical Sciences, Isfahan, Iran

Leandro R.S. Barbosa   Department of General Physics, Institute of Physics, University of São Paulo, São Paulo, Brazil; Brazilian Synchrotron Light Laboratory (LNLS), Brazilian Center for Research in Energy and Materials (CNPEM), Campinas, São Paulo, Brazil

Swati Biswas   Nanomedicine Research Laboratory, Department of Pharmacy, Birla Institute of Technology & Science-Pilani, Hyderabad Campus, Hyderabad, Telangana, India

Karine C. Castro   Department of Bioprocess and Biotechnology, School of Agriculture, Sao Paulo State University (UNESP), Botucatu, São Paulo, Brazil

Sanjay Ch   Nanomedicine Research Laboratory, Department of Pharmacy, Birla Institute of Technology & Science-Pilani, Hyderabad Campus, Hyderabad, Telangana, India

Shibam Chakraborty   Department of Zoology, Ramakrishna Mission Vidyamandira, Belur Math, Howrah, West Bengal, India

Debanik Deb   Department of Zoology, Ramakrishna Mission Vidyamandira, Belur Math, Howrah, West Bengal, India

Amany M. Diab   Faculty of Aquatic and Fisheries Sciences, Kafrelsheikh University, Kafr El Sheikh, Egypt

Douglas Dourado   Dispersed Systems Laboratory (LaSiD), Federal University of Rio Grande do Norte (UFRN), Rua Gen. Gustavo Cordeiro de Faria, SN, Natal, RN, Brazil; Department of Immunology, Aggeu Magalhães Institute (IAM), Oswaldo Cruz Foundation (FIOCRUZ), Av Professor Moraes Rego, SN, Recife, PE, Brazil

Eryvaldo Sócrates Tabosa do Egito   Dispersed Systems Laboratory (LaSiD), Federal University of Rio Grande do Norte (UFRN), Rua Gen. Gustavo Cordeiro de Faria, SN, Natal, RN, Brazil

Basant E. Elsaied   Faculty of Aquatic and Fisheries Sciences, Kafrelsheikh University, Kafr El Sheikh, Egypt

Leila Farhoudi   Nanotechnology Research Center, Pharmaceutical Technology Institute, Mashhad University of Medical Sciences, Mashhad, Iran

Danielle Teixeira Freire   Dispersed Systems Laboratory (LaSiD), Federal University of Rio Grande do Norte (UFRN), Rua Gen. Gustavo Cordeiro de Faria, SN, Natal, RN, Brazil

Hend A. Gad   Faculty of Aquatic and Fisheries Sciences, Kafrelsheikh University, Kafr El Sheikh, Egypt

Fatemeh Gheybi   Nanotechnology Research Center, Pharmaceutical Technology Institute, Mashhad University of Medical Sciences, Mashhad, Iran; Department of Medical Biotechnology and Nanotechnology, Faculty of Medicine, Mashhad University of Medical Sciences, Mashhad, Iran

Balaram Ghosh   Nanomedicine Research Laboratory, Department of Pharmacy, Birla Institute of Technology & Science-Pilani, Hyderabad Campus, Hyderabad, Telangana, India

Sumit Ghosh   Division of Molecular Medicine, Bose Institute, Kolkata, India

Tamar L. Greaves   STEM College, RMIT University, Melbourne, VIC, Australia

Shirin Hassanizadeh   Nutrition and Food Security Research Center and Department of Community Nutrition, School of Nutrition and Food Science, Isfahan University of Medical Sciences, Isfahan, Iran

Seyedeh Maryam Hosseinikhah   Nanotechnology Research Center, Pharmaceutical Technology Institute, Mashhad University of Medical Sciences, Mashhad, Iran

Tannaz Jamialahmadi   International UNESCO Center for Health-Related Basic Sciences and Human Nutrition, Mashhad University of Medical Sciences, Mashhad, Iran

Prashant Kesharwani   Department of Pharmaceutics, School of Pharmaceutical Education and Research, Jamia Hamdard, New Delhi, India

André M. Lopes   Department of Biotechnology, Lorena School of Engineering, University of São Paulo (EEL/USP), Lorena, São Paulo, Brazil

Elaheh Mirhadi   Biotechnology Research Center, Pharmaceutical Technology Institute, Mashhad University of Medical Sciences, Mashhad, Iran; Department of Biotechnology, School of Pharmacy, Mashhad University of Medical Sciences, Mashhad, Iran

Seyedeh Alia Moosavian   Nanotechnology Research Center, Pharmaceutical Technology Institute, Mashhad University of Medical Sciences, Mashhad, Iran

Neda Mostajeran   Nanotechnology Research Center, Pharmaceutical Technology Institute, Mashhad University of Medical Sciences, Mashhad, Iran; Department of Pharmaceutical Nanotechnology, School of Pharmacy, Mashhad University of Medical Sciences, Mashhad, Iran

V.G.M. Naidu   Centre for GMP Extraction Facility, National Institute of Pharmaceutical Education and Research, Guwahati, Assam, India

Matheus Cardoso de Oliveira   Dispersed Systems Laboratory (LaSiD), Federal University of Rio Grande do Norte (UFRN), Rua Gen. Gustavo Cordeiro de Faria, SN, Natal, RN, Brazil

Sri Ganga Padaga   Nanomedicine Research Laboratory, Department of Pharmacy, Birla Institute of Technology & Science-Pilani, Hyderabad Campus, Hyderabad, Telangana, India

A. Parthiban   Centre for GMP Extraction Facility, National Institute of Pharmaceutical Education and Research, Guwahati, Assam, India

Milan Paul   Nanomedicine Research Laboratory, Department of Pharmacy, Birla Institute of Technology & Science-Pilani, Hyderabad Campus, Hyderabad, Telangana, India

Daniel Torres Pereira   Dispersed Systems Laboratory (LaSiD), Federal University of Rio Grande do Norte (UFRN), Rua Gen. Gustavo Cordeiro de Faria, SN, Natal, RN, Brazil

Jyoti Punia   Centre for GMP Extraction Facility, National Institute of Pharmaceutical Education and Research, Guwahati, Assam, India

Niloufar Rahiman   Nanotechnology Research Center, Pharmaceutical Technology Institute, Mashhad University of Medical Sciences, Mashhad, Iran; Department of Pharmaceutical Nanotechnology, School of Pharmacy, Mashhad University of Medical Sciences, Mashhad, Iran

Alok Ranjan   Centre for GMP Extraction Facility, National Institute of Pharmaceutical Education and Research, Guwahati, Assam, India

Amirhossein Sahebkar   Biotechnology Research Center, Pharmaceutical Technology Institute, Mashhad University of Medical Sciences, Mashhad, Iran; Applied Biomedical Research Center, Mashhad University of Medical Sciences, Mashhad, Iran

Sepideh Salehabadi   Applied Biomedical Research Center, Mashhad University of Medical Sciences, Mashhad, Iran

Mehdi Sanati   Department of Pharmacology and Toxicology, Faculty of Pharmacy, Birjand University of Medical Sciences, Birjand, Iran; Experimental and Animal Study Center, Birjand University of Medical Sciences, Birjand, Iran

Parames C. Sil   Division of Molecular Medicine, Bose Institute, Kolkata, India

Luis E. Simental-Mendía   Biomedical Research Unit, Mexican Social Security Institute, Durango, Mexico

Meenakshi Singh   Centre for GMP Extraction Facility, National Institute of Pharmaceutical Education and Research, Guwahati, Assam, India

Aida Tasbandi   Applied Biomedical Research Center, Mashhad University of Medical Sciences, Mashhad, Iran

Ahmed A. Tayel   Faculty of Aquatic and Fisheries Sciences, Kafrelsheikh University, Kafr El Sheikh, Egypt

Fatemeh Vahdat-Lasemi   Department of Medical Biotechnology and Nanotechnology, School of Medicine, Mashhad University of Medical Sciences, Mashhad, Iran

Curcumin: Introduction, structure, and physicochemical attributes

PART

A

Curcumin: Introduction, structure, and physicochemical attributes

1

Curcumin: historical background, introduction, structure, and physicochemical attributes

Elaheh Mirhadi[1,2], Aida Tasbandi[3], Prashant Kesharwani[4], Amirhossein Sahebkar[1,3]

[1]BIOTECHNOLOGY RESEARCH CENTER, PHARMACEUTICAL TECHNOLOGY INSTITUTE, MASHHAD UNIVERSITY OF MEDICAL SCIENCES, MASHHAD, IRAN [2]DEPARTMENT OF BIOTECHNOLOGY, SCHOOL OF PHARMACY, MASHHAD UNIVERSITY OF MEDICAL SCIENCES, MASHHAD, IRAN [3]APPLIED BIOMEDICAL RESEARCH CENTER, MASHHAD UNIVERSITY OF MEDICAL SCIENCES, MASHHAD, IRAN [4]DEPARTMENT OF PHARMACEUTICS, SCHOOL OF PHARMACEUTICAL EDUCATION AND RESEARCH, JAMIA HAMDARD, NEW DELHI, INDIA

1.1 Historical background

Turmeric, the common name of *Curcuma longa,* is a spice mostly cultivated in India and other parts of Southeast Asia [1]. It has a long history of use for more than 5000 years in Traditional Chinese Medicine and Indian Ayurveda Medicine [2]. Then it was spread out from India to distant Asian countries under the Hindu religion influences [3]. In 1280 Marco Polo introduced turmeric as a vegetable that has all the saffron properties. In 1966 Burkill mentioned that it was spread to West Africa in the 13th century and to East Africa in the 17th century. Afterward, it was grown in Jamaica in 1783 [4]. Nowadays, turmeric is found all over the world in many countries including Malaysia, Myanmar, Pakistan, Philippines, Vietnam, Thailand, Korea, China, Japan, Nepal, East and West Africa, Sri Lanka, Caribbean islands, Malagasi, South Pacific Islands, and Central America. However, India is still the major producer and exporter of turmeric [5]. In Nigeria, turmeric is cultivated in about 19 states with different local names. It is called *gangamau* in Hausa, *atale pupa* in Yoruba, *ohu boboch* in Enugu (Nkanu East), *magina* in Kaduna, *onjonigho* in Cross River (Meo tribe), *turi* in Niger State, *gigir* in Tiv, and *nwandumo* in Ebonyi [6,7].

1.2 Characteristics

Turmeric is derived from the rhizome of *Curcuma longa* Linn., which belongs to the Zingiberaceae family. The genus Curcuma contains 49 genera and 1400 species and

Curcumin-Based Nanomedicines as Cancer Therapeutics. DOI: https://doi.org/10.1016/B978-0-443-15412-6.00005-2

originated in the Indo-Malayan region [8]. There are roughly 80 in the genus all over the world, 40 of which including *C. longa* belong to India. Some other sources of turmeric are *C. phaeocaulis*, *C. mangga*, *C. xanthorrhiza*, *C. aromatic*, and *C. zedoaria* [3,4]. Turmeric is grown as an annual crop with an erect aerial stem that may be two to five per plant. The height of the aerial stem bearing leaves and inflorescence differ from 90 to 100 cm. There are 7−12 leaf sheaths per plant usually green in color, which form the aerial stem. The inflorescence arising through the aerial stem is cylindrical and fleshy including a central spike of 10−15 cm length [9,10]. The best climate to culture turmeric plants is a temperature between 20°C and 30°C accompanied by a considerable amount of annual rainfall. Turmeric needs a rich and friable soil. However, it could be grown in various types of soils including sandy loam, light black, red soils, and clay loams. Turmeric is usually harvested from January to March−April. About 7-8 and 8-9 months are needed for early and medium varieties to occur in the plant to be mature. When the leaves are turning yellow and start to dry up is the best time for the crop to be harvested. At this time, leaves are cut close to the ground, the clumps are carefully lifted with a spade, and the rhizomes are gathered by handpicking. For turmeric, the number of irrigations varies from 15 to 25 times for medium-heavy soils and 35−40 times for light-texture red soils. The seed rhizomes are commonly heaped under the shade of trees or be stored in pits with sawdust [11−13].

1.3 Components

Turmeric possesses more than 100 constituents. The main component of its root is a volatile oil composed of turmerone and some other colorants namely, curcuminoids. Volatile oils include borneol, d-sabinene, zingiberene, cinol, d-α-phellandrene, and sesquiterpenes [14]. Turmerone, zingiberene, and arturmerone are the active ingredients of turmeric responsible for its flavor and aroma. About 16% of turmeric's dry weight are curcuminoids, which are formed from diarylheptanoids as the main phytoconstituents of turmeric [15]. Most of the turmeric powder contains three main compounds: diferuloylmethane (curcumin I at 94%), demethoxycurcumin (curcumin II at 6%), and bisdemethoxycurcumin (curcumin III at 3%) plus sugars, volatile oils, resins, and proteins [16]. Purest form of turmeric includes 5%−6.6% curcumin, 3.5% volatile oils, 3% mold, and 0.5% extraneous matter. Curcumene, arturmerone, germacrone, ar-curcumene, and turmerone are the examples of these compounds [17]. Moreover, some other compounds such as β-sitosterol, 2-hydroxymethyl anthraquinone, cholesterol, stigmasterol, and polysaccharides were discovered in the turmeric's rhizomes [18,19].

1.4 Benefits, pharmacological effect, and potential therapeutic effect of turmeric and its major compound curcumin

Turmeric had been numerous usages from ancient times. It has been used as an additive for its both flavor and color properties to vegetarian and nonvegetarian foods, particularly in

South Asian cuisine [20]. Turmeric powder is known as the main constituent of curry powder utilized in confectionery industries and as a functional food in the international market due to its health-promoting properties [21]. Turmeric tea has been famous in various areas of Japan, particularly in Okinawa. In some other parts of the world, turmeric is used in mustard blends, sauces, and pickles. Turmeric has also been traditionally used in many religious observances as a dye, cosmetic, and other purposes [8]. Curcumin as the main component of turmeric has been shown to exert various beneficial activities including anticardiovascular, antiinflammatory, antioxidant, antifungal, antibacterial, immunomodulating, wound healing, antiviral, immunomodulatory, radioprotective, skin protective, antiischemic, anticarcinogenic, and neuroprotective effects [22–32].

1.4.1 Antiinflammation activity

Inflammation is the immune system's response that is vital to health. Different cellular and molecular events and interactions are involved during acute inflammatory responses, leading to restoration of tissue homeostasis. Uncontrolled acute inflammation leads to various chronic inflammatory diseases [33]. Curcumin is known as a potent antiinflammatory agent and can be used to treat various inflammatory illnesses [34–37]. Antiinflammatory response of curcumin is through the production of cytokines and induction of inducible nitric oxide synthase (iNOS), cyclooxygenase-2 (COX-2), and lipooxygenase (LOX) formation [38,39]. Antiinflammatory activities of curcumin are hindered by its extreme hydrophobicity and low bioavailability. Recently, curcumin-incorporated nanoparticles have gained considerable attention by researchers to overcome such limitations. For example, alginate-curcumin conjugate micelles were applied for the treatment of ulcerative colitis, which is an idiopathic inflammatory bowel disease. These particles indicated antiinflammatory effects in Raw 264.7 cell line. Roughly 92.32% of nanoparticles reached colon after oral administration, then curcumin was released, quickly absorbed, and effectively ameliorated the colonic inflammation [40]. Fe-curcumin-based nanoparticles downregulated different substantial inflammatory cytokines such as TNF-α, IL-1β, and IL-6 in the treatment of pneumonia [41]. Another example is curcumin-loaded mesoporous calcium silicate cements that can reduce the inflammatory reaction and have the potential to be used after implantation for bone regenerative medicine and bone tissue engineering [42]. In below, some of the therapeutic and pharmacological effects of curcumin are described.

1.4.2 Antioxidant activity

In the process of cell growth in human body, oxygen consumption inherently contributes to the production of reactive oxygen species (ROS). During normal physiologic events, ROS are continuously produced and quickly start the peroxidation of membrane lipids contributing to the accumulation of lipid peroxides. ROS can also damage crucial biomolecules such as lipids, carbohydrates, proteins, and nucleic acids, and may cause DNA damage leading to mutations [43,44]. All the aerobic organisms employ antioxidant defenses, including antioxidant food constituents and antioxidant enzymes, to omit or restore the damaged molecules. Antioxidants can protect the human body by scavenging free radicals and increasing shelf life by deferring the process of lipid peroxidation [45]. Curcumin has been found to be an effective antioxidant in various in vitro assays such as reducing power, DPPH•, ABTS•$^+$, O2•$^-$, and DMPD•$^+$ radical scavenging, metal chelating activities, and hydrogen peroxide scavenging compared to other antioxidant compounds such as α-tocopherol, a natural antioxidant, butylated hydroxyanisole (BHA), butylated hydroxytoluene (BHT), and trolox. Antioxidant and radicals scavenging activity of curcumin was proved by H-atom abstraction from the free hydroxyl group. Ak, T. and İ. Gülçin concluded that the superb antioxidant properties of curcumin were due to the H-atom donation of the phenolic group [46].

1.4.3 Protective effects on cardiovascular disease

Cardiovascular diseases (CVDs) are one of the major causes of global morbidity and mortality. Aging and obesity are two main risk factors for CVDs. Aging is a nonmodifiable risk factor while obesity is a modifiable one that can lead to type 2 diabetes mellitus (T2DM). it has been reported that these two risk factors are accompanied by mitochondrial dysfunction, unbalanced reduction−oxidation situation (oxidative stress), inflammation, glucose metabolism, and altered lipid profiles. For many years, curcumin has been considered as a beneficial therapeutic agent for CVDs. A vast variety of animal and human studies have demonstrated that curcumin effectively reduces different factors that increase the risk of CVDs in both obesity and aging [47]. Reduction of vascular dysfunction, which is due to the retardation of cellular senescence and decreased oxidative stress, is observed using curcumin. It has been demonstrated that premature senescence that is induced by H_2O_2 and ROS production are ameliorated by pretreatment with curcumin in endothelial cells during 24 h, and Endothelial nitric oxide synthase activation (eNOS) and nitric oxide (NO) production are increased [48]. In addition to animal models, in human subjects, curcumin ingestion positively is associated with reduced endothelial dysfunction and improved central arterial hemodynamics in postmenopausal women [49,50]. In healthy adults, improved vascular endothelial function was observed by curcumin supplementation [51]. Curcumin acts as a protective agent, based on the upregulation of Sirtuin 1 (SIRT1) expression. Furthermore, Nrf2, as a major protective factor against both senescence and oxidative stress, is activated by curcumin through several signaling pathways [52]. In case of obesity as a risk factor for CVDs, curcumin could have a positive impact on the insulin sensitivity and glycemic status, enhances whitening of adipocytes, and decreases obesity-related adipose tissue inflammation. Therefore, the therapeutic efficacy of curcumin could be considered for the treatment of obesity [53]. Moreover, curcumin has been shown to have atheroprotective properties and decreases lipid peroxidation and elevated plasma cholesterol both of which are involved in the initiation of atherosclerosis [54,55]. As for atherosclerosis, the protective effects of curcumin in myocardial infarction (MI) and on alterations occurring upon I/R injury have been investigated in animal models. Morphological alterations of the heart were also diminished by curcumin in the isoproterenol-treated rats and infarct size of hearts from was reduced in curcumin-treated rats and mice as well [56]. Overall, curcumin as a natural constituent could be beneficially effective to prohibit CVDs; however, more standardized investigations are needed to put its full potential into clinics [47].

1.4.4 Antidiabetic properties

Curcumin and curcuminoids have been reported to have antidiabetic properties. T2DM is a common chronic metabolic disease known by persistent hyperglycemia with a 90%−95% prevalence of all diabetes cases. It is associated with the insulin signaling pathway dysfunction resulting in the insulin resistance. In addition, insulin signaling, and action suppresses glycogenolysis, and gluconeogenesis lead to reduced endogenous glucose production [57,58]. Many studies have revealed the antidiabetic properties of curcumin. Curcumin increased human peroxisome proliferator-activated receptor (PPAR)-gamma ligand-binding activity in the treatment of human adipocytes for 14 days [59,60]. Proinflammatory mediators, tumor necrosis factor-alpha (TNF-α), monocyte chemoattractant protein-1 (MCP-1), and NO levels were inhibited by curcumin [61]. Curcumin treatment has reduced the increased level of TNFα-induced IL-6 and prostaglandin E2 (PGE2) showing the ability of curcumin in adipocyte inflammatory reduction [62]. Curcumin treatment suppresses proliferative mRNAs including MMP1, MMP2, MMP3, SDF1, and VEGF as well as adipogenesis transcription factors and cytokines such as C/EBPα, C/EBPβ, PPARγ, leptin, adiponectin, and resistin [63]. Overall, curcumin decreases inflammation, adipocyte differentiation, and lipid accumulation. In case of hepatocytes, curcumin reduces cell proliferation and the expression of lipid deposition/lipogenic genes including Lpk, Scd1, Acc1, Fas, and Me1. Reduction of gluconeogenesis as well as increased glucokinase activity and glucose-6-phosphate levels by curcumin have been documented. Furthermore, IL-6, IL-1β, and TNF-α as inflammation cytokines and expression of fibrosis genes including α-SMA, collagen, and fibronectin were reduced by curcumin. Antioxidant activities of superoxide dismutase (SOD), catalase, glutathione, and GSH were increased as well [64−66]. Into the impact of curcumin on the skeletal muscle cells, improved glucose uptake and translocation of GLUT4 have been proved. Moreover, antiinflammatory effects of curcumin are through the reduction of proinflammatory mRNA and cytokine levels including TNF-α, IL-6, MCP-1, and IL-10. Anticatabolic effects of curcumin maintain skeletal muscle cells from protein degradation resulting in protein synthesis enhancement [67,68].

1.4.5 Effect on the gastrointestinal tract

Recently, curcumin's therapeutic potential to treat various gastrointestinal (GI) diseases has been demonstrated as to its incremented bioavailability in the GI tract. In addition, curcumin's therapeutic effect for preventing and treating various cancers including esophagus, stomach, intestine, pancreas, and liver has been recognized [69]. Curcumin could inhibit NF-κB activity and induce apoptosis in Flo-1 and OE33 adenocarcinoma cell lines. It also enhanced cisplatin (CDDP) and 5-fluorouracil (5-FU)-mediated chemosensitivity [70]. In another study, curcumin induced cell death in OE33 and OE19 cell lines as well as OE21 and KYSE450 squamous cell carcinoma cell lines by inhibiting the ubiquitin-proteasome system [71]. Due to the antimicrobial activity against *Helicobacter pylori*, curcumin is considered as a chemopreventive agent against *H. pylori*-induced gastric carcinogenesis [72]. It is also able to block the Rho effector rhotekin (RTKN)-mediated antiapoptotic effect in gastric cancer cells (AGS) cells [73]. It has been suggested that curcumin has chemotherapeutic effects because it can reverse the multidrug resistance in the SGC7901/VCR cell line, which is a human gastric carcinoma cell line [74]. The application of curcumin and chemotherapy at the same time may also improve the effectiveness of chemotherapeutics, providing a superb strategy in the treatment of GI cancers. For example, liposomal curcumin in combination with oxaliplatin could significantly inhibit the growth of Colo205 and LoVo xenografts and showed angiogenic effects [75]. It is also reported that curcumin significantly reduces inflammation in induced pancreatitis rats. Curcumin inhibited the proinflammatory mediator's production in various induced pancreatitis, such as cerulean or ethanol, pancreatic trypsin, neutrophil infiltration, and serum amylase [4].

1.4.6 Effect on the skin

Several documents have revealed that curcumin functions as an effective therapeutic herbal medicine in the treatment of various skin conditions including neoplastic, inflammatory, and infectious skin diseases. Curcumin has been considered as an affordable, well-tolerated, and effective agent for skin diseases treatment [76,77]. For years, curcumin has been utilized to ameliorate chronic inflammatory skin diseases like *atopic dermatitis* symptoms [78]. In psoriasis, as a chronic inflammatory, multifactorial, and multisystemic disease, curcumin suppresses the increased production of TNF-α by activated macrophages. Curcumin inhibits TNF-α promoter and impairs lipopolysaccharide (LPS) signaling, which is responsible for the induction of TNF-α production [79]. Oral administration of curcumin resulted in a significant decrease in levels of IFN-gamma, TNF-alpha, IL-2, IL-12, IL-22, and IL-23 in psoriatic mice leading to the reduction of hyperproliferation of keratinocytes [80]. Several studies have suggested that curcumin has beneficial effects in the treatment of *iatrogenic dermatitis*. Curcumin has been shown to have the potential to be used in topical applications such as epithelial cell recovery and survival in irradiated skin and it is able to decrease the expression of COX-2 and Nf-kB [81]. Curcumin plays a major role in wound healing as well. Wound healing is a dynamic biological replacement process having significant economic impact on healthcare systems, which contains three phases: (1) inflammation and hemostasis, (2) proliferation in which granulation tissue is formed, and (3) remodeling, with the formation of new epithelium and scarring [82]. As previously mentioned, curcumin reduces inflammation through the suppression of TNF-α expression and inhibition of NF-κB and LPS signaling impairment as well. Curcumin exerts it's anti-inflammatory effects through signaling pathways such as myeloid differentiation protein toll-lie receptor 4 (TLR 4) co-receptor (TLR4-MD2) and peroxisome proliferator-activated receptor-gamma (PPAR-γ) [83,84]. Studies have demonstrated the role of curcumin in the treatment of nonmelanoma skin cancer (NMSC). According to the reports, the skin of the head and neck have included the most prevalent skin cancer cases roughly 70%−80%. A main risk factor leading to NMSC is chronic sun exposure. The proinflammatory microenvironment is main outstanding features in preventing and treating cancer. Cyclooxygenases-1 (COX-1) and COX-2 enzymes play a significant role in tumor proliferation. Arachidonic acid metabolism is induced by the upregulation of COX-2 leading to prostaglandin (PG) overproduction, which consequently affects cell growth. In addition, both COX-1 and COX-2 induce the production of vascular epidermal growth factor (VEGF), which is a key factor in angiogenesis and tumor proliferation [85]. AMP-activated protein kinases (AMPK) are the factors upregulated by curcumin resulting in the inhibition of COX-2 production. It also prevents the biosynthesis of PGE2 [86]. The efficacy of curcumin in the modulating skin infection diseases has been investigated as well. Cutaneous infections are caused by microorganisms including viruses, fungi, bacteria, and parasites. These microorganisms living on the skin have been found to maintain skin homeostasis and cause cutaneous infections [87]. In this scenario, curcumin has been extensively used in clinical trials due to its beneficial antimicrobial activity and safety profile even at high doses [88]. Curcumin has been shown antimicrobial effects against *Staphylococcus aureus*, *Propionibacterium acnes*, and *Staphylococcus epidermidis* [89−91]. Curcumin encapsulated in nanoparticles has been exhibited complete prohibition of *Trychophyton rubrum* growth in vitro, which is the most frequent species of fungal pathogens causing skin infections [92].

1.4.7 Neuroprotective effect

Millions of people worldwide are suffering from neurodegenerative disorders such as Alzheimer's disease (AD), major depression, traumatic brain injury, Parkinson's disease (PD), and epilepsy with an increasing incidence rate [93,94]. Based on several studies, curcumin possesses therapeutic effects in neurological disorders such as Huntington's disease (HD), AD, PD, dementia, and multiple sclerosis due to its antiinflammatory, antioxidant, and antiprotein aggregating abilities [95−97]. It has been found that curcumin inhibits the production of PGs and inflammatory cytokines in activated microglia and astrocytes. In microglial and astrocytes cells, reduction of MCP-1, macrophage inflammatory protein (MIP-1β), IL-1β, IL-8, and TNFα has been observed [98,99]. In AD, astrocytosis, microgliosis, and the presence of proinflammatory factors in the brain lead to the deposition of amyloid-ß (Aß) peptides plaques. Curcumin binds to the Aß peptides and influences their aggregation. It inhibits the production of Aß peptide through changing the amyloid precursor protein trafficking. In addition, curcumin decreases Aß-induced toxicity by preventing JNK-3 phosphorylation. Curcumin attenuates the hyperphosphorylation of tau and enhances its clearance and reduces cholesterol levels as well [100,101]. Curcumin has also exhibited neuroprotective effects in multiple sclerosis, which is an autoimmune chronic disease affecting central nervous system through different mechanisms including antiinflammatory, antiproliferative, and antioxidant activities. It is able to adjust several molecular targets including transcriptional factors (AP-1, Nrf2, NF-κB, and STAT-1, -3, -4), inflammatory cytokines (TNFα, interleukin, and chemokine ligand), enzymes (OH-1, LOX, XO, COX-2, and iNOS), growth factors and receptors such as TLRs, TGF-α, TGF-β, and proteins (PG, CRP, caspase-3, -9, myosin light chain, Bcl-2,), and protein kinase (MAPK, JNK, JAK, and AK) [102].

1.4.8 Hepatoprotective effect

A number of studies have considered the hepatoprotective effects of curcumin [103–105]. Curcumin has been found as a promising agent for preventing liver disorders related to oxidative stress through the reduction of AST, ALT, and alkaline phosphatase levels; glutathione peroxidase (GPx), glutathione-S-transferase (GST), glutathione reductase (GR), SOD, and catalase (CAT) augmentation; NO suppression; and inhibition of ROS production [106–108]. Furthermore, curcumin treatment in chronic iron-overloaded male rats led to increased endogenous antioxidant levels such as glutathione (GSH), SOD, ascorbic acid, and CAT [109]. Curcumin administration led to increased expression of antioxidant enzymes, mitochondrial dysfunction attenuation, and inhibition of NF-kB and transient receptor potential melastatin 2 (TRPM2) channels [110,111]. Curcumin administration in alcoholic fatty liver mice led to the attenuation of hepatocyte necroptosis, suppression of ethanol-induced pathway, antioxidant signaling pathway, inhibition of glyoxylate, pyruvate metabolisms and dicarboxylate, as well as genes expression detoxifying through the ERK/p38-MAPK pathway [112–114].

1.4.9 Anticancer effect

Numerous studies have revealed that curcumin indicates anticancer effects in various types of cancers through suppressing cell proliferation and metastasis as well as inducing cell death [115–118]. Curcumin also shows protective effects against cancer formation. Some targets attributed to the effects of curcumin are NF-κB, activating protein-1 (AP-1), β-catenin, early growth response (EGR), epidermal growth factor receptors (EGFR), cyclin B1, and cyclin-dependent kinase 2 (CDk2) [119]. The antiproliferative effect of curcumin is related to its ability to regulate the cell cycle, protein kinases, and transcription factors, including NF-κB. Proinflammatory cytokines including TNF-α, IL-1, IL-2, IL-6, and MCP-1 involved in various cancers are regulated by NF-κB [120,121]. Curcumin inhibited the proliferation of melanoma cells through the NF-κB blockage [122]. AP-1 is a dimeric transcription factor responsible for managing cellular processes including cell proliferation, differentiation, progression, and metastasis related to various cancers. Curcumin dose-dependently could inhibit AP-1 with the IC50 values of 100 μM [123]. Mitogens, injury, differentiation, and stress activate EGR-1 that regulates the expression of p21, p53, phosphatase and tensin homolog (PTEN), and Gadd45 associated to the control of growth and apoptosis [124]. In human metastatic nonsmall-cell lung carcinoma (NSCLC) and colon cancer cells, curcumin suppressed proliferation and cell growth respectively through the inhibition of EGR-1 [125,126]. Curcumin inhibited cell growth through the suppression of Wnt/β-catenin pathway as well. The β-catenin is present in cell membrane, cytoplasm, and nucleus, and most of all in the cell membrane. Phosphorylation of GSK-3β regulates intracellular levels of beta-catenin. This phosphorylation was suppressed by curcumin in LNCaP prostate cancer cells induced the degradation of beta-catenin, which consequently affect the cell proliferation [127]. Nanotechnology has played an important role in improving the therapeutic index and pharmacokinetic parameters of curcumin [128]. Bi et al. exhibited that pharmacokinetic profiles of curcumin nanosuspension differ when it is administered in various sizes of 20, 70, or 200 nm. Maximum concentration of curcumin nanosuspensions in plasma observed with the size of 20 nm 5 min after administration [129]. Conventional nanosystems are especially appropriate for class IV drugs including curcumin and improve their solubilization, and permeation leading to enhanced pharmacokinetics. The role of curcumin in the treatment of various cancers has been detected including breast, skin, pancreas, cervix, colon, prostate, head, and neck cancers [130]. Curcumin nanocrystals, nanocrystals, and nanosuspensions are conventional nanosystems that are used to enhance pharmacokinetic parameters of curcumin leading to improved efficacy [131–133]. Various nanoparticles have been utilized to enhance curcumin therapeutic efficacy as well. Curcumin-loaded solid lipid nanoparticles (SLNP) have shown more cytotoxicity, cellular uptake, and induced apoptosis than free curcumin against MDA-MB-231 cells [134]. Curcumin-based SLN increased pharmacokinetic parameters and anticancer activity in combination with resveratrol and gelucire against human colon cancer HCT-116 cells [135]. CUR-loaded nanostructured lipid carriers (NLC) with a greater stability and higher loading capacity over to SLNs increased curcumin permeation coefficient and improved cellular uptake and cytotoxicity against HCT-116 cell line [136]. PEGylated liposomes containing curcumin-doxorubicin inhibited C26 cell proliferation as well as production of angiogenic/inflammatory proteins through a NF-κB-dependent manner [137]. Polymeric nanoparticles including ethyl acrylate copolymer, methyl methacrylate, amphiphilic poly-β-amino ester copolymer, and poly lactic-co-glycolic acid (PLGA) containing curcumin alone or in combination with doxorubicin revealed higher release of drug in acidic conditions than pH 7.4 and more inhibition of cell proliferation, migration, and invasion [138]. Curcumin- and docetaxel-loaded lipid–polymer hybrid nanoparticles were applied in PC3-bearing mice xenografts, which is a model of human prostate cancer. The results showed inhibition of tumor growth and any obvious side effects were not reported [139]. Nanoemulsions with the average size of <200 nm composed of an oil phase in an aqueous phase have been utilized for encapsulating bioactive agents such as curcumin [140,141]. Encapsulation of curcumin in nanoemulsions increased its solubility by 1400-fold [142]. Curcumin-loaded nanoemulsions have been found to have antiangiogenic effect by the inhibition of new vessel formation and reduction of microvessel density in mice [143].

1.4.10 Antimicrobial properties

Curcumin's antibacterial activity was first shown in 1949, which exhibited the antibacterial effect of curcumin against 56 bacterial and fungal taxa [144]. Modern studies have also demonstrated that curcumin has strong antimicrobial activity despite its scant solubility, bioavailability, and pharmacokinetic behavior [145]. Experimental data have demonstrated that the hydroxyl and methoxy groups of curcumin are associated to the antimicrobial activity [146]. It has been reported that curcumin has antibiofilm activity through the removal of already-formed biofilms and inhibition of bacterial quorum-sensing systems [147,148]. Curcumin has a photodynamic action against both biofilm and planktonic forms of bacteria through the production of cytotoxic ROS [149]. It has been shown to have beneficial effects against

Pseudomonas aeruginosa, Proteus mirabilis, Escherichia coli, and *Serratia marcescens* as Gram-negative uropathogens [150]. Several studies have exhibited that curcumin has synergistic anti-microbial effect with antibiotics and antifungals against *P. aeruginosa, Candida albicans,* methicillin-resistant *S. aureus,* and enterotoxigenic *E. coli* [151−154]. Transformation of curcumin into nanocrystals with or without the stabilizer enhances water dispersibility and colloidal stability leading to improvement of curcumin antimicrobial activity. Mean inhibitory concentration (MIC) for nanocurcumin (nanocrystals or nanocapsules) against a variety of bacteria and fungi has been shown to be lower compared to curcumin [155].

1.5 Toxicity

Based on the preclinical and clinical studies, no serious toxicity concerns have been observed with the usual consumption of turmeric or curcumin [156,157]. As it has been demonstrated by clinical trials the curcumin intakes at a dosage of 8 g per day are well tolerated and an intake of 12 g/day has no adverse effects [158−161]. This relatively low toxicity is because of low bioavailability of turmeric, which is related to its low solubility in water as well as rapid degradation in the GI tract [158,162,163]. Hydrophobic structure of curcumin molecule limits its absorption from the gut. Moreover, the portion that is absorbed transforms to glucuronide and sulfate conjugates during processes occurring in the GI tract and liver. In addition, curcumin is rapidly eliminated from the gut [158]. There has been also a wide variety of animal studies indicated the lack of significant toxicity of curcumin [164]. In some studies, doses of administered curcumin reached as high as 50,000-ppm turmeric oleoresin in the diet or up to 3.5−5.0 g/kg body weight [164−166]. There is a study on the consumption of supplemental doses of turmeric for 4 weeks leading to increased risk of kidney stone development and elevation of urinary oxalate levels [167]. Another study reported that 300 mg/d consumption of curcumin for 6 days reduced the bioavailability of talinolol, which is a drug for the treatment of hypertension and coronary heart failure [168]. Totally, it can be concluded that turmeric and nonmutagenic and nongenotoxic agents are safe to be consumed. However, further studies on various formulations of curcumin are needed and possible curcumin−drug interactions should be considered.

1.6 Conclusion

Curcumin, the active constituent of turmeric, has a long history of use as a food dye and culinary spice and more important as a constituent for medications in traditional Ayurveda and Chinese medicine. Curcumin is a light-yellow spice extracted from the rhizome of *Curcuma longa Linn.* Along the ages, progress in science and technology has exploited curcumin in a vast range of applications related to food and health. Herein, we discussed various pharmacological effects of curcumin including antioxidant, antidiabetic, antiinflammatory, neuroprotective, hepatoprotective, anticancer, and antimicrobial effects as well as its effects on the skin, GI tract, and CVD. It has been confirmed that curcumin as a pleiotropic molecule can modulate intracellular signaling pathways contributing to the control of cell growth, inflammation, and apoptosis. The beneficial activities of curcumin are associated to its complex chemistry as well as its potential to affect multiple signaling pathways including cytoprotective pathways based on Nrf2; survival pathways related to NF-κB, Akt, and growth factors; angiogenic and metastatic pathways. Curcumin exhibits antioxidant activity as it is a hydrogen donor and free radical scavenger. We also discussed that nanoparticle-encapsulated curcumin can enhance its bioavailability and pharmacokinetics compared to conventional curcumin. Based on the safety evaluation studies, curcumin is well tolerated at high doses of usage without showing any toxic effects.

Conflict of interests

The authors declare no conflict of interest.

References

[1] Jurenka JS. Anti-inflammatory properties of curcumin, a major constituent of *Curcuma longa*: a review of preclinical and clinical research. Alternative Medicine Review 2009;14(2).

[2] Ammon HP, Wahl MA. Pharmacology of *Curcuma longa*. Planta Medica 1991;57(01):1−7.

[3] Ridley HN. Spices. Macmillan and Company, Limited; 1912.

[4] Velayudhan K, Dikshit N, Nizar MA. Ethnobotany of turmeric (Curcuma longa L.). Indian Journal of Traditional Knowledge 2012;11(4):607−14.

[5] Peter K. Informatics on turmeric and ginger. Indian Spices 1999;36(2&3):12−14.

[6] Nwaekpe J, Anyaegbunam H, Okoye B, Asumugha G. Promotion of turmeric for the food/pharmaceutical industry in Nigeria. American Journal of Experimental Agriculture 2015;8(6):335−41.

[7] Okechukwu AC, Adeyemi OO, Chinedu E, Peggy OC, Chukwuma NC. Multi-location evaluation of turmeric genotypes in Nigeria. Journal of Agricultural Science and Technology B. 2013;3(12B):842.

[8] Ravindran P, Babu KN, Sivaraman K. Turmeric: the genus Curcuma. CRC Press; 2007.

[9] Sasikumar B. Turmeric. Handbook of herbs and spices. Elsevier; 2012. p. 526−46.

[10] Norman J. The complete book of spices. Viking Press; 1991.

[11] Soudamini K, Kuttan R. Inhibition of chemical carcinogenesis by curcumin. Journal of Ethnopharmacology 1989;27(1-2):227−33.

[12] Aggarwal BB, Takada Y, Oommen OV. From chemoprevention to chemotherapy: common targets and common goals. Expert Opinion on Investigational Drugs 2004;13(10):1327−38.

[13] Yadav RP, Tarun G, Roshan C, Yadav P. Versatility of turmeric: a review the golden spice of life. Journal of Pharmacognosy and Phytochemistry 2017;6(1):41−6.

[14] Ohshiro M, Kuroyanagi M, Ueno A. Structures of sesquiterpenes from *Curcuma longa*. Phytochemistry 1990;29(7):2201−5.

[15] Niranjan A, Singh S, Dhiman M, Tewari S. Biochemical composition of *Curcuma longa* L. accessions. Analytical Letters 2013;46(7):1069−83.

[16] Nasri H, Sahinfard N, Rafieian M, Rafieian S, Shirzad M, Rafieian-Kopaei M. Turmeric: a spice with multifunctional medicinal properties. Journal of HerbMed Pharmacology 2014;3.

[17] Chanda S, Ramachandra T. Phytochemical and pharmacological importance of turmeric (*Curcuma longa*): a review. Research & Reviews: A Journal of Pharmacology 2019;9(1):16−23.

[18] Kapoor L. CRC Handbook of Ayurvedic medicinal plants. CRC Press; 2018.

[19] Kirtikar K, Basu B. Indian medicinal plants. 1935.

[20] Govindarajan V, Stahl WH. Turmeric—chemistry, technology, and quality. Critical Reviews in Food Science & Nutrition. 1980;12(3):199−301.

[21] Akinpelu C, Adebayo O, Adewale O, Adebisi-Adelani O. An analysis of turmeric utilisation pattern in Ekiti state. Nigeria. Nigerian Journal of Horticultural Science 2012;17(1):68−72.

[22] Nelson KM, Dahlin JL, Bisson J, Graham J, Pauli GF, Walters MA. The essential medicinal chemistry of curcumin: miniperspective. Journal of Medicinal Chemistry 2017;60(5):1620−37.

[23] Fu YS, Chen TH, Weng L, Huang L, Lai D, Weng CF. Pharmacological properties and underlying mechanisms of curcumin and prospects in medicinal potential. Biomedicine & Pharmacotherapy = Biomedecine & Pharmacotherapie 2021;141:111888.

[24] Ganji A, Farahani I, Saeedifar AM, Mosayebi G, Ghazavi A, Majeed M, et al. Protective effects of curcumin against lipopolysaccharide-induced toxicity. Current Medicinal Chemistry 2021;28(33):6915−30.

[25] Hosseini SA, Zahedipour F, Sathyapalan T, Jamialahmadi T, Sahebkar A. Pulmonary fibrosis: therapeutic and mechanistic insights into the role of phytochemicals. Biofactors (Oxford, England) 2021;47(3):250−69.

[26] Keihanian F, Saeidinia A, Bagheri RK, Johnston TP, Sahebkar A. Curcumin, hemostasis, thrombosis, and coagulation. Journal of Cellular Physiology 2018;233(6):4497−511.

[27] Mokhtari-Zaer A, Marefati N, Atkin SL, Butler AE, Sahebkar A. The protective role of curcumin in myocardial ischemia−reperfusion injury. Journal of Cellular Physiology 2018;234(1):214−22.

[28] Momtazi-Borojeni AA, Haftcheshmeh SM, Esmaeili SA, Johnston TP, Abdollahi E, Sahebkar A. Curcumin: a natural modulator of immune cells in systemic lupus erythematosus. Autoimmunity Reviews 2018;17(2):125−35.

[29] Rahimi K, Hassanzadeh K, Khanbabaei H, Haftcheshmeh SM, Ahmadi A, Izadpanah E, et al. Curcumin: a dietary phytochemical for targeting the phenotype and function of dendritic cells. Current Medicinal Chemistry 2021;28(8):1549−64.

[30] Mohammadi A, Blesso CN, Barreto GE, Banach M, Majeed M, Sahebkar A. Macrophage plasticity, polarization and function in response to curcumin, a diet-derived polyphenol, as an immunomodulatory agent. The Journal of nutritional biochemistry, 2019;66:1−16. https://doi.org/10.1016/j.jnutbio.2018.12.005.

[31] Sahebkar A. Molecular mechanisms for curcumin benefits against ischemic injury. Fertility and Sterility 2010;94(5):e75−6.

[32] Soltani S, Boozari M, Cicero AFG, Jamialahmadi T, Sahebkar A. Effects of phytochemicals on macrophage cholesterol efflux capacity: impact on atherosclerosis. Phytotherapy Research 2021;35(6):2854−78.

[33] Zhou Y, Hong Y, Huang H. Triptolide attenuates inflammatory response in membranous glomerulonephritis rat via downregulation of NF-κB signaling pathway. Kidney and Blood Pressure Research 2016;41(6):901−10.

[34] Vickers NJ. Animal communication: when i'm calling you, will you answer too? Current Biology 2017;27(14):R713−15.

[35] Dai W, Wang H, Fang J, Zhu Y, Zhou J, Wang X, et al. Curcumin provides neuroprotection in model of traumatic brain injury via the Nrf2-ARE signaling pathway. Brain Research Bulletin 2018;140:65−71.

[36] Edwards RL, Luis PB, Varuzza PV, Joseph AI, Presley SH, Chaturvedi R, et al. The anti-inflammatory activity of curcumin is mediated by its oxidative metabolites. Journal of Biological Chemistry 2017;292 (52):21243−52.

[37] Hassanzadeh S, Read MI, Bland AR, Majeed M, Jamialahmadi T, Sahebkar A. Curcumin: an inflammasome silencer. Pharmacological Research 2020;159.

[38] Karuppagounder V, Arumugam S, Thandavarayan RA, Sreedhar R, Giridharan VV, Afrin R, et al. Curcumin alleviates renal dysfunction and suppresses inflammation by shifting from M1 to M2 macrophage polarization in daunorubicin induced nephrotoxicity in rats. Cytokine 2016;84:1−9.

[39] Pulido-Moran M, Moreno-Fernandez J, Ramirez-Tortosa C, Ramirez-Tortosa M. Curcumin and health. Molecules (Basel, Switzerland) 2016;21(3):264.

[40] Wang Y, Li Y, He L, Mao B, Chen S, Martinez V, et al. Commensal flora triggered target anti-inflammation of alginate-curcumin micelle for ulcerative colitis treatment. Colloids and Surfaces B: Biointerfaces 2021;203:111756.

[41] Yuan R, Li Y, Han S, Chen X, Chen J, He J, et al. Fe-curcumin nanozyme-mediated reactive oxygen species scavenging and anti-inflammation for acute lung injury. ACS Central Science 2021;8(1):10−21.

[42] Chen Y-C, Shie M-Y, Wu Y-HA, Lee K-XA, Wei L-J, Shen Y-F. Anti-inflammation performance of curcumin-loaded mesoporous calcium silicate cement. Journal of the Formosan Medical Association 2017;116(9):679−88.

[43] Mirhadi E, Majeed M, Kesharwani P, Sahebkar A. Reactive oxygen species-responsive drug delivery systems: a new approach in nanomedicine. Current Medicinal Chemistry 2022;.

[44] Mirhadi E, Mashreghi M, Maleki MF, Alavizadeh SH, Arabi L, Badiee A, et al. Redox-sensitive nanoscale drug delivery systems for cancer treatment. International Journal of Pharmaceutics 2020;589:119882.

[45] Hunyadi A. The mechanism (s) of action of antioxidants: from scavenging reactive oxygen/nitrogen species to redox signaling and the generation of bioactive secondary metabolites. Medicinal Research Reviews 2019;39(6):2505−33.

[46] Ak T, Gülçin İ. Antioxidant and radical scavenging properties of curcumin. Chemico-Biological Interactions 2008;174(1):27−37.

[47] Cox FF, Misiou A, Vierkant A, Ale-Agha N, Grandoch M, Haendeler J, et al. Protective effects of curcumin in cardiovascular diseases—impact on oxidative stress and mitochondria. Cells. 2022;11(3):342.

[48] Sun Y, Hu X, Hu G, Xu C, Jiang H. Curcumin attenuates hydrogen peroxide-induced premature senescence via the activation of SIRT1 in human umbilical vein endothelial cells. Biological and Pharmaceutical Bulletin 2015;38(8):1134−41.

[49] Sugawara J, Akazawa N, Miyaki A, Choi Y, Tanabe Y, Imai T, et al. Effect of endurance exercise training and curcumin intake on central arterial hemodynamics in postmenopausal women: pilot study. American journal of hypertension 2012;25(6):651−6.

[50] Akazawa N, Choi Y, Miyaki A, Tanabe Y, Sugawara J, Ajisaka R, et al. Curcumin ingestion and exercise training improve vascular endothelial function in postmenopausal women. Nutrition Research 2012;32 (10):795−9.

[51] Santos-Parker JR, Strahler TR, Bassett CJ, Bispham NZ, Chonchol MB, Seals DR. Curcumin supplementation improves vascular endothelial function in healthy middle-aged and older adults by increasing nitric oxide bioavailability and reducing oxidative stress. Aging (Albany NY) 2017;9(1):187.

[52] Ashrafizadeh M, Ahmadi Z, Mohammadinejad R, Farkhondeh T, Samarghandian S. Curcumin activates the Nrf2 pathway and induces cellular protection against oxidative injury. Current Molecular Medicine 2020;20(2):116−33.

[53] Di Pierro F, Bressan A, Ranaldi D, Rapacioli G, Giacomelli L, Bertuccioli A. Potential role of bioavailable curcumin in weight loss and omental adipose tissue decrease: preliminary data of a randomized,

controlled trial in overweight people with metabolic syndrome. Preliminary Study. European Review for Medical and Pharmacological Sciences 2015;19(21):4195–202.

[54] Zou J, Zhang S, Li P, Zheng X, Feng D. Supplementation with curcumin inhibits intestinal cholesterol absorption and prevents atherosclerosis in high-fat diet–fed apolipoprotein E knockout mice. Nutrition Research 2018;56:32–40.

[55] Wan Q, Liu Z-Y, Yang Y-P, Liu S-M. Effect of curcumin on inhibiting atherogenesis by down-regulating lipocalin-2 expression in apolipoprotein E knockout mice. Bio-medical Materials and Engineering 2016;27(6):577–87.

[56] Rahnavard M, Hassanpour M, Ahmadi M, Heidarzadeh M, Amini H, Javanmard MZ, et al. Curcumin ameliorated myocardial infarction by inhibition of cardiotoxicity in the rat model. Journal of Cellular Biochemistry 2019;120(7):11965–72.

[57] Petersen MC, Shulman GI. Mechanisms of insulin action and insulin resistance. Physiological Reviews 2018;98(4):2133–223.

[58] Alam MA, Subhan N, Rahman MM, Uddin SJ, Reza HM, Sarker SD. Effect of citrus flavonoids, naringin and naringenin, on metabolic syndrome and their mechanisms of action. Advances in Nutrition 2014;5 (4):404–17.

[59] Kuroda M, Mimaki Y, Nishiyama T, Mae T, Kishida H, Tsukagawa M, et al. Hypoglycemic effects of turmeric (*Curcuma longa* L. rhizomes) on genetically diabetic KK-Ay mice. Biological and Pharmaceutical Bulletin 2005;28(5):937–9.

[60] Mohammadi E, Behnam B, Mohammadinejad R, Guest PC, Simental-Mendía LE, Sahebkar A. Antidiabetic properties of curcumin: insights on new mechanisms. Studies on Biomarkers and New Targets in Aging Research in Iran 2021;151–64.

[61] Woo H-M, Kang J-H, Kawada T, Yoo H, Sung M-K, Yu R. Active spice-derived components can inhibit inflammatory responses of adipose tissue in obesity by suppressing inflammatory actions of macrophages and release of monocyte chemoattractant protein-1 from adipocytes. Life Sciences 2007;80 (10):926–31.

[62] Gonzales AM, Orlando RA. Curcumin and resveratrol inhibit nuclear factor-kappaB-mediated cytokine expression in adipocytes. Nutrition & Metabolism 2008;5(1):1–13.

[63] Green A, Krause J, Rumberger JM. Curcumin is a direct inhibitor of glucose transport in adipocytes. Phytomedicine: International Journal of Phytotherapy and Phytopharmacology 2014;21(2):118–22.

[64] Wu B, Xiao Z, Zhang W, Chen H, Liu H, Pan J, et al. A novel resveratrol-curcumin hybrid, a19, attenuates high fat diet-induced nonalcoholic fatty liver disease. Biomedicine & Pharmacotherapy 2019;110:951–60.

[65] Lee EJ, Hwang JS, Kang ES, Lee SB, Hur J, Lee WJ, et al. Nanoemulsions improve the efficacy of turmeric in palmitate-and high fat diet-induced cellular and animal models. Biomedicine & Pharmacotherapy 2019;110:181–9.

[66] Ding X-Q, Wu W-Y, Jiao R-Q, Gu T-T, Xu Q, Pan Y, et al. Curcumin and allopurinol ameliorate fructose-induced hepatic inflammation in rats via miR-200a-mediated TXNIP/NLRP3 inflammasome inhibition. Pharmacological Research 2018;137:64–75.

[67] Chauhan P, Tamrakar AK, Mahajan S, Prasad G. Chitosan encapsulated nanocurcumin induces GLUT-4 translocation and exhibits enhanced anti-hyperglycemic function. Life Sciences 2018;213:226–35.

[68] Sadeghi A, Rostamirad A, Seyyedebrahimi S, Meshkani R. Curcumin ameliorates palmitate-induced inflammation in skeletal muscle cells by regulating JNK/NF-kB pathway and ROS production. Inflammopharmacology 2018;26(5):1265–72.

[69] Rajasekaran SA. Therapeutic potential of curcumin in gastrointestinal diseases. World journal of gastrointestinal pathophysiology 2011;2(1):1.

[70] Hartojo W, Silvers AL, Thomas DG, Seder CW, Lin L, Rao H, et al. Curcumin promotes apoptosis, increases chemosensitivity, and inhibits nuclear factor κB in esophageal adenocarcinoma. Translational Oncology 2010;3(2):99−108.

[71] O'Sullivan-Coyne G, O'sullivan G, O'Donovan T, Piwocka K, McKenna S. Curcumin induces apoptosis-independent death in oesophageal cancer cells. British Journal of Cancer 2009;101(9):1585−95.

[72] De R, Kundu P, Swarnakar S, Ramamurthy T, Chowdhury A, Nair GB, et al. Antimicrobial activity of curcumin against *Helicobacter pylori* isolates from India and during infections in mice. Antimicrobial Agents and Chemotherapy 2009;53(4):1592−7.

[73] Liu C-A, Wang M-J, Chi C-W, Wu C-W, Chen J-Y. Rho/Rhotekin-mediated NF-κB activation confers resistance to apoptosis. Oncogene 2004;23(54):8731−42.

[74] Tang X-Q, Bi H, Feng J-Q, Cao J-G. Effect of curcumin on multidrug resistance in resistant human gastric carcinoma cell line SGC7901/VCR. Acta Pharmacologica Sinica 2005;26(8):1009−16.

[75] Li L, Ahmed B, Mehta K, Kurzrock R. Liposomal curcumin with and without oxaliplatin: effects on cell growth, apoptosis, and angiogenesis in colorectal cancer. Molecular Cancer Therapeutics 2007;6(4):1276−82.

[76] Vollono L, Falconi M, Gaziano R, Iacovelli F, Dika E, Terracciano C, et al. Potential of curcumin in skin disorders. Nutrients. 2019;11(9):2169.

[77] Panahi Y, Fazlolahzadeh O, Atkin, SL, Majeed M, Butler AE, Johnston T P, Sahebkar A. Evidence of curcumin and curcumin analogue effects in skin diseases: A narrative review. Journal of cellular physiology 2019; 234(2):1165−1178.

[78] Gupta SC, Kismali G, Aggarwal BB. Curcumin, a component of turmeric: from farm to pharmacy. Biofactors (Oxford, England) 2013;39(1):2−13.

[79] Aggarwal BB, Gupta SC, Sung B. Curcumin: an orally bioavailable blocker of TNF and other pro-inflammatory biomarkers. British Journal of Pharmacology 2013;169(8):1672−92.

[80] Kurd SK, Smith N, VanVoorhees A, Troxel AB, Badmaev V, Seykora JT, et al. Oral curcumin in the treatment of moderate to severe psoriasis vulgaris: a prospective clinical trial. Journal of the American Academy of Dermatology 2008;58(4):625−31.

[81] Kim J, Park S, Jeon B-S, Jang W-S, Lee S-J, Son Y, et al. Therapeutic effect of topical application of curcumin during treatment of radiation burns in a mini-pig model. Journal of Veterinary Science 2016;17(4):435−44.

[82] Velnar T, Bailey T, Smrkolj V. The wound healing process: an overview of the cellular and molecular mechanisms. Journal of International Medical Research 2009;37(5):1528−42.

[83] Li H-Y, Yang M, Li Z, Meng Z. Curcumin inhibits angiotensin II-induced inflammation and proliferation of rat vascular smooth muscle cells by elevating PPAR-γ activity and reducing oxidative stress. International Journal of Molecular Medicine 2017;39(5):1307−16.

[84] Zhang Y, Liu Z, Wu J, Bai B, Chen H, Xiao Z, et al. New MD2 inhibitors derived from curcumin with improved anti-inflammatory activity. European Journal of Medicinal Chemistry 2018;148:291−305.

[85] Müller-Decker K. Cyclooxygenase-dependent signaling is causally linked to non-melanoma skin carcinogenesis: pharmacological, genetic, and clinical evidence. Cancer and Metastasis Reviews 2011;30(3):343−61.

[86] Koeberle A, Northoff H, Werz O. Curcumin blocks prostaglandin E2 biosynthesis through direct inhibition of the microsomal prostaglandin E2 synthase-1. Molecular Cancer Therapeutics 2009;8(8):2348−55.

[87] Grice EA, Kong HH, Conlan S, Deming CB, Davis J, Young AC, et al. Topographical and temporal diversity of the human skin microbiome. Science (New York, N.Y.) 2009;324(5931):1190−2.

[88] Zorofchian Moghadamtousi S, Abdul Kadir H, Hassandarvish P, Tajik H, Abubakar S, Zandi K. A review on antibacterial, antiviral, and antifungal activity of curcumin. BioMed Research International 2014;2014.

[89] Madan S, Nehate C, Barman TK, Rathore AS, Koul V. Design, preparation, and evaluation of liposomal gel formulations for treatment of acne: in vitro and in vivo studies. Drug Development and Industrial Pharmacy 2019;45(3):395—404.

[90] Liu C-H, Huang H-Y. Antimicrobial activity of curcumin-loaded myristic acid microemulsions against *Staphylococcus epidermidis*. Chemical and Pharmaceutical Bulletin 2012;60(9):1118—24.

[91] Baltazar LM, Krausz AE, Souza ACO, Adler BL, Landriscina A, Musaev T, et al. Trichophyton rubrum is inhibited by free and nanoparticle encapsulated curcumin by induction of nitrosative stress after photodynamic activation. PLoS One 2015;10(3):e0120179.

[92] Andrews MD, Burns M. Common tinea infections in children. American Family Physician 2008;77 (10):1415.

[93] Askarizadeh A, Barreto GE, Henney NC, Majeed M, Sahebkar A. Neuroprotection by curcumin: A review on brain delivery strategies. International Journal of Pharmaceutics 2020;585:119476.

[94] Khayatan D, Razavi SM, Arab ZN, Niknejad AH, Nouri K, Momtaz S, et al. Protective effects of curcumin against traumatic brain injury. Biomedicine and Pharmacotherapy 2022;154.

[95] Salehi B, Calina D, Docea AO, Koirala N, Aryal S, Lombardo D, et al. Curcumin's nanomedicine formulations for therapeutic application in neurological diseases. Journal of Clinical Medicine 2020;9(2):430.

[96] Teter B, Morihara T, Lim G, Chu T, Jones M, Zuo X, et al. Curcumin restores innate immune Alzheimer's disease risk gene expression to ameliorate Alzheimer pathogenesis. Neurobiology of Disease 2019;127:432—48.

[97] Song S, Nie Q, Li Z, Du G. Curcumin improves neurofunctions of 6-OHDA-induced parkinsonian rats. Pathology-Research and Practice 2016;212(4):247—51.

[98] Cianciulli A, Calvello R, Porro C, Trotta T, Salvatore R, Panaro MA. PI3k/Akt signalling pathway plays a crucial role in the anti-inflammatory effects of curcumin in LPS-activated microglia. International Immunopharmacology 2016;36:282—90.

[99] Chen N, Geng Q, Zheng J, He S, Huo X, Sun X. Suppression of the TGF-β/Smad signaling pathway and inhibition of hepatic stellate cell proliferation play a role in the hepatoprotective effects of curcumin against alcohol-induced hepatic fibrosis. International Journal of Molecular Medicine 2014;34 (4):1110—16.

[100] Ganesh P, Karthikeyan R, Muthukumaraswamy A, Anand J. A potential role of periodontal inflammation in Alzheimer's disease: a review. Oral Health & Preventive Dentistry 2017;15(1):7—12.

[101] Goozee K, Shah T, Sohrabi HR, Rainey-Smith S, Brown B, Verdile G, et al. Examining the potential clinical value of curcumin in the prevention and diagnosis of Alzheimer's disease. British Journal of Nutrition 2016;115(3):449—65.

[102] Qureshi M, Al-Suhaimi EA, Wahid F, Shehzad O, Shehzad A. Therapeutic potential of curcumin for multiple sclerosis. Neurological Sciences 2018;39(2):207—14.

[103] Macías-Pérez JR, Vázquez-López BJ, Muñoz-Ortega MH, Aldaba-Muruato LR, Martínez-Hernández SL, Sánchez-Alemán E, et al. Curcumin and α/β-adrenergic antagonists cotreatment reverse liver cirrhosis in hamsters: participation of Nrf-2 and NF-κB. Journal of Immunology Research 2019;2019.

[104] Peng X, Dai C, Liu Q, Li J, Qiu J. Curcumin attenuates on carbon tetrachloride-induced acute liver injury in mice via modulation of the Nrf2/HO-1 and TGF-β1/Smad3 pathway. Molecules (Basel, Switzerland) 2018;23(1):215.

[105] Cicero AFG, Sahebkar A, Fogacci F, Bove, M, Giovannini M, Borghi C. Effects of phytosomal curcumin on anthropometric parameters, insulin resistance, cortisolemia and non-alcoholic fatty liver disease indices: a double-blind, placebo-controlled clinical trial. European journal of nutrition, 2020;59(2), 477—483. https://doi.org/10.1007/s00394-019-01916-7.

[106] Farzaei MH, Zobeiri M, Parvizi F, El-Senduny FF, Marmouzi I, Coy-Barrera E, et al. Curcumin in liver diseases: a systematic review of the cellular mechanisms of oxidative stress and clinical perspective. Nutrients. 2018;10(7):855.

[107] Lee H-Y, Kim S-W, Lee G-H, Choi M-K, Jung H-W, Kim Y-J, et al. Turmeric extract and its active compound, curcumin, protect against chronic CCl4-induced liver damage by enhancing antioxidation. BMC Complementary and Alternative Medicine 2016;16(1):1−9.

[108] Choudhury ST, Das N, Ghosh S, Ghosh D, Chakraborty S, Ali N. Vesicular (liposomal and nanoparticulated) delivery of curcumin: a comparative study on carbon tetrachloride−mediated oxidative hepatocellular damage in rat model. International Journal of Nanomedicine 2016;11:2179.

[109] Badria FA, Ibrahim AS, Badria AF, Elmarakby AA. Curcumin attenuates iron accumulation and oxidative stress in the liver and spleen of chronic iron-overloaded rats. PLoS One 2015;10(7): e0134156.

[110] Granados-Castro LF, Rodríguez-Rangel DS, Fernández-Rojas B, León-Contreras JC, Hernández-Pando R, Medina-Campos ON, et al. Curcumin prevents paracetamol-induced liver mitochondrial alterations. Journal of Pharmacy and Pharmacology 2016;68(2):245−56.

[111] Kheradpezhouh E, Barritt GJ, Rychkov GY. Curcumin inhibits activation of TRPM2 channels in rat hepatocytes. Redox biology 2016;7:1−7.

[112] Guo C, Ma J, Zhong Q, Zhao M, Hu T, Chen T, et al. Curcumin improves alcoholic fatty liver by inhibiting fatty acid biosynthesis. Toxicology and Applied Pharmacology 2017;328:1−9.

[113] Lu C, Xu W, Zhang F, Shao J, Zheng S. Nrf2 knockdown disrupts the protective effect of curcumin on alcohol-induced hepatocyte necroptosis. Molecular Pharmaceutics 2016;13(12):4043−53.

[114] Xiong ZE, Dong WG, Wang BY, Tong QY, Li ZY. Curcumin attenuates chronic ethanol-induced liver injury by inhibition of oxidative stress via mitogen-activated protein kinase/nuclear factor E2-related factor 2 pathway in mice. Pharmacognosy Magazine 2015;11(44):707.

[115] Mohajeri M, Sahebkar A. Protective effects of curcumin against doxorubicin-induced toxicity and resistance: a review. Critical Reviews in Oncology/Hematology 2018;122:30−51.

[116] Momtazi AA, Sahebkar A. Difluorinated curcumin: a promising curcumin analogue with improved anti-tumor activity and pharmacokinetic profile. Current Pharmaceutical Design 2016;22(28):4386−97.

[117] Kuttan G, Kumar KB, Guruvayoorappan C, Kuttan R. Antitumor, anti-invasion, and antimetastatic effects of curcumin. Advances in Experimental Medicine and Biology 2007;595:173−84.

[118] Marjaneh RM, Rahmani F, Hassanian SM, Rezaei N, Hashemzehi M, Bahrami A, Ariakia F, Fiuji H, Sahebkar A, Avan A, Khazaei M. Phytosomal curcumin inhibits tumor growth in colitis-associated colorectal cancer. Journal of cellular physiology, 2018;233(10), 6785−6798. https://doi.org/10.1002/jcp.26538.

[119] Liu H-T, Ho Y-S. Anticancer effect of curcumin on breast cancer and stem cells. Food Science and Human Wellness 2018;7(2):134−7.

[120] Singh N, Baby D, Rajguru JP, Patil PB, Thakkannavar SS, Pujari VB. Inflammation and cancer. Annals of African Medicine 2019;18(3):121.

[121] Eiró N, Vizoso FJ. Inflammation and cancer. World Journal of Gastrointestinal Surgery 2012;4(3):62.

[122] Siwak DR, Shishodia S, Aggarwal BB, Kurzrock R. Curcumin-induced antiproliferative and proapoptotic effects in melanoma cells are associated with suppression of IκB kinase and nuclear factor κB activity and are independent of the B-Raf/mitogen-activated/extracellular signal-regulated protein kinase pathway and the Akt pathway. Cancer. 2005;104(4):879−90.

[123] Ruocco KM, Goncharova EI, Young MR, Colburn NH, McMahon JB, Henrich CJ. A high-throughput cell-based assay to identify specific inhibitors of transcription factor AP-1. SLAS Discovery 2007;12 (1):133−9.

[124] Choi BH, Kim CG, Bae Y-S, Lim Y, Lee YH, Shin SY. p21Waf1/Cip1 expression by curcumin in U-87MG human glioma cells: role of early growth response-1 expression. Cancer Research 2008;68(5):1369–77.

[125] Chen Q-Y, Jiao D-M, Wang L-F, Wang L, Hu H-Z, Song J, et al. Curcumin inhibits proliferation—migration of NSCLC by steering crosstalk between a Wnt signaling pathway and an adherens junction via EGR-1. Molecular Biosystems 2015;11(3):859–68.

[126] Chen A, Xu J, Johnson A. Curcumin inhibits human colon cancer cell growth by suppressing gene expression of epidermal growth factor receptor through reducing the activity of the transcription factor Egr-1. Oncogene 2006;25(2):278–87.

[127] Choi H, Lim J, Hong J. Curcumin interrupts the interaction between the androgen receptor and Wnt/β-catenin signaling pathway in LNCaP prostate cancer cells. Prostate Cancer and Prostatic Diseases 2010;13(4):343–9.

[128] Farhoudi L, Kesharwani P, Majeed M, Johnston TP, Sahebkar A. Polymeric nanomicelles of curcumin: potential applications in cancer. International Journal of Pharmaceutics 2022;121622.

[129] Bi C, Miao XQ, Chow SF, Wu WJ, Yan R, Liao Y, et al. Particle size effect of curcumin nanosuspensions on cytotoxicity, cellular internalization, in vivo pharmacokinetics and biodistribution. Nanomedicine: Nanotechnology, Biology and Medicine 2017;13(3):943–53.

[130] Ma Z, Wang N, He H, Tang X. Pharmaceutical strategies of improving oral systemic bioavailability of curcumin for clinical application. Journal of Controlled Release 2019;316:359–80.

[131] Ashif Khan M, Akhtar N, Sharma V, Pathak K. Product development studies on sonocrystallized curcumin for the treatment of gastric cancer. Pharmaceutics. 2015;7(2):43–63.

[132] Gigliobianco MR, Casadidio C, Censi R, Di Martino P. Nanocrystals of poorly soluble drugs: drug bioavailability and physicochemical stability. Pharmaceutics. 2018;10(3):134.

[133] Bolat ZB, Islek Z, Demir BN, Yilmaz EN, Sahin F, Ucisik MH. Curcumin-and piperine-loaded emulsomes as combinational treatment approach enhance the anticancer activity of curcumin on HCT116 colorectal cancer model. Frontiers in Bioengineering and Biotechnology 2020;8:50.

[134] Rompicharla SVK, Bhatt H, Shah A, Komanduri N, Vijayasarathy D, Ghosh B, et al. Formulation optimization, characterization, and evaluation of in vitro cytotoxic potential of curcumin loaded solid lipid nanoparticles for improved anticancer activity. Chemistry and Physics of Lipids 2017;208:10–18.

[135] Gumireddy A, Christman R, Kumari D, Tiwari A, North EJ, Chauhan H. Preparation, characterization, and in vitro evaluation of curcumin-and resveratrol-loaded solid lipid nanoparticles. AAPS PharmSciTech 2019;20(4):1–14.

[136] Chaharband F, Kamalinia G, Atyabi F, Mortazavi SA, Mirzaie ZH, Dinarvand R. Formulation and in vitro evaluation of curcumin-lactoferrin conjugated nanostructures for cancerous cells. Artificial Cells, Nanomedicine, and Biotechnology 2018;46(3):626–36.

[137] Sesarman A, Tefas L, Sylvester B, Licarete E, Rauca V, Luput L, et al. Anti-angiogenic and anti-inflammatory effects of long-circulating liposomes co-encapsulating curcumin and doxorubicin on C26 murine colon cancer cells. Pharmacological Reports 2018;70(2):331–9.

[138] Bonaccorso A, Pellitteri R, Ruozi B, Puglia C, Santonocito D, Pignatello R, et al. Curcumin loaded polymeric vs. lipid nanoparticles: antioxidant effect on normal and hypoxic olfactory ensheathing cells. Nanomaterials. 2021;11(1):159.

[139] Yan J, Wang Y, Zhang X, Liu S, Tian C, Wang H. Targeted nanomedicine for prostate cancer therapy: docetaxel and curcumin co-encapsulated lipid—polymer hybrid nanoparticles for the enhanced antitumor activity in vitro and in vivo. Drug Delivery 2016;23(5):1757–62.

[140] Saxena V, Hasan A, Sharma S, Pandey LM. Edible oil nanoemulsion: an organic nanoantibiotic as a potential biomolecule delivery vehicle. International Journal of Polymeric Materials and Polymeric Biomaterials 2018;67(7):410–19.

[141] Salvia-Trujillo L, Soliva-Fortuny R, Rojas-Graü MA, McClements DJ, Martín-Belloso O. Edible nanoe-mulsions as carriers of active ingredients: a review. Annual Review of Food Science and Technology 2017;8:439−66.

[142] Li J, Hwang I-C, Chen X, Park HJ. Effects of chitosan coating on curcumin loaded nano-emulsion: Study on stability and in vitro digestibility. Food Hydrocolloids 2016;60:138−47.

[143] Xiao Y, Xu C, Xiong H, Du S, Zhou J, Yin L, et al. Dose-reduction antiangiogenic curcumin-low molec-ular weight heparin nanodrugs for enhanced combinational antitumor therapy. European Journal of Pharmaceutical Sciences 2018;119:121−34.

[144] Schraufstätter E, Bernt H. Antibacterial action of curcumin and related compounds. Nature 1949;164 (4167):456−7.

[145] Kotha RR, Luthria DL. Curcumin: biological, pharmaceutical, nutraceutical, and analytical aspects. Molecules (Basel, Switzerland) 2019;24(16):2930.

[146] Han S, Yang Y. Antimicrobial activity of wool fabric treated with curcumin. Dyes and Pigments 2005;64 (2):157−61.

[147] Loo C-Y, Rohanizadeh R, Young PM, Traini D, Cavaliere R, Whitchurch CB, et al. Combination of silver nanoparticles and curcumin nanoparticles for enhanced anti-biofilm activities. Journal of Agricultural and Food Chemistry 2016;64(12):2513−22.

[148] Shukla A, Parmar P, Rao P, Goswami D, Saraf M. Twin peaks: presenting the antagonistic molecular interplay of curcumin with LasR and LuxR quorum sensing pathways. Current Microbiology 2020;77 (8):1800−10.

[149] Abdulrahman H, Misba L, Ahmad S, Khan AU. Curcumin induced photodynamic therapy mediated suppression of quorum sensing pathway of Pseudomonas aeruginosa: an approach to inhibit biofilm in vitro. Photodiagnosis and Photodynamic Therapy 2020;30:101645.

[150] Packiavathy IASV, Priya S, Pandian SK, Ravi AV. Inhibition of biofilm development of uropatho-gens by curcumin—an anti-quorum sensing agent from *Curcuma longa*. Food Chemistry 2014;148:453−60.

[151] Teow S-Y, Liew K, Ali SA, Khoo AS-B, Peh S-C. Antibacterial action of curcumin against Staphylococcus aureus: a brief review. Journal of Tropical Medicine 2016;2016.

[152] Bahari S, Zeighami H, Mirshahabi H, Roudashti S, Haghi F. Inhibition of *Pseudomonas aeruginosa* quo-rum sensing by subinhibitory concentrations of curcumin with gentamicin and azithromycin. Journal of Global Antimicrobial Resistance 2017;10:21−8.

[153] Itzia Azucena R-C, José Roberto C-L, Martin Z-R, Rafael C-Z, Leonardo H-H, Gabriela T-P, et al. Drug susceptibility testing and synergistic antibacterial activity of curcumin with antibiotics against entero-toxigenic *Escherichia coli*. Antibiotics. 2019;8(2):43.

[154] Sharma M, Manoharlal R, Negi AS, Prasad R. Synergistic anticandidal activity of pure polyphenol cur-cumin I in combination with azoles and polyenes generates reactive oxygen species leading to apopto-sis. FEMS Yeast Research 2010;10(5):570−8.

[155] da Silva AC, de Freitas Santos PD, do Prado Silva JT, Leimann FV, Bracht L, Goncalves OH. Impact of curcumin nanoformulation on its antimicrobial activity. Trends in Food Science & Technology 2018;72:74−82.

[156] Soleimani V, Sahebkar A, Hosseinzadeh H. Turmeric (*Curcuma longa*) and its major constituent (cur-cumin) as nontoxic and safe substances: review. Phytotherapy Research: PTR 2018;32(6):985−95.

[157] Heidari Z, Daei M, Boozari M, Jamialahmadi T, Sahebkar A. Curcumin supplementation in pediatric patients: a systematic review of current clinical evidence. Phytotherapy Research 2022;36(4):1442−58.

[158] Anand P, Kunnumakkara AB, Newman RA, Aggarwal BB. Bioavailability of curcumin: problems and promises. Molecular Pharmaceutics 2007;4(6):807−18.

[159] Aggarwal BB, Kumar A, Bharti AC. Anticancer potential of curcumin: preclinical and clinical studies. Anticancer Research 2003;23(1/A):363—98.

[160] Lao CD, Ruffin MT, Normolle D, Heath DD, Murray SI, Bailey JM, et al. Dose escalation of a curcuminoid formulation. BMC Complementary and Alternative Medicine 2006;6(1):1—4.

[161] Hsu C-H, Cheng A-L. Clinical studies with curcumin. Advances in Experimental Medicine and Biology 2007;471—80.

[162] Yang CS, Sang S, Lambert JD, Lee MJ. Bioavailability issues in studying the health effects of plant polyphenolic compounds. Molecular Nutrition & Food Research 2008;52(S1):S139—51.

[163] Garcea G, Jones D, Singh R, Dennison A, Farmer P, Sharma R, et al. Detection of curcumin and its metabolites in hepatic tissue and portal blood of patients following oral administration. British Journal of Cancer 2004;90(5):1011—15.

[164] Program NT. NTP toxicology and carcinogenesis studies of turmeric oleoresin (CAS No. 8024-37-1) (major component 79%-85% curcumin, CAS No. 458-37-7) in F344/N rats and B6C3F1 mice (feed studies). National Toxicology Program Technical Report Series 1993;427:1—275.

[165] Sharma RA, Euden SA, Platton SL, Cooke DN, Shafayat A, Hewitt HR, et al. Phase I clinical trial of oral curcumin: biomarkers of systemic activity and compliance. Clinical Cancer Research 2004;10 (20):6847—54.

[166] Sharma RA, Steward WP, Gescher AJ. Pharmacokinetics and pharmacodynamics of curcumin. The Molecular Targets and Therapeutic Uses of Curcumin in Health and Disease 2007;453—70.

[167] Tang M, Larson-Meyer DE, Liebman M. Effect of cinnamon and turmeric on urinary oxalate excretion, plasma lipids, and plasma glucose in healthy subjects. The American Journal of Clinical Nutrition 2008;87(5):1262—7.

[168] Juan H, Terhaag B, Cong Z, Bi-Kui Z, Rong-Hua Z, Feng W, et al. Unexpected effect of concomitantly administered curcumin on the pharmacokinetics of talinolol in healthy Chinese volunteers. European Journal of Clinical Pharmacology 2007;63(7):663—8.

2

Curcumin as a pharmaceutical leader

Fatemeh Vahdat-Lasemi[1], Prashant Kesharwani[2], Amirhossein Sahebkar[3,4]

[1]DEPARTMENT OF MEDICAL BIOTECHNOLOGY AND NANOTECHNOLOGY, SCHOOL OF MEDICINE, MASHHAD UNIVERSITY OF MEDICAL SCIENCES, MASHHAD, IRAN [2]DEPARTMENT OF PHARMACEUTICS, SCHOOL OF PHARMACEUTICAL EDUCATION AND RESEARCH, JAMIA HAMDARD, NEW DELHI, INDIA [3]BIOTECHNOLOGY RESEARCH CENTER, PHARMACEUTICAL TECHNOLOGY INSTITUTE, MASHHAD UNIVERSITY OF MEDICAL SCIENCES, MASHHAD, IRAN [4]APPLIED BIOMEDICAL RESEARCH CENTER, MASHHAD UNIVERSITY OF MEDICAL SCIENCES, MASHHAD, IRAN

2.1 Introduction

Curcumin, a natural yellow polyphenolic pigment, was isolated from the rhizome of the turmeric plant (*Curcuma longa*) by Vogel and Pelletier in 1815 for the first time [1,2]. Interestingly, curcumin is referred to as the "wonder drug of life" worldwide [3]. For thousands of years, curcumin has been utilized in Ayurveda and traditional Chinese medicine for treating digestive and liver problems, inflammatory states of different organs, bacterial infections, skin diseases, and wound healing [4,5]. Nowadays, curcumin is used as a supplement in several countries such as China, Japan, Korea, India, Pakistan, Malaysia, and Thailand. It is also added to cosmetics, curry, tea, and drinks and utilized as a coloring agent [6]. In the United States, it is also used as a dyeing agent and a preservative, and as an ingredient in butter, cheese, chips, and mustard sauce. Curcumin is commercially available in different forms such as tablets, capsules, energy drinks, ointments, cosmetics, and soaps [6]. Also, the best source of omega-3 fatty acids and alfa-linolenic is *C. longa* [7]. Curcumin has been traditionally utilized to alleviate numerous symptoms of different gastrointestinal problems, including diarrhea, indigestion, efflux, and even duodenal and stomach ulcers [8]. There are numerous in vitro and in vivo studies that support curcumin's health-beneficial impacts related principally to its potent antiinflammatory and antioxidant activities [9—11]. Also, the antiviral, antibacterial, antiparasitic, antifungal, and antiprotozoal activities of this natural molecule are shown [12—14]. The first study on the health benefits of curcumin was recorded in the 1970s [11]. This special study and studies conducted later demonstrated the fact that curcumin has multiple therapeutic activities and immense potential medicinal use [15—28]. In particular, clinical trials have demonstrated the safety and efficacy of curcumin and curcuminoids in patients with osteoarthritis disease, metabolic syndrome, nonalcoholic fatty liver disease, type 2 diabetes, chronic obstructive pulmonary disease, respiratory disease, depression and anxiety, and ulcerative colitis (UC) [29—42]. Generally, data from many in vitro, in vivo, and clinical studies have shown that

Curcumin-Based Nanomedicines as Cancer Therapeutics. DOI: https://doi.org/10.1016/B978-0-443-15412-6.00001-5

curcumin and curcuminoids are safe and well tolerated. According to research, curcumin is not poisonous or mutagenic, and has been certified by the US Food and Drug Administration as "generally recognized as safe" [43,44]. Clinical evidence points to curcumin's safety even at doses as high as 6−7 g/day. Interestingly, the safety has also been confirmed in the clinical with curcumin bioavailability-enhanced formulations that provide higher systemic concentrations of the compound [45]. Owing to the wide variety of curcumin's biological effects and its pleiotropic nature, this natural molecule has become known as a "golden molecule" by scientists. In this chapter, we focus on the central role played by curcumin in various diseases, with a specific emphasis on its effects on both animal and human levels.

2.2 Therapeutic activities of curcumin

Among the various natural medicines studied hitherto, curcumin has drawn researchers' interest due to its important medicinal benefits [46]. Curcumin has demonstrated a variety of biological functions, including cardioprotective, hepatoprotective, anticancer, antiinflammatory, antibacterial, and antimicrobial effects [47]. Scientific research has established curcumin's diverse pharmacological properties and confirmed its potency to act as an effective medicinal treatment for a wide range of disorders, such as cardiovascular diseases (CVDs), neurological disorders, cancer, gastrointestinal disorders, diabetes, osteoarthritis, respiratory diseases, and autoimmune diseases (Fig. 2−1) [1,48−51].

2.2.1 Curcumin and neurological diseases

Any diseases affecting the peripheral and central nervous systems are categorized as neurological disorders. Alzheimer's disease (AD), Parkinson's disease (PD), epilepsy, brain tumors, migraine, and nervous system traumatic disorders are among these disorders. Numerous investigations conducted on various nervous system cell types including neurons, microglia, and astrocytes have shown curcumin's neuroprotective properties [52−54]. Curcumin's ability to inhibit neurodegenerative disorders' progressions is especially due to its strong antioxidant and antiinflammatory activities [55].

AD, a progressive neurological disorder, causes the death of brain cells and brain shrinkage (atrophy). Environmental factors, especially, serious craniocerebral injuries, type 2 diabetes, CVDs, smoking, and food have a major role in the development of AD. Amyloid cascade hypothesis is the dominant theory of AD development, but at the same time, hyperphosphorylation of tau protein is important in the etiology of this disease [56]. Various in vitro and in vivo studies have demonstrated that curcumin can cross the blood−brain barrier (BBB) and bind Aβ peptides, therefore blocking peptide aggregation and fibril formation [57,58]. Even more, curcumin can enhance the phagocytosis of Aβ peptides, leading to the effective clearance of plaques and preventing peptide-induced cellular insults [57,59]. In mouse models of AD, curcumin can restore the distorted neuritic morphology surrounding Aβ plaques, reduce serum Aβ levels, and attenuate oxidative stress, inflammation, and microglia activation [60−62]. Moreover, tau protein processing and phosphorylation can be modulated by curcumin [63]. Neuroinflammation,

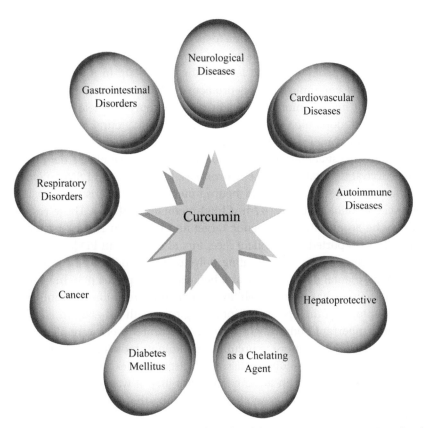

FIGURE 2–1 Schematic representation of curcumin's biological and therapeutic activities in various disorders.

another pathogenic factor in the etiology of AD, is characterized by strong cytokine production and widespread glial activation at the injury site [64]. Various studies have indicated that curcumin targets a number of inflammatory signaling pathways, like pattern recognition receptor pathways on the glial cells surface, arachidonic acid biosynthesis and metabolism, and nuclear transcription factors, thus preventing the AD progression [65–69]. In addition, oxidative stress is a key causative factor in the pathogenesis of AD [70]. Studies conducted in vitro and in vivo have shown curcumin's potent antioxidant properties [71–73]. Curcumin treatment improved learning and memory function by dramatically lowering the levels of malonyldialdehyde and superoxide anion in the hippocampus, according to a study utilizing a homocysteine-induced rat aging model [74,75].

PD, the second most common neurodegenerative disorder after AD, is characterized by the presence of α-synuclein-containing aggregates in the substantia nigra pars compacta (SNpc) and the loss of dopaminergic (DA) neurons [76,77]. Curcumin is proposed to be a useful nutraceutical and therapeutic agent for PD treatment. According to the in vitro and in vivo studies, curcumin is able to directly modulate the α-synuclein aggregation [78]. By inhibiting apoptosis, promoting microglial activation, and improving locomotion in rodents, oral and intravenous curcumin can modulate DA damage [79]. Interestingly, it is observed that curcumin suppresses the synthesis of the monoamine oxidase (MAO) enzyme, which would enhance the availability and DA level in the brain [80]. In a 6-hydroxydopamine (6-OHDA) model of PD, curcumin showed protective effects on the damaged hippocampus, leading to significant improvements in weight gain, memory and learning, neurobehavioral features, mental state, dopamine and norepinephrine levels, neural regeneration in the hippocampus tissue, and signaling pathways related to cell survival likes PI3K, BDNF, and TrkB [81]. Another study investigating the curcumin's neuroprotective effects demonstrated that it increases the survival of striatal tyrosine hydroxylase (TH) fibers and SNpc neurons, reduces aberrant turning behavior, and displays neuroprotective characteristics in part through an α7-nicotinic acetylcholine receptor (α7-nAChRs)-mediated pathway. These results show that α7-nAChR may be an effective therapeutic target and curcumin is the first naturally occurring substance to be reported to modulate receptors of nicotinic in PD [82].

Huntington's disease (HD), a devastating polyglutamine (poly Q) disorder, is marked by motor impairment, mental deterioration, and behavioral symptoms [83]. In vivo studies demonstrated that curcumin has a potent ability to reduce aggregation of Huntington's protein and improve symptoms of the disease by inhibiting cell death [84−86]. In HD flies, dysregulated lipid content, aberrant body weight, and carbohydrate levels were all successfully controlled by curcumin. Furthermore, curcumin treatment reduced high levels of reactive oxygen species (ROS) in adult adipose tissue of diseased flies and increased survival and locomotor activity in HD flies with advanced disease [87]. It was also found that curcumin's antiinflammatory and antioxidant capabilities are among the most effective ways to prevent and treat HD [88].

The therapeutic effects of curcumin have also been established for depression treatment, a neurological disorder [89]. Several preclinical studies in both rat and mice models showed that curcumin has therapeutic effects similar to conventional antidepressant drugs including fluoxetine and imipramine [90,91]. Furthermore, curcumin has been shown to boost the antiimmobility impact of subeffective doses of known antidepressants such as fluoxetine, bupropion, and venlafaxine [92]. Curcumin decreased anxiolytic behaviors and recovered tissue concentrations of serotonin (5-HT) in the amygdala, hippocampus, and striatum in rats subjected to single prolonged stress [93]. It was found that curcumin therapy altered the depression biomarkers and improved patients' moods [94,95]. In this regard, numerous studies have been carried out and have demonstrated that curcumin is an effective and safe compound for treating people with depressive disorder [96,97].

Amyotrophic lateral sclerosis (ALS) is a neurodegenerative disease characterized by the selective loss of motor neurons in the spinal cord, brainstem, and motor cortex [98]. It was demonstrated that GT863, a new curcumin derivative, dramatically delayed the progression of motor dysfunction in an ALS mouse model. Furthermore, GT863 significantly decreased highly aggregated superoxide dismutase 1 and preserved large neurons in the spinal cord of GT863-treated mice [99]. Curcumin lowered the aerobic metabolism, oxidative damage, and progression of ALS in a double-blind clinical study [100]. According to a study, curcumin-based drug delivery methods are advantageous in treating ALS, although it has been reported that curcumin has a poor solubility rate in water, poor oral bioavailability, and chemical instability in the condition of ALS disease [101,102].

In addition, Curcuma oil decreases the negative effect of ischemia by reducing oxidative and nitrosative stress. Ischemia induces mitochondrial membrane potential collapse, release of cytochrome c, altering the ratio of proteins Bax: Bcl-2, and then sequential activation of caspases causes apoptosis induction, which was strongly suppressed by Curcuma oil. So, there is evidence of Curcuma oil's strong efficacy in neuroprotection with a broad therapeutic window for decreasing ischemic brain injury [103].

2.2.2 Curcumin and cardiovascular diseases

CVD is the leading cause of death globally and one of the most serious health problems throughout the world [104]. Preclinical and clinical studies have demonstrated antiatherosclerotic, antihypercholesterolemic, and protective effects against cardiac ischemia and reperfusion of curcumin [105,106]. Curcumin suppresses inflammation, apoptosis, and oxidative stress, and has cardioprotective properties [107−109]. Furthermore, curcumin can beneficially influence the metabolism of lipoprotein because it plays a role in the increase of high-density lipoprotein (HDL) cholesterol and the decrease of triglycerides and low-density lipoprotein (LDL) cholesterol [110]. Due to its anti-CVD potential through improving the patients' lipid profiles, curcumin may be used alone or along with traditional cardiovascular medicines [111]. According to a study conducted on the curcumin efficiency on coronary artery disease patients' cardiovascular risk factors, it was found that serum levels of triglycerides, LDL, and very-low-density lipoprotein (VLDL) cholesterol were significantly reduced in people who consumed curcumin [112]. Moreover, another study has demonstrated that curcumin can be served to manage blood lipids as a safe and well-tolerable dietary supplement to statin therapy [113]. Numerous studies have also shown that curcumin possesses anticoagulant and coronary heart disease protective effects [37,114]. Cardiovascular protective properties of curcumin include lowering cholesterol and triglyceride levels, reducing LDL susceptibility to lipid peroxidation, and preventing platelet aggregation, which according to animal studies helps to fight atherosclerosis and also suppresses thromboxane formation [115−118]. Curcumin enhances plasma VLDL cholesterol, resulting in enhanced α-tocopherol levels and its mobilization from adipose tissue, which provide protection from oxidative stress occurring during the development of atherosclerosis. Nevertheless, the susceptibility of animals' fatty acids to oxidation was lower in the blood vessels [119]. Oral administration of curcumin has been reported to significantly decrease serum levels of total cholesterol and lipid peroxide while enhancing the levels of HDL cholesterol levels [120]. By increasing mitogen-activated protein kinases (MAPK), c-Jun N-terminal kinase (JNK), apoptosis signal-regulating kinase 1 (ASK1), and p38, curcumin may decrease chronic heart failure [121]. In a clinical study, curcuminoids supplementation was reported to significantly reduce serum triglyceride concentrations in healthy subjects [122]. Another clinical trial that used curcuminoids supplementation in obese subjects also revealed a similar outcome [123]. In addition, curcumin increased HDL and Apo A1 levels and reduced

LDL and Apo B levels in healthy subjects. Therefore, the low ratio of Apo B-Apo A was useful in preventing atherosclerosis [124]. Curcuminoids have been shown to considerably reduce myocardial infarction following coronary artery bypass grafting. In addition, malondialdehyde, **C-reactive protein** (CRP), and N-terminal pro-B-type natriuretic peptide levels were decreased in the curcumin-treated group [125].

2.2.3 Curcumin and gastrointestinal disorders

Curcumin effectiveness as a treatment for digestive problems has been confirmed by many studies. Preclinical studies have demonstrated its antiinflammatory activity, which potentially helps to protect the gastrointestinal tract. In addition, curcumin increases the secretion of bicarbonate, secretin, and gastrin, as well as pancreatic enzymes and gastric wall mucus [126]. It also inhibits intestinal spasms and ulcer formation induced by reserpine, indomethacin, pyloric ligation, stress, and alcohol, and improves the condition of indigestion patients [127]. In preclinical studies, curcumin was shown to successfully stop esophageal mucosal damage caused by acute reflux esophagitis [128,129]. Curcumin has been reported to protect rat's gastric mucosa from indomethacin-induced gastric ulcer, in part, by decreasing acid secretion parameters and increasing gastric mucosal barrier in addition to antiapoptotic and antioxidant effects [130]. Also, curcumin ameliorates gastric mucosal injury in rats with indomethacin-induced gastropathy through suppression of nuclear factor NF-κB and downregulation of intercellular adhesion molecule (ICAM)-1 and tumor necrosis factor (TNF)-α production [131]. It was found that curcumin is able to useful as a protective agent against the formation of gastric lesions in rats exposed to stress, partly due to the suppression of gastric secretory function [132]. In a randomized, double-blind, placebo-controlled trial, curcumin extract administration, Curcugen, to people with gastrointestinal complaints led to both a significant improvement in gastrointestinal symptoms and higher decreases in anxiety. Curcumin was well tolerated and had no serious side effects [133]. According to an animal study, oral administration of curcumin significantly reduced gastric inflammation caused by *Helicobacter pylori* (*H. pylori*) infection [134]. In a number of clinical trials, curcumin's addition to triple therapy regimens was reported to reduce oxidative stress and histological changes in chronic gastritis caused by *H. pylori* infection [135−137].

2.2.4 Curcumin and hepatoprotective

Various agents, including drugs, pollutants, alcohol, dietary components, and parasites, can induce acute and chronic liver damage, such as nonalcoholic liver disease, nonalcoholic steatohepatitis, liver fibrosis, and even cirrhosis. The hepatoprotective properties of curcumin have been widely researched [138−141]. In a study on animals, curcumin injection boosted the glutathione S-transferase (GST) and glutathione reductase (GR) levels and succinate dehydrogenase activity while reducing NADH oxidase levels. Curcumin improved the same type of hepatotoxicity by enhancing liver glutathione levels and lowering lipid peroxidase levels. It also reduced aspartate aminotransferase (AST) and alanine transaminase (ALT) activities [142]. Due to its ability to reduce the levels of AST, ALT, and alkaline phosphatase, increase levels of superoxide dismutase (SOD), GR, glutathione peroxidase (GPx),

GST, and catalase (CAT), decrease NO levels, and inhibit the generation of ROS, curcumin might be a promising treatment for the prevention of liver diseases related to oxidative stress [143]. Curcumin is able to reduce body mass index and waist circumference, improve ultrasonographic liver findings, and significantly decrease ALT and AST [144]. In addition, chronically iron-overloaded rats treated with curcumin had higher levels of endogenous antioxidants (SOD, CAT, glutathione, and ascorbic acid) in their livers [145]. Curcumin can decrease the effects of hepatoxicity induced by drugs in mice, including that caused by abusing paracetamol and streptozotocin [146,147]. Furthermore, in diabetic rats induced by streptozotocin, curcumin suppressed the levels of ASK1, IL-1β, TNF-α, and MAPK in hepatic tissue [148]. Curcumin administration leads to reduced lipogenesis, inflammation, and oxidative stress, as well as lowered HMGB1-NF-kB transmission and signaling and fibrosis in mice with nonalcoholic steatohepatitis caused by a high-fat diet and low dosage of streptozotocin [149]. Paracetamol-induced hepatotoxicity is also reduced by curcumin via suppressing transient receptor potential melastatin 2 (TRPM2) channels and NF-κB, reducing the dysfunction of mitochondria by removing free radicals, and enhancing the production of antioxidant enzymes [150,151]. Curcumin has been shown to reduce hepatocyte necroptosis, modulate pathways of antioxidant signaling, increase the expression of detoxifying genes through the ERK/p38-MAPK pathway, suppress the metabolism of pyruvate, dicarboxylate, and glyoxylate, and inhibit the ethanol-induced pathway in mice with alcoholic fatty liver [152–154]. It is reported that curcumin attenuates liver fibrosis and cirrhosis by suppressing inflammation, reducing oxidative stress, and inhibiting pathological angiogenesis [155–158]. In addition, curcumin protects against hepatitis caused by acetaminophen in mice with liver damage by reducing liver inflammation and oxidative stress, restoring hepatic glutathione levels, and improving liver injury [159]. In a clinical study, phospholipidated curcumin supplementation decreased the severity of nonalcoholic fatty liver disease and improved the ultrasonographic and biochemical indicators (such as liver transaminases and lipid profile) related to the progression of the disease. By suppressing oxidative stress, curcumin can prevent chronic bleomycin-induced hepatotoxicity and facilitate the recovery of hepatic injury [160].

2.2.5 Curcumin and respiratory disorders

Curcumin has a relaxant effect on the smooth muscles of trachea, which indicates its bronchodilatory impact in obstructive pulmonary disease patients [161]. In a respiratory disease animal model, curcumin displays a protective effect on immunomodulatory responses, airway responsiveness, lung pathological changes, and inflammatory cells and mediators [162,163]. The antiasthmatic effects of curcumin have been demonstrated in both in vivo and in vitro studies. In a guinea pig model of the ovalbumin (OVA)-induced asthma paradigm, curcumin therapy during OVA sensitization significantly reduced bronchial constriction and hyperreactivity [164]. Curcumin has also been reported to be effective in treating pneumonia and lung injury (ALI) or fatal acute respiratory distress syndrome (ARDS) caused by coronavirus infection in humans [165–168]. Patients with COVID-19 may require mechanical ventilation in more severe conditions [169]. In a preclinical study, curcumin has been found to repair ventilator-induced lung injury, reducing lung damage and edema. It was discovered that this effect was mediated by NF-κB suppression and redox balance restoration due to the recovery of total antioxidant capacity [170]. In another study for COVID-19, subjects with severe disease displayed a higher frequency of M1-type macrophages compared to patients with moderate infection or healthy control participants who displayed a higher frequency of M2-type macrophages [171]. In septic lungs, curcumin is able to increase M2 macrophages and reduce M1 macrophages, suggesting its potential impact on macrophage polarization [172].

2.2.6 Curcumin and cancer

One of the leading causes of death worldwide is cancer. The most common forms of cancer treatment are surgery, radiation therapy, and chemotherapy (cancer drugs) [173]. An active field of research is the use of natural products in cancer treatment, and curcumin is one of the most investigated natural compounds because of its several pharmacological functions and health advantages [166,174−177]. Curcumin can inhibit carcinogenesis by affecting two processes: cancer cell growth and angiogenesis. In addition, it promotes cancer cell apoptosis and suppresses cancer cell metastasis [177]. It is well recognized that angiogenesis plays a crucial role in cancer. Cancer cells actually cause the formation of new blood vessels via stimulating proangiogenic factors [178,179]. It has been demonstrated that curcumin possesses antiangiogenic effect via suppression of angiogenic factor stimulators like basic fibroblast growth factor and vascular endothelial growth factor (VEGF). Indeed, curcumin has shown the ability to downregulate the expression of VEGF by regulating NF-κB and AP-1, thereby reducing the expression of IL-8 [180]. Curcumin can suppress angiogenesis via modulation of vascular endothelial growth factor (VEGF) and PI3K/Akt signaling pathway [181]. Furthermore, it has been demonstrated that curcumin can promote the expression of tissue inhibitor of metalloproteinase-1 and inhibit the expression of MMP-2 and MMP-9, ensuring the stability and coherence of the extracellular matrix [180]. Also, curcumin is able to promote apoptosis via a p53-mediated mechanism in cancer cells. p53, one of the most critical tumor suppressor proteins, affects DNA damage and cell proliferation apoptosis [182]. Numerous studies have shown that cancer-related miRNAs interact with p53 [183,184]. It has also been reported that the proapoptotic impacts of curcumin in nonsmall cell lung cancer are dependent on miR-192-5p and miR-215, which activate p53 [184]. In other studies, it was shown that curcumin-induced apoptosis in HT-29 colon cancer cells is independent of p53 [185]. Curcumin's anticancer properties have been shown in various leukemia types when used alone and in combination with chemotherapy drugs [186]. Curcumin has potential uses to treat acute myeloid leukemia due to its ability to induce cell death via apoptosis pathway [187]. In mice with multidrug-resistant ovarian tumors, curcumin alone and in combination with docetaxel increased tumor cell apoptosis and decreased tumor cell proliferation and microvessel density [188]. In another study on rats, it was found that dietary curcumin and cisplatin could modulate fibrosarcoma tumor marker indices toward normal controls. Treatment with radiation therapy plus curcumin increased tumor cell death and decreased radioresistance, as shown by the substantial suppression of radiation-induced extracellular signal-regulated kinase (ERK). ERK and NF-κB expression [189]. Curcumin has been demonstrated to improve the overall health of people with colorectal cancer by promoting the p53 expression in tumor cells [190]. In Patients with familial adenomatous polyposis, it was found that curcumin decreases the size and number of the polyps with no substantial toxicity [191]. Also, curcumin was found to be safe and well tolerated in people with advanced pancreatic cancer, according to a phase II clinical investigation [192]. The combination treatment of curcumin with a standard dose of docetaxel has been reported to be safe and effective for the treatment of patients with advanced breast cancer [193]. A phase I/II trial in multiple myeloma patients indicated that the oral administration of curcumin together with bioperine is more effective than bioperine alone, and no curcumin-related toxicity was reported [194]. Curcumin combined with folinic acid/5-fluorouracil/oxaliplatin chemotherapy (FOLFOX) chemotherapy was shown to be a safe and tolerable treatment with the potential to help patients with metastatic colorectal cancer in a randomized controlled trial [195].

2.2.7 Curcumin and diabetes mellitus

Diabetes mellitus (DM), including type 1 (T1DM) and type 2 (T2DM), is a chronic metabolic disorder characterized by hyperglycemia due to defects in insulin secretion, insulin action, or both. It is related to long-term damage, dysfunction, and failure of different organs, including the eyes, kidneys, heart, blood vessels, and nerves [196]. Strong evidence for curcumin's effectiveness against T2DM and its complications has been provided by a number of in vivo studies [197,198]. The range of curcumin's positive effects in DM has been attributed to its ability to interact with numerous pathways and key molecules related to the pathophysiology of this disease [199–206]. An animal study showed that curcumin activates PPARγ (peroxisome proliferator-activated receptor-γ), which is a similar mechanism of action to the antidiabetic drug thiazolidinedione [207]. Also, curcumin's safety and tolerability have also been proven in a number of human patients, even at high oral doses (up to 12 g/day) [208–210]. Curcumin supplementation significantly decreased fasting glycemia, insulin resistance, and hemoglobin A1C (HbA1c) in overweight/obese T2DM patients, as well as lipoprotein lipase activity, total free fatty acids (FFAs), and serum triglyceride levels. Curcumin's ability to lower blood glucose is partially due to a reduction in serum FFA level, which may be caused by enhancing utilization and oxidation of fatty acids in tissues [208]. It has been reported that supplementing with curcumin capsules improved the antioxidant status in T2DM patients, comparable to the effects of atorvastatin [211]. Also, in T2DM patients treated with glyburide, curcumin reduced hyperglycemia and hyperlipidemia. Particularly, the triglycerides, LDL, and VLDL were markedly reduced and the HDL level increased [212]. According to the meta-analysis results, curcumin has positive effects in Asian prediabetes and T2DM patients [213].

2.2.8 Curcumin and autoimmune diseases

Autoimmune disease is one of the emerging noncommunicable disorders that occurs when the body's immune system attacks and destroys healthy body tissue by mistake [214,215]. Numerous studies on curcumin's effects on different autoimmune diseases, such as rheumatoid arthritis (RA), systemic lupus erythematosus (SLE), psoriasis, multiple sclerosis (Ms), and UC patients, have been carried out in recent years [216−218].

RA, a progressive chronic autoimmune and inflammatory disease, affects patients' ability to function and quality of life by potentially destroying their musculoskeletal system [219,220]. In RA rats, curcumin reduced the degree of joint swelling, stopped the progression of joint histopathology, and downregulated cytokines levels [221]. In another preclinical study, curcumin was demonstrated to be as effective as rapamycin at reducing ankle and joint redness and edema by targeting the mTOR (mammalian target of rapamycin) pathway as well as lowering the expression of proinflammatory cytokines IL-1β, TNF-α, MMP-1, and MMP-3 in serum and synovium [222]. In a preliminary intervention trial, patients with RA following curcumin administration showed improvements in morning joint swelling, stiffness, and walking time that were comparable to improvements after taking phenylbutazone (nonsteroidal antiinflammatory drug [NSAID]) medication [223]. Curcumin was determined to be efficient, safe, and unrelated to any side effects in individuals with active RA, in a randomized, single-blinded pilot study [224].

SLE is a chronic inflammatory autoimmune disease, affecting multiple organs and is characterized by the production of autoantibodies and the deposition of immune complexes [225]. One of the most severe manifestations of SLE is lupus nephritis that has a direct impact on patients' morbidity and death [226]. In an animal study, it has been demonstrated that curcumin oral administration can reduce kidney damage, kidney function deterioration, and autoimmune activity [227]. In lupus-prone mice, curcumin has been demonstrated to drastically decrease proteinuria and kidney inflammation. In addition, it reduced NLRP3 inflammasome activity, anti-dsDNA serum levels, and spleen size [228]. In another study, curcumin decreased proteinuria and serum levels of IgG1, IgG2a, and IgG anti-dsDNA antibodies. It also reduced the deposition of the IgG immune complex in the glomeruli and kidney inflammation [229]. Curcumin was found to dramatically lower hematuria, proteinuria, and systolic blood pressure in a small randomized and placebo-controlled trial of patients with lupus nephritis; no adverse effects of curcumin supplementation were seen [230].

Psoriasis, a chronic inflammatory hereditary skin disease, causes a rash with itchy, scaly patches, most frequently on the scalp, elbows, trunk, and knees [231]. In a mice model, curcumin improved all psoriasis indexes such as weight, redness, thickness, and lymph node weight. In addition, it decreased inflammatory factors' levels such as IL-2, IL-12, IL-22, IL-23, TNF-α, and interferon-γ (IFN-γ) [232]. Curcumin was found to be safe and well tolerated by psoriasis patients in a clinical investigation [233].

Ms, a chronic autoimmune disease, affects the central nervous system characterized by neuronal loss, gliosis, demyelination, and inflammation [234]. In mice with the experimental autoimmune encephalitis (EAE) model of Ms, curcumin has been demonstrated significantly ameliorate corpus callosum demyelination, neurobehavioral impairments, and weight loss. These outcomes were associated with enhanced activity of the antioxidant enzymes and mRNA levels suppression of proinflammatory cytokines TNF-α, IFN-γ, IL-6, and IL-17 in brain tissues [235]. In another study, curcumin treatment significantly modulated CD3 and CD4 lymphocytes' expression in the spinal cord and reduced neurological symptomatology in EAE mice.

Furthermore, in cuprizone-treated mice, curcumin improved behavioral impairments by increasing memory, motor coordination, and locomotor activity as well as restored myelination [236]. It has been reported that curcumin treatment in rats led to a reduction in the severity of EAE due to suppression of Th17 cell differentiation and proliferation caused by downregulating of IL-6, IL-21, RORγt signaling, and STAT3 phosphorylation [237].

Inflammatory bowel disease (IBD), a chronic autoimmune disease, is divided into UC and Crohn's disease, characterized by fatigue, changes in bowel habits, bloating, and abdominal pain [238]. In colitis model mice, curcumin reduced disease activity index (DAI) and histopathological score by controlling cytokine networks and preventing excessive autophagy [239]. It has been reported that curcumin with soybean oligosaccharides effectively decreased IL-8 and TNF-α expression. In addition, it significantly reduced tissue damage and colonic mucosal inflammation [240]. Curcumin has been shown to suppress the STAT3 pathway in experimental colitis, which has beneficial effects on the disease [241]. For IBD patients who had previously received standard treatment for Crohn's disease or UC, a pilot clinical study was conducted to determine the curcumin's therapeutic effects [242]. A randomized, double-blind, multicenter trial has shown that curcumin considerably lowers the morbidity related to UC by improving the endoscopic index (EI) and colitis activity index (CAI) in patients [243]. In another trial, patients with mild-to-moderate active UC responded better to the addition of curcumin to mesalamine medication than to placebo plus mesalamine, and there were no obvious side effects [244].

2.2.9 Curcumin as a chelating agent

Curcumin is able to chelate metals due to the β-diketone moiety in its structure [245]. The metal ions are essential to the body for a number of vital activities and their plasma concentration must stay within the physiological ranges to prevent adverse effects from excess and deficiency. Chelation therapy is utilized when it is necessary to decrease the body's levels of metal or increase them in a deficiency case [246−248]. By binding potentially toxic metals, neutralizing them, and removing them from the body, curcumin can also serve as a scavenge [246,249]. The chelator can also selectively deliver the metal to the cell nucleus, where it can bind to DNA and prevent cancer cell proliferation [250,251].

2.3 Conclusion

Curcumin, turmeric's main active ingredient, has a rich history of usage in cooking, textile dyeing, and cosmetics. In addition, it has been utilized in traditional Ayurvedic and Chinese medicine for a variety of medicinal preparations. Curcumin has drawn much attention in recent years because of its wide biological and pharmacological functions. Curcumin surprisingly is effective for treating, controlling, and preventing a variety of diseases like cancer, CVDs, respiratory diseases, neurological disorders, autoimmune diseases, and COVID-19 via the activation or inhibition of numerous signaling pathways, according to modern scientific studies. Also, numerous studies have shown that curcumin is safe, well tolerated, and neither toxic nor mutagenic.

Curcumin has become an attractive topic in pharmaceutical research due to its safety, low cost, and availability. However, despite the abundance of pharmacological, biological, and toxicological data on curcumin, epidemiological data and large well-designed clinical studies are required to support its effectiveness in the prevention and/or treatment of human illnesses.

Conflict of interests

The authors have no conflicts of interest to declare.

References

[1] Kunnumakkara AB, et al. Curcumin, the golden nutraceutical: multitargeting for multiple chronic diseases. British Journal of Pharmacology 2017;174(11):1325−48.

[2] Vogel A, Pelletier J. Examen chimique de la racine de Curcuma. Journal of Pharmaceutical Sciences 1815;1:289−300.

[3] Gera M, et al. Nanoformulations of curcumin: an emerging paradigm for improved remedial application. Oncotarget 2017;8(39):66680.

[4] Chainani-Wu N. Safety and anti-inflammatory activity of curcumin: a component of tumeric (Curcuma longa). The Journal of Alternative & Complementary Medicine 2003;9(1):161−8.

[5] Sharifi-Rad J, et al. Turmeric and its major compound curcumin on health: bioactive effects and safety profiles for food, pharmaceutical, biotechnological and medicinal applications. Frontiers in Pharmacology 2020;11:01021.

[6] Fuloria S, et al. A comprehensive review on the therapeutic potential of Curcuma longa Linn. in relation to its major active constituent curcumin. Frontiers in Pharmacology 2022;13:820806.

[7] Goud VK, Polasa K, Krishnaswamy K. Effect of turmeric on xenobiotic metabolising enzymes. Plant Foods for Human Nutrition (Dordrecht, Netherlands) 1993;44(1):87−92.

[8] Kwiecien S, et al. Curcumin: a potent protectant against esophageal and gastric disorders. International Journal of Molecular Sciences 2019;20(6).

[9] Hatcher H, et al. Curcumin: from ancient medicine to current clinical trials. Cellular and Molecular Life Sciences: CMLS 2008;65(11):1631−52.

[10] Marchiani A, et al. Curcumin and curcumin-like molecules: from spice to drugs. Current Medicinal Chemistry 2014;21(2):204−22.

[11] Hewlings SJ, Kalman DS. Curcumin: a review of its effects on human health. Foods 2017;6(10).

[12] Moghadamtousi SZ, et al. A review on antibacterial, antiviral, and antifungal activity of curcumin. BioMed Research International 2014;2014:186864.

[13] Praditya D, et al. Anti-infective properties of the golden spice curcumin. Frontiers in Microbiology 2019;10:912.

[14] Rai M, et al. Curcumin and curcumin-loaded nanoparticles: antipathogenic and antiparasitic activities. Expert Review of Anti-Infective Therapy 2020;18(4):367−79.

[15] Di Mario F, et al. A curcumin-based 1-week triple therapy for eradication of Helicobacter pylori infection: something to learn from failure? Helicobacter 2007;12(3):238−43.

[16] Adhvaryu MR, Reddy NM, Vakharia BC. Prevention of hepatotoxicity due to anti tuberculosis treatment: a novel integrative approach. World Journal of Gastroenterology: WJG 2008;14(30):4753.

[17] Anwar F, et al. Moringa oleifera: a food plant with multiple medicinal uses. Phytotherapy Research: An International Journal Devoted to Pharmacological and Toxicological Evaluation of Natural Product Derivatives 2007;21(1):17−25.

[18] Yanpanitch O-u, et al. Treatment of β-thalassemia/hemoglobin E with antioxidant cocktails results in decreased oxidative stress, increased hemoglobin concentration, and improvement of the hypercoagulable state. Oxidative Medicine and Cellular Longevity 2015;2015.

[19] Salehi B, et al. Cucurbits plants: a key emphasis to its pharmacological potential. Molecules (Basel, Switzerland) 2019;24(10):1854.

[20] Ghandadi M, Sahebkar A. Curcumin: an effective inhibitor of interleukin-6. Current Pharmaceutical Design 2017;23(6):921−31.

[21] Sahebkar A, et al. Effect of curcuminoids on oxidative stress: a systematic review and meta-analysis of randomized controlled trials. Journal of Functional Foods 2015;18:898−909.

[22] Abdollahi E, et al. Therapeutic effects of curcumin in inflammatory and immune-mediated diseases: A nature-made jack-of-all-trades? Journal of Cellular Physiology 2018;233(2):830−48.

[23] Tabeshpour J, Hashemzaei M, Sahebkar A. The regulatory role of curcumin on platelet functions. Journal of Cellular Biochemistry 2018;119(11):8713−22.

[24] Momtazi AA, et al. Curcumin as a MicroRNA regulator in cancer: a review. Reviews of Physiology, Biochemistry and Pharmacology 2016;171:1−38.

[25] Cicero AFG, Sahebkar A, Fogacci F, Bove M, Giovannini M, & Borghi C. (2020). Effects of phytosomal curcumin on anthropometric parameters, insulin resistance, cortisolemia and non-alcoholic fatty liver disease indices: a double-blind, placebo-controlled clinical trial. *European journal of nutrition*, *59*(2), 477−483. Available from https://doi.org/10.1007/s00394-019-01916-7.

[26] Panahi Y, Fazlolahzadeh O, Atkin SL, Majeed M, Butler AE, Johnston TP, & Sahebkar A. (2019). Evidence of curcumin and curcumin analogue effects in skin diseases: A narrative review. *Journal of cellular physiology*, *234*(2), 1165−1178. Available from https://doi.org/10.1002/jcp.27096.

[27] Mirzaei H, et al. Curcumin: a new candidate for melanoma therapy? International Journal of Cancer 2016;139(8):1683−95.

[28] Mohammadi A, Blesso CN, Barreto GE, Banach M, Majeed M, & Sahebkar A. (2019). Macrophage plasticity, polarization and function in response to curcumin, a diet-derived polyphenol, as an immunomodulatory agent. *The Journal of nutritional biochemistry*, *66*, 1−16. Available from https://doi.org/10.1016/j.jnutbio.2018.12.005.

[29] Panahi Y, et al. Effects of curcuminoids plus piperine on glycemic, hepatic and inflammatory biomarkers in patients with type 2 diabetes mellitus: a randomized double-blind placebo-controlled trial. Drug Research 2018;68(07):403−9.

[30] Lelli D, et al. Curcumin use in pulmonary diseases: state of the art and future perspectives. Pharmacological Research 2017;115:133−48.

[31] Panahi Y, et al. Investigation of the efficacy of adjunctive therapy with bioavailability-boosted curcuminoids in major depressive disorder. Phytotherapy Research 2015;29(1):17−21.

[32] Masoodi M, et al. The efficacy of curcuminoids in improvement of ulcerative colitis symptoms and patients' self-reported well-being: a randomized double-blind controlled trial. Journal of Cellular Biochemistry 2018;119(11):9552−9.

[33] Gupta SC, Patchva S, Aggarwal BB. Therapeutic roles of curcumin: lessons learned from clinical trials. The AAPS Journal 2013;15(1):195−218.

[34] Ganji A, et al. Protective effects of curcumin against lipopolysaccharide-induced toxicity. Current Medicinal Chemistry 2021;28(33):6915−30.

[35] Hassanzadeh S, et al. Curcumin: an inflammasome silencer. Pharmacological Research 2020;159.

[36] Hosseini SA, et al. Pulmonary fibrosis: therapeutic and mechanistic insights into the role of phytochemicals. Biofactors (Oxford, England) 2021;47(3):250–69.

[37] Keihanian F, et al. Curcumin, hemostasis, thrombosis, and coagulation. Journal of Cellular Physiology 2018;233(6):4497–511.

[38] Khayatan D, et al. Protective effects of curcumin against traumatic brain injury. Biomedicine and Pharmacotherapy 2022;154.

[39] Mokhtari-Zaer A, et al. The protective role of curcumin in myocardial ischemia–reperfusion injury. Journal of Cellular Physiology 2018;234(1):214–22.

[40] Rahimi K, et al. Curcumin: a dietary phytochemical for targeting the phenotype and function of dendritic cells. Current Medicinal Chemistry 2021;28(8):1549–64.

[41] Sahebkar A. Molecular mechanisms for curcumin benefits against ischemic injury. Fertility and Sterility 2010;94(5):e75–6.

[42] Soltani S, et al. Effects of phytochemicals on macrophage cholesterol efflux capacity: impact on atherosclerosis. Phytotherapy Research 2021;35(6):2854–78.

[43] Nelson KM, et al. The essential medicinal chemistry of curcumin. Journal of Medicinal Chemistry 2017;60(5):1620–37.

[44] Moghaddam NSA, et al. Hormetic effects of curcumin: what is the evidence? Journal of Cellular Physiology 2019;234(7):10060–71.

[45] Soleimani V, Sahebkar A, Hosseinzadeh H. Turmeric (Curcuma longa) and its major constituent (curcumin) as nontoxic and safe substances: review. Phytotherapy Research: PTR 2018;32(6):985–95.

[46] Prasad S, et al. Curcumin, a component of golden spice: from bedside to bench and back. Biotechnology Advances 2014;32(6):1053–64.

[47] Jyotirmayee B, Mahalik G. A review on selected pharmacological activities of Curcuma longa L. International Journal of Food Properties 2022;25(1):1377–98.

[48] Grynkiewicz G, Ślifirski P. Curcumin and curcuminoids in quest for medicinal status. Acta Biochimica Polonica 2012;59(2):201–12.

[49] Gupta SC, et al. Discovery of curcumin, a component of golden spice, and its miraculous biological activities. Clinical and Experimental Pharmacology & Physiology 2012;39(3):283–99.

[50] Heidari Z, et al. Curcumin supplementation in pediatric patients: a systematic review of current clinical evidence. Phytotherapy Research 2022;36(4):1442–58.

[51] Rahimnia AR, et al. Impact of supplementation with curcuminoids on systemic inflammation in patients with knee osteoarthritis: findings from a randomized double-blind placebo-controlled trial. Drug Research 2014;65(10):521–5.

[52] Karlstetter M, et al. Curcumin is a potent modulator of microglial gene expression and migration. Journal of Neuroinflammation 2011;8(1):1–12.

[53] Lavoie S, et al. Curcumin, quercetin, and tBHQ modulate glutathione levels in astrocytes and neurons: importance of the glutamate cysteine ligase modifier subunit. Journal of Neurochemistry 2009;108(6):1410–22.

[54] Askarizadeh A, et al. Neuroprotection by curcumin: a review on brain delivery strategies. International Journal of Pharmaceutics 2020;585:119476.

[55] Monroy A, Lithgow GJ, Alavez S. Curcumin and neurodegenerative diseases. Biofactors (Oxford, England) 2013;39(1):122–32.

[56] Tęcza P, Żylińska L. Preventive effects of curcumin and resveratrol in Alzheimer's disease. Przeglad Lekarski 2016;73(5):320–3.

[57] Yang F, et al. Curcumin inhibits formation of amyloid beta oligomers and fibrils, binds plaques, and reduces amyloid in vivo. The Journal of Biological Chemistry 2005;280(7):5892–901.

[58] Ono K, et al. Curcumin has potent anti-amyloidogenic effects for Alzheimer's beta-amyloid fibrils in vitro. Journal of Neuroscience Research 2004;75(6):742–50.

[59] Kim H, et al. Effects of naturally occurring compounds on fibril formation and oxidative stress of beta-amyloid. Journal of Agricultural and Food Chemistry 2005;53(22):8537–41.

[60] Garcia-Alloza M, et al. Curcumin labels amyloid pathology in vivo, disrupts existing plaques, and partially restores distorted neurites in an Alzheimer mouse model. Journal of Neurochemistry 2007;102 (4):1095–104.

[61] Wang YJ, et al. Consumption of grape seed extract prevents amyloid-beta deposition and attenuates inflammation in brain of an Alzheimer's disease mouse. Neurotoxicity Research 2009;15(1):3–14.

[62] Lim GP, et al. The curry spice curcumin reduces oxidative damage and amyloid pathology in an Alzheimer transgenic mouse. The Journal of Neuroscience 2001;21(21):8370–7.

[63] Tang M, Taghibiglou C. The mechanisms of action of curcumin in Alzheimer's disease. Journal of Alzheimer's Disease: JAD 2017;58(4):1003–16.

[64] Heneka MT, et al. Neuroinflammation in Alzheimer's disease. Lancet Neurology 2015;14(4):388–405.

[65] He Y, et al. Curcumin, inflammation, and chronic diseases: how are they linked? Molecules (Basel, Switzerland) 2015;20(5):9183–213.

[66] Ahmad W, et al. Effects of novel diarylpentanoid analogues of curcumin on secretory phospholipase A2, cyclooxygenases, lipo-oxygenase, and microsomal prostaglandin E synthase-1. Chemical Biology & Drug Design 2014;83(6):670–81.

[67] Innamorato NG, et al. The transcription factor Nrf2 is a therapeutic target against brain inflammation. Journal of Immunology 2008;181(1):680–9.

[68] Wang H-M, et al. PPAR-γ agonist curcumin reduces the amyloid-β-stimulated inflammatory responses in primary astrocytes. Journal of Alzheimer's Disease: JAD 2010;20(4):1189–99.

[69] Wang Y, et al. Curcumin as a potential treatment for Alzheimer's disease: a study of the effects of curcumin on hippocampal expression of glial fibrillary acidic protein. The American Journal of Chinese Medicine 2013;41(01):59–70.

[70] Nunomura A, et al. Involvement of oxidative stress in Alzheimer disease. Journal of Neuropathology and Experimental Neurology 2006;65(7):631–41.

[71] Strimpakos AS, Sharma RAJA, Signaling R. Curcumin: preventive and therapeutic properties in laboratory studies and clinical trials. Antioxidants & Redox Signaling 2008;10(3):511–46.

[72] El-Demerdash FM, et al. Ameliorating effect of curcumin on sodium arsenite-induced oxidative damage and lipid peroxidation in different rat organs. Food and Chemical Toxicology: an International Journal Published for the British Industrial Biological Research Association 2009;47(1):249–54.

[73] Dkhar P, Sharma RJIJODN. Effect of dimethylsulphoxide and curcumin on protein carbonyls and reactive oxygen species of cerebral hemispheres of mice as a function of age. International Journal of Developmental Neuroscience: the Official Journal of the International Society for Developmental Neuroscience 2010;28(5):351–7.

[74] Ataie A, et al. Neuroprotective effects of the polyphenolic antioxidant agent, curcumin, against homocysteine-induced cognitive impairment and oxidative stress in the rat. Pharmacology, Biochemistry, and Behavior 2010;96(4):378–85.

[75] Fux R, et al. Effect of acute hyperhomocysteinemia on methylation potential of erythrocytes and on DNA methylation of lymphocytes in healthy male volunteers. American Journal of Physiology. Renal Physiology 2005;289(4):F786–92.

[76] Mhyre TR, et al. Parkinson's disease. Sub-cellular Biochemistry 2012;65:389–455.

[77] Alexander GE. Biology of Parkinson's disease: pathogenesis and pathophysiology of a multisystem neurodegenerative disorder. Dialogues in Clinical Neuroscience 2004;6(3):259–80.

[78] Jangra A, et al. Piperine augments the protective effect of curcumin against lipopolysaccharide-induced neurobehavioral and neurochemical deficits in mice. Inflammation 2016;39(3):1025−38.

[79] Tripanichkul W, Jaroensuppaperch E-o. Curcumin protects nigrostriatal dopaminergic neurons and reduces glial activation in 6-hydroxydopamine hemiparkinsonian mice model. International Journal of Neuroscience 2012;122(5):263−70.

[80] Khatri DK, Juvekar AR. Kinetics of inhibition of monoamine oxidase using curcumin and ellagic acid. Pharmacogn Mag 2016;12(Suppl 2):S116−20.

[81] Yang J, et al. Neuroprotective effect of curcumin on hippocampal injury in 6-OHDA-induced Parkinson's disease rat. Pathology, Research and Practice 2014;210(6):357−62.

[82] El Nebrisi E, et al. Neuroprotective effect of curcumin on the nigrostriatal pathway in a 6-hydroxydopmine-induced rat model of Parkinson's disease is mediated by α7-nicotinic receptors. International Journal of Molecular Sciences 2020;21(19).

[83] Fatoba O, et al. Immunotherapies in Huntington's disease and α-synucleinopathies. Frontiers in Immunology 2020;11:337.

[84] Hickey MA, et al. Improvement of neuropathology and transcriptional deficits in CAG 140 knock-in mice supports a beneficial effect of dietary curcumin in Huntington's disease. Molecular Neurodegeneration 2012;7:12.

[85] Chongtham A, Agrawal N. Curcumin modulates cell death and is protective in Huntington's disease model. Scientific Reports 2016;6:18736.

[86] Verma M, et al. Curcumin prevents formation of polyglutamine aggregates by inhibiting Vps36, a component of the ESCRT-II complex. PLoS One 2012;.

[87] Aditi K, et al. Management of altered metabolic activity in drosophila model of Huntington's disease by curcumin. Experimental Biology and Medicine (Maywood) 2022;247(2):152−64.

[88] Elifani F, et al. L9 Curcumin: a natural compound to counteract the pathology of huntington's disease? BMJ Publishing Group Ltd; 2016.

[89] Zhang Y, et al. Curcumin in antidepressant treatments: an overview of potential mechanisms, pre-clinical/clinical trials and ongoing challenges. Basic & Clinical Pharmacology & Toxicology 2020;127(4):243−53.

[90] Mohammed HS, et al. Electrocortical and biochemical evaluation of antidepressant efficacy of formulated nanocurcumin. Applied Biochemistry and Biotechnology 2019;187(3):1096−112.

[91] Qi X-J, et al. Anti-depressant effect of curcumin-loaded guanidine-chitosan thermo-sensitive hydrogel by nasal delivery. Pharmaceutical Development and Technology 2020;25(3):316−25.

[92] Kulkarni SK, Bhutani MK, Bishnoi MJP. Antidepressant activity of curcumin: involvement of serotonin and dopamine system. Psychopharmacology 2008;201(3):435−42.

[93] Lee B, Lee HJE-BC, Medicine A. Systemic administration of curcumin affect anxiety-related behaviors in a rat model of posttraumatic stress disorder via activation of serotonergic systems. Evidence-Based Complementary and Alternative Medicine: eCAM 2018;2018.

[94] Lopresti AL, et al. Curcumin for the treatment of major depression: a randomised, double-blind, placebo controlled study. Journal of Affective Disorders 2014;167:368−75.

[95] Lopresti AL, et al. Curcumin and major depression: a randomised, double-blind, placebo-controlled trial investigating the potential of peripheral biomarkers to predict treatment response and antidepressant mechanisms of change. European Neuropsychopharmacology: the Journal of the European College of Neuropsychopharmacology 2015;25(1):38−50.

[96] Sanmukhani J, et al. Efficacy and safety of curcumin in major depressive disorder: a randomized controlled trial. Phytotherapy Research: PTR 2014;28(4):579−85.

...

[97] Ng QX, et al. Clinical use of curcumin in depression: a meta-analysis. Journal of the American Medical Directors Association 2017;18(6):503−8.

[98] Van den Bosch L. The causes and mechanism of selective motor neuron death in amyotrophic lateral sclerosis. Verhandelingen - Koninklijke Academie Voor Geneeskunde van Belgie 2006;68(4):249−69.

[99] Kato H, et al. Therapeutic effect of a novel curcumin derivative GT863 on a mouse model of amyotrophic lateral sclerosis. Amyotrophic Lateral Sclerosis and Frontotemporal Degeneration 2021;23:1−7.

[100] Chico L, et al. Amyotrophic lateral sclerosis and oxidative stress: a double-blind therapeutic trial after curcumin supplementation. CNS & Neurological Disorders Drug Targets 2018;17(10):767−79.

[101] Tripodo G, et al. Mesenchymal stromal cells loading curcumin-INVITE-micelles: a drug delivery system for neurodegenerative diseases. Colloids and Surfaces. B, Biointerfaces 2015;125:300−8.

[102] Rakotoarisoa M, Angelova A. Amphiphilic nanocarrier systems for curcumin delivery in neurodegenerative disorders. Medicines (Basel) 2018;5(4).

[103] Dohare P, et al. Neuroprotective efficacy and therapeutic window of curcuma oil: in rat embolic stroke model. BMC Complementary and Alternative Medicine 2008;8:55.

[104] Amini M, Zayeri F, Salehi M. Trend analysis of cardiovascular disease mortality, incidence, and mortality-to-incidence ratio: results from global burden of disease study 2017. BMC Public Health 2021;21(1):401.

[105] Gao S, et al. Curcumin ameliorates atherosclerosis in apolipoprotein E deficient asthmatic mice by regulating the balance of Th2/Treg cells. Phytomedicine: International Journal of Phytotherapy and Phytopharmacology 2019;52:129−35.

[106] Wang R, et al. Curcumin attenuates IR-induced myocardial injury by activating SIRT3. European Review for Medical and Pharmacological Sciences 2018;22(4):1150−60.

[107] Cox FF, et al. Protective effects of curcumin in cardiovascular diseases-impact on oxidative stress and mitochondria. Cells 2022;11(3).

[108] Ahmadabady S, et al. A protective effect of curcumin on cardiovascular oxidative stress indicators in systemic inflammation induced by lipopolysaccharide in rats. Biochem Biophys Rep 2021;25:100908.

[109] Pourbagher-Shahri AM, et al. Curcumin and cardiovascular diseases: focus on cellular targets and cascades. Biomedicine & Pharmacotherapy 2021;136:111214.

[110] Sahebkar A. Low-density lipoprotein is a potential target for curcumin: novel mechanistic insights. Basic & Clinical Pharmacology & Toxicology 2014;114(6):437−8.

[111] Qin S, et al. Efficacy and safety of turmeric and curcumin in lowering blood lipid levels in patients with cardiovascular risk factors: a meta-analysis of randomized controlled trials. Nutrition Journal 2017;16(1):68.

[112] Mirzabeigi P, et al. The effect of curcumin on some of traditional and non-traditional cardiovascular risk factors: a pilot randomized, double-blind, placebo-controlled trial. Iranian Journal of Pharmaceutical Research 2015;14(2):479−86.

[113] Panahi Y, et al. Curcumin as a potential candidate for treating hyperlipidemia: a review of cellular and metabolic mechanisms. Journal of Cellular Physiology 2018;233(1):141−52.

[114] Li H, et al. Curcumin, the golden spice in treating cardiovascular diseases. Biotechnology Advances 2020;38:107343.

[115] Ramírez-Tortosa MC, et al. Oral administration of a turmeric extract inhibits LDL oxidation and has hypocholesterolemic effects in rabbits with experimental atherosclerosis. Atherosclerosis 1999;147(2):371−8.

[116] Chen HW, Huang HC. Effect of curcumin on cell cycle progression and apoptosis in vascular smooth muscle cells. British Journal of Pharmacology 1998;124(6):1029−40.

[117] Srivastava KC, Bordia A, Verma SK. Curcumin, a major component of food spice turmeric (Curcuma longa) inhibits aggregation and alters eicosanoid metabolism in human blood platelets. Prostaglandins, Leukotrienes, and Essential Fatty Acids 1995;52(4):223−7.

[118] Shah BH, et al. Inhibitory effect of curcumin, a food spice from turmeric, on platelet-activating factor- and arachidonic acid-mediated platelet aggregation through inhibition of thromboxane formation and Ca2 + signaling. Biochemical Pharmacology 1999;58(7):1167−72.

[119] Quiles JL, et al. Curcuma longa extract supplementation reduces oxidative stress and attenuates aortic fatty streak development in rabbits. Arteriosclerosis, Thrombosis, and Vascular Biology 2002;22(7):1225−31.

[120] Soni KB, Kuttan R. Effect of oral curcumin administration on serum peroxides and cholesterol levels in human volunteers. Indian Journal of Physiology and Pharmacology 1992;36(4):273−5.

[121] Cao Q, et al. Dickkopf-3 upregulation mediates the cardioprotective effects of curcumin on chronic heart failure. Molecular Medicine Reports 2018;17(5):7249−57.

[122] Pungcharoenkul K, Thongnopnua PJPR. Effect of different curcuminoid supplement dosages on total in vivo antioxidant capacity and cholesterol levels of healthy human subjects. Phytotherapy Research: PTR 2011;25(11):1721−6.

[123] Mohammadi A, et al. Effects of supplementation with curcuminoids on dyslipidemia in obese patients: a randomized crossover trial. Phytotherapy Research: PTR 2013;27(3):374−9.

[124] Ramırez-Boscá A, et al. An hydroalcoholic extract of Curcuma longa lowers the apo B/apo A ratio: implications for atherogenesis prevention. Mechanisms of Ageing and Development 2000;119(1−2):41−7.

[125] Wongcharoen W, et al. Effects of curcuminoids on frequency of acute myocardial infarction after coronary artery bypass grafting. The American Journal of Cardiology 2012;110(1):40−4.

[126] Ammon HP, Wahl MA. Pharmacology of Curcuma longa. Planta Medica 1991;57(1):1−7.

[127] Rafatullah S, et al. Evaluation of turmeric (Curcuma longa) for gastric and duodenal antiulcer activity in rats. Journal of Ethnopharmacology 1990;29(1):25−34.

[128] Mahattanadul S, et al. Effects of curcumin on reflux esophagitis in rats. Journal of Natural Medicines. 2006;60(3):198−205.

[129] Mahattanadul S, et al. Comparative antiulcer effect of bisdemethoxycurcumin and curcumin in a gastric ulcer model system. Phytomedicine: International Journal of Phytotherapy and Phytopharmacology 2009;16(4):342−51.

[130] Morsy MA, El-Moselhy MAJP. Mechanisms of the protective effects of curcumin against indomethacin-induced gastric ulcer in rats. Pharmacology 2013;91(5−6):267−74.

[131] Thong-Ngam D, et al. Curcumin prevents indomethacin-induced gastropathy in rats. World Journal of Gastroenterology: WJG 2012;18(13):1479−84.

[132] He P, et al. Curcumin-induced histone acetylation inhibition improves stress-induced gastric ulcer disease in rats. Molecular Medicine Reports. 2015;11(3):1911−16.

[133] Lopresti AL, et al. Efficacy of a curcumin extract (Curcugen™) on gastrointestinal symptoms and intestinal microbiota in adults with self-reported digestive complaints: a randomised, double-blind, placebo-controlled study. BMC Complementary Medicine and Therapies. 2021;21(1):1−17.

[134] Santos AM, et al. Curcumin inhibits gastric inflammation induced by Helicobacter pylori infection in a mouse model. Nutrients 2015;7(1):306−20.

[135] Vetvicka V, Vetvickova J, Fernandez-Botran RJAOTM. Effects of curcumin on Helicobacter pylori infection. Annals of Translational Medicine 2016;4(24):479.

[136] Sarkar A, De R, Mukhopadhyay AKJWJOG. Curcumin as a potential therapeutic candidate for Helicobacter pylori associated diseases. World Journal of Gastroenterology: WJG 2016;22(9):2736.

[137] Judaki A, et al. Curcumin in combination with triple therapy regimes ameliorates oxidative stress and histopathologic changes in chronic gastritis-associated Helicobacter pylori infection. Arquivos de Gastroenterologia 2017;54:177−82.

[138] Rahmani S, et al. Treatment of non-alcoholic fatty liver disease with curcumin: a randomized placebo-controlled trial. Phytotherapy Research: PTR 2016;30(9):1540−8.

[139] Tung BT, Hai NT, Son PK. *Hepatoprotective effect of phytosome curcumin against paracetamol-induced liver toxicity in mice.*. Brazilian Journal of Pharmaceutical Sciences 2017;53.

[140] Peng X, et al. Curcumin attenuates on carbon tetrachloride-induced acute liver injury in mice via modulation of the Nrf2/HO-1 and TGF-β1/Smad3 pathway. Molecules (Basel, Switzerland) 2018;23(1):215.

[141] Macías-Pérez JR, et al. Curcumin and α/β-adrenergic antagonists cotreatment reverse liver cirrhosis in hamsters: participation of Nrf-2 and NF-κB. Journal of Immunology Research 2019;2019.

[142] Lee H-Y, et al. Turmeric extract and its active compound, curcumin, protect against chronic CCl4-induced liver damage by enhancing antioxidation. BMC Complementary and Alternative Medicine 2016;16(1):1−9.

[143] Farzaei MH, et al. Curcumin in liver diseases: a systematic review of the cellular mechanisms of oxidative stress and clinical perspective. Nutrients 2018;10(7):855.

[144] Panahi Y, et al. Efficacy and safety of phytosomal curcumin in non-alcoholic fatty liver disease: a randomized controlled trial. Drug Research 2017;67(04):244−51.

[145] Badria FA, et al. Curcumin attenuates iron accumulation and oxidative stress in the liver and spleen of chronic iron-overloaded rats. PLoS One 2015;10(7):e0134156.

[146] Sayed MM, El-Kordy EA. The protective effect of curcumin on paracetamol-induced liver damage in adult male rabbits: biochemical and histological studies. Egyptian Journal of Histology 2014;37(4):629−39.

[147] Kant V, et al. Antioxidant and anti-inflammatory potential of curcumin accelerated the cutaneous wound healing in streptozotocin-induced diabetic rats. International Immunopharmacology 2014;20 (2):322−30.

[148] Afrin R, et al. Curcumin ameliorates streptozotocin-induced liver damage through modulation of endoplasmic reticulum stress-mediated apoptosis in diabetic rats. Free Radical Research 2015;49(3):279−89.

[149] Afrin R, et al. Curcumin ameliorates liver damage and progression of NASH in NASH-HCC mouse model possibly by modulating HMGB1-NF-κB translocation. International Immunopharmacology 2017;44:174−82.

[150] Granados-Castro LF, et al. Curcumin prevents paracetamol-induced liver mitochondrial alterations. Journal of Pharmacy and Pharmacology 2016;68(2):245−56.

[151] Kheradpezhouh E, Barritt GJ, Rychkov GY. Curcumin inhibits activation of TRPM2 channels in rat hepatocytes. Redox biology 2016;7:1−7.

[152] Xiong ZE, et al. Curcumin attenuates chronic ethanol-induced liver injury by inhibition of oxidative stress via mitogen-activated protein kinase/nuclear factor E2-related factor 2 pathway in mice. Pharmacognosy Magazine 2015;11(44):707−15.

[153] Lu C, et al. Nrf2 knockdown disrupts the protective effect of curcumin on alcohol-induced hepatocyte necroptosis. Molecular Pharmaceutics 2016;13(12):4043−53.

[154] Guo C, et al. Curcumin improves alcoholic fatty liver by inhibiting fatty acid biosynthesis. Toxicology and Applied Pharmacology 2017;328:1−9.

[155] Chen N, et al. Suppression of the TGF-β/Smad signaling pathway and inhibition of hepatic stellate cell proliferation play a role in the hepatoprotective effects of curcumin against alcohol-induced hepatic fibrosis. International Journal of Molecular Medicine 2014;34(4):1110−16.

[156] Zhong W, et al. Curcumin alleviates lipopolysaccharide induced sepsis and liver failure by suppression of oxidative stress-related inflammation via PI3K/AKT and NF-κB related signaling. Biomedicine & Pharmacotherapy = Biomedecine & Pharmacotherapie 2016;83:302−13.

[157] Fu Y, et al. Curcumin protects the rat liver from CCl4-caused injury and fibrogenesis by attenuating oxidative stress and suppressing inflammation. Molecular Pharmacology 2008;73(2):399−409.

[158] Zhang F, et al. Curcumin attenuates angiogenesis in liver fibrosis and inhibits angiogenic properties of hepatic stellate cells. Journal of Cellular and Molecular Medicine 2014;18(7):1392−406.

[159] Somanawat K, Thong-Ngam D, Klaikeaw N. Curcumin attenuated paracetamol overdose induced hepa-titis. World Journal of Gastroenterology: WJG 2013;19(12):1962−7.

[160] Karamalakova YD, et al. Hepatoprotective properties of Curcuma longa L. extract in bleomycin-induced chronic hepatotoxicity. Drug Discoveries & Therapeutics 2019;13(1):9−16.

[161] Emami B, et al. Relaxant effect of Curcuma longa on rat tracheal smooth muscle and its possible mechanisms. Le Pharmacien Biologiste 2017;55(1):2248−58.

[162] Boskabady MH, Shakeri F, Naghdi F. Chapter 7 - The effects of Curcuma longa L. and its constituents in respiratory disorders and molecular mechanisms of their action. In: Atta Ur R, editor. Studies in Natural Products Chemistry. Elsevier; 2020. p. 239−69.

[163] Liu Z, Ying Y. The inhibitory effect of curcumin on virus-induced cytokine storm and its potential use in the associated severe pneumonia. Frontiers in Cell and Developmental Biology 2020;8:479.

[164] Ram A, Das M, Ghosh B. Curcumin attenuates allergen-induced airway hyperresponsiveness in sensi-tized guinea pigs. Biological and Pharmaceutical Bulletin 2003;26(7):1021−4.

[165] Pizzino G, et al. Oxidative stress: harms and benefits for human health. Oxidative Medicine and Cellular Longevity 2017;2017:8416763.

[166] Urošević M, et al. Curcumin: biological activities and modern pharmaceutical forms. Antibiotics (Basel) 2022;11(2).

[167] Thimmulappa RK, et al. Antiviral and immunomodulatory activity of curcumin: a case for prophylactic therapy for COVID-19. Heliyon 2021;7(2):e06350.

[168] Saeedi-Boroujeni A, et al. COVID-19: a case for inhibiting NLRP3 inflammasome, suppression of inflammation with curcumin? Basic & Clinical Pharmacology & Toxicology 2021;128(1):37−45.

[169] Fan E, et al. COVID-19-associated acute respiratory distress syndrome: is a different approach to man-agement warranted? Lancet Respiratory Medicine. 2020;8(8):816−21.

[170] Wang X, et al. Curcumin ameliorated ventilator-induced lung injury in rats. Biomedicine & Pharmacotherapy = Biomedecine & Pharmacotherapie 2018;98:754−61.

[171] Liao M, et al. Single-cell landscape of bronchoalveolar immune cells in patients with COVID-19. Nature Medicine 2020;26(6):842−4.

[172] Chai Y-s, et al. Curcumin regulates the differentiation of naïve CD4 + T cells and activates IL-10 immune modulation against acute lung injury in mice. Biomedicine & Pharmacotherapy = Biomedecine & Pharmacotherapie 2020;125:109946.

[173] Hay E, et al. Therapeutic effects of turmeric in several diseases: an overview. Chemico-Biological Interactions 2019;310:108729.

[174] Farhoudi L, et al. Polymeric nanomicelles of curcumin: potential applications in cancer. International Journal of Pharmaceutics 2022;617:121622.

[175] Mohajeri M, Sahebkar A. Protective effects of curcumin against doxorubicin-induced toxicity and resis-tance: a review. Critical Reviews in Oncology/Hematology 2018;122:30−51.

[176] Momtazi AA, Sahebkar A. Difluorinated curcumin: a promising curcumin analogue with improved anti-tumor activity and pharmacokinetic profile. Current Pharmaceutical Design 2016;22(28):4386−97.

[177] Deng YI, Verron E, Rohanizadeh R. Molecular mechanisms of anti-metastatic activity of curcumin. Anticancer Research 2016;36(11):5639−47.

[178] Nishida N, et al. Angiogenesis in cancer. Vascular Health and Risk Management 2006;2(3):213−19.

[179] Zuazo-Gaztelu I, Casanovas O. Unraveling the role of angiogenesis in cancer ecosystems. Frontiers in Oncology 2018;8:248.

[180] Yance Jr. DR, Sagar SM. Targeting angiogenesis with integrative cancer therapies. Integrative Cancer Therapies 2006;5(1):9−29.

[181] Binion DG, Otterson MF, Rafiee P. Curcumin inhibits VEGF-mediated angiogenesis in human intestinal microvascular endothelial cells through COX-2 and MAPK inhibition. Gut 2008;57(11):1509−17.

[182] Kandoth C, et al. Mutational landscape and significance across 12 major cancer types. Nature 2013;502 (7471):333−9.

[183] Hermeking H. p53 enters the microRNA world. Cancer Cell 2007;12(5):414−18.

[184] Ye M, et al. Curcumin promotes apoptosis by activating the p53-miR-192-5p/215-XIAP pathway in non-small cell lung cancer. Cancer Letters 2015;357(1):196−205.

[185] Watson JL, et al. Curcumin causes superoxide anion production and p53-independent apoptosis in human colon cancer cells. Cancer Letters 2010;297(1):1−8.

[186] Kouhpeikar H, et al. Curcumin as a therapeutic agent in leukemia. Journal of Cellular Physiology 2019;234(8):12404−14.

[187] Tseng YH, et al. Curcumin and tetrahydrocurcumin induce cell death in Ara-C-resistant acute myeloid leukemia. Phytotherapy Research: PTR 2019;33(4):1199−207.

[188] Lin YG, et al. Curcumin inhibits tumor growth and angiogenesis in ovarian carcinoma by targeting the nuclear factor-κB pathway. Clinical Cancer Research: An Official Journal of the American Association for Cancer Research 2007;13(11):3423−30.

[189] Mitra AK, Krishna MJJORR. In vivo modulation of signaling factors involved in cell survival. Journal of Radiation Research. 2004;45(4):491−5.

[190] He Z-Y, et al. Upregulation of p53 expression in patients with colorectal cancer by administration of curcumin. Cancer Investigation 2011;29(3):208−13.

[191] Cruz−Correa M, et al. Combination treatment with curcumin and quercetin of adenomas in familial adenomatous polyposis. Clinical Gastroenterology and Hepatology: the Official Clinical Practice Journal of the American Gastroenterological Association 2006;4(8):1035−8.

[192] Dhillon N, et al. Phase II trial of curcumin in patients with advanced pancreatic cancer. Clinical Cancer Research: an Official Journal of the American Association for Cancer Research 2008;14(14):4491−9.

[193] Bayet-Robert M, et al. Phase I dose escalation trial of docetaxel plus curcumin in patients with advanced and metastatic breast cancer. Clinical Trial 2010;9(1):8−14.

[194] Vadhan-Raj S, et al. Curcumin Downregulates NF-kB and Related Genes in Patients with Multiple Myeloma: Results of a Phase I/II Study. Blood 2007;110(11):1177.

[195] Howells LM, et al. Curcumin combined with FOLFOX chemotherapy is safe and tolerable in patients with metastatic colorectal cancer in a randomized phase IIa trial. The Journal of Nutrition 2019;149(7):1133−9.

[196] American Diabetes Association. Diagnosis and classification of diabetes mellitus. Diabetes Care 2009;32(Suppl 1):S62−7.

[197] Kelany ME, Hakami TM, Omar AH. Curcumin improves the metabolic syndrome in high-fructose-diet-fed rats: role of TNF-α, NF-κB, and oxidative stress. Canadian Journal of Physiology and Pharmacology 2017;95(2):140−50.

[198] Yekollu SK, Thomas R, O'Sullivan B. Targeting curcusomes to inflammatory dendritic cells inhibits NF-κB and improves insulin resistance in obese mice. Diabetes 2011;60(11):2928−38.

[199] Bustanji Y, et al. Inhibition of glycogen synthase kinase by curcumin: investigation by simulated molecular docking and subsequent in vitro/in vivo evaluation. Journal of Enzyme Inhibition and Medicinal Chemistry 2009;24(3):771−8.

[200] Kato M, et al. Curcumin improves glucose tolerance via stimulation of glucagon-like peptide-1 secretion. Molecular Nutrition & Food Research 2017;61(3):1600471.

[201] Ye M, et al. Curcumin improves palmitate-induced insulin resistance in human umbilical vein endothelial cells by maintaining proteostasis in endoplasmic reticulum. Frontiers in Pharmacology 2017;8:148.

[202] Karthikesan K, Pari L, Menon V. Antihyperlipidemic effect of chlorogenic acid and tetrahydrocurcumin in rats subjected to diabetogenic agents. Chemico-Biological Interactions 2010;188(3):643−50.

[203] Zheng J, et al. Curcumin, a polyphenolic curcuminoid with its protective effects and molecular mechanisms in diabetes and diabetic cardiomyopathy. Frontiers in Pharmacology 2018;9:472.

[204] Gonzales AM, Orlando RA. Curcumin and resveratrol inhibit nuclear factor-kappaB-mediated cytokine expression in adipocytes. Nutrition & Metabolism (Lond) 2008;5:17.

[205] Yu W, et al. Curcumin alleviates diabetic cardiomyopathy in experimental diabetic rats. PLoS One 2012;7(12):e52013.

[206] Jang EM, et al. Beneficial effects of curcumin on hyperlipidemia and insulin resistance in high-fat-fed hamsters. Metabolism: Clinical and Experimental 2008;57(11):1576−83.

[207] Nishiyama T, et al. Curcuminoids and sesquiterpenoids in turmeric (Curcuma longa L.) suppress an increase in blood glucose level in type 2 diabetic KK-Ay mice. Journal of Agricultural and Food Chemistry 2005;53(4):959−63.

[208] Na LX, et al. Curcuminoids exert glucose-lowering effect in type 2 diabetes by decreasing serum free fatty acids: a double-blind, placebo-controlled trial. Molecular Nutrition & Food Research 2013;57(9):1569−77.

[209] Chainani-Wu N, et al. A randomized, placebo-controlled, double-blind clinical trial of curcuminoids in oral lichen planus. Phytomedicine: International Journal of Phytotherapy and Phytopharmacology 2007;14(7−8):437−46.

[210] Hsu YC, et al. Curcuminoids-cellular uptake by human primary colon cancer cells as quantitated by a sensitive HPLC assay and its relation with the inhibition of proliferation and apoptosis. Journal of Agricultural and Food Chemistry 2007;55(20):8213−22.

[211] Usharani P, et al. Effect of NCB-02, atorvastatin and placebo on endothelial function, oxidative stress and inflammatory markers in patients with type 2 diabetes mellitus: a randomized, parallel-group, placebo-controlled, 8-week study. Drugs in R&D 2008;9(4):243−50.

[212] Neerati P, Devde R, Gangi AK. Evaluation of the effect of curcumin capsules on glyburide therapy in patients with type-2 diabetes mellitus. Phytotherapy Research: PTR 2014;28(12):1796−800.

[213] Poolsup N, et al. Effects of curcumin on glycemic control and lipid profile in prediabetes and type 2 diabetes mellitus: a systematic review and meta-analysis. PLoS One 2019;14(4):e0215840.

[214] Wang L, Wang FS, Gershwin ME. Human autoimmune diseases: a comprehensive update. Journal of Internal Medicine 2015;278(4):369−95.

[215] Jose J, et al. Pathogenesis of autoimmune diseases: a short review. Oral & Maxillofacial Pathology Journal 2014;5(1).

[216] Yang M, Akbar U, Mohan C. Curcumin in autoimmune and rheumatic diseases. Nutrients 2019;11:5.

[217] Marton LT, et al. Curcumin, autoimmune and inflammatory diseases: going beyond conventional therapy - a systematic review. Critical Reviews in Food Science and Nutrition 2022;62(8):2140−57.

[218] Momtazi-Borojeni AA, et al. Curcumin: a natural modulator of immune cells in systemic lupus erythematosus. Autoimmunity Reviews 2018;17(2):125−35.

[219] Guo Q, et al. Rheumatoid arthritis: pathological mechanisms and modern pharmacologic therapies. Bone Research 2018;6:15.

[220] Heidari B. Rheumatoid arthritis: early diagnosis and treatment outcomes. Caspian Journal of Internal Medicine 2011;2(1):161−70.

[221] Wang Q, et al. Curcumin attenuates collagen-induced rat arthritis via anti-inflammatory and apoptotic effects. International Immunopharmacology 2019;72:292−300.

[222] Dai Q, et al. Curcumin alleviates rheumatoid arthritis-induced inflammation and synovial hyperplasia by targeting mTOR pathway in rats. Drug Design, Development and Therapy 2018;12:4095−105.

[223] Dcodhar S, Sethi R, Srimal RJIJOMR. Preliminary study on antirheumatic activity of curcumin (diferuloyl methane). Indian Journal of Medical Research 2013;138(1).

[224] Chandran B, Goel AJPR. A randomized, pilot study to assess the efficacy and safety of curcumin in patients with active rheumatoid arthritis. Randomized Controlled Trial 2012;26(11):1719–25.

[225] Mok CC, Lau CS. Pathogenesis of systemic lupus erythematosus. Journal of Clinical Pathology 2003;56 (7):481–90.

[226] Agrawal N, Chiang LK, Rifkin IR. Lupus nephritis. Seminars in Nephrology 2006;26(2):95–104.

[227] Dent EL, et al. Curcumin attenuates autoimmunity and renal injury in an experimental model of systemic lupus erythematosus. Physiological Reports 2020;8(13):e14501.

[228] Zhao J, et al. Curcumin attenuates murine lupus via inhibiting NLRP3 inflammasome. International Immunopharmacology 2019;69:213–16.

[229] Lee H, et al. Curcumin attenuates lupus nephritis upon interaction with regulatory T cells in New Zealand Black/White mice. The British Journal of Nutrition 2013;110(1):69–76.

[230] Khajehdehi P, et al. Oral supplementation of turmeric decreases proteinuria, hematuria, and systolic blood pressure in patients suffering from relapsing or refractory lupus nephritis: a randomized and placebo-controlled study. Journal of Renal Nutrition: the Official Journal of the Council on Renal Nutrition of the National Kidney Foundation 2012;22(1):50–7.

[231] Armstrong AW, Read CJJ. Pathophysiology, clinical presentation, and treatment of psoriasis: a review. JAMA: The Journal of the American Medical Association 2020;323(19):1945–60.

[232] Kang D, et al. Curcumin shows excellent therapeutic effect on psoriasis in mouse model. Biochimie 2016;123:73–80.

[233] Kurd SK, et al. Oral curcumin in the treatment of moderate to severe psoriasis vulgaris: a prospective clinical trial. Journal of the American Academy of Dermatology 2008;58(4):625–31.

[234] Reich DS, Lucchinetti CF, Calabresi PA. Multiple sclerosis. The New England Journal of Medicine 2018;378(2):169–80.

[235] Esmaeilzadeh E, et al. Curcumin ameliorates experimental autoimmune encephalomyelitis in a C57BL/ 6 mouse model. Drug Development Research 2019;80(5):629–36.

[236] I EL-D, et al. Dual mechanism of action of curcumin in experimental models of multiple sclerosis. International Journal of Molecular Sciences 2022;23(15).

[237] Xie L, et al. Amelioration of experimental autoimmune encephalomyelitis by curcumin treatment through inhibition of IL-17 production. International Immunopharmacology 2009;9(5):575–81.

[238] Teruel C, Garrido E, Mesonero F. Diagnosis and management of functional symptoms in inflammatory bowel disease in remission. World Journal of Gastrointestinal Pharmacology and Therapeutics 2016;7(1):78–90.

[239] Yue W, et al. Curcumin ameliorates dextran sulfate sodium-induced colitis in mice via regulation of autophagy and intestinal immunity. The Turkish Journal of Gastroenterology: the Official Journal of Turkish Society of Gastroenterology 2019;30(3):290.

[240] Huang G, et al. Effects of curcumin plus soy oligosaccharides on intestinal flora of rats with ulcerative colitis. Cellular and Molecular Biology (Noisy-le-grand) 2017;63(7):20–5.

[241] Liu L, et al. Curcumin ameliorates dextran sulfate sodium-induced experimental colitis by blocking STAT3 signaling pathway. International Immunopharmacology 2013;17(2):314–20.

[242] Holt PR, Katz S, Kirshoff R. Curcumin therapy in inflammatory bowel disease: a pilot study. Digestive Diseases and Sciences 2005;50(11):2191–3.

[243] Hanai H, et al. Curcumin maintenance therapy for ulcerative colitis: randomized, multicenter, double-blind, placebo-controlled trial. Clinical Gastroenterology and Hepatology: the Official Clinical Practice Journal of the American Gastroenterological Association 2006;4(12):1502–6.

[244] Lang A, et al. Curcumin in combination with mesalamine induces remission in patients with mild-to-moderate ulcerative colitis in a randomized controlled trial. Clinical Gastroenterology and Hepatology: The Official Clinical Practice Journal of the American Gastroenterological Association 2015;13(8):1444–9 e1.

[245] Zhang C, et al. Curcumin decreases amyloid-beta peptide levels by attenuating the maturation of amyloid-beta precursor protein. The Journal of Biological Chemistry 2010;285(37):28472–80.

[246] Srichairatanakool S, et al. Curcumin contributes to in vitro removal of non-transferrin bound iron by deferiprone and desferrioxamine in thalassemic plasma. Medicinal Chemistry (Shariqah (United Arab Emirates)) 2007;3(5):469–74.

[247] Mary CPV, Vijayakumar S, Shankar R. Metal chelating ability and antioxidant properties of Curcumin-metal complexes - A DFT approach. Journal of Molecular Graphics & Modelling 2018;79:1–14.

[248] Ferrari E, et al. Curcumin derivatives as metal-chelating agents with potential multifunctional activity for pharmaceutical applications. Journal of Inorganic Biochemistry 2014;139:38–48.

[249] Daniel S, et al. Through metal binding, curcumin protects against lead- and cadmium-induced lipid peroxidation in rat brain homogenates and against lead-induced tissue damage in rat brain. Journal of Inorganic Biochemistry 2004;98(2):266–75.

[250] Vellampatti S, et al. Metallo-curcumin-conjugated DNA complexes induces preferential prostate cancer cells cytotoxicity and pause growth of bacterial cells. Scientific Reports 2018;8(1):14929.

[251] Tomeh MA, Hadianamrei R, Zhao X. A review of curcumin and its derivatives as anticancer agents. International Journal of Molecular Sciences 2019;20(5).

3

Chemical structure and molecular targets of curcumin for cancer therapy

Priyanka Adhikari*, Meenakshi Singh*, Jyoti Punia, Alok Ranjan,
A. Parthiban, V.G.M. Naidu

*CENTRE FOR GMP EXTRACTION FACILITY, NATIONAL INSTITUTE OF PHARMACEUTICAL
EDUCATION AND RESEARCH, GUWAHATI, ASSAM, INDIA*

3.1 Introduction

The utmost demonstrative phenolic component isolated from turmeric (*Curcuma longa*) is curcumin; it is a dynamic secondary metabolite (SMs) among the plant-based SMs, with specific reference to the plants' rhizomes [1]. Curcumin has been always forefront of prominent phytochemical for organic chemists, biotechnologists, pharmacologists, and pharmaceutical chemists because of its ability to show pleiotropic pharmacological activities, and target multiple proteins involved in different stages of cancer via various signaling pathways [1]. Curcumin displays a wide range of pharmacological activities accounting for antioxidant [2], antimicrobial [3], antidiabetic [4], and antimalarial activities [5] but its most significant property is anticancer, and curcumin's vital anticancer properties are depend mainly on the presence of the hydroxyl (OH) group of phenolics or the CH_2 (methylene) moiety of the 1,3-diketone [6]. It has been recurrently sued that curcumin is active and as well as safe for consumption. It is an appealing metabolite that has applications in plentiful industrial areas, that is, drugs, medicines, cosmeceuticals, and nutraceuticals [7]. Structure of curcumin is shown in Fig. 3−1. At the same time, curcumin has striking cytotoxic activity with programmed cell death instigation potential on a variety of cancer cell lines, because of which it is a persuasive anticancer representative, and at the same time unbeatable candidate for chemotherapy [2]. The prime advantage of curcumin is its nontoxic nature. At present, investigations are correspondingly running on in plentiful human carcinomas, for example, breast, bone, lung, hepatic, gastric, leukemia, colon, ovarian, prostate, melanoma, and pancreatic cancers [8]. As curcumin is a blockbuster anticancer drug, its chemical modifications are conveyed to increase its potential to treat dissimilar human cancer. These types

---

* Equal contribution.

Curcumin-Based Nanomedicines as Cancer Therapeutics. DOI: https://doi.org/10.1016/B978-0-443-15412-6.00011-8

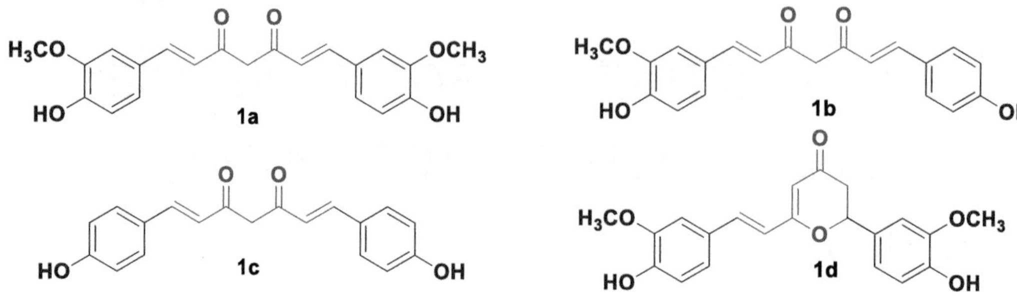

FIGURE 3–1 Chemical structures of natural products: curcumin (1a), demethoxycurcumin (1b), bisdemethoxycurcumin (1c), and cyclocurcumin (1d).

of chemical changes in curcumins are chiefly accomplished to determine molecules with alike but enhanced stability and improved anticancer possessions. Keeping curcumin's importance in mind, the present chapter gives emphasis on the significance of curcumin and their derivatives and analogs structure both natural as well as synthetic in the therapy of different types of cancers.

3.2 Chemistry of curcumin

Curcumin is an important bioactive natural product from *Curcuma longa* and it has been mainly used as a food ingredient, cosmetic, and traditional herbal medicine for centuries throughout Asia. Curcumin chemically named as diferuloylmethane, which contains 1,7-bis (4-hydroxy-3-methoxy phenyl)-1,6-heptadiene-3,5-dione, $C_{21}H_{20}O_6$ (molecular formula). It has three notable chemical moieties, such as 1,3-diketone, α, β-unsaturated double bond and ortho-methoxy phenolic group on both sides. The four important bioactive natural components are curcumin (77%) **(1a)** and its derivatives (curcuminoids) demethoxycurcumin (17%) **(1b)**, bisdemethoxycurcumin (3%), **(1c)** and cyclocurcumin **(1d)** were present in turmeric root (Fig. 3–1) [9].

Owing to β-diketone moiety in curcumin, it exits keto-enol tautomerism and the keto and enol forms are expected to be in quick equilibrium and its so-called bis-keto and enolate tautomeric structures. According to the solution nuclear magnetic resonance (NMR) investigation, the enol form of curcumin is more stable than the keto form due to the intramolecular hydrogen bonding takes place in curcumin structure (Fig. 3–2) [10–12]. The di-keto form leads in the solid phase in acidic and neutral conditions, whereas the enolic form is stable in the presence of alkaline conditions (Fig. 3–2).

3.3 Functionalities and synthesis of natural curcumin

Curcumin is a very upright anticancer agent but the chief drawback of this highly valuable drug is its solubility and stability. In addition, the limiting factors such as pharmacokinetics

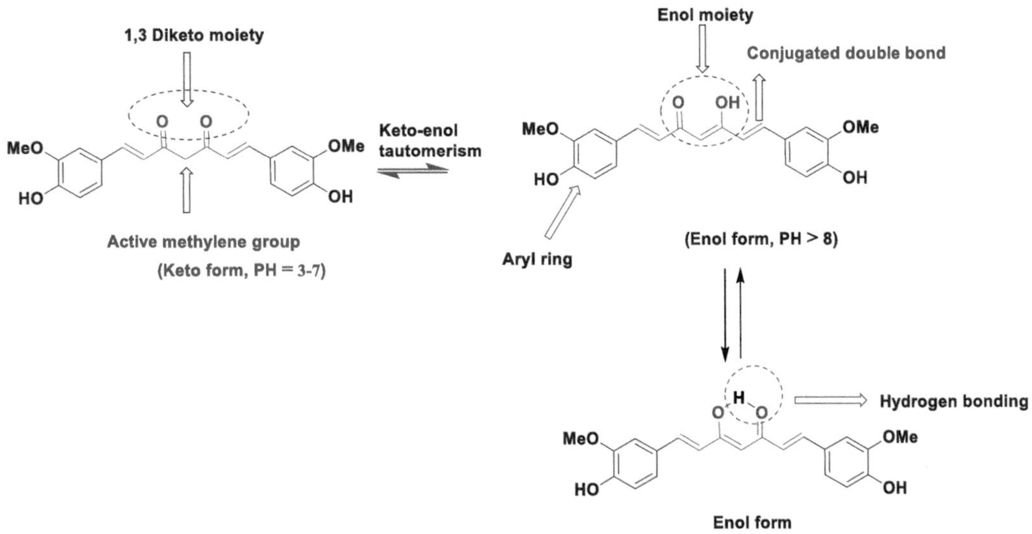

FIGURE 3–2 Keto-enol tautomerism of curcumin.

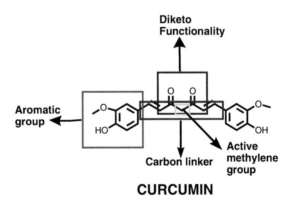

FIGURE 3–3 Structure of curcumin showing its functional sites.

and the active pharmacophore of curcumin still remain unknown [13]. In this perspective, lots of researchers are doing extensive research work, and up to now, multiple approaches are being designed on α,β-unsaturated 1,3-diketone moiety, which is known to be Michael acceptor properties and as (PAINS) interfering bioassays [10], active methylene site, carbon linker chain, and diaryl ring and their functional group (Fig. 3–3) to overcome limitation and obtaining super curcumin–based analogs [14].

The isolation and purification of curcumin from turmeric is considered as a difficult and costly procedure. In connection with this limitation, researcher has got much attention to synthesize curcumin and curcuminoids in synthetic aspects to get pure compounds with high yields and high purity. Moreover, organic synthesis affords an inexpensive and more

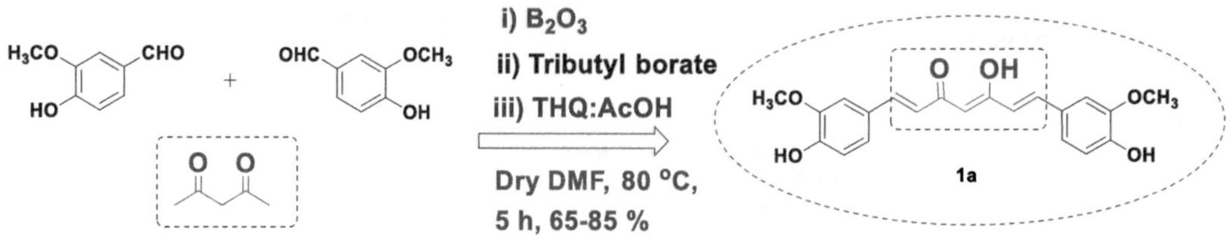

FIGURE 3–4 Synthetic scheme of natural curcumin.

efficient method to obtain bulk amounts of "natural inspired" compounds for biomedical properties than by extracting insufficient milligrams from the nature. In this regard, Babu and Rajasekharan (1994) described a novel synthetic method for the preparation of natural curcumin **1a** and its derivatives by using various substituted phenolic aldehydes, acetylacetone, and boric acid in dry N,N-dimethylformamide and followed by treated with 1,2,3,4-tetrahydroquinoline, tributyl borate, and glacial acetic acid, which was furnished curcumin as orange yellow powder in excellent yields (Fig. 3–4) [15].

One of the most favorable sites for incorporating the heterocyclic group for synthesizing the stable and potent antitumor molecules is the 1,3-dicarbonyl site in curcumin (Fig. 3–3). However, the associated drawbacks generally is the first-pass metabolism. Sametime, the PAINS-linked challenges remain unavoidable obstacles but several concepts for modification can be done by replacing or protection of oxidation sites, phenolic, enolic hydroxyls groups. Additionally, omitting its challenges causing skeleton and substitution of suitable functional group/ring to increase the sensitivity/selectivity, overcome the resistance/reoccurrence, pharmacokinetic and pharmacodynamics profile [16–18].

3.4 Curcumin revamped to super curcumin

As discussed in earlier sections, curcumin, 1,7-bis-(3-hydroxy-4-methoxyphenyl)-1,6-heptadiene-3,5-dione, is an important active molecule in *Curcuma longa* and has been utilized as a traditional herbal medicine, food additive, and cosmetic in Asian countries. Curcumin is considered as nontoxic in humans by its consumption at levels of 100 mg/day. In spite of the favorable biological activities and less toxicity of curcumin, there are some drawbacks that limit the improvement of curcumin as a better anticancer agent, which includes low bioaccessibility and instability in neutral to basic conditions. Several synthetic approaches have been found to overwhelm these problems and many synthetic analogs of curcumin have been intended and synthesized. This section describes the synthetic strategies for different curcumin derivatives and their activities performed thereafter to compare with curcumin.

3.4.1 Curcumin-based pyrazole analogs

Designed strategies for the synthesis of curcumin analogs started by targeting angiogenesis inhibitors for preventing cancer, as they can block the growth of blood vessels that support

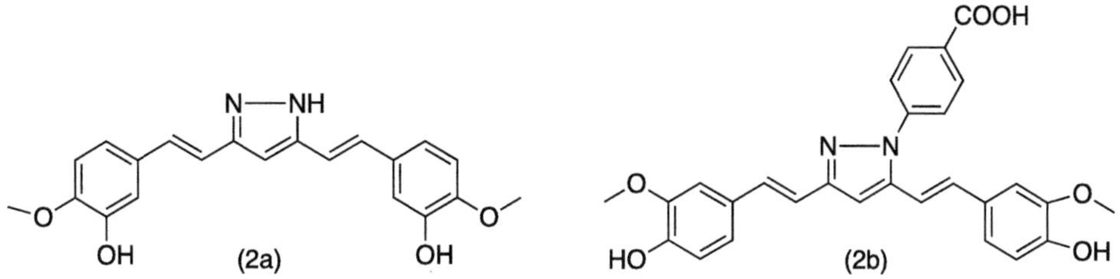

FIGURE 3–5 Structure of hydrazinocurcumin (HC) and hydrazinobenzoylcurcumin (HBC).

the tumor growth rather than targeting the tumor cells. Thus extensive research on curcumin displayed potent anticarcinogenic property against a wide range of tumors [19]. Moreover, it has been suggested that the broad spectrum of anticarcinogenic property of curcumin may be impart owing to angiogenesis inhibition [20]. Taking a cue of the above statement, researchers thought that there is a direct correlation between angiogenesis inhibitors and cancer and hence, in early, Shim et al. (2002) first synthesized a novel curcumin-based pyrazole derivative named hydrazinocurcumin (HC, **2a**) (Fig. 3−5) with other curcumin analogs. HC (**2a**) showed very potent on bovine aortic endothelial cells (IC_{50}−0.52 μM), which was 30 folds higher than the curcumin [21].

Likewise, Zhau et al. (2014) studied the role of HC on diethylnitrosamine (DEN)-induced hepatocarcinogenesis male Sprague Dawley (SD) rat model. It was evident that there were drastic changes in liver tissues, both histological and immunohistochemical, while the levels of liver marker enzymes were significantly increased, thus revealing that HC prevents hepatic cancer [11]. Furthermore, Centelles et al. (2016) explored the cytotoxicity of HC in four cancer cell lines such as MCF-7, HeLa, HEK-293, and HT-29 and it was exhibited promising activity with IC_{50} of 0.72−11.1 μM and shows HC was more active than curcumin. In the latest findings, HC at 40 μM suppressed the proliferation of hepatocellular carcinoma (HCC) cells via the p38 MAPK pathway (in vivo) [22].

Interestingly, modification of HC was studied by Zhou et al. (2015) and it was reported that HBC (Fig. 3−5) diminished human A549 nonsmall lung epithelial carcinoma cell proliferation via induction of autophagy through AMP-activated protein kinase (AMPK) signaling [23]. The connection between autophagy and apoptosis induced by HBC was distinguished. This was the first report on HBC with the dual connection of autophagy and apoptosis in A549 cells and, at the same time HBC also reported to inhibit androgen-sensitive and castration-resistant AR-positive prostate cancer [24].

In the continuing search for potent and selective cytotoxic antitumor agents, extensive research has been done on pyrazole and isoxazole derivatives of curcumin and it was reported that their activity is two or three folds higher as compared to curcumin. Curcumin had already become a very intriguing molecule that displayed potential chemopreventive and antitumor activity. However, the problem still remained in the lack of tissue bioavailability of the compounds [25]. Because of the potential biological activity, it displayed, many efforts have been made only to make a better "curcumin analog," that is equally effective or

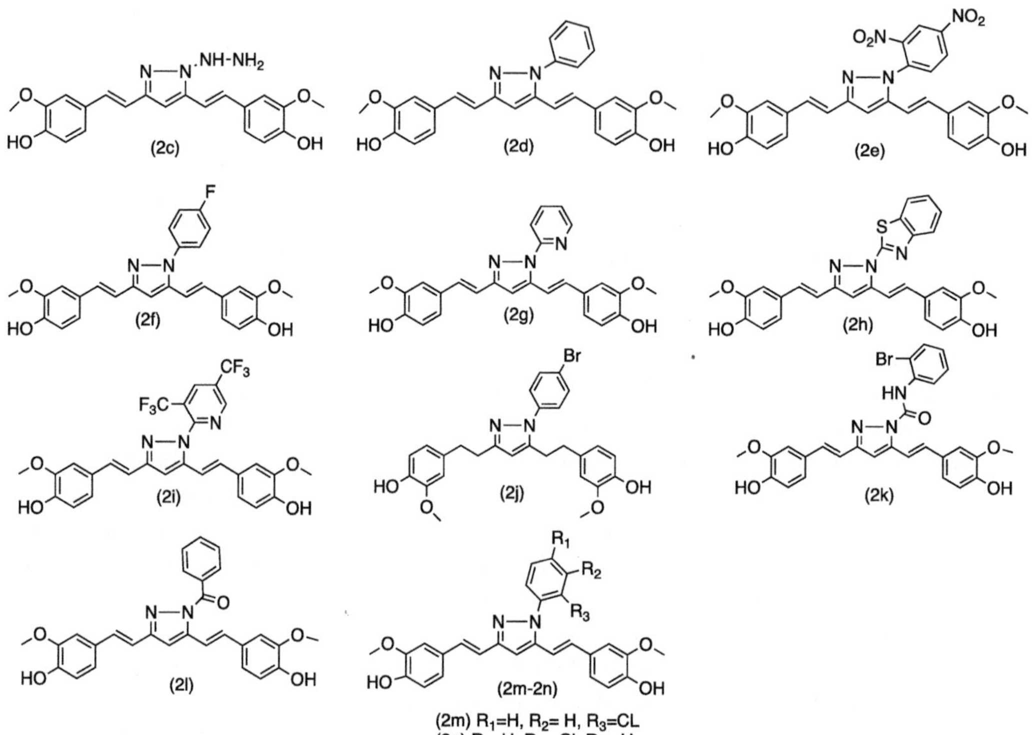

FIGURE 3–6 Structures of pyrazole analogs of curcumin.

better with increased bioavailability, which again was the purpose of the investigation. Fadda and his team did extensive work on solving the above-stated lines and synthesized a number of pyrazole and isoxazole curcumin analogs. On testing it was found that HC and **2c** were most potent on Ehrlich ascites carcinoma (EAC) and **2a**, **2b**, **2d**, and **2e** (Fig. 3–6) were active against four human cancer cell lines 9U-251 MG, HACT-15, K-562, and SKLU-1 than curcumin [26].

In continuation of this strategy, Jordan et al. (2018) described the synthesis and anti-cancer activities of pyrazole curcumin derivatives for the treatment of head and neck cancer. At low μM doses, the tested compounds were sensitive to CAL27 and UMSCC-74A cancer cells. Compound **2e** was shown promising anticancer activity against HNSCC cell lines. From the results of this study, the compounds **2 f**, **2 g**, and **2 h** were displayed good cytotoxicity activities against CAL27 oral carcinoma cancer cell [27]. Mahal et al. synthesized the series of pyrazole derivatives of curcumin metabolite (tetrahydrofuran) and these derived analogs of metabolites showed prominent anticancer activity in MCF-7 cell lines with good IC_{50} value. Out of all, the n-4-bromophenyl substituent analog **2i** was found to be the most active than the others with IC_{50} (8.0 μM A549), (9.8 μM HeLa), and (5.8 μM, MCF-7) [28]. In 2012, Kumar et al. prepared various analogs of curcumin and studied their anticancer properties against MCF-7, KB, CaCo-2, Hep G2, and WRL-68 cell lines. The anticancer activity of the pyrazole-containing curcumin compounds exhibited excellent activity due to the presence of electronegative atoms such as Br or Cl located at the para position of aryl ring. The compounds **2j**, **2k**, and **2 l** have been depicted to possess higher anticancer potential against cancer cell line KB [29]. Ahsan et al. [30] and his team synthesized more than 14 heterocyclic curcumin analogs and tested them on 60 cancerous cell lines for lung, ovarian, melanoma, renal cancer leukemia, and so on. All the designed analogs showed better activity than curcumin but compound 2 **m** showed magnificent activity, that is, 0.4 μM for SR (leukemia) and 1.73 μM for COLO 205 (colon cancer).

3.4.2 Bioisosteric-based curcumin analogs

In 2008, Simoni et al. utilized the concepts of bioisosteric to synthesize a series of curcumin analogs, where the diatonic system was extended into enaminones, oximes, and the isoxazole heterocycles [31]. The sole purpose of their experiments was to establish the structure of curcumin as a viable starting point to develop effective anticancer agents even in multidrug resistance (MDR) tumors [12]. As a result, a series of structurally related β-enamine ketone bioisoster analogs were synthesized and tested in selected cell lines (HCC HA22T/VGH cells, MCF-7 breast cancer cell line, and its MDR variant MCF-7R cell line too) and found two analogs (**2o**, **2p**) (Fig. 3−7) were known to innately produce remarkable amounts of drug resistance and antiapoptotic factors. Hence, these researchers paved a way for the better understanding of such mechanisms, which, in future, will aid in evaluating the importance of new curcumin analogs, regarding the tumor drug resistance aspect.

The selectivity and potency of pyrazoles and isoxazoles derivatives of curcumin insist on researchers seeing the effect of quinolone aromatic derivatives as they are known for their metabolic stability, binding affinity, and bonding via hydrogen bonding. Cited the importance of it, Raghawan and his team designed and synthesized 18 novel quinolone-incorporated curcumin analogs on diaryl moiety in which compound **2p** (Fig. 3−7) showed potent activity against SKOV3 cells (IC$_{50}$ 12.8 μM) than curcumin and found nontoxic to normal fibroblast cell line with the viability of 74.5% [12].

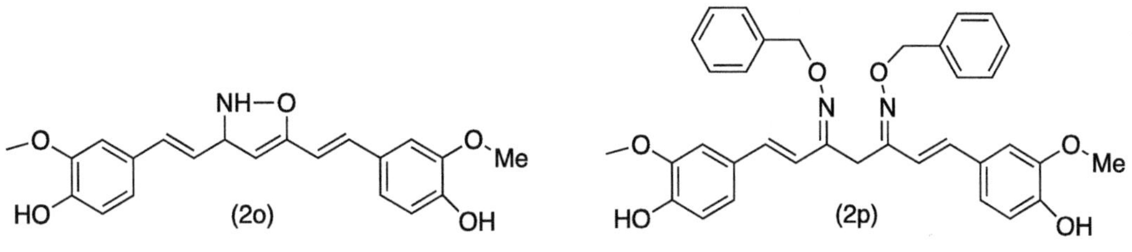

FIGURE 3-7 Structures of isoxazole and dioxime analogs of curcumin.

3.4.3 Pyrimidine-based curcumin analogs

In continuation of the exploration of different groups, Qui et al. synthesized novel pyrimidine-based curcumin derivatives and tested for two colon cancers, HT29 and HCT116, and all the prepared compounds offered better anticancer activity. However, the analogs containing the hydroxyl group (**2q**, **2r**, **2 s**, and **2t**) (Fig. 3—8) are more potent than nonhydroxylated (**2 u**, **2 v**) may be due to hydrogen bonding with protein and possess anticellular proliferation, proapoptotic and cell cycle arrest properties [32].

The compound **2w** was tested for anticancer activities against nine cancer cells (leukemia, nonsmall cell lung cancer, colon cancer, central nervous system (CNS) cancer, melanoma, ovarian cancer, renal cancer, prostate cancer, and breast cancer). Compound **2w** displayed the maximum activity against HT-29 cells (colon cancer) with a GI_{50} value of 1.30 μM and the lowest activity against NCI ADR-RES cells (ovarian cancer) with a GI_{50} value of 16.7 μM [30]. Pyrimidine derivatives **2w-2y** (Fig. 3—8) were discovered for urease enzyme inhibition studies and compound **2 y** was found to be the best molecule with an $IC_{50} = 2.44 \pm 0.07$ μM. Compound **2w** showed an IC_{50} value of 35.83 ± 0.34 μM, whereas **2x** showed no urease inhibition. In addition, pyrimidines **2w-2y** was evaluated for its antiinflammatory, antinociceptive, and cyclooxygenase-2 inhibitory properties. The compound **2x** shown 75.3% inhibition being the best active molecule based on COX-2 in vitro

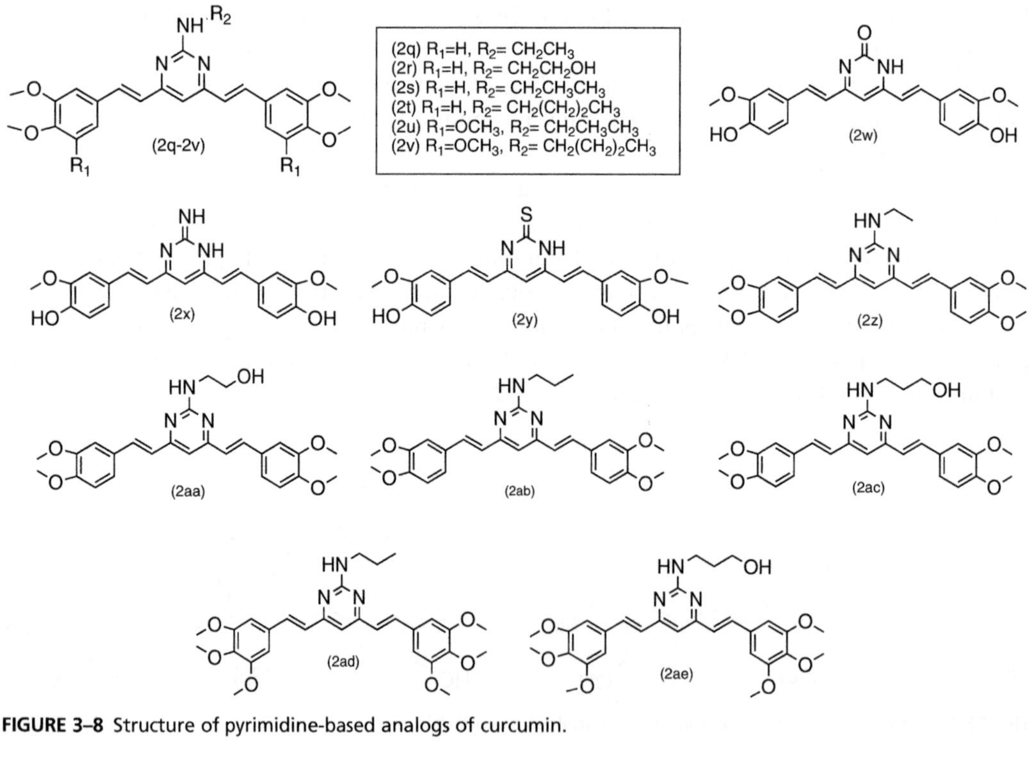

FIGURE 3–8 Structure of pyrimidine-based analogs of curcumin.

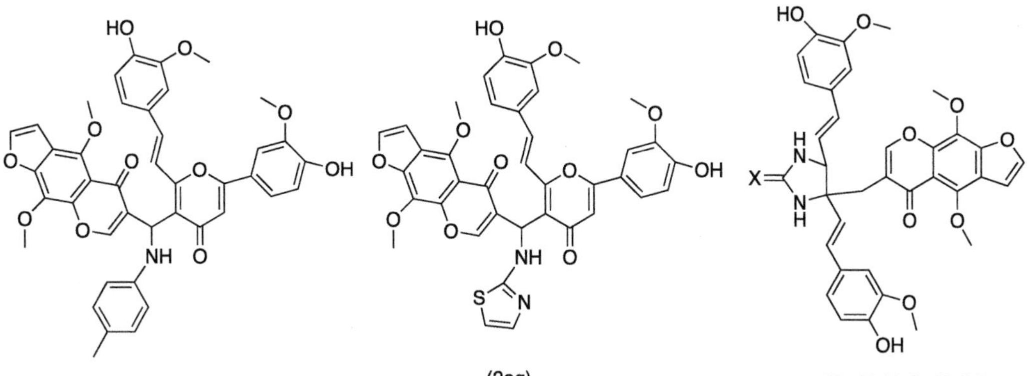

FIGURE 3–9 Structures of nonhydroxylated and hydroxylated pyrimidine-substituted curcumin.

inhibition assay [33]. Qiu et al. (2013) have synthesized a series of pyrimidine-embedded curcumin derivatives with or without hydroxyl group and improved the chemical stability and solubility of curcumin. The cell viability test shown that the three curcumin derivatives **2z**, **2aa**, and **2ab** containing hydroxyl group IC_{50} value was three- to eightfold lower than that of **2ac**, **2ad**, and **2ae** analogs (Fig. 3−8) without hydroxyl group against two colon cancer cell lines tested [32].

3.4.4 Furochromone carbaldehyde-based curcumin analogs

Chemical structures of nonhydroxylated and hydroxylated pyrimidine-substituted curcumin analogs study carried out by Borik et al. give a glance at furochromone carbaldehyde curcumin derivative using piperine as a catalyst. This one-pot condensation derivative (Fig. 3−9) reflected much more potent than curcumin on two different cancerous cell lines and **2af** and **2ai** were selectively potent on human HCC Hep G2 and **2ag** and **2ah** were active on breast carcinoma MCF-7 via inhibiting major cell cycle protein, that is, cyclin-dependent kinase 2 (CDK2), in comparison of two most-effective Food and Drug Administration (FDA)-approved anticancer reference drug (5-fluorouracil and doxorubicin) [34].

3.4.5 Bioconjugate-based curcumin analogs

Keeping in mind the bioavailability problem of curcumin, in 2005 Mishra et al. came up with an approach that makes bioconjugates of curcumin with ligands that internalize within the cellular environment. Their objective was quite clear, as they searched for ways: (1) to simplify the transmembrane passage of curcumin and also to delay its metabolism, (2) to improve the hydrophilicity of the molecule, and (3) to have a biodegradable linkage in the bioconjugate, which would provide a quick release of curcumin in an enzymatic cellular environment [35]. The study (Fig. 3−10) showed that the dipiperoyl (**2aj**) and the diglycinoyl

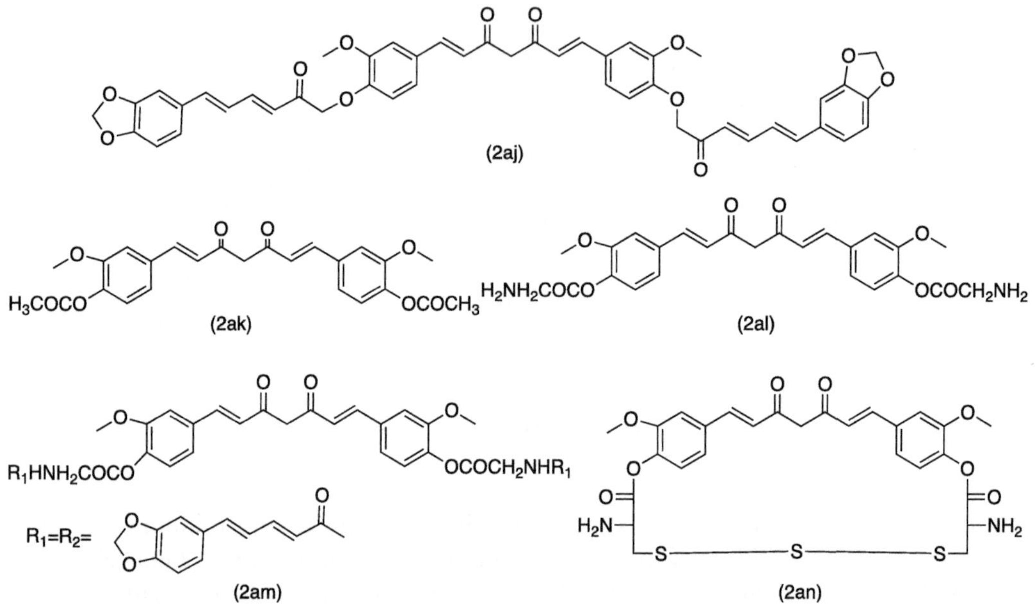

FIGURE 3–10 Structures of bioconjugate-substituted analogs of curcumin.

(**2al**) analogs of curcumin were showed more activity in affecting apoptosis of AK-5 tumor cells at lower concentrations than curcumin itself, whereas the diacetyl (**2ak**) derivative possessed slightly lower apoptotic activity. On the other hand, the diglycinoyl-dipiperoyl (**2am**) and cystinoyl (**2an**) derivatives had considerably lost its apoptotic potential. Derivatives were the most potent in the downregulation of Bcl-2, though surprisingly it was least effective in the induction of apoptosis. The anticancer activity of curcumin mainly depends on not only the nature and susceptibility of the bond between the ligands but also the chemical nature and length of the attached moiety. It was suggesting that positive role in the binding of the concerned proteins, viz., Bcl-2, Apaf-1, or the caspases. Consequentially, the apoptosis was monitored by flow cytometry and generation of intracellular ROS, generation of intracellular GSH, and inhibition of caspases was estimated for all the synthesized derivatives [35].

3.4.6 Electron-rich curcumin analogs

Further to facilitate the pharmacokinetic parameters, Amolins et al. focused on synthesizing the electron-rich curcumin analogs in which the pyrazoles and isoxazole analogs were prepared with high electron density and tested on two breast cancer cell lines. However, pyrazole and isoxazole exhibited slightly lower activities than the keto moiety (**2ao, 2ap**) (Fig. 3–11). This modification reflects the importance of the hydrogen bond framework as well as the diminished electrophilicity that maintains the antiproliferative activity [36].

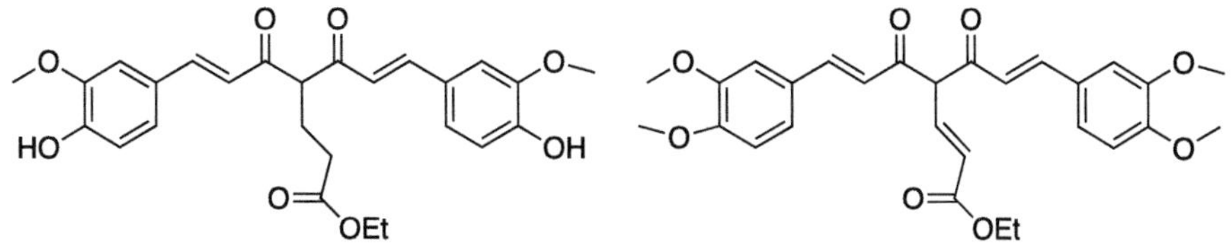

FIGURE 3–11 Structures of electron-rich analogs of curcumin.

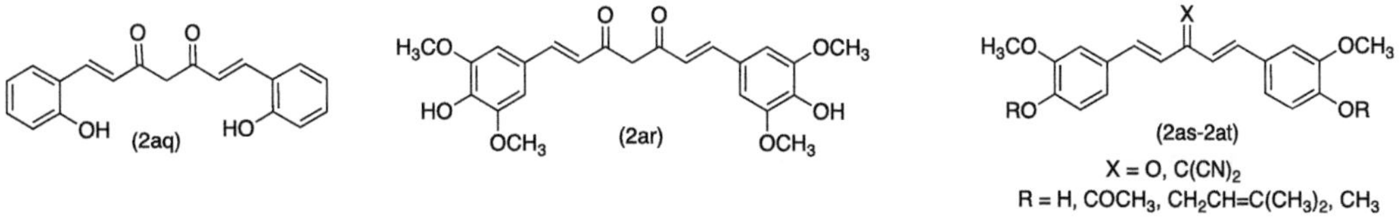

FIGURE 3–12 Structures of carbonyl analogs of curcumin.

3.4.7 Carbonyl analogs of curcumin

Kumar et al. (2014, 2015) synthesized BDMC-A (**2aq**), an analog of curcumin (Fig. 3–12), and studied their in vitro anticancer properties against breast cancer cell line, MCF-7 cells, and showed promising activities with an IC_{50} value of 15 μM and 20 μM for MCF-7, and Hep-2 cell lines, respectively, almost compared to parent curcumin (30 mM). The inhibitory activities of metastasis markers, invasion, and angiogenesis discovered that BDMC-A might have used its property by inhibiting metastatic and angiogenic trails via controlling the presence of proteins upstream to NF-kB (TGF-b, TNF-a, IL-1b, and c-Src) and NF-kB signaling cascade (c-Rel, COX-2, MMP-9, VEGF, IL-8) by upregulating TIMP-2 levels. The results of the work displayed that BDMC-A was effectively inhibited the NF-kB signaling network and interrelated markers when compared to curcumin. This better cancer activity of BDMC-A can be attained owing to the existence of hydroxyl group (OH) at the ortho position in its curcumin structure [6,37]. The di-methoxy-group-embedded curcumin (**2ar**) was synthesized and evaluated the antiproliferative property using Hep-2 cell line and matching its activity with that of parent curcumin by Kumaravel et al. (2013). The prepared methoxy-substituted curcumin exhibited greater activity with IC_{50} of 20 μM than curcumin ($IC_{50,}$ 50 μM). The flow cytometry trailed by western blot analysis was accomplished to examine the cell cycle distribution [38]. Suarez et al. (2010) synthesized the mono carbonyl derivatives of curcumin, namely, 1,5-bis(4-hydroxy-3-methoxyphenyl)-1, 4-pentadien-3-one (**2as-2at**) (Fig. 3–12). This series of prepared compounds showed excellent anticancer properties against various human cancer cell lines such as breast MCF-7, melanoma UACC-62, colon HT-29, lung carcinoma NCI-460, ovarian OVCAR-03, prostate PC-3, murine tumor cell line B16F10, renal 786-O, and leukemia K-562. All the

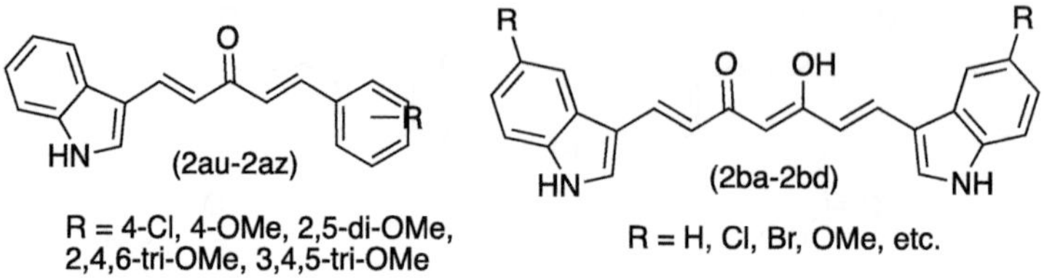

FIGURE 3–13 Structures of indole analogs of curcumin.

prepared compounds showed promising anticancer activities against colon cancer cells HT-29. However, compound **2as** was shown better activity with IC$_{50}$ values 62.3 mM for all human cancer cell lines [39].

3.4.8 Indole analogs of curcumin

The inspired indole curcumin derivatives (**2au-2az**) were synthesized and performed for their anticancer properties against different eight human cancer cell lines such as breast (MDA-MB-231, BT549, and 4T1), prostate (PC-3 and DU145), gastric (HGC-27), cervical (HeLa), and lung (A549). Among all, compounds 2,5-dimethoxy, 3,4- dimethoxy, and 3,4,5-trimethoxy substitution on aryl system of indole curcumin derivatives (**2av, 2az**) exhibited significant activities against two cells (PC-3 and BT549) with IC$_{50}$ values in the range of 3.12−6.34 mM and 4.69−8.72 mM, respectively. The best molecule 2,5-dimethoxy indole curcumin (**2av**) was also screened on RWPE-1 (normal prostate) cells and was confirmed as good than to the PC-3 cells. The compounds 2,5-dimethoxy and 3,4,5-trimethoxy indole curcumin (**2az**) were meritoriously inhibited by IC$_{50}$ values of 10.21 ± 0.10 and 8.83 ± 0.06 mM, respectively, in an assay of tubulin polymerization. Besides, DAPI and acridine orange/ethidium bromide staining studies directed **2az** molecule can make apoptosis in PC-3 cells. Moreover, flow cytometry analysis discovered that **2av** arrests PC-3 cells in the G2/M phase of the cell cycle while the compound 3,4,5-trimethoxy indole curcumin (**2az**) increase in the G2/M population [40]. The novel indole curcumin derivatives (**2ba-2bd**) (Fig. 3−13) were synthesized and studied anticancer activities against a panel of three human cancer cells, Hep-2, A549, and HeLa. Excitingly, methoxy-substituted indole curcumin (**2bd**) displayed the better anticancer property with IC$_{50}$ values of 12 μM (Hep-2), 15 μM (A549), and 4 μM (HeLa), respectively, and close to standards, doxorubicin and paclitaxel [1].

3.4.9 Ester and acid analogs of curcumin

Ferrari et al. (2013) reported a new series of ester and acid analogs of curcumin (**2be-2bi**) (Fig. 3−14) and evaluated their anticancer activity against various cancer cell lines, human colon carcinoma cells (HCT116 and LoVo) and human ovarian carcinoma cells (2008, A2780, C13, A2780/CP). When compared to acid-containing curcumin derivatives, ester curcumin compounds showed promising anticancer properties with IC$_{50}$ of 4.4 μM and 20 μM on HCT116 and LoVo cell lines, respectively [41].

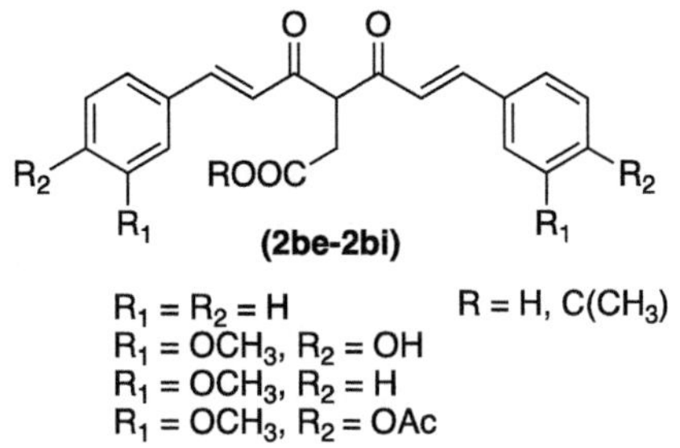

$R_1 = R_2 = H$
$R_1 = OCH_3, R_2 = OH$
$R_1 = OCH_3, R_2 = H$
$R_1 = OCH_3, R_2 = OAc$

$R = H, C(CH_3)$

FIGURE 3–14 Structures of ester and acid analogs of curcumin.

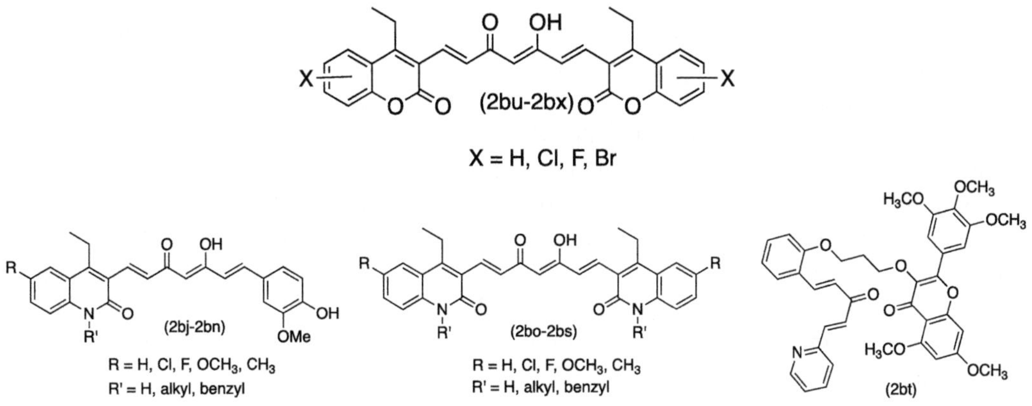

$X = H, Cl, F, Br$

$R = H, Cl, F, OCH_3, CH_3$
$R' = H, alkyl, benzyl$

$R = H, Cl, F, OCH_3, CH_3$
$R' = H, alkyl, benzyl$

FIGURE 3–15 Structures of coumarin analogs of curcumin.

3.4.10 Coumarin analogs of curcumin

Oglah et al. (2020) discovered the new coumarin-curcumin hybrids (**2bu-2bx**) (Fig. 3–15) and assessed their anticancer activity by MTT assay against MCF-7 and HeLa cancer cell lines. Among them, fluorine-substituted coumarin-curcumin (**2bw**) shown excellent activity (superior activity) with IC_{50} values of 16.687 ± 1.18 and 24.517 ± 0.85 against MCF-7 and HeLa cancer cell line than parent curcumin [42]. Raghavan et al. 2015 synthesized novel curcumin-quinolone hybrids (**2bj-2bn** and **2bo-2bs**) and evaluated their in vitro anticancer properties using MTT test against A549, MCF-7, SKOV3, and H460 cancer cells. Out of all, the compound **2bo** was found to be potent and induce apoptosis by ROS generation and seizure cell cycle progression in S and G2/M phase [42]. Wang et al. 2018 synthesized chromone-curcumin derivatives (**2bt**) and screened in vitro anticancer property in the panel of human liver cancer cell (SMMC-7721), human gastric cancer cell (SGC-7901, MGC-803), and human glioma cell (U87) and compared with standard drug doxorubicin. Among all, 5,7-dimethoxy-3-(3-(2-((1E,4E)-3-oxo-5-(pyridin-2-yl)penta-1,4-dien-1-yl)phenoxy)propoxy)-2-(3,4,5-trimethoxyphenyl)-4H-chromen-4-one (**2bt**) exhibited significant anticancer property against gastric cancer cell.

3.4.11 Hybrid analogs of curcumin

In the last few years, it has been observed by various research groups to alter/modify the core structure of curcumin to improve its drug-like properties. But still some alternative strategies are needed to be used, such as combination chemotherapy to synergize the effect and decrease the chance of tumors, reduce the cancer symptoms and death numbers, and prolong the life span [43]. Furthermore, curcumin and its analogs are being tested in combination of FDA-approved drugs, clinical trial drugs [44,45], curcumin fused or conjugated by spacer to other natural products such as carnosic acid [46], aloe vera [46], docosahexaenoic acid [46], trans-farnesylthiosalicylic acid [47], piperine [48], retinoic acid [49], α-tomatine [49], several carotenoids [50], ursolic acid [50], bicalutamide [51], quercetin [52], epigallocatechin-3-gallate, curcurbitacin B [53], rosemary [54], silymarin [55], vincristine, etoposide, carboplatin [56], etc.) for regulating various signaling pathways such as inhibiting the Bcl-2 gene [57], COX-2 [57], MMP-9/2 [58], metastatic proteins, suppressing the NF-KB [58,59], TNF-α and its regulated gene, modulate AMPK activity [58], increasing phosphorylation of ERK1/2 [60], and SAPK/JNK [60], which reducing the p65 [60], AKT/IKKa MUC1-C pathways [60], suppression of β-3 gene expression [60], suppressing the activation of JAK/STAT3/IL-8 signaling pathway [61], suppression of STAT3 [59,61] pathway, apoptosis induction via caspase-3/8 [59], Bax upregulation [59], downregulation of VEGF, VEGFR-2 expressions, upregulation of PTEN, p53, BRCA1, BRCA2, and ERCC [62]. The synergistic effects of this combination chemotherapy revealed that the antitumor effect is far greater than the effect of the native form of curcumin, showing more stability, better bioavailability, and pharmacokinetic properties [17,18].

3.5 Curcumin as tumor suppressor and its molecular targets

In the industrialized nations, one of the chief reasons of bereavement is cancer. The action that leads to cancer is forfeiture of equilibrium among cell proliferation and death of cells [63]. When the cells frolic demise because of the time off for apoptotic signals, then uncontrolled cell proliferation occurs, which leads to diverse kinds of cancer [64]. In current scenarios, the initial verdict and upsurge in healing choices have reduced the rate of death. Though, the progress in the development of resistant drugs for the treatment of cancers demands the hunt for groundbreaking and more operative medicines [65]. Curcumin is one of the most significant medicines with less side effects in the market from long time, moreover, its medicinal products are used for different cancer therapies. In cancerous cells, curcumin demonstrates tumor cascade pathways, while at the same time antitumorigenic possessions stimulated as an indication for apoptosis. These apoptotic signals are produced as two main pathways, that is, intrinsic and extrinsic [64]. The intrinsic pathway helps through stimulation of the mitochondrial membrane, which hinders the appearance of protein for antiapoptotic activities, that is, Bcl-2 and Bcl-Xl [66]. The main target molecules of curcumins anticancer activity are divided into four different categories, that is, growth factor receptor protein tyrosine, growth and metastases gene, transcription factors and

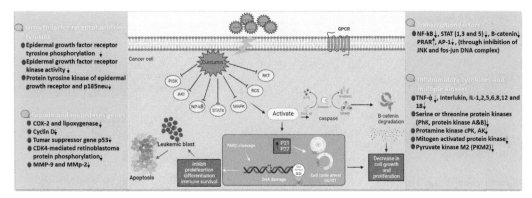

FIGURE 3-16 Curcumin target molecules for tumor suppressor and its mode of action.

inflammatory cytokines, and multiple kinases (Fig. 3–16). Dissimilar pathways of transforming gene that are jammed via curcumin, those genes exposed to constrain the epidermal growth factor receptor (EGFR), ERBB2, Wnt/β-catenin, and sonic hedgehog (SHH)/GLIs and downsignaling molecules, for example, Akt, NF-κB, and signal transducer and activator of transcription (STATs) [67]. Curcumin mainly knockouts at best place and hunk the countenance of tumor diversity encouraging trails, that is, AKT, STAT, NP-κB, MAPK, and ROS trails. It triggers the caspase path that arrest cell cycle at G0/G1, G1/S, or G2/M phase and decreases the leukemic freight by apoptosis [68]. In addition, curcumin has been testified to work on caspase-3 (mediator of apoptosis) by instigation and on the Akt/mTOR/p70S6 pathway by signal inhibition [69]. Detailed molecular targets of curcumin for curcumin anticancer potential are shown in Fig. 3–16.

Curcumin in conjugate form aim at the infested place and suppress the appearance of PI3K, AKt, NP-κB, MAPK, MAPK, ROS, and RKT tumor-encouraging pathways. Further it inhibits the appearance of mitotic properties as well p21 and p27 cyclin-dependent kinase, simultaneously as a consequence curcumin constrain cell cycle arrest G0/G1 phase, and downregulates the appearance of numerous genetic factor that intricated in the cell development, explosion, and enlargement of cancer. Downregulation/inhibition↓, upregulation/activation↑.

It is the most important point that cancer cells are fortified by liberalized signaling pathways counting detonation, programmed cell death, and angiogenesis [70,71]. In this situation, curcumin signifies as an auspicious compound as well as a functioning anticancer medicine to be used unaided or in blend with other medicines. It distresses dissimilar signaling pathways and targeted molecules intricated in the expansion of quite a lot of cancers [71]. Curcumin comes out as a very auspicious outcome in conquering cancer cells progress and explosion in numerous diverse types of cancer, that is, prostate, breast, gastric, colorectal, pancreatic, hepatic, brain, myeloma, leukemia, lymphoma, lung, and bone [8]. In melanoma healing, phytochemicals moreover control signaling trails of cell cycle or unswervingly change the controlling fragments of the cell cycles. Furthermore, the malevolence of human

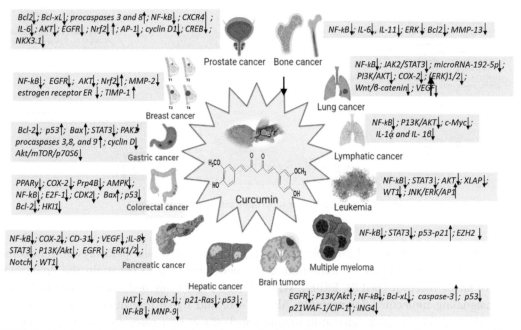

Bcl2↓; Bcl-xL↓; procaspases 3 and 8↑; NF-kB↓; CXCR4↓ ; IL-6↓; AKT↓; EGFR↓; Nrf2↓↑; AP-1↓; cyclin D1↓; CREB↓; NKX3.1↓

NF-kB↓; IL-6↓, IL-11↓; ERK↓ Bcl2↓; MMP-13↓

Prostate cancer   Bone cancer

NF-kB↓; JAK2/STAT3↓; microRNA-192-5p↓; PI3K/AKT↓; COX-2↓; (ERK)1/2↓; Wnt/β-catenin↓; VEGF↓

NF-kB↓; EGFR↓; AKT↓; Nrf2↓↑; MMP-2↓; estrogen receptor ER ↓; TIMP-1↑

Breast cancer

Lung cancer

NF-kB↓; PI3K/AKT↓; c-Myc↓; IL-1α and IL- 18↓

Lymphatic cancer

Bcl-2↑; p53↑; Bax↑; STAT3↓; PAK1↓ procaspases 3,8, and 9↑; cyclin D↓ Akt/mTOR/p70S6↓

Gastric cancer

PPARγ↓; COX-2↓; Prp4B↓; AMPK↓; NF-kB↓; E2F-1↓; CDK2↓; Bax↑; p53↓ Bcl-2↓; HKI1↓

Colorectal cancer

Curcumin

NF-kB↓; STAT3↓; AKT↓; XLAP↓; WT1↓; JNK/ERK/AP1↓

Leukemia

NF-kB↓; COX-2↓; CD-31↓ ; VEGF↓;IL-8↓ STAT3↓; P13K/Akt↓; EGFR↓; ERK1/2↓; Notch↓; WT1↓

Pancreatic cancer

NF-kB↓; STAT3↓; p53-p21↑; EZH2 ↓

Multiple myeloma

Brain tumors

Hepatic cancer

HAT↓; Notch-1↓; p21-Ras↓; p53↓; NF-kB↓; MNP-9↓

EGFR↓; P13K/Akt↑; NF-kB↓; Bcl-xL↓; caspase-3↑; p53↓ p21WAF-1/CIP-1↑; ING4↓

FIGURE 3–17 Schematic diagram showing the pathways of cell signaling for different types of cancers targeted by curcumin. ↓Downregulation/inhibition, ↑upregulation/activation, ↕modulation.

cancers rise after alterations in the DNA that straight disturb the purpose of cell cycle proteins, for example, cyclin sideways by tumor work as a suppressor of genes; for case, P53 [72]. Curcumin displays anticancer capability by directing diverse pathways for cell signaling counting growth aspects, cytokines, transcription aspects, and genes modulating cellular proliferation and apoptosis [8]. Role of curcumin in numerous cancers cell signaling pathways as modulator, regulator, and inhibitors and the details are shown in Fig. 3–17.

3.6 Curcumin for cancer therapy

3.6.1 Breast cancer

At the present time, breast cancer is the utmost common malignant tumor among the adult female and adult populace. Breast cancer is the top origin of demise owing to the incidence for women everywhere in the ecosphere [73]. In the proliferation of breast cancer cells, the key role is performed by NF-κB (proinflammatory transcription factor) [74]. Curcumin showed the aptitude to disturb the breast cancer cell production and then incursion through slowdown the regulation of genes responsible to encouraging NF-κB [75]. Same time distressing the molecular target, which is playing a role in the production of breast cancer cells, is the human epidermal growth factor receptor 2 (HER2), a tyrosine kinase (TK) receptor going to EGFR [76]. Moreover, another major molecular target is the transcription factor Nrf2, which controls diverse genes and proteins answerable for the reclamation of electrophiles and reactive oxygen species, with other properties of removal or refurbishment of their injured goods [77,78].

3.6.2 Prostate cancer

In prostate cancer, curcumin showed its healing properties by modifying several pathways of cell signaling. Curcumin mainly slows down the appearance of antiapoptotic genes Bcl-2 and Bcl-xL, in two prostate cancer cell lines, that is, human androgen-independent (DU145) and androgen-dependent (LNCaP), after that it activates procaspase-3, which leads to programmed cell death. [79]. Curcumin likewise too exaggerated the exact antigen for prostate (PSA) by slowing down the appearance of AP-1, cyclin D1, NF-κB, and cAMP response element binding (CREB). In addition, curcumin too testified to decrease the appearance of one of the androgen-receptors, that is, NKX3.1, which is basically responsible for the modulation [8].

3.6.3 Brain cancer

In humans, glioblastoma (GBM) is the utmost communal malignant brain cancer and CNS tumor [80]. During the operative procedure, that is, surgical involvement and radioactivity therapy of brain tumors and GBM, one limiting factor is the permeation of cancer cells into the healthy brain leads toward harmful paraphernalia afterward therapies [81]. Consequently, substitute treatments by means of natural derivative are getting lots of consideration. In this view, curcumins are one of the bestselling medicines with fewer side effects compared to the other orthodox actions [80]. Moreover, it was likewise reported to encourage G2/M cell cycle arrest by cumulating the protein kinase 1 (DAPK1) in U-251 malignant cell of GBM, which shows that overpowering of DAPK1 by curcumin not lone encourage cell arrest but same time constrains STAT3 and NF-κB and triggers caspase-3 [82].

3.6.4 Leukemia

Leukemia is a furthermost predominant kind of cancer everywhere in the world. Meanwhile from previous years, numerous edible foodstuffs and natural mixtures are being used for leukemia therapies. Curcumin is the main ingredient in them, it comprises dimethoxy-curcumin and bis-demethoxycurcumin, which helps in instigating the apoptosis process [83]. Wilken et al. [84] investigated the effect of curcumin on leukemic cancer; they observed that curcumin is controlling cellular propagation by encouraging apoptosis and cell cycle arrest by regulating the action of diverse tumor suppression genes, which leads to the blocking of metalloproteinases matrix. Likewise, Li et al. [85] also reported that in the K-562 cell line, curcumin inhibits the cell proliferation and clonogenicity of WT1 protein, which causes the cell cycle arrest at the G2/M phase.

3.6.5 Lung cancer

Curcumin displayed its healing competence in lung cancer therapies by downregulating the NF-κB in A549 cell lines (human lung cancer) and its major molecular targets from the signaling pathway are JAK2 and STAT3 [86]. Curcumin also reported to have proapoptotic roles in lung adenocarcinoma cells, basically it was overpowering the activities and countenance of COX-2, EGFR, and extracellular signal-regulated kinase (ERK). These all-target molecules are connected with raised caspase-mediated cell death and reduced the existence of cells from adenocarcinoma in the lungs [87]. Moreover, Jin et al. [88] investigated the curcumin anticancer activity, they noticed that it was inhibiting the cell proliferation and inducing the apoptosis of cancer cells (lung) by activating the microRNA-192-5p and inhibiting the PI3K/Akt signaling pathway [88].

3.6.6 Lymphoma

Lymphoma is a cancer that characterizes the clonal explosions of lymphocytes that are mostly organized according to their maturity and lineage (B cell, T cell, and natural killer cell). In vivo possessions of curcumin on human Burkitt's lymphoma were tested in Raji cells and it was noticed that in a xenograft mouse curcumin is downregulating the oncogene c-Myc and also upregulating the apoptotic proteins [89]. Curcumin principally distressing the lymphoma cancer by constraining the radiation-induced countenance of the molecular target of the PI3K/AKT pathway and at the same time downstream regulation of NF-κB [90].

3.6.7 Multiple myeloma

In multiple myeloma patients, curcumin reported for overpowering/suppressing IκB kinase, NF-κB, and STAT3 cell signaling pathways in peripheral blood mononuclear cells (PBMCs) [91]. Moreover, curcumin has the potential to constrain IL-6-induced STAT3 phosphorylation and consequent STAT3 nuclear translocation, which plays a significant part in the overthrow of multiple myeloma explosion [92].

3.6.8 Liver cancer

Globally, curcumin has a major therapeutic role in the treatment of HCC, usually recognized as liver cancer. It restrains MMP-9, NF-κB, COX-2 emission, encourages programmed cell death, and upsurges ROS in liver cancer cells, for example, Hep G2, HCC-SK-Hep-1, HA22T/VGH, and Hep3B [93]. Curcumin also constrains the progress of liver cancer stem cells directing the PI3K/Akt/mTOR pathway, which controls the existence, explosion, and migration of cells [94].

3.6.9 Gastric cancer

Curcumin restricts the metastasis of gastric cancer to the liver through the extenuating circulation of tumor cells in the bloodstream. It is also joint through ginsenosides that constrains liver cancer development via initiating immune escape over programmed cell death-ligand 1 (PD-L1). It also helps immune checkpoint protein in impeding angiogenesis by NF-κB-induced inflammation [95]. Curcumin also reported to reduce the appearance of cyclin D and inhibited the p21-activated kinase1 (PAK1) activity, which helps in the destruction of explosion and incursion of gastric cancer cells [96].

3.6.10 Colorectal cancer

In colorectal cancer, curcumin showed its healing accomplishment by distressing numerous pathways of cell signaling. It is reported to inhibit DMH (1,2-dimethylhydrazine)-induced rat colorectal carcinogenesis and the development of the in vitro HT-29 cell line by overpowering the pathway of PPARγ signal transduction [97]. In addition, curcumin also repressing the countenance of cyclooxygenase-2 (COX-2), p53, and pre-mRNA processing factor 4B (Prp4B) [69]. Curcumin is significantly downregulating the colorectal cancer incursion through AMPK-regulated inhibition of NF-κB, urokinase-type plasminogen activator (uPA), and matrix metalloproteinase-9 (MMP-9) [98].

3.6.11 Pancreatic cancer

Curcumin has effective cytotoxic properties on diverse pancreatic cancer cells, for example, MiaPaCa-2, PANC1, AsPC-1, and BxPC-3 [99]. In pancreatic cancer cells, curcumin has been testified to tempt the FoxO1 appearance in by acting on PI3K/Akt signaling, which instigate the cell cycle arrest and the initiation of apoptosis [100]. Furthermore, curcumin initiates programmed cell death by inhibiting the signaling of PI3K/Akt pathways and upregulating the phosphatase and TENsin (PTEN) genes [101].

3.6.12 Hepatic cancer

The dealing of hepatoma cells through curcumin controls the upsurge of ROS that affect the histone acetyltransferase (HAT), an enzyme regulating the histone acetylation in vivo. Particularly, the revelation of human hepatoma cells to curcumin significantly decreases the histone acetylation by substituting the ROS generation [102]. In human hepatoma G2 cells, curcumin encouraged DNA damage in both, that is, mitochondrial and nuclear genomes and acted as an antioxidant mediator in carcinogenesis [103].

3.7 Conclusion and future perspective

Curcumins are in the race of most successful anticancer drugs from the past time. Curcumins and their countless synthetic derivatives proved themselves are outstanding potential candidates for cancer therapies. Curcumin followed numerous cellular and molecular machinery to constrain the carcinogenic growth, due to the circumstance that no exact toxic possessions have been stated. Lots of works have been done in this field, but instead lots of areas are still need to be covered. On a positive note, this chapter has provided a careful account of the extensive efforts undertaken to transform curcumin into its various analogs, conjugates, hybrids, and combination analogs to rule out its listed drawbacks. Undoubtedly, the majority of stated analogs have shown vast enhanced antiproliferative activity on various cancers with lead drug-like properties at a nanomolar concentration as compared to respective reference molecules or curcumin. These revolutionary attempts to increase the therapeutic index of curcumin could lead to acceptance in carrying out standard clinical trial studies.

- In future, helpful sign from clinical trials on the adjunct use of curcumin, this is needed in clinical translational studies.
- More clinical trial studies are required for confirming that curcumin may upsurge existence of other treated antibiotics subjects. However, additional clinical characteristics, that is, body weight upkeep that would help in recording the helpful effect because till now no obvious opposing noxiousness has been stated.

Acknowledgment

The authors would like to thank the Department of Pharmaceuticals (Ministry of Chemicals and Fertilizers), Government of India, and the authors also thankful to the Department of Biotechnology for the financial support under the Centre of GMP Extraction Facility (BT/PR/38556/TRM/120/376/2020).

References

[1] Parthiban A, Sivasankar R, Rajdev B, Asha RN, Jeyakumar TC, Periakaruppan R, et al. Synthesis, in vitro, in silico and DFT studies of indole curcumin derivatives as potential anticancer agents. Journal of Molecular Structure 2022;1270:133885 Dec 15.

[2] Trujillo J, Chirino YI, Molina-Jijón E, Andérica-Romero AC, Tapia E, Pedraza-Chaverrí J. Renoprotective effect of the antioxidant curcumin: recent findings. Redox Biology 2013;1(1):448−56.

[3] Singh A, Singh JV, Rana A, Bhagat K, Gulati HK, Kumar R, et al. Monocarbonyl curcumin based molecular hybrids as potent antibacterial agents. ACS Omega 2019;4(7):S1−50.

[4] Wojcik M, Krawczyk M, Wozniak LA. Antidiabetic activity of curcumin: insight into its mechanisms of action. Advances in Experimental Medicine and Biology 2018;385−401 Jan 1.

[5] Dohutia C, Chetia D, Deepak Singh K. Curcumin against malaria: from traditional medicine to development of synthetic analogs; a bioorganic approach. Current Traditional Medicine 2017;2(2):124−33.

[6] Mohankumar K, Sridharan S, Pajaniradje S, Singh VK, Ronsard L, Banerjea AC, et al. Rajagopalan R. BDMC-A, an analog of curcumin, inhibits markers of invasion, angiogenesis, and metastasis in breast cancer cells via NF-κB pathway−a comparative study with curcumin. Biomedicine & Pharmacotherapy 2015;74:178−86 Aug 1.

[7] Amalraj A, Pius A, Gopi S, Gopi S. Biological activities of curcuminoids, other biomolecules from turmeric and their derivatives − a review. Journal of Traditional and Complementary Medicine 2017;7(2):205.

[8] Giordano A, Tommonaro G. Curcumin and cancer. Nutrients. 2019;11(10).

[9] Anand P, Sundaram C, Jhurani S, Kunnumakkara AB, Aggarwal BB. Curcumin and cancer: an "old-age" disease with an "age-old" solution. Cancer Letters 2008;267(1):133−64.

[10] Nelson KM, Dahlin JL, Bisson J, Graham J, Pauli GF, Walters MA. The essential medicinal chemistry of curcumin. Journal of Medicinal Chemistry 2017;60(5):1620–37.

[11] Martí-Centelles R, Falomir E, Carda M, Nieto CI, Cornago MP, Claramunt RM. Effects of curcuminoid pyrazoles on cancer cells and on the expression of telomerase related genes. Archiv der Pharmazie (Weinheim) 2016;349(7):532–8.

[12] Cheng A-L, Hsu C-H, Lin J-K, Hsu M-M, Ho Y-F, Shen T-S, et al. Phase I clinical trial of curcumin, a chemopreventive agent, in patients with high-risk or pre-malignant lesions. Anticancer Research 2001;21:2895–900.

[13] Cas MD, Ghidoni R. Dietary curcumin: correlation between bioavailability and health potential. Nutrients. 2019;11(9).

[14] Dutra LA, Ferreira de Melo TR. The paradigma of the interference in assays for natural products. Biochemical Pharmacology 2016;5(3).

[15] Babu KV, Rajasekharan KN. Simplified condition for synthesis of curcumin I and other curcuminoids. Organic Preparations and Procedures International 2009;26(6):674–7.

[16] Padhye S, Chavan D, Pandey S, Deshpande J, Swamy KV, Sarkar FH. Perspectives on chemopreventive and therapeutic potential of curcumin analogs in medicinal chemistry. Mini-Reviews in Medicinal Chemistry 2010;10(5):372–87.

[17] Zoli W, Ricotti L, Tesei A, Barzanti F, Amadori D. In vitro preclinical models for a rational design of chemo-therapy combinations in human tumors. Critical Reviews in Oncology/Hematology 2001;37(1):69–82.

[18] Liao L, Liu J, Dreaden EC, Morton SW, Shopsowitz KE, Hammond PT, et al. A convergent synthetic platform for single-nanoparticle combination cancer therapy: ratiometric loading and controlled release of cisplatin, doxorubicin, and camptothecin. Journal of the American Chemical Society 2014;136(16):5896–9.

[19] Huang MT, Ma W, Lu YP, Chang RL, Fisher C, Manchand PS, et al. Effects of curcumin, demethoxycurcumin, bisdemethoxycurcumin and tetrahydrocurcumin on 12-O-tetradecanoylphorbol-13-acetatein-duced tumor promotion. Carcinogenesis. 1995;16(10):2493–7.

[20] Mohan R, Sivak J, Ashton P, Russo LA, Pham BQ, Kasahara N, et al. Curcuminoids inhibit the angiogenic response stimulated by fibroblast growth factor-2, including expression of matrix metalloproteinase gelatinase B. Journal of Biological Chemistry 2000;275(14):10405–12.

[21] Shim JS, Kim DH, Jung HJ, Kim JH, Lim D, Lee SK, et al. Hydrazinocurcumin, a novel synthetic curcumin derivative, is a potent inhibitor of endothelial cell proliferation. Bioorganic & Medicinal Chemistry 2002;10(9):2987–92.

[22] He H, Qiao K, Wang C, Yang W, Xu Z, Zhang Z, et al. Hydrazinocurcumin induces apoptosis of hepatocellular carcinoma cells through the p38 MAPK pathway. Clinical and Translational Science 2021;14(5):2075–84.

[23] Zhou GZ, Sun GC, Zhang SN. The interplay between autophagy and apoptosis induced by one synthetic curcumin derivative hydrazinobenzoylcurcumin in A549 lung cancer cells. Journal of Biochemical and Molecular Toxicology 2015;29(6):267–73.

[24] Wu M, Kim SH, Datta I, Levin A, Dyson G, Li J, et al. Hydrazinobenzoylcurcumin inhibits androgen receptor activity and growth of castration-resistant prostate cancer in mice. Oncotarget. 2015;6(8):6136–50.

[25] Wahlström B, Blennow G. A study on the fate of curcumin in the rat. Acta Pharmacologica et Toxicologica (Copenh) 1978;43(2):86–92.

[26] Fadda AA, Badria FA, El-Attar KM. Synthesis and evaluation of curcumin analogues as cytotoxic agents. Medicinal Chemistry Research 2010;19(5):413–30.

[27] Jordan BC, Kumar B, Thilagavathi R, Yadhav A, Kumar P, Selvam C. Synthesis, evaluation of cytotoxic properties of promising curcumin analogues and investigation of possible molecular mechanisms. Chemical Biology & Drug Design 2018;91(1):332.

[28] Mahal A, Wu P, Jiang ZH, Wei X. Synthesis and cytotoxic activity of novel tetrahydrocurcumin derivatives bearing pyrazole moiety. Natural Products and Bioprospecting 2017;7(6):461–9.

[29] Kumar Dinesh, Kumar Mishra Pushpendra, Anand Anita VK, Kumar Agrawal RM Pramod. Isolation, synthesis and pharmacological evaluation of some novel curcumin derivatives as anticancer agents. Journal of Medicinal Plants Research 2012;6(14).

[30] Ahsan MJ, Khalilullah H, Yasmin S, Jadav SS, Govindasamy J. Synthesis, characterisation, and in vitro anticancer activity of curcumin analogues bearing pyrazole/pyrimidine ring targeting EGFR tyrosine kinase. BioMed Research International 2013;2013.

[31] Simoni D, Rizzi M, Rondanin R, Baruchello R, Marchetti P, Invidiata FP, et al. Antitumor effects of curcumin and structurally β-diketone modified analogs on multidrug resistant cancer cells. Bioorganic & Medicinal Chemistry Letters 2008;18(2):845–9.

[32] Qiu P, Xu L, Gao L, Zhang M, Wang S, Tong S, et al. Exploring pyrimidine-substituted curcumin analogues: design, synthesis and effects on EGFR signaling. Bioorganic & Medicinal Chemistry 2013;21 (17):5012–20.

[33] Ahmed M, Qadir MA, Hameed A, Imran M, Muddassar M. Screening of curcumin-derived isoxazole, pyrazoles, and pyrimidines for their anti-inflammatory, antinociceptive, and cyclooxygenase-2 inhibition. Chemical Biology & Drug Design 2018;91(1):338–43.

[34] Borik RM, Fawzy NM, Abu-Bakr SM, Aly MS. Design, synthesis, anticancer evaluation and docking studies of novel heterocyclic derivatives obtained via reactions involving curcumin. Molecules. 2018;23(6):1398.

[35] Mishra S, Kapoor N, Ali AM, Pardhasaradhi BVV, Kumari AL, Khar A, et al. Differential apoptotic and redox regulatory activities of curcumin and its derivatives. Free Radical Biology and Medicine 2005;38 (10):1353–60.

[36] Amolins MW, Peterson LB, Blagg BSJ. Synthesis and evaluation of electron-rich curcumin analogues. Bioorganic & Medicinal Chemistry 2009;17(1):360–7.

[37] Mohankumar K, Pajaniradje S, Sridharan S, Singh VK, Ronsard L, Banerjea AC, et al. Mechanism of apoptotic induction in human breast cancer cell, MCF-7, by an analog of curcumin in comparison with curcumin—an in vitro and in silico approach. Chemico-Biological Interactions 2014;210 (1):51–63.

[38] Kumaravel M, Sankar P, Latha P, Benson CS, Rukkumani R. Antiproliferative effects of an analog of curcumin in Hep-2 cells: a comparative study with curcumin. Natural Product Communications 2013;8 (2):183–6.

[39] Quincoces Suarez JA, Rando DG, Santos RP, Gonalves CP, Ferreira E, De Carvalho JE, et al. New antitumoral agents I: in vitro anticancer activity and in vivo acute toxicity of synthetic 1,5-bis(4-hydroxy-3-methoxyphenyl)-1,4-pentadien-3-one and derivatives. Bioorganic & Medicinal Chemistry 2010;18 (17):6275–81.

[40] Sri Ramya PV, Angapelly S, Guntuku L, Singh Digwal C, Nagendra Babu B, Naidu VGM, et al. Synthesis and biological evaluation of curcumin inspired indole analogues as tubulin polymerization inhibitors. European Journal of Medicinal Chemistry 2017;127:100–14.

[41] Ferrari E, Pignedoli F, Imbriano C, Marverti G, Basile V, Venturi E, et al. Newly synthesized curcumin derivatives: crosstalk between chemico-physical properties and biological activity. Journal of Medicinal Chemistry 2011;54(23):8066–77.

[42] Khudhayer Oglah M, Fakri Mustafa Y. Curcumin analogs: synthesis and biological activities. Medicinal Chemistry Research 2020;29(3):479–86.

[43] Ma J, Waxman DJ. Combination of antiangiogenesis with chemotherapy for more effective cancer treatment. Molecular Cancer Therapeutics 2008;7(12):3670–84.

[44] Teiten MH, Dicato M, Diederich M. Hybrid curcumin compounds: a new strategy for cancer treatment. Molecules. 2014;19(12):20839–63.

[45] Ivasiv V, Albertini C, Gonçalves AE, Rossi M, Bolognesi ML. Molecular hybridization as a tool for designing multitarget drug candidates for complex diseases. Current Topics in Medicinal Chemistry 2019;19 (19):1694–711.

[46] Einbond LS, Wu HA, Kashiwazaki R, He K, Roller M, Su T, et al. Carnosic acid inhibits the growth of ER-negative human breast cancer cells and synergizes with curcumin. Fitoterapia. 2012;83(7):1160−8.

[47] Chen Y, Zhang X, Lu J, Huang Y, Li J, Li S. Targeted delivery of curcumin to tumors via PEG-derivatized FTS-based micellar system. AAPS Journal 2014;16(3):600−8.

[48] Moorthi C, Kathiresan K. Curcumin−piperine/curcumin−quercetin/curcumin−silibinin dual drug-loaded nanoparticulate combination therapy: a novel approach to target and treat multidrug-resistant cancers. Journal of Medical Hypotheses and Ideas 2013;7(1):15−20.

[49] Thulasiraman P, McAndrews DJ, Mohiudddin IQ. Curcumin restores sensitivity to retinoic acid in triple negative breast cancer cells. BMC Cancer 2014;14(1):1−14.

[50] Linnewiel-Hermoni K, Khanin M, Danilenko M, Zango G, Amosi Y, Levy J, et al. The anti-cancer effects of carotenoids and other phytonutrients resides in their combined activity. Archives of Biochemistry and Biophysics 2015;572:28−35 Apr 15.

[51] Zhang P, Zhang X. Stimulatory effects of curcumin and quercetin on posttranslational modifications of p53 during lung carcinogenesis. Human & Experimental Toxicology 2017;37(6):618−25.

[52] Zhang JY, Lin MT, Zhou MJ, Yi T, Tang YN, Tang SL, et al. Combinational treatment of curcumin and quercetin against gastric cancer MGC-803 cells in vitro. Molecules. 2015;20(6):11524−34.

[53] Sun Y, Zhang J, Zhou J, Huang Z, Hu H, Qiao M, et al. Synergistic effect of cucurbitacin B in combination with curcumin via enhancing apoptosis induction and reversing multidrug resistance in human hepatoma cells. European Journal of Pharmacology 2015;768:28−40 Dec 5.

[54] Levine CB, Bayle J, Biourge V, Wakshlag JJ. Cellular effects of a turmeric root and rosemary leaf extract on canine neoplastic cell lines. BMC Veterinary Research 2017;13(1):1−12 Dec 13.

[55] Montgomery A, Adeyeni T, San KK, Heuertz RM, Ezekiel UR. Curcumin sensitizes silymarin to exert synergistic anticancer activity in colon cancer cells. Journal of Cancer 2016;7(10):1250−7.

[56] Sreenivasan S, Krishnakumar S. Synergistic effect of curcumin in combination with anticancer agents in human retinoblastoma cancer cell lines. Current Eye Research 2014;40(11):1153−65.

[57] Zhu DJ, Chen XW, Wang JZ, Ju Y Le, Yang MZO, Zhang WJ. Proteomic analysis identifies proteins associated with curcumin-enhancing efficacy of irinotecan-induced apoptosis of colorectal cancer LOVO cell. International Journal of Clinical and Experimental Pathology 2014;7(1):1.

[58] Aggarwal BB, Shishodia S, Takada Y, Banerjee S, Newman RA, Bueso-Ramos CE, et al. Curcumin suppresses the paclitaxel-induced nuclear factor-κB pathway in breast cancer cells and inhibits lung metastasis of human breast cancer in nude mice. Clinical Cancer Research 2005;11 (20):7490−8.

[59] Allegra A, Innao V, Russo S, Gerace D, Alonci A, Musolino C. Anticancer activity of curcumin and its analogues: preclinical and clinical studies. Cancer Investigation 2017;35(1):1−22.

[60] Li J, Xiang S, Zhang Q, Wu J, Tang Q, Zhou J, et al. Combination of curcumin and bicalutamide enhanced the growth inhibition of androgen-independent prostate cancer cells through SAPK/JNK and MEK/ERK1/2-mediated targeting NF-κB/p65 and MUC1-C. Journal of Experimental & Clinical Cancer Research 2015;34(1):1−11.

[61] Jin G, Yang Y, Liu K, Zhao J, Chen X, Liu H, et al. Combination curcumin and (−)-epigallocatechin-3-gallate inhibits colorectal carcinoma microenvironment-induced angiogenesis by JAK/STAT3/IL-8 pathway. Oncogenesis. 2017;6(10):e384.

[62] Chen X, Wang J, Fu Z, Zhu B, Wang J, Guan S, et al. Curcumin activates DNA repair pathway in bone marrow to improve carboplatin-induced myelosuppression. Scientific Reports 2017; 7(1):1−11.

[63] Wong RSY. Apoptosis in cancer: from pathogenesis to treatment. Journal of Experimental & Clinical Cancer Research 2011;30(1):1−14.

[64] Bauer JH, Helfand SL. New tricks of an old molecule: lifespan regulation by p53. Aging Cell 2006;5(5):437.

[65] Barone D, Cito L, Tommonaro G, Abate AA, Penon D, De Prisco R, et al. Antitumoral potential, antioxidant activity and carotenoid content of two Southern Italy tomato cultivars extracts: San Marzano and Corbarino. Journal of Cellular Physiology 2018;233(2):1266−77.

[66] Tuorkey M. Curcumin a potent cancer preventive agent: mechanisms of cancer cell killing. Interventional Medicine and Applied Science 2014;6(4):139.

[67] Lee WH, Loo CY, Young PM, Traini D, Mason RS, Rohanizadeh R. Recent advances in curcumin nanoformulation for cancer therapy. Expert Opinion on Drug Delivery 2014;11(8):1183−201.

[68] Tomeh MA, Hadianamrei R, Zhao X. A review of curcumin and its derivatives as anticancer agents. International Journal of Molecular Sciences. 2019;20(5).

[69] Shehzad A, Lee J, Huh TL, Lee YS. Curcumin induces apoptosis in human colorectal carcinoma (HCT-15) cells by regulating expression of Prp4 and p53. Molecules and Cells 2013;35(6):526−32.

[70] Al-Ejeh F, Kumar R, Wiegmans A, Lakhani SR, Brown MP, Khanna KK. Harnessing the complexity of DNA-damage response pathways to improve cancer treatment outcomes. Oncogene. 2010;29(46):6085−98.

[71] Udagawa T, Wood M. Tumor-stromal cell interactions and opportunities for therapeutic intervention. Current Opinion in Pharmacology 2010;10(4):369−74.

[72] Sa G, Das T. Anti cancer effects of curcumin: cycle of life and death. Cell Division 2008;3:14 Oct 3.

[73] Akram M, Iqbal M, Daniyal M, Khan AU. Awareness and current knowledge of breast cancer. Biological Research 2017;50(1):1−23.

[74] Liu Q, Loo WTY, Sze SCW, Tong Y. Curcumin inhibits cell proliferation of MDA-MB-231 and BT-483 breast cancer cells mediated by down-regulation of NFkappaB, cyclinD and MMP-1 transcription. Phytomedicine. 2009;16(10):916−22.

[75] Kim JM, Noh EM, Kwon KB, Kim JS, You YO, Hwang JK, et al. Curcumin suppresses the TPA-induced invasion through inhibition of PKCα-dependent MMP-expression in MCF-7 human breast cancer cells. Phytomedicine. 2012;19(12):1085−92.

[76] Klapper LN, Glathe S, Vaisman N, Hynes NE, Andrews GC, Sela M, et al. The erbB-2/HER2 oncoprotein of human carcinomas may function solely as a shared coreceptor for multiple stroma-derived growth factors. Proceedings of the National Academy of Sciences of the United States of America 1999;96(9):4995−5000.

[77] Kwak MK, Kensler TW. Targeting NRF2 signaling for cancer chemoprevention. Toxicology and Applied Pharmacology 2010;244(1):66.

[78] Chen B, Zhang Y, Wang Y, Rao J, Jiang X, Xu Z. Curcumin inhibits proliferation of breast cancer cells through Nrf2-mediated down-regulation of Fen1 expression. The Journal of Steroid Biochemistry and Molecular Biology 2014;143:11−18.

[79] Mukhopadhyay A, Bueso-Ramos C, Chatterjee D, Pantazis P, Aggarwal BB. Curcumin downregulates cell survival mechanisms in human prostate cancer cell lines. Oncogene. 2001;20(52):7597−609.

[80] Klinger NV, Mittal S. Therapeutic potential of curcumin for the treatment of brain tumors. Oxidative Medicine and Cellular Longevity 2016;2016.

[81] Chintala SK, Tonn JC, Rao JS. Matrix metalloproteinases and their biological function in human gliomas. International Journal of Developmental Neuroscience 1999;17(5−6):495−502.

[82] Wu B, Yao H, Wang S, Xu R. DAPK1 modulates a curcumin-induced G2/M arrest and apoptosis by regulating STAT3, NF-κB, and caspase-3 activation. Biochemical and Biophysical Research Communications 2013;434(1):75−80.

[83] Hackler L, Ózsvári B, Gyuris M, Sipos P, Fábián G, Molnár E, et al. The curcumin analog C-150, influencing NF-κB, UPR and Akt/Notch pathways has potent anticancer activity in vitro and in vivo. PLoS One 2016;11(3):e0149832.

[84] Wilken R, Veena MS, Wang MB, Srivatsan ES. Curcumin: a review of anti-cancer properties and therapeutic activity in head and neck squamous cell carcinoma. Molecular Cancer 2011;10:12 Feb 7.

[85] Li Y, Wang J, Li X, Jia Y, Huai L, He K, et al. Role of the Wilms' tumor 1 gene in the aberrant biological behavior of leukemic cells and the related mechanisms. Oncology Reports 2014;32(6):2680−6.

[86] Zhang BY, Shi YQ, Chen X, Dai J, Jiang ZF, Li N, et al. Protective effect of curcumin against formaldehyde-induced genotoxicity in A549 cell lines. Journal of Applied Toxicology 2013;33(12):1468−73.

[87] Lev-Ari S, Starr A, Vexler A, Karaush V, Loew V, Greif J, et al. Inhibition of pancreatic and lung adeno-carcinoma cell survival by curcumin is associated with increased apoptosis, down-regulation of COX-2 and EGFR and inhibition of Erk1/2 activity. Anticancer Research 2006;26(6B):4423−30.

[88] Jin H, Qiao F, Wang Y, Xu Y, Shang Y. Curcumin inhibits cell proliferation and induces apoptosis of human non-small cell lung cancer cells through the upregulation of miR-192-5p and suppression of PI3K/Akt signaling pathway. Oncology Reports 2015;34(5):2782−9.

[89] Li ZX, Ouyang KQ, Jiang X, Wang D, Hu Y. Curcumin induces apoptosis and inhibits growth of human Burkitt's lymphoma in xenograft mouse model. Molecules and Cells 2009;27(3):283−9.

[90] Qiao Q, Jiang Y, Li G. Inhibition of the PI3K/AKT-NF-κB pathway with curcumin enhanced radiation-induced apoptosis in human Burkitt's lymphoma. Journal of Pharmacological Sciences 2013;121(4):247−56.

[91] Vadhan-Raj S, Weber DM, Wang M, Giralt SA, Thomas SK, Alexanian R, et al. Curcumin downregulates NF-kB and related genes in patients with multiple myeloma: results of a phase I/II study. Blood. 2007;110(11):1177.

[92] Bharti AC, Donato N, Aggarwal BB. Curcumin (diferuloylmethane) inhibits constitutive and IL-6-inducible STAT3 phosphorylation in human multiple myeloma cells. Journal of Immunology 2003;171(7):3863−71.

[93] Darvesh AS, Aggarwal B, Bishayee A. Curcumin and liver cancer: a review. Current Pharmaceutical Biotechnology 2012;13(1):218−28.

[94] Wang J, Wang C, Bu G. Curcumin inhibits the growth of liver cancer stem cells through the phosphati-dylinositol 3-kinase/protein kinase B/mammalian target of rapamycin signaling pathway. Experimental and Therapeutic Medicine 2018;15(4):3650−8.

[95] Deng Z, Xu XY, Yunita F, Zhou Q, Wu YR, Hu YX, et al. Synergistic anti-liver cancer effects of curcumin and total ginsenosides. World Journal of Gastrointestinal Oncology 2020;12(10):1091.

[96] Cai XZ, Wang J, Li XD, Wang GL, Liu FN, Cheng MS, et al. Curcumin suppresses proliferation and inva-sion in human gastric cancer cells by downregulation of PAK1 activity and cyclin D1 expression. Cancer Biology & Therapy 2009;8(14):1360−8.

[97] Liu L, Duan C, Ma Zyi, Xu G. Curcumin inhibited rat colorectal carcinogenesis by activating PPAR-γ: an experimental study. Chinese Journal of Integrated Traditional and Western Medicine 2015;35(4):471−5.

[98] Tong W, Wang Q, Sun D, Suo J. Curcumin suppresses colon cancer cell invasion via AMPK-induced inhibition of NF-κB, uPA activator and MMP9. Oncology Letters 2016;12(5):4139−46.

[99] Bimonte S, Barbieri A, Palma G, Rea D, Luciano A, D'Aiuto M, et al. Dissecting the role of curcumin in tumour growth and angiogenesis in mouse model of human breast cancer. BioMed Research International 2015;2015.

[100] Zhao Z, Li C, Xi H, Gao Y, Xu D. Curcumin induces apoptosis in pancreatic cancer cells through the induction of forkhead box O1 and inhibition of the PI3K/Akt pathway. Molecular Medicine Reports 2015;12(4):5415−22.

[101] juan LIX, zhen LIY, ting JINC, J FAN, jun LIH. Curcumin induces apoptosis by PTEN/PI3K/AKT path-way in EC109 cells. Chinese Journal of Applied Physiology 2015;174−7.

[102] Kang J, Chen J, Shi Y, Jia J, Zhang Y. Curcumin-induced histone hypoacetylation: the role of reactive oxygen species. Biochemical Pharmacology 2005;69(8):1205−13.

[103] Cao J, Jia L, Zhou HM, Liu Y, Zhong LF. Mitochondrial and nuclear DNA damage induced by curcumin in human hepatoma G2 cells. Toxicological Sciences 2006;91(2):476−83.

4

Structural features of curcumin and its effects on cancer-related signaling pathways

Seyedeh Maryam Hosseinikhah[1], Sepideh Salehabadi[2], Prashant Kesharwani[3], Amirhossein Sahebkar[2,4]

[1]NANOTECHNOLOGY RESEARCH CENTER, PHARMACEUTICAL TECHNOLOGY INSTITUTE, MASHHAD UNIVERSITY OF MEDICAL SCIENCES, MASHHAD, IRAN [2]APPLIED BIOMEDICAL RESEARCH CENTER, MASHHAD UNIVERSITY OF MEDICAL SCIENCES, MASHHAD, IRAN [3]DEPARTMENT OF PHARMACEUTICS, SCHOOL OF PHARMACEUTICAL EDUCATION AND RESEARCH, JAMIA HAMDARD, NEW DELHI, INDIA [4]BIOTECHNOLOGY RESEARCH CENTER, PHARMACEUTICAL TECHNOLOGY INSTITUTE, MASHHAD UNIVERSITY OF MEDICAL SCIENCES, MASHHAD, IRAN

4.1 Curcumin chemistry

Curcumin (turmeric), chemically named as 1,7-Bis (4-hydroxy-3-methoxyphenyl)-1,6-hepta-dien-3,5-dione, is a culinary spice with a molecular weight of 368.38 g/mol, which is extracted from the root of *Curcuma longa* plant [1−11]. It exhibits normal keto-enol tautom-erism and antioxidant properties. In alkaline pH, curcumin exists in keto form while the enol form predominates in neutral and acidic pH media (Fig. 4−1) [12]. Curcumin can form π-π interactions due to two feruloyl moiety pairs, a nonpolar heptadiene link, a 1,3-keto-enol or diketone group, a conjugated diketone moiety, and an aromatic ring [13]. The aromatic moi-ety is responsible for π-π interactions, while the keto-enol of phenylic hydroxyl residues and phenolic sections form hydrogen links with the target macromolecules. The phenylic hydroxyl residues and the b-dicarbonyl moiety can be a hydrogen donor or acceptor [14]. In its ground state, curcumin has an estimated magnetic dipole of 10.77 D. Its logP amount is nearly 3.0 indicating a hydrophobic nature, which is therefore simply solvable in polar solvents such as ethanol, methanol, ethanol, and chloroform, among others. It only slightly dissolves in organic solvents such as cyclohexane and hexane. Currently, two noteworthy absorption bands of curcumin have been observed. The visible area of the absorption spec-trum has a wavelength between 410 and 430 nm, whereas the UV area has a wavelength of 265 nm [15]. One diketone and two phenolic parts constitute the three functional reactive groups found in curcumin (Fig. 4−1) [16]. The chemical processes linked to curcumin's

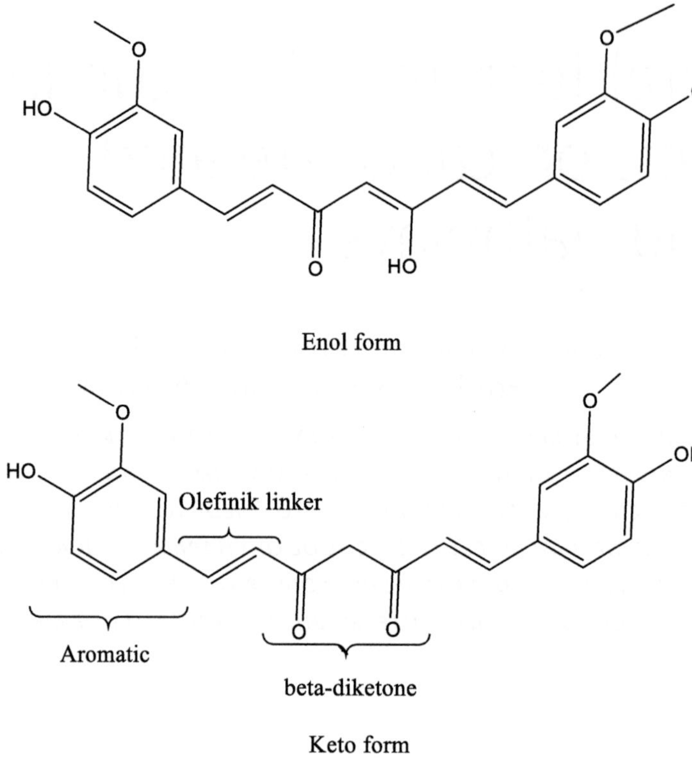

FIGURE 4–1 The keto-enol arrangement of curcumin.

biological activity include oxidation, reversible/irreversible nucleophilic addition reactions (Michael reactions), degradation, hydrolysis, and enzymatic reactions [15]. This natural substance can alter tumor microenvironments by reducing pro-inflammatory cytokines, reactive oxygen species (ROS), protein kinases, transcription factors, and oncogenes. These functions together account for the majority of curcumin's anticancer effects [17–20]. The medicinal benefits of curcumin are hypothesized to result from its effects on several therapeutically significant cancer signaling cascades including p53, PI3K, Ras, AKT, Wnt β-catenin, mTOR, and others [21]. Curcumin's therapeutic effects are considerably constrained by its low bioavailability and nonselective interaction with different molecular targets [1]. This limitation has been relatively improved by the synthesis and testing of several pharmacological analogs [1].

4.2 Changes in a structurally modified curcumin's anticancer activity

Curcumin has been shown to hinder transformation, restrain proliferation, and trigger apoptosis. Despite all these advantages, its effectiveness is still restricted due to poor absorption, weak bioavailability, and rapid removal from the circulation. Researchers are striving to generate a synthetic curcuminoid by making appropriate structural changes to concurrently increase both physicochemical characteristics and antitumor effectiveness [22]. Accordingly, Cao et al. created three classes of curcumin analogs in four cell lines (LX-2, MDA-MB-231, SMMC7221, and Hepg2) via the formation of bioactive ester bonds. These derivatives exerted noticeable effectiveness on cell death with their IC50 values from 0.18. The compound with the strongest activity is shown as compound 1 (Fig. 4–2) [23].

One of the potential restrictions associated with cancer therapy is multidrug resistance (MDR), which could be due to the upregulation of reflux pumps such as P-glycoprotein (P-gp). Lopes-Rodrigues et al. investigated the effects of several curcumin derivatives on P-gp levels. They produced a compound with the best antitumor and anti-P-gp activities. It was made utilizing curcumin, Cs_2CO_3, and Bu_4NBr in the presence of acetone and propargyl bromide (3-bromo-prop-1-yne) solution. The combination was then refluxed at 60°C for several hours (4 h) and subsequently filtered. After several washings and final recrystallization, an orange solid was produced (Compound 2, Fig. 4–2). This compound limited P-gp effect, led to cell cycle arrest at G2/M phase, and enhanced apoptosis in an MDR chronic myeloid

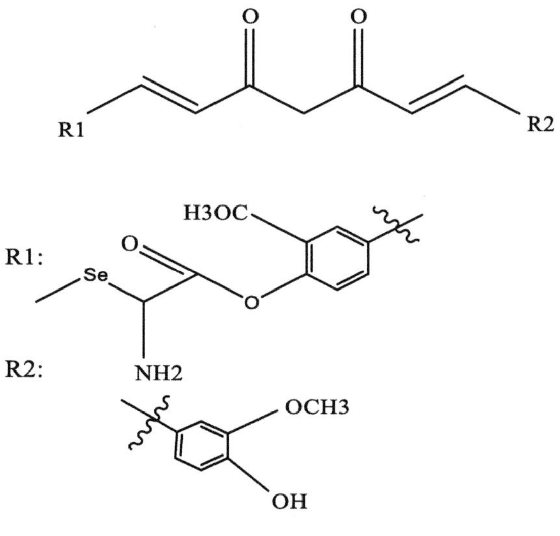

compound 1

FIGURE 4–2 Compound 1 and compound 2.

leukemia (CML) cell line [24]. Fawzi et al. made new curcumin analogs with a 3,5-dibenzylide-nepiperidin-4-one nucleus. To investigate their antitumor activity, in silico and laboratory methods were used. These compounds showed an interaction energy comparable to that of podophyllotoxin, which was performed at tubulin colchicine binding position. A tubulin polymerization experiment was conducted using some of these products on several cell lines such as human ovarian adenocarcinoma (A2780), metastatic renal adenocarcinoma (ACHN), bone metastasis of grade IV prostate cancer (PC-3), human colorectal carcinoma (HCT116), and leukemic monocyte lymphoma (U937-GTB) (Compounds A−C, Fig. 4−3). The findings revealed moderate antitumor activity by the induction of apoptosis and inactivating tubulin microtubules [25].

Ji et al. synthesized a series of 4-carbonyl-2,6-dibenzylidene cyclohexanone derivatives by aldol (a carbonyl molecule combines with an enol or enolate ion to create a β-hydroxyaldehyde) reactions. These complexes proved to block the STAT signaling pathway. A specific compound showed prominent antitumor activity against MDA-MB-231, DU145, and A549 cell lines (compound 3, Fig. 4−4). Molecular docking method also confirmed that it could inhibit STAT3 by targeting the SH2 domain [26].

Wang et al. synthesized several derivates with antitumor effects through the control of thioredoxin reductases (TrxR). Among all, one complex, 5,7-dimethoxy-3-(3-(2-((1E,4E)-3-oxo-5-(pyridin-2pyridinenta-1, Pentan-1-yl) phenoxy) propoxy)-2-(3,4,5-trimethoxyphenyl)-4Hchromen-4-one, displayed a relatively greater antitumor function (Compound 4, Fig. 4−5).

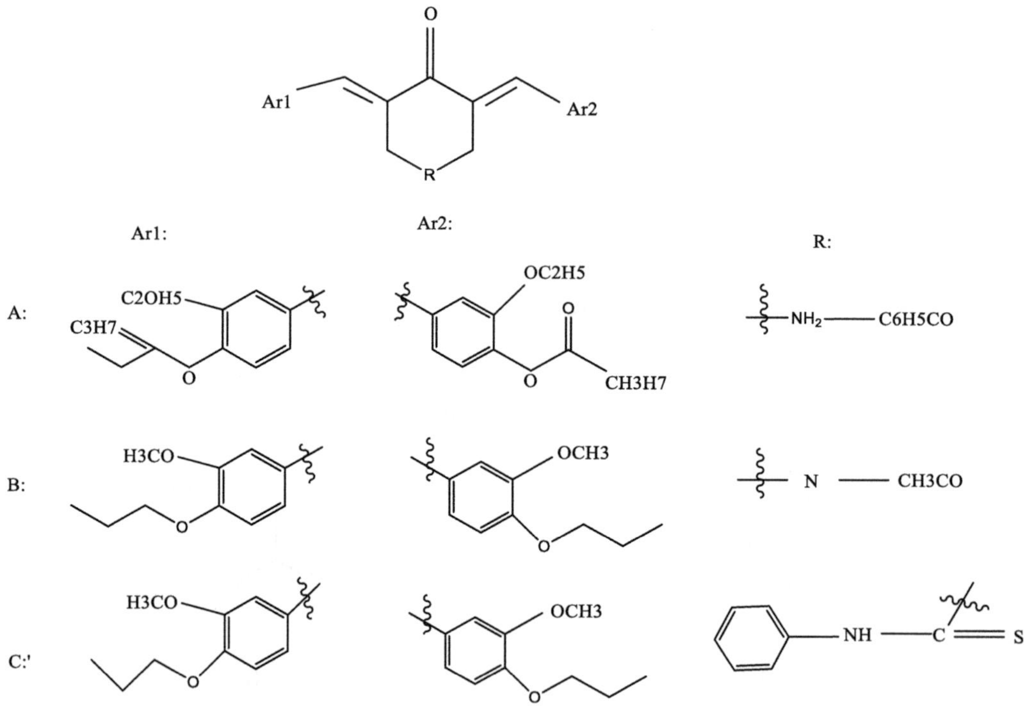

FIGURE 4-3 Compounds A−C.

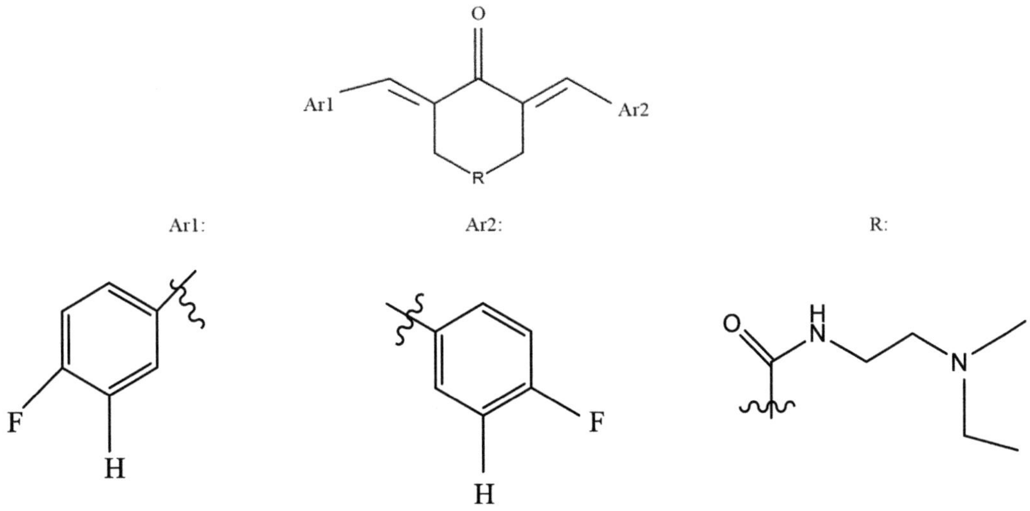

Ar1:   Ar2:   R:

FIGURE 4–4 Compound 3.

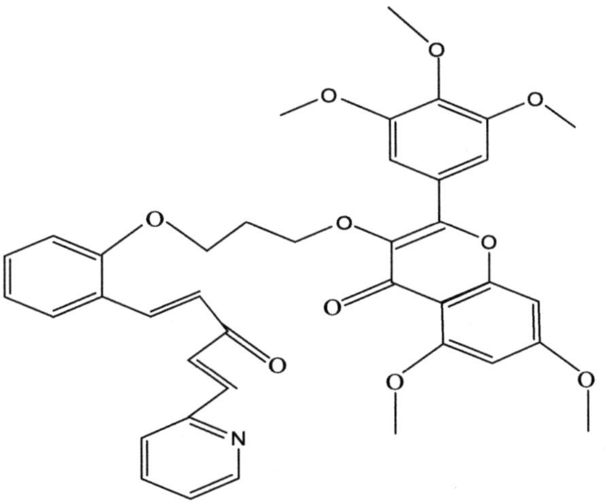

FIGURE 4–5 Compound 4.

This substance was produced by blending different chemicals (1E,4E)-1-(3,4-dimethoxyphe-nyl)-5-(4-hydroxyphenyl) penta-1,4-dien-3-one and addition of a dropwise amount of a DMF (dimethyl formamide) solution (3-bromopropoxy) 5,7-dimethoxy-2-(3,4,5-tri methoxyphenyl)-4H-chromen-4-one at 90°C for 7 hours when K_2CO_3 and DMF were present. After cooling the reaction mixture, DCM was extracted, the organic layer was washed with a strong base (NaOH) and salt (NaCl), dehydrated with anhydrous Na_2SO_4, and then purified using column chromatography. According to the anticancer assessment, this substance halted the cell cycle, disrupted mitochondrial function, and decreased TrxR function in gastric cancer (GC) cells to

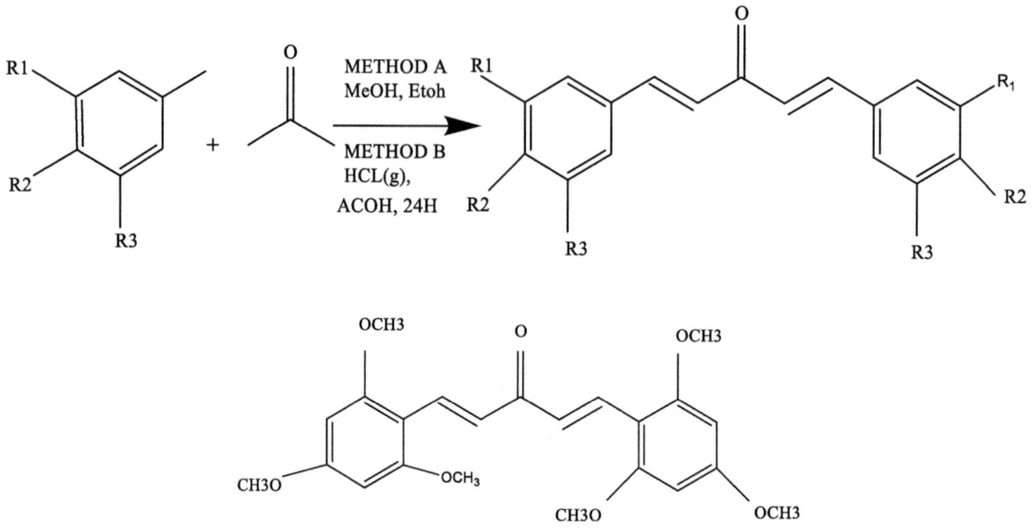

FIGURE 4–6 Synthesis of compound 5.

cause apoptosis. Findings of western blot also revealed that this compound enhanced the levels of the Bax/Bcl-2 ratio and TrxR oxidation [27] (Fig. 4–6).

Another study used condensation of acetone with the properly substituted benzaldehydes under typical protic conditions to create compound 5 [1,28]. This substance was 50 times more powerful than curcumin in inhibiting growth in both prostate and breast cancer lines, with IC50 values within the submicromolar range.

4.3 Curcumin's function on CDK inhibitors and CDK/cyclin complexes

Checkpoints control transitions between phases of cell cycle. This process is tightly regulated by cyclins, cyclin-dependent kinases (CDKs), and tumor suppressors. Cyclins are phase-specific regulatory proteins that activate CDKs when stimulated by growth factors. The cyclin-CDK complex can then phosphorylate other proteins to coordinate cell cycle progression [29]. CDK inhibitors (CDKIs), including kinase inhibitor protein (Kip), retinoblastoma protein (Rb1), p21, p27, p57, and inhibitor of CDK4 (Ink4), adversely influence the course of cell cycle [29]. CDKs are now known to have a variety of functions in both healthy and abnormal cells [30]. Malignant cells frequently have altered expression of CDKs, excessive cyclin expression, and decreased expression of CDKIs [21]. Numerous investigations have proved that curcumin affects the activity of CDKs and inhibits tumor growth. Based on the data from an ex vivo research, curcumin showed a high propensity for adenosine triphosphate (ATP) binding pocket of CDK2. In addition, the anticancer activity of curcumin was diminished in CDK2 knockout HCT116 colon cancer cells [31]. According to an in vitro study, curcumin prevented the proliferation of HCT116 colon cancer cells by halting cell cycle at G1 and decreasing the phosphorylation of Rb. Interestingly, Park et al. discovered that curcumin altered the expression of genes involved in the cell cycle using cDNA microchip. For additional validation, fluorescence-activated cell sorting (FACS) analysis and western blotting were used to assess DNA composition and expression levels of cyclins, CDKs, and CDKIs. The potential mechanisms of curcumin's antiangiogenic effects were evaluated in creation of lines of human endothelial cells (ECV304). Following curcumin administration, cell cycle was arrested at G0/G1 and/or G2/M, the levels of p21WAF1/CIP1, CDKIs, p27KIP1, and p53 were increased, and cyclin Bl and cdc2 were slightly reduced [32]. Breast cancer cells from an MCF-7 strain treated with curcumin had less cell division and their development was stalled at G1. The antiproliferative effects of curcumin were found to be mediated through upregulation of CDKIs, p53, p21, and p27 as well as proteasome-driven downregulation of cyclin E [33]. According to research by Huang et al., curcumin therapy dramatically reduced the levels of vascular endothelial growth factor (VEGF), Cyclin D1, CDK4 mRNA, and proteins in the rat liver tumor cells, protecting it against N-nitrosodiethylamine-induced hepatic damage [34]. Earlier studies demonstrated that curcumin treatment increased the proportion of MDA-MB-468 cells remained in the S and G2/M phases and had a dual effect on the development of tumor cells [35]. Similarly, SKBR-3 cells treated with 10μM curcumin were arrested at the G2/M phase and had higher levels of p21 expression, while cyclin A, B1, D1, and E levels were suppressed [36]. Curcumin also downregulated the expression of cyclin D/E in SKBR-3 and MDA-MB-231 cells [37]. It was shown that in MDA-MB-231 cells, curcumin enhanced the levels of p21, p16, and p53 while diminished cyclin E, cyclin D1, CDK2, and CDK4 levels. These effects resulted in G1/S and G2/M arrest and apoptosis, which were mediated by ROS generation and p38-MAPK stimulation [38].

4.4 P53 pathway and curcumin interaction

One of the most crucial tumor suppressors is the p53 protein, which drives a variety of biological functions such as cell division, DNA damage, and apoptosis [39]. The expression of growth arrest DNA-damage-inducible alpha (GADD45A) and p21 are increased when p53 is activated by phosphorylation of serine-15. After being exposed to 20 M curcumin for 24 h, human GC cells greatly enhanced the levels of p21 and GADD45A [40]. In addition, p21 binding to cyclin E-CDK2 or cyclin D-CDK4 complexes hinders Rb phosphorylation and hence results in cell cycle arrest at the G0/G1 phase [40]. Breast cancer cells are subjected to curcumin-mediated apoptosis through both p53-dependent and p53-independent mechanisms. That said, curcumin induced p53-dependent apoptosis and stopped cell proliferation in MCF-7 breast cancer cells [41]. Using the aggressive neuroblastoma cell line N2a, Himakshi Sidhar et al. indicated that all endogenous Bex genes were activated by curcumin in a dose- and time-dependent manner. Curcumin treatment stimulated p53 by hyperphosphorylation at serine-15, emphasizing that Bex genes are downstream targets of p53. Curcumin's ability to reexpress Bex genes functions as a tumor suppressor and may offer an alternative method of treating tumors like neuroblastomas that have Bex genes being silenced [42]. In the fibrotic liver of rats, curcumin enhanced the expression of a senescence marker known as high mobility group AT-Hook 1(Hmga1) and increased the number of senescence-associated β-galactosidase-positive hematopoietic stem cell (HSCs). It upregulated the expression of senescence markers P21, P16, and Hmga1 in cultured HSCs, which was accompanied by a decrease in the quantity of HSC activation indicators of the smooth muscle actin and procollagen. Accordingly, the P53 pharmacological inhibitor (pifithrin α (PFT-α)) or transfection with P53 siRNA was found to prevent the in vitro senescence of HSCs caused by curcumin. Additional research revealed that curcumin stimulated P53 expression via a PPARγ activation-dependent pathway. PPARγ agonist, 15d-PGJ2, significantly increased curcumin's capability to induce senescence in activated HSCs, whereas PPAR antagonist, PD68235, reversed this function [43]. Curcumin had no effect on low p53-expressing TR9 cells and immortalized human fibroblast cells (MDAH041) that lacked the p53 gene. In contrast, it had a greater impact on TR-7 and MCF-7 cells that carried the p53 gene. In addition, MCF-7 cells treated with curcumin expressed more of the proapoptotic protein Bax. These findings collectively imply that curcumin exerts its chemopreventive effects via a p53-dependent mechanism [21]. Researchers examined the biological processes underlying the anticolon cancer actions of curcumin in vitro. Curcumin was nontoxic to healthy colon epithelial cells while dose-dependently inhibited colon cancer cells' proliferation. It led to cell cycle arrest at the S phase by impeding the production of proteins such as Rb and E2F family of transcription factors. Ultimately in a xenograft mouse model, the suppressing effects of curcumin on tumor growth were assessed in vivo [44]. In another study, Allegra et al. probed into the possibility of improving the cytotoxic effects of curcumin and carfilzomib (CFZ) on in vitro grown U266 cells. Data on cell viability revealed that curcumin lessened the cytotoxic effects of CFZ. ROS contents in U266 cells increased after exposure to curcumin or CFZ; however, their synthesis did not appear to be further potentiated after starting the medication combination. It's noteworthy to mention that NF-κB nuclear accumulation was diminished after treatment with either CFZ or curcumin and was further decreased in cells treated with CFZ-curcumin combinations. This is likely because the two drugs target NF-κB using separate pathways. As a result of their experiment, both drugs were found to induce G0/G1 cell cycle arrest and p53/p21 axis activity [45]. Agarwal et al. studied the curcumin-mediated ROS production in HT-29 colon cancer cells with mutant Smd4 and p53 genes. Curcumin administration drastically promoted ROS levels, cell apoptosis, DNA fragmentation, chromatin condensation, and cell nuclear contraction of HT-29 cells in a dose- and time-dependent manner [46]. The proapoptotic properties of curcumin were investigated by Ye et al. on H460 and A427 cells. In non-small cell lung cancer (NSCLC), MiR-192−5p/215 was found to be a potential cancer restrainer. Using miRNA microarray and qPCR, miR-192−5p and miR-215 were shown to be the most responsive miRNAs to curcumin induction. Accordingly, expressions of miR-192−5p/215 in p53 wild-type A549 cells were higher than H1299 cells (p53-null) when treated with curcumin. Likewise, the tetracycline gene expression system led to conditional knockdown of p53 and notably canceled curcumin-induced miR-192−5p/215 overexpression in the p53 wild-type H460, A427, and

A549 cells [47]. These findings highlight that the proapoptotic functions of curcumin are related to miR-192−5p-215 induction and the p53-miR-192−5p-215-XIAP pathway, which are appealing targets for the treatment of non-small cell lung carcinoma [47].

4.5 Curcumin's targets in the cancer signaling pathway

Cell signaling pathways are interconnected, tightly regulated systems involving intracellular second messengers by which cellular reactions occur. Malignant cells are often associated with altered expression of signaling proteins including phosphoinositide 3-kinase (PI3K), EGFR, mammalian target of rapamycin (mTOR), Ras, Akt, NF-B, and Wingless/integrated (Wnt) and mitogen-activated protein kinases (MAPK). Consequently, targeting the main components of cell signaling pathways seems to be beneficial in cancer therapeutic strategies [48].

4.6 Activation of Ras signaling by curcumin

Ras is a small transmembrane molecule mainly involved in intracellular signal transduction, which acts via hydrolyzed enzymes called GTPase [49]. Constitutive activation of distinct Ras oncoproteins has been addressed in numerous malignancies such as the K-Ras mutation in NSCLC, H-Ras mutation in bladder and thyroid carcinoma, and the N-Ras mutation in melanoma [50,51]. Inhibition of Ras-mediated pathways has been of great therapeutic benefits in previous studies. ROS generation by curcumin downregulated the activity of matrix metalloproteinase (MMP) 2 and Bcl-2 while increased the function of Bax and caspase 3 in MCF 10 A human breast epithelial cells transformed with H-Ras [52]. Abdelmoaty et al. synthesized a brand-new curcumin derivative known as 3,5-(E)-Bis (3-methoxy)-4-hydroxhydroxybenzoate-peridipiperidineloride (C0818), which possessed anticancer effects and efficiently suppressed heat shock protein 90 (Hsp90). Their results showed that C0818 activated the mitochondrial pathway, which is a significant apoptotic pathway, to trigger ROS- and caspase-dependent death in hepatocellular carcinoma (HCC) cells. Hsp90 client proteins such as RAS, C-Raf, P-C-Raf, Erk, P-ERK, MEK, P-MEK, and Akt were also degraded by C0818 [53].

It is documented that curcumin could prevent the growth of K562 cells by downregulating p210 BCR-ABL, which in turn inhibited the Ras signal transduction pathway [54]. The progression of CML is dependent on the activation of the Breakpoint Cluster Region-Abelson (BCR-ABL) gene encoding P210 BCR-ABL molecule. Curcumin inhibited the Ras/Raf/MAPK pathway which in turn downregulated the P210 BCR-ABL overproduction [55,56]. Researchers demonstrated that curcumin-induced cell cycle arrest in AGS cells (a human gastric adenocarcinoma cell line) is mediated through the Ras/ERK signaling pathway [57].

4.7 Effect of curcumin in PI3K/AKT/mTOR signaling

A protein kinase known as mTOR is thought to be an important regulator of several cellular functions such as cell growth, proliferation, differentiation, survival, and motility [58].

Oncogenic cellular processes are associated with excessive mTOR signaling, particularly mTORC1, which represents a potential target in cancer treatment [58]. Curcumin inhibited insulin-like growth factor 1 (IGF-1)/PI3K/Akt/mTORC1 mechanism, which in turn suppressed the erythroblastosis virus transcription factor 2 and murine double minute 2 (MDM2) oncoprotein resulting in apoptosis and cell cycle arrest. In addition, curcumin increased autophagy by activating unc-51-like kinase 1, a downstream target of the IGF-1/PI3K/Akt/mTOR pathway. By suppression of F0F1-ATPase, curcumin also activated AMP-activated protein kinase, an enzyme that adversely regulates mTORC1 [58]. Borges et al. revealed that curcumin altered the expression of crucial genes that ultimately led to inhibition of PI3K-AKT-mTOR signaling pathway in head and neck carcinoma (HNC) cell lines [59]. In a different study, Liu et al. investigated the effects of multiple programmed cell deaths (PCDs) caused by curcumin on human NSCLC as well as the potential molecular pathways of apoptosis and autophagy prompted by curcumin via the PI3K/Akt/mTOR signaling pathway. They cocultured curcumin with a PI3K/Akt inhibitor (LY294002) and an mTOR inhibitor (rapamycin). Curcumin decreased the viability of A549 cells in a time- and dose-dependent manner by induction of apoptosis and autophagy via inhibition of the PI3K/Akt/mTOR signaling pathway. It also resulted in the development of fluorescent particles known as autophagic vesicles (AVs), a substantial rise in the ratio of LC3-II/LC3-I and Beclin1, as well as downregulation of p62 [60]. According to Tian et al., in N-methyl-N-nitrosourea (MNU)-induced urothelial tumor tissue and bladder cancer cells, curcumin reduced IGF1R and IRS-1 phosphorylation levels and suppressed transcription of IGF2. Their results showed that one of curcumin's modes of action is to decrease IGF2 and IGF2-mediated PI3K/AKT/mTOR signaling pathways. These findings point to a newly developed therapeutic strategy in bladder cancer induced by abnormal IGF2 activation, which is helpful for the translational use of curcumin [61]. Glioblastoma treatment still faces major challenges such as chemotherapy resistance. Hence, employing natural polyphenols could be a potential therapeutic approach [62]. Maiti et al. assessed the effects of curcumin and berberine cotreatment (SH-SY5Y) using two distinct glioblastoma cell lines, U-87MG and U-251MG, as well as human tissue-derived neuroblastoma cell lines. They evaluated c-Myc and p53 levels, as well as single and combination treatments (1:5) of solid lipid curcumin particles (SLCP) (20 M) and berberine (100 M) on cell viability. In both glioblastoma cell lines, cotreatment with SLCP and berberine led to higher DNA fragmentation and cell death but lower ATP levels and mitochondrial membrane potential as well as significantly suppressed PI3K/Akt/mTOR pathway. Therefore, combining SLCP and berberine may be a potential way to slow or cease the growth of glioblastoma. [62]. In human melanoma A375 and C8161 cell lines, both in vitro and in vivo, curcumin successfully stopped cell proliferation, reduced invasion potential, blocked cancer cells in their tracks during the G2/M cell cycle transition, and promoted autophagy. The activation of AKT, mTOR, and P70S6K proteins was also inhibited by curcumin. In light of these findings, curcumin may be a cutting-edge therapeutic possibility in the treatment of melanoma [63]. By inhibiting other signals such as the PI3K/Akt/mTOR, the NF-κB (nuclear factor-kappaB) pathways, and the sarco/endoplasmic reticulum calcium ATPase, curcumin was found to be further beneficial for the ovarian cancer (OC) [64,65]. It is remarkable that curcumin is extremely safe even at large oral doses of 12 g per day [66,67]. However, rapid metabolism and limited bioavailability are major concerns limiting its usage in medicinal applications [68]. To overcome these issues, newer strategies are being conducted such as creating analogs by modifying the primary structure or developing drug-loading nanoparticles for enhanced delivery [69,70]. That said, curcumin derivative HO-3867 exerted significantly more anticancer activities than the original compound [71]. Consequently, curcumin analogs may be major contenders in antitumor medications, particularly in the treatment of OC owing to their enhanced bioavailability.

4.8 Curcumin's effect on Wnt/β-catenin signaling pathway

By promoting cancer cell renewal, proliferation, and differentiation, the aberrant Wnt/β-catenin signaling pathway illustrates prominent functions in carcinogenesis. The therapeutic potential of drugs that target this pathway in malignancy has been highlighted by several research [72]. Curcumin appears to impede the Wnt/β-catenin pathway alongside its downstream mediators, including c-Myc and cyclin D1 [73]. In prostate cancer, interaction with coregulators including β-catenin modifies the androgen receptor's (AR) ability to regulate transcription. Curcumin may modulate the Wnt/β-catenin signaling pathway by altering interactions between AR/β-catenin contributing to a dose-dependent, substantial reduction in AR expression. In the nuclear and cytoplasmic extracts, as well as whole cell lysates, significant curcumin-induced reduction of β-catenin was observed. Further investigation found that curcumin decreased the phosphorylation of Akt and glycogen synthase kinase-3 while increased β-catenin phosphorylation. The target gene of the β-catenin/T-cell factor transcriptional complex, c-myc, and cyclin D1 were also lowered. According to these results, curcumin alters the Wnt/β-catenin signaling pathway and may be a crucial factor in mediating the inhibitory effects on lymph node carcinoma of the prostate (LNCaP) [74]. Curcumin significantly increased apoptosis in three GC cell lines of SNU-1, SNU-5, and AGS via modulating Wnt/β-catenin signaling pathway. The levels of Wnt3a, LRP6, phospho-LRP6, -catenin, phospho—catenin, C-myc, and survivin were all dramatically reduced by curcumin. It also suppressed xenograft development in vivo and decreased the target genes of Wnt/β-catenin signaling showing a promising approach in the treatment of GC [75]. One of the most prevalent malignancies and a major source of death and morbidity in women is cervical cancer [76]. Chronic inflammation promotes the production of pro-inflammatory substances such as chemokines, cytokines, oncogenes, cyclooxygenase-2 (COX-2), ROS, MMPs, intracellular signaling pathway mediators, activator protein 1 (AP-1), and signal transducer and activator of transcription 3 (STAT3), which promote tumor proliferation, invasion, angiogenesis, transformation, and metastatic spread [77–79]. In spheroids models and monolayer cell cultures, Ghasemi et al. evaluated the anticancer effects of curcumin in comparison to 5-fluorouracil in HeLa cells in cervical cancer [77]. 5-fluorouracil and curcumin caused cells to enter a G2/M cell cycle arrest followed by sub-G1 apoptosis. They demonstrated that curcumin suppressed cervical cancer cell invasion and proliferation by blocking the NF-kB and

Wnt/β-catenin pathways, suggesting additional research on the potential effects of this substance on cervical cancer treatment. [77]. By increasing miR-9 expression and blocking Wnt/β-catenin signaling, curcumin also prevented oral squamous cell carcinoma (OSCC) cell growth [80]. Likewise, miR-9 suppression increased the activity of the Wnt/β-catenin pathway while simultaneously weakened the antiproliferative effects of curcumin on OSCC cells. These findings showed that curcumin may have a therapeutic value in the treatment of OSCC. MiR-7 was found to be crucial in controlling pancreatic cell (PC) death and proliferation [81].

4.9 Role of curcumin on transcription factors in cancer

Proteins called transcription factors modulate gene expression by interacting with specific DNA segments. Under a normal physiologic state, several of these transcription factors may remain inactive and highly controlled to impede the expression of unnecessary genes. Numerous transcription factors with dysregulated functions have been found in a variety of malignancies. The growth, survival, and angiogenesis of tumor cells can all be supported by the activation or inactivation of specific transcription factors [21].

4.10 Role of curcumin in NF-κB and AP-1 signaling pathway

A group of transcription factors identified as NF-κB has been implicated in inflammation and immunological responses. Numerous medications have been tested for their ability to inhibit NF-κB protein since there is mounting evidence that abnormally and excessively active NF-κB is associated with several malignancies [82]. The synthetic aminoketone compound 3,5-bis (2-fluoro benzylidene)-4-piperidone (EF24) (C19H15F2NO) is considered one of the curcumin analogs produced by Olivera et al., which blocked NF-κB pathway and further pro-inflammatory mediators. 3,5-Bis(2-pyridinylmethylidene)-4-piperidone (EF31) is another analog that its capability to suppress NF-κB pathway has not yet been determined [83]. Mouse RAW264.7 macrophages were utilized to investigate the function of EF31 compared to a combination of EF24 and curcumin on NF-κB pathway signaling pathway. EF31 (IC50 ∼ 5 μM) exerted more effective inhibition of LPS (1 μg/mL)-induced NF-κB DNA binding than both EF24 (IC50 ∼ 35 μM) and curcumin (IC50 above 50 μM). Moreover, EF31 showed more suppression of NF-κB nuclear translocation, tumor necrosis factor-α (TNF-α), interleukin-1, interleukin-6, and other downstream inflammatory mediators. Ultimately, EF31 provoked a significant toxicity in NF-κB-dependent malignant cell lines while exhibiting extremely slight and reversible damage in RAW264.7 macrophages. These results revealed the antiinflammatory and anticancer properties of EF31 through blocking NF-κB more than EF24 or curcumin [83]. Among head and neck squamous cell carcinomas (HNSCC), laryngeal carcinoma is the most frequent and is responsible for 1% of cancer-related fatalities. Researchers investigated the function of a chemotherapeutic drug called bis-demethoxy curcumin analog (BDMC-A) compared to curcumin. BDMC-A successfully suppressed the metastatic spread of tumor cells, inhibited transcription factors such as c-Jun, STAT3, p65, PPAR-γ, NF-κB, and β-catenin which are involved in angiogenesis. It also decreased the levels of VEGF, TGF-β, IL-9, and IL-8 [84].

4.11 Role of curcumin in STAT signaling

The JAK/STAT3 signaling system is a desirable target for cancer therapy due to its ability to encourage cancer cell growth, survival, and migration [85]. STAT proteins can be activated by Janus kinase (JAK), cytokine receptors, G-protein-coupled receptors, or growth factor receptors (e.g., EGFR) through nonreceptor tyrosine kinases or by platelet-derived growth factor receptors with intrinsic tyrosine kinase activity [86,87]. Curcumin was found to bind to the JAK activation loop in a time- and concentration-dependent manner inhibiting the STAT3 signaling pathway [88]. It also inhibited the nuclear translocation of STAT3 produced by IL-6 in multiple myeloma [89]. A member of the interleukin-6 family, oncostatin M, which induced gene expression for MMP-1, MMP-3, MMP-13, and TIMP-3, was found to be decreased by curcumin. Curcumin treatment prevented IL-12-induced tyrosine phosphorylation of the transcription factors JAK2, tyrosine kinase 2, STAT3, and STAT4 in the activated T cells [90]. Cancer-associated fibroblasts (CAFs) manifested increased resistance to chemotherapy through the stimulation of the JAK2/STAT3 signaling pathway in GC cells. Combining curcumin with traditional chemotherapy could be a fruitful way to combat chemotherapy resistance in GC enriched with fibroblasts since curcumin effectively inhibited the JAK2/STAT3 signaling pathway in these cell lines [85]. In OC cells, curcumin (diferuloyl-methane) suppressed STAT3 activity, which led to less cell viability; it also disrupted PI3K/Akt and the NF-κB signaling pathways [91]. According to a mechanistic study, VEGF, B-cell lymphoma-extra-large (Bcl-xL), and cyclin D1 were all downregulated as a result of curcumin-mediated suppression of both STAT3 and JAK. In NSCLC, curcumin's antiangiogenic action was eliminated by upregulating STAT3, which makes it a promising medication in the treatment of NSCLC [92]. In laryngeal squamous cell carcinoma (LSCC), curcumin may also act as a possible angiogenesis inhibitor [93]. In small cell lung cancer (SCLC), curcumin reduced the expression of STAT3 downstream targets such as cyclin B1, Bcl-xL, survivin, VEGF, MMP-2/7, and intercellular adhesion molecule-1 (ICAM-1), which in turn reduced the proliferation, invasion, and migration of these cells [92]. The aberrant overactivation of STAT3 signaling was found in H-Ras-transformed mammary epithelial cells (H-Ras MCF10A). The potential binding site for curcumin was discovered to be the α,β-unsaturated carbonyl moieties of cysteine residue 259 of STAT, a unique residue that is essential for the function and the structure of this transcription factor. The absence of such electrophilic moieties in Tetrahydro curcumin prevented it from interacting with STAT3 and inducing apoptosis [94]. Conclusively, their research pointed out that curcumin could prevent the formation of STAT3-mediated breast carcinogenesis by directly interacting with STAT3.

4.12 Conclusions

The dietary spice turmeric contains curcumin that is a naturally occurring phenolic compound. Clinical investigations have thoroughly demonstrated curcumin's safety and efficacy [95–97]. Its role in genetically regulated highly conserved processes, such as autophagy and apoptosis, highlights its antiproliferative properties. Owing to its capability to target several cancer-related signaling pathways including PI3K/AKT, Wnt/β-catenin, MAPK, P53, JAK/STAT, and NF-κB, curcumin may serve as a promising option to minimize chemoresistance.

References

[1] Fuchs JR, Pandit B, Bhasin D, Etter JP, Regan N, Abdelhamid D, et al. Structure–activity relationship studies of curcumin analogues. Bioorganic & Medicinal Chemistry Letters 2009;19(7):2065–9.

[2] Ganji A, Farahani I, Saeedifar AM, Mosayebi G, Ghazavi A, Majeed M, et al. Protective effects of curcumin against lipopolysaccharide-induced toxicity. Current Medicinal Chemistry 2021;28(33):6915–30.

[3] Ahmadi A, Jamialahmadi T, Sahebkar A. Polyphenols and atherosclerosis: a critical review of clinical effects on LDL oxidation. Pharmacological Research 2022;184:106414. Available from: https://doi.org/10.1016/j.phrs.2022.106414.

[4] Keihanian F, Saeidinia A, Bagheri RK, Johnston TP, Sahebkar A. Curcumin, hemostasis, thrombosis, and coagulation. Journal of Cellular Physiology 2018;233(6):4497–511.

[5] Khayatan D, Razavi SM, Arab ZN, Niknejad AH, Nouri K, Momtaz S, et al. Protective effects of curcumin against traumatic brain injury. Biomedicine and Pharmacotherapy 2022;154.

[6] Mokhtari-Zaer A, Marefati N, Atkin SL, Butler AE, Sahebkar A. The protective role of curcumin in myocardial ischemia–reperfusion injury. Journal of Cellular Physiology 2018;234(1):214–22.

[7] Cicero AFG, Sahebkar A, Fogacci F, Bove M, Giovannini M, Sahebkar A. Effects of phytosomal curcumin on anthropometric parameters, insulin resistance, cortisolemia and non-alcoholic fatty liver disease indices: a double-blind, placebo-controlled clinical trial. European Journal of Nutrition 2020;59 (2):477–83. Available from: https://doi.org/10.1007/s00394-019-01916-7.

[8] Panahi Y, Sahebkar A, Amiri M, Davoudi SM, Beiraghdar F, Hoseininejad SL, et al. Improvement of sulphur mustard-induced chronic pruritus, quality of life and antioxidant status by curcumin: results of a randomised, double-blind, placebo-controlled trial. British Journal of Nutrition 2012;108(7):1272–9. Available from: https://doi.org/10.1017/S0007114511006544.

[9] Panahi Y, Fazlolahzadeh O, Atkin SL, Majeed M, Butler AE, Johnston TP, et al. Evidence of curcumin and curcumin analogue effects in skin diseases: a narrative review. Journal of Cellular Physiology 2019;234(2):1165–78. Available from: https://doi.org/10.1002/jcp.27096.

[10] Marjaneh RM, Rahmani F, Hassanian SM, Rezaei N, Hashemzehi M, Bahrami A, et al. Phytosomal curcumin inhibits tumor growth in colitis-associated colorectal cancer. Journal of Cellular Physiology 2018;233(10):6785–98. Available from: https://doi.org/10.1016/j.phrs.2022.106414.

[11] Mohammadi A, Blesso CN, Barreto GE, Banach M, Majeed M, Sahebkar A. Macrophage plasticity, polarization and function in response to curcumin, a diet-derived polyphenol, as an immunomodulatory agent. Journal of Nutritional Biochemistry 2019;66:1–16. Available from: https://doi.org/10.1016/j.jnutbio.2018.12.005.

[12] Al-Noor TH, Ali AM, Al-Sarray AJ, Al-Obaidi OH, Obeidat AI. A short review: chemistry of curcumin and its metal complex derivatives. Journal of University of Anbar for Pure Science (JUAPS) 2022;16(1).

[13] Sanphui P, Bolla G. Curcumin, a biological wonder molecule: a crystal engineering point of view. Crystal Growth & Design 2018;18(9):5690–711.

[14] Amalraj A, Pius A, Gopi S. Biological activities of curcuminoids, other biomolecules from turmeric and their derivatives—a review. Journal of Traditional and Complementary Medicine 2017;7(2): 205—33.

[15] Priyadarsini KI. The chemistry of curcumin: from extraction to therapeutic agent. Molecules (Basel, Switzerland) 2014;19(12):20091—112.

[16] Priyadarsini KI. Chemical and structural features influencing the biological activity of curcumin. Current Pharmaceutical Design 2013;19(11):2093—100.

[17] Qadir MI, Naqvi STQ, Muhammad SA. Curcumin: a polyphenol with molecular targets for cancer control. Asian Pacific Journal of Cancer Prevention: APJCP 2016;17(6):2735—9.

[18] Hassanzadeh S, Read MI, Bland AR, Majeed M, Jamialahmadi T, Sahebkar A. Curcumin: an inflammasome silencer. Pharmacological Research 2020;159.

[19] Mohajeri M, Sahebkar A. Protective effects of curcumin against doxorubicin-induced toxicity and resistance: a review. Critical Reviews in Oncology/Hematology 2018;122:30—51.

[20] Momtazi AA, Sahebkar A. Difluorinated curcumin: a promising curcumin analogue with improved antitumor activity and pharmacokinetic profile. Current Pharmaceutical Design 2016;22(28):4386—97.

[21] Kasi PD, Tamilselvam R, Skalicka-Woźniak K, Nabavi SF, Daglia M, Bishayee A, et al. Molecular targets of curcumin for cancer therapy: an updated review. Tumour Biology: the Journal of the International Society for Oncodevelopmental Biology and Medicine 2016;37(10):13017—28.

[22] Rodrigues FC, Kumar NA, Thakur G. Developments in the anticancer activity of structurally modified curcumin: an up-to-date review. European Journal of Medicinal Chemistry 2019;177:76—104.

[23] Cao Y-K, Li H-J, Song Z-F, Li Y, Huai Q-Y. Synthesis and biological evaluation of novel curcuminoid derivatives. Molecules (Basel, Switzerland) 2014;19(10):16349—72.

[24] Lopes-Rodrigues V, Oliveira A, Correia-da-Silva M, Pinto M, Lima RT, Sousa E, et al. A novel curcumin derivative which inhibits P-glycoprotein, arrests cell cycle and induces apoptosis in multidrug resistance cells. Bioorganic & Medicinal Chemistry 2017;25(2):581—96.

[25] Fawzy IM, Youssef KM, Ismail NS, Gullbo J, Abouzid KAM. Design, synthesis and biological evaluation of novel curcumin analogs with anticipated anticancer activity. Future Journal of Pharmaceutical Sciences 2015;1(1):22—31.

[26] Ji P, Yuan C, Ma S, Fan J, Fu W, Qiao C, et al. 4-Carbonyl-2, 6-dibenzylidenecyclohexanone derivatives as small molecule inhibitors of STAT3 signaling pathway. Bioorganic & Medicinal Chemistry 2016;24 (23):6174—82.

[27] Wang JQ, Wang X, Wang Y, Tang WJ, Shi JB, Liu XH. Novel curcumin analogue hybrids: synthesis and anticancer activity. European Journal of Medicinal Chemistry 2018;156:493—509.

[28] Lin L, Shi Q, Nyarko AK, Bastow KF, Wu C-C, Su C-Y, et al. Antitumor agents. 250. Design and synthesis of new curcumin analogues as potential anti-prostate cancer agents. Journal of Medicinal Chemistry 2006;49(13):3963—72.

[29] Farghadani R, Naidu RJC. Curcumin: modulator of key molecular signaling pathways in hormone-independent breast cancer. Cancers (Basel) 2 2021;13(14):3427.

[30] Sundar SN, Firestone GL. Anti-cancer dynamics of natural phytochemical inhibitors of cyclin-dependent kinases. Natural Products for Cancer Chemoprevention. Springer; 2020. p. 489—516.

[31] Lim T-G, Lee S-Y, Huang Z, Lim DY, Chen H, Jung SK, et al. Curcumin suppresses proliferation of colon cancer cells by targeting CDK2 Curcumin Inhibits CDK2 to Suppress Colon Cancer Cell Growth Cancer Prevention Research (Phila) 2014;7(4):466—74.

[32] Park M-J, Kim E-H, Park I-C, Lee H-C, Woo S-H, Lee J-Y, et al. Curcumin inhibits cell cycle progression of immortalized human umbilical vein endothelial (ECV304) cells by up-regulating cyclin-dependent kinase inhibitor, p21WAF1/CIP1, p27KIP1 and p53. International Journal of Oncology 2002;21 (2):379—83.

[33] Aggarwal BB, Banerjee S, Bharadwaj U, Sung B, Shishodia S, Sethi G. RETRACTED: curcumin induces the degradation of cyclin E expression through ubiquitin-dependent pathway and up-regulates cyclin-dependent kinase inhibitors p21 and p27 in multiple human tumor cell lines. Biochemical Pharmacology 2007; Elsevier.

[34] Huang CZ, Huang WZ, Zhang G. In vivo study on the effects of curcumin on the expression profiles of anti-tumour genes (VEGF, CyclinD1 and CDK4) in liver of rats injected with DEN. Molecular Biology Reports 2013;40(10):5825−31.

[35] Squires MS, Hudson EA, Howells L, Sale S, Houghton CE, Jones JL, et al. Relevance of mitogen activated protein kinase (MAPK) and phosphotidylinositol-3-kinase/protein kinase B (PI3K/PKB) pathways to induction of apoptosis by curcumin in breast cells. Biochemical Pharmacology 2003;65(3):361−76.

[36] Venkiteswaran S, Hsu H, Yang P, Thomas T. Curcumin interferes with HER-2 signaling in a redox-dependent manner in SK-BR-3 human breast cancer cells. Journal of Human Nutrition and Food Science 2014;2:1−8.

[37] Miller A.H., Miller A.J. CTgIN. Phase II study of curcumin vs placebo for chemotherapy-treated breast cancer patients undergoing radiotherapy. 2017.

[38] Meena R, Kumar S, Gaharwar US, Rajamani P. PLGA-CTAB curcumin nanoparticles: fabrication, characterization and molecular basis of anticancer activity in triple negative breast cancer cell lines (MDA-MB-231 cells). Biomedicine & Pharmacotherapy = Biomedecine & Pharmacotherapie 2017;94:944−54.

[39] Kandoth C, McLellan MD, Vandin F, Ye K, Niu B, Lu C, et al. Mutational landscape and significance across 12 major cancer types. Nature 2013;502(7471):333−9.

[40] Tong R, Wu X, Liu Y, Liu Y, Zhou J, Jiang X, et al. Curcumin-induced DNA demethylation in human gastric cancer cells is mediated by the DNA-damage response pathway. Oxidative Medicine and Cellular Longevity 2020;2020.

[41] Fan H, Liang Y, Jiang B, Li X, Xun H, Sun J, et al. Curcumin inhibits intracellular fatty acid synthase and induces apoptosis in human breast cancer MDA-MB-231 cells. Oncology Reports 2016;35(5):2651−6.

[42] Sidhar H, Giri RK. Induction of Bex genes by curcumin is associated with apoptosis and activation of p53 in N2a neuroblastoma cells. Scientific Reports 2017;7(1):1−19.

[43] Jin H, Lian N, Zhang F, Chen L, Chen Q, Lu C, et al. Activation of PPARγ/P53 signaling is required for curcumin to induce hepatic stellate cell senescence. Cell Death & Disease 2016;7(4):e2189 e.

[44] Li P, Pu S, Lin C, He L, Zhao H, Yang C, et al. Curcumin selectively induces colon cancer cell apoptosis and S cell cycle arrest by regulates Rb/E2F/p53 pathway. International Journal of Molecular Sciences 2022;1263:133180.

[45] Allegra A, Speciale A, Molonia MS, Guglielmo L, Musolino C, Ferlazzo G, et al. Curcumin ameliorates the in vitro efficacy of carfilzomib in human multiple myeloma U266 cells targeting p53 and NF-κB pathways. Toxicology In Vitro: an International Journal Published in Association with BIBRA 2018;47:186−94.

[46] Agarwal A, Kasinathan A, Ganesan R, Balasubramanian A, Bhaskaran J, Suresh S, et al. Curcumin induces apoptosis and cell cycle arrest via the activation of reactive oxygen species−independent mitochondrial apoptotic pathway in Smad4 and p53 mutated colon adenocarcinoma HT29 cells. Nutrition Research (New York, N.Y.) 2018;51:67−81.

[47] Ye M, Zhang J, Zhang J, Miao Q, Yao L, Zhang J. Curcumin promotes apoptosis by activating the p53-miR-192-5p/215-XIAP pathway in non-small cell lung cancer. Cancer Letters 2015;357(1):196−205.

[48] Kohno M, Pouyssegur J. Targeting the ERK signaling pathway in cancer therapy. Annals of Medicine 2006;38(3):200−11.

[49] Eisenberg S, Henis YI. Interactions of Ras proteins with the plasma membrane and their roles in signaling. Cellular Signalling 2008;20(1):31−9.

[50] Fernández-Medarde A, Santos EJ. Ras in cancer and developmental diseases. Genes & Cancer 2011;2 (3):344−58.

[51] Song X, Zhang M, Dai E, Luo Y. Molecular targets of curcumin in breast cancer. Molecular Medicine Reports 2019;19(1):23−9.

[52] Kim M-S, Kang H-J, Moon A. Inhibition of invasion and induction of apoptosis by curcumin in H-ras-transformed MCF10A human breast epithelial cells. Archives of Pharmacal Research 2001;24(4):349−54.

[53] Abdelmoaty AAA, Zhang P, Lin W, Fan Y-J, Ye S-N, Xu J-H. C0818, a novel curcumin derivative, induces ROS-dependent cytotoxicity in human hepatocellular carcinoma cells in vitro via disruption of Hsp90 function. Acta Pharmacologica Sinica 2022;43(2):446−56.

[54] Kouhpeikar H, Butler AE, Bamian F, Barreto GE, Majeed M, Sahebkar A. Curcumin as a therapeutic agent in leukemia. Journal of Cellular Physiology 2019;234(8):12404−14.

[55] Jabbour E, Kantarjian H. Chronic myeloid leukemia: 2016 update on diagnosis, therapy, and monitoring. American Journal of Hematology 2016;91(2):252−65.

[56] Zoi V, Galani V, Lianos GD, Voulgaris S, Kyritsis AP, Alexiou GA. The role of curcumin in cancer treatment. Biomedicines 2021;9(9):1086.

[57] Cao A-L, Tang Q-F, Zhou W-C, Qiu Y-Y, Hu S-J, Yin P-H. Ras/ERK signaling pathway is involved in curcumin-induced cell cycle arrest and apoptosis in human gastric carcinoma AGS cells. Journal of Asian Natural Products Research 2015;17(1):56−63.

[58] Tamaddoni A, Mohammadi E, Sedaghat F, Qujeq D, As'Habi A. The anticancer effects of curcumin via targeting the mammalian target of rapamycin complex 1 (mTORC1) signaling pathway. Pharmacological Research: the Official Journal of the Italian Pharmacological Society 2020;156:104798.

[59] Borges GA, Elias ST, Amorim B, de Lima CL, Coletta RD, Castilho RM, et al. Curcumin downregulates the PI3K−AKT−mTOR pathway and inhibits growth and progression in head and neck cancer cells. Phytotherapy Research: PTR 2020;34(12):3311−24.

[60] Liu F, Gao S, Yang Y, Zhao X, Fan Y, Ma W, et al. Antitumor activity of curcumin by modulation of apoptosis and autophagy in human lung cancer A549 cells through inhibiting PI3K/Akt/mTOR pathway. Oncology Reports 2018;39(3):1523−31.

[61] Tian B, Zhao Y, Liang T, Ye X, Li Z, Yan D, et al. Curcumin inhibits urothelial tumor development by suppressing IGF2 and IGF2-mediated PI3K/AKT/mTOR signaling pathway. Journal of Drug Targeting 2017;25(7):626−36.

[62] Maiti P, Plemmons A, Dunbar GL. Combination treatment of berberine and solid lipid curcumin particles increased cell death and inhibited PI3K/Akt/mTOR pathway of human cultured glioblastoma cells more effectively than did individual treatments. PLoS One 2019;14(12):e0225660.

[63] Zhao G, Han X, Zheng S, Li Z, Sha Y, Ni J, et al. Curcumin induces autophagy, inhibits proliferation and invasion by downregulating AKT/mTOR signaling pathway in human melanoma cells. Oncology Reports 2016;35(2):1065−74.

[64] Seo J-A, Kim B, Dhanasekaran DN, Tsang BK, Song YS. Curcumin induces apoptosis by inhibiting sarco/endoplasmic reticulum Ca^{2+} ATPase activity in ovarian cancer cells. Cancer Cells (Cold Spring Harbor, N.Y.: 1989) 2016;371(1):30−7.

[65] Lin YG, Kunnumakkara AB, Nair A, Merritt WM, Han LY, Armaiz-Pena GN, et al. Curcumin inhibits tumor growth and angiogenesis in ovarian carcinoma by targeting the nuclear factor-κB pathway. Clinical Cancer Research: an Official Journal of the American Association for Cancer Research 2007;13 (11):3423−30.

[66] Sharma RA, Euden SA, Platton SL, Cooke DN, Shafayat A, Hewitt HR, et al. Phase I clinical trial of oral curcumin: biomarkers of systemic activity and compliance. Clinical Trials 2004;10(20):6847−54.

[67] Lao CD, Ruffin MT, Normolle D, Heath DD, Murray SI, Bailey JM, et al. Dose escalation of a curcuminoid formulation. Clinical Trials 2006;6(1):1−4.

[68] Anand P, Kunnumakkara AB, Newman RA, Aggarwal BB. Bioavailability of curcumin: problems and promises. Molecular Pharmaceutics 2007;4(6):807–18.

[69] Saxena V, Hussain MD. Polymeric mixed micelles for delivery of curcumin to multidrug resistant ovarian cancer. Journal of Biomedical Nanotechnology 2013;9(7):1146–54.

[70] Mohammed ES, El-Beih NM, El-Hussieny EA, El-Ahwany E, Hassan M, Zoheiry M. Effects of free and nanoparticulate curcumin on chemically induced liver carcinoma in an animal model. Archives of Medical Science 2021;17(1):218–27.

[71] Dayton A, Selvendiran K, Kuppusamy ML, Rivera BK, Meduru S, Kálai T, et al. Cellular uptake, retention and bioabsorption of HO-3867, a fluorinated curcumin analog with potential antitumor properties. Cancer Biology & Therapy 2010;10(10):1027–32.

[72] Zhang Y, Wang X. Targeting the Wnt/β-catenin signaling pathway in cancer. Journal of Hematology & Oncology 2020;13(1):1–16.

[73] Ashrafizadeh M, Ahmadi Z, Mohamamdinejad R, Yaribeygi H, Serban M-C, Orafai HM, et al. Curcumin therapeutic modulation of the wnt signaling pathway. Current Pharmaceutical Biotechnology 2020;21 (11):1006–15.

[74] Choi H, Lim J, Hong J. Curcumin interrupts the interaction between the androgen receptor and Wnt/β-catenin signaling pathway in LNCaP prostate cancer cells. Prostate Cancer and Prostatic Diseases 2010;13(4):343–9.

[75] Zheng R, Deng Q, Liu Y, Zhao P. Curcumin inhibits gastric carcinoma cell growth and induces apoptosis by suppressing the Wnt/β-catenin signaling pathway. Medical Science Monitor: International Medical Journal of Experimental and Clinical Research 2017;23:163.

[76] Nahand JS, Taghizadeh-boroujeni S, Karimzadeh M, Borran S, Pourhanifeh MH, Moghoofei M, et al. microRNAs: new prognostic, diagnostic, and therapeutic biomarkers in cervical cancer. Journal of Cellular Physiology 2019;234(10):17064–99.

[77] Ghasemi F, Shafiee M, Banikazemi Z, Pourhanifeh MH, Khanbabaei H, Shamshirian A, et al. Curcumin inhibits NF-kB and Wnt/β-catenin pathways in cervical cancer cells. Pathology, Research and Practice 2019;215(10):152556.

[78] Sethi G, Shanmugam MK, Ramachandran L, Kumar AP, Tergaonkar V. Multifaceted link between cancer and inflammation. Bioscience Reports 2012;32(1):1–15.

[79] Siveen KS, Sikka S, Surana R, Dai X, Zhang J, Kumar AP, et al. Targeting the STAT3 signaling pathway in cancer: role of synthetic and natural inhibitors. Biochimica et Biophysica Acta 2014;1845(2):136–54.

[80] Xiao C, Wang L, Zhu L, Zhang C, Zhou J. Curcumin inhibits oral squamous cell carcinoma SCC-9 cells proliferation by regulating miR-9 expression. Biochemical and Biophysical Research Communications 2014;454(4):576–80.

[81] Ma J, Fang B, Zeng F, Pang H, Zhang J, Shi Y, et al. Curcumin inhibits cell growth and invasion through up-regulation of miR-7 in pancreatic cancer cells. Toxicology Letters 2014;231(1):82–91.

[82] Dolcet X, Llobet D, Pallares J, Matias-Guiu X. NF-kB in development and progression of human cancer. Virchows Archiv: an International Journal of Pathology 2005;446(5):475–82.

[83] Olivera A, Moore TW, Hu F, Brown AP, Sun A, Liotta DC, et al. Inhibition of the NF-κB signaling pathway by the curcumin analog, 3, 5-Bis (2-pyridinylmethylidene)-4-piperidone (EF31): anti-inflammatory and anti-cancer properties. International Immunopharmacology 2012;12(2):368–77.

[84] Mohankumar K, Francis AP, Pajaniradje S, Rajagopalan R. Synthetic curcumin analog: inhibiting the invasion, angiogenesis, and metastasis in human laryngeal carcinoma cells via NF-kB pathway. Molecular Biology Reports 2021;48(8):6065–74.

[85] Ham I-H, Wang L, Lee D, Woo J, Kim TH, Jeong HY, et al. Curcumin inhibits the cancer-associated fibroblast-derived chemoresistance of gastric cancer through the suppression of the JAK/STAT3 signaling pathway. International Journal of Oncology 2022;61(1):1–12.

[86] Yu C-L, Meyer DJ, Campbell GS, Larner AC, Carter-Su C, Schwartz J, et al. Enhanced DNA-binding activity of a Stat3-related protein in cells transformed by the Src oncoprotein. Science (New York, N.Y.) 1995;269(5220):81−3.

[87] Bromberg JF, Horvath CM, Besser D, Lathem WW, Darnell Jr JE. Stat3 activation is required for cellular transformation by v-src. Molecular and Cellular Biology 1998;18(5):2553−8.

[88] Yang C-L, Liu Y-Y, Ma Y-G, Xue Y-X, Liu D-G, Ren Y, et al. Curcumin blocks small cell lung cancer cells migration, invasion, angiogenesis, cell cycle and neoplasia through Janus kinase-STAT3 signalling pathway. PLoS One 2012;7(5):e37960.

[89] Bharti AC, Donato N, Aggarwal BB. Curcumin (diferuloylmethane) inhibits constitutive and IL-6-inducible STAT3 phosphorylation in human multiple myeloma cells. Journal of Immunology 2003;171 (7):3863−71.

[90] Natarajan C, Bright JJ. Curcumin inhibits experimental allergic encephalomyelitis by blocking IL-12 signaling through Janus kinase-STAT pathway in T lymphocytes. Journal of Immunology 2002;168 (12):6506−13.

[91] Perrone D, Ardito F, Giannatempo G, Dioguardi M, Troiano G, Lo Russo L, et al. Biological and therapeutic activities, and anticancer properties of curcumin. Experimental and Therapeutic Medicine 2015;10(5):1615−23.

[92] Wang M, Jiang S, Zhou L, Yu F, Ding H, Li P, et al. Potential mechanisms of action of curcumin for cancer prevention: focus on cellular signaling pathways and miRNAs. International Journal of Biological Sciences 2019;15(6):1200.

[93] Hu A, Huang J-J, Jin X-J, Li J-P, Tang Y-J, Huang X-F, et al. Curcumin suppresses invasiveness and vasculogenic mimicry of squamous cell carcinoma of the larynx through the inhibition of JAK-2/STAT-3 signaling pathway. American Journal of Cancer Research 2015;5(1):278.

[94] Hahn Y-I, Kim S-J, Choi B-Y, Cho K-C, Bandu R, Kim KP, et al. Curcumin interacts directly with the cysteine 259 residue of STAT3 and induces apoptosis in H-Ras transformed human mammary epithelial cells. Scientific Reports 2018;8(1):1−14.

[95] Bayet-Robert M, Kwiatowski F, Leheurteur M, Gachon F, Planchat E, Abrial C, et al. Phase I dose escalation trial of docetaxel plus curcumin in patients with advanced and metastatic breast cancer. Clinical Trials 2010;9(1):8−14.

[96] Cruz−Correa M, Shoskes DA, Sanchez P, Zhao R, Hylind LM, Wexner SD, et al. Combination treatment with curcumin and quercetin of adenomas in familial adenomatous polyposis. Clinical Trials 2006;4(8): 1035−8.

[97] Heidari Z, Daei M, Boozari M, Jamialahmadi T, Sahebkar A. Curcumin supplementation in pediatric patients: a systematic review of current clinical evidence. Phytotherapy Research 2022;36(4):1442−58.

5

An overview of cellular, molecular, and biological aspect(s) of curcumin in cancer

Atefeh Amiri[1], Amirhossein Sahebkar[2,3]

[1]DEPARTMENT OF MEDICAL BIOTECHNOLOGY AND NANOTECHNOLOGY, SCHOOL OF MEDICINE, MASHHAD UNIVERSITY OF MEDICAL SCIENCES, MASHHAD, IRAN
[2]BIOTECHNOLOGY RESEARCH CENTER, PHARMACEUTICAL TECHNOLOGY INSTITUTE, MASHHAD UNIVERSITY OF MEDICAL SCIENCES, MASHHAD, IRAN [3]APPLIED BIOMEDICAL RESEARCH CENTER, MASHHAD UNIVERSITY OF MEDICAL SCIENCES, MASHHAD, IRAN

Abbreviation

Bak	Bcl-2 homologous antagonist/killer
Bax	Bcl-2-associated X protein
BCl-2	B-cell lymphoma 2
Bcl-xL	B-cell lymphoma-extra large
bFGF	Basic fibroblast growth factor
Bim	Bcl-2 Interacting Mediator of cell death
COX-2	cyclooxygenase-2
CRABPII	Cellular retinoic acid binding proteins II
DLC1	deleted in liver cancer 1
DNMT3B	DNA methyltransferase 3 beta
DVL2	Dishevelled segment polarity protein 2
ECM	extracellular matrix
EGFR	Epidermal growth factor receptor
ERK1/2	extracellular signal-regulated kinase 1/2
EZH2	Enhancer of Zeste 2 Polycomb Repressive Complex 2
GSK-3	Glycogen synthase kinase 3
IL8	Interleukin 8
IκB	nuclear factor of kappa light polypeptide gene enhancer in B-cells inhibitor
JAK-STAT	Janus kinases - Signal transducer and activator of transcription proteins
MMP	matrix metalloproteinase
NF-κB	Nuclear factor kappa B
PA	Polyamine oxidase
PI3Ks	Phosphoinoside 3-kinases

Curcumin-Based Nanomedicines as Cancer Therapeutics. DOI: https://doi.org/10.1016/B978-0-443-15412-6.00018-0

PTEN	Phosphatase and tensin homolog
PUMA	p53 modulator of apoptosis
RARs	Retinoic acid receptors
SSAT	spermidine/spermine-N (1)-acetyltransferase
TNF	Tumor necrosis factor
VEGF	Vascular endothelial growth factor
VEGFR	Vascular endothelial growth factor receptor
XIAP	X-linked inhibitor of apoptosis protein

5.1 Introduction

Tumor development and progression are mainly associated with changes in several molecular pathways, which make cancer treatment more challenging [1]. Based on their action, existing anticancer compounds are divided into several general categories: antioxidants, antiprolifera-tives, and carcinogen-blocking agents [2]. Curcumin, a safe herbal substance with all three of these features, has attracted the attention of many researchers in recent years owing to its diversity of pharmacological activities [3−10]. Numerous clinical studies on the curcumin topic all point to the same matter [11−15].

Because of its wide range of activities, curcumin can affect almost all cancer hallmarks, including unlimited cell proliferation, drug resistance, angiogenesis, invasion, and metastasis [16−20]. Hence, curcumin has many potential targets for exerting its antitumor effects, for example, signal transductions, transcription factors, growth factors and receptors, enzymes, immune cells, inflammatory cytokines, microRNAs, exosomes, cell cycle proteins, adhesion molecules, and epigenetic factors [2,17,20−22]. Curcumin can modulate vital cellular processes based on the type and stage of cancer through the mentioned cellular targets. Induction of apoptotic pathways, reduction of survival signals, DNA damage and the cell cycle arrest, antioxidant effects, angiogenesis suppression, metastasis inhibition, and chemo-sensitization are curcumin's most important antitumor mechanisms [16,17].

Many studies have investigated the molecular mechanisms behind curcumin's anticancer effects and its ability to minimize the side effects of chemotherapy agents [23,24]. This chapter discusses some of the most crucial curcumin antitumor mechanisms, focusing on its molecular features. Examples from the in vitro and in vivo studies are also presented for further clarification.

5.2 Inducing apoptosis

Eliminating the excess, mutated, abnormal, damaged, old, and irreparable cells in the body is the critical function of a highly regulated process called apoptosis. This process is respon-sible for preserving the balance between cell death and new cell production, resulting in maintaining the integrity of organisms [17,25]. Any dysregulation or change in the natural path of this process can lead to uncontrolled cell survival, followed by pathological conditions such as autoimmunity, destructive diseases, and cancer [26−28].

It has been demonstrated that curcumin can increase apoptosis in cancer cells. A microarray study on breast cancer cells revealed that curcumin could change 104 of the 214 genes involved in apoptosis. In fact, the primary mechanism of curcumin's toxicity on cancer cells is triggering apoptosis [29]. The most prominent pathways by which curcumin induces apoptosis are highlighted below.

5.2.1 Apoptosis-related protein modulation

The B-cell lymphoma 2 (Bcl-2) family is one of the most important regulators of apoptosis. The members of this family are divided into pro- and antiapoptotic groups. The ratio between these two groups can determine cell survival or death [30]. It has been demonstrated that curcumin increases the expression of Noxa and p53 modulators of apoptosis (PUMA), which in turn activates Bim, Bak, and Bax, the proapoptotic members of the Bcl-2 family, in the prostate cancer cells. In addition, it suppresses the expression of Bcl-2 and B-cell lymphoma-extra large (Bcl-xL), the antiapoptotic members of the Bcl-2 family. As a result of the disruption of the balance between anti- and proapoptotic Bcl-2 family members, the intrinsic pathway of apoptosis starts. First, the mitochondria uptake an inflow of calcium, increasing its outer membrane's permeability. Then, the release of cytochrome C from the mitochondria triggers the caspase cascade, which results in cell death [31]. Other similar studies also showed the effect of curcumin on the Bcl-2 family. Curcumin has been found to induce apoptosis in human nonsmall cell lung cancer NCI-H460 cells by upregulating Bad and Bax proteins while downregulating Bcl-xL and X-linked inhibitor of apoptosis protein (XIAP) [32].

In addition, it has been revealed that inhibition of COX-2 expression could induce apoptosis in several different tumor types [33−35]. A study with the pancreas and lung adenocarcinoma cell lines (p34 and PC-14, respectively) found that treating these cells with curcumin inhibits the expression of COX-2, epidermal growth factor receptor (EGFR), and p-Erk1/2 (extracellular signal-regulated kinase 1/2), leading to apoptosis induction and survival reduction. Interestingly, the inhibitory effect of curcumin in the cells with higher expression of COX-2 was more significant than the COX-2-deficient cells, suggesting that at least a part of the antiapoptotic activity of curcumin in these cells is related to COX-2 [36].

Another exciting target of curcumin for apoptosis induction is AKT protein, a serine/threonine kinase. AKT is activated by phosphorylation, which stimulates antiapoptotic signals through phosphorylation/activation of some of its downstream proteins, such as nuclear factor kappa B (NF-κB), Bad, glycogen synthase kinase 3 (GSK-3), and Forkhead (FOXO1). Consequently, apoptosis cell death is stopped [37−39]. Curcumin has been found to promote apoptosis through interaction with AKT in human kidney carcinoma cells (Caki). Curcumin can suppress Bcl-2, Bcl-xL, and IAP following the AKT dephosphorylating/deactivating. Then cytochrome c is released from mitochondria, and the intrinsic pathway of apoptosis begins [40].

5.2.2 Fas-FasL interaction

One of the key mediators of apoptosis that acts through the external pathway is the Fas receptor (CD95) and its ligand (FasL). Following their interaction, the cascade of caspases is activated, and apoptosis starts [41]. Numerous studies have demonstrated the efficacy of curcumin in promoting Fas and FasL expressions. For example, in chondrosarcoma cells (JJ012 and SW1353), curcumin could increase the expression of Fas, FasL, and Dr5. Most noteworthy, in this study, animal research showed a remarkable 60% decrease in tumor volume after 21 days of treatment [42]. Curcumin has a similar effect on hepatic cancer cell line HUH7. In these cells, along with the increase in Fas and FasL expression by curcumin, increased activity of caspase-3, upregulation of p38, and PARP cleavage were also seen. These changes induce apoptosis in cancer cells through a p38-dependent pathway [43].

5.2.3 Reactive oxygen species generation

Reactive oxygen species (ROS) are a group of highly reactive molecules. The most critical ROS are hydrogen peroxide (H_2O_2), superoxide radical (O_2 •-), and hydroxyl radical (•OH). ROS can cause serious damage to biological molecules such as DNA, proteins, and lipids, depending on the concentration. ROS and mitochondria are key players in triggering apoptosis in physiological and pathological conditions. Notably, mitochondria are both the source and the target of ROS. In fact, the release of cytochrome c from mitochondria, the trigger for caspase cascade activation, is directly and indirectly mediated by ROS activity [44,45].

It has been demonstrated that curcumin can induce apoptosis by increasing ROS production, elevating intracellular calcium and endoplasmic reticulum = stress, and finally activating the caspase cascade. A similar mechanism was observed in hepatocellular carcinoma (HCC) J5 and osteosarcoma cells [32,46,47].

Curcumin has been revealed to promote apoptosis in BGC-823 gastric cancer cells through ROS-mediated activation of the ASK1-MKK4-JNK cascade. Curcumin phosphorylates the ASK1-MKK4-JNK cascade; however, ROS is responsible for its activation. Finally, the activation of this signaling pathway results in apoptosis induction [48].

Curcumin can also indirectly increase the level of ROS. It was discovered that curcumin could raise the level of polyamine catabolic enzymes such as spermidine/spermine-N (1)-acetyltransferase (SSAT) and polyamine oxidase (PAO) in a study on curcumin-resistant breast cancer cell lines (growth hormone-expressing MDA-MB-453). These enzymes can increase the amount of ROS and subsequently induce apoptosis. In this study, the inhibition of SSAT causes the production of ROS and the suppression of curcumin-induced apoptosis, which indicates the role of curcumin's executive mechanism in this cell line [49].

5.2.4 Other mechanisms

Another mechanism for inducing apoptosis is through changing the expression of miRNAs. For example, in a study on breast cancer cell line SKBR-3, it has been reported that curcumin can increase the expression of miR-15a and miR-16, which reduces Bcl-2 expression and apoptosis induction. In other cell lines from same cancer, the curcumin-mediated upregulation of miRNA-34 expression showed similar results [50,51].

A less-studied mechanism is the epigenetic control of apoptosis by curcumin. Enhancer of zeste 2 polycomb repressive complex 2 (EZH2) is an epigenetic factor overexpressed in many cancers [52]. It's expression is negatively regulated by deletion in hepatocellular carcinoma 1 (DLC1), a tumor suppressor gene. A study using breast cancer cell lines showed that the cell treatment with curcumin inhibits EZH2 and restores DLC1 expression. Following these changes, the level of Bcl-2 protein decreases and the level of caspase-9 increases, resulting in cell apoptosis [53].

In an exciting study on gastric cancer cell lines, its impact on autophagy was also investigated, in addition to curcumin's effects on apoptosis. Surprisingly, this study revealed that the apoptosis potential of curcumin diminishes by overexpression of autophagy-related proteins. In other words, the apoptosis effects of curcumin were dramatically improved when an autophagy inhibitor was added. This issue indicates a dual effect of this herbal compound that should be considered for its application in medical applications [54].

5.3 Tumor suppressor genes

Tumor suppressor genes play a crucial and undeniable role in preventing the development and progression of cancers. Any alteration or mutation in these genes can lead to their normal function loss and a pathological onset. Curcumin, as a nontoxic and low-risk substance, can be a practical approach to restore the activity of these silenced genes [28,55].

5.3.1 P53 Tumor suppressor

P53 is a vital transcription factor and tumor suppressor for the normal function of the cells. It has more than 500 gene targets, whereby it controls many fundamental processes of cells, such as signal transduction, cell cycle arrest, cellular response to DNA damage, maintenance of genome integrity, and apoptosis. So, it is unsurprising how this is called the genome guardian. Clearly, the mutation in this gene will have bad consequences on the cells, so that more than 50% of all cancers have mutations in this gene. Because of its significant role in the regulation of essential cellular pathways, p53 is a desirable target for anticancer drugs and therapeutic compounds, including curcumin [17,56–59].

A study with the stage 4 neuroblastoma cell lines found that curcumin treatment can stop the cell cycle at the G2/M phase and induce apoptosis through p53 nuclear accumulation and $p^{21WAF-1/CIP-1}$ (cyclin-dependent kinase inhibitor) and Bax induction [60]. In addition, curcumin treatment of MCF-7, the breast cancer cell line, could maximize p53 levels and induce its DNA-binding activity, followed by Bax upregulation and apoptosis promotion [61].

The molecular pathways involved in curcumin-induced p53 activity were more clarified in the gastric cancer cell line. This research also showed that curcumin activates the p53 signaling pathway by overexpressing p53 and p21, which leads to the PI3K pathway inhibition through PI3K, p-AKT, and mammalian target of rapamycin (p-mTOR) dropping [62].

The significant role of p53 in the antitumor actions of curcumin was well elucidated in different cells with various levels of p53 expression. The cells with a higher level of wild-type p53 were more sensitive to the toxic effects of curcumin than the cells with mutant or knock-out p53. Of course, the two latter also showed some toxicity, but their apoptotic index was much lower, suggesting they probably used p53-independent pathways [63].

Moreover, curcumin has been administered as a safe, natural compound in some patients with colorectal cancer (CRC). According to the molecular analyses of the samples taken from curcumin-treated patients, p53 levels increased in tumor tissues, apoptotic mediators Bcl-2 and Bax were modulated, and serum TNF-alpha levels decreased. In fact, the increased expression of the p53 molecule in tumor cells, which accelerates tumor cell apoptosis, is the mechanism by which curcumin therapy improves the general health of patients with CRC [64].

5.3.2 Phosphatase and tensin homolog

Phosphatase and tensin homolog (PTEN), another tumor suppressor, has a significant impact on controlling the cell cycle and triggering apoptosis. Mutations or changes in its expression have been seen in several cancers. PTEN acts as a major miRNA-21 target and a negative regulator of the AKT pathway by suppressing the phosphoinositide 3-kinases (PI3K) pathway [65,66]. The miR-21/PTEN/PI3K/AKT pathway is crucial for tumors' growth, invasion, and migration [67]. It has been found that high doses of curcumin in human gastric cancer cell line MGC-803 can strongly inhibitAKT, upregulate PTEN, and downregulate miRNA-21. In other words, curcumin is a negative regulator of the miR-21/PTEN/PI3K/AKT pathway [68]. It was already known that the PTEN-negative CRC cells are more sensitive to curcumin than the PTEN-positive ones. They also exhibit a different pattern of curcumin-related cell cycle arrest. In the PTEN-positive cells, curcumin reduces the phosphorylation of AKT. It increases its downstream protein activity, p21, which leads to the downregulation of cyclin 21 and CDC2, followed by the cell cycle arrest in the G2/M phase. In comparison, curcumin in the PTEN-negative cells causes a considerable elevation in AKT phosphorylation and a reduction in p21 levels, which drops cyclin D1 and cell cycle arrest in the G0/G1 phase, which could explain why they are more sensitive to curcumin [69,70].

5.3.3 RARβ

RARβ belongs to the nuclear receptor superfamily, the retinoic acid receptor (RAR) family, and the thyroid-steroid hormone receptor subfamily. This protein binds to retinoic acid (RA), the active form of vitamin A and a vital player in cellular processes such as apoptosis, cell growth, and differentiation. Actually, RARβ acts as a tumor suppressor, and its expression is disrupted in several cancers [71–73]. It has been revealed that curcumin has favorable effects on elevating RAR expression.

One of the main mechanisms of RARβ silencing is DNA hypermethylation in its promoter region, so treatment with DNA methyltransferase inhibitors can restore its expression [74]. Considering that curcumin has the potential to inhibit methylation in some cancer cell lines, its epigenetic effects on the RARβ gene were investigated. In the lung cancer cell lines, it has been shown that curcumin could diminish the mRNA expression of the DNA methyltransferase 3 beta (DNMT3N) gene, followed by hypomethylation of the RARβ promoter, which leads to its reactivation. Moreover, in vivo studies in xenograft mice bearing lung tumors treated with curcumin showed the protective effects of this compound in preventing the weight loss of mice and significantly reducing tumor growth [55]. It provides a fascinating insight into how curcumin affects epigenetic regulation.

Another study in the triple-negative breast cancer (TNBC) cells elucidated the impact of curcumin on the cellular retinoic acid binding proteins II (CRABPII)/RAR pathway (the RA-related apoptotic response pathway). RA is delivered to RARβ via the CRABPII protein, promoting apoptosis-related gene expression. This study showed that curcumin in low doses (5−10 μM) could increase the expression of CRABPII, RARβ, and RARγ. Induction of the mentioned pathway by curcumin leads to the sensitization of RA-resistant TNBC cells to RA-related apoptosis in a dose-dependent manner [75].

5.4 The survival pathways

5.4.1 Nuclear factor-kappa B

NF-κB is a crucial transcription factor whose activation can be a double-edged sword. While its controlled expression is necessary for the optimal functioning of the immune system, an abnormal increase in its expression can lead to the progression of pathological conditions such as inflammation and cancers. NF-κB promotes tumorigenesis by affecting genes involved in critical cellular processes, including survival, cell proliferation, apoptosis suppression, angiogenesis, cell migration, and metastasis. Inhibition of NF-κB can modulate all the mentioned pathways [76−78]. According to many studies, curcumin, as a multitarget compound, is one of the most effective inhibitors of this transcription factor. Curcumin inhibits NF-κB by increasing the stability of IκB, the master inhibitor of NF-κB signaling.. In most cells, NF-κB remains inactive in the cytoplasm due to binding with IκBα. IκBα is phosphorylated and degraded (by the IKK complex) in response to various triggers, leading to the unmasking of NF-κB nuclear localization signals (NLS), its translocation to the nucleus, and its activation [79−81]. In a study with a breast cancer cell line, MDA-MB-231, it was found that the treatment of cells with curcumin inhibits the phosphorylation of IκBα followed by NF-κB suppression, which in turn reduces the expression of two inflammatory cytokines, CXCL1 and CXCL2, and weakens the metastasis potential of these cells [82].

Another study focused on the impact of curcumin treatment on NF-κB activity in various ovarian cancer cell lines. The in vitro outcomes demonstrated that curcumin could reduce NF-κB activity and cell growth. The in vivo findings of this study also revealed that an oral dose of 500 mg/kg of curcumin is the most effective dose to block NF-κB and STAT3, which can subsequently restrict angiogenesis and tumor growth [83].

Interestingly, curcumin can also reduce the number of cancer stem cells (CSC) by inhibiting NF-κB. This issue was well demonstrated in a study on HCC cells treated with curcumin.

These cells were divided into curcumin-sensitive and curcumin-resistant groups. In the first case, curcumin promotes cell death, decreases CSC number, limits sphere formation, down-regulates CSC markers' expression, and suppresses tumorigenesis through NF-κB inhibition. On the contrary, an increase in CSC markers and cell growth was observed in the last group. These results show that curcumin-induced inhibition of NF-κB diminishes the population of CSC cells [84].

5.4.2 The JAK/STAT signaling pathway

It is not surprising that the JAK/STAT pathway is regarded as a potential target in cancer treatment studies, considering that it is involved both in the intrinsic onset of cancer, including cell proliferation, survival, metastasis, and so on, and in the modulation of the immune system [85,86]. This pathway transmits various signals from cytokines, growth factors, interferons, and interleukins. The binding of these ligands to JAK-associated receptors leads to the phosphorylation of specific tyrosine residues and conformational changes in these receptors, which accelerates JAK conversion to an active tyrosine kinase [87]. Activated JAK phosphorylates specific tyrosines in the cytoplasmic tail of the receptors, which leads to the binding of cytoplasmic STATs to the receptor. STAT becomes a substrate for phosphorylation by JAK. Now, phosphorylated STAT forms a dimer that can translocate to the nucleus and begins the transcription of the target genes [88].

The pivotal role of curcumin in blocking the JAK/STAT pathway is bold. According to this point, in a study, an osteosarcoma cell line, MG-63, was treated with different concentrations of curcumin. It was found that curcumin can inhibit the JAK/STAT pathway in a dose-dependent manner, which in turn leads to the suppression of cell growth and proliferation, inhibition of migration and metastasis, induction of apoptosis, and cell cycle arrest in the G0/G1 phase. The in vivo results from the xenograft mice also supported the in vitro findings [89]. In addition, in curcumin-treated lung cancer-bearing mice, the phosphorylation level of STAT3 and JAK is significantly reduced following the curcumin treatment, leading to downregulation of STAT3 downstream genes, including Bcl-xL, Cyclin D1, and vascular endothelial growth factor (VEGF). The clinical translation is reducing the size and weight of the tumor in the mice [90].

Interestingly, it has been reported that cancer-associated fibroblast (CAF) can cause drug resistance in gastric cancer cells by activating the JAK/STAT pathway. Meanwhile, curcumin can break CAF-related drug resistance by suppressing the JAK/STAT pathway [88]. In fact, by inhibiting the JAK/STAT, curcumin can access many other pathways involved in the progression of cancers. It can be advantageous in finding a suitable treatment for cancer.

5.4.3 The Wnt/β-catenin signaling pathway

The Wnt/β-catenin pathway is an evolutionarily conserved signaling axis first recognized for its significant contribution to homeostasis maintenance, tissue development, and embryogenesis. However, growing proof indicates this pathway is vital in many physiological and pathological processes, including cell proliferation and growth, cell apoptosis, cell polarity and migration, cell fate, and differentiation. Dysregulation of Wnt signaling activity encourages stem/progenitor cell malignancy, triggering aberrant differentiation and enhanced cell proliferation [91,92].

Wnt is a member of the large group of secretory glycoproteins that controls the mentioned processes using both β-catenin-dependent and independent ways [93]. The β-catenin transcription factor is one of the essential executive factors in this pathway. It is activated by binding the Wnt ligand to the related receptor, translocation to the nucleus, and promoting the expression of its downstream target genes, such as c-Myc and Cyclin D [94,95]. On the other hand, a negative regulator of β-catenin, tumor suppressor GSK3β, phosphorylates β-catenin in some specific serine residues and marks it for degradation in the proteasome [96]. Curcumin can modulate the Wnt/β-catenin pathway by affecting its different components. It has been determined that the exposure of medulloblastoma cells to curcumin increased the amount of GSK3β, followed by a decrease in the level of β-catenin and its downstream target protein, cyclin D1, which finally stopped the cell cycle at G2/M phase [97]. Axin2, an effective gene in the proliferation, apoptosis, and migration, is another crucial downstream gene of the Wnt pathway. An in vivo study with CRC-bearing mice showed that the expression level of Axin2 decreased because of curcumin-related Wnt pathway suppression, leading to the reduction of tumor size and number [98].

In summary, it is clear that Wnt is a critical player in the progression of many cancers and that its suppression by curcumin affects a broad set of genes, including disheveled segment polarity protein 2 (DVL2), β-catenin, cyclin D1, COX-2, and Axin2, and various pathological events involved in the development and progression of tumors [99].

5.5 Angiogenesis

Angiogenesis is a natural yet complicated process regulated by a wide range of precise interactions between cells, extracellular matrix (ECM), biological factors, and signals. Excessive and insufficient angiogenesis can result in major pathological disorders, so the perfect and flawless function of the regulatory mechanism is vital for the body [100,101]. One of the harmful consequences of uncontrolled angiogenesis is the growth and spread of tumors. Since cancer cells require a lot of oxygen and nutrients to survive and grow, they will undergo necrosis and even apoptosis if there is no vascular support. In fact, angiogenesis is pivotal in progressing benign tumors into malignant ones. Angiogenesis is necessary not only for tumor spreading to surrounding tissues but also for tumor metastasis. Cancer cells require new blood vessels to continue their growth in a new location away from the original place [102–104]. The importance of this process is so great that several Food and Drug Administration (FDA)-approved drugs for the treatment of cancers are angiogenesis inhibitors [105–107]. Curcumin, as an antiangiogenic agent, can affect the whole process by reducing the expression of proangiogenic genes such as VEGF, matrix metalloproteinase (MMPs), and basic fibroblast growth factor (bFGF) [108].

VEGF is a well-known vasoactive factor that acts as an endothelial cell mitogen. It can trigger the generation of new blood capillaries from surrounding existing ones (code77). Many stimulants boost the expression of this factor, including hypoxia condition, growth factors, and oncogenes [109,110]. So, it is not surprising that VEGF is the favorite of many tumor cells. VEGF predominantly encourages the formation of new blood vessels by activating Vascular endothelial growth factor receptor 2 (VEGFR-2), which is expressed on endothelial cells [111]. Vascular permeability, vascular inflammation, cell proliferation, migration, and invasion are just some of the pathways that can be triggered following the VEGFR-2 activation, which are helpful for cancer progression [112]. Curcumin, as an antiangiogenesis compound, can also intervene in this pathway. A study with VEGF-induced human umbilical vein endothelial cells (HUVEC) showed that curcumin could prevent migration and proliferation and block the VEGF-VEGFR-2 and its downstream signals, leading to apoptosis induction in these cells. In addition, in the VEGF-overexpressed tumor-bearing mice, curcumin considerably suppresses the tumor progression through modulation of the VEGF-VEGFR-2 pathway [113]. In HCC, both in vitro and in vivo, it was shown that curcumin could inhibit the expression of VEGF protein and the JAK/STAT pathway, which leads to the inhibition of growth and induction of apoptosis in the cancer cells [114]. Similar results were observed in lymphoma cells treated with the combination of curcumin and omacetaxine, where angiogenesis and growth of the curcumin-treated cells were inhibited by blocking the AKT/VEGF pathway [115]. Even in a clinical trial at phase I, after treatment of metastatic breast cancer patients with the combination of curcumin and docetaxel in three cycles, the level of serum VEGF dramatically decreased [116]. Along with the free curcumin, the antiangiogenic properties of liposomal curcumin have also been studied. As expected, this type of curcumin could also inhibit tumor growth in animal models by blocking the activity of angiogenic factors such as VEGF, CD31, and IL8 [117].

COX-2 is an inducible enzyme overexpressed in different types of human carcinomas and seems to play an essential role in the transformation of malignancies, their progression, and regression [118–120]. A study on the human CRC tissues revealed that the COX-2-positive group had higher levels of VEGF expression than the COX-2-negative group, indicating a close correlation between COX-2 and VEGF. Hence, it seems COX-2 indirectly promotes angiogenesis by affecting VEGF expression [121]. The effects of curcumin on COX-2 expression and angiogenesis were evaluated in a study with HCC cell-bearing nude mice; in comparison to the control group, the groups receiving daily oral curcumin (3000 mg/kg) demonstrated a decreased tumor neocapillary density (NCD). In addition, COX-2 and VEGF expressions in the curcumin-treated group were significantly reduced, confirming the ability of curcumin to inhibit angiogenesis [122].

5.6 Metastasis

Cancer starts as a localized disorder but has the ability to migrate, invade, and move to other organs, a process known as metastasis. Metastasis is one of the main challenges of cancer treatment and one of the main causes of cancer patients' death [123,124]. Metastasis is a complex and multistep process whose initiation and progression depend on many factors, including ECM-degrading enzymes, tissue remodeling-related cytokines, growth factors, and cell–cell adhesion proteins [125,126]. Finding a mixture that can control this process will undoubtedly be challenging and worthwhile. Curcumin has peaked the attention of numerous scientists working in this area by displaying potential antimetastatic properties. Curcumin exerts its anti-metastasis effects by changing the expression pattern of some genes involved in this process.

None of the proteins and enzymes involved in the metastasis process are as famous as MMPs. MMPs, as the proteolytic enzymes that can destroy ECM and basement membrane, are one of the most powerful enzymes involved in cancer cell metastasis. In fact, MMPs pave the way for invasion and metastasis by promoting the migration of primary tumor cells to blood vessels, the lymphatic system, and surrounding tissues [126,127]. The effect of curcumin on MMPs has been investigated in vitro and in vivo in many studies. Among the MMP subtypes, MMP-2 and MMP-9 have been studied more than others due to their pivotal role in metastasis [128,129]. For example, in an in vitro study, treatment of ER (estrogen receptor)-negative MDA-MB-231 breast cancer cell with curcumin reduced the MMP-2 expression and increased the TIMP-1 and 2 (MMP inhibitors) expression, indicating the antiinvasive effects of curcumin for this cell line [130].

Similarly, zymography and enzyme-linked immunosorbent assay (ELISA) analysis in curcumin-treated prostate cancer cells (DU-45 cells) showed decreased expression of MMP-2 and MMP-9. The same effect and tumor volume reduction were also demonstrated in the tumor-bearing mice [131]. Curcumin can also indirectly control the level of MMPs by regulating the expression of upstream genes such as NF-κB and AP-1. Due to the presence of NF-κB and AP-1 binding sites in the MMP-9 gene promoter, these transcription factors are crucial in controlling MMP-9 expression [132]. In the breast cancer cell line, MCF-7, curcumin can inhibit the TPA-induced MMP-9 expression by suppressing the activity of NF-κB and AP-1. Their suppression is actually due to curcumin inhibiting their DNA-binding activity [129]. In another study, the effects of dendrosomal curcumin (DNC) on metastatic factors were evaluated in vitro and in vivo via 4T1 breast cancer cells. The in vitro findings showed that curcumin reduced 4T1 cell growth, migration, and adhesion in a time- and dose-dependent manner, reducing cell metastasis. The in vivo results also showed improved metastatic symptoms and increased survival rate in the DNC-treated group. According to other studies, the gene expression analysis revealed a decline in NF-κB expression, followed by suppression of its specific downstream genes, including MMP-9, VEGF, and COX-2 [133].

Another factor that can promote metastasis is the presence of CSC. These cells are similar to normal stem cells, with unlimited growth, reduced adhesion ability, and increased motility. This group of cells, in combination with the epithelial-mesenchymal transition (EMT) process, can accelerate and facilitate the invasion and metastasis of the cancer cells. It has been found that curcumin can reduce the amount of metastasis in the breast cancer cell lines MCF-7 and MDA-MB-231 by changing the expression of genes involved in these pathways. The cells treated with curcumin showed decreased expression of β-catenin, vimentin, and fibronectin and increased expression of E-cadherin. At the protein level, curcumin reduced the amount of stem cell indicator proteins such as Sox-2, Nanog, and Oct-4 [134].

In addition to free curcumin, its liposomal forms are also effective in controlling metastasis, and their effects may be more than the free form. For example, in an interesting study, a dual-targeted liposome with galactose (Gal) and glycyrrhetinic acid (GA) was used for the codelivery of curcumin and capsaicin (CAPS-CUR/GA&Gal-Lip) to liver cancer cells, in vitro and in vivo. This study used the liver tumor cell line HepG2 cocultured with hepatic stellate cells (HSCs), an active player in the liver tumor microenvironment (TME), to mimic hepatic cancer TME. This cocultured model (HSCs + HepG2) has more potential for drug resistance and migration. Treating HSCs + HepG2 cells with CAPS-CUR/GA&Gal-Lip could effectively inhibit the expression of P-glycoprotein (upregulated in drug resistance cells) and vimentin (upregulated in EMT). In tumor-bearing mice, this liposomal formulation simultaneously inhibits HSCs and tumor cell metastasis, leading to decreased tumor angiogenesis, decreased ECM deposition, and increased anticancer activity [135].

5.7 Conclusion

Considering the increasing use of curcumin as a low-risk and multifunctional plant substance in many medical and pharmaceutical researches, understanding its molecular action mechanism seems even more important. Even though numerous studies have been conducted on this subject so far (partially mentioned in this chapter), there is still a long way to go before researchers can find a straightforward approach to treating cancer with curcumin. This is made a little more challenging by the complexity of the cellular and molecular environments of cancerous tissues, plus the structural-related problems of curcumin, such as low solubility and low bioavailability.

However, the significant progress in signaling pathways and their association with various medicinal compounds, including curcumin and new pharmaceutical nanocarriers, promises a bright future for using curcumin as an effective therapeutic substance in cancer treatment.

References

[1] Sever R, Brugge JS. Signal transduction in cancer. Cold Spring Harbor Perspectives in Medicine 2015;5(4).

[2] Park W, Amin AR, Chen ZG, Shin DM. New perspectives of curcumin in cancer prevention. Cancer Prevention Research (Philadelphia, Pa) 2013;6(5):387–400.

[3] Hosseini SA, Zahedipour F, Sathyapalan T, Jamialahmadi T, Sahebkar A. Pulmonary fibrosis: therapeutic and mechanistic insights into the role of phytochemicals. Biofactors (Oxford, England) 2021;47(3):250–69.

[4] Keihanian F, Saeidinia A, Bagheri RK, Johnston TP, Sahebkar A. Curcumin, hemostasis, thrombosis, and coagulation. Journal of Cellular Physiology 2018;233(6):4497–511.

[5] Khayatan D, Razavi SM, Arab ZN, Niknejad AH, Nouri K, Momtaz S, et al. Protective effects of curcumin against traumatic brain injury. Biomedicine and Pharmacotherapy 2022;154.

[6] Mokhtari-Zaer A, Marefati N, Atkin SL, Butler AE, Sahebkar A. The protective role of curcumin in myocardial ischemia–reperfusion injury. Journal of Cellular Physiology 2018;234(1):214–22.

[7] Momtazi-Borojeni AA, Haftcheshmeh SM, Esmaeili SA, Johnston TP, Abdollahi E, Sahebkar A. Curcumin: a natural modulator of immune cells in systemic lupus erythematosus. Autoimmunity Reviews 2018;17(2):125−35.

[8] Sahebkar A. Molecular mechanisms for curcumin benefits against ischemic injury. Fertility and Sterility 2010;94(5):e75−6.

[9] Panahi Y, Fazlolahzadeh O, Atkin SL, Majeed M, Butler AE, Johnston TP, & Sahebkar A. (2019). Evidence of curcumin and curcumin analogue effects in skin diseases: A narrative review. *Journal of cellular physiology*, *234*(2), 1165−1178. Available from https://doi.org/10.1002/jcp.27096.

[10] Ganji A, Farahani I, Saeedifar AM, Mosayebi G, Ghazavi A, Majeed M, et al. Protective effects of curcumin against lipopolysaccharide-induced toxicity. Current Medicinal Chemistry 2021;28(33):6915−30.

[11] Mary CPV, Vijayakumar S, Shankar R. Metal chelating ability and antioxidant properties of Curcumin-metal complexes − a DFT approach. Journal of Molecular Graphics and Modelling 2018;79:1−14.

[12] Menon VP, Sudheer AR. Antioxidant and anti-inflammatory properties of curcumin. Advances in Experimental Medicine and Biology 2007;595:105−25.

[13] Heidari Z, Daei M, Boozari M, Jamialahmadi T, Sahebkar A. Curcumin supplementation in pediatric patients: a systematic review of current clinical evidence. Phytotherapy Research 2022;36(4):1442−58.

[14] Cicero AFG, Sahebkar A, Fogacci F, Bove M, Giovannini M, & Borghi C. (2020). Effects of phytosomal curcumin on anthropometric parameters, insulin resistance, cortisolemia and non-alcoholic fatty liver disease indices: a double-blind, placebo-controlled clinical trial. *European journal of nutrition*, *59*(2), 477−483. Available from https://doi.org/10.1007/s00394-019-01916-7.

[15] Pagano E, Romano B, Izzo AA, Borrelli F. The clinical efficacy of curcumin-containing nutraceuticals: an overview of systematic reviews. Pharmacological Research: the Official Journal of the Italian Pharmacological Society 2018;134:79−91.

[16] Lin JK. Molecular targets of curcumin. Advances in Experimental Medicine and Biology 2007;595:227−43.

[17] Shishodia S. Molecular mechanisms of curcumin action: gene expression. Biofactors (Oxford, England) 2013;39(1):37−55.

[18] Mohajeri M, Sahebkar A. Protective effects of curcumin against doxorubicin-induced toxicity and resistance: a review. Critical Reviews in Oncology/Hematology 2018;122:30−51.

[19] Momtazi AA, Sahebkar A. Difluorinated curcumin: a promising curcumin analogue with improved anti-tumor activity and pharmacokinetic profile. Current Pharmaceutical Design 2016;22(28):4386−97.

[20] Marjaneh RM, Rahmani F, Hassanian SM, Rezaei N, Hashemzehi M, Bahrami A, Ariakia F, Fiuji H, Sahebkar A, Avan A, & Khazaei M. (2018). Phytosomal curcumin inhibits tumor growth in colitis-associated colorectal cancer. *Journal of cellular physiology*, *233*(10), 6785−6798. Available from https://doi.org/10.1002/jcp.26538.

[21] Hassanzadeh S, Read MI, Bland AR, Majeed M, Jamialahmadi T, Sahebkar A. Curcumin: an inflammasome silencer. Pharmacological Research 2020;159.

[22] Rahimi K, Hassanzadeh K, Khanbabaei H, Haftcheshmeh SM, Ahmadi A, Izadpanah E, et al. Curcumin: a dietary phytochemical for targeting the phenotype and function of dendritic cells. Current Medicinal Chemistry 2021;28(8):1549−64.

[23] Liu Z, Huang P, Law S, Tian H, Leung W, Xu C. Preventive effect of curcumin against chemotherapy-induced side-effects. Frontiers in Pharmacology 2018;9:1374.

[24] Abadi AJ, Mirzaei S, Mahabady MK, Hashemi F, Zabolian A, Hashemi F, et al. Curcumin and its derivatives in cancer therapy: potentiating antitumor activity of cisplatin and reducing side effects. Phytotherapy Research: PTR 2022;36(1):189−213.

[25] Liu ZG, Hsu H, Goeddel DV, Karin M. Dissection of TNF receptor 1 effector functions: JNK activation is not linked to apoptosis while NF-kappaB activation prevents cell death. Cell. 1996;87(3):565−76.

[26] Hollowood K, Macartney JC. Reduced apoptotic cell death in follicular lymphoma. The Journal of Pathology 1991;163(4):337–42.

[27] Sachs L, Lotem J. Control of programmed cell death in normal and leukemic cells: new implications for therapy. Blood 1993;82(1):15–21.

[28] Rahmani AH, Al Zohairy MA, Aly SM, Khan MA. Curcumin: a potential candidate in prevention of cancer via modulation of molecular pathways. BioMed Research International 2014;2014:761608.

[29] Ramachandran C, Rodriguez S, Ramachandran R, Raveendran Nair PK, Fonseca H, Khatib Z, et al. Expression profiles of apoptotic genes induced by curcumin in human breast cancer and mammary epithelial cell lines. Anticancer Research 2005;25(5):3293–302.

[30] Yang J, Liu X, Bhalla K, Kim CN, Ibrado AM, Cai J, et al. Prevention of apoptosis by Bcl-2: release of cytochrome c from mitochondria blocked. Science (New York, NY) 1997;275(5303):1129–32.

[31] Shankar S, Srivastava RK. Involvement of Bcl-2 family members, phosphatidylinositol 3'-kinase/AKT and mitochondrial p53 in curcumin (diferulolylmethane)-induced apoptosis in prostate cancer. International Journal of Oncology 2007;30(4):905–18.

[32] Wu SH, Hang LW, Yang JS, Chen HY, Lin HY, Chiang JH, et al. Curcumin induces apoptosis in human non-small cell lung cancer NCI-H460 cells through ER stress and caspase cascade- and mitochondria-dependent pathways. Anticancer Research 2010;30(6):2125–33.

[33] Erickson BA, Longo WE, Panesar N, Mazuski JE, Kaminski DL. The effect of selective cyclooxygenase inhibitors on intestinal epithelial cell mitogenesis. The Journal of Surgical Research 1999;81(1):101–7.

[34] Hara A, Yoshimi N, Niwa M, Ino N, Mori H. Apoptosis induced by NS-398, a selective cyclooxygenase-2 inhibitor, in human colorectal cancer cell lines. Japanese Journal of Cancer Research: Gann = Gan 1997;88(6):600–4.

[35] Sawaoka H, Kawano S, Tsuji S, Tsujii M, Gunawan ES, Takei Y, et al. Cyclooxygenase-2 inhibitors suppress the growth of gastric cancer xenografts via induction of apoptosis in nude mice. The American Journal of Physiology 1998;274(6):G1061–7.

[36] Lev-Ari S, Starr A, Vexler A, Karaush V, Loew V, Greif J, et al. Inhibition of pancreatic and lung adenocarcinoma cell survival by curcumin is associated with increased apoptosis, down-regulation of COX-2 and EGFR and inhibition of Erk1/2 activity. Anticancer Research 2006;26(6b):4423–30.

[37] Cardone MH, Roy N, Stennicke HR, Salvesen GS, Franke TF, Stanbridge E, et al. Regulation of cell death protease caspase-9 by phosphorylation. Science (New York, NY) 1998;282(5392):1318–21.

[38] Datta SR, Dudek H, Tao X, Masters S, Fu H, Gotoh Y, et al. Akt phosphorylation of BAD couples survival signals to the cell-intrinsic death machinery. Cell. 1997;91(2):231–41.

[39] Cross DA, Alessi DR, Cohen P, Andjelkovich M, Hemmings BA. Inhibition of glycogen synthase kinase-3 by insulin mediated by protein kinase B. Nature 1995;378(6559):785–9.

[40] Woo JH, Kim YH, Choi YJ, Kim DG, Lee KS, Bae JH, et al. Molecular mechanisms of curcumin-induced cytotoxicity: induction of apoptosis through generation of reactive oxygen species, down-regulation of Bcl-XL and IAP, the release of cytochrome c and inhibition of Akt. Carcinogenesis 2003;24(7):1199–208.

[41] Nagata S, Golstein P. The Fas death factor. Science (New York, NY) 1995;267(5203):1449–56.

[42] Lee HP, Li TM, Tsao JY, Fong YC, Tang CH. Curcumin induces cell apoptosis in human chondrosarcoma through extrinsic death receptor pathway. International Immunopharmacology 2012;13(2):163–9.

[43] Wang WZ, Li L, Liu MY, Jin XB, Mao JW, Pu QH, et al. Curcumin induces FasL-related apoptosis through p38 activation in human hepatocellular carcinoma Huh7 cells. Life Sciences 2013;92(6–7):352–8.

[44] Palipoch S. A review of oxidative stress in acute kidney injury: protective role of medicinal plants-derived antioxidants. African Journal of Traditional, Complementary, and Alternative Medicines: AJTCAM 2013;10(4):88–93.

[45] Simon HU, Haj-Yehia A, Levi-Schaffer F. Role of reactive oxygen species (ROS) in apoptosis induction. Apoptosis: An International Journal on Programmed Cell Death 2000;5(5):415–18.

[46] Wang WH, Chiang IT, Ding K, Chung JG, Lin WJ, Lin SS, et al. Curcumin-induced apoptosis in human hepatocellular carcinoma j5 cells: critical role of ca(+2)-dependent pathway. Evidence-Based Complementary and Alternative Medicine: eCAM 2012;2012:512907.

[47] Chang Z, Xing J, Yu X. Curcumin induces osteosarcoma MG63 cells apoptosis via ROS/Cyto-C/Caspase-3 pathway. Tumour Biology: The Journal of the International Society for Oncodevelopmental Biology and Medicine 2014;35(1):753—8.

[48] Liang T, Zhang X, Xue W, Zhao S, Zhang X, Pei J. Curcumin induced human gastric cancer BGC-823 cells apoptosis by ROS-mediated ASK1-MKK4-JNK stress signaling pathway. International Journal of Molecular Sciences 2014;15(9):15754—65.

[49] Coker-Gurkan A, Celik M, Ugur M, Arisan ED, Obakan-Yerlikaya P, Durdu ZB, et al. Curcumin inhibits autocrine growth hormone-mediated invasion and metastasis by targeting NF-κB signaling and poly-amine metabolism in breast cancer cells. Amino Acids 2018;50(8):1045—69.

[50] Yang J, Cao Y, Sun J, Zhang Y. Curcumin reduces the expression of Bcl-2 by upregulating miR-15a and miR-16 in MCF-7 cells. Medical Oncology (Northwood, London, England) 2010;27(4):1114—18.

[51] Guo J, Li W, Shi H, Xie X, Li L, Tang H, et al. Synergistic effects of curcumin with emodin against the proliferation and invasion of breast cancer cells through upregulation of miR-34a. Molecular and Cellular Biochemistry 2013;382(1—2):103—11.

[52] Chase A, Cross NC. Aberrations of EZH2 in cancer. Clinical Cancer Research: An Official Journal of the American Association for Cancer Research 2011;17(9):2613—18.

[53] Zhou X, Jiao D, Dou M, Zhang W, Lv L, Chen J, et al. Curcumin inhibits the growth of triple-negative breast cancer cells by silencing EZH2 and restoring DLC1 expression. Journal of Cellular and Molecular Medicine 2020;24(18):10648—62.

[54] Li W, Zhou Y, Yang J, Li H, Zhang H, Zheng P. Curcumin induces apoptotic cell death and protective autophagy in human gastric cancer cells. Oncology Reports 2017;37(6):3459—66.

[55] Jiang A, Wang X, Shan X, Li Y, Wang P, Jiang P, et al. Curcumin reactivates silenced tumor suppressor gene RARβ by reducing DNA methylation. Phytotherapy Research: PTR 2015;29(8):1237—45.

[56] Farghadani R, Naidu R. Curcumin: modulator of key molecular signaling pathways in hormone-independent breast cancer. Cancers. 2021;13(14).

[57] Budina-Kolomets A, Barnoud T, Murphy ME. The transcription-independent mitochondrial cell death pathway is defective in non-transformed cells containing the Pro47Ser variant of. Cancer Biology & Therapy 2018;19(11):1033—p58.

[58] Reisman D, Takahashi P, Polson A, Boggs K. Transcriptional regulation of the p53 tumor suppressor gene in S-phase of the cell-cycle and the cellular response to DNA Damage. Biochemistry Research International 2012;2012:808934.

[59] Fridman JS, Lowe SW. Control of apoptosis by p53. Oncogene 2003;22(56):9030—40.

[60] Liontas A, Yeger H. Curcumin and resveratrol induce apoptosis and nuclear translocation and activation of p53 in human neuroblastoma. Anticancer Research 2004;24(2b):987—98.

[61] Choudhuri T, Pal S, Agwarwal ML, Das T, Sa G. Curcumin induces apoptosis in human breast cancer cells through p53-dependent Bax induction. FEBS Letters 2002;512(1—3):334—40.

[62] Fu H, Wang C, Yang D, Wei Z, Xu J, Hu Z, et al. Curcumin regulates proliferation, autophagy, and apoptosis in gastric cancer cells by affecting PI3K and P53 signaling. Journal of Cellular Physiology 2018;233 (6):4634—42.

[63] Choudhuri T, Pal S, Das T, Sa G. Curcumin selectively induces apoptosis in deregulated cyclin D1-expressed cells at G2 phase of cell cycle in a p53-dependent manner. The. Journal of Biological Chemistry 2005;280(20):20059 -68.

[64] He ZY, Shi CB, Wen H, Li FL, Wang BL, Wang J. Upregulation of p53 expression in patients with colorectal cancer by administration of curcumin. Cancer Investigation 2011;29(3):208—13.

[65] Wang Z, Cai Q, Jiang Z, Liu B, Zhu Z, Li C. Prognostic role of microRNA-21 in gastric cancer: a meta-analysis. Medical Science Monitor: International Medical Journal of Experimental and Clinical Research 2014;20:1668−74.

[66] Zhang BG, Li JF, Yu BQ, Zhu ZG, Liu BY, Yan M. microRNA-21 promotes tumor proliferation and invasion in gastric cancer by targeting PTEN. Oncology Reports 2012;27(4):1019−26.

[67] Roy S, Yu Y, Padhye SB, Sarkar FH, Majumdar AP. Difluorinated-curcumin (CDF) restores PTEN expression in colon cancer cells by down-regulating miR-21. PLoS One 2013;8(7):e68543.

[68] Qiang Z, Meng L, Yi C, Yu L, Chen W, Sha W. Curcumin regulates the miR-21/PTEN/Akt pathway and acts in synergy with PD98059 to induce apoptosis of human gastric cancer MGC-803 cells. The Journal of International Medical Research 2019;47(3):1288−97.

[69] Chen L, Li WF, Wang HX, Zhao HN, Tang JJ, Wu CJ, et al. Curcumin cytotoxicity is enhanced by PTEN disruption in colorectal cancer cells. World Journal of Gastroenterology 2013;19(40):6814−24.

[70] Dvory-Sobol H, Cohen-Noyman E, Kazanov D, Figer A, Birkenfeld S, Madar-Shapiro L, et al. Celecoxib leads to G2/M arrest by induction of p21 and down-regulation of cyclin B1 expression in a p53-independent manner. European Journal of Cancer (Oxford, England: 1990) 2006;42(3):422−6.

[71] Hua F, Fang N, Li X, Zhu S, Zhang W, Gu J. A meta-analysis of the relationship between RARβ gene promoter methylation and non-small cell lung cancer. PLoS One 2014;9(5):e96163.

[72] Mattei MG, de Thé H, Mattei JF, Marchio A, Tiollais P, Dejean A. Assignment of the human hap retinoic acid receptor RAR beta gene to the p24 band of chromosome 3. Human Genetics 1988;80(2):189−90.

[73] Xu XC. Tumor-suppressive activity of retinoic acid receptor-beta in cancer. Cancer Letters 2007;253(1):14−24.

[74] Virmani AK, Rathi A, Zöchbauer-Müller S, Sacchi N, Fukuyama Y, Bryant D, et al. Promoter methylation and silencing of the retinoic acid receptor-beta gene in lung carcinomas. Journal of the National Cancer Institute 2000;92(16):1303−7.

[75] Thulasiraman P, Garriga G, Danthuluri V, McAndrews DJ, Mohiuddin IQ. Activation of the CRABPII/RAR pathway by curcumin induces retinoic acid mediated apoptosis in retinoic acid resistant breast cancer cells. Oncology Reports 2017;37(4):2007−15.

[76] Bharti AC, Aggarwal BB. Chemopreventive agents induce suppression of nuclear factor-kappaB leading to chemosensitization. Annals of the New York Academy of Sciences 2002;973:392−5.

[77] Balkwill F, Mantovani A. Inflammation and cancer: back to Virchow? Lancet (London, England) 2001;357(9255):539−45.

[78] Aggarwal BB. Nuclear factor-kappaB: the enemy within. Cancer Cell 2004;6(3):203−8.

[79] Bharti AC, Aggarwal BB. Nuclear factor-kappa B and cancer: its role in prevention and therapy. Biochemical Pharmacology 2002;64(5−6):883−8.

[80] Pahl HL. Activators and target genes of Rel/NF-kappaB transcription factors. Oncogene 1999;18(49):6853−66.

[81] Karin M. The beginning of the end: IkappaB kinase (IKK) and NF-kappaB activation. The Journal of Biological Chemistry 1999;274(39):27339−42.

[82] Bachmeier BE, Mohrenz IV, Mirisola V, Schleicher E, Romeo F, Höhneke C, et al. Curcumin downregulates the inflammatory cytokines CXCL1 and -2 in breast cancer cells via NFκB. Carcinogenesis 2008;29(4):779−89.

[83] Lin YG, Kunnumakkara AB, Nair A, Merritt WM, Han LY, Armaiz-Pena GN, et al. Curcumin inhibits tumor growth and angiogenesis in ovarian carcinoma by targeting the nuclear factor-kappaB pathway. Clinical Cancer Research: An Official Journal of the American Association for Cancer Research 2007;13(11):3423−30.

[84] Marquardt JU, Gomez-Quiroz L, Arreguin Camacho LO, Pinna F, Lee YH, Kitade M, et al. Curcumin effectively inhibits oncogenic NF-κB signaling and restrains stemness features in liver cancer. Journal of Hepatology 2015;63(3):661—9.

[85] Brooks AJ, Putoczki T. JAK-STAT signalling pathway in cancer. Cancers. 2020;12(7).

[86] Aaronson DS, Horvath CM. A road map for those who don't know JAK-STAT. Science (New York, NY) 2002;296(5573):1653—5.

[87] Brooks AJ, Dai W, O'Mara ML, Abankwa D, Chhabra Y, Pelekanos RA, et al. Mechanism of activation of protein kinase JAK2 by the growth hormone receptor. Science (New York, NY) 2014;344 (6185):1249783.

[88] Thomas SJ, Snowden JA, Zeidler MP, Danson SJ. The role of JAK/STAT signalling in the pathogenesis, prognosis and treatment of solid tumours. British Journal of Cancer 2015;113(3):365—71.

[89] Sun Y, Liu L, Wang Y, He A, Hu H, Zhang J, et al. Curcumin inhibits the proliferation and invasion of MG-63 cells through inactivation of the p-JAK2/p-STAT3 pathway. OncoTargets and Therapy 2019;12:2011—21.

[90] Xu X, Zhu Y. Curcumin inhibits human non-small cell lung cancer xenografts by targeting STAT3 pathway. American Journal of Translational Research 2017;9(8):3633—41.

[91] Zhang Y, Wang X. Targeting the Wnt/β-catenin signaling pathway in cancer. Journal of Hematology & Oncology 2020;13(1):165.

[92] Zhan T, Rindtorff N, Boutros M. Wnt signaling in cancer. Oncogene 2017;36(11):1461—73.

[93] Polakis P. Wnt signaling in cancer. Cold Spring Harbor Perspectives in Biology 2012;4:5.

[94] Kiely B, O'Donovan RT, McKenna SL, O'Sullivan GC. Beta-catenin transcriptional activity is inhibited downstream of nuclear localisation and is not influenced by IGF signalling in oesophageal cancer cells. International Journal of Cancer 2007;121(9):1903—9.

[95] Cadigan KM, Nusse R. Wnt signaling: a common theme in animal development. Genes & Development 1997;11(24):3286—305.

[96] Morin PJ. Beta-catenin signaling and cancer. BioEssays: News and Reviews in Molecular, Cellular and Developmental Biology 1999;21(12):1021—30.

[97] He M, Li Y, Zhang L, Li L, Shen Y, Lin L, et al. Curcumin suppresses cell proliferation through inhibition of the Wnt/β-catenin signaling pathway in medulloblastoma. Oncology Reports 2014;32 (1):173—80.

[98] Hao J, Dai X, Gao J, Li Y, Hou Z, Chang Z, et al. Curcumin suppresses colorectal tumorigenesis via the Wnt/β-catenin signaling pathway by downregulating Axin2. Oncology Letters 2021;21(3):186.

[99] Srivastava NS, Srivastava RAK. Curcumin and quercetin synergistically inhibit cancer cell proliferation in multiple cancer cells and modulate Wnt/β-catenin signaling and apoptotic pathways in A375 cells. Phytomedicine: International Journal of Phytotherapy and Phytopharmacology 2019;52:117—28.

[100] Karamysheva AF. Mechanisms of angiogenesis. Biochemistry. Biokhimiia 2008;73(7):751—62.

[101] Liekens S, De Clercq E, Neyts J. Angiogenesis: regulators and clinical applications. Biochemical Pharmacology 2001;61(3):253—70.

[102] Al-Ostoot FH, Salah S, Khamees HA, Khanum SA. Tumor angiogenesis: current challenges and therapeutic opportunities. Cancer Treatment and Research Communications 2021;28:100422.

[103] Huang JH, Yin XM, Xu Y, Xu CC, Lin X, Ye FB, et al. Systemic administration of exosomes released from mesenchymal stromal cells attenuates apoptosis, inflammation, and promotes angiogenesis after spinal cord injury in rats. Journal of Neurotrauma 2017;34(24):3388—96.

[104] Faraji A, Oghabi Bakhshaiesh T, Hasanvand Z, Motahari R, Nazeri E, Boshagh MA, et al. Design, synthesis and evaluation of novel thienopyrimidine-based agents bearing diaryl urea functionality as potential inhibitors of angiogenesis. European Journal of Medicinal Chemistry 2021;209:112942.

[105] Rajabi M, Mousa SA. The role of angiogenesis in cancer treatment. Biomedicines. 2017;5(2).

[106] Kulke M, Lenz HJ, Meropol NJ, Posey J, Ryan DP, Picus J, et al. A phase 2 study to evaluate the efficacy and safety of SU11248 in patients (pts) with unresectable neuroendocrine tumors (NETs). Journal of Clinical Oncology 2005;23(16_suppl):4008.

[107] Choueiri TK. Axitinib, a novel anti-angiogenic drug with promising activity in various solid tumors. Current Opinion in Investigational Drugs (London, England: 2000) 2008;9(6):658−71.

[108] Bhandarkar SS, Arbiser JL. Curcumin as an inhibitor of angiogenesis. Advances in Experimental Medicine and Biology 2007;595:185−95.

[109] Olsson AK, Dimberg A, Kreuger J, Claesson-Welsh L. VEGF receptor signalling - in control of vascular function. Nature Reviews. Molecular Cell Biology 2006;7(5):359−71.

[110] Hernández-Morales J, Hernández-Coronado CG, Guzmán A, Zamora-Gutiérrez D, Fierro F, Gutiérrez CG, et al. Hypoxia up-regulates VEGF ligand and downregulates VEGF soluble receptor mRNA expression in bovine granulosa cells in vitro. Theriogenology 2021;165:76−83.

[111] Ferrara N. Vascular endothelial growth factor: basic science and clinical progress. Endocrine Reviews 2004;25(4):581−611.

[112] Claesson-Welsh L, Welsh M. VEGFA and tumour angiogenesis. Journal of Internal Medicine 2013;273 (2):114−27.

[113] Fu Z, Chen X, Guan S, Yan Y, Lin H, Hua ZC. Curcumin inhibits angiogenesis and improves defective hematopoiesis induced by tumor-derived VEGF in tumor model through modulating VEGF-VEGFR2 signaling pathway. Oncotarget 2015;6(23):19469−82.

[114] Pan Z, Zhuang J, Ji C, Cai Z, Liao W, Huang Z. Curcumin inhibits hepatocellular carcinoma growth by targeting VEGF expression. Oncology letters 2018;15(4):4821−6.

[115] Zhang Y, Xiang J, Zhu N, Ge H, Sheng X, Deng S, et al. Curcumin in combination with omacetaxine suppress lymphoma cell growth, migration, invasion, and angiogenesis via inhibition of VEGF/Akt signaling pathway. Frontiers in Oncology 2021;11:656045.

[116] Bayet-Robert M, Kwiatkowski F, Leheurteur M, Gachon F, Planchat E, Abrial C, et al. Phase I dose escalation trial of docetaxel plus curcumin in patients with advanced and metastatic breast cancer. Cancer Biology & Therapy 2010;9(1):8−14.

[117] Li L, Ahmed B, Mehta K, Kurzrock R. Liposomal curcumin with and without oxaliplatin: effects on cell growth, apoptosis, and angiogenesis in colorectal cancer. Molecular Cancer Therapeutics 2007;6 (4):1276−82.

[118] Hida T, Kozaki K, Ito H, Miyaishi O, Tatematsu Y, Suzuki T, et al. Significant growth inhibition of human lung cancer cells both in vitro and in vivo by the combined use of a selective cyclooxygenase 2 inhibitor, JTE-522, and conventional anticancer agents. Clinical Cancer Research: An Official Journal of the American Association for Cancer Research 2002;8(7):2443−7.

[119] Kundu N, Fulton AM. Selective cyclooxygenase (COX)-1 or COX-2 inhibitors control metastatic disease in a murine model of breast cancer. Cancer Research 2002;62(8):2343−6.

[120] Bae SH, Jung ES, Park YM, Kim BS, Kim BK, Kim DG, et al. Expression of cyclooxygenase-2 (COX-2) in hepatocellular carcinoma and growth inhibition of hepatoma cell lines by a COX-2 inhibitor, NS-398. Clinical Cancer Research: An Official Journal of the American Association for Cancer Research 2001;7 (5):1410−18.

[121] Xiong B, Sun TJ, Yuan HY, Hu MB, Hu WD, Cheng FL. Cyclooxygenase-2 expression and angiogenesis in colorectal cancer. World Journal of Gastroenterology 2003;9(6):1237−40.

[122] Yoysungnoen P, Wirachwong P, Bhattarakosol P, Niimi H, Patumraj S. Effects of curcumin on tumor angiogenesis and biomarkers, COX-2 and VEGF, in hepatocellular carcinoma cell-implanted nude mice. Clinical Hemorheology and Microcirculation 2006;34(1−2):109 -15.

[123] Coghlin C, Murray GI. Current and emerging concepts in tumour metastasis. The Journal of Pathology 2010;222(1):1−15.

[124] Mehlen P, Puisieux A. Metastasis: a question of life or death. Nature Reviews. Cancer 2006;6 (6):449−58.

[125] Deng YI, Verron E, Rohanizadeh R. Molecular mechanisms of anti-metastatic activity of curcumin. Anticancer Research 2016;36(11):5639−47.

[126] Brooks SA, Lomax-Browne HJ, Carter TM, Kinch CE, Hall DM. Molecular interactions in cancer cell metastasis. Acta Histochemica 2010;112(1):3−25.

[127] Bachmeier BE, Killian PH, Melchart D. The role of curcumin in prevention and management of metastatic disease. International Journal of Molecular Sciences 2018;19(6).

[128] Lin SS, Lai KC, Hsu SC, Yang JS, Kuo CL, Lin JP, et al. Curcumin inhibits the migration and invasion of human A549 lung cancer cells through the inhibition of matrix metalloproteinase-2 and -9 and vascular endothelial growth factor (VEGF). Cancer Letters 2009;285(2):127−33.

[129] Kim JM, Noh EM, Kwon KB, Kim JS, You YO, Hwang JK, et al. Curcumin suppresses the TPA-induced invasion through inhibition of PKCα-dependent MMP-expression in MCF-7 human breast cancer cells. Phytomedicine: International Journal of Phytotherapy and Phytopharmacology 2012;19(12):1085−92.

[130] Shao ZM, Shen ZZ, Liu CH, Sartippour MR, Go VL, Heber D, et al. Curcumin exerts multiple suppressive effects on human breast carcinoma cells. International Journal of Cancer 2002;98(2):234−40.

[131] Hong JH, Ahn KS, Bae E, Jeon SS, Choi HY. The effects of curcumin on the invasiveness of prostate cancer in vitro and in vivo. Prostate Cancer and Prostatic Diseases 2006;9(2):147−52.

[132] Eberhardt W, Huwiler A, Beck KF, Walpen S, Pfeilschifter J. Amplification of IL-1 beta-induced matrix metalloproteinase-9 expression by superoxide in rat glomerular mesangial cells is mediated by increased activities of NF-kappa B and activating protein-1 and involves activation of the mitogen-activated protein kinase pathways. Journal of Immunology (Baltimore, Md: 1950) 2000;165 (10):5788−97.

[133] Farhangi B, Alizadeh AM, Khodayari H, Khodayari S, Dehghan MJ, Khori V, et al. Protective effects of dendrosomal curcumin on an animal metastatic breast tumor. European Journal of Pharmacology 2015;758:188−96.

[134] Hu C, Li M, Guo T, Wang S, Huang W, Yang K, et al. Anti-metastasis activity of curcumin against breast cancer via the inhibition of stem cell-like properties and EMT. Phytomedicine: International Journal of Phytotherapy and Phytopharmacology 2019;58:152740.

[135] Qi C, Wang D, Gong X, Zhou Q, Yue X, Li C, et al. Co-delivery of curcumin and capsaicin by dual-targeting liposomes for inhibition of aHSC-induced drug resistance and metastasis. ACS Applied Materials & Interfaces 2021;13(14):16019−35.

Smart drug delivery approaches for curcumin delivery in cancer therapy

PART

B

Smart drug delivery
approaches for curcumin
delivery in cancer therapy

Curcumin-drug conjugate-based drug delivery as cancer therapeutics

Mehdi Sanati[1,2], Amir R. Afshari[3], Tannaz Jamialahmadi[4],
Amirhossein Sahebkar[5,6]

[1]DEPARTMENT OF PHARMACOLOGY AND TOXICOLOGY, FACULTY OF PHARMACY, BIRJAND
UNIVERSITY OF MEDICAL SCIENCES, BIRJAND, IRAN [2]EXPERIMENTAL AND ANIMAL STUDY
CENTER, BIRJAND UNIVERSITY OF MEDICAL SCIENCES, BIRJAND, IRAN [3]DEPARTMENT OF
PHYSIOLOGY AND PHARMACOLOGY, FACULTY OF MEDICINE, NORTH KHORASAN
UNIVERSITY OF MEDICAL SCIENCES, BOJNURD, IRAN [4]INTERNATIONAL UNESCO CENTER FOR
HEALTH-RELATED BASIC SCIENCES AND HUMAN NUTRITION, MASHHAD UNIVERSITY OF
MEDICAL SCIENCES, MASHHAD, IRAN [5]BIOTECHNOLOGY RESEARCH CENTER,
PHARMACEUTICAL TECHNOLOGY INSTITUTE, MASHHAD UNIVERSITY OF MEDICAL SCIENCES,
MASHHAD, IRAN [6]APPLIED BIOMEDICAL RESEARCH CENTER, MASHHAD UNIVERSITY OF
MEDICAL SCIENCES, MASHHAD, IRAN

6.1 Introduction

Cancer is a challenging health issue worldwide. To date, tremendous efforts have been conducted to improve anticancer treatment approaches; however, no significant progress has been made regarding the complex pathology of cancers. Unfortunately, despite standard chemoradiation therapies, patients encounter a dismal prognosis and short survival time. In the last decade, developing drug candidates using phytochemicals has attracted lots of interest due to their multimechanism and safe function [1]. Curcumin (Cur) is a nontoxic active ingredient from *Curcuma longa* (*turmeric*), which is endowed with numerous pharmacological and therapeutic features [2−15]. Cur targets various signaling pathways and biomolecules at cellular and molecular levels in different types of cancer [16−19]. Generally, Cur is known for attenuating signal transducer and activator of transcription 3 (STAT3) and nuclear factor kappa B (NF-κB) signalings, playing critical roles in cancer cell survival, proliferation, and migration [20,21]. Unfortunately, despite the brilliant history of preclinical effectiveness, the clinical implication of Cur is confined due to its relative water insolubility and weak stability in the biological media [22,23]. In this regard, significant efforts have been accomplished to enhance Cur pharmacokinetics and pharmacodynamics; among those, conjugation-based improvements achieved substantial success. Diverse conjugates with distinct strategies (e.g., conjugating with water-soluble molecules, producing prodrugs, designing nanomicelles, and developing tumor-targeting Cur hybrids) have been originated to improve water solubility and stability, prevent biodegradation, and increase intracellular concentration [24−27]. Furthermore, conjugation with drugs or candidate anticancer drugs has been shown to promote the Cur pharmacodynamics [28]. These conjugates are tested preclinically with encouraging outcomes and need further clinical evaluations. This study summarized the advances in conjugation-based strategies to improve Cur delivery and effectiveness as cancer therapeutics.

6.2 Curcumin-drug conjugates in cancer therapy

Drug conjugation has long been considered as a unique strategy for boosting the therapeutic potential of several anticancer medications synergistically while minimizing their toxicity. The resulting hybrids exhibit notable advances in terms of pharmacokinetics and pharmacodynamics [29]. With this in mind, various investigations aimed to improve the biological properties of Cur for clinical implications. The effect of drug conjugation in enhancing Cur delivery and efficacy in cancer therapy is discussed in this chapter.

6.2.1 Improving pharmacokinetics

Cur is a promising anticancer candidate drug targeting multiple pathways in various cancer cells; however, weak water solubility and extensive metabolism restricted its bioavailability for clinical use [30,31]. Many researches have suggested manufacturing Cur hybrids to optimize Cur pharmacokinetics. For example, conjugating Cur with water-soluble molecules improves its solubility and restricts intestinal metabolism [24]. A recent study revealed that conjugating with metformin enhances Cur's stability as well as cytotoxicity against breast cancer cells [32]. Furthermore, hybrids constructed from Cur conjugating to proteins such as albumin and β-lactoglobulin have improved Cur's water solubility, stability, and anticancer effects [33,34]. Attaching to specific adjuvants has also been considered a strategy to increase Cur oral bioavailability as well as the plasma retention time. Piperine is the best-described adjutant affecting the intestinal brush border to increase Cur absorption, inhibits Cur metabolism by suppressing uridine 5'-diphospho (UDP) glucuronosyltransferases and cytochrome p450 isoenzymes, and augmenting Cur intracellular concentration via targeting P-glycoprotein (P-gp) [35,36]. In this regard, Cur-piperic acid conjugates were synthesized and tested on AK-5, MCF-7, and MDA-MB-231 cancer cells. Results demonstrated that dipiperoyl derivative permeabilized mitochondria and induced reactive oxygen species (ROS) production, leading to cytochrome C and apoptotic proteins (e.g., apoptosis-inducing factor [AIF], B-cell lymphoma 2 [bcl-2], B-cell lymphoma-extra large [Bcl-xL]) release as well as caspase-3 activation through suppressing the nuclear translocation of NF-κB [37]. Notably, demethylenated piperic acid-Cur conjugate was the most active anticancer compound among various synthesized derivatives [38]. Due to the occupation of Cur metabolic sites and inhibition of its efflux from cancerous cells, piperine only enhances the pharmacokinetics of Cur in the war against cancers.

In addition, conjugation with fatty acids like linoleic acid has been shown to improve Cur bioavailability and prolong its duration of action. Interestingly, the graphene oxide

(GFO)-linoleic-Cur conjugate showed selective accumulation and toxicity in MCF-7 cancer cells [39,40]. Besides, amino acids play the role of carriers for Cur and prevent its metabolic degradation. Among the conjugates obtained by recruiting amino acids, Cur glutamoyl derivative showed the most antiproliferative properties in HeLa and KB cancer cells, probably due to increasing Cur stability and preventing its metabolic degradation [38]. Furthermore, diglycinoyl Cur conjugates were shown to reduce cell viability and change the nuclear morphology of triple-negative breast cancer (TNBC) cells [41]. Besides inhibiting Cur degradation, amino acids (particularly proline) conjugated to Cur may bind to the Src homology (SH2) domain of the STAT3a monomer and prevent its dimerization, attenuating the expression of genes involved in cell survival and proliferation [42]. Another approach to improve the delivery of Cur into the cancerous cell is the conjugation with factors targeting P-gp. For example, Cur-loaded poly lactic-co-glycolic acid (PLGA) nanoparticles (NPs) conjugated with anti-P-gp protein has been shown to increase the cellular uptake and cytotoxicity of Cur in cancer cells with high expression of P-gp efflux protein such as KB-V1 cervical cancer cells [43]. In addition to the mentioned efforts, a variety of conjugates have been developed with different strategies, for example, developing prodrugs, designing self-assembled conjugates, creating nanosized micelles, and optimizing targeted delivery.

6.2.1.1 Producing prodrugs

One easy and inexpensive solution to overcome Cur drawbacks like poor absorption is the production of prodrugs favoring the conjugation with various polymers like PLGA, polyethylene glycol (PEG), PEG-PLGA, dextran, oligo(ethylene glycol) (OEG), and dendrimers. Broadly speaking, polymeric prodrugs of conventional drugs provide advantages such as increasing water solubility and bioavailability, preventing degradation, preserving activity during circulation, optimizing delivery to the target organ and intracellular trafficking, and overall improvement of pharmacokinetic properties [44]. The PLGA, as a biodegradable and biocompatible polymer, is frequently recruited to develop delivery systems due to its excellent properties. Conjugating Cur with PLGA was carried out to improve the bioavailability of Cur. Results demonstrated the potentiation of Cur sustainability and biological activity like caspase-mediated apoptotic effects in human colon carcinoma cells [25]. Polyamidoamine dendrimer was also synthesized and conjugated with the Cur to direct it to the mitochondria of hepatic cancer cells. This conjugation further improved the solubility and stability of Cur. In mice bearing Hepa1-6 tumor, polyamidoamine-Cur caused significant tumor suppression and extended the survival of animals compared to free Cur [45]. The conjugates result from the attachment of dendrimer with Cur also showed excellent water solubility and cytotoxicity against KBr3 and BT549 breast cancer cells [46]. Dextran is another nontoxic and available natural polymer used as a versatile scaffold to improve the biological activities of Cur by covalent grafting. Compared to Cur alone, the Cur-dextran conjugate showed noticeable cytotoxicity against cancerous cells versus fibroblast cells [47]. Cur attachment to OEG (Cur-OEG) has also been shown to form stable conjugates in aqueous conditions. The conjugate has the capability of releasing Cur at intracellular medium and suppressing multiple cancers through promoting apoptosis in vitro and in vivo. More interestingly, Cur-OEG may serve as a carrier for other chemotherapeutics like doxorubicin (DOX) and amplify their cytotoxic action [48].

However, due to the stable bindings, polymer-Cur conjugates may cause ineffective drug release at the site of action. In this regard, pH-sensitive drug conjugates have been suggested to provide effective drug release due to the acidic environment of tumors [49,50]. Zhang et al. designed a codelivery system for DOX and Cur. First, DOX is conjugated with PEG and self-assembled to produce PEG-DOX NPs. Thereafter, Cur is linked to the NPs' core via hydrophobic interaction. In the acidic medium of cancer cells, the connection between PEG and DOX breaks, releasing DOX and Cur. The conjugate system was shown to possess higher antitumor activity than each drug in HeLa and HepG2 cancer cells. Furthermore, in vivo evaluation showed protracted blood circulation time, heightened local drug accumulation, and improved tumor penetration, as well as significant tumor inhibitory property of these PEG-DOX-Cur NPs in HepG2 tumor-bearing mice [51]. Another intriguing research showed that attaching anticancer drug gemcitabine to Cur using a PEG spacer produced a conjugate with remarkable stability in aqueous buffers, noticeable tumor suppression, and lower toxicity compared to free drug congeners [52]. PEGylated Cur decorated on the surface of magnetic NPs also developed a pH-sensitive drug delivery system favoring the magnetic targeting as well as PEG conjugation to release Cur at tumor acidic conditions [53]. Strikingly, conjugating Cur on iron oxide NPs showed no negative effect on Cur functionality and magnetic property of iron oxide NPs and provided significant targeted tumor suppression as well as imaging capabilities [54,55]. Mono-PEGylation of Cur has also been shown to produce a prodrug with substantial stability at physiologic pH, releasing Cur readily in human plasma and exhibiting antitumor effects against colon, cervical, lung, and oral cavity cancer cells [56].

6.2.1.2 Producing self-assembled conjugates creating nanosized micelles

Producing Cur conjugates used for micelle formation in the biological milieu helps improve Cur biostability as well as bioavailability [26]. Micelles are capable of carrying therapeutics and delivering them to the site of action with reduced off-target toxicity [57]. For example, the conjugation of Cur with pectin has improved the pharmacokinetic properties of Cur. The Cur-pectin conjugate forms nanomicelles in the aqueous medium, improving Cur's water solubility and stability while preserving its anticancer capabilities. Notably, the Cur-pectin conjugate was shown to inhibit hepatic, breast, and cervical cancer cell proliferation better than free Cur, while it is less toxic to noncancerous cells [58]. Furthermore, attaching Cur to silica NPs has been shown to improve Cur's water solubility, bioavailability, and anticancer impacts. More interestingly, conjugating Cur-functionalized silica NPs with hyaluronic acid caused micelles formation, increasing Cur's stability and water solubility while harnessing its biological activity. The cellular uptake and toxicity of Cur in the micellar formulation were also significantly higher than free Cur in colon cancer cells [59,60]. It is worth noting that the molecular weight of hyaluronic acid is critically involved in determining the physicochemical properties and anticancer activity of the Cur-based conjugates. It has been shown that only conjugates containing hyaluronic acid with a molecular weight of less than 500 KD have improved cellular uptake and cytotoxicity in glioma cells [61]. Hybrids resulting from Cur and hydroxyethyl starch conjugation have also been shown to form nanomicelles that significantly improved Cur solubility and stability and provided a pH-dependent Cur release in cancerous cells. As proof of concept, the conjugate showed greater toxicity against HeLa and Caco-2 cancer cells compared to free Cur [62]. Another experiment co-conjugated Cur and DOX on a zwitterionic polymer. The conjugate undergoes self-assembly to form stable micelles. The micellar conjugation system showed great cytotoxicity against breast cancer cells since the codelivery of Cur and DOX improved intracellular concentration of DOX due to the Cur-mediated inhibition of drug efflux [63]. Conjugating Cur to alendronate (ALN) and hyaluronan was also exhibited to improve the targeted delivery of Cur to the bone metastasis of breast cancer. In vivo studies using the Cur-ALN-hyaluronan conjugate micelles demonstrated the accumulation of as well as cytotoxicity of Cur at the tumor site. Furthermore, in comparison to free Cur, the conjugate micelles prevent the reduction of bone density [64,65].

Micelle-forming polymer-Cur conjugates have been shown to improve the intracellular delivery of low-potency Cur. For example, Cur molecules conjugated to hydrophobic polylactic acid (PLA) and hydrophilic methoxy-PEG (mPEG) were shown to develop nanomicelles improving Cur intracellular delivery [66]. Furthermore, polyvinylpyrrolidone (PVP), due to its long history of safe usage, is engaged in enhancing Cur's bioavailability. Notably, the PVP-conjugated Cur formed nanosized micelles attenuated Cur hydrophilic degradation. The conjugate exhibited higher cytotoxicity than free Cur, which is probably related to improved aqueous solubility and drug internalization [67]. Furthermore, PVP has been shown to improve Cur's water solubility and facilitates its conjugation with gold NPs (AuNPs) in a way that the diaryl heptanoid chromophore group of Cur remains intact, which is critical for its biomedical applications [68]. In addition to synthetic polymers, natural polysaccharide conjugation is also engaged in improving the Cur delivery to the site of action. Cur has been conjugated with sodium alginate (i.e., a hydrophilic, biocompatible, and negatively charged polysaccharide) and used for producing spherical micelles. The conjugation has been shown to improve Cur's water solubility and stability [69]. Regarding the evaluations in melanoma, breast, and lung cancer cells, the cellular uptake and cytotoxicity of Cur-alginate conjugate were rapid and remarkable [70]. In vivo studies approved the safety of Cur-alginate conjugate; however, anticancer effects in colon and breast cancer animal models were moderate, which need further research and development [71]. Notably, galactosylated alginate-Cur conjugate micelles showed superior targeting as well as toxicity for HepG2 cancer cells [72]. Furthermore, conjugating Cur with chitin (a polysaccharide)-quercetin complex caused pH-dependent Cur and quercetin release in tumor environment as well as anticancer activity in vivo and in vitro [73]. The micelle-based Cur delivery will be comprehensively discussed in Chapter 10.

6.2.1.3 Producing conjugates for targeted delivery of curcumin

Another strategy to improve the Cur concentration at the site of action is conjugating with factors targeting cancer cells. Folic acid—conjugated Cur-encapsulated gum acacia microspheres have been designed for Cur delivery to the breast cancer cells. Due to the upregulated expression of folate receptors on TNBC cells, the drug conjugate targeted the cancer cells in vivo and in vitro, accompanied by improved anticancer impacts [74]. The study conducted by Ghaffari et al. also revealed that conjugation of Cur with folic acid increases its uptake by MDA-MB-468 TNBC cells [75]. Another folic acid–conjugated Cur tagged by IRMOF3 metal framework was shown to induce apoptosis in TNBC cells in vitro and in vivo, as evident by increasing the Bax/bcl-2 ratio, p53, and JNK signaling as well as reducing tumor volume [76]. Furthermore, the folic acid–conjugated Cur-entrapped PLGA-PEG NPs have been designed and tested in vivo. The conjugate was safe and improved the Cur's bioavailability and retention time. The attachment of folic acid was demonstrated to significantly increase the capability of Cur in suppressing survival signalings and its chemosensitizing effect in an immunodeficient mice model of breast cancer [77]. Conjugation of folic acid by gliadin NPs of Cur has also been shown to improve the bioavailability as well as targeting capability toward colon cancer cells [78]. Furthermore, NPs based on Cur-erlotinib (an epidermal growth factor receptor [EGFR] inhibitor) conjugate showed enhanced impacts against BxPC-3 pancreatic cancer cell survival, migration, and invasion compared to each drug alone. In vivo evaluations in a xenografted mouse model demonstrated that, due to the passive (i.e., increased penetration and retention) and active (i.e., EGFR receptor-mediated endocytosis) tumor targeting, the nanoconjugate accumulated in the tumor tissue resulting in the suppression of tumor growth and extending the survival of animals without notable adverse effects [79]. In addition, a naphthoquinone-conjugated Cur hybrid showed remarkable and selective toxic effects in OVCAR-5 and SKOV3 ovarian cancer cells. The conjugate exhibited a pH-sensitive solubility with increasing saturation solubility at the acidic condition of the tumor environment, allowing the targeted killing of cancerous cells [80].

An emerging approach for improving Cur delivery and therapeutic outcomes is the conjugation of Cur with antibodies targeting specific markers on the tumor cell. Glioma cells highly express CD^{86+} on their surface. Conjugating Cur to CD^{86+} specific antibody caused a tremendous increase in the efficacy of Cur to eradicate T98 and U87 glioma cells in vitro and decrease tumor volume in GL261-implanted mice with minimal toxicity to normal tissues [27]. Likewise, conjugating Cur with antibody against Muc18 surface antigen of melanoma cells significantly increased the impact of Cur in suppressing NF-κB signaling and prompting apoptosis to eliminate B16F10 cells in vitro and in vivo [81]. In addition, an antibody with a high affinity for human chorionic gonadotropin β (hCGβ) has been designed and conjugated with Cur to selectively eradicate hCGβ-positive cancer cells. Studies on the MOLT-4 and U-937 acute myeloid leukemia (AML) cells revealed that the immunoconjugate significantly kills both cells and leaves hCGβ-negative cells unaffected. Notably, humans suffering from cancers ectopically express hCGβ are experiencing poor prognosis [82]. Accordingly, targeting cancerous cells by monoclonal antibodies gives significant specificity and efficiency to the Cur treatment; however, the designed drugs are not economical.

6.2.2 Improving pharmacodynamics

Conjugating Cur with drugs or candidate drugs may directly potentiate or synergize the Cur anticancer dynamics. According to the literature, Cur might be helpful in photodynamic cancer therapy (PDT), in which a photosensitizing drug interacts with light and oxygen to produce ROS. Conjugating Cur with certain photosensitizers may improve its usefulness in cancer PDT.

Cerium oxide (CeO) NPs have great potential in cancer therapy as photosensitizers [83]. In this regard, a CeO NPs-Cur conjugate decreased metabolic activity, increased photosensitivity, and induced selective cytotoxicity for tumor cells under ultraviolet (UV) irradiation by promoting oxidative stress while protecting normal cells. The conjugate was also demonstrated to improve the photostability and bioaccumulation of Cur in cancerous cells [84]. Chlorin e6 is another known photosensitizer in cancer PDT. Interestingly, chlorin e6-Cur conjugates showed a remarkable photosensitizing effect in PDT of pancreatic carcinoma AsPC-1 cells. As a result, significant apoptosis was induced by reducing the Bax/bcl-2 ratio, increasing cytochrome C release, and caspase-3 cleavage. The conjugate suppressed cancer cell survival in a dose-dependent manner [85]. In addition, biocompatible transition-metal complexes, such as oxovanadium (IV) compounds, are photoactivatable chemicals that may photocleave DNA and cause cancer cell death via intrinsic mitochondrial apoptosis when exposed to near-infrared light. With this in mind, conjugating Cur with an oxovanadium (IV) moiety has been shown to increase the stability of Cur and enhance the phototoxicity following exposition to visible light. Notably, biocompatible oxovanadium (IV) complexes can potentially reduce the adverse effects of PDT, such as skin photosensitization [86–89].

Biocompatible AuNPs are promising candidates in cancer therapy due to their direct oxidative cytotoxic effects as well as controlled distribution [90,91]. Accordingly, Cur-functionalized AuNPs hybrids showed remarkable cytotoxicity against prostate cancer cells. Notably, the presence of serum proteins is necessary for the stability and biocompatibility of the conjugate [92]. Attaching Cur to ultrasmall gold nanoclusters has also been demonstrated to promote Cur-mediated apoptosis in HeLa cells while leaving normal kidney cells unaffected [93]. In addition, conjugating biosynthesized AuNPs with Cur and paclitaxel showed synergistic cytotoxic effects in TNBC cells through attenuating vascular endothelial growth factor (VEGF), cyclin-D1, and STAT3 expression and promoting caspase-9-mediated apoptosis [94]. Furthermore, the conjugation of Cur with ultrasmall gold quantum clusters was demonstrated to preserve Cur's apoptotic effect on MCF-7 breast cancer cells while not influencing NIH-3T3 normal cells. Similarly, in vivo examinations revealed that the conjugate inhibited tumor growth in MDA-MB-231 TNBC cells-implanted immunodeficient mice without significant toxicity to internal organs. However, larger AuNPs-conjugated Cur had no cytotoxic impact on cancer and normal cells, emphasizing the role of particle size [95]. In a nutshell, nanosized gold species-conjugated Cur shows great potential in treating various cancers; nevertheless, considering the physicochemical properties of AuNPs is necessary for developing the most active and safe conjugate.

A hybrid conjugate based on Cur was hypothesized to improve the therapeutic efficacy of chemotherapy in colon cancer. As mentioned, Cur not only induces the chemosensitivity of cancerous cells but also possesses multiple anticancer effects. Cur-lipid-5-fluorouracil (5-FU) conjugates probably experience better bioavailability, plasma concentration, and cellular permeation due to the better hydrophilic-lipophilic balance as well as the inhibitory action of Cur on P-gp, restricting the entry of chemotherapeutic drugs into the cancerous cells [96]. As a consequence, the hybrid compound may benefit from the anticancer and apoptotic impact of Cur and, simultaneously, the increased intracellular accumulation of cytotoxic 5-FU medicine. Moreover, a Cur-lipoic acid conjugate as a novel anticancer drug was shown to have significant cytotoxicity against U87 glioblastoma cells compared to free Cur. Lipoic acid is a natural antioxidant with established effects in inducing apoptosis and hindering cancer cell proliferation, migration, and stemness. Furthermore, a drug delivery system based on gold-iron oxide nanocomposites (Fe_3O_4@Au NCs), due to their pH-sensitive mechanism, caused the conjugate selective toxicity [97,98]. In addition, conjugating Cur with chitosan oligosaccharide was shown to create redox-sensitive nanocarriers for delivering docetaxel to glioma cells. The delivery system based on Cur conjugation produced synergistic anticancer effects [99]. Furthermore, the $Cu^{2+}/Ni^{2+}/Zn^{2+}$-Cur-conjugates incorporated into the DNA complexes as nanocarriers show a potent growth inhibitory effect in prostate cancer cells. The maximum release of Metallo-Cur conjugates was conducted in the acidic medium of tumor cells, where they produce significant ROS amounts goes beyond the oxidative thresholds of cancerous cells and induce apoptotic cell death [100]. Conjugating Cur to triazole-based moieties has also been shown to improve Cur's apoptotic effects in T acute lymphoblastic leukemia cell line [101]. Similarly, the existence of 1,2,4-triazole moieties in synthetic anticancer candidates has improved the antiproliferative effects in various cancer cell lines [102,103].

Gonadotropin-releasing hormone (GnRH) and its receptor (i.e., GnRHR) are upregulated in certain cancers. Accordingly, continuous stimulation of GnRHR using synthetic GnRH analogs has been shown to desensitize receptors and suppress the growth and proliferation of several malignant human solid tumors [104]. In this regard, Cur was conjugated with a synthetic GnRH agonist and evaluated on pancreatic cancer in vivo and in vitro. This conjugation not only delivers Cur to the specific GnRHR-positive tumor cell but also improves Cur pharmacodynamics. Results showed that the hybrid induces caspase-3 and poly(ADP-ribose) polymerase (PPAR) cleavage-mediated apoptosis in cancer cells with equal efficacy to free Cur. However, in vivo examinations demonstrated that the conjugate prevents the growth of pancreatic cancer xenografts compared to free Cur, probably due to the improved targeting of cancer cells in the biological milieu. Furthermore, conjugating GnRH agonist to Cur increased Cur's water solubility and stability in the aqueous medium [105]. Moreover, in hormone-responsive cancers, antiandrogens are capable of suppressing tumor progression. Intriguingly, conjugating Cur to the testosterone receptor antagonists such as flutamide and bicalutamide has been shown to significantly suppress the proliferation of LNCaP and PC-3 prostate cancer cells and attenuate the formation of actin-based pseudopodia implicated in tumor metastasis compared to antiandrogens alone. The conjugate improved not only the targeting of cancer cells but also therapeutic outcomes since Cur targets functional proteins in the nucleus while antiandrogens locate in the cytosol and induce irregular nuclear division as well as apoptosis [106].

Observations implying the role of Cur in sensitizing multiple myeloma cancer cells to thalidomide through suppressing NF-κB signaling led to the production of Cur-thalidomide hybrids with favorable anticancer impacts. Testing these hybrids on MM1S, RPMI18226, and U266 multiple myeloma cell lines revealed that only conjugates with 4-hydroxy-3-methoxy-phenyl ring exhibit antiproliferative effects, and their activity in producing ROS and inducing

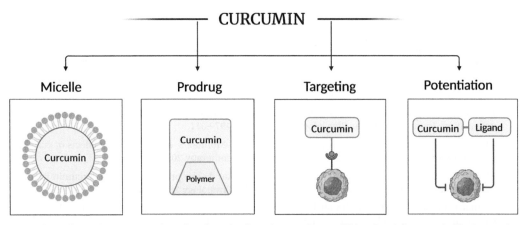

FIGURE 6–1 Schematic representation of conjugation-based strategies amplifying Cur delivery and effectiveness in cancer therapy.

apoptosis was superior to Cur alone. The conjugates also prevented the TNF-α-mediated activation of NF-κB signaling. Accordingly, the Cur-thalidomide conjugate not only preserves the properties of Cur and thalidomide but also improves their biological effects [107,108].

6.3 Conclusion

Conjugating Cur with specific bioactive or inert ligands to improve its delivery as well as anticancer effectiveness seems beneficial. As mentioned, these conjugates are designed to promote the Cur's bioavailability and delivery and potentiate its apoptotic anticancer dynamics. Preclinical reports confirm the efficacy of engineered Cur conjugates in suppressing cancer progression and invasion in vivo and in vitro; however, based on the clinicaltrials.gov information, no clinical trial has been conducted to evaluate the clinical effectiveness of these hybrids. It is also worth mentioning that the hybrid approach does not always enhance the effectiveness of Cur. For example, conjugation of paclitaxel (i.e., a natural chemotherapeutic drug) and Cur did not improve the anticancer effects of either agent [109]. Overall, in line with evaluating safe and effective current Cur conjugates in patients, there is an attractive area of research toward developing novel Cur hybrids with improved biomedical applications (Fig. 6−1).

References

[1] Zugazagoitia J, Guedes C, Ponce S, Ferrer I, Molina-Pinelo S, Paz-Ares L. Current challenges in cancer treatment. Clinical Therapeutics 2016;38(7):1551−66.

[2] Ganji A, Farahani I, Saeedifar AM, Mosayebi G, Ghazavi A, Majeed M, et al. Protective effects of curcumin against lipopolysaccharide-induced toxicity. Current Medicinal Chemistry 2021;28(33):6915−30.

[3] Hassanzadeh S, Read MI, Bland AR, Majeed M, Jamialahmadi T, Sahebkar A. Curcumin: an inflamma-some silencer. Pharmacological Research 2020;159.

[4] Heidari Z, Daei M, Boozari M, Jamialahmadi T, Sahebkar A. Curcumin supplementation in pediatric patients: a systematic review of current clinical evidence. Phytotherapy Research 2022;36(4):1442−58.

[5] Hosseini SA, Zahedipour F, Sathyapalan T, Jamialahmadi T, Sahebkar A. Pulmonary fibrosis: therapeutic and mechanistic insights into the role of phytochemicals. Biofactors (Oxford, England) 2021;47(3):250−69.

[6] Keihanian F, Saeidinia A, Bagheri RK, Johnston TP, Sahebkar A. Curcumin, hemostasis, thrombosis, and coagulation. Journal of Cellular Physiology 2018;233(6):4497−511.

[7] Khayatan D, Razavi SM, Arab ZN, Niknejad AH, Nouri K, Momtaz S, et al. Protective effects of curcumin against traumatic brain injury. Biomedicine and Pharmacotherapy 2022;154.

[8] Mokhtari-Zaer A, Marefati N, Atkin SL, Butler AE, Sahebkar A. The protective role of curcumin in myo-cardial ischemia−reperfusion injury. Journal of Cellular Physiology 2018;234(1):214−22.

[9] Momtazi-Borojeni AA, Haftcheshmeh SM, Esmaeili SA, Johnston TP, Abdollahi E, Sahebkar A. Curcumin: a natural modulator of immune cells in systemic lupus erythematosus. Autoimmunity Reviews 2018;17(2):125−35.

[10] Panahi Y, Fazlolahzadeh O, Atkin SL, Majeed M, Butler AE, Johnston TP, & Sahebkar A. (2019). Evidence of curcumin and curcumin analogue effects in skin diseases: A narrative review. J*ournal of cel-lular physiology, (2),* 1165−1178. Available from https://doi.org/10.1002/jcp.27096.

[11] Marjaneh RM, Rahmani F, Hassanian SM, Rezaei N, Hashemzehi M, Bahrami A, Ariakia F, Fiuji H, Sahebkar A, Avan A, & Khazaei M. (2018). Phytosomal curcumin inhibits tumor growth in colitis-associ-ated colorectal cancer. *Journal of cellular physiology, 233*(10), 6785−6798. Available from https://doi.org/10.1002/jcp.26538.

[12] Mohammadi A, Blesso CN, Barreto GE, Banach M, Majeed M, & Sahebkar A. (2019). Macrophage plas-ticity, polarization and function in response to curcumin, a diet-derived polyphenol, as an immunomod-ulatory agent. *The Journal of nutritional biochemistry, 66,* 1−16. Available from https://doi.org/10.1016/j.jnutbio.2018.12.005.

[13] Cicero AFG, Sahebkar A, Fogacci F, Bove M, Giovannini M, & Borghi C. (2020). Effects of phytosomal curcumin on anthropometric parameters, insulin resistance, cortisolemia and non-alcoholic fatty liver disease indices: a double-blind, placebo-controlled clinical trial. *European journal of nutrition, 59*(2), 477−483. Available from https://doi.org/10.1007/s00394-019-01916-7.

[14] Ahsan R, Arshad M, Khushtar M, Ahmad MA, Muazzam M, Akhter MS, et al. A comprehensive review on physiological effects of curcumin. Drug Research (Stuttgart) 2020;70(10):441−7.

[15] Hassanizadeh S, Shojaei M, Bagherniya M, Orekhov AN, Sahebkar A. Effect of nano-curcumin on vari-ous diseases: a comprehensive review of clinical trials. Biofactors (Oxford, England) 2023;49(3):512−33.

[16] Mohajeri M, Sahebkar A. Protective effects of curcumin against doxorubicin-induced toxicity and resis-tance: a review. Critical Reviews in Oncology/Hematology 2018;122:30−51.

[17] Momtazi AA, Sahebkar A. Difluorinated curcumin: a promising curcumin analogue with improved anti-tumor activity and pharmacokinetic profile. Current Pharmaceutical Design 2016;22(28):4386−97.

[18] Kuttan G, Kumar KB, Guruvayoorappan C, Kuttan R. Antitumor, anti-invasion, and antimetastatic effects of curcumin. Advances in Experimental Medicine and Biology 2007;595:173−84.

[19] Bar-Sela G, Epelbaum R, Schaffer M. Curcumin as an anti-cancer agent: review of the gap between basic and clinical applications. Current Medicinal Chemistry 2010;17(3):190−7.

[20] Vallianou NG, Evangelopoulos A, Schizas N, Kazazis C. Potential anticancer properties and mechanisms of action of curcumin. Anticancer Research 2015;35(2):645−51.

[21] Sa G, Das T. Anti cancer effects of curcumin: cycle of life and death. Cell Division 2008;3(1):1−14.

[22] Kasi PD, Tamilselvam R, Skalicka-Woźniak K, Nabavi SF, Daglia M, Bishayee A, et al. Molecular targets of curcumin for cancer therapy: an updated review. Tumor Biology 2016;37(10):13017—28.

[23] Mansouri K, Rasoulpoor S, Daneshkhah A, Abolfathi S, Salari N, Mohammadi M, et al. Clinical effects of curcumin in enhancing cancer therapy: a systematic review. BMC Cancer 2020;20(1):1—11.

[24] Parvathy K, Negi P, Srinivas P. Curcumin—amino acid conjugates: synthesis, antioxidant and antimutagenic attributes. Food Chemistry 2010;120(2):523—30.

[25] Waghela BN, Sharma A, Dhumale S, Pandey SM, Pathak C. Curcumin conjugated with PLGA potentiates sustainability, anti-proliferative activity and apoptosis in human colon carcinoma cells. PLoS One 2015;10(2):e0117526.

[26] Schiborr C, Kocher A, Behnam D, Jandasek J, Toelstede S, Frank J. The oral bioavailability of curcumin from micronized powder and liquid micelles is significantly increased in healthy humans and differs between sexes. Molecular Nutrition & Food Research 2014;58(3):516—27.

[27] Langone P, Debata PR, Inigo JDR, Dolai S, Mukherjee S, Halat P, et al. Coupling to a glioblastoma-directed antibody potentiates antitumor activity of curcumin. International journal of cancer 2014;135(3):710—19.

[28] Teiten M-H, Dicato M, Diederich M. Hybrid curcumin compounds: a new strategy for cancer treatment. Molecules (Basel, Switzerland) 2014;19(12):20839—63.

[29] Li WQ, Guo HF, Li LY, Zhang YF, Cui JW. The promising role of antibody drug conjugate in cancer therapy: combining targeting ability with cytotoxicity effectively. Cancer Medicine. 2021;10(14):4677—96.

[30] Anand P, Kunnumakkara AB, Newman RA, Aggarwal BB. Bioavailability of curcumin: problems and promises. Molecular Pharmaceutics 2007;4(6):807—18.

[31] Kunnumakkara AB, Bordoloi D, Harsha C, Banik K, Gupta SC, Aggarwal BB. Curcumin mediates anticancer effects by modulating multiple cell signaling pathways. Clinical Science 2017;131(15):1781—99.

[32] Perumalsamy V, Harish Kumar D, Synthesis SS. Characterisation and cytotoxic studies of novel curcumin-metformin conjugate. Journal of Young Pharmacists 2022;14(1):73.

[33] Thomas C, Pillai LS, Krishnan L. Evaluation of albuminated curcumin as soluble drug form to control growth of cancer cells in vitro. Journal of Cancer Therapy 2014;2014.

[34] Li M, Ma Y, Ngadi MO. Binding of curcumin to β-lactoglobulin and its effect on antioxidant characteristics of curcumin. Food Chemistry 2013;141(2):1504—11.

[35] Srinivasan K. Black pepper and its pungent principle-piperine: a review of diverse physiological effects. Critical Reviews in Food Science and Nutrition 2007;47(8):735—48.

[36] Shoba G, Joy D, Joseph T, Majeed M, Rajendran R, Srinivas P. Influence of piperine on the pharmacokinetics of curcumin in animals and human volunteers. Planta Medica 1998;64(04):353—6.

[37] Mishra S, Kapoor N, Ali AM, Pardhasaradhi B, Kumari AL, Khar A, et al. Differential apoptotic and redox regulatory activities of curcumin and its derivatives. Free Radical Biology and Medicine 2005;38(10):1353—60.

[38] Dubey SK, Sharma AK, Narain U, Misra K, Pati U. Design, synthesis and characterization of some bioactive conjugates of curcumin with glycine, glutamic acid, valine and demethylenated piperic acid and study of their antimicrobial and antiproliferative properties. European Journal of Medicinal Chemistry 2008;43(9):1837—46.

[39] Ku B, Zhou W, Yu F, Yao H, Yao G. Long acting curcumin derivative, preparation method and pharmaceutical use thereof. Google Patents 2013;.

[40] Razaghi M, Ramazani A, Khoobi M, Mortezazadeh T, Aksoy EA, Küçükkılınç TT. Highly fluorinated graphene oxide nanosheets for anticancer linoleic-curcumin conjugate delivery and T2-Weighted magnetic resonance imaging: in vitro and in vivo studies. Journal of Drug Delivery Science and Technology 2020;60:101967.

[41] Singh DV, Agarwal S, Singh P, Godbole MM, Misra K. Curcumin conjugates induce apoptosis via a mitochondrion dependent pathway in MCF-7 and MDA-MB-231 cell lines. Asian Pacific Journal of Cancer Prevention 2013;14(10):5797—804.

[42] Kumar A, Bora U. Molecular docking studies on inhibition of Stat3 dimerization by curcumin natural derivatives and its conjugates with amino acids. Bioinformation 2012;8(20):988.

[43] Punfa W, Yodkeeree S, Pitchakarn P, Ampasavate C, Limtrakul P. Enhancement of cellular uptake and cytotoxicity of curcumin-loaded PLGA nanoparticles by conjugation with anti-P-glycoprotein in drug resistance cancer cells. Acta Pharmacologica Sinica 2012;33(6):823−31.

[44] Khandare J, Minko T. Polymer−drug conjugates: progress in polymeric prodrugs. Progress in Polymer Science 2006;31(4):359−97.

[45] Kianamiri S, Dinari A, Sadeghizadeh M, Rezaei M, Daraei B, Bahsoun NE-H, et al. Mitochondria-targeted polyamidoamine dendrimer−curcumin construct for hepatocellular cancer treatment. Molecular Pharmaceutics 2020;17(12):4483−98.

[46] Debnath S, Saloum D, Dolai S, Sun C, Averick S, Raja K, et al. Dendrimer-curcumin conjugate: a water soluble and effective cytotoxic agent against breast cancer cell lines. Anti-Cancer Agents in Medicinal Chemistry (Formerly Current Medicinal Chemistry-Anti-Cancer Agents) 2013;13(10):1531−9.

[47] Zare M, Norouzi Sarkati M, Tashakkorian H, Partovi R, Rahaiee S. Dextran-immobilized curcumin: An efficient agent against food pathogens and cancer cells. Journal of Bioactive and Compatible Polymers 2019;34(4−5):309−20.

[48] Tang H, Murphy CJ, Zhang B, Shen Y, Sui M, Van Kirk EA, et al. Amphiphilic curcumin conjugate-forming nanoparticles as anticancer prodrug and drug carriers: in vitro and in vivo effects. Nanomedicine Nanotechnology, Biology, and Medicine 2010;5(6):855−65.

[49] Fang X-B, Zhang J-M, Xie X, Liu D, He C-W, Wan J-B, et al. pH-sensitive micelles based on acid-labile pluronic F68−curcumin conjugates for improved tumor intracellular drug delivery. International Journal of Pharmaceutics 2016;502(1−2):28−37.

[50] Liu J, Huang Y, Kumar A, Tan A, Jin S, Mozhi A, et al. pH-sensitive nano-systems for drug delivery in cancer therapy. Biotechnology Advances 2014;32(4):693−710.

[51] Zhang Y, Yang C, Wang W, Liu J, Liu Q, Huang F, et al. Co-delivery of doxorubicin and curcumin by pH-sensitive prodrug nanoparticle for combination therapy of cancer. Scientific reports 2016;6(1):1−12.

[52] Jain S, Jain R, Das M, Agrawal AK, Thanki K, Kushwah V. Combinatorial bio-conjugation of gemcitabine and curcumin enables dual drug delivery with synergistic anticancer efficacy and reduced toxicity. RSC Advances 2014;4(55):29193−201.

[53] Ayubi M, Karimi M, Abdpour S, Rostamizadeh K, Parsa M, Zamani M, et al. Magnetic nanoparticles decorated with PEGylated curcumin as dual targeted drug delivery: synthesis, toxicity and biocompatibility study. Materials Science and Engineering: C 2019;104:109810.

[54] Kitture R, Ghosh S, Kulkarni P, Liu X, Maity D, Patil S, et al. Fe3O4-citrate-curcumin: promising conjugates for superoxide scavenging, tumor suppression and cancer hyperthermia. Journal of Applied Physics 2012;111(6):064702.

[55] Yallapu MM, Othman SF, Curtis ET, Bauer NA, Chauhan N, Kumar D, et al. Curcumin-loaded magnetic nanoparticles for breast cancer therapeutics and imaging applications. International Journal of Nanomedicine 2012;7:1761.

[56] Wichitnithad W, Nimmannit U, Callery PS, Rojsitthisak P. Effects of different carboxylic ester spacers on chemical stability, release characteristics, and anticancer activity of mono-PEGylated curcumin conjugates. Journal of Pharmaceutical Sciences 2011;100(12):5206−18.

[57] Biswas S, Kumari P, Lakhani PM, Ghosh B. Recent advances in polymeric micelles for anti-cancer drug delivery. European Journal of Pharmaceutical Sciences 2016;83:184−202.

[58] Bai F, Diao J, Wang Y, Sun S, Zhang H, Liu Y, et al. A new water-soluble nanomicelle formed through self-assembly of pectin−curcumin conjugates: preparation, characterization, and anticancer activity evaluation. Journal of Agricultural and Food Chemistry 2017;65(32):6840−7.

[59] Singh SP, Sharma M, Gupta PK. Cytotoxicity of curcumin silica nanoparticle complexes conjugated with hyaluronic acid on colon cancer cells. International Journal of Biological Macromolecules 2015;74:162−70.

[60] Gangwar RK, Tomar GB, Dhumale VA, Zinjarde S, Sharma RB, Datar S. Curcumin conjugated silica nanoparticles for improving bioavailability and its anticancer applications. Journal of Agricultural and Food Chemistry 2013;61(40):9632−7.

[61] Tian C, Asghar S, Xu Y, Chen Z, Zhang M, Huang L, et al. The effect of the molecular weight of hyaluronic acid on the physicochemical characterization of hyaluronic acid-curcumin conjugates and in vitro evaluation in glioma cells. Colloids and Surfaces B: Biointerfaces 2018;165:45−55.

[62] Chen S, Wu J, Tang Q, Xu C, Huang Y, Huang D, et al. Nano-micelles based on hydroxyethyl starch-curcumin conjugates for improved stability, antioxidant and anticancer activity of curcumin. Carbohydrate Polymers 2020;228:115398.

[63] Zhao G, Sun Y, Dong X. Zwitterionic polymer micelles with dual conjugation of doxorubicin and curcumin: synergistically enhanced efficacy against multidrug-resistant tumor cells. Langmuir the ACS Journal of Surfaces and Colloids 2020;36(9):2383−95.

[64] Wang K, Guo C, Dong X, Yu Y, Wang B, Liu W, et al. In vivo evaluation of reduction-responsive alendronate-hyaluronan-curcumin polymer-drug conjugates for targeted therapy of bone metastatic breast cancer. Molecular Pharmaceutics 2018;15(7):2764−9.

[65] Kamble S, Varamini P, Müllner M, Pelras T, Rohanizadeh R. Bisphosphonate-functionalized micelles for targeted delivery of curcumin to metastatic bone cancer. Pharmaceutical Development and Technology 2020;25(9):1118−26.

[66] Yang R, Zhang S, Kong D, Gao X, Zhao Y, Wang Z. Biodegradable polymer-curcumin conjugate micelles enhance the loading and delivery of low-potency curcumin. Pharmaceutical Research 2012;29(12):3512−25.

[67] Manju S, Sreenivasan K. Synthesis and characterization of a cytotoxic cationic polyvinylpyrrolidone−curcumin conjugate. Journal of Pharmaceutical Sciences 2011;100(2):504−11.

[68] Gangwar RK, Dhumale VA, Kumari D, Nakate UT, Gosavi S, Sharma RB, et al. Conjugation of curcumin with PVP capped gold nanoparticles for improving bioavailability. Materials Science and Engineering: C. 2012;32(8):2659−63.

[69] Dey S, Sreenivasan K. Conjugation of curcumin onto alginate enhances aqueous solubility and stability of curcumin. Carbohydrate Polymers 2014;99:499−507.

[70] Lachowicz D, Karabasz A, Bzowska M, Szuwarzyński M, Karewicz A. Nowakowska M. Blood-compatible, stable micelles of sodium alginate−curcumin bioconjugate for anti-cancer applications. European Polymer Journal 2019;113:208−19.

[71] Karabasz A, Lachowicz D, Karewicz A, Mezyk-Kopec R, Stalińska K, Werner E, et al. Analysis of toxicity and anticancer activity of micelles of sodium alginate-curcumin. International Journal of Nanomedicine 2019;14:7249.

[72] Sarika P, James NR, PR AK, Raj DK. Galactosylated alginate-curcumin micelles for enhanced delivery of curcumin to hepatocytes. International Journal of Biological Macromolecules 2016;86:1−9.

[73] Singh A, Kureel AK, Dutta P, Kumar S, Rai AK. Curcumin loaded chitin-glucan quercetin conjugate: synthesis, characterization, antioxidant, in vitro release study, and anticancer activity. International Journal of Biological Macromolecules 2018;110:234−44.

[74] Pal K, Roy S, Parida PK, Dutta A, Bardhan S, Das S, et al. Folic acid conjugated curcumin loaded biopolymeric gum acacia microsphere for triple negative breast cancer therapy in invitro and invivo model. Materials Science and Engineering: C. 2019;95:204−16.

[75] Ghaffari S-B, Sarrafzadeh M-H, Fakhroueian Z, Khorramizadeh MR. Flower-like curcumin-loaded folic acid-conjugated ZnO-MPA-βcyclodextrin nanostructures enhanced anticancer activity and cellular uptake of curcumin in breast cancer cells. Materials Science and Engineering: C. 2019;103:109827.

[76] Laha D, Pal K, Chowdhuri AR, Parida PK, Sahu SK, Jana K, et al. Fabrication of curcumin-loaded folic acid-tagged metal organic framework for triple negative breast cancer therapy in in vitro and in vivo systems. New Journal of Chemistry 2019;43(1):217−29.

[77] Thulasidasan AKT, Retnakumari AP, Shankar M, Vijayakurup V, Anwar S, Thankachan S, et al. Folic acid conjugation improves the bioavailability and chemosensitizing efficacy of curcumin-encapsulated PLGA-PEG nanoparticles towards paclitaxel chemotherapy. Oncotarget. 2017;8(64):107374.

[78] Sonekar S, Mishra MK, Patel AK, Nair SK, Singh CS, Singh AK. Formulation and evaluation of folic acid conjugated gliadin nanoparticles of curcumin for targeting colon cancer cells. Journal of Applied Pharmaceutical Science 2016;6(10):068−74.

[79] Cheng C, Sui B, Wang M, Hu X, Shi S, Xu P. Carrier-free nanoassembly of curcumin−erlotinib conjugate for cancer targeted therapy. Advanced Healthcare Materials 2020;9(19):2001128.

[80] Freidus LG, Kumar P, Marimuthu T, Pradeep P, Pillay V, Choonara YE. Synthesis and properties of CurNQ for the theranostic application in ovarian cancer intervention. Molecules (Basel, Switzerland) 2020;25(19):4471.

[81] Langone P, Debata PR, Dolai S, Curcio GM, Inigo JDR, Raja K, et al. Coupling to a cancer cell-specific antibody potentiates tumoricidal properties of curcumin. International Journal of Cancer 2012;131(4): E569−78.

[82] Vyas HK, Pal R, Vishwakarma R, Lohiya NK, Talwar G. Selective killing of leukemia and lymphoma cells ectopically expressing HCGβ by a conjugate of curcumin with an antibody against HCGβ subunit. Oncology 2009;76(2):101−11.

[83] Fan Y, Li P, Hu B, Liu T, Huang Z, Shan C, et al. A smart photosensitizer−cerium oxide nanoprobe for highly selective and efficient photodynamic therapy. Inorganic Chemistry 2019;58(11):7295−302.

[84] Zholobak N, Shcherbakov A, Ivanova O, Reukov V, Baranchikov A, Ivanov V. Nanoceria-curcumin conjugate: synthesis and selective cytotoxicity against cancer cells under oxidative stress conditions. Journal of Photochemistry and Photobiology B: Biology 2020;209:111921.

[85] Jalde SS, Chauhan AK, Lee JH, Chaturvedi PK, Park J-S, Kim Y-W. Synthesis of novel Chlorin e6-curcumin conjugates as photosensitizers for photodynamic therapy against pancreatic carcinoma. European Journal of Medicinal Chemistry 2018;147:66−76.

[86] Banerjee S, Prasad P, Hussain A, Khan I, Kondaiah P, Chakravarty AR. Remarkable photocytotoxicity of curcumin in HeLa cells in visible light and arresting its degradation on oxovanadium (IV) complex formation. Chemical Communications 2012;48(62):7702−4.

[87] Prasad P, Khan I, Kondaiah P, Chakravarty AR. Mitochondria-targeting oxidovanadium (IV) complex as a near-IR light photocytotoxic agent. Chemistry−A European Journal 2013;19(51):17445−55.

[88] Banik B, Somyajit K, Nagaraju G, Chakravarty AR. Oxovanadium (IV) complexes of curcumin for cellular imaging and mitochondria targeted photocytotoxicity. Dalton Transactions 2014;43(35):13358−69.

[89] Balaji B, Somyajit K, Banik B, Nagaraju G, Chakravarty AR, Photoactivated DNA. Cleavage and anticancer activity of oxovanadium (IV) complexes of curcumin. Inorganica Chimica Acta 2013;400:142−50.

[90] Sztandera K, Gorzkiewicz M, Klajnert-Maculewicz B. Gold nanoparticles in cancer treatment. Molecular Pharmaceutics 2018;16(1):1−23.

[91] Lim Z-ZJ, Li J-EJ, Ng C-T, Yung L-YL, Bay B-H. Gold nanoparticles in cancer therapy. Acta Pharmacologica Sinica 2011;32(8):983−90.

[92] Nambiar S, Osei E, Fleck A, Darko J, Mutsaers AJ, Wettig S. Synthesis of curcumin-functionalized gold nanoparticles and cytotoxicity studies in human prostate cancer cell line. Applied Nanoscience 2018;8 (3):347−57.

[93] Govindaraju S, Rengaraj A, Arivazhagan R, Huh Y-S, Yun K. Curcumin-conjugated gold clusters for bioimaging and anticancer applications. Bioconjugate Chemistry 2018;29(2):363−70.

[94] Vemuri SK, Halder S, Banala RR, Rachamalla HK, Devraj VM, Mallarpu CS, et al. Modulatory effects of biosynthesized gold nanoparticles conjugated with curcumin and paclitaxel on tumorigenesis and metastatic pathways—in vitro and in vivo studies. International Journal of Molecular Sciences 2022;23(4):2150.

[95] Khandelwal P, Alam A, Choksi A, Chattopadhyay S, Poddar P. Retention of anticancer activity of curcumin after conjugation with fluorescent gold quantum clusters: an in vitro and in vivo xenograft study. ACS Omega 2018;3(5):4776—85.

[96] Karthika C, Sureshkumar R. Can curcumin along with chemotherapeutic drug and lipid provide an effective treatment of metastatic colon cancer and alter multidrug resistance? Medical Hypotheses 2019;132:109325.

[97] Ghorbani M, Bigdeli B, Jalili-Baleh L, Baharifar H, Akrami M, Dehghani S, et al. Curcumin-lipoic acid conjugate as a promising anticancer agent on the surface of gold-iron oxide nanocomposites: a pH-sensitive targeted drug delivery system for brain cancer theranostics. European Journal of Pharmaceutical Sciences 2018;114:175—88.

[98] Farhat D, Lincet H. Lipoic acid a multi-level molecular inhibitor of tumorigenesis. Biochimica et Biophysica Acta (BBA)-Reviews on Cancer 2020;1873(1):188317.

[99] Liu C, Gao Y, Zhao L, Wang R, Xie F, Zhai G, et al. The development of a redox-sensitive curcumin conjugated chitosan oligosaccharide nanocarrier for the efficient delivery of docetaxel to glioma cells. Annals of Translational Medicine 2022;10(6).

[100] Vellampatti S, Chandrasekaran G, Mitta SB, Lakshmanan V-K, Park SH, Metallo-curcumin-conjugated DNA. Complexes induces preferential prostate cancer cells cytotoxicity and pause growth of bacterial cells. Scientific Reports 2018;8(1):1—11.

[101] Seghetti F, Di Martino RMC, Catanzaro E, Bisi A, Gobbi S, Rampa A, et al. Curcumin-1, 2, 3-triazole conjugation for targeting the cancer apoptosis machinery. Molecules (Basel, Switzerland) 2020;25 (13):3066.

[102] Alam MM, Almalki AS, Neamatallah T, Ali NM, Malebari AM, Nazreen S. Synthesis of new 1, 3, 4-oxadiazole-incorporated 1, 2, 3-triazole moieties as potential anticancer agents targeting thymidylate synthase and their docking studies. Pharmaceuticals. 2020;13(11):390.

[103] Yadagiri B, Gurrala S, Bantu R, Nagarapu L, Polepalli S, Srujana G, et al. Synthesis and evaluation of benzosuberone embedded with 1, 3, 4-oxadiazole, 1, 3, 4-thiadiazole and 1, 2, 4-triazole moieties as new potential anti proliferative agents. Bioorganic & Medicinal Chemistry Letters 2015;25(10):2220—4.

[104] Limonta P, Marelli MM, Mai S, Motta M, Martini L, Moretti RM. GnRH receptors in cancer: from cell biology to novel targeted therapeutic strategies. Endocrine Reviews 2012;33(5):784—811.

[105] Aggarwal S, Ndinguri M, Solipuram R, Wakamatsu N, Hammer R, Ingram D, et al. [DLys6]-luteinizing hormone releasing hormone—curcumin conjugate inhibits pancreatic cancer cell growth in vitro and in vivo. International Journal of Cancer 2011;129(7):1611—23.

[106] Shi Q, Wada K, Ohkoshi E, Lin L, Huang R, Morris-Natschke SL, et al. Antitumor agents 290. Design, synthesis, and biological evaluation of new LNCaP and PC-3 cytotoxic curcumin analogs conjugated with anti-androgens. Bioorganic & Medicinal Chemistry 2012;20(13):4020—31.

[107] Sung B, Kunnumakkara AB, Sethi G, Anand P, Guha S, Aggarwal BB. Curcumin circumvents chemoresistance in vitro and potentiates the effect of thalidomide and bortezomib against human multiple myeloma in nude mice model. Molecular Cancer Therapeutics 2009;8(4):959—70.

[108] Liu K, Zhang D, Chojnacki J, Du Y, Fu H, Grant S, et al. Design and biological characterization of hybrid compounds of curcumin and thalidomide for multiple myeloma. Organic & Biomolecular Chemistry 2013;11(29):4757—63.

[109] Nakagawa-Goto K, Yamada K, Nakamura S, Chen T-H, Chiang P-C, Bastow KF, et al. Antitumor agents. 258. Syntheses and evaluation of dietary antioxidant—taxoid conjugates as novel cytotoxic agents. Bioorganic & Medicinal Chemistry Letters 2007;17(18):5204—9.

7

Curcumin microcapsule-based drug delivery as cancer therapeutics

Seyedeh Alia Moosavian[1], Sepideh Salehabadi[2], Amirhossein Sahebkar[2,3]

[1]NANOTECHNOLOGY RESEARCH CENTER, PHARMACEUTICAL TECHNOLOGY INSTITUTE, MASHHAD UNIVERSITY OF MEDICAL SCIENCES, MASHHAD, IRAN [2]APPLIED BIOMEDICAL RESEARCH CENTER, MASHHAD UNIVERSITY OF MEDICAL SCIENCES, MASHHAD, IRAN [3]BIOTECHNOLOGY RESEARCH CENTER, PHARMACEUTICAL TECHNOLOGY INSTITUTE, MASHHAD UNIVERSITY OF MEDICAL SCIENCES, MASHHAD, IRAN

7.1 Introduction

Despite significant advancements, cancer remains a major health threat in the 21st century [1]. Traditional chemotherapy is commonly employed for cancer treatment; however, the development of drug resistance and lack of sensitivity often lead to treatment failures. The combination of natural products with chemotherapeutic agents offers a promising approach to managing drug resistance and mitigating side effects. Natural products are increasingly being utilized in cancer treatment due to their accessibility, applicability, and reduced cytotoxicity, thereby enhancing treatment efficacy and reducing drug resistance [2].

Curcumin, isolated from the dried rhizomes of turmeric (*Curcuma longa*) in 1815, has garnered considerable research interest. With its wide range of therapeutic effects, including antioxidant, antiinflammatory, antimicrobial, anti-Alzheimer, antitumor, antidiabetic, and antirheumatic activities, and organ-protective properties, curcumin has been extensively studied for the treatment of various diseases [3–16].

The anticancer effects of curcumin are attributed to its modulation of various cell signaling pathways, including cytokines, inhibition of cell proliferation and growth factors, suppression of cancer cell metastasis, promotion of apoptosis pathways, and induction of autophagy (Fig. 7–1) [17–22]. However, curcumin's application in clinical settings is limited due to its low bioavailability, poor water solubility, and rapid metabolism. As a result, formulating curcumin to enhance its bioavailability and therapeutic efficacy has become a prominent topic in pharmaceutics [23,24]. Encapsulation of curcumin into nanosized particles, such as micro/nanocapsules, microspheres, liposomes, polymeric particles, mesoporous silica nanoparticles, solid lipid nanoparticles, cyclodextrins, and hydrogels, has been extensively investigated [25].

Curcumin-Based Nanomedicines as Cancer Therapeutics. DOI: https://doi.org/10.1016/B978-0-443-15412-6.00013-1

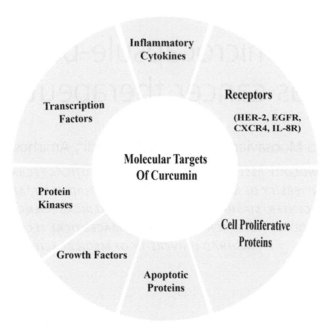

FIGURE 7–1 Molecular target of curcumin that are associated in cancer treatment.

However, in the context of curcumin delivery for cancer treatment, researchers have primarily focused on utilizing nanosized vehicles. In this review, the authors aim to present recent advancements in the development and implementation of curcumin-loaded microcapsules specifically designed for cancer therapy. These microcapsule systems have demonstrated significant efficacy both in vitro and in vivo, and they exhibit variations in terms of preparation techniques, particle size, shape, structure, chemistry, and mechanism of action. By highlighting the current opportunities and challenges associated with employing microcapsules to enhance curcumin-based cancer therapeutics, the authors provide insights into the prospects of these emerging fields. Through a comprehensive analysis, this study shed light on the potential benefits and limitations of utilizing microcapsules as a promising strategy to improve the efficacy of curcumin in cancer treatment.

7.2 Microcapsule-based drug delivery systems

Microencapsulation is a versatile process that involves the formation of microscopic particles through the application of thin coatings of wall material around different drugs [26].

The term "microencapsulation" encompasses various terms such as microcapsules, microparticles, microspheres, and microemulsions. Microcapsules typically have a well-defined core, whereas microspheres are homogeneous structures composed of an active ingredient and a matrix. The size, composition, and function of microcapsules can vary depending on the desired outcome of the encapsulated product (Fig. 7–2). The microencapsulation technique can be applied to a broad range of materials and serves various purposes, including improving stability, enhancing bioavailability, enabling targeted drug delivery, and more (Fig. 7–3).

Employing microcapsules as delivery systems provides many advantages:

1. Effective protection of the active agent from the external environment, such as enzymatic degradation.
2. Control the release rate of the encapsulated drugs.

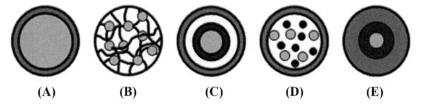

| (A) | (B) | (C) | (D) | (E) |

FIGURE 7–2 Morphologies of microcapsules: (A) single-core capsule, (B) dispersed core in polymer gel, (C) multilayer capsule, (D) dual-core capsule, and (E) single-core multishell capsule. *Reproduced from Augustin, M.A., Sanguansri, L., Lockett, T. Nano- and micro-encapsulated systems for enhancing the delivery of resveratrol. Annals of the New York Academy of Sciences 2013;1290:107–112. https://doi.org/10.1111/nyas.12130.*

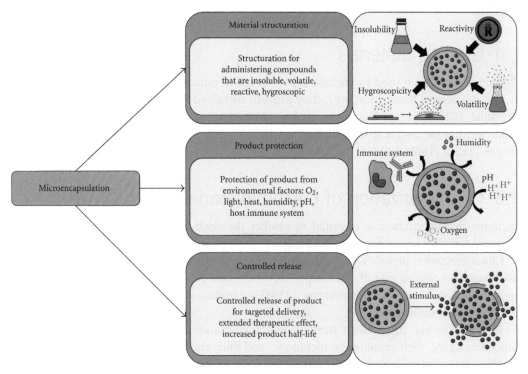

FIGURE 7–3 The main biopharmaceutical goals of microencapsulation: microencapsulation can be used to achieve material structuration, therapeutic product protection, and targeted delivery and/or controlled release of the encapsulated biotherapeutics. *Reproduced from Tomaro-Duchesneau, C., Saha, S., Malhotra, M., Kahouli, I., Prakash, S. Microencapsulation for the therapeutic delivery of drugs, live mammalian and bacterial cells, and other biopharmaceutics: current status and future directions. Journal of Pharmaceutics (Cairo). 2013;2013:103527. https://doi.org/10.1155/2013/103527. Epub 2012 Dec 4. PMID: 26555963; PMCID: PMC4595965.*

3. An easy administration (most investigated formulations are designed for oral administration).
4. Improve the delivery of active agents.

Surveying the literature shows the purpose of encapsulation of curcumin is to provide an efficient platform for improving the bioavailability of oral administrated curcumin.

7.3 Methods for microencapsulation

Various methods are available for the preparation of microcapsules. The choice of method is based on the physicochemical properties of wall material, wall–core interaction, and the desired size of microcapsules. The methods are divided into physical and chemical methods (Fig. 7–4).

1. **Physical or physicochemical methods:** Spray drying and congealing coacervation (simple or mixed methods); isoelectric precipitation; pan coating; solvent evaporation; extrusion; single and double emulsion techniques; supercritical fluid antisolvent method (SAS); nozzle vibration technology
2. **Chemical methods:** Interfacial polymerization; in situ polymerization; matrix polymerization

7.4 Coating materials

Coating materials are used to enclose active agents in microcapsules to improve their stability and delivery of them. Moreover, they provide sustained release of the core in the gastrointestinal (GI) tract or blood circulation. The type of coating ingredients affects the characteristics of microcapsules including particle size, surface charge, permeability, and release [27,28] (Table 7–1).

7.5 Characterization of curcumin-loaded microcapsules

Accurate characterization is essential to predict the shelf-life, stability, bioavailability, and potential toxicity of curcumin microcapsules.

Characterization includes state size, structure, zeta potential, morphology, encapsulation efficiency, and release rate of microcapsules, which can be studied by dynamic light scattering, transmission electron microscopy (TEM), scanning electron microscopy (SEM), and in vitro release studies [28].

In the following, the authors summarize the curcumin microcapsules that exploit as an anticancer agent, their preparation technique, and their application.

The spray-drying technique is widely used to produce microcapsules, this technique involves a cone-shaped apparatus in which a solution of active compound and coating agent is sprayed into a hot chamber, then the active ingredients are enveloped by coating

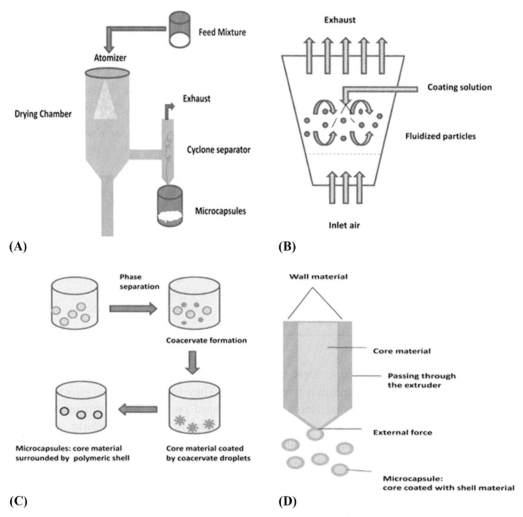

FIGURE 7–4 Different techniques of microencapsulation: (A) spray drying, (B) fluidized bed coating; (C) coacervation; and (D) extrusion. *Reproduced from Choudhury N, Meghwal M, Das K. Microencapsulation: An overview on concepts, methods, properties and applications in foods. Food Frontiers. 2021;2(4):426–-442.*

materials. This method is simple, well-established, reproducible, and cost-effective. Spray drying is one of the promising methods for plant-based material microencapsulation (Fig. 7–4A) [29]. The process of spray drying consists of four stages: (1) atomization of the liquid phase to produce nebulized particles, (2) employing hot gas to dry nebulized liquid, (3) evaporation of solvent, and (4) separation of the dried product from the drying medium [28,30–32]. This method has been extensively used to encapsulate curcumin. The major drawback of spray drying is applying high temperatures that may cause instability. However, most studies have reported curcumin microcapsules prepared by spry drying to have high thermal stability.

Table 7–1   Coating materials, their sources, properties, and the techniques they are suitable for [28].

Coating material	Source	Properties	Techniques used
Gums	Gum Arabic, sodium alginate, Carrageenan	Form soft elastic gels, poor tensile strength, hydrocolloidal	Extrusion, phase separation, spray drying, coacervation, emulsification
Carbohydrates	Starch, dextran, sucrose	Hydrocolloidal, comparatively higher tensile strength than gums	Spray drying, fluidized bed coating, extrusion, freeze drying
Proteins	Gelatin, albumin	Emulsification, gelation, foaming, and water binding capacity	Spray drying, extrusion, coacervation, freeze drying, emulsification
Lipids	Beeswax, stearic acid, phospholipids	Plasticizing properties, good barrier to gases and water vapor	Fluidized bed coating, spray chilling/cooling, extrusion
Celluloses and their derivatives	Plant cells	Hydrophilic, good film-forming ability, and surface activity	Spray drying, fluidized bed coating, extrusion, emulsification/precipitation, coacervation
Chitosan	Shells of crustaceans	Good barrier to gases and water vapor	Spray drying, coacervation

Higuita et al. investigated the effect of the preparation method and different coating materials on the stability of curcumin microcapsules. They investigated the effects of using different wall materials and drying techniques. They used gum Arabic, a mixture of maltodextrin and modified starch, and a ternary mixture of gum Arabic, maltodextrin, and modified starch as coating materials. Also, different drying methods for spray and lyophilization were utilized and their effect on the stability of prepared microcapsules was evaluated. The results indicated that curcumin powder retention during lyophilization was greater than the spray-drying method, while spray-dried microcapsules had higher retention under light exposure. They also showed the mixture of gum Arabic, modified starch, and maltodextrin microcapsules was more effective in preventing the loss of curcumin and color changes compared to other mixtures [33].

Lucas et al. prepared curcumin microcapsules by the spray-drying process and used different biopolymers such as gum Arabic, sodium alginate, and water-soluble modified chitosan as wall materials. The physicochemical properties of different formulations were analyzed by laser granulometry and by scanning electrons. The results indicate that microencapsulation of curcumin in biopolymers by spray-drying method produces 9 and 30 μm particles with 93.8% and 97.6% encapsulation efficiency. Obtained microcapsules showed controlled release properties, which made them a promising system for the delivery of curcumin [34].

In another study, curcumin was incorporated in the matrix of HI-CAP 100 (resistant starch)/maltodextrin and whey protein isolate microcapsules by spray drying to enhance its oral solubility and bioaccessibility. The results suggested this formulation is heat-stable up to 200°C and is a proper formulation for fortifying milk [35]. Bucurescu et al. used gum Arabic as a coating material for the microencapsulation of curcumin by a spray-drying technique to improve its stability and solubility in water. The aqueous solution of gum Arabic in distilled water was prepared at different concentrations and mixed with the solution of curcumin in coconut oil. The mixture was obtained by mechanical agitation (12,500 rpm for 10 min). Then the emulsion was prepared with a homogenizer. The coconut oil was chosen considering the solubility of curcumin in this oil and its potential for use as a food ingredient [36].

Wang et al. studied the efficiency of curcumin-loaded microcapsules against foodborne bacteria. They used the spray-drying method to prepare curcumin-loaded gelatin/porous starch microcapsules. They showed curcumin keeps its antimicrobial activity during the spray-drying process while its solubility improves with microencapsulation. Hence, curcumin-loaded gelatin/porous starch microcapsules could be a promising platform as a food preservative agent [37].

A novel curcumin (as a hydrophobic) encapsulation method by spray drying a warm aqueous ethanol solution with codissolved sodium caseinate was introduced by Pan and colleagues. They claimed using a warm aqueous ethanol solution increases curcumin−sodium caseinate interactions. The antioxidant and cell proliferation studies showed curcumin-encapsulated casein nanocapsules had biological activity, it could be due to better dispersibility [38].

As mentioned before, one limitation of the spray-drying technique is using high temperatures for microcapsules preparation, which can degrade the active agent. Alternative encapsulation techniques are the electrospray technique and vacuum spray-drying (VSD) methods. In electrospray, an electrostatic charge is applied in a single-step process for the conversion of liquid feed to powder at a low temperature [39]. Encapsulating therapeutic agents using electrospray results in producing monodispersed particles with controlled release characteristics [40]. This technique has been used to encapsulate curcumin in different studies [41−43].

In VSD the drying process happens under vacuum conditions and lower temperatures. This technique is the proper way to encapsulate thermos-sensitive agents [44].

Mai et al. employed polylactic acid (PLA) microcapsules as a carrier. They used one-step processing using an electrospray technique for curcumin encapsulation.

In their study, curcumin droplets were added to the PLA solution. About 20 kV voltage was applied to the mixture while it was passing through a 10-mL syringe. Curcumin-loaded microcapsules had sustained release activity for up to 200 hours and showed promising antibacterial activities against *Escherichia coli* and *Staphylococcus aureus* in vitro [45]. Yuan et al. used coaxial electrospray to produce curcumin-loaded microcapsules. Employing a coaxial needle elevates the electrical field and enhances the process' productivity and quality [46].

Hartini et al. used jelly fig pectin for microencapsulation of curcumin by VSD. Briefly, the aqueous core solution composed of curcumin, corn oil, Tween 80, and succinic acid, mixed with matrix solution (composed of jelly fig extract, dicalcium phosphate hydroxide, and sodium citrate dehydrate) and homogenized. The size of the emulsion was scaled down using sonicator. Then the VSD method was used to produce microcapsules. Their results showed the antioxidant activity of curcumin microcapsules was stable for up to 6 months [47].

Neto et al. encapsulate curcumin in psyllium husk mucilage (PHM) arabinoxylan to improve its thermal stability. They showed freeze-dried microcapsules had higher thermal stability than spray-dried ones. Since PHM is a natural product, it could be a promising encapsulating agent for curcumin in the food industry [48].

7.6 Coacervation

Coacervation is a simple, promising technique of microencapsulation that produces microcapsules with high loading efficiency. This method is a widely used method for microencapsulation in which the formation of microcapsules occurs through the phase separation of two immiscible liquid phases. In this process, the core material (e.g., drug or active compound) is dispersed or dissolved in a liquid medium, which is referred to as the core material solution. A polymer or a combination of polymers, known as the encapsulating material or wall material, is dissolved in another liquid phase called the coacervation agent or coacervating agent [30,49]. The coacervation agent is added to the core material solution under specific conditions, such as controlled temperature, pH, or the addition of salts, causing phase separation. This phase separation results in the formation of a polymer-rich coacervate phase that surrounds the core material, leading to the formation of microcapsules (Fig. 7—4C).

The coacervation method has been extensively used to develop different nanoparticle vehicles for the delivery of curcumin. Their results showed coacervation methods produce curcumin-loaded particles with proper loading efficiency and stability [50—52]. Coacervation involving only one polymeric material is called simple coacervation. In the complex coacervation method, more than one polymer is used as coating material. Shahgholian et al. used complex coacervation for the encapsulation of curcumin. Here, gum Arabic (GA) and bovine serum albumin (BSA), the two oppositely charged agents, were used for the encapsulation of curcumin [53].

Abdul Aziz et al. prepared spherical curcumin microcapsules by gelation coacervation to improve the stability and reduce the color-staining effect of curcumin [54].

Ang et al. prepared curcumin microcapsules using a complex coacervation method for the topical treatment of wounds. They increased the density of the core-shell and reduced the size of microcapsules by the addition of a cross-linker, which resulted in lower degradation rates of the curcumin [55].

7.7 Other preparation techniques

Other approaches are also employed to prepare curcumin microcapsules. Bleiel and colleagues patented a microcapsule prepared by pea protein (Shellac) for oral delivery of curcumin [56]. In the same study, chickpea protein has been employed to encapsulate curcumin to improve its bioavailability in oral administration. Microcapsules were produced using isoelectric precipitation [57]. Isoelectric precipitation is a simple and high-yield method for the encapsulation of active agents in protein shells. In this method, the wall materials are solubilized and precipitated based on the isoelectric precipitation of proteins [58]. Ariyarathna and coworkers also adopted the isoelectric precipitation method to encapsulate curcumin in a chickpea (*Cicer arietinum*) protein matrix to improve the stability and bioavailability of curcumin in the gut. They prepared a curcumin-protein homogenous solution. Then they added NaOH solution to the mixture to increase pH until the precipitation was observed. Solvent was removed by centrifugation and freeze drying. Release of curcumin from the protein matrix was slow at pH 4, and a burst release of nearly 100% was observed at pH 2 [57].

More recently, a curcumin-loaded lipid-core nanocapsule was introduced by Ortega et al. for the treatment of oral squamous cell carcinoma. Coating nanocapsules with hydrogel and chitosan makes a thermosensitive/mucoadhesive system. In vitro studies showed this formulation significantly decreases the viability of oral squamous cancer cell line [59].

Su et al. encapsulated curcumin in lotus seed protein (LSP) to achieve sustained control release at the GI tract. They conclude this platform has the potential to employ novel food-grade delivery systems [60].

7.8 Codelivery of curcumin using microcapsules

Combining curcumin with anticancer drugs or other natural products holds promise as a means to enhance therapeutic effectiveness, overcome drug resistance mechanisms, and minimize adverse effects associated with conventional chemotherapy.

Silva et al. employed the interfacial deposition of a preformed polymer technique to develop Lipid-core nanocapsules capable of coencapsulating curcumin and vitamin D3. The process involved injecting an organic phase containing the polymer, vitamin D3, and curcumin into an aqueous phase containing a surfactant. The organic solvent was subsequently eliminated through evaporation under reduced pressure. The resulting microcapsules demonstrated efficacy in the treatment of an animal model of arthritis [61]. Coradini et al. also reported the coencapsulation of curcumin and resveratrol within nanocapsules prepared via polymer interfacial deposition. They demonstrated that curcumin/resveratrol nanocapsules possessed dual antiedematogenic properties in the treatment of an animal model of arthritis [62]. Furthermore, they revealed that curcumin/resveratrol microcapsules exhibited efficient antioxidant properties [63]. In a study conducted by Friedrich et al., the dermal penetration of curcumin/resveratrol microcapsules was investigated. Their findings indicated that lipid nanocapsules show promise as a delivery system for the simultaneous dermal delivery of curcumin and resveratrol [64]. Slika et al. demonstrated that the incorporation of piperine in curcumin-encapsulated nanocapsules enhanced the bioavailability of curcumin [23].

7.9 Antitumor efficiency of curcumin microcapsules

A systematic review conducted by Oliveira et al. in 2022 analyzed the preclinical data on the antitumor efficacy of encapsulated curcumin. Their findings revealed that encapsulated curcumin effectively inhibits tumor growth (standardized mean difference (SMD): -3.03; 95% CI: -3.84, -2.21; $P < .00001$) and reduces tumor weight (SMD: -3.96; 95% CI: -6.22, -1.70; $P = .0006$) in rodents, irrespective of the specific solid tumor model used [65].

Klippstein et al. investigated the efficiency of castor curcumin-loaded oil-cored PLGA-based nanocapsules for the treatment of colon cancer in a mouse model. Their results demonstrated that these nanocapsules, utilizing castor oil as the core material, achieved a high drug-loading efficiency of curcumin, effectively delaying tumor growth in the mouse model. The exceptional loading efficiency was attributed to the superior solubility of curcumin in castor oil [66]. Previous studies have also employed oil-cored nanocapsules based on PLA [67] and poly(ε-caprolactone) (PCL) [68] to enhance curcumin loading for the treatment of B16-F10 melanoma and glioma, respectively.

7.10 Conclusion

Curcumin is widely recognized for its diverse range of effects; however, its limited bioavailability has hindered its clinical utility. An encouraging approach to overcome this challenge involves incorporating curcumin into microcapsules, which has demonstrated considerable potential in enhancing its bioavailability and effectiveness. The size range of microcapsules (ranging from 50 nm to 2 mm) allows for their administration through various routes. Numerous in vitro studies have reported the anticancer properties of curcumin microcapsules but conclusive information is derived from animal models, which are crucial for supporting the primary data. While the majority of studies have focused on developing curcumin microcapsules for oral administration as a complementary product or for use in the food industry, it is important to note that the comprehensive effects of curcumin make curcumin microcapsules applicable to both the prevention and treatment of various types of cancers. However, further clinical investigations are necessary to evaluate the safety and efficacy profile of curcumin microcapsules, whether used alone or in combination with other drugs, for cancer treatment.

References

[1] Moosavian SA, Bianconi V, Pirro M, Sahebkar A. Challenges and pitfalls in the development of liposomal delivery systems for cancer therapy. Seminars in Cancer Biology 2021;69:337−48.

[2] Newman DJ, Cragg GM. Natural products as sources of new drugs from 1981 to 2014. Journal of Natural Products. 2016;79(3):629−61.

[3] Abadi AJ, Mirzaei S, Mahabady MK, Hashemi F, Zabolian A, Hashemi F, et al. Curcumin and its derivatives in cancer therapy: potentiating antitumor activity of cisplatin and reducing side effects. Phytotherapy Research: PTR 2022;36(1):189−213.

[4] Ganji A, Farahani I, Saeedifar AM, Mosayebi G, Ghazavi A, Majeed M, et al. Protective effects of curcumin against lipopolysaccharide-induced toxicity. Current Medicinal Chemistry 2021;28(33):6915−30.

[5] Hassanzadeh S, Read MI, Bland AR, Majeed M, Jamialahmadi T, Sahebkar A. Curcumin: an inflammasome silencer. Pharmacological Research 2020;159.

[6] Panahi Y, Fazlolahzadeh O, Atkin SL, Majeed M, Butler AE, Johnston TP, et al. Evidence of curcumin and curcumin analogue effects in skin diseases: a narrative review. Journal of Cellular Physiology 2019;234(2):1165−78. Available from: https://doi.org/10.1002/jcp.27096.

[7] Hosseini SA, Zahedipour F, Sathyapalan T, Jamialahmadi T, Sahebkar A. Pulmonary fibrosis: therapeutic and mechanistic insights into the role of phytochemicals. BioFactors. 2021;47(3):250−69.

[8] Keihanian F, Saeidinia A, Bagheri RK, Johnston TP, Sahebkar A. Curcumin, hemostasis, thrombosis, and coagulation. Journal of Cellular Physiology 2018;233(6):4497−511.

[9] Khayatan D, Razavi SM, Arab ZN, Niknejad AH, Nouri K, Momtaz S, et al. Protective effects of curcumin against traumatic brain injury. Biomedicine and Pharmacotherapy 2022;154.

[10] Mokhtari-Zaer A, Marefati N, Atkin SL, Butler AE, Sahebkar A. The protective role of curcumin in myocardial ischemia−reperfusion injury. Journal of Cellular Physiology 2018;234(1):214−22.

[11] Momtazi-Borojeni AA, Haftcheshmeh SM, Esmaeili SA, Johnston TP, Abdollahi E, Sahebkar A. Curcumin: a natural modulator of immune cells in systemic lupus erythematosus. Autoimmunity Reviews 2018;17(2):125−35.

[12] Mohammadi A, Blesso CN, Barreto GE, Banach M, Majeed M, Sahebkar A. Macrophage plasticity, polarization and function in response to curcumin, a diet-derived polyphenol, as an immunomodulatory agent. The Journal of Nutritional Biochemistry 2019;66:1−16. Available from: https://doi.org/10.1016/j.jnutbio.2018.12.005.

[13] Panahi Y, Sahebkar A, Amiri M, Davoudi SM, Beiraghdar F, Hoseininejad SL, et al. Improvement of sulphur mustard-induced chronic pruritus, quality of life and antioxidant status by curcumin: results of a randomised, double-blind, placebo-controlled trial. The British Journal of Nutrition 2012;108(7):1272−9. Available from: https://doi.org/10.1017/S0007114511006544.

[14] Cicero AFG, Sahebkar A, Fogacci F, Bove M, Giovannini M, Borghi C. Effects of phytosomal curcumin on anthropometric parameters, insulin resistance, cortisolemia and non-alcoholic fatty liver disease indices: a double-blind, placebo-controlled clinical trial. European Journal of Nutrition 2020;59(2):477−83. Available from: https://doi.org/10.1007/s00394-019-01916-7.

[15] Soltani S, Boozari M, Cicero AFG, Jamialahmadi T, Sahebkar A. Effects of phytochemicals on macrophage cholesterol efflux capacity: impact on atherosclerosis. Phytotherapy Research 2021;35(6):2854−78.

[16] Rahmani AH, Alsahli MA, Aly SM, Khan MA, Aldebasi YH. Role of curcumin in disease prevention and treatment. Advanced Biomedical Research 2018;7:38.

[17] Marjaneh RM, Rahmani F, Hassanian SM, Rezaei N, Hashemzehi M, Bahrami A, et al. Phytosomal curcumin inhibits tumor growth in colitis-associated colorectal cancer. Journal of Cellular Physiology 2018;233(10):6785−98. Available from: https://doi.org/10.1002/jcp.26538.

[18] Yallapu MM, Nagesh PK, Jaggi M, Chauhan SC. Therapeutic applications of curcumin nanoformulations. The AAPS Journal 2015;17(6):1341−56.

[19] Karaboga Arslan A, Uzunhisarcikli E, Yerer M, Bishayee A. The golden spice curcumin in cancer: a perspective on finalized clinical trials during the last 10 years. Journal of Cancer Research and Therapeutics 2022;18(1):19−26.

[20] Ming T, Tao Q, Tang S, Zhao H, Yang H, Liu M, et al. Curcumin: an epigenetic regulator and its application in cancer. Biomedicine and Pharmacotherapy 2022;156.

[21] Mohajeri M, Sahebkar A. Protective effects of curcumin against doxorubicin-induced toxicity and resistance: a review. Critical Reviews in Oncology/Hematology 2018;122:30−51.

[22] Momtazi AA, Sahebkar A. Difluorinated curcumin: a promising curcumin analogue with improved antitumor activity and pharmacokinetic profile. Current Pharmaceutical Design 2016;22(28):4386−97.

[23] Slika L, Moubarak A, Borjac J, Baydoun E, Patra D. Preparation of curcumin-poly (allyl amine) hydrochloride based nanocapsules: piperine in nanocapsules accelerates encapsulation and release of curcumin and effectiveness against colon cancer cells. Materials Science and Engineering: C. 2020;109:110550.

[24] Jamwal R. Bioavailable curcumin formulations: a review of pharmacokinetic studies in healthy volunteers. Journal of Integrative Medicine 2018;16(6):367−74.

[25] Hafez Ghoran S, Calcaterra A, Abbasi M, Taktaz F, Nieselt K, Babaei E, et al. Nanoformulations: a promising adjuvant towards cancer treatment. Molecules (Basel, Switzerland) 2022;27(16).

[26] Singh MN, Hemant KS, Ram M, Shivakumar HG. Microencapsulation: a promising technique for controlled drug delivery. Research in Pharmaceutical Sciences 2010;5(2):65-77.

[27] Kurniasih RA, Dewi EN, Purnamayati L. Effect of different coating materials on the characteristics of chlorophyll microcapsules from *Caulerpa racemosa*. IOP Conference Series: Earth and Environmental Science 2018;116(1):012030.

[28] Choudhury N, Meghwal M, Das K. Microencapsulation: an overview on concepts, methods, properties and applications in foods. Food Frontiers 2021;2(4):426−42.

[29] Tang C-H, Li X-R. Microencapsulation properties of soy protein isolate: influence of preheating and/or blending with lactose. Journal of Food Engineering 2013;117(3):281−90.

[30] Gouin S. Microencapsulation: industrial appraisal of existing technologies and trends. Trends in Food Science & Technology 2004;15(7):330−47.

[31] Ahmad SU, Li B, Sun J, Arbab S, Dong Z, Cheng F, et al. Recent advances in microencapsulation of drugs for veterinary applications. Journal of Veterinary Pharmacology and Therapeutics 2021;44 (3):298−312.

[32] Guo J, Li P, Kong L, Xu B. Microencapsulation of curcumin by spray drying and freeze drying. LWT 2020;132:109892.

[33] Cano-Higuita DM, Malacrida CR, Telis VRN. Stability of curcumin microencapsulated by spray and freeze drying in binary and ternary matrices of maltodextrin, gum Arabic and modified starch. Journal of Food Processing and Preservation 2015;39(6):2049−60.

[34] Lucas J, Ralaivao M, Estevinho BN, Rocha F. A new approach for the microencapsulation of curcumin by a spray drying method, in order to value food products. Powder Technology 2020;362:428−35.

[35] Patel SS, Pushpadass HA, Franklin MEE, Battula SN, Vellingiri P. Microencapsulation of curcumin by spray drying: characterization and fortification of milk. Journal of Food Science and Technology 2022;59 (4):1326−40.

[36] Bucurescu A, Blaga AC, Estevinho BN, Rocha F. Microencapsulation of curcumin by a spray-drying technique using gum Arabic as encapsulating agent and release studies. Food and Bioprocess Technology. 2018;11(10):1795−806.

[37] Wang Y, Lu Z, Wu H, Lv F. Study on the antibiotic activity of microcapsule curcumin against foodborne pathogens. International Journal of Food Microbiology 2009;136(1):71−4.

[38] Pan K, Zhong Q, Baek SJ. Enhanced dispersibility and bioactivity of curcumin by encapsulation in casein nanocapsules. Journal of Agricultural and Food Chemistry 2013;61(25):6036−43.

[39] Laelorspoen N, Wongsasulak S, Yoovidhya T, Devahastin S. Microencapsulation of Lactobacillus acidophilus in zein−alginate core−shell microcapsules via electrospraying. Journal of Functional Foods 2014;7:342−9.

[40] Bock N, Dargaville TR, Woodruff MA. Electrospraying of polymers with therapeutic molecules: state of the art. Progress in Polymer Science 2012;37(11):1510−51.

[41] Suwantong O, Opanasopit P, Ruktanonchai U, Supaphol P. Electrospun cellulose acetate fiber mats containing curcumin and release characteristic of the herbal substance. Polymer. 2007;48(26):7546−57.

[42] Asadi M, Salami M, Hajikhani M, Emam-Djomeh Z, Aghakhani A, Ghasemi A. Electrospray production of curcumin-walnut protein nanoparticles. Food Biophysics 2021;16(1):15−26.

[43] Reddy AS, Lakshmi BA, Kim S, Kim J. Synthesis and characterization of acetyl curcumin-loaded core/shell liposome nanoparticles via an electrospray process for drug delivery, and theranostic applications. European Journal of Pharmaceutics and Biopharmaceutics 2019;142:518–30.

[44] Islam MZ, Kitamura Y, Yamano Y, Kitamura M. Effect of vacuum spray drying on the physicochemical properties, water sorption and glass transition phenomenon of orange juice powder. Journal of Food Engineering 2016;169:131–40.

[45] Mai Z, Chen J, He T, Hu Y, Dong X, Zhang H, et al. Electrospray biodegradable microcapsules loaded with curcumin for drug delivery systems with high bioactivity. RSC Advances 2017;7(3):1724–34.

[46] Yuan S, Lei F, Liu Z, Tong Q, Si T, Xu RX. Coaxial electrospray of curcumin-loaded microparticles for sustained drug release. PloS One 2015;10(7):e0132609.

[47] Hartini N, Ponrasu T, Wu JJ, Sriariyanun M, Cheng YS. Microencapsulation of curcumin in crosslinked jelly fig pectin using vacuum spray drying technique for effective drug delivery. Polymers. 2021;13(16).

[48] Monge Neto AÁ, Bergamasco RdC, de Moraes FF, Medina Neto A, Peralta RM. Development of a technique for psyllium husk mucilage purification with simultaneous microencapsulation of curcumin. PloS One 2017;12(8):e0182948.

[49] Timilsena YP, Akanbi TO, Khalid N, Adhikari B, Barrow CJ. Complex coacervation: principles, mechanisms and applications in microencapsulation. International Journal of Biological Macromolecules 2019;121:1276–86.

[50] Chirio D, Gallarate M, Peira E, Battaglia L, Serpe L, Trotta M. Formulation of curcumin-loaded solid lipid nanoparticles produced by fatty acids coacervation technique. Journal of Microencapsulation 2011;28(6):537–48.

[51] Zheng J, Gao Q, Ge G, Sun W, Van der Meeren P, Zhao M. Encapsulation behavior of curcumin in heteroprotein complex coacervates and precipitates fabricated from β-conglycinin and lysozyme. Food Hydrocolloids 2022;133:107964.

[52] Zuanon LAC, Malacrida CR, Telis VRN. Production of turmeric oleoresin microcapsules by complex coacervation with gelatin–gum Arabic. Journal of Food Process Engineering 2013;36(3):364–73.

[53] Shahgholian N, Rajabzadeh G. Fabrication and characterization of curcumin-loaded albumin/gum Arabic coacervate. Food Hydrocolloids 2016;59:17–25.

[54] Aziz HA, Peh KK, Tan YT. Solubility of core materials in aqueous polymeric solution effect on microencapsulation of curcumin. Drug Development and Industrial Pharmacy 2007;33(11):1263–72.

[55] Ang LF, Darwis Y, Por LY, Yam MF. Microencapsulation curcuminoids for effective delivery in pharmaceutical application. Pharmaceutics. 2019;11(9).

[56] MARRO S.B.K.M., Microcapsules containing curcumin, and methods for the production thereof. 2019.

[57] Ariyarathna IR, Karunaratne DN. Microencapsulation stabilizes curcumin for efficient delivery in food applications. Food Packaging and Shelf Life. 2016;10:79–86.

[58] Shi L, Beamer SK, Yang H, Jaczynski J. Micro-emulsification/encapsulation of krill oil by complex coacervation with krill protein isolated using isoelectric solubilization/precipitation. Food Chemistry 2018;244:284–91.

[59] Ortega A, da Silva AB, da Costa LM, Zatta KC, Onzi GR, da Fonseca FN, et al. Thermosensitive and mucoadhesive hydrogel containing curcumin-loaded lipid-core nanocapsules coated with chitosan for the treatment of oral squamous cell carcinoma. Drug Delivery and Translational Research 2022;.

[60] Su Y, Chen Y, Zhang L, Adhikari B, Xu B, Li J, et al. Synthesis and characterization of lotus seed protein-based curcumin microcapsules with enhanced solubility, stability, and sustained release. Journal of the Science of Food and Agriculture 2022;102(6):2220–31.

[61] da Silva JLG, Passos DF, Bernardes VM, Cabral FL, Schimites PG, Manzoni AG, et al. Co-nanoencapsulation of vitamin D3 and curcumin regulates inflammation and purine metabolism in a model of arthritis. Inflammation. 2019;42(5):1595–610.

[62] Coradini K, Friedrich RB, Fonseca FN, Vencato MS, Andrade DF, Oliveira CM, et al. A novel approach to arthritis treatment based on resveratrol and curcumin co-encapsulated in lipid-core nanocapsules: in vivo studies. European Journal of Pharmaceutical Sciences: Official Journal of the European Federation for Pharmaceutical Sciences 2015;78:163–70.

[63] Coradini K, Lima FO, Oliveira CM, Chaves PS, Athayde ML, Carvalho LM, et al. Co-encapsulation of resveratrol and curcumin in lipid-core nanocapsules improves their in vitro antioxidant effects. European Journal of Pharmaceutics and Biopharmaceutics: Official Journal of Arbeitsgemeinschaft fur Pharmazeutische Verfahrenstechnik eV 2014;88(1):178–85.

[64] Friedrich RB, Kann B, Coradini K, Offerhaus HL, Beck RC, Windbergs M. Skin penetration behavior of lipid-core nanocapsules for simultaneous delivery of resveratrol and curcumin. European Journal of Pharmaceutical Sciences: Official Journal of the European Federation for Pharmaceutical Sciences 2015;78:204–13.

[65] de Oliveira TV, Stein R, de Andrade DF, Beck RCR. Preclinical studies of the antitumor effect of curcumin-loaded polymeric nanocapsules: a systematic review and meta-analysis. Phytotherapy Research: PTR 2022;36(8):3202–14.

[66] Klippstein R, Wang JT, El-Gogary RI, Bai J, Mustafa F, Rubio N, et al. Passively targeted curcumin-loaded PEGylated PLGA nanocapsules for colon cancer therapy in vivo. Small (Weinheim an der Bergstrasse, Germany) 2015;11(36):4704–22.

[67] Mazzarino L, Silva LF, Curta JC, Licínio MA, Costa A, Pacheco LK, et al. Curcumin-loaded lipid and polymeric nanocapsules stabilized by nonionic surfactants: an in vitro and In vivo antitumor activity on B16-F10 melanoma and macrophage uptake comparative study. Journal of Biomedical Nanotechnology 2011;7(3):406–14.

[68] Zanotto-Filho A, Coradini K, Braganhol E, Schröder R, de Oliveira CM, Simões-Pires A, et al. Curcumin-loaded lipid-core nanocapsules as a strategy to improve pharmacological efficacy of curcumin in glioma treatment. European Journal of Pharmaceutics and Biopharmaceutics: Official Journal of Arbeitsgemeinschaft fur Pharmazeutische Verfahrenstechnik eV 2013;83(2):156–67.

Recent advances and regulatory aspects of gold nanoparticles

8

Nanoemulsion-based curcumin delivery systems as cancer therapeutics

Seyedeh Alia Moosavian[1], Prashant Kesharwani[2], Amirhossein Sahebkar[3,4]

1 NANOTECHNOLOGY RESEARCH CENTER, PHARMACEUTICAL TECHNOLOGY INSTITUTE, MASHHAD UNIVERSITY OF MEDICAL SCIENCES, MASHHAD, IRAN 2 DEPARTMENT OF PHARMACEUTICS, SCHOOL OF PHARMACEUTICAL EDUCATION AND RESEARCH, JAMIA HAMDARD, NEW DELHI, INDIA 3 BIOTECHNOLOGY RESEARCH CENTER, PHARMACEUTICAL TECHNOLOGY INSTITUTE, MASHHAD UNIVERSITY OF MEDICAL SCIENCES, MASHHAD, IRAN 4 APPLIED BIOMEDICAL RESEARCH CENTER, MASHHAD UNIVERSITY OF MEDICAL SCIENCES, MASHHAD, IRAN

8.1 Introduction

Curcumin, a phytochemical derived from the *Curcuma longa* L. family, has garnered significant attention as a remarkable compound due to its distinct pharmacological effects. Its IUPAC (International Union of Pure and Applied Chemistry) name is 1,7-bis(4-hydroxy-3-methoxyphenyl)hepta-1,6-diene-3,5-dione, and it has a molecular weight of 368.37 Da. Curcumin exhibits lipophilic properties and displays high solubility in organic solvents such as ethanol or acetone [1].

Numerous studies have reported that curcumin possesses a diverse pharmacological activities [2−13] and shows efficacy in combating various types of cancer [14−19]. Its cytotoxic effects on different cancer cell lines, including lung, colon, breast, and ovarian, have been extensively investigated [20−23]. Fig. 8−1 provides an overview of the molecular pathways underlying curcumin's antitumor properties [24]. Furthermore, curcumin exhibits an exceptionally favorable safety profile, positioning it as an ideal alternative for anticancer treatment. The US Food and Drug Administration (FDA) recognizes it as a generally safe product [25].

Despite its diverse functions, the limited solubility of curcumin in water hampers its applications and leads to low absorption and oral bioavailability. Extensive research has focused on enhancing the bioavailability and targeted delivery of curcumin through its incorporation into

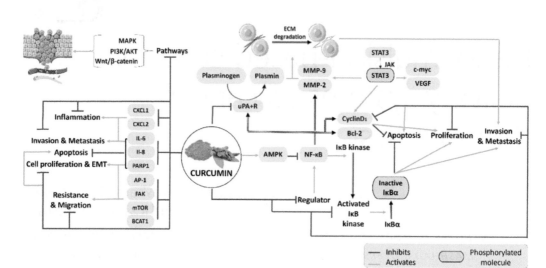

FIGURE 8–1 Molecular pathways underlying the antitumor properties of curcumin on various types of cancer [24].

nanoparticles. Numerous strategies for encapsulating curcumin have been developed to improve its bioavailability. This chapter offers a concise overview of nanoemulsion (NE) formulations of curcumin.

8.2 Nanoemulsions

Emulsions are characterized as dispersions in which the dispersed phase (internal phase) consists of small droplets distributed throughout a vehicle (external or continuous phase) with which it is immiscible [26]. NEs are emulsions that exhibit clarity or transparency, with droplet sizes typically smaller than approximately 200 nm. They can be formed as dispersions of oil droplets in water (O/W) or water droplets in oil (W/O), or as regions of water separated by an amphiphilic interfacial layer.

By virtue of their small size, NEs possess the capability to penetrate through narrow capillaries and enhance passive cellular absorption mechanisms. As a result, they have been extensively investigated as carriers for drug delivery [27,28].

8.3 Nanoemulsion structure

To design a delivery platform with the desired properties, the composition of the NE plays a critical role in regulating its physicochemical characteristics. An NE is a system that consists of two phases: a dispersed phase composed of fine droplets and a continuous phase that is stabilized by an emulsifying agent or surfactant. The attainment of a stable NE relies on maintaining a low interfacial tension, denoted as γ. However, due to the small droplet size and the large interfacial area (A) between the oil and water phases, achieving a low interfacial tension becomes challenging. Therefore, the use of a second surfactant, known as a cosurfactant, is necessary. The inclusion of cosurfactants aids in reducing the interfacial tension and promoting the stability of NE [27]. NE can be considered as oil-in-water (O/W) or as water in oil (W/O). In O/W, oil droplets are dispersed throughout the aqueous phase and in W/O, the continuous phase is the oil phase. Multiple NE systems are W/O/W or O/W/O (Fig. 8–2) [29].

8.4 Preparation of nanoemulsions

The selection of the oil phase in NEs depends on the route of administration and the desired physical properties. Hydrocarbon-based oils are commonly used in externally applied NEs, while castor oil and liquid paraffin are suitable for orally administered NEs. For parenteral administration, purified oils should be utilized. Emulsifying agents play a crucial role in stabilizing the formulation and extending its shelf life. Various types of emulsifiers, such as surfactants or biopolymers, can be used to enhance the stability of NEs. The choice of emulsifier depends on factors such as the type of emulsion to be prepared, emulsifier toxicity, and considerations of cost and availability [27,30]. In a study by Pinheiro et al., it was demonstrated how the charge of the emulsifier influences the lipid digestion process of NEs and the bioaccessibility of incorporated curcumin during in vitro digestion [31].

Several factors, including the type of surfactant, the hydrophilic-lipophilic balance (HLB) of the active agent, and the preparation method, influence the characteristic properties of NEs, such as droplet size, surface charge, and polydispersity index. Optimal stability in NEs with small droplet sizes is achieved when the HLB value of the surfactant mixture is similar to that of the active agent [32].

NEs can be fabricated using two different approaches. High-energy methods utilize mechanical energy to generate intense forces that disperse the internal phase within the continuous phase (e.g., sonication, high-pressure valve homogenizer, or microfluidizer). On the other hand, low-energy methods rely on the internal chemical energy of the oil-water-surfactant mixtures to form droplets within the continuous phase (Fig. 8–3) [33,34].

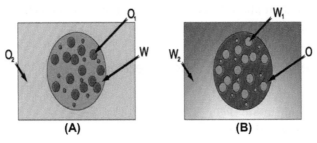

FIGURE 8–2 Schematic representation of the architectures of (A) O/W/O and (B) W/O/W multiple emulsions [29].

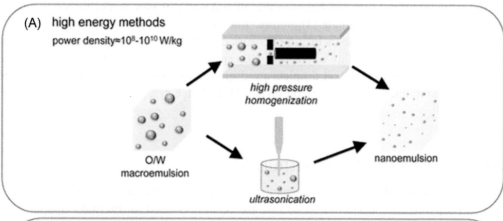

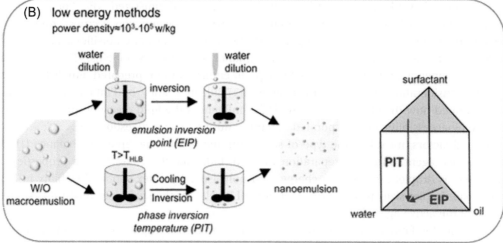

FIGURE 8–3 Schematic illustration of NEs preparation methods: (A) high-energy method and (B) low-energy method [35].

8.5 Low-energy emulsification methods

This method is founded on phase inversion or self-emulsification techniques, which encompass the following approaches:

8.5.1 Phase inversion emulsification method

- Transitional phase inversion (TPI)
- Phase inversion temperature (PIT)
- Phase inversion composition (PIC)
- Catastrophic phase inversion (CPI)
- Emulsion inversion point (EIP)

In this method, phase inversion or self-emulsification is achieved through various mechanisms, such as transitional phase changes, temperature variations, compositional adjustments, catastrophic phase shifts, and EIPs.

8.5.2 The self-nanoemulsification method

In phase inversion methods, the affinity of surfactants for either the aqueous or oil phase undergoes changes through temperature or composition variations in the NE, while other factors remain constant. PIT has been effectively utilized by Jintapattanakit and colleagues to prepare curcumin-loaded NEs. They demonstrated the potential of the PIT method in producing curcumin NEs using RH 40 as the surfactant for oral administration [36]. In the PIC method, the water-to-oil ratio is adjusted by gradually adding one phase (water or oil) to the mixture at a constant temperature to achieve the desired NE [37]. To the best of our knowledge, there have been no experiments reported on the application of this method for the preparation of curcumin NEs. Fig. 8−3 provides a schematic illustration of the low-energy methods used in this context.

8.6 High-energy emulsification methods

High-energy methods are highly effective in achieving small droplet sizes due to the utilization of mechanical devices with intense disruptive forces. Various high-energy methods have been used in the literature for the preparation of NEs, including:

- High-pressure homogenization: In this technique, the fluid is passed through a high-pressure pump, leading to the disruption of droplets. High-pressure homogenization has been extensively used in the preparation of curcumin NEs. For instance, Mistro et al. investigated the impact of high-pressure homogenization and different emulsifiers on the physicochemical properties of curcumin NEs. They demonstrated that NEs prepared with glycerol monooleate (GMO)/chitosan exhibited a reduction in droplet size of 50%−65% after three rounds of high-pressure homogenization.
- Microfluidization: Microfluidizer devices have been utilized in some studies for the production of curcumin NEs. These devices facilitate the generation of NEs with small droplet sizes.
- Ultrasonication: Ultrasonication involves the application of ultrasound energy at a controlled temperature to produce NEs. Hernández et al. studied the effects of sonication time, types of oil, and oil volume fraction on the production of curcumin-incorporated NEs. They found that increasing the sonication time resulted in a decrease in mean particle size and polydispersity index [38].

In high-pressure homogenization, the fluid passes through a high-pressure pump, which results in the disruption of droplets. This technique has been used in several studies to prepare curcumin NEs. For example, Mistro et al. investigated the impacts of the high-pressure homogenization and types of emulsifiers on the physicochemical properties of curcumin

NEs. The O/W NEs of glycerol monooleate and chitosan (GMO/chitosan) prepared by sonication and high-pressure homogenization (HPH) techniques using two different stabilizers (polyvinyl alcohol [PVA] and poloxamer 407. They showed the droplet size was reduced to 50%−65% after three rounds of high-pressure homogenization [39]. In ultrasonication, the ultrasound energy at controlled temperature is used to produce NEs. In the study of Hernández, et al., the effects of sonication time and various types of oil and oil volume fraction were investigated to produce curcumin-incorporated NEs. The increase in treatment time resulted in a decrease in mean particle size and polydispersity index [40]. Using microfluidizer device to produce curcumin NEs have been reported in some studies.

High-energy methods have been extensively explored for the preparation of curcumin-loaded NEs [41,42], demonstrating their capability to produce stable NE formulations.

In addition, membrane emulsification is another method where the dispersed phase is passed through a microporous membrane into a continuous phase while applying agitation [43].

8.7 Physicochemical characteristics of nanoemulsions

The size of NEs varies between 50 and 200 nm. The reduction in droplet size may increase the bioavailability of encapsulated compounds in NEs. The preparation method and the composition of NEs affect the size of the droplets.

Zeta potential of NEs is an important factor in the stability of NEs in storage time and its performance in blood circulation. Size, surface charge, and surface interaction of NEs with blood components should be carefully investigated.

Stability defines the shelf life of NEs. According to the FDA guidelines, size, surface charge, and encapsulation efficiency should be measured in different time points at different temperatures [44]. Drug release, encapsulation efficiency, and morphology assessment of droplets are other properties that play important role in the efficiency of NEs [45].

8.8 Advantages of nanoemulsions as delivery systems

NEs offer several advantages as delivery systems:

- Enhanced Solubility: NEs are effective in improving the solubility of lipophilic compounds. They provide a favorable environment for the solubilization of hydrophobic drugs and enhancing their bioavailability and therapeutic efficacy.
- Optical Transparency: NEs are optically transparent, making them visually appealing and suitable for applications where clarity is desired. This characteristic is particularly beneficial in formulations for topical or cosmetic products.
- High Stability: NEs exhibit high stability against flocculation or aggregation. This stability is attributed to the significant steric stabilization effect provided by the small droplet size

of NEs. The presence of surfactants or polymeric emulsifiers or stabilizers can further enhance the stability of NEs by preventing droplet coalescence.

- Minimized Ostwald Ripening: Ostwald ripening is a common instability phenomenon observed in emulsion systems, which leads to an increase in droplet size over time. NEs, with their small droplet size, are less prone to Ostwald ripening. In addition, the use of droplet stabilization techniques, such as the incorporation of surfactants or polymeric emulsifiers, can significantly reduce Ostwald ripening in NEs [46−48].

8.9 Nanoemulsions for delivery of curcumin

Studies have consistently demonstrated the beneficial effects of encapsulating curcumin in NEs. These NEs have shown improvements in solubility, bioavailability, stability, storage time, and controlled release of curcumin [49]. The small droplet size, low viscosity, and transparency of NEs make them suitable for delivering active agents via various administration routes, including oral, topical, and parenteral [50]. NEs have been extensively investigated for the delivery of various compounds, such as natural products, anticancer agents, and antibiotics [51]. In the case of curcumin, NEs have been widely used to enhance its delivery and bioavailability. Curcumin, being a lipophilic compound, is commonly encapsulated in oil-in-water (O/W) NEs. Kumar et al. demonstrated that curcumin NEs increase cellular uptake of curcumin due to sustained release in the intestine [52]. They also reported that NEs enhance the permeation of curcumin through the Caco-2 cell line, suggesting improved intestinal absorption of curcumin in vivo [53]. Zheng et al. compared the bioavailability of curcumin formulated in NEs with three commercial curcumin supplements and found significantly higher bioavailability with the NE formulation [54].

In addition to improved bioavailability, curcumin NEs have been investigated for their antiinflammatory and antioxidant properties. Wang et al. showed that curcumin encapsulated in NEs stabilized with medium-chain triglycerides (MCT) and Tween 20 significantly inhibited 12-O-tetradecanoylphorbol-13-acetate (TPA)-induced edema in mouse ears compared to curcumin solution. Their study also revealed that oral administration of curcumin NEs enhanced the antiinflammatory effect of curcumin [55]. More recently, it has been demonstrated that encapsulated curcumin in NEs efficiently ameliorates hepatic and cardiac complications and increases spermatogenesis in Wistar rats with a high-fat, high-fructose diet, as compared to curcumin powder alone. [56,57].

8.10 Parenteral curcumin nanoemulsions

The thermodynamic stability, low viscosity, transparency, high encapsulation capacity for hydrophobic drugs, and stability during sterilization make NEs a promising parenteral delivery system.

The major obstacle of parenteral administration of curcumin as a hydrophobic compound is the low concentration of curcumin that is delivered at the target site. NEs increase curcumin's half-life in blood circulation and decrease its clearance. Both O/W and W/O NEs can be administered intravenously. Surfactant toxicity could be the only limitation of parenteral NEs. Von Corsewant and Thoren used polyethylene glycol (400)/polyethylene glycol (660) 12-hydroxystearate/ethanol as a nontoxic cosurfactant to overcome the problem [58]. Hence, by selecting appropriate materials and excipients, it is possible to design NEs. Paclitaxel NEs are an example of parenteral NEs for cancer treatment [59].

8.11 Oral curcumin nanoemulsions

Oral delivery of curcumin has been a focus of many studies, with a particular interest in formulating curcumin nanoparticles in the form of NEs. This approach aims to enhance the oral bioavailability of curcumin, providing a more convenient and effective option for patients.

Incorporating curcumin into NEs offers several advantages for oral delivery. First, it improves the solubility of curcumin, which is a hydrophobic compound with limited water solubility. NEs provide a favorable environment for the dispersion of curcumin, allowing for better absorption in the gastrointestinal tract.

Another benefit of using NEs for oral delivery is the ability to bypass the first-pass effect. When curcumin is administered orally, it undergoes metabolism in the liver before reaching systemic circulation, resulting in reduced bioavailability. By encapsulating curcumin in NEs, it can be protected from metabolism during the first-pass effect, increasing its bioavailability and effectiveness.

Studies investigating the oral delivery of curcumin NEs have shown promising results in terms of improving the bioavailability and therapeutic efficacy of curcumin. These NE formulations have demonstrated enhanced absorption and increased systemic levels of curcumin, leading to improved pharmacological effects [58].

8.12 Curcumin nanoemulsions for cancer therapy

Surveying the literature shows that NEs can enhance the anticancer efficacy of curcumin in vitro and in vivo. Due to the nanoscale droplet size, NEs can be targeted to tumor tissue. The enhanced permeation and retention (EPR) is a unique phenomenon in solid tumor tissue, which is responsible for the passive accumulation of nanoparticles in tumor tissue (Fig. 8–4) [60,61].

NEs with droplet sizes smaller than 100 nm have shown the ability to accumulate in tumor environments while evading the mononuclear phagocytic system (MPS) in the liver. The small size of the NE droplets and their surface charge play a crucial role in ensuring stability during blood circulation and facilitating accumulation at the tumor site [62]. To further enhance the blood circulation stability of NEs, the surface can be coated with hydrophilic polymers such as polyethylene glycol (PEG). This coating prevents the adsorption of blood proteins and recognition by MPS cells, resulting in an extended half-life in circulation [63].

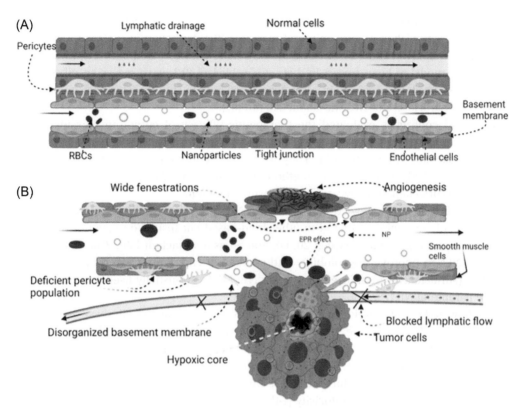

FIGURE 8–4 Schematic representation of the microenvironment of (A) healthy and (B) tumor tissues. The tumor microenvironment shows the disorganized components (hypoxic core, blocked lymphatic drainage, deficient pericyte population, disorganized basement membrane and wide fenestration) that are exploited for enhancing EPR effect. Reproduced from [60].

Active targeting of NEs can be achieved by attaching specific targeting ligands to their surfaces. These ligands enable the recognition of NEs by cancer cells, enhancing their uptake and therapeutic effect. Various targeting ligands, including folate, RGD peptide, aptamers, and monoclonal antibodies, have been explored for the targeted delivery of anticancer-encapsulated NEs [64,65]. One example of a targeting ligand is transferrin, which binds to transferrin receptors expressed on epithelial cells. Transferrin has been utilized as a targeting ligand for the delivery of solid lipid nanoparticles containing curcumin. The conjugation of transferrin to the NEs resulted in enhanced apoptosis in MCF-7 cells, demonstrating the potential of active targeting strategies in cancer therapy [66].

8.13 Passive targeting of curcumin nanoemulsions

Guerrero et al. studied the cytotoxicity effect of curcumin NEs in different cancer lines. The results showed curcumin NEs are cytotoxic against gastric (AGS), colon (HT29-ATCC, HT29-US), breast (MDA-MB-231), and melanoma (B16F10) cells. Moreover, encapsulation in NEs increases intracellular accumulation of curcumin and increases ROS formation in melanoma cells, while inhibiting cell migration and invasion. The in vivo studies showed curcumin NEs prevent metastasis in mice model of lung cancer. In their study, Miglyol 812 was used as an oil phase and Epikuron was used as a surfactant. NEs were prepared by the spontaneous emulsification method. The particle size of NEs was about 200 nm [67].

Guan and colleagues evaluated the therapeutic efficacy of curcumin NEs in the PC-3 prostate cancer cell line. Their results showed that curcumin NEs had higher cytotoxicity and cellular uptake than free curcumin. They formulated curcumin nanoemulsions through a self-microemulsifying process. In this method, they utilized MCT as the oil phase, cremophor RH 40 as the surfactant, and glycerol as the cosurfactant [68].

In 2016, **Borrin** et al. showed that curcumin NEs prepared by EIP method increase the storage time of curcumin compared to other lipid-based encapsulation systems. Soybean oil was used as an oil phase and Tween 20, 60, and 80 as a surfactant [69]. **Zou** et al. prepared curcumin NEs to improve the solubility and stability of curcumin. Corn oil (oil phase) and Tween 80 (surfactant) were utilized to prepare NE. MCTs are usually used as an oil phase to prepare parenteral NE [70−73].

Anuchapreeda et al. developed lipid NE using soybean oil as the oil phase and hydrogenated L-α-phosphatidylcholine (HEPC) as surfactant and Tween 80 and polyoxyethylene hydrogenated castor oil 60 as cosurfactants. Ultrasound was used as emulsification method to reduce the size of droplets. The curcumin-loaded NEs were cytotoxic against B16F10 (mouse melanoma cell line). Moreover, they showed that the concentration of Tween 80 in the NE did not affect the cell cytotoxicity [74].

The photosensitizing activity of curcumin NEs in photodynamic therapy in MCF-7 breast cancer cell line was investigated by **Machado** et al. They prepared curcumin using MCT and soy phospholipids as the oil phase and Poloxamer 80 as the surfactant using the spontaneous emulsification method. The results revealed that curcumin NEs decreased cell proliferation and simulated ROS production in vitro. They concluded that phototoxic effects of curcumin NEs had potential for cancer treatment [75].

Inostroza et al. showed that curcumin NEs have antiproliferative effects on gastric cancer cells (AGS). They incorporated gold nanostructures (nanospheres or nanorods) and curcumin oil-in-water nanoemulsions (CurNem) into alginate microgels using the dripping technique. The results showed that the microgels, which incorporate both gold nanostructures and NEs, not only preserve the photothermal characteristics of the gold nanostructures but also efficiently retain the curcumin nanocarriers. These findings indicate the potential for utilizing these microgels in the development of hydrogel formulations for therapeutic purposes [76].

8.14 Active targeting of curcumin nanoemulsions

To achieve the effective binding and internalization, these receptors must be exclusively expressed on cancer cells. The binding of NEs to cancer cells is mediated by ligand−receptor interactions, which result in receptor-mediated endocytosis and drug release inside the cells [60].

Simion et al. functionalized curcumin NE with cell penetration peptide to increase cellular uptake in endothelial cells and enhance the antiinflammatory effects of curcumin. Ultrasonication method was used for emulsification. Egg phosphatidylcholine (EPC), 1, 2-distearoyl-sn-glycero-3-phosphoethanolamine-N-[maleimide(polyethylene glycol)-2000] (Mal-PEG-DSPE) and 1,2-distearoyl-sn-glycero-3-phosphoethanolamine-N-[amino(polyethylene glycol)-2000] (PEG-DSPE), and soya bean oil were oil phase that contained curcumin and aqueous phase was included water, Tween 80, and/or glycerin. The results indicated that functionalized-NE highly accumulated in the liver and the lungs of C57BL6 mice after intravenous administration [77].

8.15 Curcumin coloaded nanoemulsions for cancer therapy

The anticancer effect of curcumin may be enhanced even further by combination therapy approaches, when a secondary active agent or drug candidate is administered alongside curcumin. Coloading of curcumin and chemotherapeutic agents to improve chemotherapeutic effect has been investigated in several studies. For example, combination treatments of curcumin and doxorubicin [78], gemcitabine [79], docetaxel [80], paclitaxel [81,82], camptothecin [83], cisplatin [84], and resveratrol [85] have shown promising anticancer effects. In another study, Inal et al. showed the addition of curcumin to echium oil NEs, which increased the antioxidant activity of echium oil [86].

In 2010, **Ganta** et al. studied the oral bioavailability and therapeutic efficacy of coadministration of curcumin and paclitaxel NEs in SKOV3 tumor-bearing nu/nu mice model. They found combination therapy with NE preparation improves oral bioavailability and therapeutic efficacy of paclitaxel in ovarian adenocarcinoma mice model [87]. They used omega-3 fatty acid−rich flaxseed oil as the oil phase and egg yolk lecithin and deoxycholic acid as the surfactants.

In another study, concomitant delivery of curcumin and etoposide increased cell toxicity in the PC-3 prostate cancer cell line and inhibited osteoblast differentiation of murine calvarial osteoblast [88].

Curcumin−piperine NE is another example of a combination therapy agent against various types of cancer. Piperine improves the bioavailability of curcumin while exerting no in vitro cytotoxic effects against the HCT116 Colorectal Cancer Model. Curcumin−piperine NE was more effective as compared to CUR emulsion. In addition, Curcumin−piperine NEs increased caspase 3 levels significantly compared to curcumin NE alone. The sonication was used to achieve NEs [89]. Guo and colleagues showed that coencapsulated 5-fluorouracil and curcumin NEs have a synergistic effect against liver cancer. They prepared 5-fluorouracil and curcumin O/W NEs by the emulsification method. In vivo studies in the BALB/c mice model revealed the tumor inhibition rate was significantly elevated by coadministration treatment compared to 5-fluorouracil or curcumin treatment, respectively [90].

8.16 Curcumin nanoemulsions in clinical trial

To date, no curcumin NEs have been entered into clinical trials as direct cancer therapy. Instead, some curcumin NEs are clinically examined as supplement therapy. Curcumin NEs for reducing joint pain in breast cancer survivors are in phase 1 of clinical trials (ClinicalTrial.gov ID: NCT03865992) [91]. A second clinical trial, identified by its ClinicalTrial.gov ID NCT01975363, aims to examine the effectiveness of curcumin NEs on modulating pro-inflammatory biomarkers in plasma and breast adipose tissue of obese women at high risk for developing breast cancer. This study aims to evaluate the tolerability, adherence, and safety of various doses of curcumin NEs, including 50 or 100 mg [92].

8.17 Conclusion

NEs have emerged as promising delivery systems for a wide range of substances, both hydrophilic and hydrophobic. They offer the advantage of multiple simultaneous functions and can be customized to meet specific requirements. While NEs have been extensively explored in cancer drug delivery, there are currently no FDA-approved NEs available for cancer treatment. However, due to their pharmacological and physiological benefits, a variety of nanovehicles have been investigated to enhance the bioavailability of curcumin, and NEs have emerged as one of the most extensively studied delivery systems for curcumin.

NEs have demonstrated efficient encapsulation of curcumin and improvements in its bioavailability. However, to fully harness the potential of curcumin NEs in cancer treatment, further studies are needed to evaluate the material's safety, address pharmaceutical aspects such as scale-up processes, and establish robust quality controls.

In the future, we anticipate increased clinical translation of curcumin-nanoparticle delivery systems and the widespread use of novel curcumin dosage forms as drugs or supplements in cancer treatment. Continued research and development in this field hold promise for advancing the application of curcumin NEs in clinical practice.

References

[1] Jagetia GC, Aggarwal BB. "Spicing up" of the immune system by curcumin. Journal of Clinical Immunology 2007;27(1):19–35.

[2] Ganji A, Farahani I, Saeedifar AM, Mosayebi G, Ghazavi A, Majeed M, et al. Protective effects of curcumin against lipopolysaccharide-induced toxicity. Current Medicinal Chemistry 2021;28(33):6915–30.

[3] Hassanzadeh S, Read MI, Bland AR, Majeed M, Jamialahmadi T, Sahebkar A. Curcumin: an inflammasome silencer. Pharmacological Research 2020;159.

[4] Cicero AFG, Sahebkar A, Fogacci F, Bove M, Giovannini M, Borghi C. Effects of phytosomal curcumin on anthropometric parameters, insulin resistance, cortisolemia and non-alcoholic fatty liver disease indices: a double-blind, placebo-controlled clinical trial. European Journal of Nutrition 2020;59(2):477–83. Available from: https://doi.org/10.1007/s00394-019-01916-7.

[5] Hosseini SA, Zahedipour F, Sathyapalan T, Jamialahmadi T, Sahebkar A. Pulmonary fibrosis: therapeutic and mechanistic insights into the role of phytochemicals. Biofactors (Oxford, England) 2021;47 (3):250−69.

[6] Keihanian F, Saeidinia A, Bagheri RK, Johnston TP, Sahebkar A. Curcumin, hemostasis, thrombosis, and coagulation. Journal of Cellular Physiology 2018;233(6):4497−511.

[7] Khayatan D, Razavi SM, Arab ZN, Niknejad AH, Nouri K, Momtaz S, et al. Protective effects of curcumin against traumatic brain injury. Biomedicine and Pharmacotherapy 2022;154.

[8] Mokhtari-Zaer A, Marefati N, Atkin SL, Butler AE, Sahebkar A. The protective role of curcumin in myo-cardial ischemia−reperfusion injury. Journal of Cellular Physiology 2018;234(1):214−22.

[9] Momtazi-Borojeni AA, Haftcheshmeh SM, Esmaeili SA, Johnston TP, Abdollahi E, Sahebkar A. Curcumin: a natural modulator of immune cells in systemic lupus erythematosus. Autoimmunity Reviews 2018;17(2):125−35.

[10] Rahimi K, Hassanzadeh K, Khanbabaei H, Haftcheshmeh SM, Ahmadi A, Izadpanah E, et al. Curcumin: a dietary phytochemical for targeting the phenotype and function of dendritic cells. Current Medicinal Chemistry 2021;28(8):1549−64.

[11] Panahi Y, Fazlolahzadeh O, Atkin SL, Majeed M, Butler AE, Johnston TP, et al. Evidence of curcumin and curcumin analogue effects in skin diseases: a narrative review. Journal of Cellular Physiology 2019;234(2):1165−78. Available from: https://doi.org/10.1002/jcp.27096.

[12] Sahebkar A. Molecular mechanisms for curcumin benefits against ischemic injury. Fertility and Sterility 2010;94(5):e75−6.

[13] Mohammadi A, Blesso CN, Barreto GE, Banach M, Majeed M, Sahebkar A. Macrophage plasticity, polari-zation and function in response to curcumin, a diet-derived polyphenol, as an immunomodulatory agent. Journal of Nutritional Biochemistry 2019;66:1−16. Available from: https://doi.org/10.1016/j.jnutbio.2018.12.005.

[14] Mohajeri M, Sahebkar A. Protective effects of curcumin against doxorubicin-induced toxicity and resis-tance: a review. Critical Reviews in Oncology/Hematology 2018;122:30−51.

[15] Momtazi AA, Sahebkar A. Difluorinated curcumin: a promising curcumin analogue with improved anti-tumor activity and pharmacokinetic profile. Current Pharmaceutical Design 2016;22(28):4386−97.

[16] Karaboga Arslan A, Uzunhisarcikli E, Yerer M, Bishayee A. The golden spice curcumin in cancer: A per-spective on finalized clinical trials during the last 10 years. Journal of Cancer Research and Therapeutics 2022;18(1):19−26.

[17] Ming T, Tao Q, Tang S, Zhao H, Yang H, Liu M, et al. Curcumin: an epigenetic regulator and its applica-tion in cancer. Biomedicine and Pharmacotherapy 2022;156.

[18] Mohammed ES, El-Beih NM, El-Hussieny EA, El-Ahwany E, Hassan M, Zoheiry M. Effects of free and nanoparticulate curcumin on chemically induced liver carcinoma in an animal model. Archives of Medical Science 2021;17(1):218−27.

[19] Marjaneh RM, Rahmani F, Hassanian SM, Rezaei N, Hashemzehi M, Bahrami A, et al. Phytosomal cur-cumin inhibits tumor growth in colitis-associated colorectal cancer. Journal of Cellular Physiology 2018;233(10):6785−98. Available from: https://doi.org/10.1002/jcp.26538.

[20] Namwan N, Senawong G, Phaosiri C, Kumboonma P, Somsakeesit LO, Samankul A, et al. HDAC inhibi-tory and anti-cancer activities of curcumin and curcumin derivative CU17 against human lung cancer A549 cells. Molecules (Basel, Switzerland) 2022;27(13).

[21] Fan X, Zhu M, Qiu F, Li W, Wang M, Guo Y, et al. Curcumin may be a potential adjuvant treatment drug for colon cancer by targeting CD44. International Immunopharmacology 2020;88:106991.

[22] Li M, Guo T, Lin J, Huang X, Ke Q, Wu Y, et al. Curcumin inhibits the invasion and metastasis of triple nega-tive breast cancer via Hedgehog/Gli1 signaling pathway. Journal of Ethnopharmacology 2022;283:114689.

[23] Seo JA, Kim B, Dhanasekaran DN, Tsang BK, Song YS. Curcumin induces apoptosis by inhibiting sarco/endoplasmic reticulum Ca2 + ATPase activity in ovarian cancer cells. Cancer Letters 2016;371(1):30−7.

[24] Younes M, Mardirossian R, Rizk L, Fazlian T, Khairallah JP, Sleiman C, et al. The synergistic effects of curcumin and chemotherapeutic drugs in inhibiting metastatic, invasive and proliferative pathways. Plants (Basel, Switzerland) 2022;11(16).

[25] Hewlings SJ, Kalman DS. Curcumin: a review of its effects on human health. Foods (Basel, Switzerland) 2017;6(10).

[26] Loyd Alen NP, Howard A. Pharmaceutical dosage forms and drug delivery systems. Lippincott Wiliams and Wilkins; 2009.

[27] Taylor MEAKMG. In: Eccleston GM, editor. Aulton's pharmaceutics. The design and manufacture of medicines. 5th ed. Elsevier Ltd.; 2018.

[28] Donsì F, Sessa M, Mediouni H, Mgaidi A, Ferrari G. Encapsulation of bioactive compounds in nanoemulsion-based delivery systems. Procedia Food Science 2011;1:1666−71.

[29] Mariem Ben J, Hanen F, Riadh K. Encapsulation of natural bioactive compounds: nanoemulsion formulation to enhance essential oils activities. In: Fabien S, editor. Microencapsulation. Rijeka: IntechOpen;; 2019. p. Ch. 3.

[30] Gonçalves RFS, Martins JT, Abrunhosa L, Vicente AA, Pinheiro AC. Nanoemulsions for enhancement of curcumin bioavailability and their safety evaluation: effect of emulsifier type. Nanomaterials (Basel, Switzerland) 2021;11(3).

[31] Pinheiro AC, Lad M, Silva HD, Coimbra MA, Boland M, Vicente AA. Unravelling the behaviour of curcumin nanoemulsions during in vitro digestion: effect of the surface charge. Soft Matter 2013;9 (11):3147−54.

[32] Nirmal NP, Mereddy R, Li L, Sultanbawa Y. Formulation, characterisation and antibacterial activity of lemon myrtle and anise myrtle essential oil in water nanoemulsion. Food Chemistry 2018;254:1−7.

[33] Mahdi Jafari S, He Y, Bhandari B. Nano-emulsion production by sonication and microfluidization—a comparison. International Journal of Food Properties 2006;9(3):475−85.

[34] Anandharamakrishnan C. Nanoencapsulation of food bioactive compounds. In: Anandharamakrishnan C, editor. Techniques for nanoencapsulation of food ingredients. New York, NY: Springer; 2014. p. 1−6.

[35] Gupta, A., et al. Nanoemulsions: formation, properties and applications. Soft Matter 2016;12(11): 2826−41.

[36] Jintapattanakit A, Hasan HM, Junyaprasert VB. Vegetable oil-based nanoemulsions containing curcuminoids: formation optimization by phase inversion temperature method. Journal of Drug Delivery Science and Technology 2018;44:289−97.

[37] Solans C, Solé I. Nano-emulsions: formation by low-energy methods. Current Opinion in Colloid & Interface Science 2012;17(5):246−54.

[38] Modarres-Gheisari SMM, Gavagsaz-Ghoachani R, Malaki M, Safarpour P, Zandi M. Ultrasonic nano-emulsification − a review. Ultrasonics Sonochemistry 2019;52:88−105.

[39] Mistry PH, Mohapatra SK, Dash AK. Effect of high-pressure homogenization and stabilizers on the physicochemical properties of curcumin-loaded glycerol monooleate/chitosan nanostructures. Nanomedicine (London, England) 2012;7(12):1863−76.

[40] Páez-Hernández G, Mondragón-Cortez P, Espinosa-Andrews H. Developing curcumin nanoemulsions by high-intensity methods: impact of ultrasonication and microfluidization parameters. LWT 2019;111:291−300.

[41] Artiga-Artigas M, Lanjari-Pérez Y, Martín-Belloso O. Curcumin-loaded nanoemulsions stability as affected by the nature and concentration of surfactant. Food Chemistry 2018;266:466−74.

[42] Raviadaran R, Chandran D, Shin LH, Manickam S. Optimization of palm oil in water nano-emulsion with curcumin using microfluidizer and response surface methodology. LWT 2018;96:58−65.

[43] Ahmad SU, Li B, Sun J, Arbab S, Dong Z, Cheng F, et al. Recent advances in microencapsulation of drugs for veterinary applications. Journal of Veterinary Pharmacology and Therapeutics 2021;44(3):298−312.

[44] Shakeel F, Ramadan W, Ahmed MA. Investigation of true nanoemulsions for transdermal potential of indomethacin: characterization, rheological characteristics, and ex vivo skin permeation studies. Journal of Drug Targeting 2009;17(6):435−41.

[45] Ganta S, Talekar M, Singh A, Coleman TP, Amiji MM. Nanoemulsions in translational research-opportunities and challenges in targeted cancer therapy. AAPS PharmSciTech 2014;15(3):694−708.

[46] Kim SH, Ji YS, Lee ES, Hong ST. Ostwald ripening stability of curcumin-loaded MCT nanoemulsion: influence of various emulsifiers. Preventive Nutrition and Food Science 2016;21(3):289−95.

[47] Koroleva MY, Yurtov EV. Ostwald ripening in macro- and nanoemulsions. Russian Chemical Reviews 2021;90(3):293.

[48] Anton N, Benoit J-P, Saulnier P. Design and production of nanoparticles formulated from nano-emulsion templates—a review. Journal of Controlled Release 2008;128(3):185−99.

[49] Rafiee Z, Nejatian M, Daeihamed M, Jafari SM. Application of different nanocarriers for encapsulation of curcumin. Critical Reviews in Food Science and Nutrition 2019;59(21):3468−97.

[50] Kumar M, Bishnoi RS, Shukla AK, Jain CP. Techniques for formulation of nanoemulsion drug delivery system: a review. Preventive Nutrition and Food Science 2019;24(3):225−34.

[51] Karthik P, Ezhilarasi PN, Anandharamakrishnan C. Challenges associated in stability of food grade nanoemulsions. Critical Reviews in Food Science and Nutrition 2017;57(7):1435−50.

[52] Kumar DD, Mann B, Pothuraju R, Sharma R, Bajaj R, Minaxi. Formulation and characterization of nanoencapsulated curcumin using sodium caseinate and its incorporation in ice cream. Food & Function 2016;7(1):417−24.

[53] Silva HD, Beldíková E, Poejo J, Abrunhosa L, Serra AT, Duarte CMM, et al. Evaluating the effect of chitosan layer on bioaccessibility and cellular uptake of curcumin nanoemulsions. Journal of Food Engineering 2019;243:89−100.

[54] Zheng B, Peng S, Zhang X, McClements DJ. Impact of delivery system type on curcumin bioaccessibility: comparison of curcumin-loaded nanoemulsions with commercial curcumin supplements. Journal of Agricultural and Food Chemistry 2018;66(41):10816−26.

[55] Wang X, Jiang Y, Wang YW, Huang MT, Ho CT, Huang Q. Enhancing anti-inflammation activity of curcumin through O/W nanoemulsions. Food Chemistry 2008;108(2):419−24.

[56] Nasr M, Abd-Allah H, Ahmed-Farid OAH, Bakeer RM, Hassan NS, Ahmed RF. A comparative study between curcumin and curcumin nanoemulsion on high-fat, high-fructose diet-induced impaired spermatogenesis in rats. The Journal of Pharmacy and Pharmacology 2022;74(2):268−81.

[57] Elbaset MA, Nasr M, Ibrahim BMM, Ahmed-Farid OAH, Bakeer RM, Hassan NS, et al. Curcumin nanoemulsion counteracts hepatic and cardiac complications associated with high-fat/high-fructose diet in rats. Journal of Food Biochemistry 2022;e14442.

[58] Sahu P, Das D, Mishra VK, Kashaw V, Kashaw SK. Nanoemulsion: a novel eon in cancer chemotherapy. Mini Reviews in Medicinal Chemistry 2017;17(18):1778−92.

[59] Date AA, Nagarsenker MS. Parenteral microemulsions: an overview. International Journal of Pharmaceutics 2008;355(1):19−30.

[60] Moosavian SA, Sahebkar A. Aptamer-functionalized liposomes for targeted cancer therapy. Cancer Letters 2019;448:144−54.

[61] Ejigah V, Owoseni O, Bataille-Backer P, Ogundipe OD, Fisusi FA, Adesina SK. Approaches to improve macromolecule and nanoparticle accumulation in the tumor microenvironment by the enhanced permeability and retention effect. Polymers (Basel) 2022;14(13):2601.

[62] Tagne JB, Kakumanu S, Ortiz D, Shea T, Nicolosi RJ. A nanoemulsion formulation of tamoxifen increases its efficacy in a breast cancer cell line. Molecular Pharmaceutics 2008;5(2):280—6.

[63] Allen TM, Martin FJ. Advantages of liposomal delivery systems for anthracyclines. Seminars in Oncology 2004;31(6 Suppl 13):5—15.

[64] Talekar M, Ganta S, Singh A, Amiji M, Kendall J, Denny WA, et al. Phosphatidylinositol 3-kinase inhibitor (PIK75) containing surface functionalized nanoemulsion for enhanced drug delivery, cytotoxicity and pro-apoptotic activity in ovarian cancer cells. Pharmaceutical Research 2012;29(10):2874—86.

[65] Milane L, Duan Z, Amiji M. Development of EGFR-targeted polymer blend nanocarriers for combination paclitaxel/lonidamine delivery to treat multi-drug resistance in human breast and ovarian tumor cells. Molecular Pharmaceutics 2011;8(1):185—203.

[66] Mulik RS, Mönkkönen J, Juvonen RO, Mahadik KR, Paradkar AR. Transferrin mediated solid lipid nanoparticles containing curcumin: enhanced in vitro anticancer activity by induction of apoptosis. International Journal of Pharmaceutics 2010;398(1—2):190—203.

[67] Guerrero S, Inostroza-Riquelme M, Contreras-Orellana P, Diaz-Garcia V, Lara P, Vivanco-Palma A, et al. Curcumin-loaded nanoemulsion: a new safe and effective formulation to prevent tumor reincidence and metastasis. Nanoscale 2018;10(47):22612—22.

[68] Guan YB, Zhou SY, Zhang YQ, Wang JL, Tian YD, Jia YY, et al. Therapeutic effects of curcumin nanoemulsions on prostate cancer. Journal of Huazhong University of Science and Technology - Medical Sciences 2017;37(3):371—8.

[69] Borrin TR, Georges EL, Moraes ICF, Pinho SC. Curcumin-loaded nanoemulsions produced by the emulsion inversion point (EIP) method: an evaluation of process parameters and physico-chemical stability. Journal of Food Engineering 2016;169:1—9.

[70] Sari TP, Mann B, Kumar R, Singh RRB, Sharma R, Bhardwaj M, et al. Preparation and characterization of nanoemulsion encapsulating curcumin. Food Hydrocolloids 2015;43:540—6.

[71] Abbas S, Bashari M, Akhtar W, Li WW, Zhang X. Process optimization of ultrasound-assisted curcumin nanoemulsions stabilized by OSA-modified starch. Ultrasonics Sonochemistry 2014;21(4):1265—74.

[72] Li M, Ma Y, Cui J. Whey-protein-stabilized nanoemulsions as a potential delivery system for water-insoluble curcumin. LWT - Food Science and Technology 2014;59(1):49—58.

[73] Yu H, Huang Q. Improving the oral bioavailability of curcumin using novel organogel-based nanoemulsions. Journal of Agricultural and Food Chemistry 2012;60(21):5373—9.

[74] Anuchapreeda S, Fukumori Y, Okonogi S, Ichikawa H. Preparation of lipid nanoemulsions incorporating curcumin for cancer therapy. Journal of Nanotechnology 2012;2012:270383.

[75] Machado FC, Adum de Matos RP, Primo FL, Tedesco AC, Rahal P, Calmon MF. Effect of curcumin-nanoemulsion associated with photodynamic therapy in breast adenocarcinoma cell line. Bioorganic & Medicinal Chemistry 2019;27(9):1882—90.

[76] Inostroza-Riquelme M, Vivanco A, Lara P, Guerrero S, Salas-Huenuleo E, Chamorro A, et al. Encapsulation of gold nanostructures and oil-in-water nanocarriers in microgels with biomedical potential. Molecules (Basel, Switzerland) 2018;23(5).

[77] Simion V, Stan D, Constantinescu CA, Deleanu M, Dragan E, Tucureanu MM, et al. Conjugation of curcumin-loaded lipid nanoemulsions with cell-penetrating peptides increases their cellular uptake and enhances the anti-inflammatory effects in endothelial cells. Journal of Pharmacy and Pharmacology 2016;68(2):195—207.

[78] Lv L, Qiu K, Yu X, Chen C, Qin F, Shi Y, et al. Amphiphilic copolymeric micelles for doxorubicin and curcumin co-delivery to reverse multidrug resistance in breast cancer. Journal of Biomedical Nanotechnology 2016;12(5):973−85.

[79] Dhillon N, Aggarwal BB, Newman RA, Wolff RA, Kunnumakkara AB, Abbruzzese JL, et al. Phase II trial of curcumin in patients with advanced pancreatic cancer. Clinical Cancer Research: An Official Journal of the American Association for Cancer Research 2008;14(14):4491−9.

[80] Bayet-Robert M, Kwiatkowski F, Leheurteur M, Gachon F, Planchat E, Abrial C, et al. Phase I dose escalation trial of docetaxel plus curcumin in patients with advanced and metastatic breast cancer. Cancer Biology & Therapy 2010;9(1):8−14.

[81] Ganta S, Amiji M. Coadministration of Paclitaxel and curcumin in nanoemulsion formulations to overcome multidrug resistance in tumor cells. Molecular Pharmaceutics 2009;6(3):928−39.

[82] Boztas AO, Karakuzu O, Galante G, Ugur Z, Kocabas F, Altuntas CZ, et al. Synergistic interaction of paclitaxel and curcumin with cyclodextrin polymer complexation in human cancer cells. Molecular Pharmaceutics 2013;10(7):2676−83.

[83] Xiao B, Si X, Han MK, Viennois E, Zhang M, Merlin D. Co-delivery of camptothecin and curcumin by cationic polymeric nanoparticles for synergistic colon cancer combination chemotherapy. Journal of Materials Chemistry B 2015;3(39):7724−33.

[84] Li C, Ge X, Wang L. Construction and comparison of different nanocarriers for co-delivery of cisplatin and curcumin: a synergistic combination nanotherapy for cervical cancer. Biomedicine & Pharmacotherapy 2017;86:628−36.

[85] Du Q, Hu B, An HM, Shen KP, Xu L, Deng S, et al. Synergistic anticancer effects of curcumin and resveratrol in Hepa1-6 hepatocellular carcinoma cells. Oncology Reports 2013;29(5):1851−8.

[86] Inal A, Yenipazar H, Şahin-Yeşilçubuk N. Preparation and characterization of nanoemulsions of curcumin and echium oil. Heliyon 2022;8(2):e08974.

[87] Ganta S, Devalapally H, Amiji M. Curcumin enhances oral bioavailability and anti-tumor therapeutic efficacy of paclitaxel upon administration in nanoemulsion formulation. Journal of Pharmaceutical Sciences 2010;99(11):4630−41.

[88] Shukla P, Mathur V, Kumar A, Khedgikar V, Teja VB, Chaudhary D, et al. Nanoemulsion based concomitant delivery of curcumin and etoposide: impact on cross talk between prostate cancer cells and osteoblast during metastasis. Journal of Biomedical Nanotechnology 2014;10(11):3381−91.

[89] Bolat ZB, Islek Z, Demir BN, Yilmaz EN, Sahin F, Ucisik MH. Curcumin- and piperine-loaded emulsomes as combinational treatment approach enhance the anticancer activity of curcumin on HCT116 colorectal cancer model. Frontiers in Bioengineering and Biotechnology 2020;8:50.

[90] Guo P, Pi C, Zhao S, Fu S, Yang H, Zheng X, et al. Oral co-delivery nanoemulsion of 5-fluorouracil and curcumin for synergistic effects against liver cancer. Expert Opinion on Drug Delivery 2020;17 (10):1473−84.

[91] Curcumin in reducing joint pain in breast cancer survivors with aromatase inhibitor-induced joint disease. [accessed on 19 May 2019]; Available online: https://ClinicalTrials.gov/show/NCT03865992.

[92] Pilot study of curcumin for women with obesity and high risk for breast cancer. [accessed on 19 May 2019]; Available online: https://ClinicalTrials.gov/show/NCT0197536.

9

Micelle-based curcumin delivery systems as cancer therapeutics

Niloufar Rahiman[1,2], Seyedeh Hoda Alavizadeh[1,2], Luis E. Simental-Mendía[3], Amirhossein Sahebkar[4,5]

[1]NANOTECHNOLOGY RESEARCH CENTER, PHARMACEUTICAL TECHNOLOGY INSTITUTE, MASHHAD UNIVERSITY OF MEDICAL SCIENCES, MASHHAD, IRAN [2]DEPARTMENT OF PHARMACEUTICAL NANOTECHNOLOGY, SCHOOL OF PHARMACY, MASHHAD UNIVERSITY OF MEDICAL SCIENCES, MASHHAD, IRAN [3]BIOMEDICAL RESEARCH UNIT, MEXICAN SOCIAL SECURITY INSTITUTE, DURANGO, MEXICO [4]BIOTECHNOLOGY RESEARCH CENTER, PHARMACEUTICAL TECHNOLOGY INSTITUTE, MASHHAD UNIVERSITY OF MEDICAL SCIENCES, MASHHAD, IRAN [5]APPLIED BIOMEDICAL RESEARCH CENTER, MASHHAD UNIVERSITY OF MEDICAL SCIENCES, MASHHAD, IRAN

9.1 Introduction

Curcumin has a broad application in cancer therapy, immunotherapy, and inflammatory and autoimmune disorders [1−7], and it can also be used as a conjugate to other therapeutics for treating different disorders [8−18]. Despite curcumin's superior features as an anticancer and antiinflammatory agent, its bioapplications are hindered due to low aqueous solubility and physicochemical stability, rapid systemic clearance, and low rate of cellular uptake [19].

Nanotechnology has rendered delivery carriers to become reliable for dominating these barriers [20−25]. In this regard, micelles are promising platforms with lipid-based or polymeric-based natures that usually self-assembled in aqueous solutions [26]. Micelles are able to improve curcumin's physiochemical and biological properties, thus they could significantly enhance curcumin's anticancer activity compared to free curcumin. Among them, polymeric micelles with inherent stability and ease of formation are ideal for tumor targeting with different mechanisms especially through the enhanced permeation and retention (EPR) effect [27]. In this regard, this chapter introduces different types of curcumin micelles for cancer combating with further rendering new insights in the field in terms of mechanism of action.

9.2 Lipid-based micelles

9.2.1 Traditional lipid-based micelles

Lipid-based micelles are normally formed by the self-assembly of lipid-natured molecules. The hydrophilic region faces the outside surface of the micelle and the hydrophobic molecules form the core. Traditional micelles are lipid-based with hydrophilic heads of phospholipids form the shell and the fatty acid tails of phospholipids form the hydrophobic core of the micelle, which can accommodate phytochemicals or therapeutics with various natures either hydrophilic or hydrophobic. Lipid-based traditional micelles loaded with curcumin demonstrated immunomodulatory [28], anticancer, reactive oxygen species (ROS)-scavenging, and antiinflammatory effects [1,29]. The lipid-based traditional micelles could simply form using some specific surfactants [30], fatty acids, or a salt of a fatty acid (soap) as well as phospholipids. In this case, lipid-based micelles show lower critical micelle concentration (CMC) [31]. In this section, various lipid-based curcumin micelles will be introduced and scrutinized in terms of literature description to give new insights regarding their potential efficacy in cancer management.

Cyclin D1 gene overexpression is responsible for tumorigenesis and tumor growth. Nanomicelles of curcumin have shown to potentiate cell cytotoxicity (decreased IC_{50}) and downregulate the cyclin D1 expression in esophageal squamous cell carcinoma (KYSE-30) in vitro. [32]. Due to the limited bioavailability of curcumin, micellar curcumin formulations consisting of polysorbate 80 were developed. Curcumin nanomicelles showed cytostatic and antitumor effects when administered orally in an inflammatory breast cancer SUM149 xenografts compared to free curcumin due to the bioavailability enhancement of curcumin [33].

Cisplatin is one of the most potent chemotherapeutic agents for the treatment of colon cancer. However, the acquired resistance severely restricted its clinical application. In this regard, Mohammadi et al. have investigated the antiproliferative and apoptotic effects of curcumin nanomicelles on two types of colon cancer cells (HT-29 and HCT-116), which showed comparable efficacy to cisplatin. These results validate high potency of curcumin-loaded micelles in the mitigation of various cancerous cells [34]. Gut inflammation, which is fueled by DNA damage, is considered a driving force of colorectal cancer. Chronic oral administration by a daily intake of 46 mg micellar curcumin up to 4 months in C57BL6 mice has shown to be well tolerated with high bioavailability (185-fold), resulting in reduced chemo-induced gut inflammation and reduced tumor yield and score. Colon cancer in this model was induced by azoxymethane (AOM) followed by dextran sodium sulfate (DSS) (AOM/DSS) [35].

Park et al. have developed a curcumin human serum albumin (HSA)-fatty acid (various fatty acids with 8−18 carbons) conjugate with the capability to form stable amphiphilic nanomicelles. They have used the resulting micellar curcumin to enhance curcumin solubilization, cellular uptake, and subsequent toxicity in A549 and MCF-7 cancer cell. Results indicated a significantly higher cytotoxicity and efficient cellular uptake with amphiphilic curcumin nanomicelles (especially with the nanoconjugate possessed 14 carbons in its fatty acid structure) compared to curcumin solution in vitro. The improved efficacy was attributed to the enhanced curcumin solubility by using the HSA—fatty acid carrier [36,37].

Nuclear factor-kappa B (NF-κB) pathway is extensively involved in cancer progression. NFκB mediates tumor cell proliferation, survival, and angiogenesis through controlling the expression of target genes, such as tumor necrosis factor-α (TNF-α), interleukin-6 (IL-6), and vascular endothelial growth factor (VEGF) [38]. Curcumin nanomicelles have shown to act through perturbation of Wnt/β-catenin and NF-κB pathways to suppress glioblastoma multiforme cells proliferation and invasion. Hesari et al. have investigated the curcumin nanomicelle targeting potential on these proliferative signaling pathways and compared its efficacy with erlotinib, the selective inhibitor of the epidermal growth factor receptor (EGFR) tyrosine kinase. Curcumin nanomicelles interference on NF-κB and Wnt/β-catenin pathways showed to be by decreasing p-65 expression and declining cyclin D1 expression, respectively. Furthermore, the nanomicellar curcumin exerted a considerable cytotoxicity effect and tumor shrinkage on U-373 cells compared to erlotinib [39].

Brain tumor drug delivery is mainly limited by blood—brain barrier (BBB) that prevents efficient drug penetration to the favorable regions [40]. Intranasal administration is a noninvasive approach that can circumvent BBB for treating various central nervous system disorders, especially brain tumors. The advantages of this route of administration are high absorption of low-molecular-weights lipophilic drugs, avoidance of liver first-pass effect, and fast onset of action of the administered drug [41]. D-alpha-tocopheryl polyethylene glycol-1000 succinate (TPGS)-based stable micelles of curcumin have developed for intranasal administration to enhance brain tumor targeting. The amphiphilic nature of the micelles contained hydrophobic curcumin in the core, as well as the nanoranged size of 146 nm led to the enhancement of drug permeability and bioavailability as well as bypassing BBB. Results indicated almost 380% of higher bioavailability, fourfold increase in curcumin half-life, and a significant increment in the curcumin plasma concentration when encapsulated within micelles as evaluated in rat model. The histopathological studies of sheep nasal mucosa after micelle administration also have shown no sign of destructive effect of the micellar formulations on the treated nasal mucosa [36,42].

Paclitaxel- and curcumin-loaded Soluplus (a polymeric solubilizer): TPGS mixed micelles showed higher cytotoxicity and antioxidant effect compared to Abraxane (albumin-bound paclitaxel) in SKOV-3 ovarian and MDA-MB-231 breast cancer cells. Furthermore, alleviation of paclitaxel neurotoxicity was observed as assessed in zebrafish larvae in terms of higher survival rate [43].

9.2.2 Targeted lipid-based micelles

The resistant cancer stem cells (CSCs) of breast cancer are associated with the overexpression of vasoactive intestinal peptide (VIP) receptors, so eradicating breast cancer stem cells in an efficacious and safe manner could lead to a relapse-free treatment of breast cancer [44]. CSCs are the progenitor cells available in most types of cancers. Though these cells consist of a small subpopulation of cells within the tumor environment, they are capable of regenerating malignant cells as well as fueling the growth of the cancerous cells [45]. So, sterically stabilized PEGylated micelles of curcumin (200 μg/mL concentration of curcumin) were developed with surface decoration with VIP, an overexpressed protein on the surface of CSCs. These targeted micelles were assessed in terms of efficacy on tumor-sphere model of MCF-7 enriched with CSCs, and showed notable inhibition of tumor-sphere formation (up to 20%) and anticancer effects with targeting potential of resistant MCF-7 CSCs [44].

Transferrin receptors are upregulated in various malignant tumors to provide iron requirement and increased cell survival through various cellular signaling pathways [46]. Transferrin-modified PEGylated vitamin-E-based micelles of curcumin (114 nm) have shown to improve curcumin solubility and actively target hepatic HepG2 and cervical HeLa tumor cells. The targeted micelles have also shown to enhance the interaction with overexpressed transferrin receptors, resulting in higher levels of cellular uptake and enhanced cytotoxicity compared to their nontargeted peers [47]. In spheroid model, significantly higher doses of drugs are required, compared to the monolayers, to obtain the same therapeutic response due to the limited penetration of drug molecules within the 3D structure as well as altered cellular pathways and overexpression of P-gp (P-glycoprotein). These types of transferrin-functionalized nanomicelles further demonstrated the efficacy of curcumin combination with paclitaxel on a spheroid model of ovarian cancer cells [47,48].

PEGylated PE (phosphatidylethanolamine) micelles coloaded with curcumin and doxorubicin were functionalized with anti-GLUT1 antibody. The therapeutic micelles were designed not only to specifically target cancer cells but also to decrease glucose uptake by HCT-116 human colorectal adenocarcinoma cells through inhibiting the GLUT1 transporters. At low doses of doxorubicin (0.4 mg/kg), the GLUT1-decorated micelles showed a robust killing effect on HCT-116 human colon cancer cells in vitro, with further survival enhancement on nude mice bearing HCT-116 tumors in vivo [49]. PEGylated PE-based polymeric micelles loaded with curcumin and doxorubicin were further decorated with single-chain fragment variable (scFv) of GLUT1 antibody. The resulting micelles led to about threefold higher nuclear localizations of doxorubicin in U87MG glioblastoma tumor cells. Other effects of these targeted micelles were apoptosis induction through caspase 3/7 overexpression and strong NF-κB inhibition by curcumin to dominate multidrug resistance (MDR) [50].

9.2.3 Stimuli-responsive lipid-based micelles

Stimuli-responsive micelles could be included as the family of smart micelles, which show characteristic alterations when subjected to specific environmental conditions (e.g., pH, temperature, redox potential, ultrasound, or enzymes) [51].

9.2.3.1 pH-sensitive lipid-based micelles

Micelles designed to be responsive to the specific pH values (especially acidic conditions of the tumor) can target tumoral cells to release their encapsulated drugs with maximum therapeutic impacts and minimum side effects, as this release is site specific with minimum release of drugs in off-target areas [52].

2-distearoyl-sn-glycero-3-phosphoethanolamine (DSPE)-PEG-imine-methotrexate as a self-targeting and pH-responsive prodrug was self-assembled into curcumin-loaded micelles. The self-targeting feature is attributed to the methotrexate capability in terms of possessing an affinity for folate receptors. This type of micelle can release the active form of methotrexate and curcumin more efficiently in acidic media (at pH 5) than the physiological neutral pH due to the presence of pH-sensitive imine linkage. These nanomicelles showed selective and efficient uptake by the cancer cells via folate receptor—mediated endocytosis compared to unfunctionalized peers and free drug, as well as significantly stronger cytotoxicity toward HeLa/MCF-7 cells. The in vivo tumor inhibition was also significantly more efficient in HeLa tumor-bearing nude mice [53].

9.2.3.2 Reactive oxygen species—responsive lipid-based micelles

The ROS-responsive micelles are the platforms that release their payloads in the targeted cells or tissues that overproduce ROS, especially within tumor cells possessing this feature. Some previously formed bonds such as thioether and selenide linkers in the micelle could be cleaved in the state of exposure to an ROS-containing environment, triggering content release in this way [54].

TPGS, a derivative of vitamin E, could act as both an antioxidant and surfactant to enhance the solubilization of low-aqueous-soluble agents. Curcumin solubilization has also been performed by using TPGS, which could form micelles of 12 nm size. This nanomicellar formulation with highly potent antioxidant properties is regarded as an efficient carrier to modulate the intracellular ROS levels and induce apoptosis. The oral administration of this type of curcumin micelle to rat model of colon cancer significantly enhanced curcumin oral bioavailability and inhibited colon cancer cell migration (HT-29) compared to free form of curcumin [55].

9.2.4 Chemoresistant lipid-based micelles

Multiple drug resistance as a limiting hurdle for chemotherapy is due to the overexpression of various drug efflux transporters and upregulation of numerous apoptotic inhibitory pathways within the cancerous cells. In this regard, substantial body of evidences has focused on the use of nanocarriers to dominate drug resistance through several mechanisms.

A curcumin-loaded D-α-tocopherol-lipid-based copolymeric nanomicellar system was developed by conjugating PE and D-α-tocopherol with PEG via an amino acid linkage. The copolymeric nanomicellar form of curcumin has significantly reduced P-gp drug efflux transporters expression in MDA-MB-231 drug-resistant breast cancer cells as well as melanoma cancer cells and has demonstrated a high efficacy in tumor growth suppression [56].

Another approach to combat chemotherapeutic resistance is combination therapy, which could efficiently enhance the efficacy of drugs compared to monotherapy. Combination therapy targets key pathways in a characteristically synergistic or additive manner [57]. Nanomicelle of curcumin is beneficial in suppressing the activity of NF-κB, a central protein involved in chemoresistance [58]. In a study by Eskandari et al. curcumin and pirarubicin (an anthracycline for cancer therapy) nanomicelles were distinctly prepared with DSPE-PEG_{2000} and coadministered with the aim of dominating multidrug resistance. This coadministration has shown to enhance the efficacy of treatment by suppressing P65 (a subunit of NF-κB) through curcumin as a complementary agent in MCF-7 cells, compared to pirarubicin monotherapy [59].

PEGylated-PE/vitamin E mixed micelles coloaded with curcumin and paclitaxel have also shown synergistic effects with threefold tumor inhibition potential in human ovarian adenocarcinoma. Molecular analysis indicated that the mixed micelles acted through inhibiting NF-κB and Akt signaling pathways by virtue of the curcumin moiety in dominating chemoresistance [60]. The mechanism of action by this type of curcumin-based nanomicelles is demonstrated in Fig. 9.1.

Development of chemoresistance in endometrial cancer is due to the upregulation of survivin and P-gp efflux following administration of anticancer therapeutics. In this regard, mixed micelles of curcumin were fabricated using smart surfactants including TPGS and polyethylene glycol (15)-hydroxystearate. Treatment of Ishikawa cells (endometrial adenocarcinoma) with the curcumin micelle of 13 nm in size, leads to the downregulation of survivin

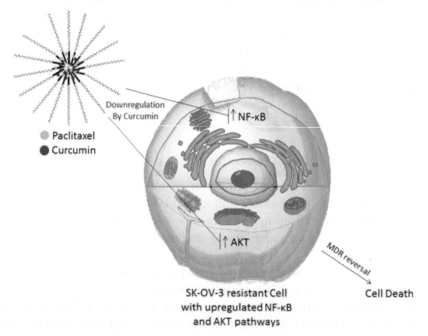

FIGURE 9.1 Curcumin- and paclitaxel-based nanomicelles and their mechanism of action in terms of affecting signaling pathways for ovarian cancer treatment. *Reproduced with permission from Abouzeid, A.H., N.R. Patel, and V.P. Torchilin, Polyethylene glycol-phosphatidylethanolamine (PEG-PE)/vitamin E micelles for co-delivery of paclitaxel and curcumin to overcome multi-drug resistance in ovarian cancer. International Journal of Pharmaceutics, 2014. 464(1--2): p. 178--184. License code: 5373610363204.*

levels, enhanced apoptosis and decreased curcumin efflux in endometrial cells. This formulation of curcumin also rendered sustained release properties of curcumin, apoptosis induction, and enhanced intracellular uptake by endometrial cells in vitro [61].

9.3 Polymeric micelles

9.3.1 Traditional polymeric micelles

Traditional polymeric micelles are micelles with polymeric base that are formed through self-assembly with the potential of encapsulating various drugs or agents. These types of polymeric micelles are simple, which means that they are not either functionalized for targeting purposes or being responsive to varying stimulants [62].

One of the most commonly used hydrophilic polymers for bioapplication purposes is poly (ethylene glycol) (PEG). Several aliphatic polyesters including poly (ε-caprolactone) (PCL), poly (D,L-lactide) (PDLLA), and poly(glycolide) (PGA) are also among the hydrophobic polymers that have been substantially investigated due to their favorable biodegradability and biocompatibility features. Since these polymers have gained Food and Drug Administration (FDA) approval for human use, several combination copolymers including mPEG-PDLLA, mPEG-PCL, and mPEG-PLGA were extensively applied for developing nanoscale drug delivery vehicles [63]. In this regard, numerous polymeric micelles of curcumin have been developed for cancer therapy that are summarized in the following sections.

In 2011, curcumin was loaded with high encapsulation efficiency (above 95%) in amphiphilic PEGylated poly (ε-caprolactone-co-p-dioxanone) micelles with a size of about 30 nm. This type of polymeric micelles significantly inhibited PC-3 human prostate cancer cells growth in a dose-dependent manner, with a controlled curcumin release pattern without any burst release [64].

To improve curcumin encapsulation, in another study, a copolymer of poly (caprolactone)-PEG-poly (caprolactone) was synthesized (83% curcumin loading efficiency). The resulting polymeric micelles 70.34 nm in size showed a sustained release pattern. In vivo investigation demonstrated the potential of these nanomicelles in reducing the tumor burden and improving the survival of animals. Furthermore, a significantly enhanced splenocyte proliferation, IFN-γ production, as well as decreased IL-4 levels were observed in PC-3 cells compared to free curcumin and empty polymeric micelles [65].

Other PEGylated PCL-based micelles were synthesized with curcumin-loaded PCL as a core encompassed by PEG as a shell. By applying this formulation, a more potent inhibitory effect on proliferation, invasion, migration, and tube formation (a criterion for angiogenesis assay) of endothelial cells was observed compared to free curcumin. Study in transgenic zebrafish model indicated an inhibition of embryonic and tumor-induced angiogenesis. These micelles also rendered higher plasma concentration of curcumin and longer plasma retention time in mice-bearing Lewis lung *carcinoma* (LL/2). Furthermore, results demonstrated a high efficiency in tumor growth inhibition and prolonging survival in metastatic models of lung cancer (either subcutaneous or pulmonary) [66]. PEGylated PCL diblock copolymers were used to develop micelles of 110 nm with negative zeta potential. Results indicated an enhanced uptake (2.95-fold higher compared to free curcumin) and considerable apoptosis induction [67]. Other PEGylated nanomicelles of ε-caprolactone loaded with curcumin showed a sustained curcumin release pattern in vitro. Animal study in mice bearing 4T1 breast tumor indicated the efficacy of nanoparticles in shrinking breast tumor growth and spontaneous pulmonary metastasis as well as increment of animal survival in vivo [68].

Some studies addressed the plasma kinetic of curcumin following encapsulation within nanomicelles. Manjili et al., for example, in a 2017 study, used PEGylated PCL diblock copolymers for curcumin loading in micellar form. This nanomicelles formulation with the size of 81 nm significantly improved curcumin pharmacokinetics in terms of increased bioavailability (53 fold), half-life (4.6 fold), and maximum concentration (7.5 fold) of curcumin in blood [69].

As already mentioned, PEG-b-PCL-based nanocarriers were extensively explored for curcumin loading; however, the loading capacity could still be improved by further conjugation of biopolymer with some lipophilic moieties. In a study by Angarita et al., the performance of PEG-b-PCL-based nanocarriers for curcumin delivery was enhanced through its conjugation with lipophilic biomolecules including cholesterol or oleic acid. Results indicated that nanomicellar conjugation with oleic acid could promote a higher curcumin release and further could improve the antitumor efficacy, whereas cholesterol conjugation did not significantly affect the curcumin release profile [70]. Curcumin-loaded polymeric micelles composed of PEGylated PCL end-capped with L-phenylalanine derivatives have also shown higher toxicity on human pancreatic SW1990 cells. The modified PEGylated PCL-based nanomicelle improved the stability of curcumin within the bloodstream and increased systemic bioavailability [71]. Star-shaped curcumin micelles formed from poly(ε-caprolactone)-b-poly (2-methacryloyloxyethyl phosphorylcholine) conjugate showed higher efficiency in killing HeLa cells and more cellular uptake compared to PEGylated micelles of poly(ε-caprolactone) [72].

Polymeric nanomicelles have widely been used for the codelivery of cytotoxic agents to the tumor site. In this contest, the PEG-PCL-based micelles were also used for combination therapy. In s study by Wang et al., the micelles coloaded with doxorubicin and curcumin exhibited a synergistic anticancer effect in LL/2 lung cancer in vivo. The involved mechanism in cancer mitigation was shown to be due to increased apoptosis as well as inhibition of tumor angiogenesis in vivo [73]. A peer similar PEGylated PCL micelle was developed for the codelivery of doxorubicin and curcumin to the tumoral cells. The double-loaded nanoparticles of 25.3 nm size demonstrated a sustained release behavior and exhibited remarkable progress in cytotoxicity apoptotic effects compared to the micellar form of each drug, primarily attributed to the enhanced cellular uptake by breast cancerous cells. The subcutaneous 4T1 breast tumor model as well as spontaneous pulmonary metastasis were effectively suppressed compared to the same dose of micellar form of each drug alone [74]. A PEGylated PCL-based nanomicelles coloaded with docetaxel and curcumin has also shown higher cytotoxicity on HeLa cells compared to either free drugs, as confirmed by significantly lower IC_{50} value [75].

Triblock copolymers of PEO and PCL cross-linked by tetraphenylethylene (TPE) as a fluorophore were self-assembled into spherical micelles for curcumin and doxorubicin loading. Both drugs showed a release pattern responsive to the acidic conditions with rapid internalization and accumulation of the block copolymer micelles into the cytoplasm and nucleus of HeLa cells. This type of micelle also showed the capability for simultaneous drug delivery to cancer cells and bioimaging [76].

PEGylated curcumin-loaded PCL-based micelles were also used to assess neovascularization inhibition. The curcumin micelles tested on C26 colon carcinoma showed noticeable tumor growth inhibition as well as improved pharmacokinetics of curcumin in vivo. Angiogenesis inhibition was confirmed in both transgenic zebrafish model and alginate-encapsulated cancer cells following intravenous administration of the curcumin micelles. In this method, a suspension of C26 colon carcinoma cells and alginate solution (1.8%) was dropped into a solution of calcium chloride to form alginate beads. The resulting beads with $1-10^5$ tumor cells/bead were subcutaneously implanted into the dorsal side of the mouse, which were used as the tumor model to assess neovascularization [77]. Other PEGylated curcumin-loaded PCL-based micelles (27 nm) have efficiently suppressed the growth of CT26 colon cancer cells in vitro due to the high rate of cellular uptake. In vivo study in mice has also demonstrated a significant antitumoral effect in the same cancer model by inhibiting tumor proliferation and angiogenesis [78].

Pluronic- and PCL-based micelles encapsulating curcumin showed favorable stability with minimal hemolysis as well as prevention of aggregation of blood components (either RBC, WBC, or platelet) that all verified their hemocompatibility. In addition, these micelles showed efficient cytotoxicity and cellular uptake by Caco2 cells. The enhanced cytotoxicity could be attributed to the presence of pluronic as well as higher solubility of curcumin, which renders its better performance as an anticancer agent [79]. Amphiphilic Pluronic F-127 (PF127)-based curcumin micelles induced apoptosis in colon adenocarcinoma, ovarian, and BGC-823 gastric cancerous cells through the downregulation of p-Rb, Blc-2, and p-AKT expression and caspase-9 activation. They also significantly enhanced the tumor cells' apoptosis and reduced VEGF expression in tumor tissues [80]. The gastric tumor cells' growth inhibition and apoptosis induction by amphiphilic PF127 micelles have shown to be through promoting ROS generation and disrupting REDOX (reduction−oxidation) equilibrium [81]. Curcumin-loaded mixed micelles of PF127 and Gelucire 44/14 (as nonionic water-dispersible surfactant) showed 55-folds enhanced oral bioavailability in rats (due to more solubilization of curcumin) and cytotoxicity (3-folds) of curcumin in A549 human lung cancer cells compared to free curcumin [82].

PF127 block copolymers loaded with curcumin demonstrated a high potency in inhibiting cell proliferation as well as the activation of NF-κB signaling, arresting the cell cycle in G0/G1 phase, improving cellular uptake of curcumin, and release of proinflammatory cytokines (e.g., IL-1β, IL-6, and IL-18). Overall, treating cancer cells with curcumin-loaded PF127 block copolymer manifests apoptotic cell death rather than necrotic [83].

Study by Lee et al. investigated the effect of the particle size on the anticancer potential of curcumin micellar nanoparticles. Therefore, polymeric curcumin nanoparticles of various sizes were synthesized using polyvinyl alcohol (PVA) and PF127 as the surfactant. Results indicated higher internalization of curcumin micellar nanoparticles within the size of 28 nm into the cell membrane, cytoplasm, and cell nucleus of the cancer cells. Furthermore, these nanoparticles were well tolerated by healthy osteoblasts even at concentrations as high as 50 μM, which validates the selective uptake of curcumin by the neoplastic cells [84].

Mixed polymeric micelles containing TPGS/F127/P123 showed selective cellular uptake of curcumin into HeLa cells, leading to a higher cytotoxicity and apoptosis as well as a significantly increased cellular sequestration at the G2/M phase of the cell cycle. Furthermore, these nanomicelles facilitated the accumulation of curcumin within the mitochondria indicated by affecting the mitochondrial membrane potential [81,85]. In a study by Riedel et al., the efficacy of paclitaxel- and curcumin-loaded Soluplus: TPGS mixed micelles was compared to Abraxane, an albumin-bound paclitaxel formulation. Results demonstrated the higher cytotoxicity and antioxidant effects of the micelles compared to Abraxane in SKOV-3 cancer cells [43]. Mixed micelles of Poloxamer 407 and TPGS encapsulating curcumin showed improved cellular uptake and cytotoxicity to multidrug-resistant ovarian cancer cells compared to free curcumin [86].

PLA-TPGS micelles were also used for curcumin and paclitaxel coloading for theranostics application. Both in vitro test on MCF-7 cells and MCF-7 spheroid model indicated an improved uptake of the resulting nanoparticles. Furthermore, results demonstrated a more efficient distribution of the nanomicelles through MCF-7 cells compared to paclitaxel, suggesting its superior potential for theranostics applications [87].

Kumari et al. showed that cholesterol conjugation to PEGylated poly (D, L-lactide) (PLA)-based polymeric micelles (169.3 nm) could result in effective nanomicelles for curcumin delivery to the cancer cells. They have shown higher cytotoxicity of the resulting polymeric micelles in MDA-MB-231 murine human breast cancer cells and B16F10 murine melanoma cells compared to free curcumin. The in vivo results also validate the reduction of tumor volume in B16F10-xenografted tumor-bearing mice compared to free curcumin [88].

Considering curcumin's potential in the mitigation of angiogenesis and its prominent role in colon cancer growth and metastasis, the efficacy of curcumin-loaded PEGylated PLA-based nanomicelles on neovascularization inhibition was investigated in the colon cancer model. The resulting nanomicelles of 30 nm in size showed sustained and slow curcumin extravasation from the blood vessels and an inhibitory effect on embryonic angiogenesis in a transgenic zebrafish and alginate-encapsulated tumor cells. As well, these micelles were also effective in suppressing the growth of subcutaneous CT26 mouse tumor models and metastasis to pulmonary tissues [89]. PEGylated PLA-based curcumin-loaded micelles with strong cytotoxicity in B16 and A375 melanoma cancer cells further restrained neovascularization in melanoma tumor tissues [90].

Polymeric micelles formed by PEG and PLA were also used for coloading curcumin and gemcitabine. The codelivery of curcumin (20 mg/kg) and gemcitabine (10 mg/kg) to the HCT-116 xenograft tumor model by using the nanomicellar system showed a significantly higher synergetic effect in terms of higher tumor growth inhibition compared to the free combination of either drugs. As well, the release of both drugs was tumor-specific as they both were released at the acidic pH of the tumor at a higher rate than neutral physiological pH [91]. Recently, PEG-PLA-based nanomicelles of 37.63 nm size were fabricated that contained curcumin and docetaxel. The resulting nanomicellar system exhibited stronger inhibition and proapoptotic effects on A2780 ovarian cancerous cells as well as inhibiting tumor proliferation and angiogenesis compared to free drugs [92].

Using biocompatible and biodegradable polymers, poly (L-lactic acid) (PLA)-based poly (anhydride-ester)-b-PEG was applied to form micellar curcumin with the aim of increasing curcumin bioavailability. The resulting micelles showed a faster rate and higher amounts of curcumin release at the acidic pH. Results also indicated higher antiangiogenesis effects on EMT6-bearing mice breast tumor model compared to free curcumin [93].

Encapsulation of curcumin in diblock copolymeric micelles of oleoyl chloride and mPEG 2000 was also performed. The resulting polymeric micelles showed an enhanced expression of Bax proapoptotic protein and decreased antiapoptotic Bcl-2 protein expression along with proliferative and angiogenic parameters in hepatocellular carcinoma and breast cancer models [94].

Alginate-based calcium cross-linked spherical micelles of curcumin were prepared, which showed a prolonged and well-controlled release pattern. The nanomicelles presented no toxicity to the peripheral blood mononuclear cells isolated from the peripheral blood of healthy donors and to the mouse primary brain endothelial cells. On the other hand, this type of micellar nanoparticles showed higher uptake efficiency in models of breast and colon cancers resulted in decreased cell viability [95].

Amphiphilic polymers based on poly(2-oxazoline) (POx) and poly(2-oxazine) (POzi) were applied to form micelles encapsulating curcumin. This formulation prevented SW480 colorectal cancer cells from adhering to the collagen scaffold, due to the antimetastatic potential of the curcumin encapsulated in the polymeric micelles. In addition, as the 3D spheroid of MDA-MB-231 triple-negative breast cancer cells requires higher concentrations of curcumin for tumor penetration and eradication, this nanomicelle could efficiently eradicate and mitigate breast tumor progression [96].

Nanogels are physically cross-linked networks with the size range of a few hundred nanometers. One of their distinctive features is their capability to swell in the aqueous media following water absorption. Nanogels have been largely used regarding their potential is responding to various stimuli as well as escaping the immune responses. One of the most compatible materials for nanogel formation is polysaccharides [97]. Setayesh et al. developed a self-assembled chondroitin-based micellar nanogel for curcumin delivery to the breast cancer cells. They used octadecylamine, which was grafted to chondroitin sulfate to form micellar nanogel capable of loading curcumin. The nanomicellar gel showed above 80% curcumin release after 70 hours. The blank nanogels showed cytocompatibility, while curcumin-loaded nanogels induced significant MCF-7 cell death after 24 hours and significantly increased the number of cells in the sub-G1 phase. The higher internalization rates of these nanomicelles were occurred through chondroitin sulfate affinity to CD44 receptors, which can support curcumin internalization [98].

In another study, a PF127-based thermogel of curcumin with micellar construction was developed as a prolonged and controlled curcumin depot for in vitro investigation and in vivo safety profile evaluation. In vitro growth inhibition study supported the cytocompatibility of bare thermogel against L929 cells. Further cellular cytotoxicity study indicated the pharmacological activity of the curcumin-loaded gel formulations against HeLa and MCF-7 cancer cells compared to free drug solution. The maximum swelling of the gel and the highest drug release were observed at pH 7.4 and 25°C owing to the relaxed gel state. Additional in vivo evaluation concerning histopathological and hematological analysis confirmed the biocompatibility of the thermogel in animal model [99].

siRNA and curcumin-loaded chitosan-cholesterol-conjugate micelles with 165 nm in size were able to efficiently condense the related siRNA due to the cationic feature of chitosan and its transfection capability. The internalization of such micelles in A549 cells occurred via clathrin-mediated endocytosis as determined by an endocytosis inhibitor agent (chlorpromazine hydrochloride) [100]. A schematic for this micelle preparation is shown in Fig. 9.2.

Stearic acid-grafted-chitosan oligosaccharide micelles loaded with curcumin showed efficient internalization by the primary colorectal cancer cells and a potent antiproliferative effect (sixfold enhanced inhibition) in vitro compared to free curcumin. Intravenous administration of these micelles marginally suppressed tumor growth without significant cytotoxicity. In addition, these micelles were effective in inhibiting $CD44^+/CD24^+$ cells' subpopulations, as markers for colorectal cancer stem cells, both in vitro and in vivo [101]. In another study, curcumin-loaded cholesterol-conjugated chitosan micelles were prepared through self-assembling and the evaluation of antitumor efficacy and antiproliferative potential was performed in the A549 3D lung cancer spheroid model. Curcumin-loaded cholesterol-conjugated chitosan micelles resulted in significantly enhanced tumor growth inhibition compared to free curcumin [102].

In a recent study, carbohydrate-based block copolymers constituted of a hydrophilic maltoheptaose block conjugated to polyisoprene were used to develop curcumin polymeric micelle. Maltoheptaose is a water-soluble and linear α-(1, 4) glucan of seven glucosyl units generated from β-cyclodextrin ring-opening; and polyisoprene is a polymer derived from isoprene found in essential oils and pheromones. This amphiphilic type of curcumin nanomicelle was effective in reducing PC-3 cell growth by reducing the viability by less than 10% at 10 μg/mL [103].

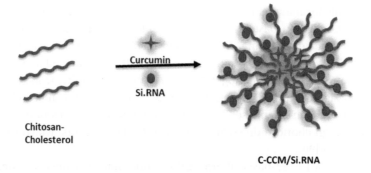

FIGURE 9.2 Synthesis of chitosan-cholesterol-conjugate containing siRNA. *Reproduced with permission from Muddineti, O.S., et al., Cholesterol-grafted chitosan micelles as a nanocarrier system for drug-siRNA co-delivery to the lung cancer cells. International Journal of Biological Macromolecules, 2018. 118: p. 857–863. License code: 5374630703576.*

PEG oleate as diblock copolymer was self-assembled to form either micelles or polymersomes loaded with curcumin (below 150 nm). Results indicated a higher efficacy of micelles compared to polymersomes in mitigating glioma cell growth [104]. The R7L10 amphiphilic peptide possessing positive charge has been used as a carrier for gene or drug delivery. The micelle formed from this peptide was loaded with curcumin and HSVtk gene. It was demonstrated that the carrier could efficiently deliver the gene to the glioblastoma animal model with the consequence of reducing the tumor size more [105].

A hydrophilic ethylene oxide-propylene oxide named Tetronic 1307 (a star-shaped block copolymer) formed curcumin and quercetin-loaded micelles by self-assembly. The nanomicellar structure, tuned with glucose incorporation to facilitate micelle formation and enhance the solubility of the loaded cargo, rendered controlled drug release with reduced toxicity in CHO-K1 ovarian cancerous cells [106].

Polymeric micelles composed of block copolymers of mPEG and N-(2-hydroxypropyl) methacrylamide (HPMA) modified with benzoyl (aromatic group) side groups were synthesized in which curcumin loading was enhanced due to the $\pi-\pi$ stacking interactions between aromatic groups of curcumin and benzoyl group of the polymer. The resulting polymer showed high retention of curcumin, favorable solubility, and controlled release of curcumin. The inhibitory bioactivity of curcumin was also higher with this construction against colon, ovarian, and leukemic cells compared to free curcumin [107].

To optimize curcumin pharmacokinetics, PEGylated HPMA-based curcumin-loaded nanomicelles were prepared. While being cytotoxic in vitro, these curcumin micelles did not inhibit tumor growth in vivo in human neuroblastoma-bearing mice model [108].

9.3.2 Targeted micelles

Active targeting involves the use of varying targeting moieties in nanomedicine to upgrade chemo- and molecular therapy of cancer by preferentially delivering the therapeutic agent to the site of action. Numerous actively targeted delivery systems have been spotted in the last decades including ligand-modified nanomedicine as well as substantial drug conjugates with monoclonal antibodies, antibody fragments, peptides, aptamers, and small molecules. To this end, long-circulating nanoparticles could effectively accumulate to the tumor site through the EPR effect, and the internalization of the nanocarriers or its attachment to vascular endothelial cells lead to increased therapeutic effect [109]. In the following section, we will summarize some studies reporting the potential of curcumin polymeric-based nanoparticulate systems in targeting various portions of the tumor using specific targeting moieties to evade the problems of limited therapeutic efficiency.

For pancreatic cancer, which may be highly resistant to chemotherapy and even nanoparticle-mediated therapies, targeted therapy could be a promising strategy [110]. Pancreatic cancers mainly overexpress CD44 receptors on their surface, which is one of the major involved receptors in MDR. In addition, cancer stem-like cells are one of the main contributing factors in acquiring multidrug-resistant phenotype. In this regard, hyaluronic acid (HA) conjugate of copoly (styrene maleic acid) formed micelles loaded with 3,4-

difluorobenzylidene curcumin; a curcumin derivative with potent anticancer activity and extended circulation half-life. This type of micelle showed dose-dependent toxicity against MiaPaCa-2 and AsPC-1 human pancreatic cancer cells and a higher internalization by triple-positive CD44$^+$/CD133$^+$/EpCAM$^+$ pancreatic cancer stem-like cells with a more pronounced activity in MiaPaCa-2 cells. In addition, a significant reduction in CD44 expression and marked inhibition of NF-κB by this curcumin-based agent could explain the significant anti-proliferative behavior [111]. The amphiphilic nature of the polymeric agent improved aqueous solubility, stability, hemocompatibility, and sustained release features of this curcumin derivative. The pharmacokinetic parameters indicated a 10-fold higher accumulation in the pancreas tissue compared to free curcumin. However, the functionalized micelles were highly more efficient in terms of targeting and eradicating pancreatic cancers due to affecting CSCs [112].

Alendronate-hyaluronic acid-octadecanoic acid (ALN-HA-C18) as a material with amphiphilic nature was also self-assembled to form the curcumin-encapsulating micelles. The resulting micelles of 118 nm size have shown the ability to deliver a substantial quantity of curcumin into the MG-63 cells compared to micelles devoid of HA. Further study has revealed great osteosarcoma tissue targeting due to the high affinity of micellar nanoparticles to the bone, leading to improvement of in vivo antitumor activity in osteosarcoma model. Thanks to the presence of HA in this micellar structure, excellent in vivo performance was attributed to the CD44 receptor targeting on osteocytes' membrane [113]. In a recent study, Kamble et al. conjugated alendronate bisphosphonate to PF127 micelles to specifically deliver curcumin to the osteolytic tumor microenvironment (TME) in the bone. This nanomicelle of 27 nm in size with positive surface charge (+2.87 mV) demonstrated rapid binding to hydroxyapatite surface of the bone, which is a promising potential for targeting bone malignancies [114].

In another study, a different approach was used for developing HA-decorated mixed nanomicelles loaded with curcumin. For this, the thin-film hydration method was first used to encapsulate curcumin within the hydrophobic core of PF127/didecyldimethylammonium bromide (PD)-mixed nanomicelles. In the next step, the positively charged surface of PD was modified by negatively charged HA through electrostatic interactions. The entrapment efficiency of curcumin within targeted nanomicelles was 95.1%. Interestingly, the average hydrodynamic size of the nanomicelles increased following HA coating (size change from 19.8 to 35.8 nm). In vitro test indicated the enhanced cytotoxicity of curcumin through HA-coated PD-mixed nanomicelles against MDA-MB-231 cancer cells compared to the nontargeted peers [115].

Various monosaccharide and disaccharide residues were also used to modify nanoparticle surface to target the encapsulated cargos to the solid tumors overexpressing glucose transporters [116]. In this framework, curcumin-loaded pristine and glucosylated polymeric micelles of poly (ethylene oxide)-poly (propylene oxide) were investigated for breast cancer targeting in vitro and in vivo. Results indicated a high potency of glucosylated polymeric micelles in terms of interaction with 4T1 breast cancer cells with enhanced aqueous solubility of curcumin to more than 50,000-fold. In addition, the glycosylation enhanced the curcumin nanomicelle internalization in these cells [117].

Folate receptors, cell-surface glycoproteins, are highly expressed in numerous cancers including breast, liver, uterus, testis, brain, colon, and lung to provide the required folate for rapidly proliferating cancer cells. The discovery of folate receptor−mediated endocytosis has opened the doors to folate-based candidates for the enhanced transfer of the therapeutic cargos to the tumors with higher expression of folate receptors. This distinct feature of the cancer cells has been extensively exploited for therapeutic and diagnostic approaches through targeting the folate receptors by various antifolate antibodies and folate-modified imaging and therapeutic nanoparticulate agents [118]. With this aim, to enhance the delivery of curcumin to the cancer cells, folate-modified PEGylated PLA-based nanomicelles of curcumin with 70 nm size were prepared. Results indicated an enhanced cytotoxicity and cellular uptake of the nanomicelles by MCF-7 and HepG2 folate receptor−positive tumor cells through folate-mediated targeting. The pharmacokinetic evaluations in rats indicated a threefold increase in the half-life, significant elongated retention time for curcumin, and a significantly higher bioavailability of curcumin following administration of this formulation compared to free curcumin [119].

A Y-shaped biotinylated folic acid−modified PEGylated PCL copolymer was fabricated to improve the therapeutic potential of curcumin. Folic acid−modified nanomicelles significantly promoted curcumin cellular uptake in HeLa and HepG2 cells compared to unmodified micelles. Furthermore, the bioactivity of the modified micelles was also improved against HeLa and HepG2 cells. The bioactivity in general was greater in HeLa cells as compared to HepG2 cells [120]. PEGylated PCL-based micelles of curcumin functionalized with folate were also used for active targeting of CT26 cells. Results indicated that the curcumin micelles inhibited CT26 cells' proliferation and angiogenesis. Moreover, a significant tumor inhibition following nanomicelles administration to colon cancer−bearing mice was observed, which was attributed to the improved bioavailability of curcumin following encapsulation within micelles [121].

Folate-conjugated poly (2-methacryloyl-oxyethyl phosphorylcholine)-PCL micelles inhibited cancer cells' proliferation through photodynamic therapy (PDT) under the state of irradiation in HeLa cells (with folate receptor overexpression) compared to HT-29 cells (lack of overexpressed folate receptor). The selective internalization of these micelles was through the receptor-mediated endocytosis pathway. They also presented about 20% higher curcumin release in acidic conditions compared to the neutral pH [122].

PEGylated PLA-based curcumin micelles functionalized with folate were synthesized, which showed an increment of curcumin solubility in aqueous medium. As the content of PLA increased in these micelles, the loading efficiency of curcumin was enhanced and the micelles grew in size. In addition, to their targeting capability, the folate-targeted micelles released curcumin more slowly compared to untargeted peers. This targeting moiety also led to a significant reduction of IC_{50} value compared to free curcumin toward HepG2 human liver hepatocellular cells [123]. Folate-decorated PEGylated PLA-based micelles of curcumin further suppressed the growth of GL261 glioma cells and promoted apoptosis. As well, tumor growth in subcutaneous and intracranial tumor models was repressed through angiogenesis and neovascularization suppression and facilitation of apoptosis in mice tumor models of glioma [124].

A block copolymer with styrene malic acid was loaded with a potent difluorinated curcumin analog and functionalized with folic acid as targeting agent. Results showed promising potential in cervical and ovarian cancer treatments in terms of increasing the number of apoptotic and necrotic cells and PTEN (phosphatase and TENsin homolog deleted on chromosome 10) tumor suppressor gene upregulation to dominate drug resistance and suppress cancer recurrence after initial treatment [125].

Anirudhan et al. have used a dual-targeting polymeric-based nanomicelles for paclitaxel and curcumin codelivery to breast cancer cells. To this aim, an HA-coated Pluronic (123/127)-mixed micelle functionalized with folic acid was developed and its anticancer activity was evaluated in MCF-7 cells. Dually targeted (CD44 and folic acid receptors) nanomicelles showed a high rate of internalization and superior anticancer effects on MCF-7 cells compared to free drug [126]. Other folate-targeted nanomicelles were synthesized by using biocompatible block copolymer of PEG and polycaprolactone using ring-opening reaction. The copolymer was then conjugated to folic acid by using a lysine linker and curcumin loading was done through nanoprecipitation method. The anticancer efficiency and biocompatibility of the nanomicelles were well proved in vitro. Animal study highlighted the potential of folic acid conjugation in improving the therapeutic efficacy of curcumin nanomicell [127].

Transferrin-conjugated PEGylated poly (D,L-Lactide) polymeric micelles loaded with curcumin (132 nm) were efficiently internalized by cervical and hepatic cancerous cells due to their high overexpression of transferrin receptors. The internalization of the micelles through clathrin-mediated endocytic pathway led to an improved growth inhibition in vitro [128]. PEGylated PLA-based curcumin-loaded micelles were also functionalized with RGD (αv3 integrin-targeted peptide). Being 20 nm in size, the resulting nanomicelles rendered sustained release and high efficiency in targeting B16 melanoma cells in mice, leading to tumor cell growth inhibition [129]. A lipo-peptide containing KKGRGDS peptide sequence as the hydrophilic heads and lauric acid as the hydrophobic tails was self-assembled into nanomicelles (30 nm) for curcumin loading. These nanomicelles were highly toxic when tested against HeLa and HepG2 cells. One explanation is that the resulting micelles could resort to the tumor-targeting functionality of RGD (Arg-Gly-Asp) section of the peptide sequence to deliver curcumin into HeLa cells due to the overexpression of integrins on these cancer cells [130].

In a recent study by Dezfouli et al., Y-shaped biotin-PEG-PCL copolymers were synthesized by a single-step nanoprecipitation method to develop a series of curcumin-loaded micelles. The resulting curcumin-loaded biotin-PEG-PCL with about 94% encapsulation efficiency showed a slower rate for curcumin release compared to nonbiotinated micelles (mPEG-PCLs). The higher uptake by MDA-MB-436 cells was also induced due to the presence of biotin. Curcumin-loaded biotin-PEG-PCL-induced apoptosis represented by the increased sub-G1 cellular population. Furthermore, the ovo chick chorioallantoic membrane (CAM) assay indicated that curcumin-bearing biotin-PEG-PCL micelles could significantly decrease both angiogenesis and proliferation of the tumor cells [120].

Octreotide-functionalized micelles of curcumin and docetaxel were used with the aim of inhibiting tumor metastasis. For this, octreotide conjugated to DSPE-mPEG and Soluplus as the surfactant formed micelles containing docetaxel and curcumin. The resulting micelles with robust cytotoxicity on A549 cells effectively inhibited vasculogenic mimicry channels. Furthermore, results indicated tumor metastasis inhibition as well as downregulated matrix metalloproteinases 2 (MMP-2) and hypoxia-inducible factor 1-alpha (HIF-1α) in the TME in A549 xenograft tumor model of nonsmall cell lung cancer [131].

In 2019, an amphiphilic polymer containing glycol chitosan (GC) and dequalinium (DQA) was fabricated by Michael addition reaction using a methyl acrylate linker. GC and DQA micelles encapsulating curcumin were prepared with the aim of targeting mitochondria. DQA lipophilic cation selective accumulation within the mitochondria could control mitochondria membrane potential. The resulted nanomicelle facilitated cellular internalization and endosomal escape without showing any significant toxicity on HeLa cells [132]. Curcumin-encapsulating chitosan-based micelles of 100 nm size showed a significant toxicity following exposure to different cervix cancerous cells compared to free curcumin [133].

9.3.3 Stimuli-responsive micelles

Stimuli-responsive micelles include a family of smart micelles, which show characteristic alterations when subjected to specific environmental conditions [51]. Stimuli-responsive nanocarriers have enticed a lot of attention in the past decades and opened a new era in cancer nanomedicine since the novel nanoparticulate materials enable a remotely controlled activation at the targeted site. The selective activation approach occurs through the exploitation of endogenous triggers including distinctive features of the TME like lowered pH, higher enzyme expression, REDOX potential, as well as remote stimuli including hyperthermia, alternating magnetic field (AMF), near-infrared (NIR), or ultrasound radiations that can trigger drugs release in a controlled manner. The key feature of the stimuli-responsive material is the structural and chemical rearrangements particularly in response to various endogenous and exogenous stimuli [134]. Numerous responsive polymeric micelles have been developed that presented controllable drug release profiles to yield the right drug concentration to the site of cancer. In the following section, we will summarize the smart polymeric nanostructures used for curcumin delivery to the cancer site.

9.3.3.1 pH sensitive

The different pathophysiological feature of the normal versus tumor tissues has been exploited for targeting smart drug delivery vehicles to the TME. Higher rate of metabolism within the tumor tissue could result in a more acidic pH compared to the normal tissues. Therefore, nanoscaled carriers with pH sensitivity are regarded as promising candidates in the context of cancer chemotherapy.

In a study by Yu et al., a size/charge switchable polymeric micelle of curcumin was developed based on amphiphilic poly (β-amino ester) derivatives. This nanomicellar structure based on amphiphilic and pH-sensitive methoxy poly (ethylene glycol)-poly (lactide)-poly (β-amino ester) (mPEG-PLA-PAE) copolymers showed an average size of 171 nm. In vitro studies indicated that mPEG-PLA-PAE micelles remain stable in murine plasma at 37°C. However, when exposed to acidic pH, micelles shrinkage led to size switching from 171.0 to 22.6 nm concomitant with surface charge increment to 24.8 mV, which resulted in a noticeable curcumin cellular uptake and cytoplasmic distribution by MCF-7 human breast cancer cells. Expectedly, enhanced chemotherapeutic efficacy of curcumin in MCF-7 tumor-bearing mice was also confirmed as reported by cancer growth inhibition of 65.6% in vivo [135]. Fig. 9.3 demonstrates the schematic mechanism of nanomicelles alteration in response to the mildly acidic TME.

A covalent conjugate of curcumin to Pluronic F68 block was synthesized via an acid-labile cis-aconitic anhydride linkage to develop an acid-responsive micellar delivery system. Results indicated negligible curcumin leakage at physiologic pH (7.4), while rapid intracellular drug release occurred within the tumor cells (pH ≤ 6.5) following the bond cleavage. Furthermore, the cytotoxicity and apoptosis against A2780 human ovarian carcinoma and SMMC 7721 hepatocellular carcinoma were improved compared to free curcumin [136]. PEGyated PCL-poly (diethylaminoethyl methacrylate) curcumin-loaded micelles have also shown to be highly pH-sensitive, releasing higher amounts of curcumin at pH 5 compared to pH 7.4 [137].

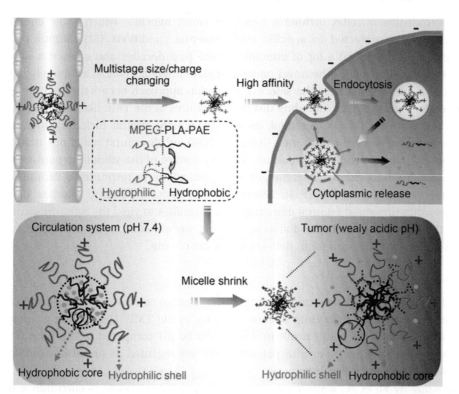

FIGURE 9.3 A schematic for the size and charge conversion of PEGylated-PLA-PAE micelles in response to the mildly acidic tumor extracellular matrix. *Reproduced with permission from Yu, Y., X. Zhang, and L. Qiu, The anti-tumor efficacy of curcumin when delivered by size/charge-changing multistage polymeric micelles based on amphiphilic poly (β-amino ester) derivates. Biomaterials, 2014. 35(10): p. 3467–3479. License code: 5365260110777.*

A large body of studies have highlighted the pivotal role of CSCs in replenishing tumor cells, inducing relapse and metastasis. Combination therapy using nanocarriers is considered a promising approach for the simultaneous removal of both CSCs and non-CSCs. In this regard, a stimuli-responsive nanomicellar system of curcumin was prepared for targeting breast cancer stem cells. The pH-sensitive PEGylated-benzoic imine-poly(γ-benzyl-L-aspartate)-b-poly(1-vinylimidazole) block copolymer-forming micelles were used for paclitaxel and curcumin codelivery. pH-responsive nanomicellar carrier was designed to stimulate intelligent switching of the surface charge from neutral to positive, de-shielding the PEG layer and inducing size reduction following extravasation. Extravasation of long-circulating nanomicelles from the leaky blood vessels was followed with deep penetration to the tumor and facilitated cellular uptake. Furthermore, combinational therapy resulted in superior tumor inhibitory effects and efficient CSCs targeting in vivo [138]. Folic acid-oligosaccharides of hyaluronan-acetal-menthone 1,2-glycerol ketal could form micellar nanoparticles for encapsulating curcumin with dual-targeting purpose (CD44 and folic acid receptors). The nanoparticle of 166.3 nm in size demonstrated favorable cellular uptake and higher release of curcumin in slightly acidic pH as well as a higher rate of tumor alleviation in MCF-7 and A549 cells [139].

One of the hurdles of conventional micelles is low drug loading efficiency, which reduces the expected therapeutic potential. Liu et al. used pH-responsive reversibly cross-linked micelles composed of PEGylated poly(2-methacrylate ethyl 5-hexynoicate) with the aim of improving curcumin loading and release profile. The curcumin micelles cross-linking with a phenol—yne click chemical click reaction improved drug loading (17.81%, wt%). The resulting switchable size cross-linked micelles turned into smaller nanomicelles following exposure to the acidic pH 5.0. Results indicated a significant toxicity of nanomicelles toward HeLa and 4T1 cells and effective internalization by the tumor cells in vivo, due to the prolonged circulation time [140]. Another curcumin micellar construction in this regard was developed by using amphiphilic poly(ethylene glycol)-block-poly(ethoxyethyl glycidyl ether) (PEG-b-PEEGE) block copolymers with acid-sensitive acetal groups that showed toxic effects on MDA-MB-231 human breast cancer cells [141]. A pH-sensitive micelle composed of glycidyl azide polymer loaded with curcumin exhibited a high level of hemocompatibility and an excellent cytotoxicity on 4T1 cancerous cells [142].

Curcumin conjugation has also been utilized as a strategy in developing targeted pH-sensitive polymeric nanocarriers for cancer therapy. Lai et al. used an acid-labile hydrazone bond for curcumin conjugation to HA to generate amphiphilic conjugates with the potential of self-assembly and nanomicellar structure formation. The drug release experiments indicate a pH-responsive release behavior and efficient internalization by 4T1 and MCF-7 cancer cells through CD44 receptor—mediated endocytosis. Animal study also demonstrated a superior tumor growth inhibitory effect attributed to selective accumulation within the tumor as well as CD44-mediated endocytosis [143]. Curcumin and paclitaxel were loaded into oligosaccharides of hyaluronan micelles (120.6 nm) via self-assembly for targeting CD44 receptor on MDA-MB-231 breast cancer cells. As already mentioned, HA is the functional material for efficiently targeting CD44 on the surface of cancer cells. These micelles were mineralized through the controlled deposition of inorganic calcium and phosphate ions on the shell and were stable at neutral pH. At pH 6.5, the inorganic minerals at the outer shell were destroyed and curcumin and paclitaxel were released in a sustained manner with high antitumor efficacy in vitro and in vivo in the MDA-MB-231-inoculated mice model [144]. Star-shaped nanomicelles coloaded with doxorubicin and curcumin (220−280 nm) showed a high rate of cytotoxicity on HeLa human cervical cancer, 786-O human renal adenocarcinoma, and HepG2 liver cancerous cells by targeting CD44 through the presence of HA. The resulting nanomicelles reduced in vivo toxicity by inhibiting drug release in systemic circulation and inducing a mass release at the weak acid environment of the tumor site [145]. Zeng et al. designed another type of pH-sensitive micelles on the basis of HA-conjugated curcumin (by pH-sensitive ester bond) and TPGS, for the delivery of dasatinib, a kinase inhibitor blocking multiplication of cancerous cells through signaling inhibition. The micelles of 66.14 nm in size were significantly cytotoxic to HepG2 cells by targeting CD44 receptors on these cells. The pH responsiveness was due to the disintegration of the mentioned ester bond at acidic tumor environment. The in vivo results indicated an efficient accumulation of these micelles at the tumor site with further significant inhibition of tumor growth in a mouse solid hepatic tumor model with the demonstration of synergistic effect of both drugs in the tumor inhibition [146].

In 2019, a triple-targeted pH-sensitive nanoactiniaes was developed for multitargeted breast cancer combinational therapy. The pH-sensitive HA-based micelles with 162.7 nm size were functionalized with folic acid and biotin for delivering curcumin and icariin (flavonol glycoside). Results indicated an efficiently boosted MCF-7 cancer cell apoptosis and cancer cell invasion inhibition in vitro, as well as an inhibitory effect on the tumors in animal model [147].

Wnt/β-catenin signaling pathway is mutated in 90% of colorectal cancers, thus its activation is essential for cancer modulation. Furthermore, since β-catenin is located in the cytoplasm and nucleus, its intracellular level is directly correlated with cell proliferation, apoptosis, and differentiation process. Polyaspartamide-based micelles consist of hydrophobic octadecylamine (C18) and hydrophilic O-(2-aminoethyl) PEG were grafted on a polysuccinimide backbone for targeting Wnt/β-catenin signaling pathway. The fabricated micelle was functionalized with folic acid on its surface, with curcumin conjugation through acid-cleavable hydrazone linkage to trigger curcumin release in a pH-sensitive manner. SW480 cells' treatment by these micelles terminated to a lower cell viability compared to nontargeted peers. These curcumin nanomicelles inhibited cyclin D1, c-myc, and Wnt/β-catenin signaling pathways in vitro in SW480 colon cancer cells [148].

The F68-acetal-PCL copolymers used for the fabrication of curcumin micelles were further functionalized with glycyrrhetinic acid. This type of micelle showed pH sensitivity due to the presence of acetal linkage as well as efficient targeting of glycyrrhetinic acid receptors on the surface of SMMC7721, HepG2, and Hepal−6 liver cancerous cells. The cytotoxicity was exerted through micelle internalization via receptor-mediated endocytosis and subsequent induced apoptosis [149].

Some studies used several pH-sensitive bonds to further improve the delivery of curcumin to the tumor cells. For example, poly(2-ethyl-2-oxazoline)-PLA-based micelles with pH-cleavable acetal and benzoic imine bonds successfully generated mixed micelles of curcumin and doxorubicin with controlled release properties. Results demonstrated a synergistically enhanced inhibition of MDA-MB-231 cell growth and metastasis in in vivo models as well as in vitro wound healing and antimigration effects. Furthermore, codelivery using the pH-labile micellar structure significantly reduced doxorubicin side effects [150].

In tumoral cell, the mitochondria are regarded as a promising subcellular organelle since cancer cell mitochondria show greater susceptibility compared with normal cells. Therefore, several therapeutic cargos capable of ROS generation could be delivered to the mitochondria of the cancer cells, leading to mitochondrial permeability modification, which significantly affect this indispensable energy supply [151]. Some studies used the potential of curcumin for mitochondrial cancer cell targeting. For example, Babikova et al. synthesized a triblock copolymer by attaching a saccharide end-functionalized PEG block through an acid-cleavable functional group to a polycationic block, with mitochondria targeting capabilities. The resulting multifunctional nanomicelles of 46 nm size showed a great potential for triggering programmed cell death and exerted a pronounced NF-κB inhibitory effect on HL-60 cells and its drug-resistant variants as compared to nonfunctionalized nanomicelles [152]. A schematic for such a micelle is presented in Fig. 9.4.

A hybrid shell/core polysaccharide-based nanoparticle-loaded curcumin was also developed, which possessed prolonged systemic circulation, mitochondrial targeting potential, and tumor-microenvironment responsiveness. In the fabrication process, a negatively charged HA derivative bearing carboxyphenylboronic acid pH-responsive bond was added to the core surface to cover the positive charges, thereby elongating blood circulation. Thanks to the presence of HA derivative, these nanomicelles were endocytosed through specific

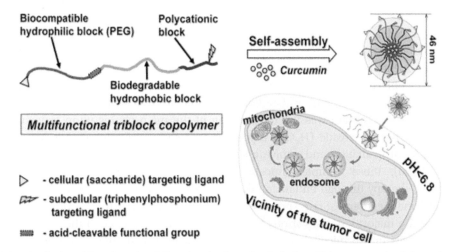

FIGURE 9.4 Synthesis and function of multifunctional polymeric micelle for efficient targeted cellular and subcellular anticancer drug delivery. *Reproduced with permission from Babikova, D., et al., Multifunctional polymer nanocarrier for efficient targeted cellular and subcellular anticancer drug delivery. ACS Biomaterials Science & Engineering, 2019. 5(5): p. 2271–2283. Copyright © 2019, American Chemical Society.*

binding to sialic acid epitope and CD44 receptors overexpressed on the tumor cells. The borate ester acid-sensitive bonds degradation led to the exposure of the cationic micelles and charge reversal from -19.47 to $+12.01$ mV, to enhance cell entry and localization within the mitochondria. This nanomicelle also showed effective tumor suppression with preferential accumulation in the pancreatic tumor model [73,153].

9.3.3.2 Reactive oxygen species/Glutathione responsive micelles

Other novel strategies in designing smart nanoscale drug delivery systems (NDDSs) responsive to the TME are based on the levels of ROS and glutathione (GSH) that have been extensively used to improve tumor targeting. Growing evidence suggests that cancer cells as well as other cells within the TME including immune cells, cancer-associated fibroblasts, and endothelial cells are a major source of ROS generation. On the other hand, substantial levels of GSH antioxidant inside the tumor cells contribute to the highly reducing environment maintaining cellular survival. The escalated ROS generation by the cancer cells as well as the reducing environment within the tumor cells serves as unique endogenous stimulants that allow for developing REDOX-responsive nanocarriers with the potential of releasing payload next to the tumor cells [154]. The ROS-responsive micelles usually composed of thioether and selenide linkers in their construction could release their payloads in the targeted tumor cells.

In this regard, an oxidation-responsive polymeric micelle of PEGylated PLG was developed for curcumin loading which was attached to two-photon aggregation-induced emission fluorogen with selenium. The nanomicelles of core-shell structure with 136 nm size demonstrated great stability in the physiological environment. On the other hand, the mild oxidative environment of the tumor caused Se oxidation to selenoxide, leading to the destruction of micellar structure and accelerated drug release. This type of nanomicelle induced apoptosis in 4T1 cancer cells and inhibited breast tumor angiogenesis and proliferation. Furthermore, the favorable aggregation-induced emission property enhanced the two-photon imaging of the cells and deeper tumor tissues [155].

Through a polycondensation reaction between curcumin, PEG chains, and oxalyl chloride, a scaffold of curcumin and oxalate linkage copolymer was synthesized. The key feature in the design of this system was the degradation of the main chains upon exposure to the exogenous hydrogen peroxide (H_2O_2), triggering complete curcumin release. Moreover, by camptothecin encapsulation and applying a near-infrared photothermal conversion reagent (namely, IR780), these complex micelles exhibited efficiency for synergistic chemo-photothermal therapy through enhancing the cytotoxicity against HeLa cells [156].

As mentioned earlier, GSH-responsive micelles are sensitive to the presence of GSH abundant in the majority of the various tumor niche. In the presence of this reducing agent, disulfide linkages in the micelle's construction are cleaved, resulting in the disassembly of the micelles construction and contents release [157]. Chen et al. used a novel strategy for developing a curcumin-loaded core cross-linked polymeric micelles by lipoic acids grafting. The micelles were functionalized within the core by disulfide linkage responding to GSH-rich environment of the tumor cells. The cross-linked PEGylated PLA-based micelle of curcumin (mPEG-PLA-(LA)4) showed a great stability under nonreductive conditions, while induced GSH-responsive cytotoxicity to MCF-7 cells [158].

Impressive expression of PD-L1 has shown to induce host immune attack evasion of the colon cancerous cells. Thus, targeting PD-L1 could restore immune function by activating cell-mediated immune responses against this type of cancer cells. Recently, a new type of curcumin polymeric micelles composed of PEGylated telodendrimer of PLA-(LA)$_4$ with 24.6 nm size was developed. This nanomicellar system capable of forming reversible disulfide cross-linked structure, exhibited superior blood stability as well as GSH-responsive release at the TME. Intravenous administration efficiently enhanced curcumin systemic bioavailability (e.g., 8.48-fold longer half-life, 7.55-fold larger AUC (area under the curve), and 94.22-fold longer mean residence time in the blood of mice). The antitumor efficacy was synergistically improved following curcumin micelles and anti-PD-1 antibody concomitant administration in MC-38 colon cancer—bearing xenograft mice. In addition, antiproliferative features of curcumin component led to downregulation of p-MEK1/2 and p-ERK1/2 expression [159].

In other study, a cystine-bridged peptide was coassembled with curcumin to form a GSH-responsive micellar structure. In the fabricated system, the hydrophilic peptide moiety enhanced curcumin water solubility, while the disulfide bond in cystine rendered curcumin release following cleavage by the GSH within the TMEs. This nanomicellal system demonstrated a higher cellular uptake and cytotoxicity toward HeLa cells accompanied by high cellular apoptosis [160].

Very recently, an amphiphilic polymeric micelle containing hydrophilic angelica polysaccharide (liver targeting agent) linked by azobenzene to ferrocene (organometallic compound with two cyclopentadienyl rings bound to a central iron atom), with arachidonic acid—modified side chain, was synthesized by Liu et al. The arachidonic acid and ferrocene moieties were used for selective enhancement of ferroptosis (an iron-dependent programmed cell death) in solid tumor, through diminishing GSH under hypoxia conditions of the TME. Furthermore, rupture of azobenzene bond contributed to curcumin release at the site of tumor. These features were terminated to the specific liver tumor cell targeting of curcumin in vitro with high efficiency in terms of inducing a higher toxicity compared to free curcumin [161]. A schematic for such micelle construction and activity is shown in Fig. 9.5.

GSH-sensitive micelles consisting of poly (allylamine hydrochloride) (PAH) (a highly cytotoxic agent) and poly (lactic-co-glycolic acid) (PLGA) conjugated through disulfide bonds were synthesized. The nanomicelles were applied for the codelivery of alpha-tocopheryl succinate (TOS) as well as curcumin. Curcumin incorporation within the core region of the micellar structure improved its bioavailability. The disulfide bond cleavage following exposure to GSH (5 mM) led to a higher rate of both curcumin and TOS release. The formulation extensively uptake with a high cytotoxicity on PAN02 pancreatic cancer cells, rendered an efficient synergetic therapy of curcumin for treating pancreatic cancer [162].

A core cross-linked micelle composed of polyethylene glycol and folic acid-polyethylene glycol as the hydrophilic moiety, pyridyl disulfide as the cross-linkable hydrophobic moiety, and disulfide bond as the cross-linker was developed. The folic acid—modified micelles of

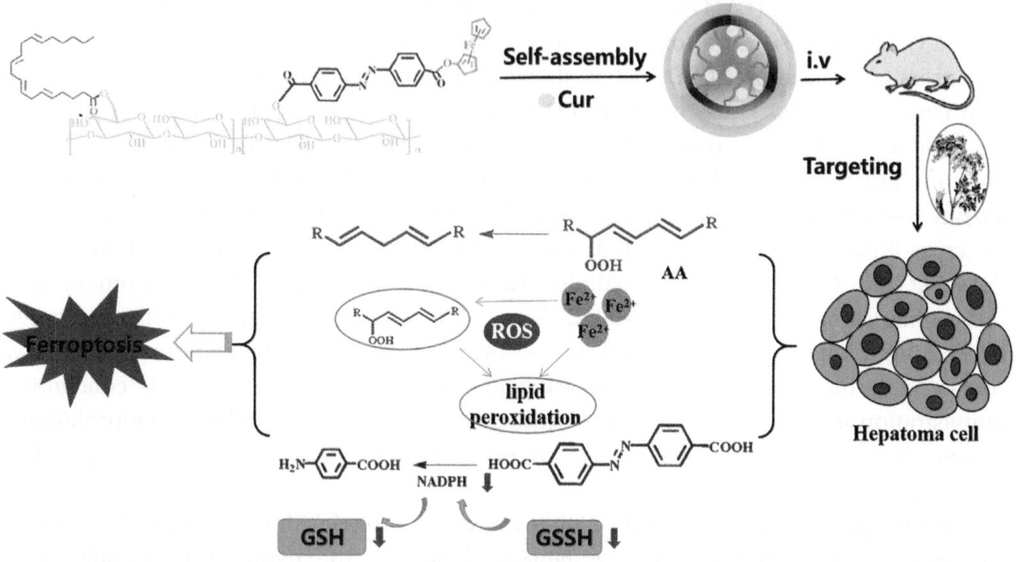

FIGURE 9.5 Design, preparation, and function of angelica polysaccharide-based curcumin micelle with glutathione sensitivity. *Reproduced with permission from Liu, X., et al., Hypoxia responsive nano-drug delivery system based on angelica polysaccharide for liver cancer therapy. Drug Delivery, 2022. 29(1): p. 138–148. Creative Commons CC BY license.*

91.2 nm size were used for curcumin loading. HeLa cells possessing a high quantity of GSH have largely captured these micelles. Both active and passive targeting as well as GSH-sensitivity were involved in the antitumoral efficacy of the crafted nanomicelle [163].

9.3.3.3 Ultrasound responsive

Ultrasound-assisted site-specific targeting is one of the promising approaches that enhance the local drug deposit at the cancer site. Pluronic P123/F127 polymeric micelles were developed with the aim of ultrasonic-triggered curcumin release. The micellar nanoparticles showed longer circulation time and enhanced curcumin uptake. Following systemic administration, the assisted focused ultrasound treatment significantly improved curcumin tumor deposition in a time-dependent manner. Results indicated a significant tumor growth suppression and tumor weight reduction (by 6.5 fold) compared to nonultrasonic conditions in breast cancer model [164]. Vitamin E succinate-grafted-polylysine micelles of curcumin showed a significantly higher rate of penetration into the deeper tumor spheroid, leading to an excellent cytotoxicity and growth inhibition in the glioma model. Furthermore, higher efficacy was observed when the micellar system was combined with ultrasound-targeted microbubble destruction, which led to a significant apoptosis induction in the tumor cells. The real-time MRI imaging indicated a complete eradication of glioma following a month posttreatment [165].

9.3.3.4 Enzyme responsive

Polymeric micelles, consist of palmitic acid as the hydrophobic and PEG as the hydrophilic moieties, were formed through self-assembling. Fourier transform infrared spectroscopy indicated the ester linkage within the conjugated structure, which can be degraded through enzymes possessing esterase activity including lipase, resulting in cargo release. The curcumin release from these nanomicelles was enzyme-triggered as confirmed by enzyme-mediated drug release by using pure lipase and HeLa cell lysate capable of degrading the micelles [166].

9.3.3.5 Dual responsive

Curcumin-loaded shell-cross-linked F127 micelles and 5-fluorouracil dispersed chitosan-dextran hydrogel with pH and REDOX-sensitivity were developed to improve the release of both drugs. Disulfide bonds within the shell of F127 micelle allowed for REDOX-sensitivity of the nanomicelle, while Schiff base bonds provided pH sensitivity of the platform. Biocompatibility assessment against HeLa cells showed low toxicity of the hydrogel platform for these cells with about 90% viability of cells. However, the potential of anticancer efficacy against these cells was not evaluated [167]. In other study, a series of amphiphilic polymers of polyoxaline-SS-poly (lactide) (PEtOx-SS-PLA) (bearing disulfide-linkes) were self-assembled into a nanomicellar system. The platform used for subsequent curcumin loading was in the range of 150−200 nm in size. The curcumin release from these nanomicelles was triggered by both reducing environment and acidic pH (5) in the C6 cells model, resulted in significant growth inhibition [168]. A schematic for such a micelle is shown in Fig. 9.6.

Hu et al. have developed folate-functionalized dual-responsive PEGylated polymeric micelles of curcumin as a smart delivery vehicle with antitumor and antiinflammatory

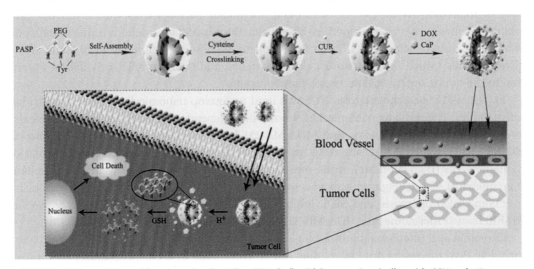

FIGURE 9.6 Self-assembly and function of polyoxaline-SS-poly (lactide) curcumin micelles with GSH and pH sensitivity. GSH, glutathione. *Reproduced with permission from Zhang, H., et al., Biodegradable reduction and pH dual-sensitive polymer micelles based on poly (2-ethyl-2-oxazoline) for efficient delivery of curcumin. RSC advances, 2020. 10(43): p. 25435−25445. Creative Commons Attribution-NonCommercial 3.0 Unported License.*

features. Nanomicellar structure consisted of two-photon fluorophore (TPF) and ibuprofen, conjugated to poly (2-azepane ethyl methacrylate) (PAEMA), showed a high loading capacity for curcumin as well as stability in physiological environment. The dual pH and GSH-responsive nanomicelles showed reassembly within the TME leading to a rapid release of ibuprofen (Ibup) and further curcumin release. The nanomicelles also enhanced antitumor efficacy on 4T1 cells in vitro and in vivo and ameliorated antiinflammatory functions on RAW 264.7 cells. The potency of this type of nanoparticle was confirmed in terms of the capability of two-photon cell and deep bioimaging as well as cancer therapy [169].

Dual stimuli-responsive curcumin nanomicelles were fabricated for simultaneous CD44 receptor and mitochondria targeting. The pH and REDOX-responsive TPP-oHSM nanomicelles were fabricated by triphenylphosphonium (TPP)/oligomeric hyaluronic acid (oHA)/ disulfide-menthone 1,2-glycerol ketal (SM) amphiphilic block copolymer. The ketal bonds were sensitive to the acidic pH of the tumor site, and lipophilic cationic triphenylphosphine and triphenylmethylphosphonium were used for mitochondria targeting. Results indicated an enhanced nanomicellar penetration and effective targeting of MCF-7 and MDA-MB breast cancer cells owing to targeting mitochondria and CD44 receptor [170].

9.3.4 Chemoresistant polymeric micelles (multidrug resistance)

The efficacy of conventional chemotherapy is largely affected by varying intrinsic or acquired drug resistance mechanisms, resulting in treatment failure. In the past decades, nanotechnology endowed with tremendous advancement to overcome tumor drug resistance. Despite numerous advantages of nanoparticles, several pathophysiological barriers within the TME, including tumor distribution, penetration, and intracellular trafficking, severely limit the efficacy of treatment. As previously mentioned, intelligent nanoparticles with distinctive and adaptable physicochemical properties have been introduced to ameliorate the therapeutic efficacy of nanomedicine [171,172]. In the following section, we will summarize some of the advancements in this field to combat drug resistance and to more efficiently deliver curcumin to the tumor site by exploiting polymeric micelles.

In 2018, PEGylated cholesterol/α-TOS was used to develop nanomicellar curcumin following self-assembly. The resulting nanomicelles showed dose-dependent cellular uptake and cytotoxicity in B16F10 murine melanoma and MDA-MB-231 human breast cancer cells. The improved efficacy was in terms of reversing drug resistance by denoting significantly higher retention of rhodamine-123 (P-gp substrate) in the resistant B16F10 cells compared to verapamil (standard P-gp inhibitor). The synergic anticancer activity of curcumin was also demonstrated by inducing α-TOS-mediated apoptosis, and MDR inhibition in A549 lung cancer 3D spheroids as well as B16F10 murine melanoma and MDA-MB-231 human breast cancer cell monolayers [173].

Curcumin as a promising pharmacological agent has shown to downregulate MDR proteins including P-gp mediating drug efflux thus can be considered as a chemosensitizer to improve chemotherapeutics potential in combatting MDR. A REDOX-sensitive micelle was fabricated for the codelivery of doxorubicin, and curcumin as a chemosensitizer, by using a zwitterionic polymer named poly (carboxybetaine). This nanomicelle enhanced MCF-7 cellular uptake and significantly reduced the IC_{50} value. Furthermore, curcumin inhibition of doxorubicin efflux led to a higher intracellular doxorubicin concentration and exerted synergistic anticancer effects for dominating MDR [174]. Chondroitin sulfate-based polymeric micelles functionalized with RVG (rabies viral glycoprotein) polypeptide (derived from neurotropic rabies virus) were also fabricated for curcumin and doxorubicin coloading. Chondroitin sulfate conjugation with curcumin through disulfide bound gave the micellar system REDOX-sensitivity properties. This curcumin nanomicellar system suppressed the main efflux proteins in doxorubicin-resistant glioma cells, while RVG functionalization facilitated BBB penetration and drug release upon stimulation by the high concentration of GSH in the glioblastoma region. Results indicated an enhanced brain accumulation and in vivo tumor inhibition as well as a higher survival rate without systemic toxicity following treatment with the multifunctional system [175].

PEGylated PLA-based micelles were synthesized for the codelivery of doxorubicin, and curcumin as a chemosensitizer, to dominate MDR in breast cancer. The polymeric micelles showed superiority to free doxorubicin, combination of doxorubicin and curcumin, and doxorubicin-loaded micelles in proliferation inhibition of MCF-7 cells. This could be attributed to the higher cellular uptake, lower doxorubicin efflux, and higher efficacy in downregulating P-gp and ATP activity inhibition. Furthermore, enhanced tumor accumulation of these micelles was observed, which led to a significant inhibitory effect on tumor growth in the xenograft model of drug-resistant MCF-7 [176].

Folate-targeted PEGylated nanomicelles (90 nm) and HA-vitamin E succinate nanomicelles (224 nm) were loaded with both doxorubicin and curcumin to combat against MDR in MCF-7 cells. The targeted nanomicelles induced an efficient internalization of doxorubicin through energy-dependent and caveolae-mediated endocytosis and a significant cell apoptosis and reduced cellular efflux. HA-vitamin E succinate nanomicelles also reversed MDR effects by targeting CD44 through HA moiety. A significant synergistic antitumor efficacy in suppressing breast tumor in mice model of MCF-7 and 4T1 was also indicated in terms of the mentioned nanomicellar formulation [177]. Other peer formulations coloaded with doxorubicin and curcumin were synthesized, which contained vitamin E succinate-grafted PEG-micelles and HA-based micelles to enhance antitumor effects and overcome MDR. Vitamin E-grafted micellar system demonstrated higher efficacy in terms of higher cytotoxicity and MDR reversal compared to conventional micelles in chemoresistant MCF-7 cells. Both EPR enhancement through PEG moiety and CD44-active targeting through HA component improved the tumor biodistribution of nanomicelles. Curcumin combination has also showed to reduce doxorubicin side effects in 4T1 tumor-bearing mice. Overall, there was no significant difference between the efficacy of the two micellar systems delivering doxorubicin and curcumin in vivo [178]. In another study, a micellar structure of HA-vitamin E succinate graft copolymer was used for synergistic codelivery of curcumin and doxorubicin to improve antitumor efficacy in doxorubicin-resistant MCF-7 breast cancer models. The nanomicelles showed a significant cytotoxicity and apoptosis-inducing activity, and noticeably reversed MDR effects via CD44 targeting and synergic codelivery of drugs in DOX-resistant MCF-7/Adr cells. In vivo study indicated an efficient inhibition of tumor growth in 4T1 tumor-bearing mice and alleviation of doxorubicin cardiotoxicity through the targeting potential of the nanomicelles [179].

In a study by Wang et al., codelivery of doxorubicin and curcumin was tested using micellar nanoparticle comprising $TPGS_{2000}$ and PEG_{2000}-DSPE diblock polymers as (MDR) modulator. The micelles with 13.76 nm size showed considerable synergetic cytotoxicity effect by reversing MDR in MCF-7/Adr cells. Furthermore, tumor suppression in 4T1-bearing mice highlighted the potential of codelivery based on nanoparticles as a robust approach in improving antitumor efficacy [180]. D-tocopheryl PEG1000 succinate (TPGS1000) as an amphiphilic copolymer was used to form micelles containing both curcumin and doxorubicin to overcome MDR in A549 lung tumor-induced mice. Both TPGS1000 and curcumin aided for synergistically reversing doxorubicin resistance in A549 tumor cells. The micelles also increased the plasma concentration of both drugs and prolonged the blood circulation time, which enhanced their efficacy compared to either free drugs [181].

By using curcumin and quercetin in combination with doxorubicin in a nanomicellar formulation, the efficacy of the combination was assessed to combat against drug resistance. The synergetic effect of curcumin and quercetin reduced doxorubicin dosing through chemosensitization and camouflaged doxorubicin cardiotoxic effects in mice inoculated with ES2-Luc or A2780ADR ovarian cancerous cells [182].

Paclitaxel, as a widely used chemotherapeutic agent, has developed resistance against cancers due to the activation of NF-κB. It was indicated that this chemoresistance could be mitigated by codelivering curcumin as both NF-κB suppressor and apoptosis inducer. In this regard, PEGylated PCL-based micelles containing both paclitaxel and curcumin with 38 nm size showed an extended-release profile for these two drugs. Furthermore, results demonstrated apoptosis induction and antiangiogenic properties both in vitro and in vivo in CT26 cells [183]. As another combinational chemotherapy platform for MDR domination, PEGylated micelles of PCL loaded with platinum and curcumin have also shown a synergetic effect in terms of cancer inhibition in A2780 human ovarian cancer cells [184].

9.4 Future insights

Curcumin has demonstrated great potential to circumvent challenges related to conventional chemotherapeutics for the treatment of cancers or varying resistant tumors. To the best of our knowledge, almost all curcumin nanomicelles could act as curcumin solubilizers in aqueous medium, and by switching this highly lipophilic compound to a more bioavailable compound, higher efficacy in tumor alleviation is attained. Furthermore, it is noteworthy that curcumin encapsulation within micelles, either lipid- or polymeric-based, leads to an improvement in its pharmacokinetic features.

In the various sections of this chapter, a number of curcumin micelles have been introduced and their mechanism of action and potential for managing various types of tumors with different targeting potentials have been analyzed. These nanoscaled micelles are promising for improving cytotoxicity against different types of tumors, cellular uptake, as well as specific targeting of signaling pathways involved in the tumor formation.

The limited use of these micelles is primarily due to concerns regarding their potential risks including toxicity and biocompatibility issues for clinical applications. In this regard, it is important to consider the nature and composition of the micelle (especially polymers as most of them are not considered organic), total size and charge, ligands and targeting moieties, and release profiles of curcumin from the micelles before in vivo usages or further clinical trials (Tables 9.1 and 9.2).

Table 9.1 A summary of lipid-based micelles properties.

Main component of micelles	Surface modification/ type of stimulus	In vitro/ in vivo	Cancer cell types	References
SinaCurcumin	—	In vitro	Esophageal squamous cell carcinoma (KYSE-30)	[32]
Polysorbate 80		In vivo	Breast cancer cell (SUM149)	[33]
ND[a]		In vivo	Colon cancer cells (HT-29 and Hct116)	[34]
HSA[b]-fatty acid conjugate		In vitro	Lung carcinoma (A549)/breast cancer cells (MCF-7)	[36,37]
SinaCurcumin		In vitro	Glioblastoma (U-373)	[39]
TPGS[c]		In vivo	Brain cancer cells (U87-MG)	[36,42]
Soluplus/TPGS		In vivo	Ovarian cancer cells (SKOV-3)/ breast cancer cells (MDA-MB-231)	[43]
DSPE[d]/PEG[e]$_{2000}$	VIP[f] (targeting agent)	In vitro	Breast cancer cells (MCF-7)	[44]
PEG/vitamin-E	Transferrin (targeting agent)	In vitro	Hepatic tumor cells (HepG2)/ cervical tumor cells (HeLa)	[47,48]
PEG/vitamin-E		In vivo	Human colorectal adenocarcinoma cells (HCT-116)	[49]
PEG/vitamin-E	GLUT1 antibody (targeting agent)	In vitro	Glioblastoma cells (U87MG)	[50]
DSPE-PEG	pH-responsive	In vivo	Cervical tumor cells (HeLa)/ breast cancer cells (MCF-7)	[53]
TPGS	ROS[g]-responsive	In vitro	Colon cancer cell (HT-29)	[55]
D-α-tocopherol conjugated to PE[h]	Chemoresistant	In vitro	Breast cancer cells (MDA-MB-231)/ melanoma cancer cells (B16F10)	[56]
DSPE-PEG$_{2000}$		In vitro	Breast cancer cells (MCF-7)	[59]
PEG/PE/vitamin E		In vitro	Human ovarian adenocarcinoma (t SK-OV-3)	[60]
TPGS/PEG (15)-hydroxystearate		In vitro	Ishikawa cells (endometrial adenocarcinoma)	[61]

[a]Not defined.
[b]Human serum albumin.
[c]Tocopherol polyethylene glycol succinate.
[d]1, 2-Distearoyl-sn-glycero-3-phosphoethanolamine.
[e]Poly(ethylene glycol).
[f]Vasoactive intestinal peptide.
[g]Reactive oxygen species.
[h]Phosphatidyl ethanolamine.

Table 9.2 A summary of polymeric micelles properties.

Polymer nature	Surface modification/ type of stimulus	In vitro/in vivo	Cancer cell types	References
PEG[a]/PCL[b]	–	In vitro	Human prostate cancer cells (PC-3)	[64,65]
		In vivo	Lewis lung carcinoma (LL2)	[66]
		In vivo	Breast tumor (4T1)	[68]
		In vivo	–	[69]
		In vivo	Human pancreatic cells (SW1990)	[71]
		In vivo	Lung cancer (LL2)	[73]
		In vivo	Breast tumor (4T1)	[74]
		In vitro	Cervical cancer cells (HeLa)	[75]
		In vivo	Colon carcinoma (C26/CT26)	[77,78]
PCL(2-methacryloyloxyethyl phosphorylcholine) conjugate		In vitro	Cervical cancer cells (HeLa)	[72]
PEO[c]/PCL cross-linked by TPE[d]		In vitro	Colorectal adenocarcinoma (Caco2)	[76]
Pluronic/PCL		In vitro	Colon-adenocarcinoma (C26)/Cervical cancer cells	[79]
PF127[e]		In vitro	Colon-adenocarcinoma (C26)/Cervical cancer cells (HeLa)/Gastric cancerous cells (BGC-823)	[80]
PF127		In vitro	Gastric cancerous cells (SGC-7901 and BGC-823)	[81]
PF127/Gelucire 44/14		In vivo	Human lung cancer (A549)	[82]
PF127		In vitro	Human breast adenocarcinoma cells (MCF-7)	[83]
PVA[f]/PF127		In vitro	Osteoblasts	[84]
TPGS[g]/F127/P123		In vitro	Cervical cancer cells (HeLa)	[81,85]
Soluplus: TPGS		In vitro	Ovarian cancer cells (SKOV-3)	[43]
Poloxamer 407/TPGS		In vitro	Ovarian cancer cells (NCI/ADRRES)	[86]
PLA[h]/TPGS		In vitro	Breast cancer cells (MCF-7)	[87]
PEG/PLA		In vitro	Breast cancer cells (MDA-MB-231)	[88]
		In vivo	Melanoma cancer cells (B16F10)	[88]
		In vivo	Colon carcinoma cells (CT26)	[89]
		In vitro	Melanoma cancer cells (B16 /A375)	[90]
		In vivo	Human colon cancer (HCT-116)	[91]
		In vivo	Ovarian cancerous cell (A2780)	[92]
		In vivo	Breast tumor (EMT6)	[93]
Leoyl chloride/mPEG 2000		In vivo	Hepatocellular carcinoma (HuH-7)	[93]
		In vivo	Breast cancer (4T1)	[94]

Material	Targeting	In vitro/In vivo	Cancer type (cells)	Reference
Alginate-based calcium		In vitro	Breast cancer (4T1)	[95]
POx/POz[i][j]		In vitro	Colon cancer (CT26-CEA)	[96]
			Colorectal cancer cells (SW480)	
			Breast cancer cells (MDA-MB-231)	
Octadecylamine/chondroitin sulfate		In vitro	Breast cancer cells (MCF-7 cells)	[98]
Pluronic127		In vivo	Lung cancer cells (L929)/Cervical cancer cells (HeLa)/Breast cancer cells (MCF-7)	[99]
Chitosan-cholesterol conjugate		In vitro	Lung carcinoma (A549 cells)	[100]
Stearic acid-grafted-chitosan oligosaccharide		In vivo	Colorectal cancer stem cells	[101]
Cholesterol-conjugated chitosan		In vitro	Lung cancer (A549)	[102]
Maltoheptaose		In vitro	Prostate cancer cell (PC-3 cell)	[103]
PEG oleate		In vitro	Glioma cell (U87MG)	[104]
R7L10 peptide		In vivo	Glioblastoma (C6)	[105]
Ethylene oxide-propylene oxide (Tetronic 1307)		In vitro	Ovarian cancerous cells (CHO-K1)	[106]
PEG/HPMA[k]		In vitro	Human ovarian carcinoma (OVCAR-3)/human colorectal adenocarcinoma (Caco-2)/ human lymphoblastic leukemia (Molt-4)	[107]
PEG/HPMA		In vivo	Neuroblastoma (Neuro2A)	[108]
Hyaluronic acid conjugate of co-poly (styrene maleic acid)	Targeting CD44	In vitro	Pancreatic cancer (MiaPaCa-2 / AsPC-1)	[111]
Alendronate-hyaluronic acid-octadecanoic acid		In vivo	Osteosarcoma cells (MG-63)	[113]
Hyaluronic acid/pluronic F127/didecyldimethylammonium bromide		In vitro	Breast cancer cell (MDA-MB-231)	[115]
Pluronic F127	Targeting hydroxyapatite surface of the bone	In vitro	Osteosarcoma	[114]
Poly (ethylene oxide)-poly (propylene oxide)	Targeting glucose transporters	In vivo	Breast cancer cells (4T1)	[117]
PEG/PLA	Targeting folate receptors	In vivo	Breast cancer cells (MCF-7) liver hepatocellular cells (HepG2)	[119]
PEG/PCL		In vitro	HeLa hepatocellular cells (HepG2)	[120]
PEG/PCL		In vivo	Colon cancer cells (CT26)	[121]
Poly (2-methacryloyl-oxyethyl phosphorylcholine)/PCL		In vitro	Human colorectal adenocarcinoma (HT-29)	[122]
PEG/PLA		In vitro	Hepatocellular cells (HepG2)	[123]

(Continued)

Table 9.2 (Continued)

Polymer nature	Surface modification/type of stimulus	In vitro/in vivo	Cancer cell types	References
PEG/PLA		In vivo	glioma cells (GL261)	[124]
Styrene malic acid		In vitro	Cervical (HeLa) and ovarian cancer cells (SKOV-3)	[125]
PEG/PCL		In vivo	Breast cancer	[127]
Hyaluronic acid-coated pluronic (123/127)	Targeting CD44 and folate receptors	In vivo	Breast cancer cells (MCF-7)	[126]
PEGylated poly (D,L-Lactide)	Targeting transferrin receptors	In vitro	Cervical and hepatic cancerous cells	[128]
PEG/PLA	Targeting RGD	In vivo	Melanoma cells (B16)	[129]
KKGRGDS peptide/lauric acid		In vitro	Cervical (HeLa) and hepatic cancerous cells (HepG2)	[130]
PEG/PCL	Targeting biotin	In vitro	Cervical (HeLa) and hepatic cancerous cells (HepG2)	[120]
PEG/Soluplus	Octreotide-functionalized	In vivo	Lung carcinoma (A549)	[131]
Glycol chitosan/dequalinium	Targeting mitochondria	In vitro	Human cervical cancer (HeLa)	[132]
Chitosan	pH-sensitive	In vitro	Cervix cancerous cells	[133]
PEG/PLA/PAE		In vivo	Human breast cancer (MCF-7)	[135]
PF68		In vitro	Human ovarian carcinoma (A2780)/hepatocellular carcinoma (SMMC 7721)	[136]
PEG/benzoic imine-poly(γ-benzyl-L-aspartate)-b-poly(1-vinylimidazole)		In vivo	CSC's	[138]
PEG/poly(2-methacrylate ethyl 5-hexynoicate)		In vivo	Human cervical cancer (HeLa)/human breast cancer (4T1)	[140]
Glycidyl azide		In vitro	Human breast cancer (4T1)	[142]
PEG/PEEGE		In vitro	Human breast cancer cells (MDA-MB-231)	[141]
PEG/PLA		In vitro	Acute myeloid leukemia (HL-60 cells)	[152]
Poly(2-ethyl-2-oxazoline)/PLA		In vivo	Human breast cancer cells (MDA-MB-231)	[150]
Oligosaccharides of hyaluronan-acetal-menthone 1,2-glycerol ketal	pH-sensitive/Targeting CD44 and folate receptors	In vitro	Human breast cancer cells (MCF-7/4T1) and lung carcinoma (A549) human cervical cancer (HeLa)	[139]
Hyaluronic acid	pH-sensitive /Targeting CD44	In vivo	Human breast cancer (4T1 and MCF-7)	[143]
Hyaluronic acid		In vivo	Breast cancer cells (MDA-MB-231)	[144]
Hyaluronic acid		In vitro		[145]

Hyaluronic acid/TPGS		In vivo	Human cervical cancer (HeLa)/human renal adenocarcinoma (786-O)/liver cancerous cells (HepG2)	[146]
Hyaluronic acid	pH-sensitive/Targeting folate and biotin and CD44 receptors	In vivo	Liver cancerous cells (HepG2) / Pancreatic tumor (PANC-1)	[73,153]
Hyaluronic acid		In vivo	Human breast cancer (MCF-7)	[147]
Octadecylamine/O-(2-aminoethyl)/PEG/polysuccinimide	pH-sensitive/Targeting folate receptor	In vitro	Colon cancer cells (SW480)	[148]
F68-acetal/PCL	pH-sensitive/targeting glycyrrhetinic acid receptors	In vitro	Liver cancerous cells (HepG2/Hepa1–6/SMMC7721)	[149]
PEG/PLG	ROS-sensitive	In vitro	Human breast cancer (4T1)	[155]
PEG/oxalyl chloride		In vitro	Human cervical cancer (HeLa)	[156]
PEG/PLA	Glutathione-responsive	In vitro	Human breast cancer (MCF-7)	[158]
PEG/PLA-(LA)$_4$		In vivo	Colon cancer (MC-38)	[159]
Cystine-bridged peptide lysin-bridged peptide		In vivo	Human cervical cancer (HeLa)	[160]
Angelica polysaccharide/ferrocene/arachidonic acid		In vitro	Liver tumor cell (HepG2)	[161]
PAH[m]/PLGA[n]	Targeting folate receptors/glutathione-responsive	In vitro	Pancreatic cancer cells (PANO2)	[162]
PEG/ N-(2-(2-pyridyl disulfide) ethyl methacrylamide (DS) and S-1-dodecyl-S-(α,α′-dimethyl-α″-acetic acid) trithiocarbonate		In vivo	Human cervical cancer (HeLa)	[163]
Pluronic P123/F127	Ultrasound-responsive	In vivo	Breast cancer cells (MDA-MB-231 / 4T1)	[164]
Vitamin E succinate/polylysine		In vivo	Glioma (C6)	[165]
PEG/palmitic acid	Enzyme-responsive	In vitro	Human cervical cancer (HeLa)	[166]
F127/chitosan/dextran	pH sensitivity/Redox-sensitivity	In vitro	Human cervical cancer (HeLa)	[167]
Polyoxaline/poly (lactide)		In vitro	Glioma cells (C6)	[168]
TPP/hyaluronic acid		In vivo	Breast cancer cells (MCF-7 /MDA-MB)	[170]
PAEMA[o]	pH sensitivity/Glutathione-sensitivity	In vivo	4T1 cells	[169]
PEG/cholesterol/α-tocopheryl succinate	Chemoresistant	In vitro	Murine melanoma (B16F10)/human breast cancer cell (MDA-MB-231)/lung cancer (A549)	[173]
TPGS$_{2000}$/PEG$_{2000}$		In vivo	Lung cancer (A549)	[181]
PF127		In vivo		[182]

(Continued)

Table 9.2 (Continued)

Polymer nature	Surface modification/ type of stimulus	In vitro/in vivo	Cancer cell types	References
			Human ovarian clear cell carcinoma cells (ES2)/ ovarian cancerous cells (A2780ADR)	
PEG/PCL		In vivo	Colon cancer cells (CT26)	[183]
PEG/PCL		In vitro	Human ovarian cancer cells (A2780)	[184]
PEG/PLA		In vivo	Breast cancer (MCF-7)	[176]
Poly (carboxybetaine)	Chemoresistant/ REDOX-sensitive	In vitro	Breast cancer (MCF-7)	[174]
Chondroitin sulfate	Chemoresistant/REDOX-sensitive/Targeting RVG polypeptide	In vivo	Glioblastoma (C6)	[175]
PEG/hyaluronic acid/vitamin E succinate	Chemoresistant/ Targeting folate receptors/Targeting CD44	In vitro	Breast cancer (MCF-7/ 4T1)	[177]
vitamin E succinate/PEG/hyaluronic acid	Chemoresistant/ Targeting CD44	In vivo	Breast cancer (MCF-7/ 4T1)	[178]
Hyaluronic acid/vitamin E succinate		In vivo	Breast cancer (MCF-7)	[179]

[a]Poly(ethylene glycol).
[b]Polycaprolactone.
[c]Polyethylene oxide.
[d]Tetraphenylethylene.
[e]Pluronic F-127.
[f]Polyvinyl alcohol.
[g]Tocopherol polyethylene glycol succinate.
[h]Polylactic acid.
[i]Poly(2-oxazoline).
[j]Poly(2-oxazine).
[k]N-(2-hydroxypropyl) methacrylamide.
[l]Cancer stem cell.
[m]Poly (allylamine hydrochloride).
[n]Poly (lactic-co-glycolic acid).
[o]Poly (2-azepane ethyl methacrylate).

References

[1] Rahiman N, et al. Curcumin-based nanotechnology approaches and therapeutics in restoration of auto-immune diseases. Journal of Controlled Release 2022;348:264−86.

[2] Hassanzadeh S, et al. Curcumin: an inflammasome silencer. Pharmacological Research 2020;159.

[3] Mohajeri M, Sahebkar A. Protective effects of curcumin against doxorubicin-induced toxicity and resistance: a review. Critical Reviews in Oncology/Hematology 2018;122:30−51.

[4] Momtazi AA, Sahebkar A. Difluorinated curcumin: a promising curcumin analogue with improved antitumor activity and pharmacokinetic profile. Current Pharmaceutical Design 2016;22(28):4386−97.

[5] Momtazi-Borojeni AA, et al. Curcumin: a natural modulator of immune cells in systemic lupus erythematosus. Autoimmunity Reviews 2018;17(2):125−35.

[6] Vallianou NG, et al. Potential anticancer properties and mechanisms of action of curcumin. Anticancer Research 2015;35(2):645−51.

[7] Mohammed ES, et al. Effects of free and nanoparticulate curcumin on chemically induced liver carcinoma in an animal model. Archives of Medical Science 2021;17(1):218−27.

[8] Wu Q, et al. Nanoscale formulations: incorporating curcumin into combination strategies for the treatment of lung cancer. Drug Design, Development and Therapy 2021;15:2695.

[9] Marjaneh RM, Rahmani F, Hassanian SM, Rezaei N, Hashemzehi M, Bahrami A, Ariakia F, Fiuji H, Sahebkar A, Avan A, & Khazaei M. (2018). Phytosomal curcumin inhibits tumor growth in colitis-associated colorectal cancer. *Journal of cellular physiology*, *233*(10):6785−6798. Available from https://doi.org/10.1002/jcp.26538.

[10] Heidari Z, et al. Curcumin supplementation in pediatric patients: a systematic review of current clinical evidence. Phytotherapy Research 2022;36(4):1442−58.

[11] Hosseini SA, et al. Pulmonary fibrosis: therapeutic and mechanistic insights into the role of phytochemicals. Biofactors (Oxford, England) 2021;47(3):250−69.

[12] Keihanian F, et al. Curcumin, hemostasis, thrombosis, and coagulation. Journal of Cellular Physiology 2018;233(6):4497−511.

[13] Khayatan D, et al. Protective effects of curcumin against traumatic brain injury. Biomedicine and Pharmacotherapy 2022;154.

[14] Mokhtari-Zaer A, et al. The protective role of curcumin in myocardial ischemia−reperfusion injury. Journal of Cellular Physiology 2018;234(1):214−22.

[15] Cicero AFG, Sahebkar A, Fogacci F, Bove M, Giovannini M, & Borghi C. (2020). Effects of phytosomal curcumin on anthropometric parameters, insulin resistance, cortisolemia and non-alcoholic fatty liver disease indices: a double-blind, placebo-controlled clinical trial. *European journal of nutrition*, *59*(2), 477−483. Available from https://doi.org/10.1007/s00394-019-01916-7.

[16] Panahi Y, Fazlolahzadeh O, Atkin SL, Majeed M, Butler AE, Johnston TP, & Sahebkar A. (2019). Evidence of curcumin and curcumin analogue effects in skin diseases: A narrative review. *Journal of cellular physiology*, *234*(2), 1165−1178. Available from https://doi.org/10.1002/jcp.27096.

[17] Sahebkar A. Molecular mechanisms for curcumin benefits against ischemic injury. Fertility and Sterility 2010;94(5):e75−6.

[18] Mohammadi A, Blesso CN, Barreto GE, Banach M, Majeed M, & Sahebkar A. (2019). Macrophage plasticity, polarization and function in response to curcumin, a diet-derived polyphenol, as an immunomodulatory agent. *The Journal of nutritional biochemistry*, *66*, 1−16. https://doi.org/10.1016/j.jnutbio.2018.12.005.

[19] Lee W-H, et al. Recent advances in curcumin nanoformulation for cancer therapy. Expert Opinion on Drug Delivery 2014;11(8):1183−201.

[20] Chavda VP, et al. Current status of cancer nanotheranostics: emerging strategies for cancer management. Nanotheranostics 2023;7(4):368−79.

[21] Jiang T, et al. Nanotechnology-enabled gene delivery for cancer and other genetic diseases. Expert
Opinion on Drug Delivery 2023;20(4):523−40.

[22] Luo H, et al. Exosome-based nanoimmunotherapy targeting TAMs, a promising strategy for glioma. Cell
Death & Disease 2023;14(4):235.

[23] Patel P, et al. Nanotheranostics for Diagnosis and Treatment of Breast Cancer. Current Pharmaceutical
Design 2023;29(10):732−47.

[24] Wei F, et al. Recent progress in metal complexes functionalized nanomaterials for photodynamic therapy. Chemical Communications (Camb) 2023;59(46):6956−68.

[25] Goradel NH, et al. Regulation of tumor angiogenesis by microRNAs: state of the art. Journal of Cellular
Physiology 2019;234(2):1099−110.

[26] Shetab Boushehri MA, Dietrich D, Lamprecht A. Nanotechnology as a platform for the development of
injectable parenteral formulations: a comprehensive review of the know-hows and state of the art.
Pharmaceutics 2020;12(6):510.

[27] Farhoudi L, et al. Polymeric nanomicelles of curcumin: potential applications in cancer. International
Journal of Pharmaceutics 2022;121622.

[28] Rahiman N, et al. Recent advancements in nanoparticle-mediated approaches for restoration of multiple
sclerosis. Journal of Controlled Release 2022;.

[29] Park W, et al. New perspectives of curcumin in cancer prevention. Cancer Prevention Research 2013;6
(5):387−400.

[30] Priya LB, Baskaran R, Padma VV. Phytonanoconjugates in oral medicine. Nanostructures for oral medicine. Elsevier; 2017. p. 639−68.

[31] Hanafy NA, El-Kemary M, Leporatti S. Micelles structure development as a strategy to improve smart
cancer therapy. Cancers 2018;10(7):238.

[32] Hosseini S, et al. An in vitro study on curcumin delivery by nano-micelles for esophageal squamous cell
carcinoma (KYSE-30). Reports of Biochemistry & Molecular Biology 2018;6(2):137.

[33] Wang G, Sukumar S. Characteristics and antitumor activity of polysorbate 80 curcumin micelles preparation by cloud point cooling. Journal of Drug Delivery Science and Technology 2020;59:101871.

[34] Mohammadi H, et al. Evaluation of curcumin nano-micelle on proliferation and apoptosis of HT29 and
Hct116 colon cancer cell lines. Middle East Journal of Cancer 2022;13(1):99−109.

[35] Seiwert N, et al. Curcumin administered as micellar solution suppresses intestinal inflammation and
colorectal carcinogenesis. Nutrition and Cancer 2021;73(4):686−93.

[36] Zendedel E, et al. Cytotoxic effects investigation of nanomicelle and free curcuminoids against cancer
and normal cells. Nanomedicine Research Journal 2019;4(2):63−8.

[37] Park C, et al. Fatty acid chain length impacts nanonizing capacity of albumin-fatty acid nanomicelles:
enhanced physicochemical property and cellular delivery of poorly water-soluble drug. European
Journal of Pharmaceutics and Biopharmaceutics 2020;152:257−69.

[38] Xia L, et al. Role of the NFκB-signaling pathway in cancer. OncoTargets and therapy 2018;11:2063.

[39] Hesari A, et al. Effect of curcumin on glioblastoma cells. Journal of Cellular Physiology 2019;234
(7):10281−8.

[40] Le Bras A. Local drug delivery to brain tumor. Nature Publishing Group; 2020.

[41] Grassin-Delyle S, et al. Intranasal drug delivery: an efficient and non-invasive route for systemic administration: focus on opioids. Pharmacology & Therapeutics 2012;134(3):366−79.

[42] Keshari P, Sonar Y, Mahajan H. Curcumin loaded TPGS micelles for nose to brain drug delivery: in vitro and in vivo studies. Materials Technology 2019;34(7):423–32.

[43] Riedel J, et al. Paclitaxel and curcumin co-loaded mixed micelles: Improving in vitro efficacy and reducing toxicity against Abraxane®. Journal of Drug Delivery Science and Technology 2021;62:102343.

[44] Gülçür E, et al. Curcumin in VIP-targeted sterically stabilized phospholipid nanomicelles: a novel therapeutic approach for breast cancer and breast cancer stem cells. Drug Delivery and Translational Research 2013;3(6):562–74.

[45] Yu Z, et al. Cancer stem cells. The International Journal of Biochemistry & Cell Biology 2012;44 (12):2144–51.

[46] Zhang C, Zhang F. Iron homeostasis and tumorigenesis: molecular mechanisms and therapeutic opportunities. Protein & Cell 2015;6(2):88–100.

[47] Muddineti OS, et al. Transferrin-modified vitamin-E/lipid based polymeric micelles for improved tumor targeting and anticancer effect of curcumin. Pharmaceutical Research 2018;35(5):1–14.

[48] Sarisozen C, Abouzeid AH, Torchilin VP. The effect of co-delivery of paclitaxel and curcumin by transferrin-targeted PEG-PE-based mixed micelles on resistant ovarian cancer in 3-D spheroids and in vivo tumors. European Journal of Pharmaceutics and Biopharmaceutics 2014;88(2):539–50.

[49] Abouzeid AH, et al. Anti-cancer activity of anti-GLUT1 antibody-targeted polymeric micelles co-loaded with curcumin and doxorubicin. Journal of Drug Targeting 2013;21(10):994–1000.

[50] Sarisozen C, et al. Nanomedicine based curcumin and doxorubicin combination treatment of glioblastoma with scFv-targeted micelles: in vitro evaluation on 2D and 3D tumor models. European Journal of Pharmaceutics and Biopharmaceutics 2016;108:54–67.

[51] Nair HA, Rajawat GS, Nagarsenker MS. Stimuli-responsive micelles: a nanoplatform for therapeutic and diagnostic applications. Drug targeting and stimuli sensitive drug delivery systems. Elsevier; 2018. p. 303–42.

[52] Karimi M, et al. pH-Sensitive stimulus-responsive nanocarriers for targeted delivery of therapeutic agents. Wiley Interdisciplinary Reviews: Nanomedicine and Nanobiotechnology 2016;8(5):696–716.

[53] Xie J, et al. Design of pH-sensitive methotrexate prodrug-targeted curcumin nanoparticles for efficient dual-drug delivery and combination cancer therapy. International Journal of Nanomedicine 2018;13:1381.

[54] Tao W, He Z. ROS-responsive drug delivery systems for biomedical applications. Asian Journal of Pharmaceutical Sciences 2018;13(2):101–12.

[55] Li H, et al. Synthesis of TPGS/curcumin nanoparticles by thin-film hydration and evaluation of their anti-colon cancer efficacy in vitro and in vivo. Frontiers in Pharmacology 2019;10:769.

[56] Muddineti OS, et al. d-α-Tocopheryl succinate/phosphatidyl ethanolamine conjugated amphiphilic polymer-based nanomicellar system for the efficient delivery of curcumin and to overcome multiple drug resistance in cancer. ACS Applied Materials & Interfaces 2017;9(20):16778–92.

[57] Mokhtari RB, et al. Combination therapy in combating cancer. Oncotarget 2017;8(23):38022.

[58] Godwin P, et al. Targeting nuclear factor-kappa B to overcome resistance to chemotherapy. Frontiers in Oncology 2013;3:120.

[59] Eskandari Z, et al. NF-kappa B inhibition activity of curcumin-loaded sterically stabilized micelles and its up-regulator effect on enhancement of cytotoxicity of a new nano-pirarubicin formulation in the treatment of breast cancer. Records of Natural Products 2019;13(5).

[60] Abouzeid AH, Patel NR, Torchilin VP. Polyethylene glycol-phosphatidylethanolamine (PEG-PE)/vitamin E micelles for co-delivery of paclitaxel and curcumin to overcome multi-drug resistance in ovarian cancer. International Journal of Pharmaceutics 2014;464(1–2):178–84.

[61] Kumar A, et al. Enhanced apoptosis, survivin down-regulation and assisted immunochemotherapy by curcumin loaded amphiphilic mixed micelles for subjugating endometrial cancer. Nanomedicine: Nanotechnology, Biology and Medicine 2017;13(6):1953−63.

[62] Kedar U, et al. Advances in polymeric micelles for drug delivery and tumor targeting. Nanomedicine: Nanotechnology, Biology and Medicine 2010;6(6):714−29.

[63] Chu B, et al. Synthesis, characterization and drug loading property of Monomethoxy-Poly (ethylene glycol)-Poly (ε-caprolactone)-Poly (D, L-lactide)(MPEG-PCLA) copolymers. Scientific Reports 2016;6 (1):1−15.

[64] Song L, et al. Polymeric micelles for parenteral delivery of curcumin: preparation, characterization and in vitro evaluation. Colloids and Surfaces A: Physicochemical and Engineering Aspects 2011;390 (1−3):25−32.

[65] Manjili HK, et al. Poly (caprolactone)−poly (ethylene glycol)−poly (caprolactone)(PCL−PEG−PCL) nanoparticles: a valuable and efficient system for in vitro and in vivo delivery of curcumin. RSC Advances 2016;6(17):14403−15.

[66] Gong C, et al. Improving antiangiogenesis and anti-tumor activity of curcumin by biodegradable polymeric micelles. Biomaterials 2013;34(4):1413−32.

[67] Mohanty C, et al. Curcumin-encapsulated MePEG/PCL diblock copolymeric micelles: a novel controlled delivery vehicle for cancer therapy. Nanomedicine: Nanotechnology, Biology, and Medicine 2010;5 (3):433−49.

[68] Liu L, et al. Curcumin loaded polymeric micelles inhibit breast tumor growth and spontaneous pulmonary metastasis. International Journal of Pharmaceutics 2013;443(1−2):175−82.

[69] Manjili HK, et al. Pharmacokinetics and in vivo delivery of curcumin by copolymeric mPEG-PCL micelles. European Journal of Pharmaceutics and Biopharmaceutics 2017;116:17−30.

[70] Angarita AV, Umaña-Perez A, Perez LD. Enhancing the performance of PEG-b-PCL-based nanocarriers for curcumin through its conjugation with lipophilic biomolecules. Journal of Bioactive and Compatible Polymers 2020;35(4−5):399−413.

[71] Gong F, et al. Curcumin-loaded blood-stable polymeric micelles for enhancing therapeutic effect on erythroleukemia. Molecular Pharmaceutics 2017;14(8):2585−94.

[72] Huang L, et al. Uptake enhancement of curcumin encapsulated into phosphatidylcholine-shielding micelles by cancer cells. Journal of Biomaterials Science, Polymer Edition 2014;25(13):1407−24.

[73] Wang B-L, et al. Codelivery of curcumin and doxorubicin by MPEG-PCL results in improved efficacy of systemically administered chemotherapy in mice with lung cancer. International Journal of Nanomedicine 2013;8:3521.

[74] Sun L, et al. Co-delivery of doxorubicin and curcumin by polymeric micelles for improving antitumor efficacy on breast carcinoma. RSC Advances 2014;4(87):46737−50.

[75] Le TTD, et al. Docetaxel and curcumin-containing poly (ethylene glycol)-block-poly (ε-caprolactone) polymer micelles. Advances in Natural Sciences: Nanoscience and Nanotechnology 2013;4(2):025006.

[76] Kulkarni B, et al. AIE-based fluorescent triblock copolymer micelles for simultaneous drug delivery and intracellular imaging. Biomacromolecules 2021;22(12):5243−55.

[77] Gou M, et al. Curcumin-loaded biodegradable polymeric micelles for colon cancer therapy in vitro and in vivo. Nanoscale 2011;3(4):1558−67.

[78] Yang X, et al. Curcumin-encapsulated polymeric micelles suppress the development of colon cancer in vitro and in vivo. Scientific Reports 2015;5(1):1−15.

[79] Raveendran R, Bhuvaneshwar G, Sharma CP. In vitro cytotoxicity and cellular uptake of curcumin-loaded Pluronic/Polycaprolactone micelles in colorectal adenocarcinoma cells. Journal of Biomaterials Applications 2013;27(7):811−27.

[80] Li X, et al. Preparation of curcumin micelles and the in vitro and in vivo evaluation for cancer therapy. Journal of Biomedical Nanotechnology 2014;10(8):1458−68.

[81] Lin X, et al. Curcumin micelles suppress gastric tumor cell growth by upregulating ROS generation, disrupting redox equilibrium and affecting mitochondrial bioenergetics. Food & Function 2020;11(5):4146−59.

[82] Patil S, et al. Enhanced oral bioavailability and anticancer activity of novel curcumin loaded mixed micelles in human lung cancer cells. Phytomedicine: International Journal of Phytotherapy and Phytopharmacology 2015;22(12):1103−11.

[83] Vaidya FU, et al. Pluronic micelles encapsulated curcumin manifests apoptotic cell death and inhibits pro-inflammatory cytokines in human breast adenocarcinoma cells. Cancer Reports 2019;2(1):e1133.

[84] Lee W-H, et al. Fabrication of curcumin micellar nanoparticles with enhanced anti-cancer activity. Journal of Biomedical Nanotechnology 2015;11(6):1093−105.

[85] Wang J, et al. Curcumin-loaded TPGS/F127/P123 mixed polymeric micelles for cervical cancer therapy: formulation, characterization, and in vitro and in vivo evaluation. Journal of Biomedical Nanotechnology 2017;13(12):1631−46.

[86] Saxena V, Hussain MD. Polymeric mixed micelles for delivery of curcumin to multidrug resistant ovarian cancer. Journal of Biomedical Nanotechnology 2013;9(7):1146−54.

[87] Nguyen HN, et al. *Curcumin as fluorescent probe for directly monitoring in vitro uptake of curcumin combined paclitaxel loaded PLA-TPGS nanoparticles*. Advances in Natural. Sciences: Nanoscience and Nanotechnology 2016;7(2):025001.

[88] Kumari P, et al. Cholesterol-conjugated poly (D, L-lactide)-based micelles as a nanocarrier system for effective delivery of curcumin in cancer therapy. Drug Delivery 2017;24(1):209−23.

[89] Gao X, et al. Improving the anti-colon cancer activity of curcumin with biodegradable nano-micelles. Journal of Materials Chemistry B 2013;1(42):5778−90.

[90] Wang B, et al. Improving anti-melanoma effect of curcumin by biodegradable nanoparticles. Oncotarget 2017;8(65):108624.

[91] Tan M, Luo J, Tian Y. Delivering curcumin and gemcitabine in one nanoparticle platform for colon cancer therapy. RSC Advances 2014;4(106):61948−59.

[92] Hu Y, et al. Co-delivery of docetaxel and curcumin via nanomicelles for enhancing anti-ovarian cancer treatment. International Journal of Nanomedicine 2020;15:9703.

[93] Lv L, et al. Enhancing curcumin anticancer efficacy through di-block copolymer micelle encapsulation. Journal of Biomedical Nanotechnology 2014;10(2):179−93.

[94] Alizadeh AM, et al. Encapsulation of curcumin in diblock copolymer micelles for cancer therapy. BioMed Research International 2015; **2015**.

[95] Lachowicz D, et al. Blood-compatible, stable micelles of sodium alginate−curcumin bioconjugate for anti-cancer applications. European Polymer Journal 2019;113:208−19.

[96] Lübtow MM, et al. Drug induced micellization into ultra-high capacity and stable curcumin nanoformulations: physico-chemical characterization and evaluation in 2D and 3D in vitro models. Journal of Controlled Release 2019;303:162−80.

[97] Muraoka D, et al. Self-assembled polysaccharide nanogel delivery system for overcoming tumor immune resistance. Journal of Controlled Release 2022;347:175−82.

[98] Setayesh A, Bagheri F, Boddohi S. Self-assembled formation of chondroitin sulfate-based micellar nanogel for curcumin delivery to breast cancer cells. International Journal of Biological Macromolecules 2020;161:771−8.

[99] Khan S, et al. A difunctional Pluronic® 127-based in situ formed injectable thermogels as prolonged and controlled curcumin depot, fabrication, in vitro characterization and in vivo safety evaluation. Journal of Biomaterials Science, Polymer Edition 2021;32(3):281−319.

[100] Muddineti OS, et al. Cholesterol-grafted chitosan micelles as a nanocarrier system for drug-siRNA co-delivery to the lung cancer cells. International Journal of Biological Macromolecules 2018;118:857—63.

[101] Wang K, et al. Novel micelle formulation of curcumin for enhancing antitumor activity and inhibiting colorectal cancer stem cells. International Journal of Nanomedicine 2012;7:4487.

[102] Muddineti OS, et al. Curcumin-loaded chitosan—cholesterol micelles: evaluation in monolayers and 3D cancer spheroid model. Nanomedicine: Nanotechnology, Biology, and Medicine 2017;12 (12):1435—53.

[103] Caldas BS, et al. Drug carrier systems made from self-assembled glyco-nanoparticles of maltoheptaose-b-polyisoprene enhanced the distribution and activity of curcumin against cancer cells. Journal of Molecular Liquids 2020;309:113022.

[104] Erfani-Moghadam V, et al. A novel diblock of copolymer of (monomethoxy poly [ethylene glycol]-oleate) with a small hydrophobic fraction to make stable micelles/polymersomes for curcumin delivery to cancer cells. International Journal of Nanomedicine 2014;9:5541—54.

[105] Park JH, Han J, Lee M. Thymidine kinase gene delivery using curcumin loaded peptide micelles as a combination therapy for glioblastoma. Pharmaceutical Research 2015;32(2):528—37.

[106] Patidar P, et al. Glucose triggered enhanced solubilisation, release and cytotoxicity of poorly water soluble anti-cancer drugs fromT1307 micelles. Journal of Biotechnology 2017;254:43—50.

[107] Naksuriya O, et al. HPMA-based polymeric micelles for curcumin solubilization and inhibition of cancer cell growth. European Journal of Pharmaceutics and Biopharmaceutics 2015;94:501—12.

[108] Bagheri M, et al. In vitro and in vivo studies on HPMA-based polymeric micelles loaded with curcumin. Molecular Pharmaceutics 2021;18(3):1247—63.

[109] Wang Z, Meng F, Zhong Z. Emerging targeted drug delivery strategies toward ovarian cancer. Advanced Drug Delivery Reviews 2021;113969 113969.

[110] Mohammadzadeh V, et al. Novel EPR-enhanced strategies for targeted drug delivery in pancreatic cancer: an update. Journal of Drug Delivery Science and Technology 2022;103459.

[111] Kesharwani P, et al. Hyaluronic acid engineered nanomicelles loaded with 3, 4-difluorobenzylidene curcumin for targeted killing of CD44 + stem-like pancreatic cancer cells. Biomacromolecules 2015;16 (9):3042—53.

[112] Kesharwani P, et al. Parenterally administrable nano-micelles of 3, 4-difluorobenzylidene curcumin for treating pancreatic cancer. Colloids and Surfaces B: Biointerfaces 2015;132:138—45.

[113] Xi Y, et al. Dual targeting curcumin loaded alendronate-hyaluronan-octadecanoic acid micelles for improving osteosarcoma therapy. International Journal of Nanomedicine 2019;14:6425.

[114] Kamble S, et al. Bisphosphonate-functionalized micelles for targeted delivery of curcumin to metastatic bone cancer. Pharmaceutical Development and Technology 2020;25(9):1118—26.

[115] Soleymani M, Velashjerdi M, Asgari M. Preparation of hyaluronic acid-decorated mixed nanomicelles for targeted delivery of hydrophobic drugs to CD44-overexpressing cancer cells. International Journal of Pharmaceutics 2021;592:120052.

[116] Ancey PB, Contat C, Meylan E. Glucose transporters in cancer—from tumor cells to the tumor microenvironment. The FEBS Journal 2018;285(16):2926—43.

[117] Lecot N, et al. Glucosylated polymeric micelles actively target a breast cancer model. Advanced Therapeutics 2021;4(1):2000010.

[118] Chen C, et al. Structural basis for molecular recognition of folic acid by folate receptors. Nature 2013;500(7463):486—9.

[119] Yang C, et al. Development of a folate-modified curcumin loaded micelle delivery system for cancer targeting. Colloids and Surfaces B: Biointerfaces 2014;121:206—13.

[120] Feng R, et al. Y-shaped folic acid-conjugated PEG-PCL copolymeric micelles for delivery of curcumin. Anti-Cancer Agents in Medicinal Chemistry (Formerly Current Medicinal Chemistry-Anti-Cancer Agents) 2017;17(4):599−607.

[121] Hu Y, et al. Tumor targeted curcumin delivery by folate-modified MPEG-PCL self-assembly micelles for colorectal cancer therapy. International Journal of Nanomedicine 2020;15:1239.

[122] Lin YH, Chen C-Y. Folate-targeted curcumin-encapsulated micellar nanosystem for chemotherapy and curcumin-mediated photodynamic therapy. Polymers 2020;12(10):2280.

[123] Phan QT, et al. Characteristics and cytotoxicity of folate-modified curcumin-loaded PLA-PEG micellar nano systems with various PLA: PEG ratios. International Journal of Pharmaceutics 2016;507 (1−2):32−40.

[124] He Y, et al. Anti-glioma effect with targeting therapy using folate modified nano-micelles delivery curcumin. Journal of Biomedical Nanotechnology 2020;16(1):1−13.

[125] Luong D, et al. Folic acid conjugated polymeric micelles loaded with a curcumin difluorinated analog for targeting cervical and ovarian cancers. Colloids and Surfaces B: Biointerfaces 2017;157:490−502.

[126] Anirudhan T, Varghese S, Manjusha V. Hyaluronic acid coated Pluronic F127/Pluronic P123 mixed micelle for targeted delivery of paclitaxel and curcumin. International Journal of Biological Macromolecules 2021;192:950−7.

[127] Zamani M, et al. Targeted drug delivery via folate decorated nanocarriers based on linear polymer for treatment of breast cancer. Pharmaceutical Development and Technology 2022;27(1):19−24.

[128] Kumari P, et al. Transferrin-anchored poly (lactide) based micelles to improve anticancer activity of curcumin in hepatic and cervical cancer cell monolayers and 3D spheroids. International Journal of Biological Macromolecules 2018;116:1196−213.

[129] Zhao L, et al. Development of RGD-functionalized PEG-PLA micelles for delivery of curcumin. Journal of Biomedical Nanotechnology 2015;11(3):436−46.

[130] Liang J, et al. Enhanced solubility and targeted delivery of curcumin by lipopeptide micelles. Journal of Biomaterials Science, Polymer Edition 2015;26(6):369−83.

[131] An Q, et al. Development and characterization of octreotide-modified curcumin plus docetaxel micelles for potential treatment of non-small-cell lung cancer. Pharmaceutical Development and Technology 2019;24(9):1164−74.

[132] Mallick S, et al. Self-assembled nanoparticles composed of glycol chitosan-dequalinium for mitochondria-targeted drug delivery. International Journal of Biological Macromolecules 2019;132:451−60.

[133] Sajomsang W, et al. Synthesis and anticervical cancer activity of novel pH responsive micelles for oral curcumin delivery. International Journal of Pharmaceutics 2014;477(1−2):261−72.

[134] Li F, et al. Stimuli-responsive nano-assemblies for remotely controlled drug delivery. Journal of Controlled Release 2020;322:566−92.

[135] Yu Y, Zhang X, Qiu L. The anti-tumor efficacy of curcumin when delivered by size/charge-changing multistage polymeric micelles based on amphiphilic poly (β-amino ester) derivates. Biomaterials 2014;35(10):3467−79.

[136] Fang X-B, et al. pH-sensitive micelles based on acid-labile pluronic F68−curcumin conjugates for improved tumor intracellular drug delivery. International Journal of Pharmaceutics 2016;502 (1−2):28−37.

[137] Li Y, et al. pH responsive micelles based on copolymers mPEG-PCL-PDEA: The relationship between composition and properties. Colloids and Surfaces B: Biointerfaces 2017;154:397−407.

[138] Yang Z, et al. pH multistage responsive micellar system with charge-switch and PEG layer detachment for co-delivery of paclitaxel and curcumin to synergistically eliminate breast cancer stem cells. Biomaterials 2017;147:53−67.

[139] Chen D, et al. Design and evaluation of dual CD44 receptor and folate receptor-targeting double-smart pH-response multifunctional nanocarrier. Journal of Nanoparticle Research 2017;19(12):1–11.

[140] Liu Y, et al. pH-responsive reversibly cross-linked micelles by phenol–yne click via curcumin as a drug delivery system in cancer chemotherapy. Journal of Materials Chemistry B 2019;7(24):3884–93.

[141] Illy N, et al. pH-sensitive poly (ethylene glycol)/poly (ethoxyethyl glycidyl ether) block copolymers: synthesis, characterization, encapsulation, and delivery of a hydrophobic drug. Macromolecular Chemistry and Physics 2019;220(16):1900210.

[142] Rashidzadeh H, et al. pH-sensitive curcumin conjugated micelles for tumor triggered drug delivery. Journal of Biomaterials Science, Polymer Edition 2021;32(3):320–36.

[143] Lai H, et al. pH-responsive hyaluronic acid-based nanoparticles for targeted curcumin delivery and enhanced cancer therapy. Colloids and Surfaces B: Biointerfaces 2021;198:111455.

[144] Chen D, et al. Novel CD44 receptor targeting multifunctional "nano-eggs" based on double pH-sensitive nanoparticles for co-delivery of curcumin and paclitaxel to cancer cells and cancer stem cells. Journal of Nanoparticle Research 2015;17(10):1–10.

[145] Bai F, et al. Cross-linking of hyaluronic acid by curcumin analogue to construct nanomicelles for delivering anticancer drug. Journal of Molecular Liquids 2019;288:111079.

[146] Zeng X, et al. Construction of pH-sensitive targeted micelle system co-delivery with curcumin and dasatinib and evaluation of anti-liver cancer. Drug Delivery 2022;29(1):792–806.

[147] Liu M, et al. Novel multifunctional triple folic acid, biotin and CD44 targeting pH-sensitive nano-actiniaes for breast cancer combinational therapy. Drug Delivery 2019;26(1):1002–16.

[148] Le TT, Kim D. Folate-PEG/Hyd-curcumin/C18-g-PSI micelles for site specific delivery of curcumin to colon cancer cells via Wnt/β-catenin signaling pathway. Materials Science and Engineering: C 2019;101:464–71.

[149] Song J, et al. Glycyrrhetinic acid modified and pH-sensitive mixed micelles improve the anticancer effect of curcumin in hepatoma carcinoma cells. RSC Advances 2019;9(68):40131–45.

[150] Zhou Y, et al. Multi pH-sensitive polymer–drug conjugate mixed micelles for efficient co-delivery of doxorubicin and curcumin to synergistically suppress tumor metastasis. Biomaterials Science 2020;8(18):5029–46.

[151] Fu X, et al. Precise design strategies of nanomedicine for improving cancer therapeutic efficacy using subcellular targeting. Signal Transduction and Targeted Therapy 2020;5(1):1–15.

[152] Babikova D, et al. Multifunctional polymer nanocarrier for efficient targeted cellular and subcellular anticancer drug delivery. ACS Biomaterials Science & Engineering 2019;5(5):2271–83.

[153] Fang L, et al. Novel mitochondrial targeting charge-reversal polysaccharide hybrid shell/core nanoparticles for prolonged systemic circulation and antitumor drug delivery. Drug Delivery 2019;26(1):1125–39.

[154] Li Y, et al. Anticancer nanomedicines harnessing tumor microenvironmental components. Expert Opinion on Drug Delivery 2022;19(4):337–54.

[155] He H, et al. Oxidation-responsive and aggregation-induced emission polymeric micelles with two-photon excitation for cancer therapy and bioimaging. ACS Biomaterials Science & Engineering 2019;5(5):2577–86.

[156] Qiao Z, et al. Completely degradable backbone-type hydrogen peroxide responsive curcumin copolymer: Synthesis and synergistic anticancer investigation. Polymer Chemistry 2019;10(31):4305–13.

[157] Lee P-Y, et al. Nanogels comprising reduction-cleavable polymers for glutathione-induced intracellular curcumin delivery. Journal of Polymer Research 2017;24(5):1–10.

[158] Chen D, et al. Preparation and characterization of glutathione-responsive polymeric micelles functionalized with core cross-linked disulfide linkage for curcumin delivery. Journal of Polymer Research 2019;26(5):1–12.

[159] Gong F, et al. Synergistic effect of the anti-PD-1 antibody with blood stable and reduction sensitive curcumin micelles on colon cancer. Drug Delivery 2021;28(1):930−42.

[160] Dai Y, et al. Co-assembly of curcumin and a cystine bridged peptide to construct tumor-responsive nano-micelles for efficient chemotherapy. Journal of Materials Chemistry B 2020;8(9):1944−51.

[161] Liu X, et al. Hypoxia responsive nano-drug delivery system based on angelica polysaccharide for liver cancer therapy. Drug Delivery 2022;29(1):138−48.

[162] Debele TA, et al. Combination delivery of alpha-tocopheryl succinate and curcumin using a GSH-sensitive micelle (PAH-SS-PLGA) to treat pancreatic cancer. Pharmaceutics 2020;12(8):778.

[163] Zhang Y, et al. Folic acid-targeted disulfide-based cross-linking micelle for enhanced drug encapsulation stability and site-specific drug delivery against tumors. International Journal of Nanomedicine 2016;11:1119.

[164] Wu P, et al. Ultrasound-responsive polymeric micelles for sonoporation-assisted site-specific therapeutic action. ACS Applied Materials & Interfaces 2017;9(31):25706−16.

[165] Xu H-L, et al. Therapeutic supermolecular micelles of vitamin E succinate-grafted ε-polylysine as potential carriers for curcumin: enhancing tumour penetration and improving therapeutic effect on glioma. Colloids and Surfaces B: Biinterfaces 2017;158:295−307.

[166] Sahu A, et al. Synthesis of novel biodegradable and self-assembling methoxy poly (ethylene glycol)−palmitate nanocarrier for curcumin delivery to cancer cells. Acta Biomaterialia 2008;4(6):1752−61.

[167] Gao N, et al. Injectable shell-crosslinked F127 micelle/hydrogel composites with pH and redox sensitivity for combined release of anticancer drugs. Chemical Engineering Journal 2016;287:20−9.

[168] Zhang H, et al. Biodegradable reduction and pH dual-sensitive polymer micelles based on poly (2-ethyl-2-oxazoline) for efficient delivery of curcumin. RSC Advances 2020;10(43):25435−45.

[169] Hu J, et al. A two-photon fluorophore labeled multi-functional drug carrier for targeting cancer therapy, inflammation restraint and AIE active bioimaging. Journal of Materials Chemistry B 2019;7(24):3894−908.

[170] Qi M, et al. Enhanced in vitro and in vivo anticancer properties by using a nanocarrier for co-delivery of antitumor polypeptide and curcumin. Journal of Biomedical Nanotechnology 2018;14(1):139−49.

[171] Basha M. Nanotechnology as a promising strategy for anticancer drug delivery. Current Drug Delivery 2018;15(4):497−509.

[172] Gao Y, et al. Targeted cancer therapy; nanotechnology approaches for overcoming drug resistance. Current Medicinal Chemistry 2015;22(11):1335−47.

[173] Muddineti OS, et al. Cholesterol and vitamin E-conjugated PEGylated polymeric micelles for efficient delivery and enhanced anticancer activity of curcumin: evaluation in 2D monolayers and 3D spheroids. Artificial Cells, Nanomedicine, and Biotechnology 2018;46(sup1):773−86.

[174] Zhao G, Sun Y, Dong X. Zwitterionic polymer micelles with dual conjugation of doxorubicin and curcumin: synergistically enhanced efficacy against multidrug-resistant tumor cells. Langmuir: the ACS Journal of Surfaces and Colloids 2020;36(9):2383−95.

[175] Xu J, et al. RVG-functionalized reduction sensitive micelles for the effective accumulation of doxorubicin in brain. Journal of Nanobiotechnology 2021;19(1):1−16.

[176] Lv L, et al. Amphiphilic copolymeric micelles for doxorubicin and curcumin co-delivery to reverse multidrug resistance in breast cancer. Journal of Biomedical Nanotechnology 2016;12(5):973−85.

[177] Huang S, et al. PEGylated doxorubicin micelles loaded with curcumin exerting synergic effects on multidrug resistant tumor cells. Journal of Nanoscience and Nanotechnology 2017;17(5):2873−80.

[178] Wang J, et al. Comparison of hyaluronic acid-based micelles and polyethylene glycol-based micelles on reversal of multidrug resistance and enhanced anticancer efficacy in vitro and in vivo. Drug Delivery 2018;25(1):330−40.

[179] Ma W, et al. Co-assembly of doxorubicin and curcumin targeted micelles for synergistic delivery and improving anti-tumor efficacy. European Journal of Pharmaceutics and Biopharmaceutics 2017;112:209−23.

[180] Wang J, Ma W, Tu P. Synergistically improved anti-tumor efficacy by co-delivery doxorubicin and curcumin polymeric micelles. Macromolecular Bioscience 2015;15(9):1252−61.

[181] Gu Y, et al. Nanomicelles loaded with doxorubicin and curcumin for alleviating multidrug resistance in lung cancer. International Journal of Nanomedicine 2016;11:5757.

[182] Al Fatease A, et al. Chemosensitization and mitigation of Adriamycin-induced cardiotoxicity using combinational polymeric micelles for co-delivery of quercetin/resveratrol and resveratrol/curcumin in ovarian cancer. Nanomedicine: Nanotechnology, Biology and Medicine 2019;19:39−48.

[183] Gao X, et al. Combined delivery and anti-cancer activity of paclitaxel and curcumin using polymeric micelles. Journal of Biomedical Nanotechnology 2015;11(4):578−89.

[184] Scarano W, De Souza P, Stenzel MH. Dual-drug delivery of curcumin and platinum drugs in polymeric micelles enhances the synergistic effects: a double act for the treatment of multidrug-resistant cancer. Biomaterials Science 2015;3(1):163−74.

10

Liposome-based curcumin delivery systems as cancer therapeutics

Neda Mostajeran[1,2], Seyedeh Hoda Alavizadeh[1,2], Fatemeh Gheybi[1,3], Amirhossein Sahebkar[4,5]

[1]NANOTECHNOLOGY RESEARCH CENTER, PHARMACEUTICAL TECHNOLOGY INSTITUTE, MASHHAD UNIVERSITY OF MEDICAL SCIENCES, MASHHAD, IRAN [2]DEPARTMENT OF PHARMACEUTICAL NANOTECHNOLOGY, SCHOOL OF PHARMACY, MASHHAD UNIVERSITY OF MEDICAL SCIENCES, MASHHAD, IRAN [3]DEPARTMENT OF MEDICAL BIOTECHNOLOGY AND NANOTECHNOLOGY, FACULTY OF MEDICINE, MASHHAD UNIVERSITY OF MEDICAL SCIENCES, MASHHAD, IRAN [4]BIOTECHNOLOGY RESEARCH CENTER, PHARMACEUTICAL TECHNOLOGY INSTITUTE, MASHHAD UNIVERSITY OF MEDICAL SCIENCES, MASHHAD, IRAN [5]APPLIED BIOMEDICAL RESEARCH CENTER, MASHHAD UNIVERSITY OF MEDICAL SCIENCES, MASHHAD, IRAN

10.1 Introduction

Curcumin (CUR) is a polyphenolic phytochemical derived from turmeric and has been shown to exert extensive pharmacological effects against various diseases [1−12]. Notably, CUR serves as a promising phytochemical with chemoprotective and chemotherapeutic potential. CUR bioapplications have been widely explored in the treatment of liver, breast, ovarian, prostate, pancreatic, liver, and colorectal cancers, among others [13−17]. Several underlying mechanisms have been recognized to facilitate CUR's anticancer capacity including affecting vital cancer-related transduction and inflammatory pathways, leading to the subsequent cell cycle arrest and apoptotic induction [13,14,18,19].

Kinetic behavior of CUR is the central weak point limiting its application, since this compound is chemically unstable, has poor aqueous solubility, and undergoes rapid metabolism. Many approaches have been exploited to overcome the shortcomings of CUR including introducing synthetic CUR analogs, combination therapy with chemotherapeutic agents as well as applying numerous novel drug carriers to overcome the pharmacokinetic limitations of CUR's systemic and oral administration [20,21].

CUR analog including IND-4, FLLL, GO-Y030, and C086 have demonstrated improved cytotoxicity. CUR combination with many other therapeutics such as tolfenamic acid, 5-fluorouracil, resveratrol, and dasatinib have also showed to enhance cytotoxicity and

Curcumin-Based Nanomedicines as Cancer Therapeutics. DOI: https://doi.org/10.1016/B978-0-443-15412-6.00014-3

therapeutic potential in cancer therapy. This chapter focuses on the CUR encapsulation within liposomes as a widespread drug delivery system in the treatment of various cancers, which can be considered as an alternative strategy to improve CUR therapeutic efficacy [22].

10.2 Conventional liposomes

Liposomes are a family of spherical structures comprised of lipid bilayers surrounding an encapsulated aqueous phase in the center. Since their discovery in 1965, liposomes have been extensively used as versatile therapeutic vehicles due to their biocompatible and biodegradable features. The main benefits of nanoliposomes include their capability to encase hydrophilic moieties (drugs, DNA, RNA, etc.) in their inner aqueous core and hydrophobic agents within their lipidic bilayers. Other advantages include controlled release properties, stability, safety, and targeting pathophysiological and inflammatory sites including cancer tissues [23,24].

Conventional liposomes are defined as liposomes that are typically composed of phospholipids (neutral and/or negatively charged) and/or cholesterol, mostly used in earlier research on liposomes as a drug-carrier system. Conventional liposomes can vary widely in their physicochemical properties including size, lipid composition, surface charge, and the number and fluidity of the phospholipid bilayers [25]. One of the main shortcomings of conventional liposomes is their relatively short blood circulation time. When administered in vivo by a variety of parenteral routes, often through intravenous administration, they show a strong tendency to accumulate rapidly in the phagocytic cells of the mononuclear phagocyte system (MPS), also often referred to as the reticuloendothelial system (RES) [26]. Indeed, conventional liposomes opsonization by plasma proteins, results in their quick capture by the RES. The major RES organs include liver and spleen and the primary reasons for the preponderance of particles in these organs are the abundance of MPS macrophages and their rich blood supply [25]. Conventional liposomes have been used for antigen delivery approaches and liposome-based vaccines have proved effective in experimental models against viral, bacterial, and parasitic infections [27−29] as well as against tumors [30]. Several liposomal vaccines have been tested in humans, and one of these, a liposomal hepatitis-A vaccine, has received marketing approval in Switzerland [31,32].

Unwanted RES uptake of liposomes especially during chemotherapy may cause depletion of macrophages as one of the prime host defense soldiers, resulting in immune system impairment as well as treatment failure [33]. RES uptake, however, depends on the physicochemical features of the liposome including size, surface potential, and lipid composition can occur within several minutes following administration to clear the liposomes from the blood circulation. For instance, liposomes 400 nm in diameter are quickly removed from the circulation, while liposomes less than 200 nm in size can circulate longer within bloodstream [34−36].

Stealth liposomes were developed by coating liposome surface with hydrophilic polymers by incorporating amphipathic polyethylene glycol (PEG) derivatives like lipid derivative of PEG into liposomes. This modification extends the blood circulation half-life of stealth liposomes to several hours as compared to less than a few minutes in conventional liposomes [37]. Uptake inhibition of liposomes by the RES system concomitant with reduced drug leakage while in circulation has resulted in considerable pharmacological properties [38]. These stealth carriers improved extravasation and enhanced localization within the tumors and other inflammatory tissues.

Indeed, the enhanced permeability and retention (EPR) of nanoparticles into the tumor has long stood as one of the central principles for the delivery of therapeutics to the cancer site. EPR holds the promise of safe and effective therapy by allowing preferential access of the particles to the tumor by virtue of their small size and extended circulation time. Following the discovery of EPR by Maeda in the mid-1980s, this phenomenon appeared to be a neat rationale for justifying the promising evidence from the preclinical and clinical studies of Doxil [39]. This PEGylated liposomal form of doxorubicin (DOX) has proved successful results in clinical trials and received FDA approval in 1995 for the treatment of AIDS-related Kaposi sarcoma (ARKS), as the first clinically approved nano-sized drug carrier [40]. Under the label Doxil in the United States and Caelyx in Europe, other applications include refractory ovarian cancer and multiple myeloma [41]. Other examples of conventional liposomes include an amphotericin B-incorporate liposome, Ambisome (Nexstar, Boulder, CO, USA), which has been employed as an antifungal drug, and Myocet (Elan Pharma Inc., Princeton, NJ, USA), liposome-containing DOX, adopted for the treatment of metastatic breast cancer [42]. Myocet is a non-PEGylated liposomal DOX formulation with substantially different pharmacokinetic features from Doxil/Caelyx, including circulation half-life, stability of the formulation, and drug release pattern [43]. Myocet releases a huge amounts of drug content within an hour and less than 10% of the original dose remains in the circulation following 24 h of administration while more than half of the Doxil DOX contents can remain in the circulation 48–72 h following administration [44]. This difference actually justifies the importance of formulation design of liposomes for bioapplication.

The role of CUR (diferuloylmethane), a proapoptotic compound, for the treatment of cancer has been an area of growing interest. CUR in its free form is poorly absorbed from the gastrointestinal tract and therefore has limited clinical efficacy. Some studies have investigated the combination therapy with intact CUR to overcome chemoresistance and to sensitize cancer cells to chemotherapy. Paclitaxel (PTX), a microtubule-targeting antineoplastic agent, is highly efficacious against a wide spectrum of human cancers. However, dose-limiting toxicities and occurrence of drug resistance impede its clinical applications. It was previously shown that CUR could enhance PTX-induced cytotoxicity in vitro through the downregulation of nuclear factor (NF)-κB and Akt pathways [45]. Sreekanth et al. examined the underlying molecular mechanisms of CUR and PTX synergic action in vivo. Mouse cervical multistage squamous cell carcinoma model and a xenograft model of human cervical cancer were used for this investigation. Combination therapy with CUR and PTX reduced tumor incidence and induced tumor shrinkage in mice compared to the individual treatment with PTX. Molecular analysis revealed that CUR augments PTX antitumor activity by downregulating the antiapoptotic and survival signals including NF-κB, Akt, and mitogen-activated protein kinases that play pivotal roles in cancer proliferation, survival, angiogenesis, and metastasis. Furthermore, it was shown that preexposure of the carcinoma cells to CUR could potentiate PTX-induced apoptosis [46]. Developing the use of carriers provides a strong rationale for further investigation of such combination strategies, which could potentiate the therapeutic index of either therapeutic agent. In the following sections, we summarized the application of CUR conventional liposomes for the treatment of various malignancies.

10.2.1 Skin cancer (melanoma)

Liposomes are widely used as carriers, most notably in their application for topical delivery of a variety of drugs due to their small size, biodegradability, and low toxicity [47]. Results from several studies demonstrated that liposomes bear the potential to enhance drug penetration into the skin layers, improving therapeutic effectiveness, reducing side effects, and further acting as local depots for the sustained release of drugs [48,49]. Phospholipids composition of liposomes has also shown to directly influence the penetration behavior of liposomes [50]. Yan Chen et al. investigated the efficacy of various phospholipid compositions on the transdermal delivery potential of curcumin liposomes (CL). In vitro skin permeation study and in vivo antineoplastic activity revealed that C-SPC-L (curcumin-loaded soybean phosphatidyl choline liposomes) has significantly promoted drug permeation deposition and antimelanoma activity, followed by C-EPC-L (curcumin-loaded egg yolk phosphatidyl Choline liposomes), and C-HSPC-L (curcumin-loaded hydrogenated soybean phosphatidyl choline liposomes) and CUR solution. Results indicated a higher in vitro release of CUR and an improved skin penetration by C-SPC-L compared to other liposomal formulations. Furthermore, the C-SPC-L formulation showed a higher inhibitory activity on B16BL6 melanoma cells and significantly suppressed tumor growth in mice model of melanoma cancer. The aforementioned results suggested that C-SPC-liposome could be a promising transdermal carrier for the delivery of CUR in the treatment of skin cancer [50].

10.2.2 Pancreatic cancer

NF-κB comprises a family of transcription factors that play fundamental roles in multiple physiological and pathological processes including inflammation, cell proliferation, differentiation, and survival [51]. NF-κB constitutive activation in cancer cells is associated with cancer cell proliferation [52]. Liposomal curcumin (Lip-cur) interference with NF-κB signaling pathways has led to the suppression of tumor growth and invasiveness. Lan Li et al. have shown that Lip-cur could decrease the expression of NF-κB-regulated gene products, including cyclo-oxygenase-2 (COX-2) and interleukin-8 (IL-8) in pancreatic carcinoma cells. Further in vitro results indicated a concentration- and time-dependent antiproliferative and proapoptotic effect on the cancer cells. The activity of Lip-cur was greater than that of free CUR at equimolar concentrations. In vivo CL suppressed pancreatic tumor burden growth in murine xenograft model and inhibited tumor angiogenesis [53]. Lip-cur has also shown NF-κB machinery downregulation, suppressed growth, and induced apoptosis of human pancreatic cells in vitro as well as antitumor and antiangiogenesis effects in vivo [54]. This experiment provides a rationale for systemic delivery of phytochemical using liposomes.

Amalendu P. Ranjan et al. have used pancreatic cancer cells in vitro and xenograft mouse model to assess the therapeutic efficacy of Lip-cur. Toxicity study indicated an in vitro IC_{50} value of 17.5 μM. Pancreatic xenograft model in nude mice represented a significant tumor growth inhibition following i.p. administration of Lip-cur (20 mg/kg, three times a week for 4 weeks). Immunohistochemistry study revealed a robust antiangiogenic effect as shown by downregulated vascular endothelial growth factor (VEGF) and annexin A2 proteins [55].

In a study by Mohamed Mahmud et al., varying CUR-loaded liposomal formulations were developed by using different lipids and drug to lipid ratios. The formulations were assessed regarding size, shape, surface charge, and stability at two temperatures (4°C and 37°C). PEGylated, cholesterol-free HSPC (hydrogenated soya PC)-based liposomal formulation with 0.05/10 drug to lipid molar ratio showed 96% CUR incorporation efficiency with favorable stability. All Lip-cur formulations showed considerable toxicity on AsPC-1 and BxPC-3 cancer cells, while did not significantly affect the viability of NHDF normal cells. Significant changes in the cell morphology including irregularity in the cellular shape, cell shrinking, cytoplasmic blebbing, as well as phosphatidylserine exposure on the outer cell membrane were observed following treatment. Results also demonstrated intracellular reactive oxygen species (ROS) generation and significant activity in 3/7 caspases. Though no in vivo experiment was performed, release study indicated a slow leakage of the loaded CUR in the human plasma, which is expected to improve the targeting capacity of liposomes by the EPR effect [56].

The minimum effective dose (MED) and optimum-dosing schedule of Lip-cur were evaluated in a xenograft model of athymic nude mice bearing MiaPaCa-2 human pancreatic cancer cells. For MED, mice received Lip-cur at 1−40 mg/kg through tail vein injection three times weekly for 28 days. For the optimum-dosing schedule, three different additional schedules were evaluated and compared to three times weekly dosing including (1) daily (5 days per week), (2) every-four-day, and (3) weekly for 28 days. Results indicated that Lip-cur at 20 mg/kg has significantly decreased tumor growth. MED of 20 mg/kg was further used for the optimal dosing schedule evaluation. Daily dosing and three times per week dosing showed greater tumor growth inhibition, with no discernible difference compared to once-weekly or every-four-day dosing. No toxicity was observed at any doses or schedules. The finding of this study merits further preclinical studies to define the safety and tolerability of Lip-cur in other animal models [57].

10.2.3 Liver cancer

Hepatocellular carcinoma (HCC) is a leading cause of death in the world. Transcatheter embolization (TAE) is an extensively used procedure in the treatment of nonsurgical HCC. In 2019 a study was conducted to investigate the efficacy of Lip-cur on HCC following TAE. For this, the HepG2 cells were cultured under hypoxic condition (1% O_2) and then were treated with CL in vitro. CL have clearly reduced the cell viability and promoted cell apoptosis in G1 phase through regulating the apoptosis-related molecules. For in vivo study, VX2 rabbits were distributed into three groups of control (saline embolization), lipiodol embolization as well as lipiodol embolization and CL treatment. CUR liposomal treatment has obviously inhibited the tumor growth and ameliorated neoplasia in the animal model. Pathological investigation demonstrated that CL treatment could decrease the microvessel density (MVD) and VEGF expression, and increase cancer liver cells apoptosis. The hypoxia-inducible factor-1α (HIF-1α) and survivin expression were suppressed following treatment with Lip-cur in hypoxic cells as well as in VX2 rabbit liver tissues [58].

Cisplatin (CDDP) is one of the most applicable chemotherapeutic agents used in the treatment of solid tumors. CDDP's poor efficacy in HCC is mainly attributed to severe toxicity and drug resistance. CUR has already shown to improve the chemosensitivity by regulating several cancer-related signaling pathways. In 2018 Yao Cheng et al. used a combination strategy for efficacious codelivery of CDDP and CUR to HCC to overcome the poor outcome of CDDP therapy. The reverse microemulsion and film dispersion method were used to prepare CDDP-CUR coloaded liposomes (CDDP/Lip-cur), resulting in liposomes with an average diameter of 294.6 $\pm$ 14.8 nm and homogenous size distribution. In vitro cytotoxicity study indicated a synergistic cell killing potential against HepG2 cells following CDDP/Lip-cur exposure at the optimal 1:8 ratio of CDDP and CUR, respectively. Furthermore, CDDP/Lip-cur treatment led to an increased intracellular ROS levels in HepG2 cells. Therapeutic efficacy study demonstrated an elongated retention time ($t_{1/2} = 2.38$ h) and significant tumor shrinkage in mouse hepatoma H22 and human HCC HepG2 xenograft models and less CDDP distribution in the normal vital organs compared to the tumor tissue [59]. CUR and tetrandrine encapsulation within liposomes bearing either DSPE-mPEG$_{2000}$ or Tween 80 showed no significant toxicity on zebrafish liver, while the liposomes indicated a robust cytotoxic effect on a variety of cancer cells including MDA-MB-231, HepG2, HGC-27, and HCT11 [60].

10.2.4 Colorectal cancer

In 2007 Lan Li et al. evaluated the Lip-cur antitumor activity in colorectal cancer and compared its efficacy with oxaliplatin, a standard chemotherapy used in the treatment of this malignancy. In vitro treatment with Lip-cur induced a dose-dependent growth inhibition and apoptosis in LoVo and Colo205 human colorectal cancer cells. There was also a synergistic effect between Lip-cur and oxaliplatin at 4:1 molar ratio, respectively, in LoVo cells. PARP cleavage as determined by western blot analysis in colon cancer cells indicated a dose-dependent effect following exposure to oxaliplatin, Lip-cur, or Lip-cur and oxaliplatin combination. In vivo significant tumor shrinkage was observed in Colo205 and LoVo xenografts mouse models, and the tumor growth inhibition of Lip-cur was greater compared to that of oxaliplatin in Colo205-bearing animals. Tumors from animals treated with combination therapy with Lip-cur showed a significant antiangiogenic effect by attenuating CD31 endothelial marker, VEGF, and IL-8 expression. This study established a combination approach based on Lip-cur and oxaliplatin for the treatment of colorectal cancer [61].

In 2018 Alina Sesarman et al. prepared long-circulating liposomes (LCL) loaded with curcumin and doxorubicin (LCL-CURC-DOX) to explore antitumor efficacy of coencapsulation and to dominate the limitations regarding the side effects and resistance. The cytotoxicity of CURC-DOX coencapsulated LCL on C26 cells exceeded compared to either administered agent in the free form. Notably, results indicated that LCL-CURC-DOX could dramatically inhibit NF-κB-dependent angiogenic/inflammatory protein levels compared to the free agents, however, did not affect ROS production or AP-1 c-Jun activation [62]. In a recent study, the same group used LCL-CURC-DOX to explore the antitumor efficacy of coencapsulation and the effect on DOX toxicity in colon cancer models. So, two animal models were used to assess the biodistribution and pharmacokinetic of the dual-loaded liposomes. BALB/c mice bearing C26 colon tumors received two i.v. doses of LCL-CURC-DOX at 2.5 and 5 mg/kg of DOX and CURC, respectively, and healthy rats were administered a single i.v. injection of the liposome at 1 mg/kg DOX. Results revealed that the pharmacokinetics and biodistribution of DOX were significantly improved and further investigation on the markers of cardiac and hepatic oxidative status demonstrated an alleviation of the DOX-associated adverse effects due to the antioxidative nature of the encapsulated CUR [63].

In another study in 2011, CUR was incorporated into egg-phosphatidylcholine (EPC) liposomes (1:14 drug to lipid molar ratio) with an encapsulation efficiency of approximately 85%. The Lip-cur formulation was lyophilized to preserve its stability and the subsequent reconstitution resulted in the original liposomal suspension. The release profile in fetal bovine serum (FBS) indicated a maximum of 14% CUR leakage at 96 hours of incubation. The liposomal formulation found to be more potent against HCT116 and HCT15 colon cancer cells with multidrug resistance (MDR) phenotype [64].

Yu-Ling Lin et al. applied a hybrid cationic liposome-PEG-PEI complex (LPPC) (270 nm, 40% encapsulation efficiency) for CUR delivery to the colon cancer cells. Cytotoxicity of CUR/LPPC complex has shown to be greater compared to free CUR by 5- and 20-fold when tested on CUR-sensitive and CUR-resistant cells, respectively. Further study indicated a rapid accumulation of CUR/LPPC within the cells leading to G2/M phase cell cycle arrest and apoptosis. In vivo study in mice bearing CT-26 or B16F10 tumor cells demonstrated that administration of CUR/LPPC could inhibit tumor growth by 60%–90% [65]. Quercetin-modified Lip-cur has also demonstrated promising feature as an anticancer therapeutic agent. In vitro study indicated that quercetin-decorated liposomes improved cytotoxicity of the liposomal carrier against HT-29 and HCT-15 cells. Furthermore, liposomes modification with quercetin prolonged the animal life span and improved the body weight of the lymphoma-bearing mice compared to nonmodified liposomes [66].

10.2.5 Stomach cancer

In a recent 2020 paper, a fibronectin-coated electroconductive platform was introduced as a detection tool to precisely evaluate the anticancer effects of phytochemicals with low toxicity. In this study, the novel cell-based electrochemical sensing platform was utilized to investigate the potential toxicity of CUR-nanoliposomes (curcumin-NLC) toward human stomach cancer cells (MKN-28). The platform was designed to enable cancer cell adhesion and growth on the chip surface to provide real-time monitoring of the cell behavior quantitatively. The biocompatibility and electroconductivity of the used electrodes were adjusted by optimizing gold nanostructure density and surface coating with some extracellular matrix

(ECM) proteins. Results indicated that at $10-100\ \mu M$, both free CUR and curcumin-NLC exerted toxic effects on MKN-28 cells. Findings also demonstrated the higher sensitivity of electrochemical sensing by $1.7-2$ times compared to conventional colorimetric assay [67].

10.2.6 Head and neck squamous carcinoma

Head and neck squamous cell carcinoma (HNSCC) is the sixth most common cancer worldwide, with 600,000 new cases every year and 50% 5-year survival following chemotherapy. Drug resistance is one of the main reason of treatment failure, thus finding alternative strategies to overcome drug resistance is required to improve HNSCC therapy. In 2015 Basak et al. packaged curcumin-difluorinated (CDF), a synthetic analog of CUR, into liposomes to evaluate its efficacy on growth inhibition of CCL-23R and UM-SCC-1R CDDP-resistant HNSCC cells. Treatment of the resistant cells in vitro with liposomal CDF followed by CDDP resulted in a significant growth inhibition. The nude mice xenograft study showed a significant tumor growth suppression of UM-SCC-1R model as well as a remarkable reduced CD44 expression, indicating the inhibitory effects of liposomal CDF combination with CDDP on cancer stem cells (CSCs). Results demonstrated that delivery of CDF through liposomes in combination with chemotherapeutics may be an effective approach to combat drug resistance [68].

In another study, treatment with Lip-cur showed a significant growth suppression of CAL27 and UM-SCC1 HNSCC in vitro and in vivo. Additionally, Lip-cur treatment suppressed NF-κB signaling activation without affecting the expression of pAKT or its downstream target phospho-S6 kinase. Expression of cyclin D1, COX-2, matrix metalloproteinase-9, Bcl-2, Bcl-xL, Mcl-1L, and Mcl-1S were significantly decreased, laying emphasis on the effect of CUR on NF-κB pathway. Tumor burden of HNSCC xenograft mouse model was suppressed 3.5 weeks following treatment with i.v. Lip-cur, and there was no demonstrable tissue toxicity upon autopsy. Tumors immunohistochemistry analysis further confirmed NF-κB inhibition without affecting the pAKT expression, suggesting that Lip-cur as a nontoxic therapeutic agent may work via an AKT-independent pathway in HNSCC [69].

10.2.7 Breast cancer

Chemoresistance is one of the biggest hurdles in treating breast cancers. There are emerging evidence presenting CUR potential in combating resistance to classical chemotherapeutic agents. Furthermore, codelivery of varying chemotherapeutics by using a nanoscale vehicle could significantly regulate the colocalization of the therapeutic agent within the targeted tissue, thus promoting the antitumor efficacy. In 2021 Mahmoudi et al. have developed a dual-loaded CDDP-CUR nanoliposomal carrier (Cur-Cis@NLP) for the treatment of breast cancer cells. In vitro study indicated that Cur-Cis@NLP has remarkably inhibited breast cancer cells growth (82.5%) compared to free and liposomal CDDP. Furthermore, combination index value of Cur-Cis@NLP was <1, confirming the synergetic action of the dual-targeted delivery system. Flow cytometry analysis showed a 10-fold increase in cell apoptosis with Cur-Cis@NLPs in vitro compared to liposomal CDDP. On the whole, this study highlighted a notable synergistic activity following CUR and CDDP codelivery by using liposomal carrier [70].

In 2017 *Siying Zhou et al.* also comprehensively investigated the role of Lip-cur on chemosensitivity of Adr-resistant MCF-7 human breast cancer cells (MCF-7/Adr) by exploring dysregulated and differentially expressed microRNAs. The results indicated that Lip-cur could affect the sensitivity of MCF-7/Adr cells to DOX by modifying the expression of microRNAs. For example, miR-29b-1-5p lowered expression was associated with decreased IC$_{50}$ while its higher expression weakened Lip-cur effect on Adr-resistance. Furthermore, they have reported that 20 target genes (mRNAs) of each dysregulated miRNA neither were predicted by prediction algorithms nor were differentially expressed in the microarray. Results also indicated that several signaling pathways including MAPK, mTOR, PI3K-Akt, AMPK, TNF, Ras, and numerous target genes such as PPARG, RRM2, SRSF1, and EPAS1 were involved in breast cancer cells' drug resistance to Adr. On the whole, this study provides insights into the role of miRNA expression in acquiring resistance to Adr, and to the fact that Lip-cur could alter resistance by affecting miRNA signaling pathways in breast cancer MCF-7 cells [71].

The instability of liposome matrices, leading to drug leakage, is one of the hurdles that limit their applications. Thus surface coating using polymers has advanced the field and showed to prevent drug release. In a very recent study in 2022, Alaa K Othman et al. fabricated a variety of CUR nanocapsules by using 1,2-dimyristoyl-*sn-glycero*-3-phosphocholine (DMPC) and surface coating with poly(diallyldimethylammonium)chloride (PDAA) polymer and silica. Interestingly, entrapment efficiency, release pattern, and liposome stability of the surface-coated liposomes showed a significant improvement compared to the noncoated liposomes. CUR diffusion from the coated nanocapsules has dramatically decreased with increasing the number of layers and followed the Higuchi model [72]. In other study in 2017, Riwang Li et al. utilized a thiol-derivatised chitosan (CSSH) for CL surface coating. The resulting liposomes (Lip-cur-CSSH) with 406.0 nm size and 93.95% encapsulation efficiency demonstrated slower release pattern at pH 5.5 and 7.4 compared to noncoated Lip-cur. The stability was also improved at room temperature and at higher temperature as determined by the differential scanning calorimetry (DSC) assay. CL at 200 μM showed dramatic growth-inhibitory effects on MCF-7 cells. On the whole, it seemingly that liposome proper surface coating could significantly contribute to the stability and functions thus improving its bioapplications [73].

Mahmoud Hasan et al. have used another approach to improve the liposome stability. They have developed CUR-encapsulated chitosan-coated nanoliposomes derived from three natural lecithin sources with nanometric scale (around 120 nm) and negative surface charge (approximately −40 mV). Among the three lecithins used for liposome preparation, salmon lecithin demonstrated the greatest growth inhibition on MCF-7 cells at an equimolar concentration of CUR. The soya- and rapeseed-derived lecithins presented a similar growth-inhibitory action on the tumor cells. Modifying the nanoliposomes with chitosan coating resulted in a more efficient loading of CUR (88% in chitosan-coated liposomes vs 65% in noncoated liposomes) and a stronger cytotoxicity on MCF-7 breast cancer cells [74].

In another study, hybrid polymer-lipid nanoparticles were used for the codelivery of PTX and CUR to the breast tumor. To do this, PTX-bearing albumin nanoparticles (APN) were encapsulated within CL through the thin-film hydration technique. The resulting nano-sized

CL-APN hybrid polymer-lipid showed dramatically superior cytotoxicity compared to the cocktail combination at lower doses. CL-APN acted as an NF-κB inhibitor due to the presence of CUR and significantly induced early and late apoptosis, robust G2/M arrest, and cell sequestration with subG1 [75].

10.2.8 Endometrial carcinoma

As already mentioned, NF-κB is one the leading and extensively studied pathways contributing to the cancer cell proliferation and differentiation. In a recent study, the efficacy of CUR liposomal formulation was assessed on modulating such a pathway in endometrial carcinoma (EC). In vitro study revealed a dose-dependent inhibition of Ishikawa and HEC-1 endometrial cancer cell motility and proliferation and apoptosis induction. Treatment with Lip-cur has also shown a significant inhibitory effect on the activation and/or expression of NF-κB, caspase-3, as well as matrix metallopeptidase 9 (MMP-9). Investigation on the safety profile of the fabricated liposomes in zebrafish model revealed no considerable toxicity and treatment efficacy in a zebrafish transplantation model of EC tumor demonstrated reduced tumor burden and downregulated NF-κB expression [76].

10.2.9 Prostate cancer

The chemopreventive role of CUR or resveratrol encapsulating liposomes alone and in combination was tested in prostate cancer model. In vitro assays using PTEN-CaP8 prostate cancer cells indicated synergistic effects of Lip-cur and resveratrol on the cell growth and apoptosis. Several molecular targets including pAkt, cyclin D1, mammalian target of rapamycin, and androgen receptor (AR) were downregulated by using the combination of Lip-cur and resveratrol. Results clearly suggested that phytochemicals in combination could reduce prostate cancer incidence due to the loss of the *PTEN* tumor suppressor gene. High performance liquid chromotagraphy (HPLC) analysis revealed a significant increase in the CUR levels in serum and prostate tissues of B6C3F1/J mice following CUR and resveratrol liposomes coadministration. Combination of the two liposomes has significantly decreased prostatic adenocarcinoma in vivo. Findings of this study provide promising evidence on the combination of phytochemicals using a favorable carrier system to treat prostate cancer [77].

Rajesh L. Thangapazham et al. investigated the effect of Lip-cur on LNCaP (lymph node carcinoma of the prostate) and C4-2B human prostate cancer cells. Results indicated that Lip-cur incubation with the prostate cancer cells exerted significant antiproliferative activity. Free CUR, on the other hand, demonstrated the same antitumor activity at significantly higher concentrations ($>50\ \mu$M). Results also highlighted higher sensitivity of LNCaP prostate cancer cells compared to C4-2B toward this proliferation inhibition [78].

10.2.10 Osteosarcoma

The delivery of CUR in the liposomal form has been explored to treat osteosarcoma (OS). Since CUR is water insoluble, an effective delivery option could be through its encapsulation in cyclodextrins followed by a second encapsulation within liposomes. Santosh S. Dhule et al. have evaluated the Lip-cur potential against cancer models of mesenchymal (OS) and epithelial origins (breast cancer). The 2-hydroxypropyl-γ-cyclodextrin/Lip-cur complex showed promising anticancer potential both in vitro and in vivo against KHOS OS and MCF-7 breast cancer cells. An interesting aspect is that Lip-cur could initiate the caspase cascade that leads to apoptotic cell death in vitro compared to DMSO-CUR induced autophagy-induced cell death. In addition, the efficiency of the Lip-cur formulation in vivo using a xenograft OS model also confirmed the same result. CUR-loaded γ-cyclodextrin liposomes indicated significant potential as delivery vehicles for the treatment of cancers of different tissue origins [79]. Also in A-459 lung and SW-620 colon cancer cells, β-cyclodextrin/Lip-cur complex showed significant efficiency in inhibiting cell proliferation [80].

10.2.11 Lung cancer

There are strong evidences that CUR could noticeably reduce tumor burden, inhibit tumor growth and metastasis, and combat drug resistance by sensitizing cells to chemotherapeutics in lung cancer. CUR incorporated in Krill oil liposomes (marinosomes) is regarded as low-cost and readily available nutraceutical with the cancer targeting potential. Ibrahim et al. developed CUR-loaded marinosomes (CURMs) with favorable physicochemical and oxidative stability even after 8 weeks' storage at 4°C. CURMs released 30% of the CUR contents following 72 h incubation in vitro in culture conditions at 37°C. Furthermore, CURMs indicated a powerful antioxidant activity ($EC_{50} \doteqdot 4\,\mu g/mL$) with maximum cytotoxic effect on A549 lung cancer cells (IC_{50}; $11.7 \pm 0.24\,\mu g/mL$) after 72 h of incubation. CURMs also showed a significant inhibitory action on the proliferation of HUVECs in a dose-dependent manner (IC_{50} of $2.64 \pm 0.21\,\mu g/mL$). On the whole, this study indicated CURMs as promising drug delivery carrier to target cancer disease [81].

Combination therapy with other chemotherapeutics or varying cancer treatment options has been widely exploited by using various nanocarriers to extend the CUR therapeutic applications [82]. For example, coadministration of CUR and bromocriptine in a liposomal platform was done to treat lung cancer. Results indicated that liposomal nanocarriers enhanced the solubility and bioavailability of both drugs and improved anticancer activity in QU-DB human lung cancer cells without affecting normal cells [83]. In 2020 Qi Zhou and et al. have embedded both gefitinib (GFT) and CUR within liposomes to investigate if the combination could dominate MDR. The results showed that GFT/CL of 130 nm size and negative zeta potential of -22.2 mV slowly released the entrapped drugs in a biphasic pattern and showed a higher uptake by GFT-resistant cells [84].

Li-Qiang Wang et al. used combination therapy with hyperthermia to improve the antitumor efficacy of Lip-cur. For this, they have assessed toxicity and in vivo experiment using C57BL/6 and BALB/c mice-bearing LL/2 murin Lewis lung tumor. Therefore, Lip-cur (10 mg/kg) was i.v. injected once daily for 14 days followed by an hour of hyperthermia twice a week by immersing tumor-bearing legs in a water bath for 60 minutes. For in vitro study, treatment with Lip-cur at 2.5−10 μg/mL was followed by heating in a 42°C incubator for 60 minutes. Results indicated that Lip-cur could exert inhibitory effects on the proliferation of LL/2 murin Lewis lung cancer cells and induce cell cycle arrest and apoptosis. Therapeutic efficacy study also indicated the superior antitumor efficacy of the combination therapy with hyperthermia leading to the tumor shrinkage and prolonged survival as well as further angiogenesis inhibition [85].

One of the dose-limiting toxicity during thoracic radiotherapy is radiation pneumonitis (RP). In 2012 the protective role of Lip-cur in combination with radiotherapy was explored against thoracic irradiation following intravenous administration in mice model. Lip-cur treatment inhibited the NF-κB pathway and reduced tumor necrosis factor-α, interleukin (IL)-6, IL-8, and transforming growth factor-β inflammatory factors expression. Notably, combination therapy with Lip-cur in LL/2 murine lung carcinoma induced a significant intratumoral apoptosis and microvessel response to irradiation and dramatically suppressed tumor growth. Overall, results highlighted the potential of Lip-cur systemic administration in mitigating RP, alleviating lung fibrosis, and empowering irradiation effect on LL/2 cells [86].

The applications of nanocarriers in general could promote CUR pharmacokinetic features and broaden novel directions in the application of CUR in vast areas including drug delivery, biotechnology, nutraceutical, and food industries [87]. Malignant pleural effusion (MPE) is a pathological condition associated with fluid accumulation in the pleural cavity due to lung, pleura, and mediastinal lymph node malignancies.

To explore CUR's potential in treating MPE, the CUR pharmacokinetic and safety profile was investigated following intrapleural and intravenous administration of its liposomal form. For this, Ashleigh Hocking et al. used Fischer 344 rats and administered Lip-cur at 16 mg/kg by either intrapleural injection or intravenous infusion. Results indicated no pleural or lung toxicity following CUR-encapsulated liposome administration. While intrapleural administration did not affect red blood cell morphology, echinocytosis was observed right after and at 1.5 hours after intravenous infusion of the Lip-cur. On the whole, direct administration of liposomal curcumin into the pleural cavity proved to be a safe alternative treatment compared to intravenous infusion in pleural tumors [88].

Recently, Tongtong Zhanga et al. introduced a novel application of Lip-cur in the treatment of primary lung cancer. They have developed a Lip-cur dry powder inhaler (LCD) with an aerodynamic diameter of 5.81 μm and a fine particle fraction of 46.71%, which fitted pulmonary delivery. CL uptake was significantly improved compared to free CUR by A549 human lung cancer cells. Furthermore, Lip-cur showed greater cytotoxicity on A549 cells compared to normal BEAS-2B human bronchial epithelial cells. LCDs, CUR powders, as well as gemcitabine were directly sprayed into the trachea of rat model bearing lung cancer. LCDs demonstrated high anticancer activity regarding the tissue pathology and the expression of several cancer-associated markers including VEGF, malondialdehyde, TNF-α, caspase-3, and BCL-2. Results of this study have highlighted LCDs as the promising inhalation treatment for lung cancer [89].

10.3 Actively targeted liposome

Active targeting is based on modifying nanoparticles using various targeting moieties to reinforce preferential delivery of the therapeutic agent to the specific cancer cells. Substantial number of actively targeted delivery systems have been presented including surface-modified drug delivery systems, varying drug conjugates with monoclonal antibodies, antibody fragments, peptides, aptamers, and small molecules. In this approach, EPR-mediated accumulation of long-circulating nanocarriers within the tumor microenvironment is followed by selective cellular internalization or attachment to the vascular endothelial cells, which could ameliorate the outcome of therapy [90]. In the following section, we addressed several reports on the use of actively targeted liposome for efficient and selective CUR delivery to the site of tumor (Table 10–1).

10.3.1 Cervical cancer

The tumor growth highly depends on the angiogenesis, a robust consistent process that supplies essential nutrients required for the tumor cells metabolism. Therefore, identification of the features of endothelial cells and inhibiting new vessels growth is a promising research approach in cancer treatment that could render the development of antiangiogenic therapy [111].

Cationic liposomes demonstrated the potential to preferentially target the tumor endothelium, making it possible to deliver the therapeutic cargo to the angiogenic vessels and subsequently restrict tumor growth and metastasis [112]. A study in 2014 investigated the efficacy of cationic liposomes to improve the endothelium-targeting potential of CUR. For this,

Table 10–1   Actively targeted curcumin liposomes.

Cancer type	Ligands/specific moiety	Drug/treatment combination	Therapeutic model	References
Cervical	DDAB cationic lipid	–	In vitro	[91]
	Folic acid	–	In vitro	[92]
Lung	RGD peptide	Paclitaxel	In vitro/In vivo	[93]
Breast	RGD peptide	–	In vitro	[94]
	GHHNGR (an integrin-homing peptide bearing a C-end R neuropilin-1)	–	In vitro	[95]
	ZHER2:342 Affibody		In vitro	
	Trastuzumab	Resveratrol	In vitro	[96]
	Tagged-antinucleolin AS1411 aptamer (NCL)	–	In vitro	[97]
	Tuftsin (the natural macrophage-stimulating peptide)	Doxorubicin (DOX)	In vivo	[98]
				[99]
Hepatocellular	Glycyrrhetinic acid (GA) and galactose (Gal)	Capsaicin (CAPS)	In vitro/In vivo	[100]
	Gal-Mor (Galactose-Morpholine)	–	In vitro/In vivo	[101]
	Hyaluronic acid (HA) and glycyrrhetinic acid (GA)	Aprepitant (APR)	In vitro/In vivo	[102]
Leukemia	Hyaluronan (HA)	–	In vivo	[103]
Skin	RGDGWK-lipopeptide	Homoserine-based C8-ceramide analog	In vitro/In vivo	[104]
Osteosarcoma	Folic acid	–	In vitro/In vivo	[105,106]
Pancreatic	EGF (Epidermal growth factor receptor)	–	In vitro	[107]
Prostate	Aptamer A15	–	In vitro/In vivo	[108]
Brain	RDP peptide	–	In vitro/In vivo	[109]
	Amyloid precursor protein (APP)	–	In vivo	[110]

various liposomal formulations composed of either DDAB (didecyldimethylammonium bromide), cholesterol, or nonionic montanov82: cocoyl glucoside surfactant were fabricated. Results indicated that DDAB as an enhancer of cellular internalization could significantly potentiate cellular death in HeLa and SiHa cervical cancer cells. Furthermore, it was concluded that the anticancer activity of Lip-cur formulations bearing DDAB was greater compared to DDAB-free liposomes. Cholesterol incorporation has also showed to improve CUR encasement within liposomes [91].

Recently, Wang et al. explored the efficacy of folic acid (FA)-modified CUR liposomes (LPs) using HeLa cells cervical cancer model. The optimized liposomes of 112.3 nm and zeta potential of -15.3 mV showed 87.6% and 7.9% of encapsulation efficiency and drug loading, respectively. FA-modified CUR liposomes significantly inhibited HeLa cells proliferation and exerted a superior antitumor effect in vivo compared to the nonmodified peers [92].

10.3.2 Lung cancer

In 2018 PTX and CUR coloaded liposomes were prepared and modified with RGD tripeptide to explore the efficacy in lung cancer. Targeted liposomes showed a sustained-release property in vitro (in ethanol 50%, v/v) and superior antiproliferative activity on A549 lung cancer cells. In vivo study also demonstrated that codelivery of PTX and CUR using RGD-targeted liposome could exert a higher synergistic tumor inhibitory effect in nude mice transplanted with A549 human adenocarcinoma cells. However, there was no significant difference in terms of pharmacokinetic profile between the modified and nonmodified liposomes [93].

10.3.3 Breast cancer

Varying Lip-cur preparations were targeted using several peptide moieties, antibodies, and aptamers and their efficacy was investigated in breast cancer model. Previously, the effect of RGD-modified liposomal curcumin (RGD-Lip-Cur) in MCF-7 breast cancer cells was investigated. In vitro bioactivity of the fabricated liposomes showed a significant cytotoxicity on MCF-7 cells at $4-32$ µg/mL compared to nontargeted counterparts. Furthermore, apoptosis induction and caspase-3/7 activation were significant following RGD-Lip-Cur treatment compared to Lip-Cur and free curcumin in MCF-7 breast cancer cells [94]. Sogol Kangarlou et al. have also decorated the CUR nanoliposomes with an integrin-homing peptide bearing a C-end R neuropilin-1 targeting motif to specifically target the endothelial cells and facilitate receptor-mediated internalization. For this, GHHNGR (glycine-histidine-histidine-asparagine-glycine-arginine) was synthesized by F-moc chemistry on 2-chlorotrityl chloride resin and was then conjugated to oleic acid. To prepare liposomes, the resulting lipoyl-peptide units, lecithin, and Tween 80 ($0-75$ mole%) were used and CUR entrapment was mediated through a pH-switch loading method. Nanoliposomal of less than 50 nm comprised of oleyl-peptide, lecithin, and Tween 80 at 1:1:0.75 mole ratio indicated maximum CUR entrapment of 15.5% w/w. The oleyl-peptide unit hemolytic activity at up to 10-fold of its experimental concentration was negligible ($<1.5\%$). The targeted CL induced a significant cancer cell death in MCF-7 and MDA-MB-468 cells with IC_{50} values of 3.8 and 5.4 μM, respectively. The successful therapeutic potential of the decorated CL was in part attributed to the targeting of integrin and neuropilin-1 receptors [95].

Human epidermal growth factor receptor 2 (HER 2) is also a promising candidate in treating many cancers including breast cancer. In a recent paper, Moballegh-Nasery et al. used ZHER2:342 Affibody-decorated liposome to explore its efficacy against SKBR3 and MCF-7 breast cancer cells. Soybeans lecetin and cholesterol were used for liposome preparation, and C-terminal cysteine residue of affibody ZHER2:342 moiety was used for liposome conjugation. Findings indicated that HER2-decorated liposomes of about 150 nm improved CUR bioactivity on both cancerous cells resulting in apoptosis induction independent of the levels of HER2 expression [96]. In 2013 Angela Catania et al. developed the immune-liposome of CUR and/or resveratrol and assessed their potential in inhibiting the growth of human breast cancer cells overexpressing HER2 receptors. Resveratrol is a natural compound with noticeable cytotoxicity activity against numerous cancer cells; however, like CUR, its poor physicochemical features including negligible absorption and bioavailability are limiting its bioapplication. The immune-liposomes bearing trastuzumab displayed a dramatic antiproliferative effect in HER2-positive human breast cancer cells compared to their nontargeted peers. Lip-cur uptake was also significantly enhanced as confirmed by ImageStream technique. The considerable efficacy of the immune-liposomes encapsulating both resveratrol and CUR revealed a multitargeted mechanism that needs further studies regarding the molecular mechanism [97].

In a recent study, cholesterol-tagged-antinucleolin AS1411 aptamer (NCL) was used for CL surface decoration. To achieve this aim, a novel postinsertion approach was exploited by utilizing cholesterol as a wedge to incorporate aptamer into the surface of the liposome bilayer. Using flow cytometry, MCF-7 and MDA-MB-231 human breast cancer cellular uptake of liposomes was significantly improved with aptamer-decorated liposomes. Additionally, confocal laser scanning microscopy (CLSM) confirmed endocytosis of liposomes into the breast cancer cells' cytoplasm, leading to a prominent toxicity toward cancer cells [98].

Tuftsin, the natural macrophage-stimulating peptide was used for modifying the surface of liposomes loaded with DOX and/or CUR. To do this, the aforementioned peptide was attached through its C-terminus to a palmitoyl residue (Thr-Lys-Pro-Arg-CO-NH-$(CH_2)_2$-NH-$COC_{15}H_{31}$, P. Tuft) to enable liposome bilayer grafting. Ehrlich ascites carcinoma (EAC) tumor-induced mice model was used to investigate the liposomal formulation toxicity and anticancer activity. Palmitoyl tuftsin—grafted dual-drug-loaded liposomes demonstrated a significant reduction in the tumor burden compared to the single drug-loaded formulation, which was revealed to be associated with p53-mediated apoptotic pathway. Furthermore, liposomal formulations showed to be nontoxic at the specified dose of 10 mg/kg [99].

10.3.4 Hepatocellular carcinoma

Activated hepatic stellate cells (aHSCs) in the liver tumor microenvironment (TME) have shown to contribute significantly to the development of liver cancer. A recent 2021 study has presented the potential of aHSCs and tumor cells dual-targeting using an established cocultured model and a promising approach for the treatment of liver cancer. In this study, Cuiping Qi et al. have developed a noble multifunctional liposomes (CAPS-CUR/GA&Gal-Lip) for the codelivery of CUR and capsaicin (CAPS). To achieve double targeting of the liver cancer cells, they have decorated the liposomes with glycyrrhetinic acid (GA) and galactose (Gal) as targeting ligands, which could accelerate cancer cell uptake of the liposomes. As mentioned earlier, a novel HSCs-HepG2 human hepatoma cell cocultured model was established to empower drug resistance and cancer cell migration through upregulating P-glycoprotein (P-gp) and Vimentin expression and further simulate real TME. Results demonstrated a dramatic inhibition of tumor cell growth and migration following CAPS-CUR/GA&Gal-Lip exposure to the cocultured cells. The therapeutic potential of the double-targeted system was assessed using three models including subcutaneous H22 mouse hepatom-, H22 + m-HSC mouse hepatic stellate-, and orthotopic H22 cells-bearing mice. CAPS-CUR/GA&Gal-Lip treatment presented less ECM deposition, reduced angiogenesis, and significant tumoricidal effect compared to the non-Gal-modified Lip. It was concluded that the promising efficacy of the double-functionalized delivery system was attributed to the simultaneous targeting of both hepatic cancer and stellate cells, leading to the tumor cells growth and metastasis inhibition [100].

One of the intracellular CUR targets that facilitate cancer cell apoptosis is the lysosomal permeabilization pathway. In a recent study by Wang et al., a novel dually targeted liposome encapsulating CUR (Gal-Mor-LPs) was developed. In this design, the galactose group (Gal) was suited for targeting asialoglycoprotein receptor (ASGPR) overexpressed on the HCC cells, while the morpholine group was incorporated to target the lysosome. The dual-targeted Gal-Mor-LPs have shown a remarkable hepatic targeting potential, which was significantly greater compared to galactose-decorated liposomes. This was obviously due to the presence of morpholine group that targets acidic lysosome following Gal-Mor-LPs treatment. In vitro study also indicated a competitive inhibition of Gal-Mor-LPs endocytosis in the presence of galactose, which laid emphasis on the fact that the galactose-modified Lip-cur entrance was facilitated through ASGPR-mediated pathway. In vivo investigation has also revealed that Gal-Mor-LPs could successfully reduce the tumor burden in animal model, which was significantly greater compared to galactose-modified liposomes. In general, this study indicated that the dual-targeted CL could boost the antitumor efficacy by directly targeting hepatic cancer cells as well as the lysosome compartment within the cells [101] (Fig. 10–1).

There are increasing evidence that substance P (SP) secretion from peripheral nerves within the TME could cause a shift from quiescent hepatic stellate cells (HSCs) to cancer-associated fibroblasts (CAFs). In a recent study, targeting "SP-HSCs-HCC" axis was exploited as an effective strategy to inhibit tumor growth and metastasis. Therefore, liposomes coencapsulating aprepitant (APR) and CUR, and decorated with hyaluronic acid (HA) and GA (CUR-APR/HA&GA-LPs) were prepared wherein APR was chosen to block SP/neurokinin-1 receptor (NK-1R) while CUR was opted as the cytotoxic agent. In this study, "SP + HSCs + HCC" coculture model was established to simulate TME. Findings indicated simultaneous uptake of CUR-APR/HA&GA-LPs by both CAFs and HCC and a remarkable tumor cell migration inhibition. Therapeutic potential of the fabricated carrier in

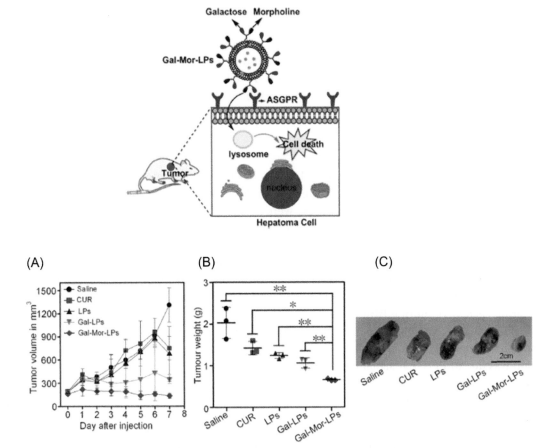

FIGURE 10–1 Schematic illustration of curcumin-loaded liposomes constructed by galactose-morpholine-modified lipid materials with hepatic and lysosomal dual-targeting efficacy, in which galactose group can recognize ASGPR of hepatoma cells and morpholine group can target to lysosome, in vivo antitumor efficacy. (A) The tumor volumes of mice treated with saline, free curcumin (CUR), LPs, Gal-LPs, and Gal-Mor-LPs during 7 days. (B) The tumor weights of different groups at the end of treatment. (C) Images of tumors from different groups at the end of treatment (scale bar, 2 cm). *ASGPR*, Asialoglycoprotein receptor; *Gal-Mor*, galactose-Morpholine; *LPs*, liposomes *Reproduced with permission from Wang Y, Ding R, Zhang Z, Zhong C, Wang J, Wang M. Curcumin-loaded liposomes with the hepatic and lysosomal dual-targeted effects for therapy of hepatocellular carcinoma. International Journal of Pharmaceutics. 2021;602:120628. License code: 5378600011837.*

"SP + m-HSCs + HCC" coimplanted mice model revealed a notable tumor inhibition, reduced ECM deposition and tumor angiogenesis following treatment with the dual-loaded CUR-APR/HA&GA-LPs [102].

10.3.5 Acute myeloid leukemia

In a study by Dan Sun et al., the therapeutic potential and molecular mechanism of targeted Lip-cur were assessed in acute myeloid leukemia (AML). Hyaluronan was used to modify liposomal surface (HA-Cur-LPs) for CD44-specific targeting on the AML cell surface. HA-Cur-LPs demonstrated stability and favorable affinity to CD44 receptors, resulting in increased cellular uptake and subsequent AML cell proliferation inhibition. Antitumor efficacy data indicated the capability of targeted liposome (50 mg/kg of CL every 2 days for 2 weeks) in prohibiting AML progression in KG-1 cell-implanted model. HA-Cur-LPs has shown to inhibit Akt/ERK pathway and downregulate DNMT1 expression leading to DNA hypomethylation and reactivation of tumor suppressor genes including miR-223 [103].

10.3.6 Skin cancer

In a prior study, the anticancer potential of homoserine-based ceramides in combination with CUR using liposomes was investigated to dominate MDR. To this aim, four serine- and homoserine-based C8-ceramide analogs were synthesized and along with PEGylated RGDGWK-lipopeptide and various lipids were incorporated within liposomes to enhance tumor endothelial cells targeting. To prepare coencapsulated liposomes, CUR was added to the aforementioned lipid mixture at 15:1 (w/w) lipid/CUR ratio. The liposomal formulation bearing homoserine-based C8-ceramide analog with oleyl chain improved antiproliferation activities in vitro using HUVEC, B16F10, and CHO cells. Animal study in C57BL/6 J mice bearing aggressive murine B16F10 melanoma tumor indicated a synergistic therapeutic benefit following the codelivery of CUR-homoserine-based ceramide combination. Further to a significant tumor growth inhibition, study findings demonstrated that tumor growth suppression was due to PI3K-Akt signaling pathway inhibition [104].

10.3.7 Osteosarcoma

CUR and C6 ceramide (C6) water-insoluble drugs loaded within the lipid bilayer of liposomes demonstrated 1.5 times higher toxicity against MG-63 and KHOS OS cells compared to CL. Furthermore, C6-CL showed less toxicity on untransformed primary human cells (human mesenchymal stem cells) compared to OS cells. Cell cycle assays indicated that C6-CL resulted in cell sequestration in G2/M phases due to the increased expression levels of cyclin D1 and B1. A human OS xenograft indicated that the C6-CUR-FA liposomes (tagged with folate [FA]) improved the plasma half-life and significantly reduced tumor burden [105]. In 2020 a folated pluronic F127 (FA-F127) moiety was developed to modify liposomes surface. For this, FA linking to pluronic F127 was enhanced via the terminal OH group (FA-F127) and the structure was used for liposome preparation (cur-FA-F127-Lps). Findings indicated the bioactivity of cur-FA-F127-Lps toward KB cells compared to nonfolated-decorated F127 liposomes (cur-F127-Lps) [106].

10.3.8 Pancreatic cancer

Epidermal growth factor receptor (EGFR) is a potential target for targeted cancer therapy specifically in pancreatic tumors. In 2018 Uyen Minh Le et al. investigated the potential of epidermal growth factor-decorated liposomal curcumin (EGF-LP-Cur) on EGFR-expressing BxPC-3,

Panc-1, and Mia Paca-2 human pancreatic cancer cells. The stable liposomal formulation demonstrated superior cytotoxicity on BxPC-3 compared to other cells. Findings further indicated that the CUR cellular uptake was attributed to EGFR-mediated internalization [107].

10.3.9 Prostate cancer

A CUR-loaded CD133 aptamer A15 liposome was designed to improve prostate cancer therapy. The stable spherical liposomes of <100 nm size indicated an initial burst release within 2 h followed by continuous release over 48 h. In vitro findings revealed that both A15-decorated and unmodified Lip-cur showed similar toxicity profiles at the same concentrations while A15-CUR LPs showed greater cellular internalization in DU145 cells compared to others. In vivo investigation using DU145 prostate carcinoma-bearing mice indicated a dramatic tumor suppression compared to controls [108]. In 2008 Rajesh L. Thangapazham et al. used liposomes decorated with prostate membrane-specific antigen-specific antibodies for prostate cancer therapy. Findings indicated 70%−80% proliferation inhibition of LNCaP on C4-2B human prostate cancer cells after treatment with Lip-cur of dimyristoyl phosphatidyl choline (DMPC) and cholesterol, wherein free CUR exerted similar effects at 10-fold higher concentrations (>50 UM) [78].

10.3.10 Brain tumors

Glioma comprising about 30% of all brain tumors is the most aggressive brain tumor recognized in humans. One of the main hurdles in the treatment of brain tumors is the low penetration of chemotherapeutics through blood−brain barrier (BBB). BBB is composed of many components including the endothelial layer that limits the transition of xenobiotic within the circulation to the central nervous system (CNS). Similarly, this protective interface prevents the penetration of therapeutics into the brain tissue. In 2018 a novel CUR nanoliposome was developed by RDP brain-targeting peptide conjugation for glioma therapy. In vitro study indicated apoptosis induction due to cell cycle arrest at the S phase and liposomal uptake by U251MG human glioma cells through acetylcholine receptor-mediated endocytosis pathway. To induce glioma in mice model, U251MG cells were transplanted into the mice striatum. Intravenous administration of RDP-modified liposomes (RCL) in these glioma-bearing mice demonstrated elongated survival time from 23 to 33 days [109] (Fig. 10−2). In 2021 Martin Gabay et al. used a short peptide sequence (of five amino acids [RERMS]) present in the amyloid precursor protein (APP) for triple-drug targeting to BBB. The APP-targeted liposomes were loaded with temozolomide (TMZ), CUR, and DOX anticancer agents to specifically target BBB transporters system. Labeled and decorated liposomes showed a higher penetration to the brain by 35% compared to nontargeted liposomes. Investigation in SCID mouse model of human U87 glioblastoma developed by intracranial injection of the tumor cells indicated that targeted liposomes have substantially limited tumor growth and prolonged mice survival by 45%−70% [110].

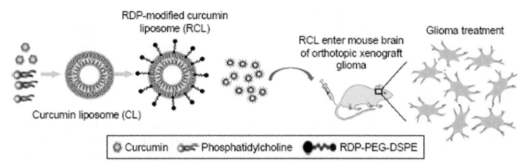

FIGURE 10–2 Schematic representing the efficacy of RDP-modified curcumin nanoliposomes (RCL) for glioma therapy. Curcumin nanoliposomes were prepared by using thin-film hydration method. Intravenous administration of RCL prolonged the survival of mice bearing glioma tumor. *Reproduced from Zhao M, Zhao M, Fu C, Yu Y, Fu A. Targeted therapy of intracranial glioma model mice with curcumin nanoliposomes. International Journal of Nanomedicine 2018;13:1601-1610. https://doi.org/10.2147/IJN.S157019. PMID: 29588587; PMCID: PMC5858816.*

10.4 Physical stimuli-responsive curcumin liposomal delivery systems

Stimuli-responsive delivery vehicles have opened a new era in cancer therapy by using specific nanoparticulate materials with the capability to remotely control carrier activation at the tumor site. Various distinctive endogenous features of the TME including lowered pH, higher enzyme expression, REDOX potential, as well as exogenous stimulants like hyperthermia, alternating magnetic field (AMF), near-infrared (NIR), or ultrasound radiations have been used to induce drug release in the specific site. The key to the controlled-manner drug release of the stimuli-responsive material is structural modification particularly in response to the stimulus [113]. Responsive liposomes presented controllable drug release to deliver considerable amounts of drug to the cancer site. In the following section, we will address few smart CLs that have been developed for targeted cancer therapy (Table 10−2).

10.4.1 Skin cancer

Overexpression of numerous oncogenic signaling molecules including STAT3 has shown to greatly contribute to the development of skin cancer. Cationic liposomes have been utilized for topical iontophoretic-assisted codelivery of small molecule and siRNA to the skin diseases. Anup Jose et al. have studied the codelivery of CUR and STAT3 siRNA by using liposomes to treat skin cancer in combination with noninvasive topical iontophoretic application. For this, CUR was first encapsulated within DOTAP-based cationic liposomes followed by subsequent complexion with STAT3 siRNA. CUR-encapsulated cationic liposomes complexed with STAT3 siRNA were tested on A431 human epidermoid cancer cells. Results indicated preferential and rapid uptake of CUR-loaded liposome−siRNA complex by the cancer cells through clathrin-mediated endocytosis pathway. The codelivery system has significantly inhibited cancer cell proliferation and ameliorated apoptosis compared to

Table 10–2   Curcumin stimuli-responsive liposomes.

Cancer type	Stimulus	Drug/treatment combination	Therapeutic model	References
Skin	Topical iontophoretic	STAT3 siRNA	In vitro/In vivo	[114]
			In vitro/In vivo	[115]
	Photothermal therapy (NIR light)	Gold coverage	In vitro	[116]
	pH-responsive component (Citraconic anhydride 98% (CA))		In vitro	[117]
Pancreatic	pH-sensitive component	Gemcitabine	In vitro/In vivo	[118]
Breast	Thermosensitive hydrogel	–	In vitro/In vivo	[119]
	Ultrasound-responsive bubble generating (ammonium bicarbonate)	–	In vitro/In vivo	[120]
Colon	pH-sensitive component (CaCO$_3$)	–	In vivo	[121]

free CUR and STAT3 siRNA. Furthermore, topical application of iontophoresis has significantly improved skin penetration of the dual nano-complex through viable epidermis [114]. The same group investigated the efficacy of iontophoretic-mediated codelivery of CUR and anti-STAT3 siRNA by using cationic liposomes against mouse skin cancer. Cell viability studies against B16F10 mouse melanoma cells confirmed the successful codelivery of CUR and STAT3 siRNA and cancer cell growth inhibition compared to Lip-cur or STAT3 siRNA alone. Iontophoresis application (0.47 mA/cm^2) enabled a deep penetration of CUR-loaded liposomes into the skin (160 μm). The in vivo efficacy study in a mouse model of melanoma skin cancer indicated a significant tumor inhibition following liposomal codelivery of CUR and STAT3 siRNA using liposomes. Furthermore, the iontophoretic-assisted administration of CUR-loaded liposome-siRNA complex showed similar efficacy in tumor inhibitory effect as well as STAT3 protein suppression compared to intratumoral administration [115].

In 2018 Singh et al. fabricated a biodegradable Lip-cur coated with gold nanoparticles (Au-Lipos Cur NPs) as an adjuvant for in situ photothermal therapy. The gold coverage enhanced specific absorption of NIR light (780 nm) by virtue of surface plasmon resonance (SPR), which was subsequently converted to heat. Upon laser irradiation, Au-Lipos Cur nanoparticles enhanced heat generation, leading to CUR release due to the destabilization of the liposomal core. Au-Lipos Cur NPs indicated a noticeable uptake by B16F10 melanoma cells, enhanced cancer cell cytotoxicity, and irreversible cellular damage upon laser irradiation owing to the CUR content [116].

A novel biocompatible stealth-nanoliposome with or without pH-responsive polymeric coating was developed by Zarrabi et al. to deliver CUR to the cancer site. Citraconic anhydride 98% (CA) was used as a pH-responsive component contributing to the smart feature of nanoliposome. For this purpose, CA attachment to the PEG and DSPE was done through two different chemical reactions including amidation and esterification, resulting in the (DSPE-citraconic-PEG [DSPE-CIT-PEG]) final product. Field emission-scanning electron microscopy

(FE-SEM) results indicated an average size of about 50 nm and 74% entrapment efficiency for noncoated liposome while it was about 40 nm and 84% for PEGylated liposomes. Drug release also indicated a controllable pattern in pH-responsive polymeric-coated stealth-liposome compared to noncoated one. Bioactivity assessment revealed significant toxicity of the CUR-loaded carriers on the cancer cells [117].

10.4.2 Pancreatic cancer

In 2021 Hongtao Xu et al. have used a PEGylated pH-sensitive liposome (PSL) dually loaded with gemcitabine and CUR to dominate gemcitabine-resistance in pancreatic ductal adeno-carcinoma (PDAC). The rationale was the CUR's capacity in inhibiting the multidrug resistance protein 5 (MRP5) efflux transporter in PDAC cells. For this, they have first fabricated and characterized liposomes bearing gemcitabine in the core and hydrophobic CUR located within the bilayers. Results indicated that CUR incorporation to the PSL bilayers at 0.2−1 mol% has slightly decreased the pH reactivity of the PSL. In vitro assay has demonstrated that coloading dramatically improved gemcitabine cellular internalization in a concentration-dependent pattern, leading to a synergistic toxicity toward MIA PaCa-2 cells. Animal kinetic study revealed a remarkable reduction in the drugs' plasma clearance as well as the volume of distribution (V_d) accompanied with a three- to fourfold higher area-under-the-concentration-time curves when compared to the free drugs. Possible explanation includes the CUR-associated MRP5 inhibition, which promoted gemcitabine intracellular concentration and eventually increased gemcitabine plasma levels, contributing to the much higher drug concentrations for further distribution to the targeted site. On the whole, the codelivery of CUR with gemcitabine using liposomes has dramatically ameliorated the pharmacokinetics for both drugs [118].

10.4.3 Breast cancer

In 2020 an injectable in situ forming thermosensitive hydrogel of CUR was designed as a scaffold for tissue regeneration applications following breast tumor resection. Riwang Li et al. have developed this thermosensitive hydrogel by using liposomes as CUR carrier. They first prepared liposomal curcumin (Lip-cur) that was then coated with thiolated chitosan (CSSH) to form liposome-based hydrogel (CSSH/Lip-cur gel). The distinctive feature of the liposomal hydrogel was its rapid switching from a fluidic phase at room temperature to gel at 37°C. The thermosensitive CSSH/Lip-cur gel demonstrated almost 32% release at 12 h. While liposomal hydrogels showed favorable cytocompatibility, the cytotoxicity study after CUR loading has revealed a dramatic MCF-7 cell killing following 72 h incubation. The efficacy of injectable in situ forming hydrogel was proved in an in vivo breast cancer recurrence experiment. Results showed that the liposomal hydrogel could inhibit cancer recurrence after tumor resection, and repair the tissue defect in CSSH/Lip-cur gel group. Overall, the results of this study demonstrated the capability of CUR liposomal hydrogels in continuous drug delivery and exerting antitumor efficacy [119].

In 2018 Andrew Shore et al. developed a novel ultrasound-responsive bubble-generating liposome bearing CUR with the aim of reducing the cost of precursors. The conventional precursor's applicability is limited due to low stability and drug encapsulation potential as well as drug release efficiency. Thus 1,3-ditetradecanamidopropan-2-yl-(2-hydroxyethyl) hydrogen phosphite (DPHP) and 2-((4-aminophenyl)dimethylammonio)ethyl-(1,3-dipalmita-midopropan-2-yl) phosphate (AEDP) were utilized as the precursors and bubble generation was mediated through ammonium bicarbonate incorporation within the liposome core. The liposomes were used as contrast agents in ultrasound imaging due to the hyperechogenic nature of the generated bubbles.

The liposomes were also tagged with FA−cholesterol and fluorescein dye−cholesterol conjugates, which facilitate fluorescence imaging agents. Results indicated that the bubble-generating liposomes were stable with good cytocompatibility and prolonged circulation. The toxicity of the resulting liposomes was assessed in MCF-7, Hep G2, and HEK cells [120].

10.4.4 Colon cancer

In 2019 Yi Chen et al. introduced an innovative approach to develop pH-sensitive $CaCO_3$-encapsulated liposomes for colon cancer therapy. The dual-loaded liposomes with encapsulated $CaCO_3$ and curcumin (LCC) showed pH-selective swelling when exposed to the acidic environment, thus releasing the encapsulated CUR. This swelling behavior and lysosomal escape further enhanced CUR accumulation within the cytosol. Therapeutic efficacy study revealed LCC-favorable antitumor effect in colorectal cancer model induced by azoxymethane (AOM)/dextran sodium sulfate (DSS). On the whole, the solubility and intracellular delivery of CUR were substantially improved by $CaCO_3$ coencapsulation within liposomes making this carrier as an ideal therapeutic option for further bioapplications [121].

10.5 Microfluidic

As mentioned in earlier reports, the use of nano-based carriers including liposomes has substantially improved CUR physicochemical features; however, there are still needs for scalable and reproducible manufacturing techniques. In 2019 Nobuhito Hamano et al. fabricated curcumin liposomal formulation (Lipo-Cur) by using an automated microfluidic technology. The resulting Lipo-Cur, 120 nm in diameter, increased the CUR aqueous solubility by 700-fold and showed a favorable loading capacity of 17 wt.%. Coadministration of the liposomes with CDDP in multiple tumor-bearing mice model has dramatically ameliorated CDDP antitumor potential and reduced off-target toxicity including the nephrotoxicity [122]. Very recently, a novel microfluidic swirl mixer with 3D mixing chamber structures was developed for larger scale (up to 320 mL/min or 20 L/h) production of liposomes under varying processing conditions. This approach was successful resulting in favorable productivity and control on liposomal size and physicochemical properties compared to conventional techniques. In vitro investigation using cancer cells revealed the potential of liposomes in CUR delivery to the cancer cells [123].

10.6 Tissue engineering

The basis of tissue engineering is developing 3DP scaffolds with an interconnected porous network that could fabricate implants by providing new tissue ingrowth interlocking between the scaffold and the surrounding host tissue. Naboneeta Sarkar et al. investigated the efficacy of CUR-incorporated liposome in fabricating a 3DP scaffold on both human fetal osteoblast cells (hFOB) and human OS (MG-63) cells. Lip-cur release from the 3DP scaffold exerted significant cytotoxicity in vitro on OS (bone cancer) cells, while it ameliorated osteoblast (healthy bone cell) cell proliferation. The potential of the bifunctional scaffold in killing bone cancer cells, while preserving bone cell viability offers novel approaches for treating bone defects following tumor resection [124].

10.7 Clinical studies

The safety and tolerability of increasing doses of Lip-cur were investigated in metastatic cancer patients in a phase-1 dose-escalation study in 2018. So, to run a phase 1, single-center, open-label clinical study, metastatic cancer patients were administered intravenous infusion of Lip-cur weekly for 8 weeks. Thirty-two patients received an initial dose of 100 mg/m^2 over 8 h followed by a dose increment to 300 mg/m^2 over 6 h. Treatment of patients with Lip-cur at 100 and 300 mg/m^2 over 8 h demonstrated no dose-limiting toxicity in 26 patients. Regarding higher doses of 300 mg/m^2 over 6 h, out of six treated patients, one developed hemolysis and three others had hemoglobin decreases > 2 g/dL without signs of hemolysis. CUR concentrations remained stable in plasma during infusion, which was then followed by a rapid decline, resulting in negligible CUR levels after the infusion. No significant antitumor therapeutic outcome was detected and transient clinical benefit along with significant tumor marker responses was seen in only two patients. Results indicated a maximum tolerated dose of Lip-cur at 300 mg/m^2 over 6 h, which was recommended for further anticancer clinical studies [125]. Another phase 1, open-label, single-center, uncontrolled, dose-escalation study is conducted to investigate the tolerability and kinetics of a single dose of Lip-cur in MPE patients. To determine the maximum tolerated dose, Lip-cur will be directly administered to the tumor via tunneled indwelling pleural catheter (TIPC). A 3 + 3 expanded cohort for dose-escalation levels will be considered and patients will receive Lip-cur (LipoCurc, SignPath Pharma) as a sequential enrolling case series at 100, 200, and 300 mg/m^2. Primary endpoints will be the maximum tolerated dose and the feasibility of the administration route while the secondary endpoints include CUR kinetic in plasma and the pleural fluid, patients' median overall survival, and the effects on the quality of life [126].

10.8 Future insights

CUR inclusion within liposomes has emerged as a way in circumventing various challenges associated with its pharmacokinetic features. In this chapter, a number of studies investigating Lip-cur's potential and the mechanism involved in managing various types of cancers including skin, pancreatic, liver, colorectal, breast, prostate, OS, lung, and head and neck squamous carcinoma have been comprehensively explored. The findings of these studies defined the safety and tolerability of Lip-cur in various animal models.

The liposomal carrier demonstrated to be promising in improving the toxicity of CUR or its combination against varying types of cancer, as well as improving targeting signaling pathways like NF-κB involved in tumor progress and metastasis. Most of the explored liposomes were conventional carriers and in some limited studies, targeting ligands including RGD tripeptide and galactose group were incorporated in liposomes to improve its targeting potential in specific cancers with promising results. Several combinations of Lip-cur with chemotherapeutics including oxaliplatin, CDDP, resveratrol, and PTX proved the potential of Lip-cur in dominating MDR phenotype in cancer cells. Furthermore, some limited studies revealed the potential of Lip-cur in improving the skin penetration using iontophoretic in skin cancer model or as an adjuvant for in situ photothermal therapy.

Though FDA-approved liposomal drug carriers have been extensively used in clinics, there is still no Lip-cur available in the market. The limited use of these liposomes is possibly due to concerns regarding their encapsulation potential, stability issues, and release kinetics. It is pivotal to take into consideration that the composition of the liposomes, the loading method, size, and surface charge and the type of targeting moieties could affect liposomes' bioapplications.

References

[1] Ganji A, Farahani I, Saeedifar AM, Mosayebi G, Ghazavi A, Majeed M, et al. Protective effects of curcumin against lipopolysaccharide-induced toxicity. Current Medicinal Chemistry 2021;28(33):6915–30.

[2] Hassanzadeh S, Read MI, Bland AR, Majeed M, Jamialahmadi T, Sahebkar A. Curcumin: an inflammasome silencer. Pharmacological Research 2020;159.

[3] Panahi Y, Sahebkar A, Amiri M, Davoudi SM, Beiraghdar F, Hoseininejad SL, et al. Improvement of sulphur mustard-induced chronic pruritus, quality of life and antioxidant status by curcumin: results of a randomised, double-blind, placebo-controlled trial. The British Journal of Nutrition 2012;108(7):1272–9. Available from: https://doi.org/10.1017/S0007114511006544.

[4] Hosseini SA, Zahedipour F, Sathyapalan T, Jamialahmadi T, Sahebkar A. Pulmonary fibrosis: therapeutic and mechanistic insights into the role of phytochemicals. Biofactors (Oxford, England) 2021;47 (3):250–69.

[5] Keihanian F, Saeidinia A, Bagheri RK, Johnston TP, Sahebkar A. Curcumin, hemostasis, thrombosis, and coagulation. Journal of Cellular Physiology 2018;233(6):4497–511.

[6] Khayatan D, Razavi SM, Arab ZN, Niknejad AH, Nouri K, Momtaz S, et al. Protective effects of curcumin against traumatic brain injury. Biomedicine and Pharmacotherapy 2022;154.

[7] Mokhtari-Zaer A, Marefati N, Atkin SL, Butler AE, Sahebkar A. The protective role of curcumin in myocardial ischemia–reperfusion injury. Journal of Cellular Physiology 2018;234(1):214–22.

[8] Momtazi-Borojeni AA, Haftcheshmeh SM, Esmaeili SA, Johnston TP, Abdollahi E, Sahebkar A. Curcumin: a natural modulator of immune cells in systemic lupus erythematosus. Autoimmunity Reviews 2018;17 (2):125–35.

[9] Cicero AFG, Sahebkar A, Fogacci F, Bove M, Giovannini M, Borghi C. Effects of phytosomal curcumin on anthropometric parameters, insulin resistance, cortisolemia and non-alcoholic fatty liver disease indices:

a double-blind, placebo-controlled clinical trial. European Journal of Nutrition 2020;59(2):477–83. Available from: https://doi.org/10.1007/s00394-019-01916-7.

[10] Panahi Y, Fazlolahzadeh O, Atkin SL, Majeed M, Butler AE, Johnston TP, et al. Evidence of curcumin and curcumin analogue effects in skin diseases: a narrative review. Journal of Cellular Physiology 2019;234(2):1165–78. Available from: https://doi.org/10.1002/jcp.27096.

[11] Sahebkar A. Molecular mechanisms for curcumin benefits against ischemic injury. Fertility and Sterility 2010;94(5):e75–6.

[12] Mohammadi A, Blesso CN, Barreto GE, Banach M, Majeed M, Sahebkar A. Macrophage plasticity, polarization and function in response to curcumin, a diet-derived polyphenol, as an immunomodulatory agent. The Journal of Nutritional Biochemistry 2019;66:1–6. Available from: https://doi.org/10.1016/j.jnutbio.2018.12.005.

[13] Vallianou NG, Evangelopoulos A, Schizas N, Kazazis C. Potential anticancer properties and mechanisms of action of curcumin. Anticancer Research 2015;35(2):645–51.

[14] Wilken R, Veena MS, Wang MB, Srivatsan ES. Curcumin: a review of anti-cancer properties and therapeutic activity in head and neck squamous cell carcinoma. Molecular Cancer 2011;10:12.

[15] Zhang X, Zhu L, Wang X, Zhang H, Wang L, Xia L. Basic research on curcumin in cervical cancer: progress and perspectives. Biomedicine & Pharmacotherapy 2023;162:114590.

[16] Mohammed ES, El-Beih NM, El-Hussieny EA, El-Ahwany E, Hassan M, Zoheiry M. Effects of free and nanoparticulate curcumin on chemically induced liver carcinoma in an animal model. Archives of Medical Science 2021;17(1):218–27.

[17] Marjaneh RM, Rahmani F, Hassanian SM, Rezaei N, Hashemzehi M, Bahrami A, et al. Phytosomal curcumin inhibits tumor growth in colitis-associated colorectal cancer. Journal of Cellular Physiology 2018;233(10):6785–98. Available from: https://doi.org/10.1002/jcp.26538.

[18] Mohajeri M, Sahebkar A. Protective effects of curcumin against doxorubicin-induced toxicity and resistance: a review. Critical Reviews in Oncology/Hematology 2018;122:30–51.

[19] Momtazi AA, Sahebkar A. Difluorinated curcumin: a promising curcumin analogue with improved anti-tumor activity and pharmacokinetic profile. Current Pharmaceutical Design 2016;22(28):4386–4397.

[20] Jamwal R. Bioavailable curcumin formulations: a review of pharmacokinetic studies in healthy volunteers. Journal of Integrative Medicine 2018;16(6):367–74.

[21] Bolger GT, Pucaj K, Minta YO, Sordillo P. Relationship between the in vitro efficacy, pharmacokinetics and in vivo efficacy of curcumin. Biochemical Pharmacology 2022;205:115251.

[22] Selvam C, Prabu SL, Jordan BC, Purushothaman Y, Umamaheswari A, Zare MSH, et al. Molecular mechanisms of curcumin and its analogs in colon cancer prevention and treatment. Life Sciences 2019;239:117032.

[23] Senapati S, Mahanta A, Kumar S, Maiti P. Controlled drug delivery vehicles for cancer treatment and their performance. Signal Transduction and Targeted Therapy 2018;3:7.

[24] Torchilin V. Recent advances with liposomes as pharmaceutical carriers. Nature Reviews. Drug Discovery 2005;4(2):145–60.

[25] Storm G, Crommelin DJ. Liposomes: quo vadis? Pharmaceutical Science & Technology Today 1998;1(1):19–31.

[26] Gabizon A, Goren D, Cohen R, Barenholz Y. Development of liposomal anthracyclines: from basics to clinical applications. Journal of Controlled Release: Official Journal of the Controlled Release Society 1998;53(1-3):275–9.

[27] Alving CR. Liposomal vaccines: clinical status and immunological presentation for humoral and cellular immunity. Annals of the New York Academy of Sciences 1995;754:143–52.

[28] Gregoriadis G. Liposomes as immunoadjuvants and vaccine carriers: antigen entrapment. Immunomethods 1994;4(3):210−16.

[29] Kersten GF, Crommelin DJ. Liposomes and ISCOMS as vaccine formulations. Biochimica et Biophysica Acta (BBA)-Reviews on Biomembranes 1995;1241(2):117−38.

[30] Bergers J, Den Otter W, Crommelin D. Vesicles for tumour-associated antigen presentation to induce protective immunity: preparation, characterization and enhancement of the immune response by immunomodulators. Journal of Controlled Release 1994;29(3):317−27.

[31] Glück R. Liposomal presentation of antigens for human vaccines. Vaccine Design 1995;325−45.

[32] Glück R, Mischler R, Brantschen S, Just M, Althaus B, Cryz S. Immunopotentiating reconstituted influenza virus virosome vaccine delivery system for immunization against hepatitis A. The Journal of Clinical Investigation 1992;90(6):2491−5.

[33] Daemen T, Hofstede G, Ten Kate M, Bakker-Woudenberg I, Scherphof G. Liposomal doxorubicin-induced toxicity: depletion and impairment of phagocytic activity of liver macrophages. International Journal of Cancer 1995;61(5):716−21.

[34] Maruyama K. Intracellular targeting delivery of liposomal drugs to solid tumors based on EPR effects. Advanced Drug Delivery Reviews 2010;63(3):161−9.

[35] Maruyama K, Yuda T, Okamoto A, Kojima S, Suginaka A, Iwatsuru M. Prolonged circulation time in vivo of large unilamellar liposomes composed of distearoyl phosphatidylcholine and cholesterol containing amphipathic poly (ethylene glycol). Biochimica et Biophysica Acta 1992;1128(1):44−9.

[36] Liu D, Mori A, Huang L. Role of liposome size and RES blockade in controlling biodistribution and tumor uptake of GM1-containing liposomes. Biochimica et Biophysica Acta 1992;1104(1):95−101.

[37] Klibanov A, Maruyama K, Torchilin V, Huang L. Amphipathic polyethyleneglycols effectively prolong the circulation time of liposomes. FEBS Letters 1990;268(1):235−7.

[38] Gabizon A. Liposome circulation time and tumor targeting: implications for cancer chemotherapy. Advanced Drug Delivery Reviews 1995;16(2-3):285−94.

[39] Nichols JW, Bae YH. EPR: Evidence and fallacy. Journal of Controlled Release 2014;190:451−64.

[40] Barenholz YC. Doxil®—the first FDA-approved nano-drug: lessons learned. Journal of Controlled Release 2012;160(2):117−34.

[41] Barenholz YC. Doxil®—the first FDA-approved nano-drug: from an idea to a product. Handbook of harnessing biomaterials in nanomedicine. Jenny Stanford Publishing; 2021. p. 463−528.

[42] Sharma VK, Agrawal MK. A historical perspective of liposomes-a bio nanomaterial. Materials Today: Proceedings 2021;45:2963−6.

[43] Waterhouse DN, Tardi PG, Mayer LD, Bally MB. A comparison of liposomal formulations of doxorubicin with drug administered in free form. Drug safety 2001;24(12):903−20.

[44] Amantea M, Newman M, Sullivan T, Forrest A, Working P. Relationship of dose intensity to the induction of palmar-plantar erythrodysesthia by pegylated liposomal doxorubicin in dogs. Human & Experimental Toxicology 1999;18(1):17−26.

[45] Bava SV, Puliappadamba VT, Deepti A, Nair A, Karunagaran D, Anto RJ. Sensitization of taxol-induced apoptosis by curcumin involves down-regulation of nuclear factor-κB and the serine/threonine kinase Akt and is independent of tubulin polymerization. Journal of Biological Chemistry 2005;280(8):6301−8.

[46] Sreekanth C, Bava S, Sreekumar E, Anto R. Molecular evidences for the chemosensitizing efficacy of liposomal curcumin in paclitaxel chemotherapy in mouse models of cervical cancer. Oncogene 2011;30 (28):3139−52.

[47] Muthu M.S., Singh S. Targeted nanomedicines: effective treatment modalities for cancer, AIDS and brain disorders. 2009.

[48] Mura P, Maestrelli F, González-Rodríguez ML, Michelacci I, Ghelardini C, Rabasco AM. Development, characterization and in vivo evaluation of benzocaine-loaded liposomes. European Journal of Pharmaceutics and Biopharmaceutics 2007;67(1):86−95.

[49] Seth AK, Misra A, Umrigar D. Topical liposomal gel of idoxuridine for the treatment of herpes simplex: pharmaceutical and clinical implications. Pharmaceutical Development and Technology 2005;9 (3):277−89.

[50] Chen Y, Wu Q, Zhang Z, Yuan L, Liu X, Zhou L. Preparation of curcumin-loaded liposomes and evaluation of their skin permeation and pharmacodynamics. Molecules (Basel, Switzerland) 2012;17 (5):5972−87.

[51] Oeckinghaus A, Ghosh S. The NF-kappaB family of transcription factors and its regulation. Cold Spring Harbor Perspectives in Biology 2009;1(4) a000034-a.

[52] Xia Y, Shen S, Verma I. NF-κB, an active player in human cancers. Cancer Immunology Research; a Journal of Science and its Applications 2014;2(9):823−30.

[53] Kurzrock R, Li L. Liposome-encapsulated curcumin: in vitro and in vivo effects on proliferation, apoptosis, signaling, and angiogenesis. Journal of Clinical Oncology 2005;23(16_suppl):4091.

[54] Li L, Braiteh FS, Kurzrock R. Liposome-encapsulated curcumin: in vitro and in vivo effects on proliferation, apoptosis, signaling, and angiogenesis. Cancer: Interdisciplinary International Journal of the American Cancer Society 2005;104(6):1322−31.

[55] Ranjan AP, Mukerjee A, Helson L, Gupta R, Vishwanatha JK. Efficacy of liposomal curcumin in a human pancreatic tumor xenograft model: inhibition of tumor growth and angiogenesis. Anticancer Research 2013;33(9):3603−9.

[56] Mahmud M, Piwoni A, Filiczak N, Janicka M, Gubernator J. Long-circulating curcumin-loaded liposome formulations with high incorporation efficiency, stability and anticancer activity towards pancreatic adenocarcinoma cell lines in vitro. PLoS One 2016;11(12):e0167787.

[57] Mach CM, Mathew L, Mosley SA, Kurzrock R, Smith JA. Determination of minimum effective dose and optimal dosing schedule for liposomal curcumin in a xenograft human pancreatic cancer model. Anticancer Research 2009;29(6):1895−9.

[58] Zhang X, Dai F, Chen J, Xie X, Xu H, Bai C, et al. Antitumor effect of curcumin liposome after transcatheter arterial embolization in VX2 rabbits. Cancer Biology & Therapy 2019;20(5):642−52.

[59] Cheng Y, Zhao P, Wu S, Yang T, Chen Y, Zhang X, et al. Cisplatin and curcumin co-loaded nano-liposomes for the treatment of hepatocellular carcinoma. International Journal of Pharmaceutics 2018;545 (1-2):261−73.

[60] Song J-W, Liu Y-S, Guo Y-R, Zhong W-X, Guo Y-P, Guo L. Nano−liposomes double loaded with curcumin and tetrandrine: preparation, characterization, hepatotoxicity and anti-tumor effects. International Journal of Molecular Sciences 2022;23(12):6858.

[61] Li L, Ahmed B, Mehta K, Kurzrock R. Liposomal curcumin with and without oxaliplatin: effects on cell growth, apoptosis, and angiogenesis in colorectal cancer. Molecular Cancer Therapeutics 2007;6 (4):1276−82.

[62] Sesarman A, Tefas L, Sylvester B, Licarete E, Rauca V, Luput L, et al. Anti-angiogenic and anti-inflammatory effects of long-circulating liposomes co-encapsulating curcumin and doxorubicin on C26 murine colon cancer cells. Pharmacological Reports 2018;70(2):331−9.

[63] Sesarman A, Muntean D, Abrudan B, Tefas L, Sylvester B, Licarete E, et al. Improved pharmacokinetics and reduced side effects of doxorubicin therapy by liposomal co-encapsulation with curcumin. Journal of Liposome Research 2021;31(1):1−10.

[64] Pandelidou M, Dimas K, Georgopoulos A, Hatziantoniou S, Demetzos C. Preparation and characterization of lyophilised egg PC liposomes incorporating curcumin and evaluation of its activity against colorectal cancer cell lines. Journal of Nanoscience and Nanotechnology 2011;11(2):1259−66.

[65] Lin Y-L, Liu Y-K, Tsai N-M, Hsieh J-H, Chen C-H, Lin C-M, et al. A Lipo-PEG-PEI complex for encapsulating curcumin that enhances its antitumor effects on curcumin-sensitive and curcumin-resistance cells. Nanomedicine: Nanotechnology, Biology and Medicine 2012;8(3):318−27.

[66] Ravichandiran V, Masilamani K, Senthilnathan B, Maheshwaran A, Wui Wong T, Roy P. Quercetin-decorated curcumin liposome design for cancer therapy: in-vitro and in-vivo studies. Current Drug Delivery 2017;14(8):1053−9.

[67] Angeline N, Suhito IR, Kim C-H, Hong G-P, Park CG, Bhang SH, et al. A fibronectin-coated gold nanostructure composite for electrochemical detection of effects of curcumin-carrying nanoliposomes on human stomach cancer cells. Analyst. 2020;145(2):675−84.

[68] Basak SK, Zinabadi A, Wu AW, Venkatesan N, Duarte VM, Kang JJ, et al. Liposome encapsulated curcumin-difluorinated (CDF) inhibits the growth of cisplatin resistant head and neck cancer stem cells. Oncotarget. 2015;6(21):18504.

[69] Wang D, Veena MS, Stevenson K, Tang C, Ho B, Suh JD, et al. Liposome-encapsulated curcumin suppresses growth of head and neck squamous cell carcinoma in vitro and in xenografts through the inhibition of nuclear factor κB by an AKT-independent pathway. Clinical Cancer Research 2008;14(19):6228−36.

[70] Mahmoudi R, Hassandokht F, Ardakani MT, Karimi B, Roustazadeh A, Tarvirdipour S, et al. Intercalation of curcumin into liposomal chemotherapeutic agent augments apoptosis in breast cancer cells. Journal of Biomaterials Applications 2021;35(8):1005−18.

[71] Zhou S, Li J, Xu H, Zhang S, Chen X, Chen W, et al. Liposomal curcumin alters chemosensitivity of breast cancer cells to Adriamycin via regulating microRNA expression. Gene 2017;622:1−12.

[72] Othman AK, El Kurdi R, Badran A, Mesmar J, Baydoun E, Patra D. Liposome-based nanocapsules for the controlled release of dietary curcumin: PDDA and silica nanoparticle-coated DMPC liposomes enhance the fluorescence efficiency and anticancer activity of curcumin. RSC Advances 2022;12(18):11282−92.

[73] Li R, Deng L, Cai Z, Zhang S, Wang K, Li L, et al. Liposomes coated with thiolated chitosan as drug carriers of curcumin. Materials Science and Engineering: C. 2017;80:156−64.

[74] Hasan M, Elkhoury K, Belhaj N, Kahn C, Tamayol A, Barberi-Heyob M, et al. Growth-inhibitory effect of chitosan-coated liposomes encapsulating curcumin on MCF-7 breast cancer cells. Marine Drugs 2020;18(4):217.

[75] Ruttala HB, Ko YT. Liposomal co-delivery of curcumin and albumin/paclitaxel nanoparticle for enhanced synergistic antitumor efficacy. Colloids and Surfaces B: Biointerfaces 2015;128:419−26.

[76] Xu H, Gong Z, Zhou S, Yang S, Wang D, Chen X, et al. Liposomal curcumin targeting endometrial cancer through the NF-κB pathway. Cellular Physiology and Biochemistry 2018;48(2):569−82.

[77] Narayanan NK, Nargi D, Randolph C, Narayanan BA. Liposome encapsulation of curcumin and resveratrol in combination reduces prostate cancer incidence in PTEN knockout mice. International Journal of Cancer 2009;125(1):1−8.

[78] Thangapazham RL, Puri A, Tele S, Blumenthal R, Maheshwari RK. Evaluation of a nanotechnology-based carrier for delivery of curcumin in prostate cancer cells. International Journal of Oncology 2008;32(5):1119−23.

[79] Dhule SS, Penfornis P, Frazier T, Walker R, Feldman J, Tan G, et al. Curcumin-loaded γ-cyclodextrin liposomal nanoparticles as delivery vehicles for osteosarcoma. Nanomedicine: Nanotechnology, Biology and Medicine 2012;8(4):440−51.

[80] Rahman S, Cao S, Steadman KJ, Wei M, Parekh HS. Native and β-cyclodextrin-enclosed curcumin: entrapment within liposomes and their in vitro cytotoxicity in lung and colon cancer. Drug Delivery 2012;19(7):346−53.

[81] Ibrahim S, Tagami T, Kishi T, Ozeki T. Curcumin marinosomes as promising nano-drug delivery system for lung cancer. International Journal of Pharmaceutics 2018;540(1-2):40−9.

[82] Wu Q, Ou H, Shang Y, Zhang X, Wu J, Fan F. Nanoscale formulations: incorporating curcumin into combination strategies for the treatment of lung cancer. Drug Design, Development and Therapy 2021;15:2695.

[83] Sheikhpour M, Sadeghizadeh M, Yazdian F, Mansoori A, Asadi H, Movafagh A, et al. Co-administration of curcumin and bromocriptine nano-liposomes for induction of apoptosis in lung cancer cells. Iranian Biomedical Journal 2020;24(1):24.

[84] Zhou Q, Fu Z. In vitro and in vivo study of a novel liposome-mediated dual drug delivery for synergistic lung cancer therapy via oral administration. OncoTargets and Therapy 2020;13:12695.

[85] Tang J-C, Shi H-S, Wan L-Q, Wang Y-S, Wei Y-Q. Enhanced antitumor effect of curcumin liposomes with local hyperthermia in the LL/2 model. Asian Pacific Journal of Cancer Prevention 2013;14 (4):2307−10.

[86] Shi H-S, Gao X, Li D, Zhang Q-W, Wang Y-S, Zheng Y, et al. A systemic administration of liposomal curcumin inhibits radiation pneumonitis and sensitizes lung carcinoma to radiation. International Journal of Nanomedicine 2012;7:2601.

[87] Hardwick J, Taylor J, Mehta M, Satija S, Paudel KR, Hansbro PM, et al. Targeting cancer using curcumin encapsulated vesicular drug delivery systems. Current Pharmaceutical Design 2021;27(1):2−14.

[88] Hocking A, Tommasi S, Sordillo P, Klebe S. The safety and exploration of the pharmacokinetics of intrapleural liposomal curcumin. International Journal of Nanomedicine 2020;15:943.

[89] Zhang T, Chen Y, Ge Y, Hu Y, Li M, Jin Y. Inhalation treatment of primary lung cancer using liposomal curcumin dry powder inhalers. Acta Pharmaceutica Sinica B. 2018;8(3):440−8.

[90] Wang Z, Meng F, Zhong Z. Emerging targeted drug delivery strategies toward ovarian cancer. Advanced Drug Delivery Reviews 2021;113969.

[91] Saengkrit N, Saesoo S, Srinuanchai W, Phunpee S, Ruktanonchai UR. Influence of curcumin-loaded cationic liposome on anticancer activity for cervical cancer therapy. Colloids and Surfaces B: Biointerfaces 2014;114:349−56.

[92] Wang W-Y, Cao Y-X, Zhou X, Wei B. Delivery of folic acid-modified liposomal curcumin for targeted cervical carcinoma therapy. Drug Design, Development and Therapy 2019;13:2205.

[93] Jiang K, Shen M, Xu W. Arginine, glycine, aspartic acid peptide-modified paclitaxel and curcumin co-loaded liposome for the treatment of lung cancer: in vitro/vivo evaluation. International Journal of Nanomedicine 2018;13:2561.

[94] Mahmoudi R, Ashraf Mirahmadi-Babaheidri S, Delaviz H, Fouani MH, Alipour M, Jafari Barmak M, et al. RGD peptide-mediated liposomal curcumin targeted delivery to breast cancer cells. Journal of Biomaterials Applications 2021;35(7):743−53.

[95] Kangarlou S, Ramezanpour S, Balalaie S, Roudbar Mohammadi S, Haririan I. Curcumin-loaded nanoliposomes linked to homing peptides for integrin targeting and neuropilin-1-mediated internalization. Pharmaceutical Biology 2017;55(1):277−85.

[96] Moballegh-Nasery M, Mandegary A, Eslaminejad T, Zeinali M, Pardakhti A, Behnam B, et al. Cytotoxicity evaluation of curcumin-loaded affibody-decorated liposomes against breast cancerous cell lines. Journal of Liposome Research 2021;31(2):189−94.

[97] Catania A, Barrajón-Catalán E, Nicolosi S, Cicirata F, Micol V. Immunoliposome encapsulation increases cytotoxic activity and selectivity of curcumin and resveratrol against HER2 overexpressing human breast cancer cells. Breast Cancer Research and Treatment 2013;141(1):55−65.

[98] Nsairat H, Mahmoud IS, Odeh F, Abuarqoub D, Al-Azzawi H, Zaza R, et al. Grafting of anti-nucleolin aptamer into preformed and remotely loaded liposomes through aptamer-cholesterol post-insertion. RSC Advances 2020;10(59):36219−29.

[99] Murugesan K, Srinivasan P, Mahadeva R, Gupta CM, Haq W. Tuftsin-bearing liposomes co-encapsulated with doxorubicin and curcumin efficiently inhibit EAC tumor growth in mice. International Journal of Nanomedicine 2020;15:10547.

[100] Qi C, Wang D, Gong X, Zhou Q, Yue X, Li C, et al. Co-delivery of curcumin and capsaicin by dual-targeting liposomes for inhibition of aHSC-induced drug resistance and metastasis. ACS Applied Materials & Interfaces 2021;13(14):16019−35.

[101] Wang Y, Ding R, Zhang Z, Zhong C, Wang J, Wang M. Curcumin-loaded liposomes with the hepatic and lysosomal dual-targeted effects for therapy of hepatocellular carcinoma. International Journal of Pharmaceutics 2021;602:120628.

[102] Li Y, Wu J, Lu Q, Liu X, Wen J, Qi X, et al. GA&HA-modified liposomes for co-delivery of aprepitant and curcumin to inhibit drug-resistance and metastasis of hepatocellular carcinoma. International Journal of Nanomedicine 2022;17:2559.

[103] Sun D, Zhou J-K, Zhao L, Zheng Z-Y, Li J, Pu W, et al. Novel curcumin liposome modified with hyaluronan targeting CD44 plays an anti-leukemic role in acute myeloid leukemia in vitro and in vivo. ACS Applied Materials & Interfaces 2017;9(20):16857−68.

[104] Barui S, Saha S, Yakati V, Chaudhuri A. Systemic codelivery of a homoserine derived ceramide analogue and curcumin to tumor vasculature inhibits mouse tumor growth. Molecular Pharmaceutics 2016;13(2):404−19.

[105] Dhule SS, Penfornis P, He J, Harris MR, Terry T, John V, et al. The combined effect of encapsulating curcumin and C6 ceramide in liposomal nanoparticles against osteosarcoma. Molecular Pharmaceutics 2014;11(2):417−27.

[106] Li Z, Xiong X, Peng S, Chen X, Liu W, Liu C. Novel folated pluronic F127 modified liposomes for delivery of curcumin: preparation, release, and cytotoxicity. Journal of Microencapsulation 2020;37 (3):220−9.

[107] Le UM, Hartman A, Pillai G. Enhanced selective cellular uptake and cytotoxicity of epidermal growth factor-conjugated liposomes containing curcumin on EGFR-overexpressed pancreatic cancer cells. Journal of Drug Targeting 2018;26(8):676−83.

[108] Ma Q, Qian W, Tao W, Zhou Y, Xue B. Delivery of curcumin nanoliposomes using surface modified with CD133 aptamers for prostate cancer. Drug Design, Development and Therapy 2019;13:4021.

[109] Zhao M, Zhao M, Fu C, Yu Y, Fu A. Targeted therapy of intracranial glioma model mice with curcumin nanoliposomes. International Journal of Nanomedicine 2018;13:1601.

[110] Gabay M, Weizman A, Zeineh N, Kahana M, Obeid F, Allon N, et al. Liposomal carrier conjugated to APP-derived peptide for brain cancer treatment. Cellular and Molecular Neurobiology 2021;41 (5):1019−29.

[111] Xu Z, Guo C, Ye Q, Shi Y, Sun Y, Zhang J, et al. Endothelial deletion of SHP2 suppresses tumor angiogenesis and promotes vascular normalization. Nature Communications 2021;12(1):1−15.

[112] Sakurai Y, Akita H, Harashima H. Targeting tumor endothelial cells with nanoparticles. International Journal of Molecular Sciences 2019;20(23):5819.

[113] Li F, Qin Y, Lee J, Liao H, Wang N, Davis TP, et al. Stimuli-responsive nano-assemblies for remotely controlled drug delivery. Journal of Controlled Release 2020;322:566−92.

[114] Jose A, Labala S, Venuganti VVK. Co-delivery of curcumin and STAT3 siRNA using deformable cationic liposomes to treat skin cancer. Journal of Drug Targeting 2017;25(4):330−41.

[115] Jose A, Labala S, Ninave KM, Gade SK, Venuganti VVK. Effective skin cancer treatment by topical co-delivery of curcumin and STAT3 siRNA using cationic liposomes. AAPS PharmSciTech 2018;19 (1):166−75.

[116] Singh SP, Alvi SB, Pemmaraju DB, Singh AD, Manda SV, Srivastava R, et al. NIR triggered liposome gold nanoparticles entrapping curcumin as in situ adjuvant for photothermal treatment of skin cancer. International Journal of Biological Macromolecules 2018;110:375−82.

[117] Zarrabi A, Zarepour A, Khosravi A, Alimohammadi Z, Thakur VK. Synthesis of curcumin loaded smart pH-responsive stealth liposome as a novel nanocarrier for cancer treatment. Fibers 2021;9(3):19.

[118] Xu H, Li Y, Paxton JW, Wu Z. Co-delivery using pH-sensitive liposomes to pancreatic cancer cells: the effects of curcumin on cellular concentration and pharmacokinetics of gemcitabine. Pharmaceutical Research 2021;38(7):1209–19.

[119] Li R, Lin Z, Zhang Q, Zhang Y, Liu Y, Lyu Y, et al. Injectable and in situ-formable thiolated chitosan-coated liposomal hydrogels as curcumin carriers for prevention of in vivo breast cancer recurrence. ACS Applied Materials & Interfaces 2020;12(15):17936–48.

[120] Shore A. Retraction: creation of ultrasound and temperature-triggered bubble liposomes from economical precursors to enhance the therapeutic efficacy of curcumin in cancer cells. RSC Advances 2018;8 (69):39786.

[121] Chen Y, Du Q, Guo Q, Huang J, Liu L, Shen X, et al. AW/O emulsion mediated film dispersion method for curcumin encapsulated pH-sensitive liposomes in the colon tumor treatment. Drug Development and Industrial Pharmacy 2019;45(2):282–91.

[122] Hamano N, Böttger R, Lee SE, Yang Y, Kulkarni JA, Ip S, et al. Robust microfluidic technology and new lipid composition for fabrication of curcumin-loaded liposomes: effect on the anticancer activity and safety of cisplatin. Molecular Pharmaceutics 2019;16(9):3957–67.

[123] Xu R, Tomeh MA, Ye S, Zhang P, Lv S, You R, et al. Novel microfluidic swirl mixers for scalable formulation of curcumin loaded liposomes for cancer therapy. International Journal of Pharmaceutics 2022;121857.

[124] Sarkar N, Bose S. Liposome-encapsulated curcumin-loaded 3D printed scaffold for bone tissue engineering. ACS Applied Materials & Interfaces 2019;11(19):17184–92.

[125] Greil R, Greil-Ressler S, Weiss L, Schönlieb C, Magnes T, Radl B, et al. A phase 1 dose-escalation study on the safety, tolerability and activity of liposomal curcumin (Lipocurc™) in patients with locally advanced or metastatic cancer. Cancer Chemotherapy and Pharmacology 2018;82(4):695–706.

[126] Hocking AJ, Farrall AL, Newhouse S, Sordillo P, Greco K, Karapetis CS, et al. Study protocol of a phase 1 clinical trial establishing the safety of intrapleural administration of liposomal curcumin: curcumin as a palliative treatment for malignant pleural effusion (IPAL-MPE). BMJ Open 2021;11(3):e047075.

11

Inorganic nanoparticle-based curcumin delivery as cancer therapeutics

Leila Farhoudi[1], Tannaz Jamialahmadi[2], Amirhossein Sahebkar[3,4]

[1]NANOTECHNOLOGY RESEARCH CENTER, PHARMACEUTICAL TECHNOLOGY INSTITUTE, MASHHAD UNIVERSITY OF MEDICAL SCIENCES, MASHHAD, IRAN [2]INTERNATIONAL UNESCO CENTER FOR HEALTH-RELATED BASIC SCIENCES AND HUMAN NUTRITION, MASHHAD UNIVERSITY OF MEDICAL SCIENCES, MASHHAD, IRAN [3]BIOTECHNOLOGY RESEARCH CENTER, PHARMACEUTICAL TECHNOLOGY INSTITUTE, MASHHAD UNIVERSITY OF MEDICAL SCIENCES, MASHHAD, IRAN [4]APPLIED BIOMEDICAL RESEARCH CENTER, MASHHAD UNIVERSITY OF MEDICAL SCIENCES, MASHHAD, IRAN

11.1 Introduction

Due to the existing limitations in the current chemotherapeutic methods, innovative approaches like nanobiotechnology are being explored as suitable alternatives in prevention, diagnosis, treatment, and follow-up of many malignancies [1,2,3]. Nanoparticles (NPs) have improved physicochemical properties as well as optical, magnetic, and biomedical features due to their appropriate size and morphology [4]. They remain in the blood circulation for a prolonged period of time and reach the target, which is tissue facilitated by the enhanced permeability and retention (EPR) effect [5−7]. Inorganic NP formulations such as metal dioxide, gold nanoparticles (AuNPs), and mesoporous silica possess enhanced stability, tunable morphology, potent magnetic and electrical properties, as well as highly intact framework within the bloodstream compared to organic compounds [8].

Curcumin is a yellow phenolic compound that belongs to the family of ginger. Based on the biopharmaceutics classification system (BCS), it is a class IV component [9]. A wide range of pharmacological activities have been reported for curcumin, which include anticancer, antioxidant [10], and antiinflammatory properties, among others [11−33]. Curcumin's inhibitory roles in cancer are mainly exerted at the cellular level through modulating the signaling pathways [34,35]. Apart from a myriad of desirable features, curcumin's administration has faced some challenges due to its short elimination half-life and poor bioavailability [11,36]. Recent advances made by the NPs have improved the bioactivity of medications by extending their half-life and controlling their release rate in a target tissue [37]. Here, the authors have collected most of the recent studies on curcumin delivery in treatment of malignancies using different inorganic NPs.

11.1.1 Inorganic nanoparticles

Inorganic NPs on the scale of a nanometer are biocompatible and nontoxic products with high drug loading and stability compared to organic NPs [38]. Smaller dimensions contribute to a large surface to volume ratio increasing the reactivity with the corresponding atom. Due to their unique magnetic, optical, and electrical properties, they can be utilized in drug delivery, cancer treatment, magnetic resonance imaging (MRI), and tissue engineering [39]. They are successfully used in functionalizing strategies such as thermal heating for AuNPs. It is documented that they possess the capacity to respond to external stimuli like near-infrared (NIR) light or magnetic field to improve drug release and imaging [40,41]. Their advantages such as simple preparation, biocompatibility, controllable structure, and optical properties [42] have attracted researchers to focus on their biomedical application particularly in cancer therapy.

11.2 Different types of inorganic nanoparticles

11.2.1 Metal oxide nanoparticle

Specific characteristics of metal oxide NPs include simple preparation, high stability, easy fabrication for a desired size, shape, and porosity, and functionalized with other molecules due to negative charge [43]. Owing to these advantages, they have been applied in diagnostic purposes such as tumor imaging, as molecular markers, and as photosensitizers in photodynamic therapy [44]. Different types of metal oxides such as TiO_2, ZnO, Fe_3O_4, CuO, and CeO_2 that are used for curcumin delivery are introduced in the following sections.

11.2.1.1 TiO_2

Application of TiO_2 in biomedical research is due to its notable properties such as stability, low toxicity, high opacity, biocompatibility, conductivity, and low cost [45,46]. When exposed to UV light, the electrons in TiO_2 valence band can be stimulated and subsequently shift toward the conduction band, resulting in the production of electron-hole pairs, which can then interact with the nearby O_2 and H_2O to produce reactive oxygen species (ROS) [47]. Since UV light is not appropriate for photodynamic therapy (PDT) due to its low tumor penetration, different researches have addressed TiO_2-based NPs for visible-light-driven PDT applications [48]. Mesoporous silica was embedded in TiO_2 as a sonosensitizer agent with encapsulation of curcumin coated with polyethylenimine (PEI) and targeted with folic acid (CUR@PEI-FA-DSTNs). Curcumin was released after sonodynamic therapy by ROS-mediated degradation of PEI dendrimer generated by TiO_2. The cellular uptake and antitumor study of the targeting ligand demonstrated a potent nanocarrier with greater effects of chemotherapy in combination with sonodynamic therapy [49]. Similarly, loading of curcumin inside TiO_2 showed highly effective inhibition of HeLa tumor cells [50]. In another study, folic acid (FA)-targeted PEGylation TiO_2 was prepared by emulsion-evaporation-solidification method at low temperatures. The synthesized NP was loaded with curcumin and salvianolic acid B for evaluation of synergistic effect in breast cancer. The findings showed a higher cellular uptake and accumulation of the NP in MDA-MB-231 and MCF-7 cell lines. This in vivo study exhibited the enhanced ability of FA-NP to penetrate and accumulate in tumor site and inhibit tumor growth [51].

The cyclodextrin-based polymer was used to generate curcumin-modified TiO_2 nanoarrays in the treatment of osteosarcoma. In this study, polydopamine-assisted film was implanted on the surface of TiO_2 as the first coating layer. Curcumin subsequently induced apoptosis in osteosarcoma MG63 cell lines [52].

11.2.1.2 ZnO

ZnO is a biocompatible NP that is over 10 nm and its safety is confirmed by the FDA [53]. ZnO was coated with chitosan to increase the stability and solubility of NP composite. Curcumin was loaded in NP by the coprecipitation method. At tumor $pH \sim (5-6$ phenyl), ZnO dissolved quickly into Zn^{2+} ions. Significant toxicity derived from higher dissolution rates and increased ion release primarily affected cancer cells. Detection of less toxicity in the physiologic media suggested that the damaged cells caused by ZnCur nanocomposite were repaired during subsequent cell divisions [54]. Targeting of ZnO with carboxymethyl chitosan for delivery of curcumin showed higher accumulation of NP in monkey kidney cancer cell lines (MA104). This in vitro study showed faster diffusion of curcumin in acidic media, which was attributed to the protonation of amine groups. Higher internalization and cytotoxicity confirmed the presence of curcumin and its effects in cancer therapy [55]. A chitosan-phenodione-coated CuO with the particle size of $100-200$ nm was tested in three types of cancer cells (HeLa, breast, and skin). The IC_{50} concentration results were around 14, 19, and 12 µg/mL, respectively. The results demonstrated favorable curcumin release within the tumor microenvironment [56]. Treatment with a curcumin-loaded ZnO that was fabricated with phenylboronic acid (PBA) showed a completely disturbed morphology of tumor tissue. Besides the higher levels of proapoptotic proteins following administration of Zno-PBA-Cur NPs revealed the ability of these NPs to activate the intrinsic apoptotic pathway [57]. In an interesting study, a nonspherical flower structure of ZnO with β-cyclodextrin functionalized by 3-mercaptopropionic acid (MPA) resulted in increased cellular uptake of curcumin and enhanced anticancer efficacy against MDA-MB-231 breast cancer cells [58].

11.2.1.3 Cerium oxide

Cerium oxide (CeO_2) NP consists of a core called Ce, which is surrounded by oxygen lattice. CeO_2 has direct cytotoxicity by generation of ROS and induction of apoptosis by targeting mitochondria [59,60]. It has dual activities based on the pH of the target tissue. CeO_2 could either act as an ROS scavenge in normal tissue (pH = 7.4) or generate ROS in cancer tissues (pH = 5.5−6.5) [61,62]. Curcumin-loaded combination of CeO_2 and SiO_2 with modifying PEG (CeO_2@SiO_2-PEG [CSPNPs]) demonstrated effective protection against $HepG_2$ and HeLa cells [63].

11.2.1.4 Superparamagnetic iron oxide nanoparticles

Superparamagnetic iron oxide NPs (SPIONs) are used in processes such as drug delivery, bioimaging, and cell detection, among others [64]. The phenomenon of magnetic hyperthermia related to SPIONs is the conversion of energy into heat when in a magnetic field. Codelivery of curcumin and paclitaxel (PTX) was done by FA-targeted Fe_3O_4 NPs. FA was joined to Pluronic F-127 via diethylene glycol bis (3-aminopropyl) ether spacer. Cellular uptake and cytotoxicity of the nanoformulation against MCF-7 cell line were promoted by active FA and passive magnetic field targeting. Lower IC_{50} value PTX-cur-OAMNPPF127FA under an external magnetic field was observed [65]. Similarly, the synergistic effects of curcumin and 5FU by decoration of human serum albumin-coated Fe_3O_4 NPs and targeting FA (C-MNP-HSA-FA) were evaluated in the treatment of breast cancer. In the presence of a magnetic field, affinity of NP for receptor-mediated endocytosis and the cytotoxicity of the composite drugs were further increased [66]. In another study, PEGylated poly amidoamine (PAMAM) dendrimer generation 3 with Fe_3O_4 entrapped in the core containing FA as targeting ligand and curcumin was incorporated (FA-mPEG-PAMAM G3-CUR@SPIONs). Fe_3O_4 acts as a hyperthermia agent and generates heat in the target tissue upon stimulation by an alternating magnetic field (AMF) contributing to thermo chemotherapy. The chemotherapy with magnetic hyperthermia remarkably enhanced the diagnosis and therapeutic performance. FA-targeted SPION dendrimer in combination with AMF increased cellular uptake of NP facilitated by FA receptor and induced apoptosis. In conclusion, increased concentration of curcumin and SPION may result in excess heat generation efficacy in combination with AMF [67]. In a study by Saikia et al., Fe_3O_4 NP coated with aminated starch in conjugation of FA showed higher inhibition of MCF-7 and $HepG_2$ cell lines [68]. B-CD by functionalizing the surface of Fe_3O_4 (DOX-CUR/β-CD-Fe_3O_4) increased the loading content of curcumin and Doxorubicin as well as uptake of NP on MCF-7, which resulted in decreasing tumor volume with magnetic field treatment [69]. It was revealed that Fe_3O_4 NPs coated with β-CD and Pluronic F-68 clearly enhanced cellular uptake and accumulation of curcumin using magnetic field [70]. In another study, β-CD and Pluronic polymer F-127 coated Fe_3O_4 for hyperthermia MRI. The biocompatible formulation with curcumin exhibited equivalent inhibitory effects on breast, ovary, and prostate cancer cells. The NP size had a suitable surface area to generate heat. With a further increase in the concentration of formulation, a continuous increase in temperature was observed [71]. Chitosan as a cationic targeting biopolymer ligand is well known in drug delivery. Chitosan as shell coated surface of Fe_3O_4 NP was used to evaluate the cytotoxicity of curcumin-CS-Fe_3O_4 against A549 cell lines (with IC_{50} value of 11.37 $\mu g\ mL^{-1}$ for curcumin-CS-Fe_3O_4 and 73.03 $\mu g\ mL^{-1}$ for free curcumin) [72]. Hamed Nosrati et al. prepared Fe_3O_4 as core and bovine serum albumin as shell that coated the NP. Evaluation of curcumin-magnetic biomimetic NP exhibited a significant reduction in cell survival [73] (Table 11−1).

11.2.2 Mesoporous silica nanoparticles

Distinct properties of mesoporous silica nanoparticles (MSN) such as homogeneous size (2−20 nm), high surface area, and pore volume have made them ideal NPs for drug

Table 11–1 Summary of characterization of metal oxides nanoparticles.

			Outcome	Size	Zeta	References
TiO$_2$	Breast cancer	FA-PEG-TiO$_2$		18.01 ± 0.79	−7.80 ± 2.01	[51]
ZnO	B16F10 melanoma cancer cell line	ZnO-Cur-chitosan	Curcumin's therapeutic efficacy and bioavailability are increased, resulting in tumor growth.	161	20.4	[54]
	Kidney cancer cell (MA104)	ZnO-o-CMCS-Cur		40	–	[55]
Fe$_3$O$_4$	MCF-7	PTX-cur-OAMNPPF127FA	Better cytotoxicity and higher cellular uptake with combination drugs and targeting of folic acid could be utilized for MDR cancer treatment.	94.2 ± 6.3	− 25.5	[65]
	MCF-7	(Cur-MNP-HSA-FA)		108.4	− 49.1	[66]
	MCF-7	FA-mPEG-PAMAM G3-		∼ 20–90	–	[67]
	HepG2 and MCF-7	CUR@SPIONs		42.9 ± 0.03	–	[68]
	HFF2 and MCF-7	ZnO-aminated starch/Fe$_3$O$_4$	Increase the cellular uptake	56 ± 11.43	− 10.1	[73]
	MDA-MB-231	F@BSA@CUR NPs	Increase antitumor activity	123	− 0.66	[70]
	A2780CP (ovarian), MDA-MB-231 (breast), PC-3 (prostate)	B-CD-F68 polymer/Fe$_3$O$_4$	Increase cytotoxicity due to sustained drug release	174.47 ± 2.41	− 18.85	[71]
		B-CD-F-127 polymer/Fe$_3$O$_4$	Effect cell colony and reduced cell viability Superior hyperthermia effect in compare CD and pure magnetic nanoparticle			

delivery. The porocity of mesoporouse can host a variety of agents like drugs or proteins [74]. MSN dissolution rate is affected by particle characteristics such as pore size, surface area, and functionalization, as well as degradation characteristics including pH, temperature, and concentration. Therefore, its dissolution rate could be variable from few hours to several weeks [75]. One of the main benefits of MSN is to minimize the limitations in the administration of some medications including low solubility, narrow therapeutic window, and adverse effects. MSN was surface-modified with m-PEG-KIT-6 and Gu to increase curcumin loading and the interaction between curcumin and Guanidyl group. This NP with pH-responsive characteristics as well as highly programmed release and penetrability was used in vitro for breast cancer cell lines [76]. Also, β-cyclodextrin functionalized PEGylated KIT-6 with NH functional group was synthesized as a pH-sensitive carrier. Under acidic conditions, curcumin release was increased [77]. Curcumin as a photosensitizer agent was loaded in the PEG-surface of mesoporous. Upon irradiation, the result of cytotoxicity of MSN-PEG@Cur was evaluated against HeLa cancer cells and showed a quick reaction with oxygen to effectively produce cytotoxic ROS. This NP could be a promising vehicle for curcumin-mediated PDT [78]. In vivo study of curcumin-mesoporous NP that was modified with PEG and conjugated with transferrin (Tf) to target the pancreatic cancer cell significantly inhibited tumor growth and minimized distant metastasis [79]. The goal in target drug delivery is to enhance drug concentration in the right tissue to maximize its efficacy. The targeting moieties like hyaluronic acid as a biodegradable and biocompatible glycosaminoglycan cooperates with the receptors on the surface of CD44 cells to facilitate cell entry via hyaluronic acid—mediated endocytosis. In an interesting study, hyaluronic acid—functionalized mesoporous NP was used for curcumin delivery to the breast cancer cells. Results showed decreased tumor mass and enhanced apoptosis, which was attributed to the improved bioavailability of targeting mesoporous NP [80]. Based on the physiological condition of the tumor microenvironment, some drug delivery systems (DDS) are designed to respond to environmental stimuli. For example, in a study, MSN coated with tannic acid-Fe (III) complex glutathione (GSH) was designed. The structure triggered curcumin release in response to pH variation and altered GSH concentrations. A sustained release of curcumin was detected in physiologic media [81]. By functionalizing amine groups at the surface of MSN encapsulated by curcumin, sustained release of curcumin was evaluated in different media such as simulated gastric fluid (SGF), simulated colon fluid (SCF), simulated body fluids (SBF), and intestinal (SIF). Under acidic pH, the burst release and release rate of curcumin into SGF was decreased due to interaction of hydrogen bonds between curcumin and surface MSN molecules indicating a protective effect of pH-responsive MSNs [82]. In another study, curcumin and guanidine-loaded hallow MSNs increased the phosphorylation of oncogenic proteins (such as c-Raf (Ser249), Akt (Ser473), PTEN (Ser380), PDK1 (Ser241), and GSK-3β (Ser9)), which resulted in cell death in MCF-7 breast cancer [83]. Similarly, combination of curcumin and gallium (III) nitrate in hollow MSNs with 3-aminopropyl triethoxysilane (APTES) showed induction of apoptosis through the mitochondrial intrinsic pathway [84].

11.2.3 Gold nanoparticles

AuNPs are metal-based NPs with favorable characteristics including photothermal and optical properties, adjustable surface and shape, high quality, controllable size, and facile synthesis [85,86]. They have been developed in different sizes and shapes such as gold silica nanoshells, gold nanosphere, gold nanorod, hollow gold nanoshells, gold nanocages, and gold nanostars [87]. AuNPs have been used as drug delivery and photothermal agents due to their biocompatibility, simple preparation, and optical properties; they are particularly useful in protodermal cancer therapy (PTT) using surface plasmon resonance (SPR). The cytotoxic effects of AuNPs were first discovered by Huang et al., when Au-Cur NPs induced enhanced cytotoxicity in 4T1 breast cancer cell lines under 808 nm laser light radiation [88,89]. Other than PTT, AuNPs have also been applied in DDS by functionalizing gated onto the inner shell via an acid-cleavable hydrazine linkage to achieve the target site and remotely control drug delivery. In a study by M. Ghorbani et al., an AuNP functionalized with GSH as the targeting ligand for targeting the brain. Lipophilic acid (LA) was also used as a linker conjugated to curcumin. Both LA-curcumin and GSH were then attached to Au-iron oxide NPs. The enhanced cellular uptake of Fe_3O_4@Au-LA-CUR/GSH NCs demonstrated the therapeutics efficacy of GSH against cancer cells. In terms of diagnostic applications, in vitro MRI studies revealed the acceptable magnetic property and selective targeting ability of this NP to implying its potential role as a negative MRI contrast agent [90]. A dual-responsive cleavable nanosystem for synergetic NIR-triggered PDT/PTT was studied. Curcumin-loaded gold nanorods (AuNRs) that were encapsulated with upconverting nanoparticles (UCNPs) and phenylboronic double ester (PBE) on the outer shell were applied. The nanoplatform AuNRs/Cur/UCNPs@PBE with ROS and pH-responsive properties and the synergistic effects of PPT/PDT exhibited improved intracellular accumulation within cancer cells [91]. In an animal study, curcumin was encapsulated into chitosan-graft-poly (N-vinyl caprolactam) NPs containing Au-curcumin-TRC NPs. Compared to free curcumin with a short half-life, circulation of these NPs was increased up to a week and maximum curcumin concentrations were found in tumor cells [92]. The synergistic effects of curcumin and Au combination in breast cancer were found to be mediated by ROS generation, which in turn activated the apoptotic pathway without exerting any toxicity in normal tissues [93]. To evaluate radiation therapy for cancer, AuNPs were encapsulated into polymeric m-PEG that covalently conjugated to curcumin. Following X-ray irradiation, secondary and auger electrons were generated that led to the production of large numbers of ROS within the cells. Cotreatment with mPEG-CUR@Au and X-ray was associated with decreased tumor volume with no significant loss of body weight [94]. In another study, three types of cyclodextrin (α, β, and γ) were conjugated with PEGylated AuNPs. Although the encapsulation efficiency was different, the in vitro results of cur-CD-GNPs exhibited similar cytotoxicity among all three. This NP improved the solubility of curcumin and could be potentially used in cancer imaging and treatment [95]. A curcumin-AuNP was designed which was then equipped with a surface of polymeric dendrimer G5 conjugated to aptamer MUC-1. Findings revealed facilitated cellular uptake and cytotoxicity within the C26 and HT29 cells through aptamer MUC-1-mediated targeting pathway. The hybrid theranostic platform was also used for CT scan imaging [96].

11.2.4 Quantum dot nanoparticles

Quantum dots (QDs) ranging from 2 to 20 nm are nanocrystals with a core consisting of magnetic metals, noble metals, and semiconductors such as CdTe/CdSe [97]. QDs are promising nanoprobes in biological and imaging applications. Compared with fluorescent dyes, QDs have some advantages including high photostability, broad absorption spectra, and photoluminescence excitation (PLE) as well as narrow and sharp spectra [98]. Indeed, QDs seem to be appealing compounds in cancer treatment and nanobiotechnology. Besides, the incorporation of protective materials such as Zinc sulfide (ZnS) has somewhat overcome the concerns regarding the possible toxicity of QDs (e.g., CdSe QDs) [99,100]. CdSe core/ZnS shell QDs in combination with UV irradiation were found to induce apoptosis in HL-60 cell lines [101]. Also, curcumin-loaded QDs showed growth inhibition in colon cancer [102]. In another research, the COOH group of poly(lactic-co-glycolic acid) (PLGA) NPs was modified and upon activation, QDs were added. The efficacy on the two cell lines (BCBL-1 and HBL-6) of the primary effusion lymphoma (PEL) showed significantly decreased cell viability. In addition, the confocal microscopy findings confirmed that curcumin release markedly altered cell proliferation [103]. In fluorescent and flow cytometry studies, curcumin-loaded graphene QDs conjugated with glucosamine revealed stronger cellular uptake mediated through glucosamine receptor [104]. Multidrug resistance (MDR) mechanisms in cancer cells reduce penetration of drugs via different routes such as Pg-P and NF-kB and PI3K pathways [105]. Curcumin is shown to downregulate the NF-kB and PI3K pathways and suppress the Pg-P expression [11]. In this regard, curcumin was incorporated into a disulfide-linked hydrophobic backbone of a PEGylated amphiphilic diblock copolymer (biotin poly(ethylene glycol)−poly(curcumin-dithio dipropionic acid)). Biotin binds to its receptors that are overexpressed on the surface of cancer cells. The Fe_3O_4 NP was also added to guide the delivery of this multifunction NP toward target tissues. Combination of PTX and curcumin led to the downregulation of Pg-P and accumulation of PTX in MDR cancer cells (MCF-7/ADR). Meanwhile, to trace NP delivery, Cd^{2+}-free $CuInS_2$/ZnS core/shell QDs were encapsulated. Conclusively, PTX/MNPs/QDs@Biotin−PEG−PCDA NPs provided efficient intracellular uptake and GSH-trigger to release simultaneous synergic for overcoming drug resistance [106].

11.2.5 Upconversion nanoparticle

Upconvertion nanoparticles (UNPCs) are inorganic, luminescent NPs with the ability to convert the long-wavelength infrared photon into a short-wavelength photon. In this process, which is called antistockes shift luminescence, the NP absorbs photon energy that is lower than the emitted photon energy [107,108]. Biologic application of some materials with florescent properties such as dyes or QDs is restricted due to their penetration depth and poor signal-to-noise ratio [109]. Therefore, the distinct properties of UCNPs seem to open new windows to imaging probes and DDS to be used as theranostic agents especially in cancer treatment.

Hexagonal NaYF4:Yb, Er/Tm UCNPs were synthesized and PLGA—curcumin was encapsulated within UCNPs. The results of imaging studies and in vitro distribution of UCNPs in rat C6 glioma cells demonstrated a desired accumulation of UCNPs in tumor spheroids [110]. Zhang et al. synthesized NIR-triggered core-satellite UCNPs conjugated with curcumin as potential photosensitizer carriers. The NP was successfully applied for PDT in deep tumor tissue with a long excitation wavelength (980 nm) and also induced immunotherapeutic effects by simultaneous upregulation of HIF-1α [111]. In another study, UV-responsive spiropyran was immobilized on MSN-coated UCNPs with the incorporation of curcumin. Upon NIR, spiropyran converted the UV emission light and turned to open state that ultimately facilitated drug release. Moreover, UCNPs generated UV/visible, which led to the production of ROS by interaction between curcumin and oxygen and significant therapeutic efficacy in breast cancer 4T1 cell lines [112].

Codelivery of curcumin and doxorubicin (DOX) by UCNPs was also investigated. Hexagonal NaYF4:Yb/Er UCNPs were synthesized and coated with porous silica and amine groups. Further release of DOX and curcumin at acidic pH indicated the pH-sensitive mechanism of DOX-CCM-loaded UCNP@mSiO$_2$. The better cellular uptake was observed possibly due to the protonation of amine groups [113].

11.3 Conclusion

Application of nanobiotechnology-based concepts in drug delivery has provided promising tools in the treatment of cancer. In this study, the authors discussed a variety of inorganic NPs for the delivery of curcumin and evaluated its antitumor properties, as well as photothermal and photodynamic properties of these compounds in therapeutic approaches. Many formulations of curcumin have not been evaluated in clinical trials. Indeed, the future success of NP-based curcumin delivery requires enough preclinical experiments to achieve better stability and pharmacokinetic parameters to treat cancer in real tumor microenvironment.

References

[1] Amekyeh H, Alkhader E, Sabra R, Billa N. Prospects of curcumin nanoformulations in cancer management. Molecules (Basel, Switzerland) 2022;27(2):361.

[2] van der Meel R, Sulheim E, Shi Y, Kiessling F, Mulder WJ, Lammers T. Smart cancer nanomedicine. Nature Nanotechnology 2019;14(11):1007—17.

[3] Chaturvedi VK, Singh A, Singh VK, Singh MP. Cancer nanotechnology: a new revolution for cancer diagnosis and therapy. Current Drug Metabolism 2019;20(6):416—29.

[4] Saravanan A, Kumar PS, Karishma S, Vo D-VN, Jeevanantham S, Yaashikaa P, et al. A review on biosynthesis of metal nanoparticles and its environmental applications. Chemosphere 2021;264:128580.

[5] Kalyane D, Raval N, Maheshwari R, Tambe V, Kalia K, Tekade RK, et al. Employment of enhanced permeability and retention effect (EPR): nanoparticle-based precision tools for targeting of therapeutic and diagnostic agent in cancer. Materials Science and Engineering: C 2019;98:1252—76.

[6] Goradel NH, Mohammadi N, Haghi-Aminjan H, Farhood B, Negahdari B, Sahebkar A. Regulation of tumor angiogenesis by microRNAs: state of the art. Journal of Cellular Physiology 2019;234(2):1099—110.

[7] Shi Y, van der Meel R, Chen X, Lammers T. The EPR effect and beyond: strategies to improve tumor targeting and cancer nanomedicine treatment efficacy. Theranostics 2020;10(17):7921—4. Available from: https://doi.org/10.7150/thno.49577.

[8] Paul W, Sharma CP. JBomim. Inorganic nanoparticles for targeted drug delivery. 2020:333-373.

[9] Farhoudi L, Kesharwani P, Majeed M, Johnston TP, Sahebkar A. Polymeric nanomicelles of curcumin: potential applications in cancer. International Journal of Pharmaceutics 2022;121622.

[10] Ghareghomi S, Rahban M, Moosavi-Movahedi Z, Habibi-Rezaei M, Saso L, Moosavi-Movahedi AA. The potential role of curcumin in modulating the master antioxidant pathway in diabetic hypoxia-induced complications. Molecules 2021;26(24):7658.

[11] Abd El-Hack ME, El-Saadony MT, Swelum AA, Arif M, Abo Ghanima MM, Shukry M, et al. Curcumin, the active substance of turmeric: its effects on health and ways to improve its bioavailability. Journal of the Science of Food and Agriculture 2021;101(14):5747—62.

[12] Marjaneh, R.M., Rahmani, F., Hassanian, S.M., Rezaei, N., Hashemzehi, M., Bahrami, A., et al. Phytosomal curcumin inhibits tumor growth in colitis-associated colorectal cancer. Journal of Cellular Physiology, 2018;233(10):6785—6798. Available from: https://doi.org/10.1002/jcp.26538.

[13] Panahi Y, Sahebkar A, Amiri M, Davoudi SM, Beiraghdar F, Hoseininejad SL, et al. Improvement of sulphur mustard-induced chronic pruritus, quality of life and antioxidant status by curcumin: results of a randomised, double-blind, placebo-controlled trial. The British Journal of Nutrition 2012;108(7):1272—9. Available from: https://doi.org/10.1017/S0007114511006544.

[14] Ganji A, Farahani I, Saeedifar AM, Mosayebi G, Ghazavi A, Majeed M, et al. Protective effects of curcumin against lipopolysaccharide-induced toxicity. Current Medicinal Chemistry 2021;28(33):6915—30.

[15] Hassanzadeh S, Read MI, Bland AR, Majeed M, Jamialahmadi T, Sahebkar A. Curcumin: an inflammasome silencer. Pharmacological Research 2020;159.

[16] Heidari Z, Daei M, Boozari M, Jamialahmadi T, Sahebkar A. Curcumin supplementation in pediatric patients: a systematic review of current clinical evidence. Phytotherapy Research 2022;36(4):1442—58.

[17] Hosseini SA, Zahedipour F, Sathyapalan T, Jamialahmadi T, Sahebkar A. Pulmonary fibrosis: therapeutic and mechanistic insights into the role of phytochemicals. Biofactors (Oxford, England) 2021;47 (3):250—69.

[18] Keihanian F, Saeidinia A, Bagheri RK, Johnston TP, Sahebkar A. Curcumin, hemostasis, thrombosis, and coagulation. Journal of Cellular Physiology 2018;233(6):4497—511.

[19] Khayatan D, Razavi SM, Arab ZN, Niknejad AH, Nouri K, Momtaz S, et al. Protective effects of curcumin against traumatic brain injury. Biomedicine and Pharmacotherapy 2022;154.

[20] Mokhtari-Zaer A, Marefati N, Atkin SL, Butler AE, Sahebkar A. The protective role of curcumin in myocardial ischemia—reperfusion injury. Journal of Cellular Physiology 2018;234(1):214—22.

[21] Momtazi-Borojeni AA, Haftcheshmeh SM, Esmaeili SA, Johnston TP, Abdollahi E, Sahebkar A. Curcumin: a natural modulator of immune cells in systemic lupus erythematosus. Autoimmunity Reviews 2018;17(2):125—35.

[22] Rahimi K, Hassanzadeh K, Khanbabaei H, Haftcheshmeh SM, Ahmadi A, Izadpanah E, et al. Curcumin: a dietary phytochemical for targeting the phenotype and function of dendritic cells. Current Medicinal Chemistry 2021;28(8):1549—64.

[23] Panahi Y, Fazlolahzadeh O, Atkin SL, Majeed M, Butler AE, Johnston TP, et al. Evidence of curcumin and curcumin analogue effects in skin diseases: a narrative review. Journal of Cellular Physiology 2019;234(2):1165—78. Available from: https://doi.org/10.1002/jcp.27096.

[24] Mohammadi A, Blesso CN, Barreto GE, Banach M, Majeed M, Sahebkar A. Macrophage plasticity, polarization and function in response to curcumin, a diet-derived polyphenol, as an immunomodulatory

agent. The Journal of Nutritional Biochemistry 2019;66:1−16. Available from: https://doi.org/10.1016/j.
jnutbio.2018.12.005.

[25] Cicero AFG, Sahebkar A, Fogacci F, Bove M, Giovannini M, Borghi C. Effects of phytosomal curcumin
on anthropometric parameters, insulin resistance, cortisolemia and non-alcoholic fatty liver disease
indices: a double-blind, placebo-controlled clinical trial. European Journal of Nutrition 2020;59
(2):477−83. Available from: https://doi.org/10.1007/s00394-019-01916-7.

[26] Naksuriya O, Okonogi S, Schiffelers RM, Hennink WE. Curcumin nanoformulations: a review of pharmaceutical properties and preclinical studies and clinical data related to cancer treatment. Biomaterials
2014;35(10):3365−83.

[27] Shetty NP, Prabhakaran M, Srivastava AK. Pleiotropic nature of curcumin in targeting multiple
apoptotic-mediated factors and related strategies to treat gastric cancer: a review. Phytotherapy
Research: PTR 2021;35(10):5397−416.

[28] Malik P, Hoidal JR, Mukherjee TK. Recent advances in curcumin treated non-small cell lung cancers: an impe-
tus of pleiotropic traits and nanocarrier aided delive ry. Current Medicinal Chemistry 2021;28(16):3061−106.

[29] Mohajeri M, Sahebkar A. Protective effects of curcumin against doxorubicin-induced toxicity and resistance: a review. Critical Reviews in Oncology/Hematology 2018;122:30−51.

[30] Momtazi AA, Sahebkar A. Difluorinated curcumin: a promising curcumin analogue with improved antitumor activity and pharmacokinetic profile. Current Pharmaceutical Design 2016;22(28):4386−97.

[31] Mohammed ES, El-Beih NM, El-Hussieny EA, El-Ahwany E, Hassan M, Zoheiry M. Effects of free and
nanoparticulate curcumin on chemically induced liver carcinoma in an animal model. Archives of
Medical Science 2021;17(1):218−27.

[32] Mbese Z, Khwaza V, Aderibigbe BA. Curcumin and its derivatives as potential therapeutic agents in
prostate, colon and breast cancers. Molecules (Basel, Switzerland) 2019;24(23):4386.

[33] Zhang M, Zhang X, Tian T, Zhang Q, Wen Y, Zhu J, et al. Anti-inflammatory activity of curcumin-loaded
tetrahedral framework nucleic acids on acute gouty arthritis. Bioactive Materials 2022;8:368−80.

[34] Vadukoot AK, Mottemmal S, Vekaria PH. Curcumin as a potential therapeutic agent in certain cancer
types. Cureus. 2022;14(3):e22825.

[35] Li P, Pu S, Lin C, He L, Zhao H, Yang C, et al. Curcumin selectively induces colon cancer cell apoptosis
and S cell cycle arrest by regulates Rb/E2F/p53 pathway. Journal of Molecular Structure
2022;1263:133180.

[36] Ahmadian E, Dizaj SM, Sharifi S, Shahi S, Khalilov R, Eftekhari A, et al. The potential of nanomaterials
in theranostics of oral squamous cell carcinoma: Recent progress. Trends in Analytical Chemistry
2019;116:167−76.

[37] Maleki Dizaj S, Alipour M, Dalir Abdolahinia E, Ahmadian E, Eftekhari A, Forouhandeh H, et al.
Curcumin nanoformulations: beneficial nanomedicine against cancer. Phytotherapy research: PTR
2022;36(3):1156−81.

[38] Kango S, Kalia S, Celli A, Njuguna J, Habibi Y, Kumar R. Surface modification of inorganic nanoparticles
for development of organic−inorganic nanocomposites—a review. Progress in Polymer Science 2013;38
(8):1232−61.

[39] Huang H-C, Barua S, Sharma G, Dey SK, Rege K. Inorganic nanoparticles for cancer imaging and therapy. Journal of Controlled Release 2011;155(3):344−57.

[40] Takahashi K, Yasui H, Taki S, Shimizu M, Koike C, Taki K, et al. Near-infrared-induced drug release
from antibody−drug double conjugates exerts a cytotoxic photo-bystander effect. Bioengineering &
Translational Medicine 2022;e10388.

[41] Li D, He S, Wu Y, Liu J, Liu Q, Chang B, et al. Excretable lanthanide nanoparticle for biomedical imaging
and surgical navigation in the second near-infrared window. Advanced Science 2019;6(23):1902042.

[42] Liu Q, Kim YJ, Im GB, Zhu J, Wu Y, Liu Y, et al. Inorganic nanoparticles applied as functional therapeutics. Advanced Functional Materials 2021;31(12):2008171.

[43] Sanchez-Moreno P, Ortega-Vinuesa JL, Peula-Garcia JM, Marchal JA, Boulaiz H. Smart drug-delivery systems for cancer nanotherapy. Current Drug Targets 2018;19(4):339−59.

[44] Falcaro P, Ricco R, Yazdi A, Imaz I, Furukawa S, Maspoch D, et al. Application of metal and metal oxide nanoparticles@ MOFs. 2016;307:237-54.

[45] Akasaka H, Mukumoto N, Nakayama M, Wang T, Yada R, Shimizu Y, et al. Investigation of the potential of using TiO$_2$ nanoparticles as a contrast agent in computed tomography and magnetic resonance imaging. 2020;10(8):3143-8.

[46] Dessai S, Ayyanar M, Amalraj S, Khanal P, Vijayakumar S, Gurav N, et al. Bioflavonoid mediated synthesis of TiO$_2$ nanoparticles: characterization and their biomedical applications. Materials Letters 2022;311:131639.

[47] Jiménez VA, Moreno N, Guzmán L, Torres CC, Campos CH, Alderete JB. Visible-light-responsive folate-conjugated titania and alumina nanotubes for photodynamic therapy applications. JJoMS 2020;55 (16):6976−91.

[48] Youssef Z, Jouan-Hureaux V, Colombeau L, Arnoux P, Moussaron A, Baros F, et al. Titania and silica nanoparticles coupled to Chlorin e6 for anti-cancer photodynamic therapy. 2018;22:115-26.

[49] Malekmohammadi S, Hadadzadeh H, Rezakhani S, Amirghofran Z. Design and synthesis of gatekeeper coated dendritic silica/titania mesoporous nanoparticles with sustained and controlled drug release properties for targeted synergetic chemo-sonodynamic therapy. JABS, Engineering 2019;5(9):4405−15.

[50] Aljubouri F. The formation, structure, and electronic properties of TiO$_2$ nanoparticles drug delivery conjugated with curcumin (theoretical and experimental study) address for correspondence. JIJNS 2018;8:14354.

[51] Ding L, Li J, Huang R, Liu Z, Li C, Yao S, et al. Salvianolic acid B protects against myocardial damage caused by nanocarrier TiO$_2$; and synergistic anti-breast carcinoma effect with curcumin via codelivery system of folic acid-targeted and polyethylene glycol-modified TiO$_2$ nanoparticles. 2016;11:5709.

[52] Zhang M, Zhang J, Chen J, Zeng Y, Zhu Z, Wan Y. Fabrication of curcumin-modified TiO$_2$ Nanoarrays via cyclodextrin based polymer functional coatings for osteosarcoma therapy. Advanced Healthcare Materials. 2019;8(23):1901031.

[53] Jin S-E, Jin H-EJP. Synthesis, characterization, and three-dimensional structure generation of zinc oxide-based nanomedicine for biomedical applications. 2019;11(11):575.

[54] Deshpande SS, Veeragoni D, Rachamalla HK, Misra S. Anticancer properties of ZnO-curcumin nanocomposite against melanoma cancer and its genotoxicity profiling. JJoDDS, Technology 2022;103703.

[55] Upadhyaya L, Singh J, Agarwal V, Pandey AC, Verma SP, Das P, et al. Efficient water soluble nanostructured ZnO grafted O-carboxymethyl chitosan/curcumin-nanocomposite for cancer therapy. Process Biochemistry 2015;50(4):678−88.

[56] Sriram K, Maheswari PU, Ezhilarasu A, Begum KMMS, Arthanareeswaran G. CuO-loaded hydrophobically modified chitosan as hybrid carrier for curcumin delivery and anticancer activity. Asia-Pacific Journal of Chemical Engineering 2017;12(6):858−71.

[57] Kundu M, Sadhukhan P, Ghosh N, Chatterjee S, Manna P, Das J, et al. pH-responsive and targeted delivery of curcumin via phenylboronic acid-functionalized ZnO nanoparticles for breast cancer therapy. 2019;18:161-72.

[58] Ghaffari S-B, Sarrafzadeh M-H, Fakhroueian Z, Khorramizadeh MR. C E. Flower-like curcumin-loaded folic acid-conjugated ZnO-MPA-βcyclodextrin nanostructures enhanced anticancer activity and cellular uptake of curcumin in breast cancer cells. JMS 2019;103:109827.

[59] Popova NR, Popov AL, Shcherbakov AB, Ivanov VKJHф. Layer-by-layer capsules as smart delivery systems of CeO$_2$ nanoparticle-based theranostic agents. химия, математика 2017;8(2):282−9.

[60] Javad Farhangi M, Es-Haghi A, Taghavizadeh Yazdi ME, Rahdar A, Baino F. MOF-mediated synthesis of CuO/CeO$_2$ composite nanoparticles: characterization and estimation of the cellular toxicity against breast cancer cell line (MCF-7). JJoFB. 2021;12(4):53.

[61] Tapeinos C, Battaglini M, Prato M, La Rosa G, Scarpellini A, Ciofani G. CeO$_2$ nanoparticles-loaded pH-responsive microparticles with antitumoral properties as therapeutic modulators for osteosarcoma. JAo 2018;3(8):8952−62.

[62] Li H, Liu C, Zeng Y-P, Hao Y-H, Huang J-W, Yang Z-Y, et al. Nanoceria-mediated drug delivery for targeted photodynamic therapy on drug-resistant breast cancer. 2016;8(46):31510-23.

[63] Chen Z, Xu L, Gao X, Wang C, Li R, Xu J, et al. A multifunctional CeO$_2$@ SiO$_2$-PEG nanoparticle carrier for delivery of food derived proanthocyanidin and curcumin as effective antioxidant, neuroprotective and anticancer agent. 2020;137:109674.

[64] Xiao Y, Du J. Superparamagnetic nanoparticles for biomedical applications. JJoMCB 2020;8(3):354−67.

[65] Hiremath CG, Heggnnavar GB, Kariduraganavar MY, Hiremath MB. Co-delivery of paclitaxel and curcumin to foliate positive cancer cells using Pluronic-coated iron oxide nanoparticles. JPib 2019;8(3):155−68.

[66] Hiremath CG, Kariduraganavar MY, Hiremath MB. Synergistic delivery of 5-fluorouracil and curcumin using human serum albumin-coated iron oxide nanoparticles by folic acid targeting. JPiB 2018;7(4):297−306.

[67] Montazerabadi A, Beik J, Irajirad R, Attaran N, Khaledi S, Ghaznavi H, et al. Folate-modified and curcumin-loaded dendritic magnetite nanocarriers for the targeted thermo-chemotherapy of cancer cells. 2019;47(1):330-40.

[68] Saikia C, Das MK, Ramteke A, Maji TK. Evaluation of folic acid tagged aminated starch/ZnO coated iron oxide nanoparticles as targeted curcumin delivery system. JCp 2017;157:391−9.

[69] Rastegar R, Akbari Javar H, Khoobi M, Dehghan Kelishadi P, Hossein Yousefi G, Doosti M, et al. Evaluation of a novel biocompatible magnetic nanomedicine based on beta-cyclodextrin, loaded doxorubicin-curcumin for overcoming chemoresistance in breast cancer. 2018;46(sup2):207-16.

[70] Yallapu MM, Othman SF, Curtis ET, Bauer NA, Chauhan N, Kumar D, et al. Curcumin-loaded magnetic nanoparticles for breast cancer therapeutics and imaging applications. 2012;7:1761.

[71] Yallapu MM, Othman SF, Curtis ET, Gupta BK, Jaggi M, Chauhan SC. Multi-functional magnetic nanoparticles for magnetic resonance imaging and cancer therapy. JB 2011;32(7):1890−905.

[72] Pham XN, Nguyen TP, Pham TN, Tran TTN, Tran TVT. Synthesis and characterization of chitosan-coated magnetite nanoparticles and their application in curcumin drug delivery. JAiNSN, Nanotechnology 2016;7(4):045010.

[73] Nosrati H, Sefidi N, Sharafi A, Danafar H, Manjili HK. Bovine serum albumin (BSA) coated iron oxide magnetic nanoparticles as biocompatible carriers for curcumin-anticancer drug. Bioorganic Chemistry 2018;76:501−9.

[74] Vallet-Regi M, Rámila A, Del Real R, Pérez-Pariente J. A new property of MCM-41: drug delivery system. JCoM 2001;13(2):308−11.

[75] Manzano M, Vallet-Regí M. Mesoporous silica nanoparticles for drug delivery. JAfm 2020;30(2):1902634.

[76] Ma'Mani L, Nikzad S, Kheiri-Manjili H, Al-Musawi S, Saeedi M, Askarlou S, et al. Curcumin-loaded guanidine functionalized PEGylated I3ad mesoporous silica nanoparticles KIT-6: practical strategy for the breast cancer therapy. European Journal of Medicinal Chemistry 2014;83:646−54.

[77] Abdous B, Sajjadi SM, Ma'mani L. β-Cyclodextrin modified mesoporous silica nanoparticles as a nanocarrier: response surface methodology to investigate and optimize loading and release processes for curcumin delivery. JJoAB 2017;15(3):210−18.

[78] Kuang G, Zhang Q, He S, Liu Y. Curcumin-loaded PEGylated mesoporous silica nanoparticles for effective photodynamic therapy. RSC advances 2020;10(41):24624−30.

[79] RS P, Mal A, Valvi SK, Srivastava R, De A, Bandyopadhyaya R. Noninvasive preclinical evaluation of targeted nanoparticles for the delivery of curcumin in treating pancreatic cancer. JAABM 2020;3 (7):4643−54.

[80] Ghosh S, Dutta S, Sarkar A, Kundu M, Sil PC. Targeted delivery of curcumin in breast cancer cells via hyaluronic acid modified mesoporous silica nanoparticle to enhance anticancer efficiency. JC, Biointerfaces SB 2021;197:111404.

[81] Kim S, Philippot S, Fontanay S, Duval RE, Lamouroux E, Canilho N, et al. pH-and glutathione-responsive release of curcumin from mesoporous silica nanoparticles coated using tannic acid−Fe (iii) complex. 2015;5(110):90550-8.

[82] Bolouki A, Rashidi L, Vasheghani-Farahani E, Piravi-Vanak Z. Study of mesoporous silica nanoparticles as nanocarriers for sustained release of curcumin. JIJoN, Nanotechnology 2015;11(3):139−46.

[83] Viswanathan TM, Chitradevi K, Zochedh A, Vijayabhaskar R, Sukumaran S, Kunjiappan S, et al. Guanidine−curcumin complex-loaded amine-functionalised hollow mesoporous silica nanoparticles for breast cancer therapy. 2022;14(14):3490.

[84] Mohan Viswanathan T, Krishnakumar V, Senthilkumar D, Chitradevi K, Vijayabhaskar R, Rajesh Kannan V, et al. Combinatorial delivery of gallium (III) nitrate and curcumin complex-loaded hollow mesoporous silica nanoparticles for breast cancer treatment. 2022;12(9):1472.

[85] Turkevich J, Stevenson PC, Hillier J. A study of the nucleation and growth processes in the synthesis of colloidal gold. JDotFS 1951;11:55−75.

[86] De Roo J. JCoM. Chemical considerations for colloidal nanocrystal synthesis. 2022.

[87] Liu Y, Crawford BM, Vo-Dinh T. Gold nanoparticles-mediated photothermal therapy and immunotherapy. JI. 2018;10(13):1175−88.

[88] Huang X, El-Sayed IH, Qian W, El-Sayed MA. Cancer cell imaging and photothermal therapy in the near-infrared region by using gold nanorods. JJotACS 2006;128(6):2115−20.

[89] Rahimi-Moghaddam F, Sattarahmady N, Azarpira N. Gold-curcumin nanostructure in photo-thermal therapy on breast cancer cell line: 650 and 808 nm diode lasers as light sources. JJoBP, Engineering 2019;9(4):473.

[90] Ghorbani M, Bigdeli B, Jalili-Baleh L, Baharifar H, Akrami M, Dehghani S, et al. Curcumin-lipoic acid conjugate as a promising anticancer agent on the surface of gold-iron oxide nanocomposites: A pH-sensitive targeted drug delivery system for brain cancer theranostics. 2018;114:175-88.

[91] Zhong Y, Zhang X, Yang L, Liang F, Zhang J, Jiang Y, et al. Hierarchical dual-responsive cleavable nanosystem for synergetic photodynamic/photothermal therapy against melanoma. 2021;131:112524.

[92] Rejinold NS, Thomas RG, Muthiah M, Chennazhi K, Manzoor K, Park I-K, et al. Anti-cancer, pharmacokinetics and tumor localization studies of pH-. RF-and thermo-responsive nanoparticles 2015;74:249−62.

[93] Kondath S, Rajaram R, Anantanarayanan RJI, Chemistry N-M. Curcumin reduced gold nanoparticles synergistically induces ROS mediated apoptosis in MCF-7 cancer cells. 2020;51(5):601−613.

[94] Nosrati H, Seidi F, Hosseinmirzaei A, Mousazadeh N, Mohammadi A, Ghaffarlou M, et al. Prodrug polymeric nanoconjugates encapsulating gold nanoparticles for enhanced X-ray radiation therapy in breast cancer. 2022;11(3):2102321.

[95] Hoshikawa A, Nagira M, Tane M, Fukushige K, Tagami T, Ozeki TJB, et al. Preparation of curcumin-containing α-, β-, and γ-cyclodextrin/polyethyleneglycol-conjugated gold multifunctional nanoparticles and their in vitro cytotoxic effects on A549 cells. 2018;41(6):908-14.

[96] Alibolandi M, Hoseini F, Mohammadi M, Ramezani P, Einafshar E, Taghdisi SM, et al. Curcumin-entrapped MUC-1 aptamer targeted dendrimer-gold hybrid nanostructure as a theranostic system for colon adenocarcinoma. 2018;549(1−2):67−75.

[97] Drbohlavova J, Adam V, Kizek R, Hubalek J. Quantum dots—characterization, preparation and usage in biological systems. International journal of molecular sciences 2009;10(2):656−73.

[98] Fang B, Xiong Q, Duan H, Xiong Y, Lai W. Tailored quantum dots for enhancing sensing performance of lateral flow immunoassay. JTTiAC 2022;116754.

[99] Kays JC, Saeboe AM, Toufanian R, Kurant DE, Dennis AM. Shell-free copper indium sulfide quantum dots induce toxicity in vitro and in vivo. JNl 2020;20(3):1980−91.

[100] Sukhanova A, Bozrova S, Gerasimovich E, Baryshnikova M, Sokolova Z, Samokhvalov P, et al. Dependence of quantum dot toxicity in vitro on their size. Chemical Composition, and Surface Charge 2022;12(16):2734.

[101] Goo S, Choi YJ, Lee Y, Lee S, Chung HW. Selective effects of curcumin on CdSe/ZnS quantum-dot-induced phototoxicity using UVA irradiation in normal human lymphocytes and leukemia cells. JTR 2013;29(1):35−42.

[102] Khan FA, Lammari N, Muhammad Siar AS, Alkhater KM, Asiri S, Akhtar S, et al. Quantum dots encapsulated with curcumin inhibit the growth of colon cancer, breast cancer and bacterial cells. 2020;15 (10):969-80.

[103] Belletti D, Riva G, Luppi M, Tosi G, Forni F, Vandelli MA, et al. Anticancer drug-loaded quantum dots engineered polymeric nanoparticles: diagnosis/therapy combined approach. 2017;107:230-9.

[104] Ghanbari N, Salehi Z, Khodadadi AA, Shokrgozar MA, Saboury AA. C E. Glucosamine-conjugated graphene quantum dots as versatile and pH-sensitive nanocarriers for enhanced delivery of curcumin targeting to breast cancer. JMS 2021;121:111809.

[105] Farghadani R, Naidu R. Curcumin as an enhancer of therapeutic efficiency of chemotherapy drugs in breast cancer. JIJoMS 2022;23(4):2144.

[106] Wang J, Wang F, Li F, Zhang W, Shen Y, Zhou D, et al. A multifunctional poly (curcumin) nanomedicine for dual-modal targeted delivery, intracellular responsive release, dual-drug treatment and imaging of multidrug resistant cancer cells. 2016;4(17):2954-62.

[107] Hong E, Liu L, Bai L, Xia C, Gao L, Zhang L, et al. Control synthesis, subtle surface modification of rare-earth-doped upconversion nanoparticles and their applications in cancer diagnosis and treatment. Materials Science and Engineering: C. 2019;105:110097.

[108] Wilhelm S. Perspectives for upconverting nanoparticles. ACS Nano 2017;11(11):10644−53.

[109] Muhr V, Wilhelm S, Hirsch T, Wolfbeis OS. Upconversion nanoparticles: from hydrophobic to hydrophilic surfaces. Accounts of Chemical Research 2014;47(12):3481−93.

[110] Lakshmanan A, Akasov RA, Sholina NV, Demina PA, Generalova AN, Gangadharan A, et al. Nanocurcumin-loaded UCNPs for cancer theranostics: physicochemical properties, in vitro toxicity, and in vivo imaging studies. Nanomaterials. 2021;11(9):2234.

[111] Zhang L-J, Huang R, Shen Y-W, Liu J, Wu Y, Jin J-M, et al. Enhanced anti-tumor efficacy by inhibiting HIF-1α to reprogram TAMs via core-satellite upconverting nanoparticles with curcumin mediated photodynamic therapy. Biomaterials Science. 2021;9(19):6403−15.

[112] Liu C, Zhang Y, Liu M, Chen Z, Lin Y, Li W, et al. A NIR-controlled cage mimicking system for hydrophobic drug mediated cancer therapy. 2017;139:151-62.

[113] Reddy KL, Sharma PK, Singh A, Kumar A, Shankar KR, Singh Y, et al. Amine-functionalized, porous silica-coated NaYF4: Yb/Er upconversion nanophosphors for efficient delivery of doxorubicin and curcumin. 2019;96:86-95.

12

PLGA nanoparticle-based curcumin delivery as cancer therapeutics

Anis Askarizadeh[1], Amirhossein Sahebkar[2,3]

[1]MARINE PHARMACEUTICAL SCIENCE RESEARCH CENTER, AHVAZ JUNDISHAPUR UNIVERSITY OF MEDICAL SCIENCES, AHVAZ, IRAN [2]BIOTECHNOLOGY RESEARCH CENTER, PHARMACEUTICAL TECHNOLOGY INSTITUTE, MASHHAD UNIVERSITY OF MEDICAL SCIENCES, MASHHAD, IRAN [3]APPLIED BIOMEDICAL RESEARCH CENTER, MASHHAD UNIVERSITY OF MEDICAL SCIENCES, MASHHAD, IRAN

12.1 Introduction

Despite there being major breakthroughs in cancer therapy, cancer has remained as a serious global fatal concern about public health [1]. It is estimated that 19.3 million new cases have been detected and approximately 10 million people died in 2020, thereby being the second leading cause of death worldwide [2]. The increasing rate of cancer occurrence will exacerbate the current world health problem; expectedly, cancer-related mortality will rise by more than 13 million people per annum till 2030 [3,4]. Cancer is characterized by improper cell proliferation involving several deregulated signaling pathways of apoptosis, angiogenesis, and proliferation [5,6]. Early diagnosis and effective treatment procedures are of great importance in cancer treatment. However, surgery and chemo/radiotherapy as standard cancer treatment modalities have posed many challenges associated with multidrug resistance and severe side effects on healthy tissues [7,8].

Alongside conventional chemically synthesized chemotherapeutic agents, chemical plants with different modes of action, such as *Catharanthus roseus, Cephalotaxus* species, *Taxus brevifolia, Betula alba, Erythroxylum previllei,* and *Curcuma longa,* have been approved to be promising in the treatment of varied diseases such as cancer [9,10]. Up to now, particular attention has been paid to curcumin (Cur) extracted from *Curcuma longa* owing to its pharmacological effects, such as antiinflammation, antioxidant, antiischemic, antithrombotic, antifibrotic, and anticancer activities [11−24]. Among the multiple pharmacological effects, the anticancer effect of Cur has become a central issue for many researchers. Mounting evidence has suggested that the anticancer effect of Cur is related to the apoptotic induction in cancer cells, regulation of cell cycle, suppression of angiogenesis, tumor metastasis, and increment of chemotherapy sensitivity [10,25−28]. Despite its promising biological activity, several drawbacks, including low aqueous solubility, physicochemical instability, light and

Curcumin-Based Nanomedicines as Cancer Therapeutics. DOI: https://doi.org/10.1016/B978-0-443-15412-6.00015-5

pH sensitivity, low bioavailability, and poor pharmacokinetics, have challenged Cur's clinical application. Hence, there is an emergency need for developing ways to improve Cur bioavailability and therapeutic efficacy [29−33]. In an attempt to address these problems, nanomaterials hold obvious benefits as drug delivery vehicles for Cur encapsulation, reducing its degradation and improving Cur solubility and bioavailability [31].

Among the nanoparticulate delivery systems, polymeric nanoparticles (NPs) offer immense potential for different applications of targeting, imaging, diagnostics, and therapy [34−36]. Polymeric NPs composed of poly(D, L-lactide-co-glycolide) (PLGA) have been more interesting because of their inimitable physicochemical properties such as regular morphology, high stability, small and tunable particle size, large surface area, simple surface modification, desirable pharmacokinetic profile, excellent biodegradability, and biocompatibility [37−41]. PLGA is approved by the Food and Drug Administration (FDA) and the European Medicines Agency (EMA) for human application [42]. In the body, upon the aqueous condition, PLGA is hydrolyzed and degraded to biodegradable metabolite monomers, glycolic acid and lactic acid, which can be converted to carbon dioxide and water, leading to low systemic toxicity [43]. The proportion of lactic acid and glycolic acid in polymer composition, glass transition temperature (Tg) of polymer, the molecular weight of polymer, and manufacturing process directly affect the degradation time of polymer, consequently, determining the drug release rate from polymer [44−46]. The encapsulated drug inside PLGA NPs is released in a sustainable manner through diffusion or polymer matrix degradation [47]. Several approaches have been suggested to prepare PLGA NPs. Relying on the preparation procedure, the final structure of polymers in terms of size, shape, homogeneity, and stability may differ. The emulsification evaporation, salting out, nanoprecipitation, and microfluidics-assisted methods are the most commonly used approaches to synthesize PLGA-based drug delivery systems [45].

This chapter is focused on providing comprehensive insight into the provision and development of Cur-loaded PLGA NPs for cancer therapy. The implication from in vitro and in vivo tests is that the benefit of Cur-loaded PLGA NPs to several types of cancer needs to be considered in the light of a possible improvement in antitumor efficacy, tumor-specificity, and cytotoxicity effect in cancer cells.

12.2 Curcumin-PLGA nanoparticles in cancer therapy

To achieve desirable efficacy, reaching the drugs-loaded PLGA NPs to the targeted site and minimizing side effects in normal tissues are of great importance. Also, drug activity and administrated doses should be remained intact in the bloodstream before reaching the tumor site [48]. Passive and active targeting are the ways of delivering Cur-loaded PLGA NPs to the tumors.

In passive targeting, the accumulation of PLGA-based NPs in the tumors is driven by the enhanced permeability and retention (EPR) effect, allowing NPs with a size in the 10−100 nm range to extravasate through the permeable vasculature and penetrate to cancer lesions [49,50]. For active targeting, divers targeting ligands are introduced on the surface of PLGA NPs, enhancing their tumor-targeting ability and selectivity for tumor sites [45]. In the following sections, the application of Cur-loaded PLGA NPs in the treatment of several cancers is discussed. The physicochemical properties and the in vitro and in vivo outcomes of formulations are presented in Tables 12−1−12−3.

12.3 Breast cancer

Breast cancer is the most prevalent malignancy experienced by women around the world. It is estimated that 2.3 million cases are diagnosed in 2020. This cancer is recently ranked as the fifth leading cause of mortality worldwide, accounting for 685,000 deaths [105].

Regarding the anticancer activity of Cur, the efficacy of Cur-PLGA NPs was assessed in MDA-MB-231 breast cancer cells [51,52]. It was found that Cur-loaded PLGA NPs improved the therapeutic efficacy of Cur in MDA-MB-231 breast cancer cells [51,52]. This nanoformulation showed improved efficacy in terms of cellular uptake, antiproliferative effect, apoptosis induction, and antimetastatic properties compared to free Cur.

There has been evidence that Cur arrests the cell cycle in various cancer cells [106−109]. Moreover, Cur-loaded PLGA NPs have been demonstrated to be efficient against MCF-7 breast cancer cells by the G2/M blocking mechanism [53]. Intracellular release of Cur from PLGA NPs prevents the proliferation of MCF-7 cells. DNA analysis recognized the pivotal role of G2/M blocking played by Cur in cell cycle arresting in the MCF-7 cell line.

Positive-charged Cur nanoparticles (CN) utilizing PLGA and CTAB (hexadecyltrimethylammonium bromide) were fabricated to test the effectiveness of these particles in treating triple-negative breast cancer (TNBC) [54]. Electrostatic interaction of cationic CN with negatively charged membrane cells and continuous absorption of CN through an energy-dependent transport mechanism such as endocytosis by the clathrin pathway mediated greater internalization of NPs than free Cur. The higher cellular incorporation and extended presence of Cur in cells appear to be the cause of increased cytotoxicity and apoptosis of CN. ROS production and consequently DNA damage are the reasons behind apoptosis.

Surface modification of NPs provides the opportunity to allow for targeted drug delivery, minimizing dose requirements and adverse effects, and improving therapeutic efficacy. They can also help to improve the drug's pharmacokinetic, pharmacodynamic, and physical and biochemical characteristics [110].

The common approaches taken for modifying the NP's surface are coating them with surfactants or hydrophilic bioadhesive polymers and adding biodegradable copolymers with hydrophilic components in their structure. To improve the drug solubilization, coated Cur-loaded PLGA NPs with dextran, chitosan (CS), and polyethylene glycol (PEG), as well as emulsifier TPGS (tocopherol poly (ethylene glycol)1000 succinate), have been synthesized [55]. TGPS-coated, Dextran-coated, TGPS-dextran-coated, and TGPS-PEG-coated particles performed better in cell viability and apoptosis assays. It can be deduced that surface modification of PLGA NPs using various coating agent combinations might enhance drug delivery and improve therapeutics more effectively in breast cancer cells.

Table 12–1 Physicochemical properties of PLGA nanoparticles as delivery systems for curcumin.

Formulation	Preparation method	Size (nm)	Zeta potential (mV)	EE%	Surface modification/Target	References
Cur-PLGA (50:50) NP	Nanoprecipitation	76.2 ± 5.36	0.06 ± 0.01	89.53 ± 3.26	NO	[51]
Cur-PLGA (50:50) NP	Solvent evaporation technique	188	−3.22	79	NO	[52]
Cur-PLGA (50:50) NP	Single emulsion	133.2 ± 4.3	−30.2 ± 3.7	80	NO	[53]
Cur-PLGA (50:50) NP	Nanoprecipitation	81.05 ± 3.85	+31.8	21.8	CTAB	[54]
Cur-PLGA (60/40) NP	Emulsion solvent evaporation	~141−198.5	7.94−40.47	80−89	Chitosan/Dextran/PEG/ emulsifier TPGS	[55]
PLGA (50:50)	Solvent displacement	270.2, 267.4, 275.4	N. A.	41.02, 47.2, 42.76	PEG + FA or HA or Tf	[56]
FA-Cur-PLGA particles	Double emulsion	863.5	−6.8	97	FA	[57]
Cur-PLGA (50:50) NP	Emulsification/solvent evaporation	128.5 ± 1.3	N. A.	79.5 ± 1.56	PEG + Fab'	[58]
Cur-PLGA (50:50) NP	Nanoprecipitation	72	N. A.	N. A.	N. A.	[59]
Cur-PLGA (50:50)/(75:25) NPs	Solvent evaporation	PLGA (50:50): 129.7 ± 9.6; PLGA (75:25): 191.1 ± 9.8	N. A.	PLGA (50:50): 90.03 ± 1.35; PLGA (75:25): 74.73 ± 2.71	NO	[60]
APgp-Cur-PLGA NP	Nanoprecipitation	132.4 ± 1.5	−40.3 ± 6.1	60	APgp	[61]
Cur-PLGA (50:50) NP	Single emulsion-solvent evaporation	219.6 ± 1.6	−36.8	74.4 ± 8.2;	NO	[62]
Cur-PLGA (75:25)-based polymeric oil-cored nanocapsules (NCs)	Nanoprecipitation	150.5 ± 4.7	−37.2	92.3 ±1.6	PEG + oil core materials (castor oil, soybean oil, and miglyol812 oil)	[63]
Cur-PLGA (50:50) NP	Emulsification/solvent evaporation	CS-NP: 252 ± 3; WGA-NP: 227 ± 3; GE11-NP: 209 ± 2	CS-NP: 32.9 ± 1.7; WGA-NP: −20.5 ± 0.8; GE11-NP: −10.8 ± 0.9	CS-NP: 54 ± 2; WGA-NP: 66 ± 1; GE11-NP: 62 ± 2	CS, WGA, GE11 peptide	[64]
Cur-PLGA (50:50) NP	Nanoprecipitation	90.2 ± 1.9	−36.3 ± 4.2	89.98 ± 3.8	PEG/Lecthin/RNA aptamers	[65]
Cur-PLGA (50:50) NP	S/O/W emulsion	45	N. A.	90.88 ± 0.14	NO	[66]
Cur-PLGA (50:50) NP	S/O/W emulsion	136	N. A.	97 ± 0.45	NO	[67]
Cur-PLGA (50:50) NP	Nanoprecipitation	N. A.	N. A.	N. A.	PSMA MAb (prostate-specific membrane antigen)	[68]

Formulation	Method	Size	Zeta potential	Encapsulation efficiency	Surface modification	Reference
Cur-PLGA (50:50) NP	Modified spontaneous emulsification solvent diffusion	189.7	N. A.	33.5	NO	[69]
Cur-PLGA (50:50) NP	Nanoprecipitation	162 ± 3	−34.3 ± 1.2	93.8 ± 1.5	RBCM	[70]
Cur-PLGA NP	Emulsification-solvent evaporation	110.6 ± 2.3	−23.6	83.2 ± 2.7	TPGS	[71]
Cur-PLGA NP	Nanoprecipitation	97.3 ± 1.7	N. A.	80.52 ± 2.39	PEG + cHP	[72]
Cur- PLGA (85:15)-DSPE-PEG NPs	Emulsion sonication method	196 ± 4.8	N. A.	35 ± 1.2	NO	[73]
Cur-PLGA (50:50) NP	Microfluidic-assisted nanoprecipitation	30–70	−44 to −58	55–67	NO	[74]
Cur-PLGA (75:25) NP	Emulsion solvent evaporation	180	N. A.	93.7	NO	[75]
Cur-PLGA (75:25) NP	Single emulsion solvent evaporation	246.4 ± 4.9	N. A.	90.5 ± 3.0	NO	[76]
Cur-PLGA NP	Nanoprecipitation	62 ± 0.03	−23.9	95.7	NO	[77]
CS-Cur-PEG-PLGA NPs	Emulsification/solvent evaporation	264	+19.1	60	PEG + chitosan	[78]
Cur-PLGA-C NPs	Emulsification-solvent evaporation	202.5 ± 16.3	−0.67 ± 1.23	41.99 ± 0.14	Cholesterol	[79]
Cur-CTP-NPFs	Poly dimethyl siloxane (PDMS) cast molding technique	20	N. A.	N. A.	TPGS	[80]
Cur-RGD–lpNPs	Double emulsion/solvent evaporation	216.6 ± 4.7	−0.23 ± 0.12	96.0 ± 0.6	Arg-Gly-Asp (RGD) peptide /mPEG–cholesterol	[81]
GANT61-Cur-PLGA NPs	Emulsion-solvent evaporation	347.4 ± 2.75	−21.3 ± 0.23	GANT61: 98.3 ± 0.33 Curcumin: 99.97 ± 0.09	NO	[82]
Cur/Met-PEG-PLGA NPs	Double emulsion (W/O/W)	257 ± 11.38	−3.2 ± 1.2	Met: 75.15 Cur: 80.5	PEG	[83]
Cur-PLGA (50:50) NP	Emulsion solvent evaporation	157 ± 14.5	−28.56 ± 2.6	89.23 ± 1.19	Annexin A2 antibody	[84]
MTX/Cur-PLGA NPs	Double emulsion solvent evaporation	148.3 ± 4.07	−3.41 ±0.8	MTX: 71.32 ±7.8 Cur: 85.64 ±6.3	NO	[85]
Cur-PLGA NPs	Emulsion–diffusion–evaporation	201.8 ± 6.0	−5.43 ± 0.67	80.4 ± 10.6	NO	[86]
Cur-PLGA NPs	Emulsion–diffusion–evaporation	201.8 ± 6.0	−5.43 ± 0.67	80.4 ± 10.6	NO	[87]

(Continued)

Table 12–1 (Continued)

Formulation	Preparation method	Size (nm)	Zeta potential (mV)	EE%	Surface modification/Target	References
SH-ASA/Cur- mPEG-PLGA NPs	O/W single-emulsion solvent evaporation	122.3 ± 6.8	N. A.	SH-ASA: 83.17 ± 3.04 Cur: 87.3 ± 3.68	PEG	[88]
Paclitaxel-curcumin -PLGA-phospholipid-PEG NPs	Nanoprecipitation	94.3	− 31.6	86.87	PEG	[89]
GE11-DTX-Cur NPs	Solvent displacement	166.7 ± 4.5	− 37.5 ± 3.3	DTX: 91.4 ± 4.2 Cur: 87.5 ± 3.9	GE11	[90]
FA-Cur-PEG-PLGA(50:50) NPs	Emulsion-solvent evaporation	100–200	N. A.	N. A.	FA	[91]
Chr/Cur PLGA NPs	Oil-in-water (O/W) emulsion-solvent evaporation	257 ± 11.38	−2.8 ± 1.2	Chr: 83.5 Cur: 78.27	NO	[92]
HA-CPT/Cur PLGA NPs	O/W emulsion-solvent evaporation	289	− 10	CPT:38.0 ± 4.1 Cur: 35.7 ± 1.1	HA	[93]
CDDP-PLGA (75:25)/Cur LBL NPs	Solvent diffusion	179.6 ± 6.7	− 29.9 ± 3.2	CDDP: 85.6 ± 3.9 Cur: 82.1 ± 2.8	NO	[94]
HER2-SPION-Cur-PLGA (50:50) NPs	Solvent evaporation technique	150–200	N. A.	N. A.	HER2 + SPION	[95]
Apt-Cur-SPION-PLGA NPs	Solvent evaporation	150	N. A.	N. A.	Aptamer AS1411 + SPION	[96]
Tf-THC PEG-PLGA NPs	Double-emulsion method	255.77 ± 6.15	−16.80 ± 0.87	THC: 63.72 ±4.36 Dox: 85.57 ± 2.95	PEG/Tf	[97]
MAb-Cur-PLGA NPs	Emulsion sonication method	196 ± 4.8	N. A.	35 ± 1.2	Anti-EGFRvIII MAb	[98]
BDMC-PLGA (75:25) (50:50) /(75:25) NPs	Nanoprecipitation	<200	− 9.25 to −13.23	~98%	PEG 4000, Pluronic F68, Tween 80	[99]
DMC-loaded PLGA (50:50) NPs	Emulsification solvent evaporation/diffusion	158.5 ± 9.8	N. A.	88.85	NO	[100]
ICA-PLGA (75:25) NPs	Solvent precipitation	50–150	N. A.	74	NO	[101]
ACPCSL NPs	Electron spray	410–450 ± 10 nm	N. A.	N. A.	NO	[102]

EE, encapsulation efficacy; O/W, oil-in-water; ACPCSL NPs, ((1E,6E)-3,5-dioxohepta-1,6-diene-1,7-diyl) bis (2-methoxy-4,1-phenylene) diacetate acetyl curcumin (AC)-loaded PLGA core/shell liposome nanoparticles; APgp; anti-P-glycoprotein; BDMC, Bisdemethoxycurcumin; C, cholesterol; CDDP, cisplatin; cHP, c(RGDf(N-me)VK)-C; Chr, chrysin; CPT, camptothecin; CS, chitosan; CTAB, hexadecyltrimethylammonium bromide; CTP-NPFs, TPGS stabilized PLGA nanopatterened films; DMC, Demethoxycurcumin; Dox, Doxorubicin; DSPE, 1,2-distearoyl-snglycero-3-phosphoethanolamine-N-[amino (PEG)-2000]; DTX, Docetaxel; FA, Folic Acid; Fab'; antigen-binding fragments cut from Trastuzumab; HA, Hyaluronic acid; HER2, Human epidermal growth factor receptor 2; ICA, indole-curcumin analog; lpNPs, Lipid-shell and polymer core nanoparticles; Met, Metformin; MTX, Methotrexate; N. A., Not available; PEG, polyethylene glycol; PLGA, poly (D, L-lactide-co-glycolide); RBCM, red blood cell membranes; SH-ASA, H2S-releasing prodrug SH-aspirin; SPION, Superparamagnetic iron oxide nanoparticles; Tf, transferrin; THC, tetrahydrocurcumin; TPGS, Tocopherol Poly (Ethylene Glycol)1000 Succinate, DEX; WGA, wheat germ agglutinin.

Table 12-2 Pharmacological effects of curcumin-PLGA NPs in vitro.

Formulation	Cell line	Model	Effect	References
Cur-PLGA NPs	MDA-MB-231	Human breast cancer cell line	Increased cellular uptake by six-fold and higher antiproliferative effect and enhanced apoptosis as compared to free curcumin.	[51]
Cur-PLGA NPs	MDA-MB-231	Human breast cancer cell line	Curcumin encapsulation into PLGA NPs decreased cell viability, invasion, and metastasis in comparison with free curcumin.	[52]
Cur-PLGA NPs	MCF-7	HER2-positive human breast cancer cell line	Intracellular release of curcumin facilitated the blockage of G2/M phase and arrested cell cycle.	[53]
CTAB/Cur-PLGA NPs	MDA-MB-231	Human breast cancer cell line	Higher internalization and apoptosis was observed by NPs than free curcumin. Curcumin caused cell cycle arrested by reduction in the expressions of cell progression inducers such as CDK-2, CDK-4, cyclin D1, and cyclin E1as and by enhanced expression of p53 protein, p21waf1/cip1, and p16/INK4a involving in DNA damage process.	[54]
CS or DEX or PEG/Cur-PLGA NPs	MCF-7	HER2-positive human breast cancer cell line	The apoptotic potential of PLGA-Cur-DEX-TPGS and PLGA-Cur-PEG-TPGS was higher in comparison with free curcumin and other formulations. PLGA-Cur-DEX-TPGS showed the highest cellular uptake than other formulations and free curcumin.	[55]
PEG + FA or HA or Tf Cur-PLGA nanoparticles	MDA-MB-231	Human breast cancer cell line	HA and FA conjugated PLGA nanoparticles showed more cytotoxicity than Tf conjugated on triple-negative MDA-MB-231 breast cancer cells. Targeted PLGA nanoparticles facilitated high rate of curcumin internalization into cancer cell compared to nontargeted ones.	[56]
FA-Cur-PLGA particles	MDA-MB 468, MDA-MB-231, MCF-7, 4T1	Human and mice triple-negative breast cancer cell lines	FA-conjugated curcumin PLGA particles showed more cytotoxicity in MDA-MB 468 and 4T1 cells than nontargeted PLGA particles. These particles induced apoptosis in MDA-MB 468 cells thorough the p-Akt-dependent pathways, upregulating cleaved caspase-3 and p27 protein, and downregulating Bcl2 protein.	[57]
Fab′-PEG-PLGA NPs	BT-474/MDA-MB-231	HER2 + breast cancer cell/HER2 − breast cancer cell line	Fab′ and TMAB NPs had higher uptake in BT-474 via receptor-mediated endocytosis than MDA-MB-231 cells. Fab′ NP efficiently penetrates into BT-474 than TMAB.	[58]
Cur-PLGA NP	A2780CP	Ovarian cancer cell line	Curcumin-PLGA showed increased cellular uptake, cytotoxicity, and apoptosis in A2780CP cell lines as compared to free curcumin.	[51]

(Continued)

Table 12–2 (Continued)

Formulation	Cell line	Model	Effect	References
Cur-PLGA NP	A2780CP	Ovarian cancer cell line	Pretreatment with curcumin increased chemo/radio-sensitization in A2780CP cancer cells via downregulation of Bcl-XL and Mcl-1 expression, and reduced the dose of cisplatin and radiation needed to suppress tumor growth.	[59]
Cur-PLGA NP	HeLa	Human cervical cancer cell	Enhanced cellular uptake and cytotoxicity of curcumin nanoparticles compared to free curcumin. Cur-PLGA NPs (50:50) showed superior efficacy than Cur-PLGA NPs (25:75). The PLGA combination used did not affect the cellular uptake.	[60]
Cur-PLGA NP	Caski and SiHa	Cervical cancer cell	Nano-Cur caused greater interaction with the cell surface and consequently facilitated drug internalization, cellular uptake, apoptosis induction, and reduced clonogenic potential of cervical cancer cells as compared to free curcumin.	[103]
APgp-Cur-PLGA NP	KB-V1 and KB-3–1	Cervical cancer cell	Higher cell interaction and cellular uptake of APgp-Cur-PLGA NP in KB-V1 cells than KB-3–1 cells. APgp-Cur-PLGA NP effectively induced cell death as compared to free curcumin and nontargeted nanoparticles.	[61]
Cur-PLGA NP	HT-29	Human Caucasian colon adenocarcinoma cell	Enhance cellular uptake of curcumin-PLGA nanoparticles	[62]
NCs	CT26	Murine colon carcinoma cell	The high drug loading was obtained by castor oil core. Efficient internalization, apoptosis, and cell cycle blocking were obtained by NCs in CT26 cell as compared to free drug.	[63]
CS/WGA/ GE11 peptide/Cur-PLGA NP	HT29	Human Caucasian colon adenocarcinoma cell	WGA and GE11-curcumin PLGA NPs increased mucoadhesivity by 2.3-fold and twofold compared to noncoated NPs. Also, cellular interaction of WGA and GE11 targeted NPs were about 10- and 5-fold higher than noncoated NPs.	[64]
Apt-Cur-NPs	HT29	Human Caucasian colon adenocarcinoma cell	Increased binding, cellular uptake, and cytotoxicity in HT29 cells in comparison with control group.	[65]
Cur-PLGA NP	LNCaP, PC3, DU-145	Prostate cancer cell	Enhanced cellular uptake of curcumin NPs in three different cell lines and more cytotoxic effects of NPs in prostate cancer cell compared to nontumorigenic cells (PWR1E).	[66]
Cur-PLGA NP	PC3	Prostate cancer cell	A significant reduction in cell viability and cell growth was observed by curcumin-PLGA NPs in PC3 cells in comparison with cells treated with free curcumin.	[67]

NP	Cell line	Cell type	Description	Ref.
PSMA Mab-Cur-PLGA NP	C4–2, PC-3, DU-145	Prostate cancer cell	Enhanced cellular uptake is mediated by clathrin and caveolae pathways. High accumulation and retention of Cur-PLGA NP than free curcumin in DU-145 and C4–2 cells while PC-3 showed less retention for both free curcumin and curcumin-PLGA NPs.	[68]
Cur-PLGA NP RBCM-p-PLGA@Cur NPs	HL60, HepG2 H22	Human hepatocyte carcinoma cell Mouse hepatocellular carcinoma cell	Enhance apoptosis and cytotoxicity in HL60 and HepG2 cell lines. Higher cellular uptake for RBCM-p-PLGA@Cur NPs compared to noncoated NPs. Above 50 µg/mL Cur, RBCM-p-PLGA@Cur NPs showed substantial inhibitory effect in cells than noncoated NPs and free curcumin.	[69] [70]
Cur-PLGA-TPGS NPs	HepG2	Human hepatocyte carcinoma cell	Higher internalization for Cur-PLGA-TPGS NPs than free Curcumin.	[71]
cHP-PEG-Cur-PLGA NPs	C6	Rat glioma cell	Due to the ability of cHP targeted NPs to bind to $\alpha V\beta 3$-integrin, they showed more toxicity effect in c6 cells than HeLa (integrin negative) cells. Also, cellular uptake was improved via receptor-mediated endocytosis.	[72]
Cur-PLGA NP	BCL2 (S70A) Jurkat	Human T-cell leukemia	Cur-PLGA NP enhanced cellular uptake, cell toxicity, and antitumor effect against Jurkat cells, compared to free curcumin.	[74]
Cur-PLGA NP	CAR (CAL27-cisplatin resistant)/HGFs/OKs	Human oral cancer/normal human gingival fibroblasts/normal human oral keratinocytes	Cur-PLGA NP showed no cytotoxicity effect on normal cells, but considerably reduced cell viability of CAL27 cancer cells. These NPs induced apoptosis via activation of caspases -3, -9, cytochrome c and Bax, and downregulation of Bcl-2 and ROS production. Also, suppression of the multiple drug resistance of CAL27-cisplatin-resistant cells was observed.	[75]
Cur-PLGA NP	U2OS	Human osteosarcoma cell	Enhanced cellular uptake and toxicity in cells treated with Cur-PLGA NP. Apoptosis induction in U2OS cells through the activation of aspase-3/7 and caspase-9, related to Akt-Bad signaling pathway.	[76]
Cur-PLGA NP	Hep-2	Human laryngeal squamous carcinoma cell	In a comparative study, curcumin nanoparticles were more efficient in inducing apoptosis in initial 24 h than long-term assay (48 h), while 5-fluorouracil nanoparticles induced higher apoptosis in long term.	[77]
CS-Cur-PEG-PLGA NPs	PANC-1/Mia Paca-2	Human pancreatic cancer cell	Increased cellular uptake, cytotoxicity, antiinvasive, antimigratory, and apoptosis induction by CS-Cur-PEG-PLGA NPs compared to free curcumin.	[78]

(Continued)

Table 12–2 (Continued)

Formulation	Cell line	Model	Effect	References
Cur-PLGA-C NPs	Hep-2	Human laryngeal squamous carcinoma cell	Cholesterol modification enhanced cellular uptake of nanoparticles, in comparison with nanoparticles without cholesterol. This is may be due to cholesterol interaction with cellular membrane leading to enhanced endocytosis.	[79]
Cur-CTP-NPFs	A431	Human epidermoid skin carcinoma	Cur-CTP-NPFs exhibited higher growth inhibitory effect and caused greater cytotoxicity by disrupting mitochondrial membrane potential (MMP) against A431 than the unpattern films.	[80]
Cur-RGD–IpNPs	B16	Human melanoma cells	Results showed that Cur-RGD–IpNPs were more effective in suppressing tumor growth in B16 cells.	[81]
GANT61-Cur-PLGA NPs	MCF-7	HER2-positive Human breast cancer cell	Successful internalization of the GANT61-curcumin PLGA NPs even at a low concentration (20 μg/mL), more cytotoxicity of GANT61-curcumin PLGA NPs compared to single-drug NPs, induction of autophagy and apoptosis in MCF-7 cell, lower rate of in vitro tumor relapse in cells treated with GANT61-curcumin PLGA NPs than single-drug NPs.	[82]
Cur/Met-PEG-PLGA NPs	T47D	Human breast cancer cell	Enhanced synergistic antiproliferative effect and inhibition of hTERT gene expression in Cur/Met-PEG-PLGA NPs in comparison with free combination (Cur-Met).	[83]
AnxA2-CPNPs	MCF10A, MCF10AT, MCF10CA1a	Human breast cancer cell	AnxA2-CPNPs decreased cancer invasion confirmed by a reduction in plasminogen-plasmin conversion and the considerably lower wound closure (wound scratch assay) in MCF10AT and MCF10CA1a cells in comparison with untreated control cells.	[84]
MTX/Cur-PLGA NPs	SK-Br-3	Human breast adenocarcinoma cell	MTX/Cur-PLGA NPs after 24 and 48 hours had lower IC_{50} than MTX-NPs.	[85]
Cur-PLGA NP	SK-OV-3	Human ovarian adenocarcinoma cell	Improved serum stability, haemocompatibility, and cellular uptake of curcumin after encapsulation into polymeric NPs. Higher ROS generation by curcumin-PLGA NPs than free curcumin and blank NPs after PDT.	[87]
SH-ASA/Cur-mPEG-PLGA NPs	SKOV3, ES-2	Human ovarian cancer cell	Enhanced cellular uptake, synergistic anticancer effects on ES-2 and SKOV3, and activation of the mitochondrial apoptosis pathway.	[88]

Formulation	Cell model	Cell type	Findings	Ref.
Paclitaxel/curcumin-PLGA-phospholipid-PEG NPs	A2780	Human ovarian cancer cell	Curcumin-PLGA NPs significantly alleviated P-gp level of the drug-resistant cell line.	[89]
GE11-DTX-Cur PLGANPs	LNCaP	Human prostate cancer	DTX-Cur NPs showed lower IC$_{50}$ value compared to free drugs or mono capsulated NPs.	[90]
FA-Cur-PEG-PLGANPs	HeLa	Human cervical cancer cell	Paclitaxel-induced cytotoxicity, chromatin condensation, and caspase cleavage is increased more efficiently by FA-Cur-PEG-PLGANPs in HeLa cells than free curcumin.	[91]
Chr/Cur PLGA NPs	Caco-2	Human colorectal cancer cell	Chr/Cur PLGA NPs showed a more synergistic antiproliferative effect and considerable inhibited cell growth than the free drugs. Also, the synergic effect of Chr/Cur PLGA NPs in the downregulation of hTERT gene expression was observed.	[92]
HA-CPT/Cur PLGA NPs	C26	Mouse colon adenocarcinoma cell	The HA-CPT/CUR-NPs showed excellent colon cancer cell-targeting potential and had clear synergistic effects against Colon-26 cells. Higher cellular uptake ability of HA-CPT/Cur PLGA NPs than unmodified NPs. HA-CPT/Cur PLGA NPs were entered to cells through endocytosis pathway.	[93]
CDDP-PLGA/Cur LBL NPs	A549, NCI-H1299,	Human lung carcinoma cell	CDDP-PLGA/Cur LBL NPs could significantly enhance in vitro cytotoxicity in comparison with free drug and single-drug-loaded LBL NPs.	[94]
HER2-SPION-Cur-PLGA NPs	PANC-1/ MIA PaCa-2	Human pancreatic cancer cell	In the presence of an external magnetic field, HER2 targeted NPs demonstrated ameliorated cellular uptake and cytotoxicity compared to nontargeted NPs.	[95]
Apt-Cur-SPION-PLGA NPs	PANC-1/ MIA PaCa-2	Human pancreatic cancer cell	Higher cellular uptake of AS1411 aptamer-targeted NPs due to high selectivity to nucleolin receptor overexpressing in pancreatic cancer cell. Photothermal ablation of cancer cells upon laser irradiation of Apt-Cur-SPION-PLGA.	[96]
Cur PLGA-PEG-Fe$_3$O$_4$ NPs	A549	Human lung carcinoma cell	More cytotoxic effect and reduced hTERT gene expression in nanoparticles as compared to free curcumin.	[104]
Tf-THC/Dox PEG-PLGA NPs	C6	Rat glioma cell	Tf-targeted NPs exhibited greater and faster cellular uptake than nontargeted NPs. Tf-THC/Cur-PLGA NPs improved cytotoxicity and apoptotic effect. Clonogenic survival assay confirmed that THC sensitized the C6 cells to radiation.	[97]

(Continued)

Table 12–2 (Continued)

Formulation	Cell line	Model	Effect	References
MAb-Cur-PLGA NPs	DKMG/EGFRvIII/DK-MG^{low}	Human glioblastoma cell line	MAb-Cur-PLGA NPs showed more cytotoxicity in DKMG/EGFRvIII cells than DK-MG^{low} (low express of EGFRvIII).	[98]
BDMC-PLGA NPs	HepG-2	Human liver carcinoma cell	The Pluronic F68-coated PLGA NPs were more cytotoxic than free BDMC and uncoated PLGA NPs.	[99]
DMC-PLGA NPs	DU-145, MDA-MB-231, MiaPaCa	Human prostate cancer, human breast cancer, human pancreas cancer cells	High cellular uptake of NPs in all cell lines	[100]
ICA-PLGA NPs	SW480	Human colon cancer cell	Drugs-loaded NPs induced nuclear fragmentation and apoptosis, cell cycle arrested, and downregulated Cyclooxygenase-2.	[101]
ACPCSLNPs	HeLa/HDFa	Human cervical cancer cell/human dermal fibroblasts	The results revealed that ACPCSLNPs are considerably toxic against HeLa cells but nontoxic to the normal HDFa cells.	[102]

ACPCSLNPs, ((1E,6E)-3,5-dioxohepta-1,6-diene-1,7-diyl) bis (2-methoxy-4,1-phenylene) diacetate acetyl curcumin (AC)-loaded PLGA core/shell liposome nanoparticles; AnxA2, Annexin A2 antibody; APgp, anti-P-glycoprotein; Apt, Aptamer; BDMC, Bisdemethoxycurcumin; C, cholesterol; CDDP, cisplatin; cHP, c(RGDf(N-me)VK)-C; Met, Metformin; Chr, chrysin; CPT, camptothecin; CS, chitosan; CTAB, hexadecyltrimethylammonium bromide; CTP-NPFs, TPGS stabilized PLGA nanopatterened films; DEX, dextran; Dox, doxorubicin; FA, folic acid; Fab′, antigen-binding fragments cut from Trastuzumab; HA, hyaluronic acid; ICA, indole-curcumin analog; MAb, monoclonal antibody against EGFRv; Met, Metformin; MTX, Methotrexate; NCs, curcumin-loaded PLGA-based polymeric oil-cored nanocapsules; NP, nanoparticle; PDT, photodynamic therapy; PEG, polyethylene glycol; PLGA, polyD, L-lactide-co-glycolide); RBCM, red blood cell membranes; SH-ASA, H2S-releasing prodrug SH-aspirin; Tf, transferrin; THC, tetrahydrocurcumin; TPGS, tocopherol poly (ethylene glycol)1000 succinate; WGA, wheat germ agglutinin.

Table 12–3 Pharmacological effects of curcumin-PLGA NPs in vivo.

Formulation	Animal model	Dose	Type of disease	Treatment duration	Route of administration	Effect	References
FA-Cur-PLGA particles	Female Balb/c mice	2000 µg/kg	Triple-negative breast cancer	Triple dose	N. A.	Tumor volume was significantly reduced in mice treated with FA-conjugated curcumin PLGA particles in comparison with nontargeted particles and untreated groups.	[57]
Fab'-PEG-PLGA NPs	Sprague-Dawley rats/BALB/c mice	4 mg/kg	Breast cancer	Single dose	Intravenous	Fab'-PEG-PLGA NPs increased half-life (t1/2) and AUC0-t by 5.3-fold and 1.76-fold than TMAB-Cur-NPs, respectively. Also, Fab'-PEG-PLGA NPs showed higher tumor accumulation relative to TMAB-Cur-NPs.	[58]
Cur-PLGA NP	NSG mice	100 µg/mice	Cervical cancer	Single dose	Intratumoral	Nano-CUR effectively reduced tumor growth through suppressing the expression of HPV oncoproteins such as E6/E7 and Ki67, modulating miRNA-21 and miRNA-214.	[103]
NCs	Female Balb/c mice	16 mg /kg	Colorectal cancer	Multiple injections (four doses)	Intravenous	High tumor accumulation and reduced tumor growth.	[63]
CS/WGA/GE11 peptide/Cur-PLGA NP	Female BALB/c	200 µL	Colorectal cancer	Single dose	Oral	Upon oral administration, WGA-curcumin PLGA NPs were adsorbed in the gastrointestinal tracts of mice, showing promising potential for selective delivery to the colon.	[64]

(Continued)

Table 12–3 (Continued)

Formulation	Animal model	Dose	Type of disease	Treatment duration	Route of administration	Effect	References
Apt-Cur-PLGA NP	Male Sprague Dawley rats	4 mg/kg	Colorectal cancer	Single dose	Intravenous	Free curcumin was cleared from blood after 6 h of administration, while curcumin NPs were detectable for over 24 h. Moreover, encapsulation of curcumin into NPs improved bioavailability and half-time of curcumin by three- and six-fold, respectively.	[65]
PSMA Mab-Cur-PLGA NP	C4–2 xenograft mouse model.	25 mg/mice	Prostate cancer	Single dose	Intratumoral	Enhanced antitumor effect was obtained by PSMA Mab-Cur-PLGA NP treatment.	[68]
RBCM-p-PLGA@Cur NPs	ICR female mice	2 mg/kg	Liver cancer	Every 2 days for 16 days	Intravenous	Reduced tumor volume, mass, and lower cytotoxicity were observed in mice treated with RBCM-p-PLGA@Cur NPs.	[70]
Cur-PLGA-TPGS NPs	Kunming strain mice	10 mg/kg	Liver cancer	10 times in 20 days	Intravenous	Tumor growth inhibition and decrease in tumor size compared to free curcumin and Cur-PLGA NP.	[71]
cHP-PEG-Cur-PLGA NPs	Male SD rats	300 µg/kg	Glioma	Single dose	Intravenous	Increase penetration and accumulation of targeted NPs in tumor.	[72]
Cur-PLGA-DSPE-PEG NPs	Female Wistar rats	25 µM curcumin	Glioblastoma	Single dose	Intravenous/ intratumoral	Intratumoral administration of NPs showed the more effective antitumor activity than intravenous route.	[73]
Cur-PLGA-C NPs	Female BALB/c nude mice	83.6 mg/kg	Laryngeal cancer	Single dose	Intravenous	Ameliorated tumor targetability of PLGA-C NPs compared to PLGA NPs group	[79]

Formulation	Animal model	Dose	Cancer type	Dosing schedule	Route	Observations	Ref.
Cur-CTP-NPFs	Swiss Albino mice	—	—	—	—	Cur-CTP-NPFs effectively suppressed progression of skin cancer in mice.	[80]
Cur-RGD–IpNPs	BALB/c mice	25 mg/kg	Melanoma	Every 3 days for 21 days	Intraperitoneal	After 9 days of treatment, Cur-RGD–IpNPs reduced tumor growth rate with no weight loss compared to free curcumin. Immunofluorescent and immunohistochemical evaluations in Cur-RGD–IpNPs group revealed more apoptosis induction and reduced angiogenesis in tumor tissue.	[81]
AnxA2-CPNPs	BALB/c nude mice	20 mg/kg	Breast cancer	Three times a week	Intravenous	Reduced expression of NF-κB subunits and EGFR in tumor tissues, which in turn decreased angiogenesis and metastasis potential of cancer cells. Higher accumulation of AnxA2-CPNPs in tumor compared to nontargeted NP. Significant tumor regression and decreased tumor volume in mice treated with AnxA2-CPNPs when compared to nontargeted group.	[84]
MTX/Cur-PLGA NPs	Female Sprague Dawley rats	5 mg MTX and 2.5 mg Cur	Brest cancer	Once a week for 4 weeks	Intravenous	MTX/Cur-PLGA NPs treatment reduced tumor size.	[85]

(Continued)

Table 12–3 (Continued)

Formulation	Animal model	Dose	Type of disease	Treatment duration	Route of administration	Effect	References
GE11-DTX-Cur PLGANPs	Balb/c nude mice	DTX: 10 mg/kg Cur: 100 mg/kg	Prostate cancer	Every 3 days	Intravenous	GE11-DTX-Cur PLGANPs showed was effective in reducing tumor progression during 21 days	[90]
FA-Cur-PEG-PLGANPs	NOD-SCID mice	Paclitaxel: 10 mg/kg Cur: 25 mg/kg	Cervical cancer	Paclitaxel: twice weekly Cur: alternate days	Intraperitoneal	Increased chemosensitization potential toward paclitaxel and tumor reduction was observed in mice treated with FA-Cur-PEG-PLGANPs.	[91]
CDDP-PLG A/Cur LBL NPs	BALB/c nude mice	10 mg/kg	Lung cancer	Multiple dose	Intravenous	The most considerable antitumor proficiency was obtained by CDDP-PLG A/Cur LBL NPs, which was higher than free CDDP/Cur and CDDP/Cur LBL NPs.	[94]
Tf-THC/Dox PEG-PLGA NPs	Nude mice	5 mg/kg.	Glioma	Five times followed by 3 Gy of radiation	Intravenous	The synergistic effect of THC and curcumin substantially inhibited tumor growth in comparison with saline group, confirming that THC was successful at tumor sensitization to radiation.	[97]
DMC-PLGA NPs	Male Sprague Dawley rats	7.5 mg/kg	—	Single dose	Intravenous	Pharmacokinetic profile of DMC-PLGA NPs demonstrated two compartmental model with the AUC0-∞ being 6.139 mg/L/h.	[100]

AUC0-∞, area under the curve; BW, body weight; C, cholesterol; CDDP, cisplatin; cHP, c(RGDf(N-me)VK)-C; CS, chitosan; CTP-NPFs, TPGS stabilized PLGA nanopatterened films; DMC, demethoxycurcumin; Dox, doxorubicin; DSPE, 1,2-distearoyl-snglycero-3-phosphoethanolamine-N-[amino(PEG)-2000]; FA, folic acid; Fab', antigen-binding fragments cut from Trastuzumab; MTX, methotrexate; N. A., not available; NCs, curcumin-loaded PLGA-based polymeric oil-cored nanocapsules; NP, nanoparticle; NSG, NOD scid gamma; PLGA, polydD, L-lactide-co-glycolide); THC, tetrahydrocurcumin; WGA, wheat germ agglutinin.

It has been argued that hyaluronic acid (HA), transferrin (Tf) [56], and folic acid (FA) [56,57] have served as an ideal target ligand for Cur-loaded PLGA NPs in triple negative breast cancer (TNBC) treatment. TNBC is the most challenging subclass of breast cancer, lacking receptors of estrogen and progesterone (ER and PR) and HER2 gene amplification, and accounted for 15%−20% of newly diagnosed breast carcinoma [111]. Generally, TNBC is an aggressive breast cancer with a poor clinical outcome occurring in youthful women and is identified by the high rate of relapse and great potential for metastasis [112]. Folate receptors are highly presented on the surface of a variety of cancer cells, including colorectal, lung, breast, kidney, epithelial, ovarian, and brain tumors [113]. These receptors are either absent or limited expression on the normal cell surfaces. This issue makes FA an ideal targeting ligand for specifically targeting cancer cells [114−116]. FA is a massively overexpressed receptor on the surface of TNBC cells, even though they are well-known for lacking a variety of molecular targets on their membrane [117−119]. The FA-conjugated-Cur PLGA particles cause ROS-mediated DNA damage and mitochondrial membrane perturbing, followed by cell apoptosis that was higher than nontargeted Cur PLGA particles [57]. The results of in vivo experiment conducted in triple-negative breast tumor-bearing mice confirmed that the FA-conjugated-Cur PLGA particles considerably reduced the volume of tumor compared to empty particles and nontargeted Cur particles. A comparative study found that the ligand-PEG-Cur-PLGA-NPs (with either HA or FA) have higher efficacy in MDA-MB-231 TNBC cells compared to Tf-conjugated-PEG-Cur-PLGA NPs [56]. The rationale could be that the MDA-MB-231 cells express a higher level of CD44 and FA receptors than Tf receptors, which makes HA or FA-PEG-Cur-PLGA NPs more effective at targeting cancer cells.

Trastuzumab (Herceptin, TMAB), a humanized monoclonal antibody, is a first-line option for human epidermal growth factor (HER2)-positive breast cancer [120]. The fragment antigen-binding region (Fab′) specifically interacts with subdomain IV of the HER2 receptor, inducing antibody-dependent cellular cytotoxicity, inhibiting of cell proliferation, and tumor angiogenesis [121]. TMAB is a large molecule (185 kDa) that comes with several limitations, such as slow penetration to solid tumors, nonuniform distribution at the target site, and rapid recognition by the reticuloendothelial system [122,123]. Hence, the small-molecule fragment Fab′ was conjugated to Cur-loaded PEG-PLGA NPs to obtain immunized NPs with high efficacy in HER2-overexpressing cells [58]. Pharmacokinetics and biodistribution evaluations in vivo affirmed that Fab′-PEG-PLGA NPs increased half-life and area under the blood concentration−time curve by 5.3-fold and 1.76-fold than TMAB-Cur-NPs, respectively. Also, Fab′-PEG-PLGA NPs significantly accumulated in tumors relative to TMAB-Cur-NPs.

12.4 Ovarian cancer

Ovarian cancer is one of the most deadly types of gynecologic malignancies in women with a poor prognosis, which causes 5% of cancer mortality in women [124]. A total of 240,000 women suffer from ovarian cancer yearly, ranking it the 11th most-frequent malignancy among female patients and the fifth reason for mortality in women [86,125].

The potential utility of Cur-PLGA NPs for ovarian cancer therapy has been proposed in several studies. In 2010 the efficacy of Cur-PLGA NPs was jointly investigated in breast cancer and A2780CP ovarian cancer cell lines [51]. Consistent with the mentioned results for the breast cancer cells, the Cur-PLGA NPs increased cellular uptake, cytotoxicity, and cell apoptosis in ovarian cancer cells compared to free Cur. Resistance to conventional platinum-based therapies is a major reason for reduced survival and high recurrence rates in patients diagnosed with ovarian cancer [126,127].

Cur is expected potentially minimize drug resistance and increase sensitization of ovarian cancer cells to chemo-/radiotherapy [128−130]. A study investigated the Cur-PLGA NPs regarding the effect of Cur pretreatment to induce chemo/radio-sensitization in A2780CP ovarian cancer cells, aiming to suppress tumor growth [59]. A2780CP ovarian cancer cells were pretreated with Cur and, then, were exposed to cisplatin or radiation. Cur pretreatment considerably prohibited proliferation and the clonogenic ability of cells and increased the cytotoxicity of cisplatin, when compared to each agent treatment alone. Also, Cur-pretreatment lessened the required dose of radiation and cisplatin to prevent cell growth. The observed results could be attributed to Cur's potential to lower the expression of Mcl-1 and Bcl-XL, two pro-survival proteins, resulting in cell apoptosis induction in cells after cisplatin treatment.

12.5 Cervical cancer

Cervical cancer, as the third most-frequent cancer in women, seems to be a main cause of the disorder and death-related cancer worldwide, with 529,800 new patients and 275,100 dying per annum [131]. Cervical cancer, similar to other types of cancer, is a chronic and complicated process that is driven by diverse external environmental effects, and inherited genetic factors [132]. Human papillomavirus (HPV) is known as a primary causative environmental risk factor in cervical cancer. HPV is linked to more than 90% of cervical cancer [133].

In an attempt to investigate the efficacy of the Cur-PLGA NPs in cervical cancer therapy, Nair et al. [60] showed that Cur-PLGA NPs were effectively taken up by HeLa cells and exert more cytotoxicity effects compared to free Cur.

Another study reported that the Cur-PLGA NPs are capable of inhibiting cellular proliferation, inducing apoptosis, and cell cycle arresting in the G1-S transition phase in Caski and SiHa cervical cancer cells [103]. In vivo studies following intratumoral administration exhibited that tumor burden was considerably reduced by modulating oncogenic miRNA-21, repressing nuclear β-catenin, and suppressing the expression of HPV oncoproteins such as E6/E7 and Ki67 in tumor tissue.

Punfa and colleagues developed PLGA NPs conjugated to anti-P-glycoprotein and evaluated their cytotoxicity and cellular uptake in cervical cancer cell lines, KB-3−1 (low expression of P-gp) and KB-V1 (high expression of P-gp) [61]. The results confirmed that in comparison with free Cur and bare NPs, conjugation of Cur-PLGA NPs to anti-P-glycoprotein successfully improved the efficacy of Cur in KB-V1 cancer cells.

12.6 Colorectal cancer

Colorectal cancer, the third most popular detected cancer, is classified as the second leading cause of cancer fatality (9.4% of total cancer deaths) [105].

It is reported that PLGA NPs effectively increased the cellular uptake of Cur in HT-29 colon adenocarcinoma cells compared to free Cur [62]. The improved cellular uptake could be ascribed to the tiny size of NPs and their cell internalization through clathrin-mediated endocytosis and fluid-phase pinocytosis, allowing the escape of NPs from endolysosomes and enter the cytoplasm.

Klippstein et al. developed Cur-loaded PLGA-based polymeric oil-cored nanocapsules (NCs) and performed in vivo evaluations to confirm their efficacy for colon cancer therapy [63]. Upon systemic administration, NCs passively accumulated in CT26 tumors and delayed tumor progression.

To create Cur-loaded modified PLGA NPs for selective delivery of Cur to the gastrointestinal tract, the surface of the NPs was functionalized with three different ligands, including CS, GE11 peptide, and wheat germ agglutinin (WGA) [64]. WGA, a small lectin protein, reversibly and nonenzymatically binds to sialic acid and N-acetyl-D-glucosamine on the surface of human colonocytes and colon cancer cells [134]. GE11 is a small peptide possessing high affinity against epidermal growth factor receptor (EGFR), which is significantly upregulated on the surface of different human cancer cells, including ovarian, esophageal, breast, non-small cell lung cancer, colorectal, and stomach cancer cells [135,136]. In vivo imaging of BALB/c mice orally administrated with targeted and noncoated Cur-PLGA NPs provided evidence that prepared NPs stayed in the stomach up to 6 h postinjection. Despite the clearance of noncoated and GE11-Cur-PLGA NPs without attendance in the colon, WGA-Cur-PLGA NPs were traced in the colon, indicating WGA-mediated efficient adsorption with the gastrointestinal tracts.

Cur-loaded PLGA-lecithin-PEG hybrid NPs modified with Aptamers (Apt) against epithelial cell adhesion molecule (EpCAM) [65] were tested for specific delivery to colorectal cancer cells. The study of the pharmacokinetic behavior of NPs and free Cur after intravenous administrations revealed that the bioavailability of Cur-NPs was enhanced by threefold toward free Cur. Overall, surface modification of NPs with EpCAM Apt enables them to increase cellular binding and uptake, thus improving selective drug delivery to colorectal cancer cells.

12.7 Prostate cancer

Prostate cancer, the fifth prominent cause of cancer mortality, is considered the most common cancer in the male population in the world, with highly variable clinical presentation and outcomes [137].

In 2009 the potential of Cur-loaded PLGA NPs was investigated in prostate cancer therapy regarding their efficacy against LNCaP, PC3, and DU-145 prostate cancer cells [66]. The results indicated that Cur-loaded PLGA NPs increased cellular uptake and cytotoxicity in all three cancer cells.

The more cytotoxicity of Cur-PLGA NPs in prostate cancer cells compared to nontumorigenic cells (PWR1E) is attributed to the Cur capability for cellular apoptosis induction in increasingly proliferating cancer cells, which is amplified by utilizing Cur-loaded NPs.

In another study, Cur-loaded PLGA NPs were designed and evaluated in vitro, suggesting the utility of Cur-PLGA NPs in treating prostate cancer [67]. Cells treated with Cur-PLGA NPs have undergone cell death through type I cell death (apoptosis) and type II programmed cell death (autophagy/necrosis). Generally, Cur-loaded PLGA NPs showed significant apoptosis, cytotoxicity, and antiproliferative effects on PC-3 cells when compared to cells treated with free Cur.

Yallapu and colleagues functionalized Cur-loaded PLGA NPs with an anti-PSMA antibody to enhance tumor targeting for prostate cancer therapy [68]. In vitro results exhibited that Cur-PLGA NPs have more anticancer efficacy over free Cur by regulating STAT3 and AKT pathways and inducing cell apoptosis. Also, Cur-PLGA NPs inhibit prostate cancer progression and metastasis through upregulation of miR-205 and downregulation of miR-21. C4−2 xenograft mice administrated with PSMA Mab-Cur-PLGA NPs improved specific binding to C4−2 and anticancer effect compared to nontargeted Cur-PLGA NPs and free Cur.

12.8 Liver cancer

Liver cancer is the seventh most prevalent cancer and the fourth cause of cancer mortality worldwide [138].

Hepatitis C virus and B virus (HCV and HBV) infection, smoking, alcohol drinking, and extended exposure to Aflatoxin are the essential risk factors to cause liver cancer [139]. Cholangiocarcinoma and hepatocellular carcinoma (HCC) are considered the main classes of liver cancer [138].

To assay the antitumor activity of Cur on liver cancer, one group designed optimized Cur-PLGA NPs [69]. Results indicated that Cur-PLGA NPs effectively increased cytotoxicity and apoptosis in HL60 and HepG2 cells compared to free Cur.

Xie et al. [70] proposed the modification of Cur-loaded porous PLGA NPs with red blood cell membranes (RBCM) to mimic biological conditions and cloak porous NPs (RBCM-p-PLGA@Cur NPs). The efficacy of these NPs has been investigated both in vitro and in vivo, using H22 hepatocyte cancer cells and a xenograft mouse model. In vitro studies showed that RBCM-p-PLGA@Cur NPs caused greater cellular uptake and cytotoxicity in H22 cells than noncoated NPs and free Cur. The antitumor test performed in H22 tumor-bearing ICR mice demonstrated a reduction in tumor size, mass, lower systemic toxicity, and tumor cells apoptosis induction in mice treated with RBCM-p-PLGA@Cur NPs in comparison with free Cur, noncoated NPs, and saline group. It is thought that the erythrocyte protein, CD47, enables NPs to evade phagocytosis by disguising, which consequently enhances cellular uptake and preferential accumulation in the tumors. In another study, Cur-loaded (PLGA/TPGS) NPs were used as a delivery system for liver cancer therapy [71]. Cur-loaded (PLGA/TPGS) NPs were administrated intravenously, and more enormous amount of Cur was detected in the liver than in other organs and blood with no liver tissue damage. These results indicated the safety of Cur-loaded (PLGA/TPGS) NPs as a platform for liver targeting. Also, Cur-loaded (PLGA/TPGS) NPs substantially diminish tumor volume and have better antitumor effects than free Cur and Cur-PLGA NPs.

12.9 Brain cancer

Brain and central nervous system (CNS) tumors can be considered a formidable and invasive form of cancer. Out of all diagnosed primary CNS tumors, over 80% is allocated to brain tumor [140]. The annual incidence of brain cancer is approximately 300,000 new cases and 241,000 deaths around the world in 2018 [141]. Although advances in medical care continue, survival time for patients diagnosed with brain tumors is low and seldom exceeds 16 months [142]. The blood–brain barrier (BBB) as a selective barrier limits the chemotherapeutic agents' access to the tumor, thereby reducing the therapeutic efficacy and completely destroying the tumor cells. However, a possible solution to this issue could be to use nano-carriers to ease drug penetration across the BBB [143,144].

In this context, Zhang et al. offered Cur-loaded-PEG-PLGA NPs modified with cyclic hexa-peptide c(RGDf(N-me)VK)-C (cHP) with an objective to increase the affinity for highly overex-pressed integrins cells and ensure the brain targeting capability [72]. In vivo studies confirmed that cHP conjugation improved the penetration and accumulation of NPs in the brain of the rat.

An investigation was carried out to develop Cur-PEG-PLGA and 1,2-distearoyl-snglycero-3-phosphoethanolamine-N-[amino(PEG)-2000] (DSPE) hybrid NPs for in vivo evaluation in the RG2 mice glioblastoma tumor model [73]. In vivo results revealed the superiority of the intratumoral injection of Cur-loaded NPs over the intravenous route to obtain the favorable antitumor activity. The main reason for this is that an inadequate amount of NPs successfully across the BBB upon intravenous injection.

12.10 Other types of cancers

In addition to the abovementioned cancers, there are several published studies describing the key role of Cur-loaded PLGA NPs in successfully combating other types of cancers in in vitro and in vivo experiments.

In vitro evaluation of Cur-loaded PLGA NPs was carried out to confirm the efficiency and specificity in Jurkat human T-cell leukemia [74], CAR (CAL27-cisplatin resistant) human oral cancer [75], U2OS human osteosarcoma [76], Hep-2 human laryngeal squamous carcinoma [77], and Mia Paca-2 and PANC-1 human pancreatic cancer cells [78].

An investigation was performed to fabricate PLGA-cholesterol (PLGA-C)-based NPs for Cur delivery in Hep-2 tumor-xenografted mice model [79]. In vivo biodistribution study showed the ameliorated tumor targetability of PLGA-C NPs compared to PLGA NPs group, indicating the higher presence of cholesterol in cancer tissue and cells than normal ones, which operates as a receptor for cholesterol-rich NPs.

In the field of skin cancer therapy, Cur-TPGS stabilized PLGA nanopatterned films (CTP-NPFs) [80] and Cur-encapsulated hybrid cholesterol-PEG-PLGA NPs modified with Arg−Gly−Asp (RGD) (Cur-RGD−lpNPs) [81] presented promising in vivo therapeutic outcome for skin cancer treatment.

12.11 Combination therapy

Cancers are thought to be a multifactorial process and are related to the combined effects of many factors, mutational variants, and general heterogeneity. Therefore, cancer treatment approaches based on conventional monotherapies seem to be insufficient and there is a need to develop adaptive therapies [145]. Combination therapy has appeared as a successful strategy for effective cancer therapy, offering several advantages of enhancing therapeutic efficacy due to the synergistic or augmentative effects, decreasing side effects by minimizing the therapeutic dose of a single drug, and overcoming drug resistance [146]. Several researches have assessed the therapeutic efficacy of Cur combined with other chemotherapy agents, immunomodulators, or different strategies such as photodynamic therapy (PDT), radiation therapy, and magnetic guidance.

Hedgehog (Hh) and EGFR are two of the basic pathways initiating tumorigenesis and malignant transformation of breast cancer cells [147,148]. Borah and colleagues [82] offered synergistically the downregulation of the Hh/Gli and EGFR signaling pathways for breast cancer treatment by encapsulating an EGFR inhibitor Cur and GANT61, selective inhibitor of Hh/Gli, into PLGA NPs. In vitro results indicated that GANT61-Cur-PLGA NPs, due to the blockage of two signaling pathways simultaneously, enhanced antitumor effects in MCF-7 breast cancer cells.

In another study, coencapsulation of metformin (Met) and Cur in PEGylated PLGA NPs (Cur/Met-PEG-PLGA NPs) showed a more synergistic antiproliferative effect and knocking down of hTERT gene expression in T47D human breast cancer cell line in relative to free drug and mono encapsulated NPs [83].

Annexin A2 (AnxA2) is a tumor-associated protein mediating the proliferation, invasion, and metastasis processes of tumors in various types of cancers, including gliomas, hepatoma, pancreatic, ovarian, breast, and nasopharyngeal carcinoma [149−155].

Considering the modulating role of AnxA2 in breast cancer metastasis, Mukerjee et al. [84] exploited the combinatorial anticancer and antiangiogenic potential of AnxA2 antibody-conjugated Cur-loaded PLGA NPs (AnxA2-CPNP) against metastatic breast cancer. According to in vivo studies, higher accumulation, and retention of AnxA2-CPNP in the tumor for an extended time than nontargeted NPs, improved antitumor efficacy and angiogenesis reduction around the tumor in mice treated with AnxA2-CPNP was observed. These results indicated that AnxA2 antibody conjugation confers targeting potential to the NPs, which consequently leads to enhanced cellular uptake in cancer cells, substantial tumor accumulation, and decreased tumor burden.

In a study conducted by Vakilinezhad and colleagues [85], it was shown that coencapsulation of methotrexate (MTX) and Cur in PLGA NPs could delay tumor progression and eliminate tumors in tumor-bearing mice.

PDT is a valuable and noninvasive treatment modality, applied in the treatment of various types of cancers that relies on the systemic or local administration of a drug as a photosensitive compound followed by local illumination of the pathological tissue area [156,157]. The photosensitizer molecule accumulating in pathological tissues is exposed to a proper power, duration, and specific light wavelength, initiating the molecule excitation to singlet or triplet. This process leads to selective tissue damage by inducing apoptosis and cell death [158−160]. The initial investigation of the photobiological and photokilling ability of Cur comes back to 1987 [161,162]. Considering all the evidence, it seems that Cur is an efficient photosensitizer with a wide absorption spectrum (300−500 nm) coupled with possible advantages of photodynamic potential that can bring in the treatment of various diseases [163−165].

Recently, the combination of light-emitting diode (LED)-based PDT and Cur-PLGA NPs was proposed for the ovarian cancer therapy [87]. Regarding the crucial role of ROS generation in PDT therapy, Cur-PLGA NPs generated higher ROS levels than free Cur and blank PLGA NPs upon irradiation. Also, photo-demolition and nuclear perforation of cells indicated more cellular uptake of Cur-PLGA NPs than free Cur.

There have been reports on the use of prodrug SH-aspirin (SH-ASA)-Cur coencapsulated into m-PEG-PLGA NPs [88] and paclitaxel-Cur co-encapsulated PLGA-phospholipid-PEG NPs [89] for ovarian cancer therapy and were found to be effective in preventing the progression of ovarian carcinoma cell line.

A dual-targeted delivery system, EGFR peptide decorated PLGA NPs codelivering pH-sensitive curcumin (Cur) prodrug and docetaxel (DTX) (GE11-DTX-Cur PLGA NPs), was designed for the prostate cancer treatment [90]. In vivo antitumor results exhibited that free Cur prodrug had better performance than free Cur attributed to the cleavage of pH-sensitive bond and triggered Cur release in the acidic pH of intracellular tumor environment. Also, GE11-DTX-Cur PLGA NPs were more effective in reducing tumor progression than free drugs and nontargeted NPs.

In the context of the chemosensitizing potential of Cur, Cur-entrapped in PEG-PLGA NPs conjugated with FA (FA-Cur-PEG-PLGA NPs) have been proven to be successful in enhancing chemosensitization effects toward paclitaxel in cervical cancer xenograft NOD-SCID mice model [91].

Two studies have shown the beneficial effects of combination chemotherapy using chrysin (Chr)/Cur-coencapsulated-PLGA NPs (Cur/Chr PLGA NPs) [92] and HA-modified camptothecin (CPT)/Cur-loaded PLGA NPs (HA-Cur/CPT PLGA NPs) [93] for colon cancer therapy.

In a study, researchers planned cisplatin prodrug (CDDP-PLGA) and Cur coencapsulated layer-by-layer (LBL), lipid-polymer hybrid NPs (CDDP-PLGA/Cur LBL NPs) with the aim of combination therapy of lung cancer [94]. In vivo antitumor efficacy assessment showed that CDDP-PLGA/Cur LBL NPs can efficiently fight against A549 tumor cells. LBL NPs were found to be protective shells preventing the dissociation of CDDP and Cur in the bloodstream and providing high tumor accumulation.

To obtain theragnostic purpose, Cur and superparamagnetic iron oxide NPs (SPIONs) were coencapsulated into PLGA NPs modified with HER2 and examined for pancreatic cancer therapy [95]. In the attendance of an external magnetic field, the Cur-HER2-SPION-PLGA NPs augmented cellular uptake and antiproliferative activity attributed to the synergistic therapeutic efficacy of the Cur and active magnetic targeting, leading to a promising approach for the treatment of pancreatic cancer.

A multifunctional AS1411Apt-conjugated PLGA NP was synthesized for the simultaneous delivery of Cur, and SPION (Apt-Cur-SPION-PLGA NPs), with the aim of combining magnetic resonance imaging (MRI) and photothermal capabilities in one system [96]. Based on a photothermal study, NIR-laser irradiation of Apt-Cur-SPION-PLGA NPs can produce sufficient heat for photothermal ablation of cancer cells, causing necrotic cell death with no side effect on healthy cells out of the laser irradiation zone. It should be noted that temperature rise was not observed in Cur-PLGA NPs and empty PLGA NPs.

Another attempt has been made to develop a magnetic nanocarrier platform to allow for the coencapsulation of Cur and Fe_3O_4 inside PEG-PLGA NPs [104]. Compared to free Cur, Cur-PLGA-PEG-Fe3O4 NPs caused a more time-dependent cytotoxic effect and a further decline in the hTERT gene expression in the A549 lung cancer cell line.

In a study conducted by the Zhang group, Tf-modified PEG-PLGA NPs delivering tetrahydrocurcumin (THC) and doxorubicin (Dox) effects were established for the chemoradiotherapy of glioma [97]. In both C6 subcutaneously grafted mice models and orthotopic C6 glioma models, Tf-THC/Dox PEG-PLGANPs combined with radiation showed favorable antitumor efficacy, indicating THC was successful for sensitizing tumor to radiation. In another attempt, the use of anti-EGFRvIII MAb conjugated to Cur-loaded PLGA NPs in combination with PDT represented that these NPs were more photocytotoxic in DKMG/EGFRvIII human glioblastoma cells than Cur-PLGA NPs [98]. It can be attributed to enhanced cellular uptake of targeted NPs through receptor-mediated endocytosis.

12.11.1 Curcumin analogs for cancer treatment

As mentioned earlier, Cur application is challenged by some drawbacks, including poor stability, solubility, and in vivo bioavailability. Therefore, Cur analogs with higher stability can be considered as a possible solution to these problems. Cur analogs are generally classified into natural analogs and synthetic analogs. Besides Cur, bisdemethoxycurcumin (BDMC) and demethoxycurcumin (DMC) are the other natural active components in turmeric [166].

BDMC has shown more stability than Cur and DMC with antitumor effects applying several mechanisms, including apoptosis induction, cell proliferation, invasion, migration, and tumor development inhibition in cancer cells [167,168].

Moving ahead in this context, BDMC-loaded PLGA NPs were synthesized and coated with different coating agents such as Pluronic F68, PEG 4000, and Tween 80 [99]. The Pluronic F68-coated PLGA NPs exhibited the highest cytotoxicity in HepG-2 in comparison with free BDMC and uncoated PLGA NPs.

In another study, intravenous administration of DMC-loaded PLGA NPs provided a higher area under the curve (AUC0-∞) than previously reported work [100].

Based on the earlier study [169] showing the superiority of the indole analog of Cur over Cur in repressing the growth of the SW480 human colon cancer cell line, the same group further investigated the potency of Cur and indole-curcumin analog (ICA)−encapsulated polysorbate 80-stabilized PLGA NPs in SW480 cell lines [101]. In another study, ((1E,6E)-3,5-dioxohepta-1,6-diene-1,7-diyl) bis (2-methoxy-4,1-phenylene) diacetate acetyl curcumin (AC)-loaded PLGA core/shell liposome NPs (ACPCSLNPs) were developed and evaluated their anticancer effect on the HeLa cell line [102].

12.12 Conclusion

Cancer, as the main cause of mortality and morbidity, is becoming increasingly prevalent around the world and the urgent need to introduce promising therapeutic agents seems set to continue in the future. Cur is a hydrophobic phenol isolated from the rhizomes of *Curcuma longa* L. possessing a broad range of biological activities and its anticancer potential is highly regarded. However, several drawbacks, such as poor bioavailability and solubility, hindered its clinical application. One way around this problem could be utilizing polymeric-based PLGA NPs to ameliorate the physicochemical properties of Cur. Evidence presented in this chapter have proved that PLGA NPs provide the possibility to enhance Cur solubility, sustained release of Cur into cells over time, and facilitate Cur internalization through the endocytosis pathway. In all studies, Cur-encapsulated PLGA NPs performed in a better way than free Cur reflecting that Cur entrapment in PLGA NPs capable of reaching the cancer cells in an active form and exert their anticancer potential. Furthermore, surface modification with various highly overexpressed ligands over cancer cells and another polymeric coating such as PEG, dextran, and CS have enabled PLGA NPs to site-selective delivery of Cur and enhanced its therapeutic efficacy for cancer therapy.

Collectively, although Cur-encapsulated PLGA NPs have opened up the promising way toward successful cancer therapy, further investigations are required to translate clinical application.

References

[1] Yu S, Chen Z, Zeng X, Chen X, Gu Z. Advances in nanomedicine for cancer starvation therapy. Theranostics. 2019;9(26):8026.

[2] Abbasi Kajani A, Haghjooy Javanmard S, Asadnia M, Razmjou A. Recent advances in nanomaterials development for nanomedicine and cancer. ACS Applied Bio Materials 2021;4(8):5908−25.

[3] Chaturvedi VK, Singh A, Singh VK, Singh MP. Cancer nanotechnology: a new revolution for cancer diagnosis and therapy. Current Drug Metabolism 2019;20(6):416−29.

[4] Jemal A, Bray F, Center MM, Ferlay J, Ward E, Forman D. Global cancer statistics. CA: A Cancer Journal for Clinicians 2011;61(2):69−90.

[5] Krieghoff-Henning E, Folkerts J, Penzkofer A, Weg-Remers S. Cancer—an overview. Medizinische Monatsschrift fur Pharmazeuten 2017;40(2):48—54.

[6] Giordano A, Tommonaro G. Curcumin and cancer. Nutrients 2019;11(10):2376.

[7] Liao J, Jia Y, Wu Y, Shi K, Yang D, Li P, et al. Physical-, chemical-, and biological-responsive nanomedicine for cancer therapy. Wiley Interdisciplinary Reviews: Nanomedicine and Nanobiotechnology 2020;12(1):e1581.

[8] Amini P, Mirtavoos-Mahyari H, Motevaseli E, Shabeeb D, Musa AE, Cheki M, et al. Mechanisms for radioprotection by melatonin; can it be used as a radiation countermeasure? Current Molecular Pharmacology 2019;12(1):2—11.

[9] Tomeh MA, Hadianamrei R, Zhao X. A review of curcumin and its derivatives as anticancer agents. International Journal of Molecular Sciences 2019;20(5):1033.

[10] Mirzaei H, Masoudifar A, Sahebkar A, Zare N, Sadri Nahand J, Rashidi B, et al. MicroRNA: a novel target of curcumin in cancer therapy. Journal of Cellular Physiology 2018;233(4):3004—15.

[11] Nagahama K, Utsumi T, Kumano T, Maekawa S, Oyama N, Kawakami J. Discovery of a new function of curcumin which enhances its anticancer therapeutic potency. Scientific Reports 2016;6(1):1—14.

[12] Ganji A, Farahani I, Saeedifar AM, Mosayebi G, Ghazavi A, Majeed M, et al. Protective effects of curcumin against lipopolysaccharide-induced toxicity. Current Medicinal Chemistry 2021;28(33):6915—30.

[13] Hassanzadeh S, Read MI, Bland AR, Majeed M, Jamialahmadi T, Sahebkar A. Curcumin: an inflammasome silencer. Pharmacological Research 2020;159.

[14] Cicero AFG, Sahebkar A, Fogacci F, Bove M, Giovannini M, Borghi C. Effects of phytosomal curcumin on anthropometric parameters, insulin resistance, cortisolemia and non-alcoholic fatty liver disease indices: a double-blind, placebo-controlled clinical trial. European Journal of Nutrition 2020;59 (2):447—83. Available from: https://doi.org/10.1007/s00394-019-01916-7.

[15] Hosseini SA, Zahedipour F, Sathyapalan T, Jamialahmadi T, Sahebkar A. Pulmonary fibrosis: therapeutic and mechanistic insights into the role of phytochemicals. Biofactors (Oxford, England) 2021;47(3):250—69.

[16] Keihanian F, Saeidinia A, Bagheri RK, Johnston TP, Sahebkar A. Curcumin, hemostasis, thrombosis, and coagulation. Journal of Cellular Physiology 2018;233(6):4497—511.

[17] Khayatan D, Razavi SM, Arab ZN, Niknejad AH, Nouri K, Momtaz S, et al. Protective effects of curcumin against traumatic brain injury. Biomedicine and Pharmacotherapy 2022;154.

[18] Mokhtari-Zaer A, Marefati N, Atkin SL, Butler AE, Sahebkar A. The protective role of curcumin in myocardial ischemia—reperfusion injury. Journal of Cellular Physiology 2018;234(1):214—22.

[19] Momtazi-Borojeni AA, Haftcheshmeh SM, Esmaeili SA, Johnston TP, Abdollahi E, Sahebkar A. Curcumin: a natural modulator of immune cells in systemic lupus erythematosus. Autoimmunity Reviews 2018;17(2):125—35.

[20] Rahimi K, Hassanzadeh K, Khanbabaei H, Haftcheshmeh SM, Ahmadi A, Izadpanah E, et al. Curcumin: a dietary phytochemical for targeting the phenotype and function of dendritic cells. Current Medicinal Chemistry 2021;28(8):1549—64.

[21] Panahi Y, Fazlolahzadeh O, Atkin SL, Majeed M, Butler AE, Johnston TP, et al. Evidence of curcumin and curcumin analogue effects in skin diseases: a narrative review. Journal of Cellular Physiology 2019;234(2):1165—78. Available from: https://doi.org/10.1002/jcp.27096.

[22] Sahebkar A. Molecular mechanisms for curcumin benefits against ischemic injury. Fertility and Sterility 2010;94(5):e75—6.

[23] Soltani S, Boozari M, Cicero AFG, Jamialahmadi T, Sahebkar A. Effects of phytochemicals on macrophage cholesterol efflux capacity: impact on atherosclerosis. Phytotherapy Research 2021;35(6):2854—78.

[24] Mohammadi A, Blesso CN, Barreto GE, Banach M, Majeed M, Sahebkar A. Macrophage plasticity, polarization and function in response to curcumin, a diet-derived polyphenol, as an immunomodulatory agent. The Journal of Nutritional Biochemistry 2019;66:1—16. Available from: https://doi.org/10.1016/j.jnutbio.2018.12.005.

[25] Shakeri A, Ward N, Panahi Y, Sahebkar A. Anti-angiogenic activity of curcumin in cancer therapy: a narrative review. Current Vascular Pharmacology 2019;17(3):262−9.

[26] Mohajeri M, Sahebkar A. Protective effects of curcumin against doxorubicin-induced toxicity and resistance: a review. Critical Reviews in Oncology/Hematology 2018;122:30−51.

[27] Momtazi AA, Sahebkar A. Difluorinated curcumin: a promising curcumin analogue with improved antitumor activity and pharmacokinetic profile. Current Pharmaceutical Design 2016;22(28):4386−97.

[28] Marjaneh RM, Rahmani F, Hassanian SM, Rezaei N, Hashemzehi M, Bahrami A, et al. Phytosomal curcumin inhibits tumor growth in colitis-associated colorectal cancer. Journal of Cellular Physiology 2018;233(10):6785−98. Available from: https://doi.org/10.1002/jcp.26538.

[29] Khurana A, Ho C-T. High performance liquid chromatographic analysis of curcuminoids and their photo-oxidative decomposition compounds in *Curcuma longa* L. Journal of Liquid Chromatography 1988;11(11):2295−304.

[30] Mirzaei H, Shakeri A, Rashidi B, Jalili A, Banikazemi Z, Sahebkar A. Phytosomal curcumin: a review of pharmacokinetic, experimental and clinical studies. Biomedicine & Pharmacotherapy 2017;85:102−12.

[31] Chen Y, Lu Y, Lee RJ, Xiang G. Nano encapsulated curcumin: and its potential for biomedical applications. International Journal of Nanomedicine 2020;15:3099.

[32] Wu W, Shen J, Banerjee P, Zhou S. Water-dispersible multifunctional hybrid nanogels for combined curcumin and photothermal therapy. Biomaterials 2011;32(2):598−609.

[33] Mohammed ES, El-Beih NM, El-Hussieny EA, El-Ahwany E, Hassan M, Zoheiry M. Effects of free and nanoparticulate curcumin on chemically induced liver carcinoma in an animal model. Archives of Medical Science 2021;17(1):218−27.

[34] Acharya S, Sahoo SK. PLGA nanoparticles containing various anticancer agents and tumour delivery by EPR effect. Advanced Drug Delivery Reviews 2011;63(3):170−83.

[35] Hashemi Goradel N, Ghiyami-Hour F, Jahangiri S, Negahdari B, Sahebkar A, Masoudifar A, et al. Nanoparticles as new tools for inhibition of cancer angiogenesis. Journal of Cellular Physiology 2018;233 (4):2902−10. Available from: https://doi.org/10.1002/jcp.26029.

[36] Sanati M, Afshari AR, Aminyavari S, Kesharwani P, Jamialahmadi T, Sahebkar A. RGD-engineered nanoparticles as an innovative drug delivery system in cancer therapy. Journal of Drug Delivery Science and Technology 2023;84104562. Available from: https://doi.org/10.1016/j.jddst.2023.104562.

[37] Deng L, Li L, Yang H, Li L, Zhao F, Wu C, et al. Development and optimization of doxorubicin loaded poly (lactic-co-glycolic acid) nanobubbles for drug delivery into HeLa cells. Journal of Nanoscience and Nanotechnology 2014;14(4):2947−54.

[38] Shen X, Li T, Chen Z, Geng Y, Xie X, Li S, et al. Luminescent/magnetic PLGA-based hybrid nanocomposites: a smart nanocarrier system for targeted codelivery and dual-modality imaging in cancer theranostics. International Journal of Nanomedicine 2017;12:4299.

[39] Shen X, Li T, Chen Z, Xie X, Zhang H, Feng Y, et al. NIR-light-triggered anticancer strategy for dual-modality imaging-guided combination therapy via a bioinspired hybrid PLGA nanoplatform. Molecular Pharmaceutics 2019;16(3):1367−84.

[40] Yang H, Deng L, Li T, Shen X, Yan J, Zuo L, et al. Multifunctional PLGA nanobubbles as theranostic agents: combining doxorubicin and P-gp siRNA co-delivery into human breast cancer cells and ultrasound cellular imaging. Journal of Biomedical Nanotechnology 2015;11(12):2124−36.

[41] Yang H, Shen X, Yan J, Xie X, Chen Z, Li T, et al. Charge-reversal-functionalized PLGA nanobubbles as theranostic agents for ultrasonic-imaging-guided combination therapy. Biomaterials Science 2018;6 (9):2426−39.

[42] Kapoor DN, Bhatia A, Kaur R, Sharma R, Kaur G, Dhawan S. PLGA: a unique polymer for drug delivery. Therapeutic Delivery 2015;6(1):41−58.

[43] da Silva Feltrin F, Agner T, Sayer C, Lona LMF. Curcumin encapsulation in functional PLGA nanoparticles: a promising strategy for cancer therapies. Advances in Colloid and Interface Science 2021;102582.

[44] Lü J-M, Wang X, Marin-Muller C, Wang H, Lin PH, Yao Q, et al. Current advances in research and clinical applications of PLGA-based nanotechnology. Expert Review of Molecular Diagnostics 2009;9(4):325−41.

[45] Rezvantalab S, Drude NI, Moraveji MK, Güvener N, Koons EK, Shi Y, et al. PLGA-based nanoparticles in cancer treatment. Frontiers in Pharmacology 2018;9:1260.

[46] Park K, Otte A, Sharifi F, Garner J, Skidmore S, Park H, et al. Potential roles of the glass transition temperature of PLGA microparticles in drug release kinetics. Molecular Pharmaceutics 2020;18(1):18−32.

[47] Parveen S, Sahoo SK. Polymeric nanoparticles for cancer therapy. Journal of Drug Targeting 2008;16(2):108−23.

[48] Shen X, Li T, Xie X, Feng Y, Chen Z, Yang H, et al. PLGA-based drug delivery systems for remotely triggered cancer therapeutic and diagnostic applications. Frontiers in Bioengineering and Biotechnology 2020;8:381.

[49] Maeda H, Nakamura H, Fang J. The EPR effect for macromolecular drug delivery to solid tumors: improvement of tumor uptake, lowering of systemic toxicity, and distinct tumor imaging in vivo. Advanced Drug Delivery Reviews 2013;65(1):71−9.

[50] Varani M, Galli F, Capriotti G, Mattei M, Cicconi R, Campagna G, et al. Theranostic designed near-infrared fluorescent poly (lactic-co-glycolic acid) nanoparticles and preliminary studies with functionalized VEGF-nanoparticles. Journal of Clinical Medicine 2020;9(6):1750.

[51] Yallapu MM, Gupta BK, Jaggi M, Chauhan SC. Fabrication of curcumin encapsulated PLGA nanoparticles for improved therapeutic effects in metastatic cancer cells. Journal of Colloid and Interface Science 2010;351(1):19−29.

[52] Sharma A, Hawthorne S, Jha SK, Jha NK, Kumar D, Girgis S, et al. Effects of curcumin-loaded poly (lactic-co-glycolic acid) nanoparticles in MDA-MB231 human breast cancer cells. Nanomedicine: Nanotechnology, Biology, and Medicine 2021;16(20):1763−73.

[53] Verderio P, Bonetti P, Colombo M, Pandolfi L, Prosperi D. Intracellular drug release from curcumin-loaded PLGA nanoparticles induces G2/M block in breast cancer cells. Biomacromolecules 2013;14(3):672−82.

[54] Meena R, Kumar S, Gaharwar US, Rajamani P. PLGA-CTAB curcumin nanoparticles: fabrication, characterization and molecular basis of anticancer activity in triple negative breast cancer cell lines (MDA-MB-231 cells). Biomedicine & Pharmacotherapy 2017;94:944−54.

[55] Sampath M, Pichaimani A, Kumpati P, Sengottuvelan B. The remarkable role of emulsifier and chitosan, dextran and PEG as capping agents in the enhanced delivery of curcumin by nanoparticles in breast cancer cells. International Journal of Biological Macromolecules 2020;162:748−61.

[56] Prabhuraj R, Bomb K, Srivastava R, Bandyopadhyaya R. Selection of superior targeting ligands using PEGylated PLGA nanoparticles for delivery of curcumin in the treatment of triple-negative breast cancer cells. Journal of Drug Delivery Science and Technology 2020;57:101722.

[57] Pal K, Laha D, Parida PK, Roy S, Bardhan S, Dutta A, et al. An in vivo study for targeted delivery of curcumin in human triple negative breast carcinoma cells using biocompatible PLGA microspheres conjugated with folic acid. Journal of Nanoscience and Nanotechnology 2019;19(7):3720−33.

[58] Duan D, Wang A, Ni L, Zhang L, Yan X, Jiang Y, et al. Trastuzumab-and Fab′ fragment-modified curcumin PEG-PLGA nanoparticles: preparation and evaluation in vitro and in vivo. International Journal of Nanomedicine 2018;13:1831.

[59] Yallapu MM, Maher DM, Sundram V, Bell MC, Jaggi M, Chauhan SC. Curcumin induces chemo/radio-sensitization in ovarian cancer cells and curcumin nanoparticles inhibit ovarian cancer cell growth. Journal of Ovarian Research 2010;3(1):1−12.

[60] Nair KL, Thulasidasan AKT, Deepa G, Anto RJ, Kumar GV. Purely aqueous PLGA nanoparticulate formulations of curcumin exhibit enhanced anticancer activity with dependence on the combination of the carrier. International Journal of Pharmaceutics 2012;425(1−2):44−52.

[61] Punfa W, Yodkeeree S, Pitchakarn P, Ampasavate C, Limtrakul P. Enhancement of cellular uptake and cytotoxicity of curcumin-loaded PLGA nanoparticles by conjugation with anti-P-glycoprotein in drug resistance cancer cells. Acta Pharmacologica Sinica 2012;33(6):823−31.

[62] Akl MA, Kartal-Hodzic A, Oksanen T, Ismael HR, Afouna MM, Yliperttula M, et al. Factorial design formulation optimization and in vitro characterization of curcumin-loaded PLGA nanoparticles for colon delivery. Journal of Drug Delivery Science and Technology 2016;32:10−20.

[63] Klippstein R, Wang JTW, El-Gogary RI, Bai J, Mustafa F, Rubio N, et al. Passively targeted curcumin-loaded pegylated PLGA nanocapsules for colon cancer therapy in vivo. Small (Weinheim an der Bergstrasse, Germany) 2015;11(36):4704−22.

[64] Akl MA, Kartal-Hodzic A, Suutari T, Oksanen T, Montagner IM, Rosato A, et al. Real-time label-free targeting assessment and in vitro characterization of curcumin-loaded poly-lactic-co-glycolic acid nanoparticles for oral colon targeting. ACS Omega 2019;4(16):16878−90.

[65] Li L, Xiang D, Shigdar S, Yang W, Li Q, Lin J, et al. Epithelial cell adhesion molecule aptamer functionalized PLGA-lecithin-curcumin-PEG nanoparticles for targeted drug delivery to human colorectal adenocarcinoma cells. International Journal of Nanomedicine 2014;9:1083.

[66] Mukerjee A, Vishwanatha JK. Formulation, characterization and evaluation of curcumin-loaded PLGA nanospheres for cancer therapy. Anticancer Research 2009;29(10):3867−75.

[67] Azandeh SS, Abbaspour M, Khodadadi A, Khorsandi L, Orazizadeh M, Heidari-Moghadam A. Anticancer activity of curcumin-loaded PLGA nanoparticles on PC3 prostate cancer cells. Iranian Journal of Pharmaceutical Research: IJPR 2017;16(3):868.

[68] Yallapu MM, Khan S, Maher DM, Ebeling MC, Sundram V, Chauhan N, et al. Anti-cancer activity of curcumin loaded nanoparticles in prostate cancer. Biomaterials 2014;35(30):8635−48.

[69] Chen C, Yang W, Wang D-T, Chen C-L, Zhuang Q-Y, Kong X-D. A modified spontaneous emulsification solvent diffusion method for the preparation of curcumin-loaded PLGA nanoparticles with enhanced in vitro anti-tumor activity. Frontiers of Materials Science 2014;8(4):332−42.

[70] Xie X, Wang H, Williams GR, Yang Y, Zheng Y, Wu J, et al. Erythrocyte membrane cloaked curcumin-loaded nanoparticles for enhanced chemotherapy. Pharmaceutics. 2019;11(9):429.

[71] Chen X-p Li Y, Zhang Y, G-w Li. Formulation, characterization and evaluation of curcumin-loaded PLGA-TPGS nanoparticles for liver cancer treatment. Drug Design, Development and Therapy 2019;13:3569.

[72] Zhang X, Li X, Hua H, Wang A, Liu W, Li Y, et al. Cyclic hexapeptide-conjugated nanoparticles enhance curcumin delivery to glioma tumor cells and tissue. International Journal of Nanomedicine 2017;12:5717.

[73] Orunoğlu M, Kaffashi A, Pehlivan SB, Şahin S, Söylemezoğlu F, Oğuz KK, et al. Effects of curcumin-loaded PLGA nanoparticles on the RG2 rat glioma model. Materials Science and Engineering: C. 2017;78:32−8.

[74] Leung MH, Shen AQ. Microfluidic assisted nanoprecipitation of PLGA nanoparticles for curcumin delivery to leukemia Jurkat cells. Langmuir: the ACS Journal of Surfaces and Colloids 2018;34(13):3961−70.

[75] Chang P-Y, Peng S-F, Lee C-Y, Lu C-C, Tsai S-C, Shieh T-M, et al. Curcumin-loaded nanoparticles induce apoptotic cell death through regulation of the function of MDR1 and reactive oxygen species in cisplatin-resistant CAR human oral cancer cells. International Journal of Oncology 2013;43(4):1141−50.

[76] Peng S-F, Lee C-Y, Hour M-J, Tsai S-C, Kuo D-H, Chen F-A, et al. Curcumin-loaded nanoparticles enhance apoptotic cell death of U2OS human osteosarcoma cells through the Akt-Bad signaling pathway. International Journal of Oncology 2014;44(1):238−46.

[77] Masloub SM, Elmalahy MH, Sabry D, Mohamed WS, Ahmed SH. Comparative evaluation of PLGA nanoparticle delivery system for 5-fluorouracil and curcumin on squamous cell carcinoma. Archives of Oral Biology 2016;64:1−10.

[78] Arya G, Das M, Sahoo SK. Evaluation of curcumin loaded chitosan/PEG blended PLGA nanoparticles for effective treatment of pancreatic cancer. Biomedicine & Pharmacotherapy 2018;102:555−66.

[79] Lee J-J, Lee SY, Park J-H, Kim D-D, Cho H-J. Cholesterol-modified poly (lactide-co-glycolide) nanoparticles for tumor-targeted drug delivery. International Journal of Pharmaceutics 2016;509(1−2):483−91.

[80] Malathi S, Pavithra P, Sridevi S, Verma RS. Fabrication of nanopatterned PLGA films of curcumin and TPGS for skin cancer. International Journal of Pharmaceutics 2020;578:119100.

[81] Zhao Y, Lin D, Wu F, Guo L, He G, Ouyang L, et al. Discovery and in vivo evaluation of novel RGD-modified lipid-polymer hybrid nanoparticles for targeted drug delivery. International Journal of Molecular Sciences 2014;15(10):17565−76.

[82] Borah A, Pillai SC, Rochani AK, Palaninathan V, Nakajima Y, Maekawa T, et al. GANT61 and curcumin-loaded PLGA nanoparticles for GLI1 and PI3K/Akt-mediated inhibition in breast adenocarcinoma. Nanotechnology 2020;31(18):185102.

[83] Farajzadeh R, Pilehvar-Soltanahmadi Y, Dadashpour M, Javidfar S, Lotfi-Attari J, Sadeghzadeh H, et al. Nano-encapsulated metformin-curcumin in PLGA/PEG inhibits synergistically growth and hTERT gene expression in human breast cancer cells. Artificial Cells, Nanomedicine, and Biotechnology 2018;46(5):917−25.

[84] Mukerjee A, Ranjan AP, Vishwanatha JK. Targeted nanocurcumin therapy using annexin A2 antibody improves tumor accumulation and therapeutic efficacy against highly metastatic breast cancer. Journal of Biomedical Nanotechnology 2016;12(7):1374−92.

[85] Vakilinezhad MA, Amini A, Dara T, Alipour S. Methotrexate and curcumin co-encapsulated PLGA nanoparticles as a potential breast cancer therapeutic system: in vitro and in vivo evaluation. Colloids and Surfaces B: Biointerfaces 2019;184:110515.

[86] Morand S, Devanaboyina M, Staats H, Stanbery L, Nemunaitis J. Ovarian cancer immunotherapy and personalized medicine. International Journal of Molecular Sciences 2021;22(12):6532.

[87] Duse L, Agel MR, Pinnapireddy SR, Schäfer J, Selo MA, Ehrhardt C, et al. Photodynamic therapy of ovarian carcinoma cells with curcumin-loaded biodegradable polymeric nanoparticles. Pharmaceutics. 2019;11(6):282.

[88] Zhou L, Duan X, Zeng S, Men K, Zhang X, Yang L, et al. Codelivery of SH-aspirin and curcumin by mPEG-PLGA nanoparticles enhanced antitumor activity by inducing mitochondrial apoptosis. International Journal of Nanomedicine 2015;10:5205.

[89] Liu Z, Zhu Y-Y, Li Z-Y, Ning S-Q. Evaluation of the efficacy of paclitaxel with curcumin combination in ovarian cancer cells. Oncology Letters 2016;12(5):3944−8.

[90] Yan J, Wang Y, Jia Y, Liu S, Tian C, Pan W, et al. Co-delivery of docetaxel and curcumin prodrug via dual-targeted nanoparticles with synergistic antitumor activity against prostate cancer. Biomedicine & Pharmacotherapy 2017;88:374−83.

[91] Thulasidasan AKT, Retnakumari AP, Shankar M, Vijayakurup V, Anwar S, Thankachan S, et al. Folic acid conjugation improves the bioavailability and chemosensitizing efficacy of curcumin-encapsulated PLGA-PEG nanoparticles towards paclitaxel chemotherapy. Oncotarget. 2017;8(64):107374.

[92] Lotfi-Attari J, Pilehvar-Soltanahmadi Y, Dadashpour M, Alipour S, Farajzadeh R, Javidfar S, et al. Co-delivery of curcumin and chrysin by polymeric nanoparticles inhibit synergistically growth and hTERT gene expression in human colorectal cancer cells. Nutrition and Cancer 2017;69(8):1290−9.

[93] Xiao B, Han MK, Viennois E, Wang L, Zhang M, Si X, et al. Hyaluronic acid-functionalized polymeric nanoparticles for colon cancer-targeted combination chemotherapy. Nanoscale. 2015;7(42):17745−55.

[94] Hong Y, Che S, Hui B, Wang X, Zhang X, Ma H. Combination therapy of lung cancer using layer-by-layer cisplatin prodrug and curcumin co-encapsulated nanomedicine. Drug Design, Development and Therapy 2020;14:2263.

[95] Sivakumar B, Aswathy RG, Nagaoka Y, Iwai S, Hasumura T, Venugopal K, et al. Augmented cellular uptake and antiproliferation against pancreatic cancer cells induced by targeted curcumin and SPION encapsulated PLGA nanoformulation. Materials Express 2014;4(3):183−95.

[96] Sivakumar B, Aswathy RG, Romero-Aburto R, Mitcham T, Mitchel KA, Nagaoka Y, et al. Highly versatile SPION encapsulated PLGA nanoparticles as photothermal ablators of cancer cells and as multimodal imaging agents. Biomaterials Science 2017;5(3):432−43.

[97] Zhang X, Zhao L, Zhai G, Ji J, Liu A. Multifunctional polyethylene glycol (PEG)-poly (lactic-co-glycolic acid)(PLGA)-based nanoparticles loading doxorubicin and tetrahydrocurcumin for combined chemoradiotherapy of glioma. Medical Science Monitor: International Medical Journal of Experimental and Clinical Research 2019;25:9737.

[98] Jamali Z, Khoobi M, Hejazi SM, Eivazi N, Abdolahpour S, Imanparast F, et al. Evaluation of targeted curcumin (CUR) loaded PLGA nanoparticles for in vitro photodynamic therapy on human glioblastoma cell line. Photodiagnosis and Photodynamic Therapy 2018;23:190−201.

[99] Mehanny M, Hathout RM, Geneidi AS, Mansour S. Studying the effect of physically-adsorbed coating polymers on the cytotoxic activity of optimized bisdemethoxycurcumin loaded-PLGA nanoparticles. Journal of Biomedical Materials Research. Part A 2017;105(5):1433−45.

[100] Ranjan AP, Mukerjee A, Helson L, Vishwanatha JK. Scale up, optimization and stability analysis of curcumin C3 complex-loaded nanoparticles for cancer therapy. Journal of Nanobiotechnology 2012;10(1):1−18.

[101] Sufi SA, Hoda M, Pajaniradje S, Mukherjee V, Coumar SM, Rajagopalan R. Enhanced drug retention, sustained release, and anti-cancer potential of curcumin and indole-curcumin analog-loaded polysorbate 80-stabilizied PLGA nanoparticles in colon cancer cell line SW480. International Journal of Pharmaceutics 2020;588:119738.

[102] Reddy AS, Lakshmi BA, Kim S, Kim J. Synthesis and characterization of acetyl curcumin-loaded core/shell liposome nanoparticles via an electrospray process for drug delivery, and theranostic applications. European Journal of Pharmaceutics and Biopharmaceutics 2019;142:518−30.

[103] Zaman MS, Chauhan N, Yallapu MM, Gara RK, Maher DM, Kumari S, et al. Curcumin nanoformulation for cervical cancer treatment. Scientific Reports 2016;6(1):1−14.

[104] Sadeghzadeh H, Pilehvar-Soltanahmadi Y, Akbarzadeh A, Dariushnejad H, Sanjarian F, Zarghami N. The effects of nanoencapsulated curcumin-Fe3O4 on proliferation and hTERT gene expression in lung cancer cells. Anti-Cancer Agents in Medicinal Chemistry (Formerly Current Medicinal Chemistry-Anti-Cancer Agents) 2017;17(10):1363−73.

[105] Sung H, Ferlay J, Siegel RL, Laversanne M, Soerjomataram I, Jemal A, et al. Global cancer statistics 2020: GLOBOCAN estimates of incidence and mortality worldwide for 36 cancers in 185 countries. CA: A Cancer Journal for Clinicians 2021;71(3):209−49.

[106] Blakemore LM, Boes C, Cordell R, Manson MM. Curcumin-induced mitotic arrest is characterized by spindle abnormalities, defects in chromosomal congression and DNA damage. Carcinogenesis 2013;34(2):351−60.

[107] Hu A, Huang J-J, Zhang J-F, Dai W-J, Li R-L, Lu Z-Y, et al. Curcumin induces G2/M cell cycle arrest and apoptosis of head and neck squamous cell carcinoma in vitro and in vivo through ATM/Chk2/p53-dependent pathway. Oncotarget 2017;8(31):50747.

[108] Berrak Ö, Akkoç Y, Arısan ED, Çoker-Gürkan A, Obakan-Yerlikaya P, Palavan-Ünsal N. The inhibition of PI3K and NFκB promoted curcumin-induced cell cycle arrest at G2/M via altering polyamine metabolism in Bcl-2 overexpressing MCF-7 breast cancer cells. Biomedicine & Pharmacotherapy 2016;77:150−60.

[109] Basha R, Connelly SF, Sankpal UT, Nagaraju GP, Patel H, Vishwanatha JK, et al. Small molecule tolfenamic acid and dietary spice curcumin treatment enhances antiproliferative effect in pancreatic cancer cells via suppressing Sp1, disrupting NF-kB translocation to nucleus and cell cycle phase distribution. The Journal of Nutritional Biochemistry 2016;31:77−87.

[110] Joshi G, Patel M, Chaudhary D, Sawant K. Preparation and surface modification of polymeric nanoparticles for drug delivery: state of the art. Recent Patents on Drug Delivery & Formulation 2020;14(3):201−13.

[111] Pathology of triple negative breast cancer. In: Borri F, Granaglia A, editors. Seminars in cancer biology. Elsevier; 2021.

[112] Deepak K, Vempati R, Nagaraju GP, Dasari VR, Nagini S, Rao D, et al. Tumor microenvironment: challenges and opportunities in targeting metastasis of triple negative breast cancer. Pharmacological Research 2020;153:104683.

[113] Pal K, Roy S, Parida PK, Dutta A, Bardhan S, Das S, et al. Folic acid conjugated curcumin loaded biopolymeric gum acacia microsphere for triple negative breast cancer therapy in invitro and invivo model. Materials Science and Engineering: C. 2019;95:204–16.

[114] Kefayat A, Ghahremani F, Motaghi H, Amouheidari A. Ultra-small but ultra-effective: folic acid-targeted gold nanoclusters for enhancement of intracranial glioma tumor radiation therapy efficacy. Nanomedicine: Nanotechnology, Biology and Medicine 2019;16:173–84.

[115] Xu L, Bai Q, Zhang X, Yang H. Folate-mediated chemotherapy and diagnostics: an updated review and outlook. Journal of Controlled Release 2017;252:73–82.

[116] Kefayat A, Hosseini M, Ghahremani F, Jolfaie NA, Rafienia M. Biodegradable and biocompatible subcutaneous implants consisted of pH-sensitive mebendazole-loaded/folic acid-targeted chitosan nanoparticles for murine triple-negative breast cancer treatment. Journal of Nanobiotechnology 2022;20(1):1–16.

[117] Paulmurugan R, Bhethanabotla R, Mishra K, Devulapally R, Foygel K, Sekar TV, et al. Folate receptor−targeted polymeric micellar nanocarriers for delivery of orlistat as a repurposed drug against triple-negative breast cancer in vivo delivery of orlistat as cancer therapeutic. Molecular Cancer Therapeutics 2016;15(2):221–31.

[118] Necela BM, Crozier JA, Andorfer CA, Lewis-Tuffin L, Kachergus JM, Geiger XJ, et al. Folate receptor-α (FOLR1) expression and function in triple negative tumors. PLoS One 2015;10(3):e0122209.

[119] O'Shannessy DJ, Somers EB, Maltzman J, Smale R, Fu Y-S. Folate receptor alpha (FRA) expression in breast cancer: identification of a new molecular subtype and association with triple negative disease. Springerplus. 2012;1(1):1–9.

[120] Yamashita T, Masuda N, Saji S, Araki K, Ito Y, Takano T, et al. Trastuzumab, pertuzumab, and eribulin mesylate versus trastuzumab, pertuzumab, and a taxane as a first-line or second-line treatment for HER2-positive, locally advanced or metastatic breast cancer: study protocol for a randomized controlled, non-inferiority, phase III trial in Japan (JBCRG-M06/EMERALD). Trials 2020;21(1):1–9.

[121] Sakai A, de Sousa Mesquita AP, de Castro Levatti EV, Straus AH, Nader HB, Lopes CC, et al. Interaction of trastuzumab with biomembrane models at air-water interfaces mimicking cancer cell surfaces. Biochimica et Biophysica Acta (BBA)-Biomembranes 2019;1861(10):182992.

[122] Kenanova V, Olafsen T, Crow DM, Sundaresan G, Subbarayan M, Carter NH, et al. Tailoring the pharmacokinetics and positron emission tomography imaging properties of anti−carcinoembryonic antigen single-chain Fv-Fc antibody fragments. Cancer Research 2005;65(2):622–31.

[123] Béduneau A, Saulnier P, Hindré F, Clavreul A, Leroux J-C, Benoit J-P. Design of targeted lipid nanocapsules by conjugation of whole antibodies and antibody Fab' fragments. Biomaterials 2007;28(33):4978–90.

[124] Shimizu A, Sawada K, Kimura T. Pathophysiological role and potential therapeutic exploitation of exosomes in ovarian cancer. Cells 2020;9(4):814.

[125] Siegel RL, Miller KD, Jemal A. Cancer statistics, 2019. CA: A Cancer Journal for Clinicians 2019;69(1):7–34.

[126] Muñoz-Galván S, Carnero A. Targeting cancer stem cells to overcome therapy resistance in ovarian cancer. Cells 2020;9(6):1402.

[127] van Zyl B, Tang D, Bowden NA. Biomarkers of platinum resistance in ovarian cancer: what can we use to improve treatment. Endocrine-Related Cancer 2018;25(5):R303–18.

[128] Kuhar M, Imran S, Singh N. Curcumin and quercetin combined with cisplatin to induce apoptosis in human laryngeal carcinoma Hep-2 cells through the mitochondrial pathway. Journal of Molecular Cancer 2007;3(4):121–8.

[129] Chendil D, Ranga RS, Meigooni D, Sathishkumar S, Ahmed MM. Curcumin confers radiosensitizing effect in prostate cancer cell line PC-3. Oncogene 2004;23(8):1599–607.

[130] Chirnomas D, Taniguchi T, de la Vega M, Vaidya AP, Vasserman M, Hartman A-R, et al. Chemosensitization to cisplatin by inhibitors of the Fanconi anemia/BRCA pathway. Molecular Cancer Therapeutics 2006;5(4):952−61.

[131] Hu Z, Ma D. The precision prevention and therapy of HPV-related cervical cancer: new concepts and clinical implications. Cancer Medicine 2018;7(10):5217−36.

[132] Shi Y, Li L, Hu Z, Li S, Wang S, Liu J, et al. A genome-wide association study identifies two new cervical cancer susceptibility loci at 4q12 and 17q12. Nature Genetics 2013;45(8):918−22.

[133] Marquina G, Manzano A, Casado A. Targeted agents in cervical cancer: beyond bevacizumab. Current Oncology Reports 2018;20(5):1−10.

[134] Beckmann HS, Möller HM, Wittmann V. High-affinity multivalent wheat germ agglutinin ligands by one-pot click reaction. Beilstein Journal of Organic Chemistry 2012;8(1):819−26.

[135] Li K, Pang L, Pan X, Fan S, Wang X, Wang Q, et al. GE11 modified PLGA/TPGS nanoparticles targeting delivery of salinomycin to breast cancer cells. Technology in Cancer Research & Treatment 2021;20 15330338211004954.

[136] Brand TM, Iida M, Luthar N, Starr MM, Huppert EJ, Wheeler DL. Nuclear EGFR as a molecular target in cancer. Radiotherapy and Oncology 2013;108(3):370−7.

[137] Rosellini M, Santoni M, Mollica V, Rizzo A, Cimadamore A, Scarpelli M, et al. Treating prostate cancer by antibody−drug conjugates. International Journal of Molecular Sciences 2021;22(4):1551.

[138] Ghafouri-Fard S, Tamizkar KH, Hussen BM, Taheri M. MicroRNA signature in liver cancer. Pathology-Research and Practice 2021;219:153369.

[139] Mohammadian M, Mahdavifar N, Mohammadian-Hafshejani A, Salehiniya H. Liver cancer in the world: epidemiology, incidence, mortality and risk factors. World Cancer Research Journal 2018;5(2).

[140] Bhatt A, Gurnany E, Modi A, Gulbake A, Jain A. Theranostic potential of targeted nanoparticles for brain cancer. Mini Reviews in Medicinal Chemistry 2017;17(18):1758−77.

[141] Zhao M, Liu Y, Ding G, Qu D, Qu H. Online database for brain cancer-implicated genes: exploring the subtype-specific mechanisms of brain cancer. BMC Genomics 2021;22(1):1−11.

[142] Tang W, Fan W, Lau J, Deng L, Shen Z, Chen X. Emerging blood−brain-barrier-crossing nanotechnology for brain cancer theranostics. Chemical Society Reviews 2019;48(11):2967−3014.

[143] Askarizadeh A, Barreto GE, Henney NC, Majeed M, Sahebkar A. Neuroprotection by curcumin: a review on brain delivery strategies. International Journal of Pharmaceutics 2020;585:119476.

[144] Zhao M, van Straten D, Broekman ML, Préat V, Schiffelers RM. Nanocarrier-based drug combination therapy for glioblastoma. Theranostics. 2020;10(3):1355.

[145] Xiao B, Ma L, Merlin D. Nanoparticle-mediated co-delivery of chemotherapeutic agent and siRNA for combination cancer therapy. Expert Opinion on Drug Delivery 2017;14(1):65−73.

[146] Aumeeruddy MZ, Mahomoodally MF. Combating breast cancer using combination therapy with 3 phytochemicals: piperine, sulforaphane, and thymoquinone. Cancer 2019;125(10):1600−11.

[147] Kyriakopoulou K, Kefali E, Piperigkou Z, Bassiony H, Karamanos NK. Advances in targeting epidermal growth factor receptor signaling pathway in mammary cancer. Cellular Signalling 2018;51:99−109.

[148] Memmi EM, Sanarico AG, Giacobbe A, Peschiaroli A, Frezza V, Cicalese A, et al. p63 Sustains self-renewal of mammary cancer stem cells through regulation of Sonic Hedgehog signaling. Proceedings of the National Academy of Sciences 2015;112(11):3499−504.

[149] Chen C-Y, Lin Y-S, Chen C-H, Chen Y-J. Annexin A2-mediated cancer progression and therapeutic resistance in nasopharyngeal carcinoma. Journal of Biomedical Science 2018;25(1):1−10.

[150] Chen C-Y, Lin Y-S, Chen C-L, Chao P-Z, Chiou J-F, Kuo C-C, et al. Targeting annexin A2 reduces tumorigenesis and therapeutic resistance of nasopharyngeal carcinoma. Oncotarget. 2015;6(29):26946.

[151] Lokman NA, Elder AS, Ween MP, Pyragius CE, Hoffmann P, Oehler MK, et al. Annexin A2 is regulated by ovarian cancer-peritoneal cell interactions and promotes metastasis. Oncotarget. 2013;4(8):1199.

[152] Zhai H, Acharya S, Gravanis I, Mehmood S, Seidman RJ, Shroyer KR, et al. Annexin A2 promotes glioma cell invasion and tumor progression. Journal of Neuroscience 2011;31(40):14346−60.

[153] Zhang H-J, Yao D-F, Yao M, Huang H, Wang L, Yan M-J, et al. Annexin A2 silencing inhibits invasion, migration, and tumorigenic potential of hepatoma cells. World Journal of Gastroenterology: WJG 2013;19(24):3792.

[154] Zheng L, Foley K, Huang L, Leubner A, Mo G, Olino K, et al. Tyrosine 23 phosphorylation-dependent cell-surface localization of annexin A2 is required for invasion and metastases of pancreatic cancer. PLoS One 2011;6(4):e19390.

[155] Sharma MR, Koltowski L, Ownbey RT, Tuszynski GP, Sharma MC. Angiogenesis-associated protein annexin II in breast cancer: selective expression in invasive breast cancer and contribution to tumor invasion and progression. Experimental and Molecular Pathology 2006;81(2):146−56.

[156] Yang D, Lei S, Pan K, Chen T, Lin J, Ni G, et al. Application of photodynamic therapy in immune-related diseases. Photodiagnosis and Photodynamic Therapy 2021;34:102318.

[157] Donohoe C, Senge MO, Arnaut LG, Gomes-da-Silva LC. Cell death in photodynamic therapy: from oxidative stress to anti-tumor immunity. Biochimica et Biophysica Acta (BBA)-Reviews on Cancer 2019;1872(2):188308.

[158] Abrahamse H, Hamblin MR. New photosensitizers for photodynamic therapy. Biochemical Journal 2016;473(4):347−64.

[159] Kwiatkowski S, Knap B, Przystupski D, Saczko J, Kędzierska E, Knap-Czop K, et al. Photodynamic therapy—mechanisms, photosensitizers and combinations. Biomedicine & pharmacotherapy 2018;106:1098−107.

[160] Huang L, Asghar S, Zhu T, Ye P, Hu Z, Chen Z, et al. Advances in chlorin-based photodynamic therapy with nanoparticle delivery system for cancer treatment. Expert Opinion on Drug Delivery 2021;18(10):1473−500.

[161] Kazantzis K, Koutsonikoli K, Mavroidi B, Zachariadis M, Alexiou P, Pelecanou M, et al. Curcumin derivatives as photosensitizers in photodynamic therapy: photophysical properties and in vitro studies with prostate cancer cells. Photochemical & Photobiological Sciences 2020;19(2):193−206.

[162] Dahl TA, McGowan WM, Shand MA, Srinivasan VS. Photokilling of bacteria by the natural dye curcumin. Archives of Microbiology 1989;151(2):183−5.

[163] Sreedhar A, Sarkar I, Rajan P, Pai J, Malagi S, Kamath V, et al. Comparative evaluation of the efficacy of curcumin gel with and without photo activation as an adjunct to scaling and root planing in the treatment of chronic periodontitis: a split mouth clinical and microbiological study. Journal of Natural Science, Biology, and Medicine 2015;6(Suppl 1):S102.

[164] Priyadarsini KI. Photophysics, photochemistry and photobiology of curcumin: studies from organic solutions, bio-mimetics and living cells. Journal of Photochemistry and Photobiology C: Photochemistry Reviews 2009;10(2):81−95.

[165] Haukvik T, Bruzell E, Kristensen S, Tønnesen H. Photokilling of bacteria by curcumin in selected polyethylene glycol 400 (PEG 400) preparations. Studies on curcumin and curcuminoids, XLI. Die Pharmazie-An. International Journal of Pharmaceutical Sciences 2010;65(8):600−6.

[166] Zhao S, Pi C, Ye Y, Zhao L, Wei Y. Recent advances of analogues of curcumin for treatment of cancer. European Journal of Medicinal Chemistry 2019;180:524−35.

[167] Pei H, Yang Y, Cui L, Yang J, Li X, Yang Y, et al. Bisdemethoxycurcumin inhibits ovarian cancer via reducing oxidative stress mediated MMPs expressions. Scientific reports 2016;6(1):1−8.

[168] Ramezani M, Hatamipour M, Sahebkar A. Promising anti-tumor properties of bisdemethoxycurcumin: a naturally occurring curcumin analogue. Journal of Cellular Physiology 2018;233(2):880−7.

[169] Sufi SA, Adigopula LN, Syed SB, Mukherjee V, Coumar MS, Rao HSP, et al. In-silico and in-vitro anti-cancer potential of a curcumin analogue (1E, 6E)-1, 7-di (1H-indol-3-yl) hepta-1, 6-diene-3, 5-dione. Biomedicine & Pharmacotherapy 2017;85:389−98.

13

Polymersomes-based curcumin delivery as cancer therapeutics

Karine C. Castro[1], Leandro R.S. Barbosa[2,3], Tamar L. Greaves[4], André M. Lopes[5]

[1]DEPARTMENT OF BIOPROCESS AND BIOTECHNOLOGY, SCHOOL OF AGRICULTURE, SAO PAULO STATE UNIVERSITY (UNESP), BOTUCATU, SÃO PAULO, BRAZIL [2]DEPARTMENT OF GENERAL PHYSICS, INSTITUTE OF PHYSICS, UNIVERSITY OF SÃO PAULO, SÃO PAULO, BRAZIL [3]BRAZILIAN SYNCHROTRON LIGHT LABORATORY (LNLS), BRAZILIAN CENTER FOR RESEARCH IN ENERGY AND MATERIALS (CNPEM), CAMPINAS, SÃO PAULO, BRAZIL [4]STEM COLLEGE, RMIT UNIVERSITY, MELBOURNE, VIC, AUSTRALIA [5]DEPARTMENT OF BIOTECHNOLOGY, LORENA SCHOOL OF ENGINEERING, UNIVERSITY OF SÃO PAULO (EEL/USP), LORENA, SÃO PAULO, BRAZIL

List of abbreviations

ABC Amphiphilic block copolymers
AS Angiostatin
CUR Curcumin
DDS Drug delivery systems
DL Drug loading
DOX Doxorubicin
EE Encapsulation efficiency
GSH Glutathione
IC_{50} Half maximal inhibitory concentration
MDR Multidrug resistance effect
MTX Methotrexate
PDI Polydispersity
PEG Poly(ethylene glycol)
PLA Polylactide
PSs Polymersomes (*i.e.*, polymeric vesicles)

13.1 Introduction

Research and development of innovative nanometric materials has recently resulted in several advances that are impacting the way cancer is being treated. Among the numerous existing nanomaterials proposed for drug delivery, a significant number are based on amphi-philic block copolymers (ABC). Drug delivery systems (DDS) based on ABC are reported to increase the solubility of chemotherapeutic agents (or anticancer drugs), protecting them against hydrolysis, enzymatic degradation, and/or conjugation with biomolecules impairing their activity, among others. These can be aimed toward prolonging drug release and/or tar-geted delivery (*e.g.*, employing further intracellular release or cellular delivery mechanisms). An optimal nanoformulation should be capable of retaining the drug for the required period while releasing it in therapeutic concentrations at the required site [1,2].

The ABC can self-assemble in solution into core-shell architectures with distinct size and shape. One of the forms that can be acquired in solution is vesicular, often referred to as polymeric vesicles. The first mention of the term "polymeric vesicles" happened a little over two decades ago by Discher et al. [3], and they are also known as polymersomes (PSs), which is the term the authors use in this chapter. PSs are analogous to liposomes, and composed of ABC comprising of covalently connected homopolymer blocks (Fig. 13–1A) [4–6].

Different preparation techniques combined with the diversity of copolymers can lead to the formation of PSs with sizes ranging from nm to μm, with relative particle size dis-tributions [4,7]. In particular, several procedures have been used to fabricate PSs, includ-ing hydration of a thin copolymer film, solvent switch, microfluidic platform, nanoprecipitation, centrifugation, and phase inversion [7–10]. In contrast, film rehydra-tion and solvent exchange methods are more effective for obtaining nanometer-sized PSs, which need additional processes to obtain nanoformulations with narrow-size distri-butions, and in this case, the main processes employed are sonication, filtration, centrifu-gation, or extrusion [7,10,11].

PSs are spherical nanostructures consisting of bilayer membranes, where the structure of bilayer is composed of hydrophilic polymers on the inner and outer regions, with hydropho-bic polymers incorporated between them [4,7,12]. In general, the hydrophilic (polar) parts have favorable contact with water molecules while the opposite occurs for the hydrophobic (apolar) parts. The balance of these interactions favors the formation of self-assembled struc-tures of higher order, which are maintained by intermolecular or noncovalent interactions, with their structure controlled by the polar/apolar molar ratio. A basic way to understand the geometry of PSs is through the calculation of the critical packing parameter (or shape factor), p, which is given in Eq. (13–1) [13]:

$$p = \frac{v}{al} \qquad (13-1)$$

where v, l, and a represent the volume and length of the extended hydrophobic block and the optimum surface area per molecule of the headgroups. As a general rule, spherical micelles (high curvature) are generated when $p < 1/3$, cylindrical micelles are formed when $1/3 \leq p < 1/2$, and PSs for copolymers when $1/2 \leq p < 1$. For the later, the repulsive contact between the aqueous medium and the hydrophobic parts cause the membranes to fold into closed structures to minimize surface energy, giving rise to these vesicles [7,13].

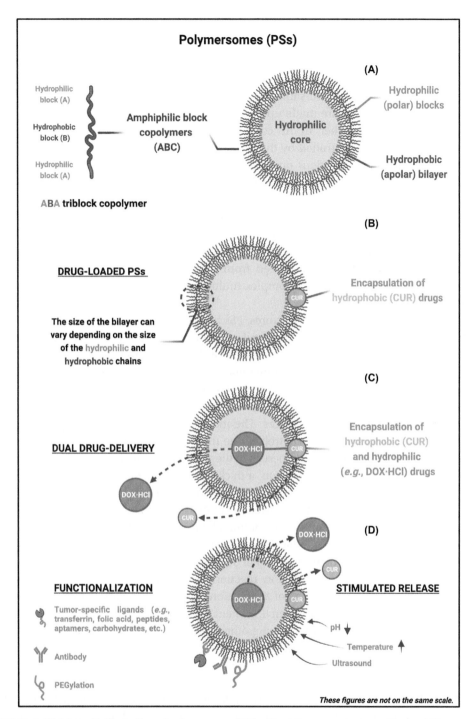

FIGURE 13–1 **(A)** Schematic illustration of polymersomes (PSs) with a bilayer membrane and hydrophilic core composed of amphiphilic block copolymers (ABC), in this case, represented by ABA triblock copolymers. **(B)** Curcumin (CUR) encapsulation can be individually loaded in the bilayer membrane and/or **(C)** additional drugs (e.g., DOX hydrochloride [DOX · HCl]) can be coencapsulated into hydrophilic core, for dual-controlled release purposes. **(D)** Functionalization can be used to increase the selectivity toward the target tissue (tumor cells), improve the effectiveness, and reduce adverse effects, and stimulated release approaches can be used to control the release of the drugs (e.g., reducing the pH and raising the temperature). Figure developed based on D'Angelo et al. [2].

As mentioned earlier, amphiphilic molecules can have a broad range of structures, and among the existing classes, the versatile structure of copolymers are of interest for the design of vesicles. These structures are made up of blocks in sequence, random, or grafted between one monomer type and another. In this context, ABC are highly useful, as the final structures can be finely adjusted or controlled by the synthesis technique [14]. For ABC, the final packing parameter is highly dependent on the ratio of the hydrophilic/hydrophobic blocks, as mentioned earlier. For example, some experimental studies emphasized that a poly(ethylene oxide) (PEO) (also known as PEG)-based system can form spherical micelles with a PEG volume fraction (f) > 50%, cylindrical micelles (40% < f < 50%), and vesicles (25% < f < 40%) [3,7,15]. PSs can be fabricated not only from AB-type diblock copolymer molecules (*i.e.*, A and B refer to hydrophilic and hydrophobic blocks, respectively) producing a bilayer-like structure but they can also be assembled from diblock or triblock (ABA) copolymers (as shown in Fig. 13−1A) or even more complex multiblock copolymers, which can be linear or grafted structures [4,16−18].

Compared to other existing nanostructures, PSs have some interesting advantages. For example, PSs can encapsulate hydrophilic molecules (including biomolecules such as proteins or enzymes) in their core and hydrophobic molecules within the membrane (*i.e.*, bilayer), whereas micelles encapsulate only hydrophobic compounds [5,19,20]. Despite the structural similarity to liposomes, PSs have many properties that make them more attractive, such as greater tenacity and flexibility in terms of chemical manipulation, less permeability to water, and robustness, which allow tolerance for greater pressures. The molecular weight of the hydrophobic block in the PSs is primarily responsible for controlling the thickness of the bilayer. For this reason, the thickness determines the important properties of these nanostructures, such as elasticity, permeability, and mechanical stability. In addition, a thicker membrane makes PSs more resistant and stable than liposomes, and the fact that the ABC are formed by different chain lengths provide them with tailorable physicochemical diversity [3,19,21,22]. For more comparative aspects between PSs and liposomes, the authors recommend the excellent following works [23,24].

Another outstanding feature is that PSs are also highly versatile due to their ability to be manipulated with high sensitivity by external stimuli such as pH, magnetic fields, temperature, radiation, and oxidation−reduction reactions [25]. This response to external stimuli leads to PSs having a very wide range of applications, especially in cancer therapy. This strategy is interesting because the tumor environment has unique characteristics such as enzymatic activity, pH, and temperature, among others, which can act as a trigger (*i.e.*, stimulus) for sustained and controlled release of a chemotherapeutic agent at the target region. Specifically, antigens or receptors that are overexpressed distinguish tumor cells from normal (or healthy) cells and favor the interaction of conjugated or functionalized platforms (PSs) with affinity ligands of tumor cells. For example, it is known that tumor cells are able to adapt to an environment with a lower concentration of oxygen and nutrients and that tumor cells are present in a more acidic environment (reaching pH values between 4.0 and 6.0) and with temperatures higher than physiological ones (between 40°C and 44°C). Therefore, PSs have immense potential to be employed using responsive approaches (*e.g.*, pH- and temperature-responsiveness) [26−31].

13.2 Polymersomes as nanoformulations for curcumin delivery

Curcumin (CUR), a bioactive drug with significant potential, is among the candidate drugs for cancer therapy. CUR is a bioactive compound present in the tuberous root of turmeric (*Curcuma longa* Linn.). This powerful polyphenol has been the subject of a vast number of studies due to its antioxidant and antiinflammatory characteristics, in addition to its action as an antitumor, antibacterial, antiviral, and antifungal agent [1]. The chemotherapeutic effect of CUR is closely linked to its antiinflammatory response, that is, its ability to act on cellular chemical pathways reducing inflammation; in addition, CUR can inhibit the production of free radicals, protecting cells from oxidative stress. This enables it to potentially prevent the formation of a variety of diseases. It has been reported that CUR can also inhibit tumor necrosis factor-α (TNF-α) and interleukin 1 (IL-1), IL-6, IL-8, and IL-12 production. On the other hand, the administration or feeding of CUR is hampered due to some challenges, such as its low solubility in an aqueous environment, and chemical instability, which results in rapid metabolism, photochemical degradation, and low bioavailability [1,32].

The encapsulation of CUR in PSs is an excellent approach to enhance the activity of CUR as a chemotherapeutic agent (Fig. 13−1B), this not only increases the CUR solubility in the bloodstream, facilitates its absorption by the body, but also preserves it from degradation. Another advantageous feature is that PSs can provide high capacity to encapsulate CUR, and since chemotherapeutic agents usually have a hydrophobic fraction, it is worth noting that thicker membranes exhibit better trapping efficiency for hydrophobic drugs [4,21].

In this sense, several works have been developed using PSs to encapsulate CUR. For example, Pakizehkar et al. [33] proposed poly(ethylene glycol)$_{400}$-oleate-based PSs for CUR encapsulation. In that study a mean vesicle size of 259.5 nm was obtained, polydispersity (PDI) of 0.465, and ζ potential of −8.74 mV, while the encapsulation parameters (*i.e.*, drug loading [DL] and encapsulation efficiency [EE]) were 16.08% and 97.18%, respectively. The results showed that PSs with a half maximal inhibitory concentration ($IC_{50} = 14$ µg/mL) raised apoptosis and induced S-phase arrest in the treatment of human colorectal adenocarcinoma (HT29) cells. In addition, the flow cytometry assay demonstrated a reduction in cancer stemness markers [33].

Cao et al. [34] synthesized PSs based on poly(1-*O*-methacryloyl-β-D-fructopyranose)-*b*-poly (methyl methacrylate) for CUR encapsulation. Microscopy studies showed that the presence of CUR can induce morphological changes in the type of nanostructure, from cylindrical micelles (without CUR) to PSs. The results showed that CUR-loaded PSs size could be influenced by the CUR concentration. The vesicle size reduced from 272 to 263 nm when the concentration of the drug increased from 0.37 to 0.75 mg/mL, and similarly the PDI changed from 0.118 to 0.124 and the ζ potential from −22.6 to −19.5 mV. Regarding CUR encapsulation, EE and DL changed from 36.5% to 20.8% and 6.8% to 7.8%, respectively. The authors pointed out a change in the morphology of the structures as a function of the CUR concentration, which results in a variation/transition from cylindrical micelles to PSs. The IC_{50} values varied from 15.2 to 148.3 µM, when the CUR concentration increased from 0.0061 to 0.0374 mg/mL. Both the shape of the nanoformulation and the hydration of the shell were influenced by the presence of CUR. For example, by raising the CUR concentration, dehydration of the nanostructure shell was observed, corresponding with a lower nanostructure uptake by noncancerous RAW 264.7 and human breast cancer (MCF-7) cells. Thus, these groups demonstrated that CUR can affect the profile of the nanoformulation in regard to shape and shell hydration, and most importantly that these influence the biological performance [34].

In another interesting work, Erfani-Moghadam et al. [35] proposed nanoformulations containing micelles and PSs based on monomethoxy poly(ethylene glycol)-oleate (mPEG-OA) for CUR encapsulation applied to brain carcinoma (U87MG) cells. The average size of the micelles and PSs was 18.33 and 99.40 nm, with ζ potential of -32.6 mV. The results exhibited a monodispersity characteristic of mPEG-OA nanoformulations when stored for 7 days at room temperatures (average PDI of 0.182 with 100% of PSs having an average size of 100 nm). Regarding encapsulation, *EE* and *DL* were determined at 87.1% and 5.22%, respectively. *In vitro* cytotoxicity against U87MG cells showed an IC_{50} of 48 μM for free CUR solution, whereas IC_{50} values for CUR-loaded mPEG-OA at 24 h and 48 h after treatment were reduced to 24 and 15.5 μM, respectively. Also, the empty mPEG-OA nanoformulation did not present significant toxicity, even at a nanoformulation concentration of 50 μM. Further studies should be applied to evaluate the profile of the mPEG-OA nanoformulation in terms of *in vivo* improvement of the CUR efficacy. On the other hand, these groups concluded that the mPEG-OA nanoformulations can be considered as a safe nanoformulation for the delivery of CUR and other hydrophobic molecules [35].

Damera et al. [31] prepared PSs based on Pluronics F127 and F108 for CUR delivery. The PSs were conjugated (or functionalized) with a specific ligand for tumor cells (phenylboronic acid [PBA]) to evaluate the conjugation in the membrane fluidity, characterizing the samples using the technique of fluorescence recovery after photobleaching. The average size of the PSs was between 10 and 50 μm, and the *EE* values for the nanoformulations consisting of F108-PBA and F127-PBA PSs were 53% and 82%, respectively. A possible explanation for the difference observed in the *EE* values of PSs fabricated with the different copolymers is their different numbers of hydrophobic (PPO) blocks [*i.e.*, 65 units for F127 (PEO_{100}-PPO_{65}-PEO_{100}) *vs* 50 units for F018 (PEO_{133}-PPO_{50}-PEO_{133})], which directly impacts the PSs bilayer size. Free CUR evaluated at pH 5.0 and 7.0 showed fast release without considerable differences in regard to pH, and after 12 h around 100% of CUR was released. In contrast, for the F127-PBA PSs, after 40 h the release was 73% and 50% at pH 5.0 and 7.0, respectively, while for the F108-PBA PSs, the release profiles at pH 5.0 and 7.0 were 55% and 47%, respectively. The authors noted that PSs can be used as an alternative DDS for targeted release of chemotherapeutic agent (CUR) when triggered by acid conditions present in tumor cells [31].

13.3 Polymersomes for dual-drug delivery using responsiveness or surface functionalization

Here, we describe the possibility of PSs codelivering CUR in conjunction with other drugs applied to cancer therapy (Fig. 13–1C). The versatility of coencapsulating two or more types of drugs is an interesting strategy for cancer therapy, as it is often necessary to simultaneously deliver several drugs that work synergistically, mainly to avoid the multidrug resistance (MDR) effect. Particularly, this effect is related to the fact that tumor cells can become resistant to the chemotherapeutic agents administered, which can make treatment unfeasible. This effect is complex and involves several mechanisms, such as changes in the drug target region, augmented drug efflux, as well as decreased drug uptake. For this reason, the nanoencapsulation of two or more drugs can prevent this effect or even reverse the P-gp efflux process from tumor cells, restoring the action of the chemotherapeutic agents during the therapy [10,36,37]. On the other hand, the encapsulation and delivery of drugs with different chemical properties by a single nanostructure is still challenging because nanoformulations can be detrimentally affected by *DL*. Hydrophobic chemotherapeutic agents, which are the vast majority, still have problems of low bioavailability, low half-life in the bloodstream, as well as fast elimination from the body [10,38]. All these considerations can be overcome when PSs are employed, and some works have demonstrated the success of these nanoformulations, which will be outlined in this section.

For example, Curcio et al. [39] fabricated PSs composed of carboxyl-terminated PEG, which were trialed for the dual-drug delivery of CUR and methotrexate (MTX). The pH-responsive PSs nanoformulation had an average size of 70 nm and a PDI of less than 0.300. The drug encapsulation showed high *EE* values: 93% and 91% for MTX and CUR, respectively. For MTX-encapsulated PSs, a slow release at pH 7.4 was observed with a maximum value of relative release (M_{max}) of 0.44, whereas incubation at acid conditions (pH 5.0) stimulated/triggered a considerable raise in MTX release (M_{max} of 0.91). For CUR, lower kinetic parameters of release were obtained (M_{max} of 0.46 and 0.57 at pH 7.4 and 5.0, respectively), possibly because there were greater interactions of the hydrophobic drug with the polymeric compartments (*i.e.*, bilayer region), these drug interaction-nanoformulation, caused the release behavior for CUR to be less affected by pH fluctuations. The authors demonstrated that the drug-encapsulated PSs exhibited improved cytotoxic potential against breast cancer (MCF-7) cells and were considered to be quite hemocompatible. Moreover, pH-responsive PSs can be a smart and efficient platform for combinatorial (dual-drug delivery) and targeted chemotherapy [39].

Cao et al. [40] studied poly(ethylene glycol)-*b*-poly(ε-caprolactone)-based PSs (PEG-PCL-PSs) to coencapsulate CUR and angiostatin (AS), where the PSs were 153 nm in size and had a neutral ζ potential (-0.22 mV). The *DL* and *EE* values were 4.37% and 48.1% for CUR and 5.7% and 62.7% for AS, respectively. For AS encapsulation, *EE* values were higher than CUR, and this performance can be related to the large aqueous core in the PSs. A sustained release of coencapsulated AS and CUR from PEG-PCL-PSs nanoformulation at pH 7.4 (*i.e.*, physiological conditions) could be observed. For example, the AS and CUR release was 50.7% and 59.8% at 24 h, respectively, followed by a slow and steady release. The amount of CUR and AS released was about 67.9% and 62.4% at the end of the test (72 h), respectively. *In vitro* assays with endothelial (HMEC-1) cells showed that the AS-CUR-PSs nanoformulation increased the inhibition of endothelial cell proliferation. The study of angiogenesis inhibition by the chick chorioallantoic membrane assay showed inhibition and formation of branches and new blood vessels reaching 76.1% with AS-CUR-PSs nanoformulation, compared to 46.1% (AS-PSs) and 56.3% (CUR-PSs). The anti-angiogenic potential of the AS-CUR-PSs indicates its ability to inhibit the formation of new blood capillaries. Dual-delivery of AS and CUR by PSs is a potential approach for the synergistic improvement of antitumor activity, and therefore could show immense potential in the near future in this field [40].

Cui et al. [41] synthesized PSs composed of benzimidazole ended PEG-PCL and chitosan-graft-β-cyclodextrin for the codelivery of CUR and DOX applied to human cervical cancer cells (HeLa). The vesicle size was 100 nm and the ζ potential was $+18.2$ mV. The encapsulation parameters of DL and EE were 20.2% and 42.2% for CUR and 38.4% and 88.4% for DOX, respectively. The authors pointed out that the sustained drug release was pH and temperature dependent. The DOX release was 47.2% into the surroundings at pH 7.2, and approximately 100% of DOX was released while at pH 5.2, while for CUR the release was 36.5% and 76.3% at pH 7.2 and 5.2, respectively. Regarding temperature, DOX release was 56.5% at 25°C, which increased to 89.6% when the temperature was raised to 40°C. Similarly, the release of CUR was 32.5% and 66.8% at 25°C and 40°C, respectively. Cytotoxicity assays performed with HeLa cells revealed that PSs displayed reasonable biocompatibility, and coencapsulated drugs in PSs showed good efficacy in cellular inhibition, around 76.5% at the highest dose of the drug (200 μg/mL), while for free CUR + DOX blend, the cellular inhibition was observed to be 71.5% (for the highest dose administered). Decreasing the pH to acidic conditions, or increasing the temperature, led to rapid and controllable release of both drugs, and thus these PSs can be employed in the area of smart DDS for dual-drug delivery in cancer therapy [41].

Another important strategy, as mentioned earlier, is that PSs can be functionalized/conjugated/decorated with specific ligands (i.e., proteins, peptides, enzymes, monoclonal antibodies, antibody fragments, small organic molecules, carbohydrates, and aptamers) on their surface, which are used to bind to specific receptors of cancer cells (as highlighted in Fig. 13–1D), improving the targeting and cellular absorption of the chemotherapeutic agents [42]. PSs functionalized on the surface with cell-specific targeting ligands obtained the loading capacity of polymeric hydrophilic and hydrophobic regions, robustness of the PSs, combined with the possibility of using, for example, antibodies that have high site-specific affinity [43,44]. For instance, PSs decorated with the trastuzumab antibody loaded with maghemite nanoparticles have already been used, particularly for breast tumors, aiming to design a new magnetic resonance image contrast agent [45]. Other examples, like targeting peptides (e.g., RGD, GE11, NLS, ApoE, Tet-1, among others) and pH-sensitive fusogenic have been designed primarily to deliver smart PSs to specific cells or organelles and/or to improve its penetration into the tumor applied to diagnostic or therapeutic approaches [46–49]. The decoration of PSs with aptamer AS1411 (i.e., a 26-mer DNA aptamer) on their surface is another interesting example, which may be useful for targeting applications. This aptamer binds specifically to nucleolin, and certain types of cancer overexpress this compound on the surface of the tumor cell (such as breast cancer cells), which may considerably enhance endocytosis in this cell type [43–52]. Some of these approaches are already being used, and many related ones can be employed in the near future, for dual-delivery of CUR and other chemotherapeutic agents from DDS-based PSs.

In this way, Anajafi et al. [53] developed a nuclear-localized matrix metalloproteinase-7 (MMP-7) isozyme, of redox-sensitive PSs, conjugating the vesicles to a protected nuclear localization peptide (i.e., simian virus 40 [SV40] T-antigen derived peptide). The PSs were based on PEG-PLA for the encapsulation of captisol-CUR (i.e., CUR complexed with sulfobutyl-β-cyclodextrin) and doxorubicin (DOX). The mean diameter of the PSs was 143 nm with a PDI of 0.200. The ζ potential was measured before and after peptide conjugation and was found to be -13.8 and -16.6 mV, respectively. The *EE* of captisol-CUR and DOX was 47% and 56%, respectively. The authors studied the release process separately and the assays were performed in the presence of the enzyme MMP-7 and glutathione (GSH) at concentrations of 50 μM, 10 mM, and 50 mM. The captisol-CUR showed no significant release subsequent to 50 μM and 10 mM GSH treatment. Nevertheless, the addition of 50 mM GSH triggered a 45% release of captisol-CUR. The same occurred with the release of DOX, the PSs released around 94% with 50 mM GSH. The *in vitro* cytotoxicity assays were performed against pancreatic cancer (BxPC-3) cells (that overexpress the enzyme MMP-7) and normal (bEnd-3) cells. It was found from these assays that combining the two drugs encapsulated into PSs containing the SV40 peptide on their surface considerably reduced the cell viability of BxPC-3 cells (65%), and for comparison the normal cell viability was 88%. In contrast, when the two drugs were encapsulated into PSs without the peptide, the nanoformulations showed low toxicity to BxPC-3 cells (cell viability of 87%) and high toxicity to normal cells (cell viability of 67%). Therefore, smart DDS may be better and more effective when compared to current trigger-release nanoformulations for several tumors, mainly pancreatic cancer [53].

Some polymers/copolymers or other amphiphilic molecules employed in the fabrication of PSs are also responsible for their overall responsiveness to external stimuli (Fig. 13.1D), which facilitates targeted drug delivery, making them smart and highly accurate nanoformulations to attack tumor cells. In this context, Sarkar et al. [54] synthesized amphiphile-containing naphthalimide-containing azo-based self-assembled (NI-Azo) PSs, where the azo moiety acted as the stimulus-responsive junction, loaded with CUR. The average diameter of the PSs and *DL* were 300 nm and 49%, respectively. CUR-loaded NI-Azo PSs killed melanoma cancer (B16F10) cells via the early apoptotic pathway in a $CoCl_2$-induced hypoxic environment, with 2.4-fold greater efficiency than free CUR. The efficiency of cancer cell killing by CUR-loaded NI-Azo PSs was 1.9- and 4.5-fold higher compared to NIH 3T3 cells (mouse embryonic fibroblasts) in hypoxic and normoxic environments, respectively [54].

A thermoresponsive biodegradable hydrogel based on poly(ε-caprolactone-*co*-lactide)-*b*-poly (ethylene glycol)-*b*-poly(ε-caprolactone-*co*-lactide) containing mPEG-*b*-PLA PSs loaded with CUR was developed by Babaei et al. [55] for glioma tumor cells (C6) application. The PSs had an average diameter of 188.6 nm, low PDI of 0.100, and ζ potential of -15 mV, with *EE* value of 68.6%. *In vitro* release studies of hydrogel-PSs-CUR and PSs-CUR suggested a higher release rate —these nanoformulations displayed an initial burst release of approximately 14.5% and 24.5% for hydrogel-PSs-CUR and PSs-CUR in the first 5 h, respectively. After 10 days, the PSs-CUR sample released 66.7%, while the hydrogel-PSs-CUR sample only released 39%. *In vivo* studies in mice were based on changes in ectopic glioma tumor (C6) size over 15 days. After 15 days, the size of the tumor was evaluated, and the results showed that saline, hydrogel-CUR, and blank hydrogel increased the tumor volume 20-, 12.1-, and 12.4-fold compared to the first day, respectively. On the other hand, hydrogel-PSs-CUR nanoformulation suppressed tumor growth, and the tumor volume only exhibited around fourfold increase compared to the original tumor size. The results showed that the developed platform (hydrogel-PSs-CUR) is an interesting strategy to sustain the therapeutic effect of CUR at the target site [55].

PSs based on poly(ethylene glycol)$_{40}$-stearate and keratin for encapsulation of CUR and MTX were developed with redox-responsive properties by Curcio et al. [56]. The mean diameter and PDI were 134 nm and 0.250, with *EE* values of 80% and 85% for MTX and CUR, respectively. Results showed that PSs when stored in a medium comprising a GSH concentration mimetic to that of the intracellular environment had pronounced responsiveness and actionable drug release profiles. *In vitro* studies performed with human cervical cancer (HeLa) cells established the cytotoxic efficacy of the PSs, indicating that they are promising as nanoformulations for chemotherapeutic agents [56].

The main relevant studies describing the composition, production method, strategy or approach used, and the type of tumor cell evaluated regarding to CUR-loaded PSs applied for cancer therapy are summarized in Table 13−1.

Table 13–1 Key studies employed with curcumin (CUR)-loaded polymersomes (PSs) applied to cancer therapy.

PSs composition	Production method	Chemotherapeutic agent encapsulated	Stimulus-responsive PSs	Evaluated cell type	References
PEG$_{400}$-OA	Solvent evaporation/ water (or buffer) addition	CUR	NA	Colorectal adenocarcinoma (HT29) cells	[33]
Poly(1-*O*-MAFru)$_{36}$-*b*-PMMA$_{192}$	Solvent solubilization/ water (or buffer) addition	CUR	NA	Breast cancer (MCF-7) cells	[34]
mPEG-OA	Solvent evaporation/ water (or buffer) addition	CUR	NA	Glioblastoma tumor (U87MG) cells	[35]
NI-Azo	Solvent solubilization/ water (or buffer) addition	CUR	Hypoxia-responsive	Melanoma tumor (B16F10) cells	[54]
mPEG-PLA	Nanoprecipitation	CUR	Thermoresponsive	Glioma tumor (C6) cells	[55]
F127, F108, and PBA	Thin-layer evaporation method	CUR	pH-responsive	NA	[31]
Dual-drug release approach					
Carboxyl-terminated PEG	Solvent evaporation/ water (or buffer) addition	CUR and MTX	pH-responsive	Breast cancer (MCF-10A and MCF-7) cells	[39]
PEG-PCL		CUR and AS	NA	Endothelial (HMEC-1) cells	[40]
PEG-PLA-SV40	Solvent exchange	Captisol-CUR and DOX	Nuclear localizing peptide-conjugated and redox-sensitive	Pancreatic cancer (BxPC-3) cells	[53]
Ker-*g*-PEG$_{40}$ST	Solvent evaporation/ water (or buffer) addition	CUR and MTX	Redox-responsive	Cervical cancer (HeLa) cells	[56]
CS-*g*-CD-PEG-*b*-PCL-BM	Host−guest interactions	CUR and DOX	Thermo- and pH-responsive		[41]

AS, angiostatin; CS-*g*-CD-PEG-*b*-PCL-BM, chitosan-graft-β-cyclodextrin and benzimidazole ended poly(ethylene glycol)-*b*-poly(ε-caprolactone); DOX, doxorubicin; F127, PEO$_{100}$-PPO$_{65}$-PEO$_{100}$; F108, PEO$_{133}$-PPO$_{50}$-PEO$_{133}$; Ker-*g*-PEG$_{40}$ST, keratin grafted with polyethylene glycol$_{40}$ stearate; mPEG-OA, monomethoxy poly(ethylene glycol)-oleate; mPEG-PLA, polyethylene glycol-*b*-polylactide; MTX, methotrexate; NA, not applicable; NI-Azo, naphthalimide-based azo moiety containing amphiphile; PBA, phenylboronic acid; PEG, poly(ethylene glycol); PEG$_{400}$-OA, Polyethylene glycol $_{400}$-oleate; PEG-PCL, poly(ethylene glycol)-*b*-poly(ε-caprolactone); PEG-PLA-SV40, poly(ethylene glycol)-*b*-poly(lactic acid)-simian virus 40 T-antigen derived peptide; Poly(1-*O*-MAFru)$_{36}$-*b*-PMMA$_{192}$, poly(1-*O*-methacryloyl-β-D-fructopyranose)$_{36}$-*b*-poly(methyl methacrylate)$_{192}$.

13.4 Final considerations

Cancer remains one of the deadliest disorders, and effective treatments are still needed. In this sense, several chemotherapeutic agents show improved therapeutic outcomes against cancer when loaded into DDS, in contrast to their free counterparts. In particular, PSs are multipurpose nanostructures with an aptitude toward incorporating wide-ranging hydrophobic and hydrophilic drugs and have been established as efficient DDS over the last 20 years [2,57]. In this chapter, although there are still only preliminary results with the encapsulation of CUR (and dual-drug delivery of other drugs) into PSs, the results demonstrate the real impact and the immense potential that these platforms present for the treatment of cancer. In fact, there is still much to be done in this field, especially with respect to the development of PSs responsive to external stimuli, in addition to understanding their mechanisms of action *in vivo*, as an important path to reducing side effects in cancer therapies. Deepening research on poorly studied PSs can be a promising path not only for the discovery of new properties but also for consolidating the approach of these DDS *in vivo*. The use of PSs will potentially increase in the near future, mainly for their cargo capacity (*i.e.*, codelivery drugs), fabrication of new polymers/copolymers with responsive approaches, as well as novel targeting ligands functionalization to improve targeted and controlled drug delivery.

Acknowledgments

This study was funded by the State of São Paulo Research Foundation (FAPESP/Brazil, processes #2020/03727−2, #2019/08549−8, #2018/10799−0, and #2017/10789−1), National Council for Scientific and Technological Development (CNPq/Brazil), and Coordination for Higher Level Graduate Improvements (CAPES/Brazil, finance code 001). The Fig. 13−1 was created with BioRender.

References

[1] D'Angelo NA, Noronha MA, Kurnik IS, Câmara MCC, Vieira JM, Abrunhosa L, et al. Curcumin encapsulation in nanostructures for cancer therapy: a 10-year overview. International Journal of Pharmaceutics 2021;604. Available from: https://doi.org/10.1016/j.ijpharm.2021.120534.

[2] D'Angelo NA, Noronha MA, Câmara MCC, Kurnik IS, Feng C, Araujo VHS, et al. Doxorubicin nanoformulations on therapy against cancer: an overview from the last 10 years. Biomaterials Advances 2022;133:112623. Available from: https://doi.org/10.1016/J.MSEC.2021.112623.

[3] Discher BM, Won Y-Y, Ege DS, Lee JC-M, Bates FS, Discher DE, et al. Polymersomes: tough vesicles made from diblock copolymers. Science (New York, N.Y.) 1979;284(1999):1143−6. Available from: https://doi.org/10.1126/science.284.5417.1143.

[4] Meerovich I, Dash AK. Polymersomes for drug delivery and other biomedical applications. Materials for Biomedical Engineering 2019;269−309. Available from: https://doi.org/10.1016/B978-0-12-818433-2.00008-X.

[5] Pachioni-Vasconcelos JA, Lopes AM, Apolinário AC, Valenzuela-Oses JK, Costa JSR, Nascimento LO, et al. Nanostructures for protein drug delivery. Biomaterials Science 2016;4:205−18. Available from: https://doi.org/10.1039/C5BM00360A.

[6] Müller LK, Landfester K. Natural liposomes and synthetic polymeric structures for biomedical applications. Biochemical and Biophysical Research Communications 2015;468:411−18. Available from: https://doi.org/10.1016/J.BBRC.2015.08.088.

[7] Guan L, Rizzello L, Battaglia G. Polymersomes and their applications in cancer delivery and therapy. Nanomedicine: Nanotechnology, Biology, and Medicine 2015;10:2757−80. Available from: https://doi.org/10.2217/nnm.15.110.

[8] Battaglia G, Ryan AJ. Pathways of polymeric vesicle formation. The Journal of Physical Chemistry. B 2006;110:10272−9. Available from: https://doi.org/10.1021/jp060728n.

[9] Lefley J, Waldron C, Becer CR. Macromolecular design and preparation of polymersomes. Polymer Chemistry 2020;11:7124−36. Available from: https://doi.org/10.1039/D0PY01247E.

[10] D'Angelo NA, Câmara MCC, Noronha MA, Grotto D, Chorilli M, Lourenço FR, et al. Development of PEG-PCL-based polymersomes through design of experiments for co-encapsulation of vemurafenib and doxorubicin as chemotherapeutic drugs. Journal of Molecular Liquids 2022;349:118166. Available from: https://doi.org/10.1016/J.MOLLIQ.2021.118166.

[11] Marguet M, Bonduelle C, Lecommandoux S. Multicompartmentalized polymeric systems: towards biomimetic cellular structure and function. Chemical Society Reviews 2013;42:512−29. Available from: https://doi.org/10.1039/c2cs35312a.

[12] Misra C, Paul RK, Thotakura N, Raza K. Biodegradable self-assembled nanocarriers as the drug delivery vehicles. Nanoparticle Therapeutics 2022;293−325. Available from: https://doi.org/10.1016/B978-0-12-820757-4.00007-7.

[13] Israelachvili J. The science and applications of emulsions—an overview. Colloids and Surfaces. A, Physicochemical and Engineering Aspects 1994;91:1−8. Available from: https://doi.org/10.1016/0927-7757(94)02743-9.

[14] Smart T, Lomas H, Massignani M, Flores-Merino Mv, Perez LR, Battaglia G. Block copolymer nanostructures. Nano Today 2008;3:38−46. Available from: https://doi.org/10.1016/S1748-0132(08)70043-4.

[15] Christian DA, Cai S, Bowen DM, Kim Y, Pajerowski JD, Discher DE. Polymersome carriers: from self-assembly to siRNA and protein therapeutics. European Journal of Pharmaceutics and Biopharmaceutics 2009;71:463−74. Available from: https://doi.org/10.1016/J.EJPB.2008.09.025.

[16] Hasannia M, Aliabadi A, Abnous K, Taghdisi SM, Ramezani M, Alibolandi M. Synthesis of block copolymers used in polymersome fabrication: application in drug delivery. Journal of Controlled Release 2022;341:95−117. Available from: https://doi.org/10.1016/J.JCONREL.2021.11.010.

[17] Matyjaszewski K, Tsarevsky Nv. Nanostructured functional materials prepared by atom transfer radical polymerization. Nature Chemistry 2009;1:276−88. Available from: https://doi.org/10.1038/nchem.257.

[18] Adams ML, Lavasanifar A, Kwon GS. Amphiphilic block copolymers for drug delivery. Journal of Pharmaceutical Sciences 2003;92:1343−55. Available from: https://doi.org/10.1002/JPS.10397.

[19] Meng F, Zhong Z, Feijen J. Stimuli-responsive polymersomes for programmed drug delivery. Biomacromolecules 2009;10:197−209. Available from: https://doi.org/10.1021/bm801127d.

[20] Pachioni-Vasconcelos JA, Apolinário AC, Lopes AM, Pessoa A, Barbosa LRS, Rangel-Yagui CO. Compartmentalization of therapeutic proteins into semi-crystalline PEG-PCL polymersomes. Soft Matter 2021;19:222−30. Available from: https://doi.org/10.1080/1539445X.2020.1812643.

[21] Araste F, Aliabadi A, Abnous K, Taghdisi SM, Ramezani M, Alibolandi M. Self-assembled polymeric vesicles: focus on polymersomes in cancer treatment. Journal of Controlled Release 2021;330:502−28. Available from: https://doi.org/10.1016/j.jconrel.2020.12.027.

[22] Antonietti M, Förster S. Vesicles and liposomes: a self-assembly principle beyond lipids. Advanced Materials 2003;15:1323−33. Available from: https://doi.org/10.1002/adma.200300010.

[23] Kauscher U, Holme MN, Björnmalm M, Stevens MM. Physical stimuli-responsive vesicles in drug delivery: beyond liposomes and polymersomes. Advanced Drug Delivery Reviews 2019;138:259−75. Available from: https://doi.org/10.1016/J.ADDR.2018.10.012.

[24] Rideau E, Dimova R, Schwille P, Wurm FR, Landfester K. Liposomes and polymersomes: a comparative review towards cell mimicking. Chemical Society Reviews 2018;47:8572−610. Available from: https://doi.org/10.1039/C8CS00162F.

[25] Khan MI, Hossain MI, Hossain MK, Rubel MHK, Hossain KM, Mahfuz AMUB, et al. Recent progress in nanostructured smart drug delivery systems for cancer therapy: a review. ACS Applied Bio Materials 2022;5:971−1012. Available from: https://doi.org/10.1021/acsabm.2c00002.

[26] Emami Nejad A, Najafgholian S, Rostami A, Sistani A, Shojaeifar S, Esparvarinha M, et al. The role of hypoxia in the tumor microenvironment and development of cancer stem cell: a novel approach to developing treatment. Cancer Cell International 2021;21. Available from: https://doi.org/10.1186/s12935-020-01719-5.

[27] Jing X, Yang F, Shao C, Wei K, Xie M, Shen H, et al. Role of hypoxia in cancer therapy by regulating the tumor microenvironment. Molecular Cancer 2019;18. Available from: https://doi.org/10.1186/s12943-019-1089-9.

[28] Gao C, Tang F, Gong G, Zhang J, Hoi MPM, Lee SMY, et al. PH-Responsive prodrug nanoparticles based on a sodium alginate derivative for selective co-release of doxorubicin and curcumin into tumor cells. Nanoscale 2017;9:12533−42. Available from: https://doi.org/10.1039/c7nr03611f.

[29] Alsuraifi A, Curtis A, Lamprou DA, Hoskins C. Stimuli responsive polymeric systems for cancer therapy. Pharmaceutics 2018;10. Available from: https://doi.org/10.3390/pharmaceutics10030136.

[30] Chen W, Meng F, Cheng R, Zhong Z. pH-Sensitive degradable polymersomes for triggered release of anticancer drugs: a comparative study with micelles. Journal of Controlled Release 2010;142:40−6. Available from: https://doi.org/10.1016/J.JCONREL.2009.09.023.

[31] Damera DP, Nag A. Exploring the membrane fluidity of phenyl boronic acid functionalized polymersomes using the FRAP technique and their application in the pH-sensitive release of curcumin. New Journal of Chemistry 2022;46:11329−40. Available from: https://doi.org/10.1039/D2NJ01330D.

[32] Alves RC, Fernandes RP, Fonseca-Santos B, Victorelli FD, Chorilli M. A critical review of the properties and analytical methods for the determination of curcumin in biological and pharmaceutical matrices. Critical Reviews in Analytical Chemistry 2019;49:138−49. Available from: https://doi.org/10.1080/10408347.2018.1489216.

[33] Pakizehkar S, Ranji N, Sohi AN, Sadeghizadeh M. Polymersome-assisted delivery of curcumin: a suitable approach to decrease cancer stemness markers and regulate miRNAs expression in HT29 colorectal cancer cells. Polymers for Advanced Technologies 2020;31:160−77. Available from: https://doi.org/10.1002/pat.4759.

[34] Cao C, Zhao J, Chen F, Lu M, Khine YY, Macmillan A, et al. Drug-induced morphology transition of self-assembled glycopolymers: insight into the drug−polymer interaction. Chemistry of Materials 2018;30:5227−36. Available from: https://doi.org/10.1021/acs.chemmater.8b01882.

[35] Erfani-Moghadam V, Nomani A, Zamani M, Yazdani Y, Najafi F, Sadeghizadeh M. A novel diblock copolymer of (monomethoxy poly [ethylene glycol]-oleate) with a small hydrophobic fraction to make stable micelles/polymersomes for curcumin delivery to cancer cells. International Journal of Nanomedicine 2014;9:5541−54. Available from: https://doi.org/10.2147/IJN.S63762.

[36] Lôbo GCNB, Paiva KLR, Silva ALG, Simões MM, Radicchi MA, Báo SN. Nanocarriers used in drug delivery to enhance immune system in cancer therapy. Pharmaceutics 2021;13:1167. Available from: https://doi.org/10.3390/pharmaceutics13081167.

[37] Brigger I, Dubernet C, Couvreur P. Nanoparticles in cancer therapy and diagnosis. Advanced Drug Delivery Reviews 2002;54:631−51. Available from: https://doi.org/10.1016/S0169-409X(02)00044-3.

[38] Zhang H, Cui W, Qu X, Wu H, Qu L, Zhang X, et al. Photothermal-responsive nanosized hybrid polymersome as versatile therapeutics codelivery nanovehicle for effective tumor suppression. Proceedings of the National Academy of Sciences of the United States of America 2019;116:7744−9. Available from: https://doi.org/10.1073/pnas.1817251116.

[39] Curcio M, Mauro L, Naimo GD, Amantea D, Cirillo G, Tavano L, et al. Facile synthesis of pH-responsive polymersomes based on lipidized PEG for intracellular co-delivery of curcumin and methotrexate. Colloids and Surfaces. B, Biointerfaces 2018;167:568−76. Available from: https://doi.org/10.1016/j.colsurfb.2018.04.057.

[40] Cao Y, Li Y, Wu Y, Li W, Yu C, Huang Y, et al. Co-delivery of angiostatin and curcumin by a biodegradable polymersome for antiangiogenic therapy. RSC Advances 2016;6:105442−8. Available from: https://doi.org/10.1039/c6ra24426b.

[41] Cui X, Wang N, Wang H, Li G, Tao Q. pH sensitive supramolecular vesicles from cyclodextrin graft copolymer and benzimidazole ended block copolymer as dual drug carriers. International Journal of Polymeric Materials and Polymeric Biomaterials 2019;68:733−40. Available from: https://doi.org/10.1080/00914037.2018.1493686.

[42] Sharma AK, Prasher P, Aljabali AA, Mishra V, Gandhi H, Kumar S, et al. Emerging era of "somes": polymersomes as versatile drug delivery carrier for cancer diagnostics and therapy. Drug Delivery and Translational Research 2020;10:1171−90. Available from: https://doi.org/10.1007/s13346-020-00789-2.

[43] Meyer CE, Abram S-L, Craciun I, Palivan CG. Biomolecule−polymer hybrid compartments: combining the best of both worlds. Physical Chemistry Chemical Physics 2020;22:11197−218. Available from: https://doi.org/10.1039/D0CP00693A.

[44] Simón-Gracia L, Scodeller P, Fuentes SS, Vallejo VG, Ríos X, San Sebastián E, et al. Application of polymersomes engineered to target p32 protein for detection of small breast tumors in mice. Oncotarget 2018;9:18682−97. Available from: https://doi.org/10.18632/oncotarget.24588.

[45] Pourtau L, Oliveira H, Thevenot J, Wan Y, Brisson AR, Sandre O, et al. Antibody-functionalized magnetic polymersomes: in vivo targeting and imaging of bone metastases using high resolution MRI. Advanced Healthcare Materials 2013;2:1420−4. Available from: https://doi.org/10.1002/adhm.201300061.

[46] Li X, Zhu X, Qiu L. Constructing aptamer anchored nanovesicles for enhanced tumor penetration and cellular uptake of water soluble chemotherapeutics. Acta Biomaterialia 2016;35:269−79. Available from: https://doi.org/10.1016/j.actbio.2016.02.012.

[47] Jiang Y, Zhang J, Meng F, Zhong Z. Apolipoprotein E peptide-directed chimeric polymersomes mediate an ultrahigh-efficiency targeted protein therapy for glioblastoma. ACS Nano 2018;12:11070−9. Available from: https://doi.org/10.1021/acsnano.8b05265.

[48] Yao P, Zhang Y, Meng H, Sun H, Zhong Z. Smart polymersomes dually functionalized with cRGD and fusogenic GALA peptides enable specific and high-efficiency cytosolic delivery of apoptotic proteins. Biomacromolecules 2019;20:184−91. Available from: https://doi.org/10.1021/acs.biomac.8b01243.

[49] Pawar PV, Gohil SV, Jain JP, Kumar N. Functionalized polymersomes for biomedical applications. Polymer Chemistry 2013;4:3160. Available from: https://doi.org/10.1039/c3py00023k.

[50] Singh V, Md S, Alhakamy NA, Kesharwani P. Taxanes loaded polymersomes as an emerging polymeric nanocarrier for cancer therapy. European Polymer Journal 2022;162:110883. Available from: https://doi.org/10.1016/J.EURPOLYMJ.2021.110883.

[51] Scheerstra JF, Wauters AC, Tel J, Abdelmohsen LKEA, van Hest JCM. Polymersomes as a potential platform for cancer immunotherapy. Materials Today Advances. 2022;13:100203. Available from: https://doi.org/10.1016/J.MTADV.2021.100203.

[52] Alhaj-Suliman SO, Wafa EI, Salem AK. Engineering nanosystems to overcome barriers to cancer diagnosis and treatment. Advanced Drug Delivery Reviews 2022;189:114482. Available from: https://doi.org/10.1016/J.ADDR.2022.114482.

[53] Anajafi T, Yu J, Sedigh A, Haldar MK, Muhonen WW, Oberlander S, et al. Nuclear localizing peptide-conjugated, redox-sensitive polymersomes for delivering curcumin and doxorubicin to pancreatic cancer microtumors. Molecular Pharmaceutics 2017;14:1916−28. Available from: https://doi.org/10.1021/acs.molpharmaceut.7b00014.

[54] Sarkar D, Chowdhury M, Das PK. Naphthalimide-based azo-functionalized supramolecular vesicle in hypoxia-responsive drug delivery. Langmuir: The ACS Journal of Surfaces and Colloids 2022;38:3480−92. Available from: https://doi.org/10.1021/acs.langmuir.1c03334.

[55] Babaei M, Davoodi J, Dehghan R, Zahiri M, Abnous K, Taghdisi SM, et al. Thermosensitive composite hydrogel incorporated with curcumin-loaded nanopolymersomes for prolonged and localized treatment of glioma. Journal of Drug Delivery Science and Technology 2020;59. Available from: https://doi.org/10.1016/j.jddst.2020.101885.

[56] Curcio M, Blanco-Fernandez B, Diaz-Gomez L, Concheiro A, Alvarez-Lorenzo C. Hydrophobically modified keratin vesicles for GSH-responsive intracellular drug release. Bioconjugate Chemistry 2015;26:1900−7. Available from: https://doi.org/10.1021/acs.bioconjchem.5b00289.

[57] Castro KC, Coco JC, Santos EM, Ataide JA, Martinez RM, Nascimento MHM, et al. Pluronic® triblock copolymer-based nanoformulations for cancer therapy: A 10-year overview. Journal of Controlled Release 2023;353:802−22. Available from: https://doi.org/10.1016/j.jconrel.2022.12.017.

Recent advances in nanocurcumin delivery in cancer therapy

Recent advances in
nanocurcumin delivery in
cancer therapy

14

Biopolymer-based formulations for curcumin delivery toward cancer management

Hend A. Gad, Amany M. Diab, Basant E. Elsaied, Ahmed A. Tayel

FACULTY OF AQUATIC AND FISHERIES SCIENCES, KAFRELSHEIKH UNIVERSITY, KAFR EL SHEIKH, EGYPT

14.1 Introduction

A natural yellow-orange dye called curcumin (CUR) (diferuloylmethane; see Fig. 14−1) that is originated from the rhizome of the East Indian plant *Curcuma longa Linn*. However, dimethyl-sulfoxide, ethanol, and other organic solvents can dissolve CUR. It is not soluble in ether or water. It has a molecular weight of 368.37 and a melting point of 183°C. Turmeric, demethoxy curcumin, and bisdemethoxy curcumin (collectively known as curcuminoid) are the three primary ingredients of commercial CUR (Fig. 14−1). In a curcuminoids extract, CUR makes up 60%−70% of the weight of the turmeric, whereas demethoxy and bisdemethoxy curcumin make up more minor amounts (20%−27% and 10%−15%), respectively [1] (Table 14−1).

Although the multicomponent nature of "CUR" is well established, it is not always clear how certain structures are unambiguously assigned in a given preparation. While many in vitro studies use pure, synthetic CUR, the bulk of in vivo researches and clinical investigations use a mixture of curcuminoids. It is difficult to think of solubilized CUR as a single chemical in vitro or in vivo due to its dynamic character. The structure of CUR is frequently cited as a designated active ingredient that should be investigated for therapeutic benefit, possibly by default, regardless of the sources used in the majority of studies. It is also the compound that is utilized as a suggested "lead" structure for the medicinal chemistry investigations. Instead of attempting to examine the potential therapeutic effects of even more complex turmeric extracts or preparations, this mini-perspective will focus on the value claimed for the chemical structure of the extract's main component, CUR [2]. CUR produces superoxide in toluene and ethanol through photolysis. In acetonitrile, however, it quenches superoxide ions [3]. CUR is also phototoxic to mammalian cells, as demonstrated by a rat basophilic leukemia cell model, and its phototoxicity also requires the presence of oxygen [4]. Because CUR's spectral and photochemical characteristics change depending on the environment, there is a possibility of additional or alternative paths for the execution of photodynamic

Curcumin-Based Nanomedicines as Cancer Therapeutics. DOI: https://doi.org/10.1016/B978-0-443-15412-6.00009-X

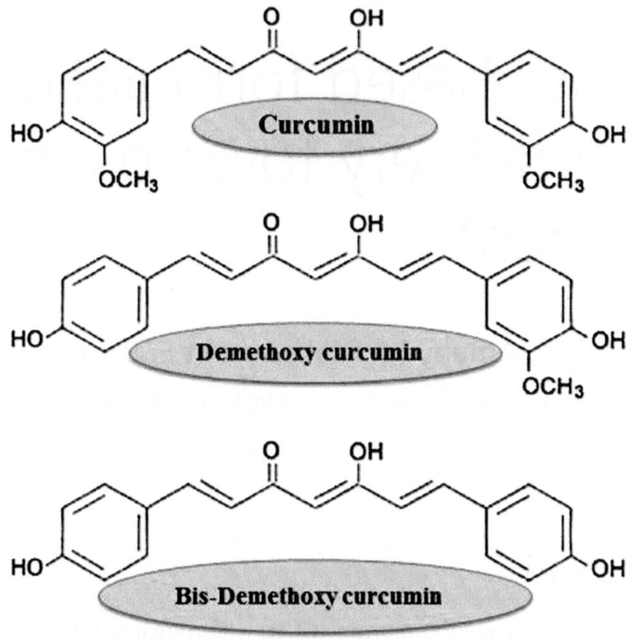

FIGURE 14–1 Major phyto-constituents of extracts of *Curcuma longa*. Compounds curcumin, demethoxy curcumin, and bisdemethoxy curcumin, often grouped together as "curcuminoids".

Table 14–1   Major components of *Curcuma longa* L.

Constituents	Composition
Curcuminoids	1%−6% (w/w)
Carbohydrates	60%−70% (w/w)
Moisture	6%−13% (w/w)
Fat	5%−10% (w/w)
Essential oil (volatile)	3%−7% (w/w)
Fiber	2%−7% (w/w)
Mineral substance	3%−7% (w/w)
Protein	6−8 (w/w)

effects. For instance, CUR produces reduced forms of molecular oxygen and singlet oxygen under a variety of situations that are important to the cellular environment. The CUR seems to have a number of appealing properties from the perspective of drug discovery. The compounds are "generally recognized as safe" (GRAS) by the Food and Drug Administration (FDA) as a food additive at doses up to 20 mg per serving, according to a profusion of papers claiming a wide diversity of biological actions [5]. When exposed to sunshine, CUR degrades significantly more quickly [6,7]. One common finding is that stains caused by CUR or turmeric can be swiftly erased with sunlight exposure.

Vanillin, ferulic acid, and other tiny phenols are the colorless compounds discovered during the photodegradation of CUR, demonstrating a similar product distribution during photochemical breakdown as in chemical degradation in solution. The excited states of CUR are formed during this photodegradation process. According to some findings, the photobiological and photodynamic activity of CUR is actually caused by the generation of singlet oxygen and other reactive oxygen species (ROS) by CUR upon photoexcitation [8]. In this situation, CUR must enter its triplet excited state before degrading after photoexcitation [6]. According to photophysical studies, the life span of CUR's triplet excited state is measured in microseconds, which suggests that the degradation process could move along quickly and compete with singlet oxygen generation. The removal of turmeric stains from cotton garments can be accomplished with this technique because the photodegradation is increased in the presence of TiO_2 nanoparticles (NPs) [9]. Condensation/addition reactions have been used to create chemically modified CUR derivatives, such as semicarbazone derivatives and oxime derivatives of CUR [10,11]. The anticancer activity of these stable products that were separately prepared has been tested. These compounds are reportedly more cytotoxic to cancer cells than free CUR in the majority of these trials. This leads the authors to hypothesize that CUR's glutathione conjugate may also have cytotoxic properties and contribute to the substance's overall antitumor effect.

14.2 Curcumin bioavailability

CUR is nontoxic and has recently attracted a lot of attention as a potential anticancer agent. Due to its substantial first-pass metabolism and poor water solubility, its principal drawback is its limited oral bioavailability [12−17]. It is widely known that the enhanced retention and permeability properties of nanomaterials may encourage the absorption of chemotherapeutic drugs in cancer regions. For instance, micelles, dendrimers, carbon nanotubes, and liposomes have been used as carriers for SN38, doxorubicin, paclitaxel, and cisplatin to raise medication concentrations in tumors and reduce adverse effects [17−22]. One advantage of using nanomaterials as drug carriers is the improved solubility of chemotherapeutic medicines. Self-assembling peptide nanofibers have drawn a lot of interest because of their excellent biocompatibility, simplicity in modification, and adaptability in terms of design using a "bottom-up" methodology [23,24]. They are frequently utilized in a variety of cell cultures and drug delivery methods to increase a hydrophobic medication's solubility, increase in accumulating material at the cancerous location, and lessen negative effects [25].

Paclitaxel, camptothecin, and ellipticine are examples of hydrophobic antitumor medications encased in peptide nanofibers that have demonstrated increased anticancer effects [26−28]. Studies have shown that peptide nanofibers' two-dimensional structure is preferable to NPs' three-dimensional structure for drug delivery. In fact, Wagh et al. showed that peptide-based nanofibers outperform spherical nanomaterials poly[lactic-co-glycolic acid] (PLGA), (gold, polystyrene, cadmium and selenium quantum dots), carbon rods, and spherical nanomaterials in terms of biocompatibility, tumors targeting, and rate of removal [29]. CUR has recently received a lot of research attention, and many synthetic analogs have been created and tested for possible pharmacological properties [30−37]. Some analogs have demonstrated promising features in a variety of cancer cell lines and models. According to a recent study, molecules linked to CUR that contain a benzyl piperidone have improved the biological activity and absorption [38,39]. CUR analogs may have anticancer effects, according to other studies [40−44]. The bioavailability of CUR has been significantly improved by the integration of CUR into nanoformulations (NF) for improved water solubility. Their extended release formulae and better degree of compatibility appear to provide significant prospects for their actions in vivo, as evidenced by improved CUR transport and cell concentrations in vitro [45−47].

14.3 Curcumin's absorption and stability

CUR's solubility, stability, and subsequent in vivo bioavailability are some of the main obstacles preventing it from being used as a medicinal agent from the lab to the bedside. Since CUR is photosensitive, the pH of the solvent medium is a key factor in determining how soluble it is [41]. To improve the drug's solubility and ability to dissolve, a number of solubilizing strategies have been developed, including the use of surfactants, polymeric conjugates, water-soluble carriers, and solid dispersions [48,49]. The main techniques being researched in the current decade involve using simple/complex formation to incorporate therapeutic proteins and medications into different polymers, micelle generation, and nanoconversion using polymers and microspheres [50]. Given that they increase blood circulation time, biopolymer micelles are currently a rapidly expanding sector in the delivery of nutraceuticals or medications. Hydrophobically modified starch (HMS) has recently been demonstrated to produce micelles in aqueous solution [51]. Because of its combination with cyclodextrin (Cd), CUR is at least 104 times more soluble in acid than it was before.

The influence of charge, cavity size, and bulkiness of the Cd side chains on the stability factor are the reasons for higher solubility and slower degradation [52]. In addition, when compared to pure water, the solubility of CUR in HMS micelles is nearly 1700-fold higher. It has been demonstrated that small-molecule surfactants, including cetyltri-methyl-ammonium bromide (CTAB), enhance CUR stability [53]. By giving rats an injection of piperine (Pip) followed by CUR, Shoba et al. demonstrated that a stabilizing agent could enhance the bioavailability of CUR. Following Pip injection, the serum concentration rises, and the healthy human volunteers show the same tendency [54]. It is unclear how concurrent delivery works to increase serum concentration and the molecular processes that lead to drug stability in vivo. In addition, Pip alters the way a variety of medicines are metabolized [55,56]. Free radical polymerization is used to create graft-vinyl acetate copolymers, and the ultrasonic irradiation is used to create CUR-NPs. The positive charges on the discrete, homogeneous spheres known as NPs are present. A slower release rate of CUR is obtained because of the higher encapsulation efficiency of NPs that reached 91.6% [57]. CUR is very hydrophobic and cannot be given systemically because of this. CUR's liposomal encapsulation makes it suitable for intravenous dosage and gets over the issue of limited oral availability that restricts the use of free CUR. The composition exhibits 1wheightened resistance to the development of cancer cells, although the in vitro release is not explicable [58]. Lecithin and Tween 80 are used to create a CUR-encapsulated oil in water (O/W) microemulsion system, with ethyl oleate (EO) serving as the oil phase and lecithin and Tween 80 as the surfactants. The lecithin/Tween 80 mole ratio of the CUR microemulsion is 0.3, and the EO 10:1.7:0.4 in weight ratio is stable for 2 months with an average diameter of 71.8 $\pm$ 2.45 nm. For 48 hours, the microemulsion's structure could be diluted with aqueous buffer without causing it to break down [59]. In a different investigation, it was discovered that the CUR-phospholipid complex demonstrated a proper twofold rise in plasma concentration following oral administration in rats [60]. To increase CUR's oral bioavailability, different biodegradable NPs have been created. The CUR-encapsulated NPs withstand the test circumstances (ICH accelerated stability test settings for refrigerated items) for the 3 months that were specifically evaluated. Diffusion phenomena dominate the in vitro release, which adheres to Higuchi's release pattern. When compared to CUR delivered with Pip as an absorption enhancer, CUR-encapsulated NPs show at least a ninefold improvement in oral bioavailability, according to in vivo pharmacokinetics [61]. When gallocatechin gallate (EGCG) and CUR are encapsulated in nanoemulsions, their stability and oral bioavailability are examined and may be improved [62]. Lopes Rodrigues et al. stated that CUR can be encapsulated into polyethylene glycol-pentacosadiynoic acid (PEG-PCDA) complex to further increase CUR solubility and discovered that it was 500 times more soluble than free CUR with considerable anticancer potential [63]. Different CUR formulations and their effects are presented in Table 14—2.

14.4 Utilizing nanotechnology to create derivatives of curcuma

New formulations such as solid lipid and CUR NPs conjugates, micelles, liposomes, nanoemulsion of Cd complex, nanodisk, and nanofiber have been synthesized to improve the therapeutic action of CUR against several diseases, including the treatment and prevention of cancer [86]. Most notably, when compared to other cancer cell lines, nanoparticulate CUR was more effective than native CUR [87]. Using the emulsion and solvent evaporation approach, Mohanty et al. have created a 192-nm-sized CUR-loaded nanoparticulate delivery system that encapsulates CUR within glycerol mono-oleate-based NPs with a 90% encapsulation efficiency [88].

14.5 Combination nanomedicine with curcumin

CUR's anticancer effects were first identified in 1987 [89,90]. Its anticancer activities result from its capacity to inhibit protein kinase since apoptosis and cancer cell cycle arrest stimulate the development of death receptors and ultimately slow tumor growth [91]. One of the

Table 14–2 Some curcumin formulations [64].

S. No.	Formulation	CUR combination	Advantage	References
1	Microcapsule	Microcapsules are made by layering poly(ethylene imine) and poly (sodium 4-styrene sulfonic acid) together.	Appropriate for applications involving medication administration	[65]
		CUR-loaded bovine serum albumin gel microcapsules	Increased bioavailability, anticancer, and antioxidant effects	[66]
2	Micelles	Copolymer poly(L-lactic acid)-based poly(anhydride ester)-b-poly (ethylene glycol) (PAE-bPEG) encapsulating CUR micelle	Enhanced anticancer behavior	[67]
		CUR encapsulated within cationic micelles made of the surfactants DTAB (dodecyl trimethylammonium bromide) or CTAB (cetyl trimethylammonium bromide)	Reduces CUR's alkaline hydrolysis	[68]
3	Excipient emulsions	CUR encapsulated in copolymer micelles treated with linolenic acid	More suitable carrier for CUR delivery	[69]
		CUR in a corn oil emulsion in water as an excipient	Improved bioaccessibility	[70]
4	Liposomes (nanodelivery vehicles)	CUR-loaded liposomes	Improved antitumor action	[71–73]
5	Yeast encapsulation	Saccharomyces cerevisiae—encapsulated CUR	Because CUR was protected from oxidizing conditions, it was released slowly over time and degraded slowly.	[74]
6	Nanodisks	Apolipoprotein-stabilized disk-shaped phospholipid bilayers trapped by CUR (nanodisks)	Enhanced in vitro cell culture delivery	[75]
7	Solid dispersions	CUR-polyvinylpyrrolidone K-30 ratio of 1:6	Increased solubility and dispersion	[49]
		Mannitol and CUR-D-a-TPGS (tocopheryl polyethylene glycol 1000 succinate).	Suspension and bioavailability delivery	[76]
		CUR-PVP	Improved cell absorbency, solubility, and suspension rate	[77]
8	Encapsulation	CUR encapsulated in hydrophobically modified starch	Improved anticancer activity and solubility	[51]
		CUR encapsulated into silane-hydrogel NP	Enhanced wound healing and antibacterial action	[78]
9	Microemulsion	CUR in O/W emulsion of Tween 20 and triacylglycerol	Improved antiinflammatory activity	[79]
		CUR in transcutol P, cremophor RH 40, and capryol oil.	Enhanced oral bioavailability	[80]
10	Nanoparticulate formulation	CUR-loaded PLGA NPs (poly(D,L-lactide-co-glycolide))	Improved bioactivity in stimulating apoptosis, controlling proliferation of cancer cells, and enhanced cellular uptake	[81]
11	Complex formation	CUR with Cd	Enhancement in photochemical stability, water solubility, and hydrolytic	[52]
		CUR with c-Cd	Enhancement in the absorption of curcuminoids in wholesome humans	[82]
12	Conjugation with magnetic NPs	Fe_3O_4-CUR conjugate	Enhanced cellular uptake and water dispossibility. Potent antitumor activity.	[83–85]

Cd, cyclodextrin; CUR, curcumin; NP, nanoparticles.

main uses of nanomedicine, which is a rapidly expanding area of study, is in oncology. The fundamental issue with cancer medications is their lack of specificity, which might be fixed by creating personalized cancer treatments using nanotechnology. The US FDA has approved a number of nanoparticulate dosage forms in recent years. They function better than traditional administration techniques due to the enhanced medicine delivery, less toxicity, an improved safety profile, personalized therapy, and longer product life cycles [92] (Fig. 14−2).

14.5.1 Colorectal cancer

The third most common kind of cancer is CRC. They are difficult to cure because of their invasive characteristics, and the recurrence is frequent [93]. CUR has an impact on a number of cell signaling pathways. For instance, the Wnt signaling (WS) system, which is crucial for cell growth, the multiplication of tumor cells, the emergence of drug resistance, and the reappearance of various cancers have all been linked to abnormalities in the WS system. In spite of being exposed to anticancer medications in colon tissue, canonical WS is increased in colon cancer, causing unchecked cell proliferation and shielding cancer cells from apoptosis [94]. It is vital to note that using polymeric micelles to enhance the therapeutic efficiency of encapsulated anticancer medicines for colon cancer offers a wide range of advantages and potential [95]. CUR also acts as a strong inhibitor of the production of angiogenic growth factors, which are crucial for the development of new blood vessels. Regarding this, Zhang et al.

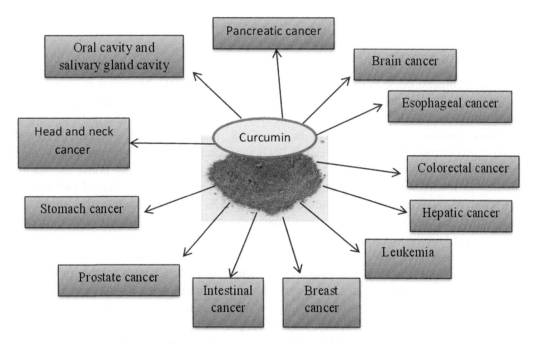

FIGURE 14–2 Curcumin plays a significant role in the treatment of multiple types of cancers.

(2015) revealed that CUR-loaded mono-methyl poly(ethylene glycol)-poly(-caprolactone) (m-PEG-PCL) polymeric micelles showed more effective angiogenesis suppression in CT-26 cancer cells than free CUR [96].

14.5.2 Breast cancer

The most prevalent cancer and the second leading cause of death for women globally is breast cancer [97]. Antiestrogens are frequently used as a treatment for breast cancer, which has an estrogen receptor (ER) positivity rate of more than 50%. CUR, which has been used to treat breast cancer, has an impact on a variety of intracellular signaling pathways, including receptors, cytokines, enzymes, and growth factors [98]. In one investigation, four T1 cells were used to test CUR's anticancer efficacy while it was enclosed in polymeric micelles. With a substantially lower IC50 than that of free CUR, nanosized CUR/polymeric micelles significantly inhibited the growth of 4 T1 cells while also inducing apoptosis in these cells [99]. CUR-loaded polymeric micelles showed excellent anticancer potential in vitro and in vivo in another investigation using the 4 T1 cancer cell line. When compared to the apoptotic score for free CUR (9.42; 2.13%), the apoptotic index for CUR micelles (15.77; 2.74%) was higher. A decrease in the spontaneous lung metastasis of 4 T1 breast cancer cells was also seen in this investigation using CUR/polymeric micelles. Thus nanosized polymeric micelles appeared to enhance the overall availability of CUR relative to free CUR to suppress tumor cell proliferation [100].

14.5.3 Liver cancer

The second biggest cause of death worldwide is liver cancer [101]. According to several studies, CUR has therapeutic benefits for malignant hepatoma. The death receptor route and the death receptor-independent pathway are the two main apoptotic signaling pathways that its anticancer action can activate [102]. In one work, multiarmed poly-ethylenimine-g-poly (-benzyl-oxy-carbonyl-L-lysine) s (PEZ-alt-PEG) super-amphiphiles were created to enhance the thermodynamic stability of polymeric micelles and to dramatically boost the loading capacity of hydrophobic medicines, such as CUR. The impact of CUR-loaded PEZ-alt-PEG polymeric micelles on human hepatoma (HepG2) cells was examined in this study. The amount of HepG2 cells that underwent apoptosis when exposed to the CUR-polymeric micelles was found to be higher than the amount of HepG2 cells that underwent apoptosis when exposed to free CUR. The PEZ-alt-PEG polymer micelles were used, which dramatically increased the absorption of CUR by cells and had a considerable inhibitory effect on the development of HepG2 cells. Because of their high thermodynamic stability, high drug-loading capacity, improved pharmacodynamic effects, and enhanced drug uptake, these authors came to the conclusion that PEZ-alt-PEG polymeric micelles could potentially serve as effective nanocarriers for drugs like CUR that are poorly water soluble [103].

14.5.4 Lung cancer

The most prevalent invasive tumor and one of the main causes of death worldwide is lung cancer [104]. CUR not only has anticancer properties such as preventing metastasis, invasion, and cell proliferation, but also it can trigger apoptosis and control the expression of microRNA [105]. A thin film approach was used to create MPEG-PLA/CUR-polymeric micelles in a study on the relationship between CUR and lung cancer. The impact of the m-PEG-PLA/CUR-polymeric micelles on in vitro cultured A-549 lung cancer cells was examined. These micelles promoted the death of A-549 cells, lowered the expression of the proliferative protein Bcl-2, and elevated the expression of the Bax protein. Results of cytotoxicity tests showed that A-549 lung cancer cells were killed by m-PEG-PLA-CUR polymeric micelles. In addition, CUR-loaded polymeric micelles reduced the expression of matrix metalloproteinase (MMP)-2 and MMP-9, which decreased the ability of A-549 cells to metastatically spread [106,107].

14.5.5 Cervical cancer

The human papillomavirus (HPV)—particularly types HPV16 and HPV18—causes cervical cancer [108]. The absence of the oncoprotein E2 causes the integration of HPV-DNA into the host genome in malignant tumors. E6 and E7, which are crucial in the development of cervical malignancies brought on by HPV infection, are ultimately upregulated as a result of this process [109]. Critical proteins in cell signaling pathways, such as the tumor suppressor protein (P53) and the retinoblastoma gene product (pRb), are deregulated as a result of these two viral oncoproteins, E6 and E7 [99]. CUR-loaded TPGS/F127/P123-mixed polymeric micelles can be successfully targeted (localized) within these organelles, as seen by the staining of the mitochondria in HeLa cells. Wang et al. looked at how CUR-polymeric micelles affected mitochondrial membrane potential, a crucial metric for determining whether or not the mitochondria are functioning normally. These scientists demonstrated that after treating HeLa cells with CUR-polymeric micelles, the membrane potential significantly decreased. Their findings seem to indicate that the mitochondrial-mediated apoptosis pathway may be involved in the apoptosis of the HeLa cells [110].

14.5.6 Leukemia

According to Sahlol et al. (2020), leukemia is the malignancy of white blood cells (WBCs). Depending on the kind of blood cell involved, there are several different varieties of leukemia, including acute myeloid leukemia (AML) [111], acute lymphoblastic leukemia (ALL), chronic myeloid leukemia (CML), and chronic lymphoblastic leukemia (CLL) [112]. By inducing apoptosis through the overexpression of BAX, CUR has the ability to drastically inhibit the development of leukemia cells [113]. CUR also works to stop cell division by preventing the expression of BCR-ABL, FLT3-ITD, and WT1. The overexpression of these genes aids in leukemia diagnosis and progression assessment. One of the overexpressed markers on the surface of leukemia cells is FL3 [114]. In one investigation, CUR-loaded FLT3-targeted micelles displayed higher cytotoxicity against FLT3-ITD-mutant MV4-11 cells in addition to a faster rate of cellular absorption. These findings illustrated FLT3 surface-specificity on micelles. It was indicated that this discovery was likely connected to an intracellular concentration of CUR close to the saturation concentration even though the cytotoxicity associated with nontargeted CUR micelles demonstrated a higher degree of cytotoxicity than the targeted micelles [115]. In another work, FLT3 overexpressing EoL-1 leukemic cells exhibited improved cellular absorption of CUR-loaded micelles [116]. Finally, cationic polymeric micelles containing CUR have been examined in both human multiple myeloma cell line U-266 and K-562 cells derived from CML. The interaction between the negatively charged cell surface and the positively charged micelles resulted in increased cellular absorption and greater cytotoxicity to both cell lines, according to the findings [117].

14.5.7 Ovarian cancer

Another significant cause of death for women is ovarian cancer [118]. Because ovarian cancer has no symptoms in its early stages, early identification is challenging. As a result, it is frequently discovered after it is well advanced, which is ultimately linked to a higher incidence of cancer relapse, metastasis, and chemoresistance. These changes are associated with the Wnt/ß-catenin signaling pathway—controlled epithelial-mesenchymal transition (EMT) process [119]. Notably, it is understood that ovarian cancer has dysregulated WS, one of the most significant signaling pathways in carcinogenesis [120]. The ß-catenin protein expression and migration are inhibited by CUR via DNA methylation alteration, which is known to have inhibitory action in terms of cancer cell growth and proliferation. In addition, this organic substance has the ability to reverse ovarian cancer's multidrug resistance [121,122].

14.6 Different types of curcumin delivery systems used in cancer therapy

To enhance CUR characteristics and targetability, numerous CUR delivery methods have been created using various nanotechnologies. The rational design of NF should take into account a number of variables to increase the effectiveness and cellular targeting of anticancer medicines. These elements include the surface characteristics, size, targeting ligands, and shape of the NPs as shown in Fig. 14–3. A list of the most popular CUR delivery systems is introduced in this section.

14.6.1 Polymeric nanoparticles

To improve the biological activity of NF for CUR drug delivery, various polymers have been used [123]. Biodegradable and biocompatible polymers are chosen in medication delivery systems due to the lower risk of toxicity [124]. Drug delivery has consequently seen a rise in the use of biodegradable polymers that are synthetic like PLGA (poly(D, L-lactic-co-glycolic acid)) and natural polymers like chitosan and silk fibroin (SF) [125–127]. PLGA-CUR NF was

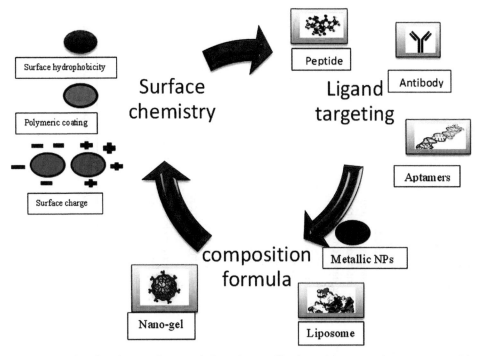

FIGURE 14–3 Examples of modern NP design techniques being utilized to enhance targeting. *NP*, nanoparticle.

discovered to be equally efficacious as CUR at a 15-fold lower dose by inhibiting mRNAs for inflammatory cytokines (CXCR3 and CXCL10) and elevating antiinflammatory cytokine interleukin-10 (IL-10) in the brain [128]. When injected with the alkaloid compound Pip in a rat research, CUR-PLGA nanospheres had a ninefold higher bioavailability than untreated CUR. On the other hand, CUR/Pip coadministration boosted CUR activity by preventing hepatic and intestinal deactivation [61]. In a different investigation, the anticancer properties of CUR-NPs and CUR-NPs coupled to anti-Pgp (P-glycoprotein) (CUR-NPs-APgp) were compared. The latter formulation showed noticeably higher specific binding to cervical cancer cells KB-3-1 than CUR-NPs, although with less effective entrapment [129]. To enclose dimethyl CUR (ASC-J9), spherical PLGA nanospheres were also developed and tested in breast cancer cells. The proliferation of estrogen-dependent MCF-7 cancer cells might be inhibited by the release of ASC-J9 from the PLGA nanospheres intracellularly [130].

14.6.2 Liposomes nanoscale

One of the best anticancer medication delivery techniques is emerging: liposomes. Recent improvements in liposome formulations have improved the treatment of drug-resistant tumors and decreased toxicity [131]. A liposome is a good transporter for both hydrophobic and hydrophilic chemicals because it consists of an aqueous core and a phospholipid bilayer shell. Several liposome preparations have been used to encapsulate CUR (Table 14–3).

Table 14-3 Recent examples of curcumin delivery methods [132].

Nanoformulation	Application	Outcome	Particle size	References
CUR nanoemulsion	Human ovarian adenocarcinoma cells (SKV3)	Improved cytotoxicity	<200 nm	[14]
CUR-loaded chitin nanogels	Human dermal fibroblasts (HDF) and human skin melanoma (A385)	Certain toxicity in melanoma of skin (lower toxicity in HDF)	70–80 nm	[133]
Liposome-encapsulated CUR	Neck squamous cell carcinoma (HNSCC) cell lines (CAL27 and UM-SCC1) and head cancer	Growth control both in vitro and in vivo	Not reported	[134]
CUR–chitosan NPs	Melanomas	Improved anticancer activity	100–250 nm	[135]
CUR-cross-linked polymeric nanogels	Pancreatic and breast cancers	Increased stability and anticancer activity	10–200 nm	[133]
CUR-loaded lipo-PEG f -PEI g complexes	Colon carcinoma (CT-26) cells and melanoma (B16F10)	Increased cytotoxicity	269 nm	[136]
CUR-loaded lipid-core nanocapsules	U251MG glioma cell lines and Rat C6	Extended survival and reduced cancer size	196 ± 1.4 nm	[137]
CUR-loaded magnetic silk NPs	Human breast cancer (MDA-MB-231) cells	Inhibition of growth and improved cellular uptake	100–350 nm	[127]
CUR-PLGA e NPs	Erythro-leukemia type 562 cells	Enhanced leukemia control	248 ± 1.6 nm	[138]
Apo-E h peptide-functionalized CUR-loaded liposomes	RBE4 cell monolayer	Improved capillary endothelium accumulation in brain	132 nm	[139]
CUR-loaded liposomal PMSA a antibodies	CUR-loaded liposomal PMSA a antibodies 100–150 nm; human prostate cancer (LNCa, C4–2B)	Improved antiproliferative targeting and efficacy	100–150 nm	[71]
CUR-loaded liposomes coated with N-dodecyl chitosan-HPTMA d chloride	Murine melanoma (B16F10) cells and murine fibroblasts (NIH3T3)	Certain toxicity in murine melanoma (but not in fibroblasts)	73 nm	[140]
CUR/MPEG b -PCL c micelles	Colon carcinoma (C-26) cells	Improved growth inhibition of cancer	27 ± 1.3 nm	[141]

PMSA, prostate membrane specific antigen; *MPEG*, mono-methoxy poly ethylene glycol; *PCL*, poly-caprolactone); *HPTMA*, N-[(2-hydroxy-3-trimethylamine) propyl; *PLGA*, poly-lactic-co-glycolic acid; *PEG*, poly ethylene glycol; *PEI*, polyethyleneimine; *Apo-E*, apolipoprotein E; *CUR*, curcumin; *NP*, nanoparticle.

CUR is soluble in the liposomal lipid bilayer made up of dihexyl phosphate, cholesterol, and egg yolk phosphatidylcholine (EYPC). It was shown that the amount of loaded CUR stabilized by this preparation correlated with its content [142]. Another work used HPTMA (N-dodecyl chitosan-N-[(2-hydroxy-3-trimethylamine) propyl]) chloride to coat liposomes with a lipid-polymer conjugate. Cationic polyethyleneimine (PEI) and PEG have also been used to create positively charged nanoliposomes for CUR delivery. This formulation beat unprocessed CUR in a number of cell lines, including human HepG2 hepatocellular carcinoma, A549 lung carcinoma, HT29 colorectal carcinoma, and cervical cancer [143], despite having poor encapsulation efficiency (45%). In a fascinating study, Fujita et al. [144] utilized CUR to regulate the release of s-RNA during liposomal gene delivery. Due to CUR's dose-dependent increase in liposomal permeability, s-RNA release assumed a bell-shaped pattern when it was introduced to the liposomal solution. This study used CUR-loaded liposomes to inhibit macrophage IL-6 synthesis. A lipid mixture consisting of DPPC (1, 2-dipalmitoyl-sn-glycero-3-phosphocholine), DPPS (1, 2-dipalmitoyl-sn-glycero-3-phospho-L-serine sodium salt), and cholesterol was combined with CUR solution and human serum albumin (HSA) solution. The intended system greatly lowered the IL-6 and the overall quantity of macrophages [145].

14.6.3 Nanogels

Few researches have examined CUR nanogel delivery in cancer therapy, despite the fact that hydrogels and nanogels have drawn a lot of attention as prospective drug delivery systems in the past 10 years. Recently, a number of polymeric hydrogel NP systems were created using artificial or natural polymers. The most researched natural polymers for creating nanogels for drug delivery include chitosan, alginate, and chitin [146]. The most widely used synthetic polymers are polyethylene, polyvinyl alcohol (PVA), oxide (PEO), polyvinylpyrrolidone (PVP), polyethylene, and poly-N-isopropyl-acrylamide (PNIAA) [147]. Biocompatibility and biodegradability are the two key benefits of natural hydrogels over synthetic ones when it comes to drug administration [133,147]. In addition, nanogels offer unique properties such a porous structure for drug loading and release and a large surface area for drug trapping [133,148]. To treat skin cancer, a CUR-loaded chitin nanogel was used as a transdermal system, and it showed stronger specific toxicity toward human skin melanoma (A375) cells than toward human dermal fibroblast (HDF) cells while retaining CUR's anticancer efficacy [133]. A hybrid nanogel system made of alginate, pluronic polymers, and chitosan was created in a different study using the polycationic crosslinking process and evaluated on a HeLa cell line [149]. Extremely high entrapment effectiveness was shown by this delivery system, and cells treated with synthetic CUR proliferated at a significantly higher rate than cells treated with free CUR.

14.6.4 Peptide and protein formulations

In the delivery of CUR drugs, hydrogels and polymeric materials have shown promising effects. The toxicity of unreacted monomers, postcrosslinking shrinkage or fragility of polymer gels, and the fast discharge of a significant portion of the loaded drug during the initial burst release in drug carrier are some constraints that have come to light in clinical applications [150]. To overcome these restrictions, self-assembling peptide systems have been developed. Peptides have various benefits when used in drug delivery systems, including biocompatibility, desired hydrophilicity, and easy processing [151]. In a recent work, the physical characteristics and therapeutic effectiveness of a CUR-loaded, self-assembling (MAX8) peptide (-hairpin) hydrogel system were examined. This recently designed method offers better delivery, CUR stabilization, and controlled drug release by altering the MAX8 peptide concentration [152]. The capacity of an amphiphilic polypeptide (-casein) to self-assemble into micelles is another illustration. The hydrophobic core of casein micelles was encased by CUR, increasing its water solubility by 2500 times [46]. HSA is one of the most often used proteins in NP synthesis because of its outstanding biocompatibility [153]. The process of making CUR-loaded HSA NPs involved mixing an aqueous HSA solution (to cross-link the HSA molecules) with CUR that had been dissolved in chloroform. This formulation enhanced CUR solubility by 300 times but only managed a 7.2% loading efficiency, most likely because CUR was trapped by hydrophobic interactions within the hydrophobic cavity of albumin [154]. Due to its outstanding biocompatibility and extensive list of biomedical applications, the SF protein has recently attracted a great deal of attention [155]. Since the FDA approved it, a number of studies have been carried out to look at its potential uses in drug delivery [156]. Magnetic silk nanoparticles (MSPs) were used to deliver CUR to MDA-MB-231 breast cancer cells. These particles, as depicted in Fig. 14−4, were produced by salting out silk from its helix form to its sheet (insoluble) form, producing a hydrophobic surface for CUR loading. The developed NF was able to target the target tissue using an external magnetic field, obtain a tiny particle size (100−350 nm), and internalize cells.

14.6.5 Cyclodextrin complexes

Cds are cyclic oligosaccharides that have an exterior layer that is hydrophilic and a lipophilic core. These complexes have a number of advantageous drug delivery characteristics, such as bioavailability, increased solubility, and stability of the loaded drug. In terms of water solubility and molecular weight, natural Cds, chemically altered Cds, and polymerized Cds are all distinct [157]. Cd complexes can also come in a variety of forms, including inclusion complexes and self-assembled Cds (Fig. 14−5). In a few investigations, Cds have been used as CUR delivery vehicles to prevent degradation, increase bioavailability, and lessen nonselective toxicity [158]. A -Cd-CUR self-assembling preparation improved the CUR absorption by DU145 prostate cancer cells as compared to untreated CUR [158].

14.7 Biopolymer-based techniques for nanoencapsulation of curcumin

One of the greatest materials for synthesizing NPs is biopolymers. Numerous methods, including emulsion crosslinking, spray drying, ionic gelation, complicated coacervations, solvent evaporation, and solvent displacement, are used in the synthesis of NF [159]. Biopolymers are made from living organisms as opposed to synthetic polymers, and they

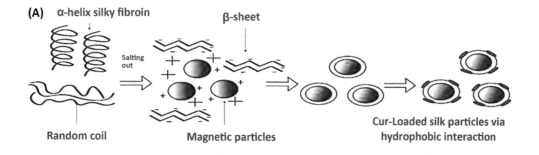

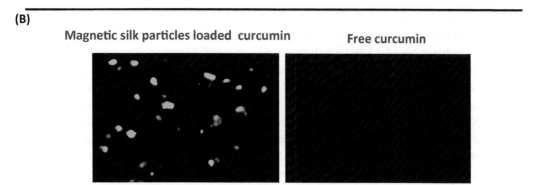

FIGURE 14–4 (A) Generating magnetic silk particles (MSP) for the delivery of curcumin. (B) Sample microscopic pictures of MDA-MB-231 cells after they were treated with free curcumin and MSP that had been loaded with curcumin, demonstrating a notable improvement in curcumin cellular uptake [123].

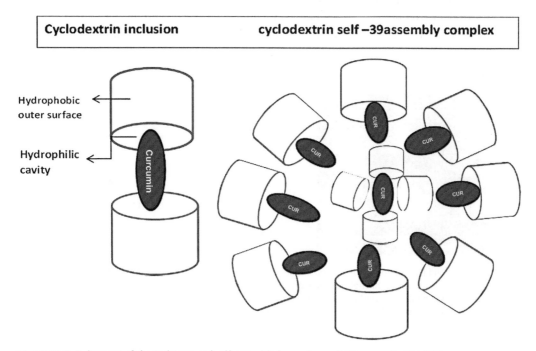

FIGURE 14–5 A diagram of the inclusion and self-assembled complexes of Cd-curcumin (CD-CUR).

have a good safety profile as well as a high rate of biodegradability and biocompatibility [160]. Due to these distinctive qualities, biopolymer-based NF is used in a variety of in vitro and in vivo investigations [161]. Drug delivery could make use of biopolymers as chitosan, polyhydroxyalkanoates, polylactic acid (PLA), and cellulose [162]. The in vitro cytocompatibility and dissolve rate of polymeric NPs loaded with CUR were examined by Umerska and colleagues, who found that these NPs had improved redispersibility after high bioavailability, freeze-drying, and quick CUR release [163]. In a different work, Medel et al. (2017) created polymeric NPs loaded with CUR-bortezomib and evaluated their anticancer effectiveness. Methoxy-poly(ethylene glycol)-block-polylactic acid (m-PEG-b-PLA) di-block copolymers were used in the study [164]. The resultant NPs enhanced the anticancer properties of CUR, and the combination of CUR with bortezomib showed a strong synergistic impact. The buildup of photosensitizers in healthy tissues commonly results in the bad side effects of photodynamic therapy. The physiochemical characteristics of CUR, particularly serum stability and light stability, have been enhanced by its encapsulation in biodegradable polymeric (PLGA) NPs. In addition, the CUR formulation permitted the use of a larger CUR concentration, leading to better anticancer effects (Fig. 14–6) [166]. Investigated was the surface coating of PEG and chitosan on CUR-loaded PLGA NPs. Synthetic NF was more hazardous than free CUR, prevented pancreatic tumor invasion and migration to a greater extent, and had larger levels of apoptotic effects [167]. In addition, CUR-loaded folate-modified chitosan NPs have been synthesized, and their effectiveness against breast cancer has been investigated. It was shown that the amount of CUR released from the NPs increases with decreasing pH. These NPs may also have potential for drug delivery systems in the treatment of breast cancer, according to cell proliferation assays [167]. In addition, CUR-loaded 2-ethyl-2-oxazoline-grad-2-(4-dodecyloxyphenyl)-2-oxazoline copolymer NPs were synthesized, with the ability to control solvent hydrogen binding and polarity influencing the copolymer's self-assembly

(A)   **(B)**

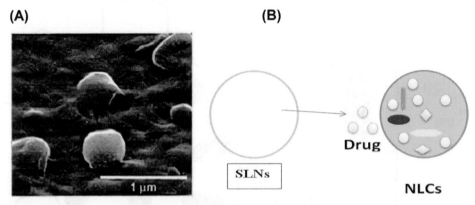

FIGURE 14–6 (A) Solid lipid nanoparticles (SLNs) images captured by scanning electron microscopy. (B) Due to the crystallization process occurring throughout the storage circumstances, SLNs have a higher drug expulsion and loading capacity than nanostructured lipid carriers (NLCs) (per the terms and conditions of the Creative Commons Attribution [CC BY] license) [165].

characteristics. In both the free and CUR-loaded NP synthesis, solvents were a key component. To increase NP stability, polymers were used in the CUR loading process. CUR's solubility greatly improved as well. Produced CUR-loaded (EtOx-gradDPOx) copolymer NPs showed minimal toxicity, concentration-dependent absorption, and excellent stability by HeLa and U87 MG cells [168].

14.8 Anticarcinogenesis mechanisms of curcumin

The majority of malignancies, including colon, oral, breast, lung, and pancreatic prostate cancers, have been proven to respond favorably to CUR [169–174]. Several proteins, including STAT3, activated protein 1 (AP-1), NF-B, and epidermal growth response (Egr-1), all of which are crucial in preoplastic and malignant pathways, are susceptible to being influenced by CUR. Cancer cells in CUR apoptosis and die as a result of CUR's regulation of the expression of genes such Bcl-2, Bcl-xL, cyclin D1, MMP-9, and cyclooxygenase 2 (COX-2) [175–177]. By blocking signals in the STAT3 and AP-1 pathways, CUR reduces the development of cancerous cells. By controlling the epidermal growth factor receptor, CUR also reduces Egr-1 activity in intestinal cancer cells [175,177]. In addition, CUR reduces the expression of the p53 tumor inhibitor gene, modifies the antiapoptotic Bcl-2 or Bcl-xL genes, and activates the cell death signal to suppress cell proliferation in the G2 stage [178]. To improve CUR bioavailability and transport to target tissues, CUR NF is utilized [179]. Over the years, numerous NF have been investigated to help CUR spread to tumors. The main purposes of NF are to make CUR more consistently delivered and to make it more water soluble [180,181]. The therapeutic efficacy of CUR in a nanocarrier for cancer may ideally be increased over free CUR while still being nontoxic to healthy cells [124]. To date, lipid-based NPs (such as liposomes, nanostructured lipid carriers, and solid lipid NPs), Cd, meso-porous silica, nanogels, gold NPs, polymeric NPs, and micelles have all been investigated for use in the therapy of cancer.

14.9 Curcumin combination therapy's drawbacks and future aspects

14.9.1 Challenges with curcumin combination therapy

The examination of multiple barriers is necessary for efficient anticancer combination therapy. Preliminary studies demand exact tuning of an ideal mass ratio (ratio-metric dosage) of each drug in a combination based on individual drug efficacy and pharmacokinetic (PK) characteristics [182]. Combination formulation is made more challenging by CUR's limited bioavailability and poor absorption [178]. One of the main difficulties in the construction of nonsite-specific combination NPs is the off-site effects brought on by activity on healthy cells. On the other hand, a number of chemotherapeutic NF has added folate or other particular antigens to enhance the site specificity for cytotoxic drug delivery to tumor cells.

As seen in Fig. 14–7, a possible CUR combination NPs with paclitaxel delivery method might be further expanded into combination chemotherapy to obtain the highest level of therapeutic efficacy. In addition, each formulation needs to undergo extensive testing for both short- and long-term toxicity due to the fact that some of the components used to create NF are hazardous. Since the most popular way for giving NF is intravenously, toxicity associated with the interaction of blood vessel endothelial cells and nanocarrier should be taken into account [184]. Other crucial factors to take into account for nanocarrier-based combination therapy include the quality by design criteria, logically based on size, and the surface physicochemical characteristics of the materials to be manufactured [185] (Fig. 14–8).

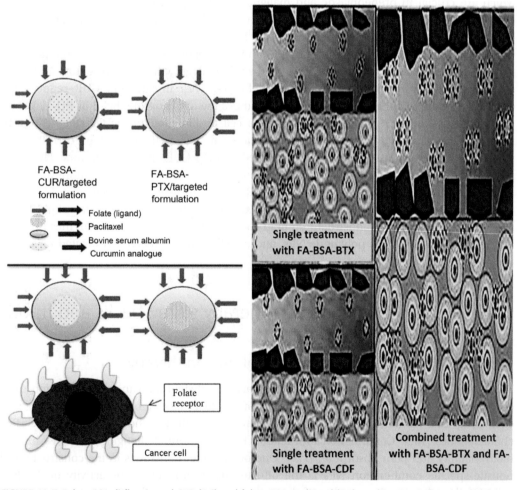

FIGURE 14–7 Folate-BSA-di-fluorinated CUR (T C) and folate-BSA-paclitaxel (T P) combination index plots [183].

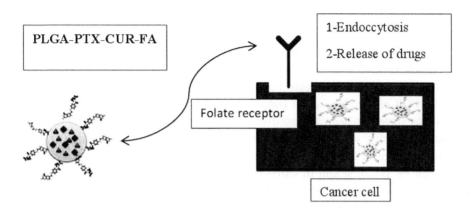

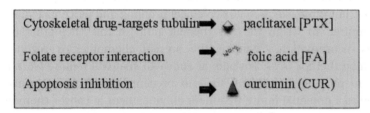

FIGURE 14–8 A putative paclitaxel (PTX) and curcumin nanoparticle (NP) mechanism of action is shown. They have been shown to interact with the folate receptor, which causes the PLGA-FA-PTX lipid nanocarrier to end up in the body [183].

14.9.2 Conclusion and future directions

Around the world, the delivery of anticancer medications in nanoencapsulated form with CUR as an adjuvant is beginning to outperform monotherapy. In addition to the chemosensitizing synergism and tissue specificity it offers, combination therapy is now recognized for its ability to address multidrug resistance and provide effective treatment plans. Although the in vitro and in vivo research being done now presents a positive picture, much more work needs to be done before this therapy can be scaled up to safe dose forms for use in people. The most challenging task from a pharmaceutical perspective is changing CUR from its natural form to a formulation-relevant derivative that is more stable and has more "drug-like properties." In one such approach, poly(CUR-di-thiodipropionic acid) PCDA coating on NPs was utilized. This coating was made of disulfide bond linked mono-CUR, which breaks down at a much higher glutathione (GSH) concentration in the cytoplasm than in the extracellular environment, leading to GSH-responsive release of CUR and changing CUR's original form into a more readily usable form for formulation.

Other sophisticated fabrications, such as prodrug approach, cocrystallization of CUR, polymer coating, and complexation, would need time and money inputs, both of which are typical offsets for the pharmaceutical industry. Therefore, more study is needed to determine how to incorporate CUR into a delivery system that can be optimized for best use, compensating the financial input. The absence of target-specific features is another significant obstacle to this method's adoption by humans. Potential solutions to these problems include ligand attachment, PEG of NPs, tissue-specific coating, and future external techniques like electrophoresis and iontophoresis. Further research should be done on human dose optimization for CUR either alone or in conjunction with other medications. Since no commercial medications have yet been released onto the market, dosing would be a significant rate-limiting step in this scenario. In vitro dose−response studies, potential FDA approval, and preclinical or clinical data backups must be in place before those negotiations can even start. A thorough PK profiling and in vitro−in vivo correlation (IVIVC) for the medication combinations are necessary to advance up the ladder. Furthermore, before dosage design, the anti-cancer effect of the combination NPs must be tested in actual cancer situations. The efficiency of these formulations is frequently influenced by the altered vasculature found in cancer tumors. Many of the developmental doses discussed in the preceding work have undergone toxicity studies, but more extensive toxicological profiling and percentage damage to healthy tissue are required to weigh the risk−benefit ratio of this chemotherapeutic approach and justify its incorporation. Changing the present chemotherapy regimen to nanoparticulate CUR combo therapy is a translational endeavor that will require work from fundamental molecular to pharmaceutical and then to preclinical and clinical trials. To finally create this strategy as a potential future treatment enhancement in cancer chemotherapy, significant efforts from existing possibilities with CUR combination NPs are necessary.

References

[1] Aggarwal BB, Kumar A, Bharti AC. Anticancer potential of curcumin: preclinical and clinical studies. Anticancer Research 2003;23(1/A):363−98.

[2] Nelson KM, Dahlin JL, Bisson J, Graham J, Pauli GF, Walters MA. The essential medicinal chemistry of curcumin: miniperspective. Journal of Medicinal Chemistry 2017;60(5):1620−37.

[3] Toniolo R, Di Narda F, Susmel S, Martelli M, Martelli L, Bontempelli G. Quenching of superoxide ions by curcumin. A mechanistic study in acetonitrile. Annali di Chimica 2002;92(3):281−8.

[4] Dahll TA, Bilski P, Reszka KJ, Chignell CF. Photocytotoxicity of curcumin. Photochemistry and Photobiology 1994;59(3):290−4.

[5] Food and Drug Administration Office of Food Additive Safety. Agency Response Letter GRAS Notice No. Grn 000460. U.S. Food and Drug Administration, 2013.

[6] Priyadarsini KI. Photophysics, photochemistry and photobiology of curcumin: studies from organic solutions, bio-mimetics and living cells. Journal of Photochemistry and Photobiology C: Photochemistry Reviews 2009;10(2):81−95.

[7] Khurana A, Ho CT. High performance liquid chromatographic analysis of curcuminoids and their photo-oxidative decomposition compounds in *Curcuma longa* L. Journal of Liquid Chromatography 1988;11(11):2295−304.

[8] Tønnesen HH, De Vries H, Karlsen J, Van Henegouwen GB. Studies on curcumin and curcuminoids IX: investigation of the photobiological activity of curcumin using bacterial indicator systems. Journal of Pharmaceutical Sciences 1987;76(5):371−3.

[9] Singh U, Verma S, Ghosh HN, Rath MC, Priyadarsini KI, Sharma A, et al. Photo-degradation of curcumin in the presence of TiO_2 nanoparticles: fundamentals and application. Journal of Molecular Catalysis A: Chemical 2010;318(1−2):106−11.

[10] Dutta S, Padhye S, Priyadarsini KI, Newton C. Antioxidant and antiproliferative activity of curcumin semicarbazone. Bioorganic & Medicinal Chemistry Letters 2005;15(11):2738−44.

[11] Simoni D, Rizzi M, Rondanin R, Baruchello R, Marchetti P, Invidiata FP, et al. Antitumor effects of curcumin and structurally β-diketone modified analogs on multidrug resistant cancer cells. Bioorganic & Medicinal Chemistry Letters 2008;18(2):845−9.

[12] Dhillon N, Aggarwal BB, Newman RA, Wolff RA, Kunnumakkara AB, Abbruzzese JL, et al. Phase II trial of curcumin in patients with advanced pancreatic cancer. Clinical Cancer Research 2008;14(14):4491−9.

[13] Zlotogorski A, Dayan A, Dayan D, Chaushu G, Salo T, Vered M. Nutraceuticals as new treatment approaches for oral cancer−I: curcumin. Oral Oncology 2013;49(3):187−91.

[14] Adams BK, Ferstl EM, Davis MC, Herold M, Kurtkaya S, Camalier RF, et al. Synthesis and biological evaluation of novel curcumin analogs as anti-cancer and anti-angiogenesis agents. Bioorganic & Medicinal Chemistry 2004;12(14):3871−83.

[15] Lee KH, Aziz FHA, Syahida A, Abas F, Shaari K, Israf DA, et al. Synthesis and biological evaluation of curcumin-like diarylpentanoid analogues for anti-inflammatory, antioxidant and anti-tyrosinase activities. European Journal of Medicinal Chemistry 2009;44(8):3195−200.

[16] Zhao C, Yang J, Wang Y, Liang D, Yang X, Li X, et al. Synthesis of mono-carbonyl analogues of curcumin and their effects on inhibition of cytokine release in LPS-stimulated RAW 264.7 macrophages. Bioorganic & Medicinal Chemistry 2010;18(7):2388−93.

[17] Bala V, Rao S, Boyd BJ, Prestidge CA. Prodrug and nanomedicine approaches for the delivery of the camptothecin analogue SN38. Journal of Controlled Release 2013;172(1):48−61.

[18] Das M, Singh RP, Datir SR, Jain S. Intranuclear drug delivery and effective in vivo cancer therapy via estradiol−PEG-appended multiwalled carbon nanotubes. Molecular Pharmaceutics 2013;10(9):3404−16.

[19] Teow HM, Zhou Z, Najlah M, Yusof SR, Abbott NJ, D'Emanuele A. Delivery of paclitaxel across cellular barriers using a dendrimer-based nanocarrier. International Journal of Pharmaceutics 2013;441 (1−2):701−11.

[20] Qi X, Li N, Gu H, Xu Y, Xu Y, Jiao Y, et al. Amphiphilic oligomer-based micelles as cisplatin nanocarriers for cancer therapy. Nanoscale 2013;5(19):8925−9.

[21] Arzuman L, Beale P, Chan C, Yu JQ, Huq F. Synergism from combinations of tris (benzimidazole) monochloroplatinum (II) chloride with capsaicin, quercetin, curcumin and cisplatin in human ovarian cancer cell lines. Anticancer Research 2014;34(10):5453−64.

[22] Huq F, Yu JQ, Beale P, Chan C, Arzuman L, Nessa MU, et al. Combinations of platinums and selected phytochemicals as a means of overcoming resistance in ovarian cancer. Anticancer Research 2014;34 (1):541−5.

[23] Nune M, Kumaraswamy P, Maheswari Krishnan U, Sethuraman S. Self-assembling peptide nanofibrous scaffolds for tissue engineering: novel approaches and strategies for effective functional regeneration. Current Protein and Peptide Science 2013;14(1):70−84.

[24] Hu Y, Wang H, Wang J, Wang S, Liao W, Yang Y, et al. Supramolecular hydrogels inspired by collagen for tissue engineering. Organic & Biomolecular Chemistry 2010;8(14):3267−71.

[25] Wang H, Wei J, Yang C, Zhao H, Li D, Yin Z, et al. The inhibition of tumor growth and metastasis by self-assembled nanofibers of taxol. Biomaterials 2012;33(24):5848−53.

[26] Zhang P, Cheetham AG, Lin YA, Cui H. Self-assembled Tat nanofibers as effective drug carrier and transporter. ACS Nano 2013;7(7):5965−77.

[27] Soukasene S, Toft DJ, Moyer TJ, Lu H, Lee HK, Standley SM, et al. Antitumor activity of peptide amphiphile nanofiber-encapsulated camptothecin. ACS Nano 2011;5(11):9113−21.

[28] Cho H, Indig GL, Weichert J, Shin HC, Kwon GS. In vivo cancer imaging by poly (ethylene glycol)-b-poly (ε-caprolactone) micelles containing a near-infrared probe. Nanomedicine: Nanotechnology, Biology and Medicine 2012;8(2):228—36.

[29] Wagh A, Singh J, Qian S, Law B. A short circulating peptide nanofiber as a carrier for tumoral delivery. Nanomedicine: Nanotechnology, Biology and Medicine 2013;9(4):449—57.

[30] Yadav B, Taurin S, Rosengren RJ, Schumacher M, Diederich M, Somers-Edgar TJ, et al. Synthesis and cytotoxic potential of heterocyclic cyclohexanone analogues of curcumin. Bioorganic & Medicinal Chemistry 2010;18(18):6701—7.

[31] Sun A, Shoji M, Lu YJ, Liotta DC, Snyder JP. Synthesis of EF24 — tripeptide chloromethyl ketone: a novel curcumin-related anticancer drug delivery system. Journal of Medicinal Chemistry 2006;49(11):3153—8.

[32] Somers-Edgar TJ, Taurin S, Larsen L, Chandramouli A, Nelson MA, Rosengren RJ. Mechanisms for the activity of heterocyclic cyclohexanone curcumin derivatives in estrogen receptor negative human breast cancer cell lines. Investigational New Drugs 2011;29(1):87—97.

[33] Robinson TP, Ehlers T, Hubbard Iv RB, Bai X, Arbiser JL, Goldsmith DJ, et al. Design, synthesis, and biological evaluation of angiogenesis inhibitors: aromatic enone and dienone analogues of curcumin. Bioorganic & Medicinal Chemistry Letters 2003;13(1):115—17.

[34] Ohori H, Yamakoshi H, Tomizawa M, Shibuya M, Kakudo Y, Takahashi A, et al. Synthesis and biological analysis of new curcumin analogues bearing an enhanced potential for the medicinal treatment of cancer. Molecular Cancer Therapeutics 2006;5(10):2563—71.

[35] Subramaniam D, May R, Sureban SM, Lee KB, George R, Kuppusamy P, et al. Diphenyl difluoroketone: a curcumin derivative with potent in vivo anticancer activity. Cancer Research 2008;68(6):1962—9.

[36] Liang G, Shao L, Wang Y, Zhao C, Chu Y, Xiao J, et al. Exploration and synthesis of curcumin analogues with improved structural stability both in vitro and in vivo as cytotoxic agents. Bioorganic & Medicinal Chemistry 2009;17(6):2623—31.

[37] Karthikeyan NS, Sathiyanarayanan KI, Aravindan PG, Giridharan P. Synthesis, crystal structure, and anticancer properties of cyclic monocarbonyl analogs of curcumin. Medicinal Chemistry Research 2011;20(1):81—7.

[38] Dayton A, Selvendiran K, Kuppusamy ML, Rivera BK, Meduru S, Kálai T, et al. Cellular uptake, retention and bioabsorption of HO-3867, a fluorinated curcumin analog with potential antitumor properties. Cancer Biology & Therapy 2010;10(10):1027—32.

[39] Lee HE, Choi ES, Jung JY, You MJ, Kim LH, Cho SD. Inhibition of specificity protein 1 by dibenzylideneacetone, a curcumin analogue, induces apoptosis in mucoepidermoid carcinomas and tumor xenografts through Bim and truncated Bid. Oral Oncology 2014;50(3):189—95.

[40] Novaković M, Pešić M, Trifunović S, Vučković I, Todorović N, Podolski-Renić A, et al. Diarylheptanoids from the bark of black alder inhibit the growth of sensitive and multi-drug resistant non-small cell lung carcinoma cells. Phytochemistry 2014;97:46—54.

[41] Rahman SMH, Telny TC, Ravi TK, Kuppusamy S. Role of surfactant and pH in dissolution of curcumin. Indian Journal of Pharmaceutical Sciences 2009;71(2):139.

[42] Zheng A, Li H, Wang X, Feng Z, Xu J, Cao K, et al. Anticancer effect of a curcumin derivative B63: ROS production and mitochondrial dysfunction. Current Cancer Drug Targets 2014;14(2):156—66.

[43] Ucisik MH, Küpcü S, Schuster B, Sleytr UB. Characterization of curcuemulsomes: nanoformulation for enhanced solubility and delivery of curcumin. Journal of Nanobiotechnology 2013;11(1):1—13.

[44] Sahu A, Kasoju N, Goswami P, Bora U. Encapsulation of curcumin in Pluronic block copolymer micelles for drug delivery applications. Journal of Biomaterials Applications 2011;25(6):619—39.

[45] Basniwal RK, Khosla R, Jain N. Improving the anticancer activity of curcumin using nanocurcumin dispersion in water. Nutrition and Cancer 2014;66(6):1015—22.

[46] Esmaili M, Ghaffari SM, Moosavi-Movahedi Z, Atri MS, Sharifizadeh A, Farhadi M, et al. Beta casein-micelle as a nano vehicle for solubility enhancement of curcumin; food industry application. LWT-Food Science and Technology 2011;44(10):2166−72.

[47] Anuchapreeda S, Fukumori Y, Okonogi S, Ichikawa H. Preparation of lipid nanoemulsions incorporating curcumin for cancer therapy. Journal of Nanotechnology 2012;2012.

[48] Yoo SD, Lee SH, Kang E, Jun H, Jung JY, Park JW, et al. Bioavailability of itraconazole in rats and rabbits after administration of tablets containing solid dispersion particles. Drug Development and Industrial Pharmacy 2000;26(1):27−34.

[49] Kaewnopparat N, Kaewnopparat S, Jangwang A, Maneenaun D, Chuchome T, Panichayupakaranant P. Increased solubility, dissolution and physicochemical studies of curcumin-polyvinylpyrrolidone K-30 solid dispersions. World Academy of Science, Engineering and Technology 2009;55:229−34.

[50] Reddy PD, Swarnalatha D. Recent advances in novel drug delivery systems. International Journal of Research in Ayurveda and Pharmacy 2003;1(2):316−26.

[51] Yu H, Huang Q. Enhanced in vitro anti-cancer activity of curcumin encapsulated in hydrophobically modified starch. Food Chemistry 2010;119(2):669−74.

[52] Tønnesen HH, Másson M, Loftsson T. Studies of curcumin and curcuminoids. XXVII. Cyclodextrin complexation: solubility, chemical and photochemical stability. International Journal of Pharmaceutics 2002;244(1−2):127−35. Available from: https://doi.org/10.1016/s0378-5173(02)00323-x.

[53] Iwunze MO. Binding and distribution characteristics of curcumin solubilized in CTAB micelle. Journal of Molecular Liquids 2004;111(1−3):161−5.

[54] Shoba G, Joy D, Joseph T, Majeed M, Rajendran R, Srinivas PSSR. Influence of piperine on the pharmacokinetics of curcumin in animals and human volunteers. Planta Medica 1998;64(04):353−6.

[55] Bano G, Raina RK, Zutshi U, Bedi KL, Johri RK, Sharma SC. Effect of piperine on bioavailability and pharmacokinetics of propranolol and theophylline in healthy volunteers. European Journal of Clinical Pharmacology 1991;41(6):615−17.

[56] Velpandian T, Jasuja R, Bhardwaj RK, Jaiswal J, Gupta SK. Piperine in food: interference in the pharmacokinetics of phenytoin. European Journal of Drug Metabolism and Pharmacokinetics 2001;26(4):241−7.

[57] Liu ZJ, Han G, Yu JG, Dai HG. Preparation and drug releasing property of curcumin nanoparticles. Zhong yao cai = Zhongyaocai = Journal of Chinese Medicinal Materials 2009;32(2):277−9.

[58] Li L, Braiteh FS, Kurzrock R. Liposome-encapsulated curcumin: in vitro and in vivo effects on proliferation, apoptosis, signaling, and angiogenesis. *Cancer: Interdisciplinary*. International Journal of the American Cancer Society 2005;104(6):1322−31.

[59] Lin CC, Lin HY, Chen HC, Yu MW, Lee MH. Stability and characterisation of phospholipid-based curcumin-encapsulated microemulsions. Food Chemistry 2009;116(4):923−8.

[60] Liu A, Lou H, Zhao L, Fan P. Validated LC/MS/MS assay for curcumin and tetrahydrocurcumin in rat plasma and application to pharmacokinetic study of phospholipid complex of curcumin. Journal of Pharmaceutical and Biomedical Analysis 2006;40(3):720−7.

[61] Shaikh J, Ankola DD, Beniwal V, Singh D, Kumar MR. Nanoparticle encapsulation improves oral bioavailability of curcumin by at least 9-fold when compared to curcumin administered with piperine as absorption enhancer. European Journal of Pharmaceutical Sciences 2009;37(3−4):223−30.

[62] Wang, X, Wang, YW, & Huang Q. (2009). Enhancing stability and oral bioavailability of polyphenols using nanoemulsions.

[63] Lopes-Rodrigues V, Sousa E, Vasconcelos MH. Curcumin as a modulator of P-glycoprotein in cancer: challenges and perspectives. Pharmaceuticals 2016;9(4):71.

[64] Sivasami P, Hemalatha T. Augmentation of therapeutic potential of curcumin using nanotechnology: current perspectives. Artificial Cells, Nanomedicine, and Biotechnology 2018;46(sup1):1004−15.

[65] Paşcalău V, Soritau O, Popa F, Pavel C, Coman V, Perhaita I, et al. Curcumin delivered through bovine serum albumin/polysaccharides multilayered microcapsules. Journal of Biomaterials Applications 2016;30(6):857−72.

[66] Ghosh M, Singh AT, Xu W, Sulchek T, Gordon LI, Ryan RO. Curcumin nanodisks: formulation and characterization. Nanomedicine: Nanotechnology, Biology and Medicine 2011;7(2):162−7.

[67] Lv L, Shen Y, Liu J, Wang F, Li M, Li M, et al. Enhancing curcumin anticancer efficacy through di-block copolymer micelle encapsulation. Journal of Biomedical Nanotechnology 2014;10(2):179−93.

[68] Leung MH, Colangelo H, Kee TW. Encapsulation of curcumin in cationic micelles suppresses alkaline hydrolysis. Langmuir the ACS Journal of Surfaces and Colloids 2008;24(11):5672−5.

[69] Song Z, Zhu W, Liu N, Yang F, Feng R. Linolenic acid-modified PEG-PCL micelles for curcumin delivery. International Journal of Pharmaceutics 2014;471(1−2):312−21.

[70] Zou L, Zheng B, Liu W, Liu C, Xiao H, McClements DJ. Enhancing nutraceutical bioavailability using excipient emulsions: influence of lipid droplet size on solubility and bioaccessibility of powdered curcumin. Journal of Functional Foods 2015;15:72−83.

[71] Thangapazham RL, Puri A, Tele S, Blumenthal R, Maheshwari RK. Evaluation of a nanotechnology-based carrier for delivery of curcumin in prostate cancer cells. International Journal of Oncology 2008;32(5):1119−23.

[72] Saengkrit N, Saesoo S, Srinuanchai W, Phunpee S, Ruktanonchai UR. Influence of curcumin-loaded cationic liposome on anticancer activity for cervical cancer therapy. Colloids and Surfaces B: Biointerfaces 2014;114:349−56.

[73] Dai F, Zhang X, Shen W, Chen J, Liu L, Gao G. Liposomal curcumin inhibits hypoxia-induced angiogenesis after transcatheter arterial embolization in VX2 rabbit liver tumors. OncoTargets and Therapy 2015;8:2601.

[74] Paramera EI, Konteles SJ, Karathanos VT. Stability and release properties of curcumin encapsulated in *Saccharomyces cerevisiae*, β-cyclodextrin and modified starch. Food Chemistry 2011;125(3):913−22.

[75] Manju S, Sreenivasan K. Hollow microcapsules built by layer by layer assembly for the encapsulation and sustained release of curcumin. Colloids and Surfaces B: Biointerfaces 2011;82(2):588−93.

[76] Song IS, Cha JS, Choi MK. Characterization, in vivo and in vitro evaluation of solid dispersion of curcumin containing d-α-tocopheryl polyethylene glycol 1000 succinate and mannitol. Molecules (Basel, Switzerland) 2016;21(10):1386.

[77] Paradkar A, Ambike AA, Jadhav BK, Mahadik KR. Characterization of curcumin−PVP solid dispersion obtained by spray drying. International Journal of Pharmaceutics 2004;271(1−2):281−6.

[78] Krausz AE, Adler BL, Cabral V, Navati M, Doerner J, Charafeddine RA, et al. Curcumin-encapsulated nanoparticles as innovative antimicrobial and wound healing agent. Nanomedicine: Nanotechnology, Biology and Medicine 2015;11(1):195−206.

[79] Wang X, Jiang Y, Wang YW, Huang MT, Ho CT, Huang Q. Enhancing anti-inflammation activity of curcumin through O/W nanoemulsions. Food Chemistry 2008;108(2):419−24.

[80] Hu L, Jia Y, Niu F, Jia Z, Yang X, Jiao K. Preparation and enhancement of oral bioavailability of curcumin using microemulsions vehicle. Journal of Agricultural and Food Chemistry 2012;60(29):7137−41.

[81] Nair KL, Thulasidasan AKT, Deepa G, Anto RJ, Kumar GV. Purely aqueous PLGA nanoparticulate formulations of curcumin exhibit enhanced anticancer activity with dependence on the combination of the carrier. International Journal of Pharmaceutics 2012;425(1−2):44−52.

[82] Purpura M, Lowery RP, Wilson JM, Mannan H, Münch G, Razmovski-Naumovski V. Analysis of different innovative formulations of curcumin for improved relative oral bioavailability in human subjects. European Journal of Nutrition 2018;57(3):929−38.

[83] Dai Tran L, Hoang NMT, Mai TT, Tran HV, Nguyen NT, Tran TD, et al. Nanosized magnetofluorescent Fe_3O_4−curcumin conjugate for multimodal monitoring and drug targeting. Colloids and Surfaces A: Physicochemical and Engineering Aspects 2010;371(1−3):104−12.

[84] Mancarella S, Greco V, Baldassarre F, Vergara D, Maffia M, Leporatti S. Polymer-coated magnetic nanoparticles for curcumin delivery to cancer cells. Macromolecular Bioscience 2015;15(10):1365−74.

[85] Yallapu MM, Othman SF, Curtis ET, Bauer NA, Chauhan N, Kumar D, et al. Curcumin-loaded magnetic nanoparticles for breast cancer therapeutics and imaging applications. International Journal of Nanomedicine 2012;7:1761.

[86] Gafner S, Lee SK, Cuendet M, Barthélémy S, Vergnes L, Labidalle S, et al. Biologic evaluation of curcumin and structural derivatives in cancer chemoprevention model systems. Phytochemistry 2004;65 (21):2849−59.

[87] Fidelis GK, Louis H, Tizhe TF, Onoshe S. Curcumin and curcumin-based derivatives as anti-cancer agents: recent nano-synthetic methodologies and anti-cancer therapeutic mechanisms. Journal of Medicinal and Chemical Sciences 2019;2(2):59−63.

[88] Mohanty C, Sahoo SK. The in vitro stability and in vivo pharmacokinetics of curcumin prepared as an aqueous nanoparticulate formulation. Biomaterials 2010;31(25):6597−611.

[89] Gaurisankar S, Tanya D, Shuvomoy B, Juni C. Curcumin: from exotic spice to modern anticancer drug. Al Ameen Journal of Medical Sciences 2010;3(1):21−37.

[90] Zhao S, Pi C, Ye Y, Zhao L, Wei Y. Recent advances of analogues of curcumin for treatment of cancer. European Journal of Medicinal Chemistry 2019;180:524−35.

[91] Lee DS, Lee MK, Kim JH. Curcumin induces cell cycle arrest and apoptosis in human osteosarcoma (HOS) cells. Anticancer Research 2009;29(12):5039−44.

[92] Zhang Y, Chan HF, Leong KW. Advanced materials and processing for drug delivery: the past and the future. Advanced Drug Delivery Reviews 2013;65(1):104−20.

[93] Kim SE, Paik HY, Yoon H, Lee JE, Kim N, Sung MK. Sex-and gender-specific disparities in colorectal cancer risk. World Journal of Gastroenterology: WJG 2015;21(17):5167.

[94] Deitrick J, Pruitt WM. Wnt/β catenin-mediated signaling commonly altered in colorectal cancer. Progress in Molecular Biology and Translational Science 2016;144:49−68.

[95] Woraphatphadung T, Sajomsang W, Gonil P, Saesoo S, Opanasopit P. Synthesis and characterization of pH-responsive N-naphthyl-N, O-succinyl chitosan micelles for oral meloxicam delivery. Carbohydrate Polymers 2015;121:99−106.

[96] Zhang W, Cui T, Liu L, Wu Q, Sun L, Li L, et al. Improving anti-tumor activity of curcumin by polymeric micelles in thermosensitive hydrogel system in colorectal peritoneal carcinomatosis model. Journal of Biomedical Nanotechnology 2015;11(7):1173−82.

[97] Kumar P, Kadakol A, Krishna Shasthrula P, Arunrao Mundhe N, Sudhir Jamdade V, C Barua C, et al. Curcumin as an adjuvant to breast cancer treatment. Anti-Cancer Agents in Medicinal Chemistry (Formerly Current Medicinal Chemistry-Anti-Cancer Agents) 2015;15(5):647−56.

[98] Wang Y, Yu J, Cui R, Lin J, Ding X. Curcumin in treating breast cancer: A review. Journal of Laboratory Automation 2016;21(6):723−31.

[99] Lin M, Ye M, Zhou J, Wang ZP, Zhu X. Recent advances on the molecular mechanism of cervical carcinogenesis based on systems biology technologies. Computational and Structural Biotechnology Journal 2019;17:241−50.

[100] Liu L, Sun L, Wu Q, Guo W, Li L, Chen Y, et al. Curcumin loaded polymeric micelles inhibit breast tumor growth and spontaneous pulmonary metastasis. International Journal of Pharmaceutics 2013;443(1−2):175−82.

[101] Wu K, Ding J, Chen C, Sun W, Ning BF, Wen W, et al. Hepatic transforming growth factor beta gives rise to tumor-initiating cells and promotes liver cancer development. Hepatology (Baltimore, Md.) 2012;56(6):2255−67.

[102] Gupta S. Molecular steps of death receptor and mitochondrial pathways of apoptosis. Life Sciences 2001;69(25−26):2957−64.

[103] Lu C, Jiang L, Xu W, Yu F, Xia W, Pan M, et al. Poly (ethylene glycol) crosslinked multi-armed poly (ε-benzyloxycarbonyl-L-lysine) s as super-amphiphiles: synthesis, self-assembly, and evaluation as efficient delivery systems for poorly water-soluble drugs. Colloids and Surfaces B: Biointerfaces 2019;182:110384.

[104] Hirsch FR, Scagliotti GV, Mulshine JL, Kwon R, Curran Jr WJ, Wu YL, et al. Lung cancer: current therapies and new targeted treatments. The Lancet 2017;389(10066):299–311.

[105] Wan Mohd Tajuddin WNB, Lajis NH, Abas F, Othman I, Naidu R. Mechanistic understanding of curcumin's therapeutic effects in lung cancer. Nutrients 2019;11(12):2989.

[106] Chen HW, Lee JY, Huang JY, Wang CC, Chen WJ, Su SF, et al. Curcumin inhibits lung cancer cell invasion and metastasis through the tumor suppressor HLJ1. Cancer Research 2008;68(18):7428–38.

[107] Zhu W-T, Liu S-Y, Wu L, Xu H-L, Wang J, Ni G-X, et al. Delivery of curcumin by directed self-assembled micelles enhances therapeutic treatment of non-small-cell lung cancer. International Journal of Nanomedicine. 2017;12:2621.

[108] Wang P, Liu S, Cheng B, Wu X, Ding S, Wu D, et al. Expression of cyclin D1 in cervical intraepithelial neoplasia and squamous cell carcinoma and its relationship with HPV16 E7 gene. Zhonghua Bing li xue za zhi = Chinese Journal of Pathology 2015;44(12):884–8.

[109] Gupta S, Gupta MK. Possible role of nanocarriers in drug delivery against cervical cancer. Nano Reviews & Experiments 2017;8(1):1335567.

[110] Wang J, Liu Q, Yang L, Xia X, Zhu R, Chen S, et al. Curcumin-loaded TPGS/F127/P123 mixed polymeric micelles for cervical cancer therapy: formulation, characterization, and in vitro and in vivo evaluation. Journal of Biomedical Nanotechnology 2017;13(12):1631–46.

[111] Sahlol AT, Kollmannsberger P, Ewees AA. Efficient classification of white blood cell leukemia with improved swarm optimization of deep features. Scientific Reports 2020;10(1):1–11.

[112] Kouhpeikar H, Butler AE, Bamian F, Barreto GE, Majeed M, Sahebkar A. Curcumin as a therapeutic agent in leukemia. Journal of Cellular Physiology 2019;234(8):12404–14.

[113] Zoi V, Galani V, Lianos GD, Voulgaris S, Kyritsis AP, Alexiou GA. The role of curcumin in cancer treatment. Biomedicines 2021;9(9):1086.

[114] Rafiq S, Raza MH, Younas M, Naeem F, Adeeb R, Iqbal J, et al. Molecular targets of curcumin and future therapeutic role in leukemia. Journal of Biosciences and Medicines 2018;6(04):33.

[115] Tima S, Anuchapreeda S, Ampasavate C, Berkland C, Okonogi S. Stable curcumin-loaded polymeric micellar formulation for enhancing cellular uptake and cytotoxicity to FLT3 overexpressing EoL-1 leukemic cells. European Journal of Pharmaceutics and Biopharmaceutics 2017;114:57–68.

[116] Tima S, Okonogi S, Ampasavate C, Berkland C, Anuchapreeda S. FLT3-specific curcumin micelles enhance activity of curcumin on FLT3-ITD overexpressing MV4-11 leukemic cells. Drug Development and Industrial Pharmacy 2019;45(3):498–505.

[117] Yoncheva K, Kamenova K, Perperieva T, Hadjimitova V, Donchev P, Kaloyanov K, et al. Cationic triblock copolymer micelles enhance antioxidant activity, intracellular uptake and cytotoxicity of curcumin. International Journal of Pharmaceutics 2015;490(1–2):298–307.

[118] Yallapu MM, Jaggi M, Chauhan SC. Scope of nanotechnology in ovarian cancer therapeutics. Journal of Ovarian Research 2010;3(1):1–10.

[119] Feng YL, Chen DQ, Vaziri ND, Guo Y, Zhao YY. Small molecule inhibitors of epithelial-mesenchymal transition for the treatment of cancer and fibrosis. Medicinal Research Reviews 2020;40(1):54–78.

[120] Vergara D, Merlot B, Lucot JP, Collinet P, Vinatier D, Fournier I, et al. Epithelial–mesenchymal transition in ovarian cancer. Cancer Letters 2010;291(1):59–66.

[121] He M, Li Y, Zhang L, Li L, Shen Y, Lin L, et al. Curcumin suppresses cell proliferation through inhibition of the Wnt/β-catenin signaling pathway in medulloblastoma. Oncology Reports 2014;32(1):173–80.

[122] Yen HY, Tsao CW, Lin YW, Kuo CC, Tsao CH, Liu CY. Regulation of carcinogenesis and modulation through Wnt/β-catenin signaling by curcumin in an ovarian cancer cell line. Scientific Reports 2019;9 (1):1−14.

[123] Tomeh MA, Hadianamrei R, Zhao X. A review of curcumin and its derivatives as anticancer agents. International Journal of Molecular Sciences 2019;20(5):1033. Available from: https://doi.org/10.3390/ijms20051033.

[124] Naksuriya O, Okonogi S, Schiffelers RM, Hennink WE. Curcumin nanoformulations: a review of pharmaceutical properties and preclinical studies and clinical data related to cancer treatment. Biomaterials 2014;35(10):3365−83.

[125] Danhier F, Ansorena E, Silva JM, Coco R, Le Breton A, Préat V. PLGA-based nanoparticles: an overview of biomedical applications. Journal of Controlled Release 2012;161(2):505−22.

[126] Fredenberg S, Wahlgren M, Reslow M, Axelsson A. The mechanisms of drug release in poly (lactic-co-glycolic acid)-based drug delivery systems—a review. International Journal of Pharmaceutics 2011;415 (1−2):34−52.

[127] Song W, Muthana M, Mukherjee J, Falconer RJ, Biggs CA, Zhao X. Magnetic-silk core−shell nanoparticles as potential carriers for targeted delivery of curcumin into human breast cancer cells. ACS Biomaterials Science & Engineering 2017;3(6):1027−38.

[128] Dende C, Meena J, Nagarajan P, Nagaraj VA, Panda AK, Padmanaban G. Nanocurcumin is superior to native curcumin in preventing degenerative changes in experimental cerebral malaria. Scientific Reports 2017;7(1):1−12.

[129] Punfa W, Yodkeeree S, Pitchakarn P, Ampasavate C, Limtrakul P. Enhancement of cellular uptake and cytotoxicity of curcumin-loaded PLGA nanoparticles by conjugation with anti-P-glycoprotein in drug resistance cancer cells. Acta Pharmacologica Sinica 2012;33(6):823−31.

[130] Verderio P, Pandolfi L, Mazzucchelli S, Marinozzi MR, Vanna R, Gramatica F, et al. Antiproliferative effect of ASC-J9 delivered by PLGA nanoparticles against estrogen-dependent breast cancer cells. Molecular Pharmaceutics 2014;11(8):2864−75.

[131] Malam Y, Loizidou M, Seifalian AM. Liposomes and nanoparticles: nanosized vehicles for drug delivery in cancer. Trends in Pharmacological Sciences 2009;30(11):592−9.

[132] Sun M, Su X, Ding B, He X, Liu X, Yu A, et al. Advances in nanotechnology-based delivery systems for curcumin. Nanomedicine Nanotechnology, Biology, and Medicine 2012;7(7):1085−100.

[133] Mangalathillam S, Rejinold NS, Nair A, Lakshmanan VK, Nair SV, Jayakumar R. Curcumin loaded chitin nanogels for skin cancer treatment via the transdermal route. Nanoscale 2012;4(1):239−50.

[134] Wang D, Veena MS, Stevenson K, Tang C, Ho B, Suh JD, et al. Liposome-encapsulated curcumin suppresses growth of head and neck squamous cell carcinoma in vitro and in xenografts through the inhibition of nuclear factor κB by an AKT-independent pathway. Clinical Cancer Research 2008;14 (19):6228−36.

[135] Li X, Chen S, Zhang B, Li M, Diao K, Zhang Z, et al. In situ injectable nano-composite hydrogel composed of curcumin, N, O-carboxymethyl chitosan and oxidized alginate for wound healing application. International Journal of Pharmaceutics 2012;437(1−2):110−19.

[136] Lin YL, Liu YK, Tsai NM, Hsieh JH, Chen CH, Lin CM, et al. A Lipo-PEG-PEI complex for encapsulating curcumin that enhances its antitumor effects on curcumin-sensitive and curcumin-resistance cells. Nanomedicine: Nanotechnology, Biology and Medicine 2012;8(3):318−27.

[137] Zanotto-Filho A, Coradini K, Braganhol E, Schröder R, De Oliveira CM, Simões-Pires A, et al. Curcumin-loaded lipid-core nanocapsules as a strategy to improve pharmacological efficacy of curcumin in glioma treatment. European Journal of Pharmaceutics and Biopharmaceutics 2013;83 (2):156−67.

[138] Ganta S, Amiji M. Coadminstration of paclitaxel and curcumin in nanoemulsion formulations to overcome multidrug resistance in tumor cells. Molecular Pharmaceutics 2009;6(3):928−39.

[139] Re F, Cambianica I, Zona C, Sesana S, Gregori M, Rigolio R, et al. Functionalization of liposomes with ApoE-derived peptides at different density affects cellular uptake and drug transport across a blood-brain barrier model. Nanomedicine: Nanotechnology, Biology and Medicine 2011;7(5):551−9.

[140] Karewicz A, Bielska D, Loboda A, Gzyl-Malcher B, Bednar J, Jozkowicz A, et al. Curcumin-containing liposomes stabilized by thin layers of chitosan derivatives. Colloids and Surfaces B: Biointerfaces 2013;109:307−16.

[141] Gou M, Men K, Shi H, Xiang M, Zhang J, Song J, et al. Curcumin-loaded biodegradable polymeric micelles for colon cancer therapy in vitro and in vivo. Nanoscale 2011;3(4):1558−67.

[142] Karewicz A, Bielska D, Gzyl-Malcher B, Kepczynski M, Lach R, Nowakowska M. Interaction of curcumin with lipid monolayers and liposomal bilayers. Colloids and Surfaces B: Biointerfaces 2011;88 (1):231−9.

[143] Li X, Nan K, Li L, Zhang Z, Chen H. In vivo evaluation of curcumin nanoformulation loaded methoxy poly (ethylene glycol)-graft-chitosan composite film for wound healing application. Carbohydrate Polymers 2012;88(1):84−90.

[144] Fujita K, Hiramatsu Y, Minematsu H, Somiya M, Kuroda SI, Seno M, et al. Release of siRNA from liposomes induced by curcumin. Journal of Nanotechnology 2016;2016.

[145] Amano C, Minematsu H, Fujita K, Iwashita S, Adachi M, Igarashi K, et al. Nanoparticles containing curcumin useful for suppressing macrophages in vivo in mice. PLoS One 2015;10(9):e0137207.

[146] Lee WH, Loo CY, Young PM, Traini D, Mason RS, Rohanizadeh R. Recent advances in curcumin nanoformulation for cancer therapy. Expert Opinion on Drug Delivery 2014;11(8):1183−201.

[147] Hamidi M, Azadi A, Rafiei P. Hydrogel nanoparticles in drug delivery. Advanced Drug Delivery Reviews 2008;60(15):1638−49.

[148] Stuart MAC, Huck WT, Genzer J, Müller M, Ober C, Stamm M, et al. Emerging applications of stimuli-responsive polymer materials. Nature Materials 2010;9(2):101−13.

[149] Das RK, Kasoju N, Bora U. Encapsulation of curcumin in alginate-chitosan-pluronic composite nanoparticles for delivery to cancer cells. Nanomedicine: Nanotechnology, Biology and Medicine 2010;6 (1):153−60.

[150] Hatefi A, Amsden B. Biodegradable injectable in situ forming drug delivery systems. Journal of Controlled Release 2002;80(1−3):9−28.

[151] Chung HJ, Park TG. Self-assembled and nanostructured hydrogels for drug delivery and tissue engineering. Nano Today 2009;4(5):429−37.

[152] Altunbas A, Lee SJ, Rajasekaran SA, Schneider JP, Pochan DJ. Encapsulation of curcumin in self-assembling peptide hydrogels as injectable drug delivery vehicles. Biomaterials 2011;32(25):5906−14.

[153] Lomis N, Westfall S, Farahdel L, Malhotra M, Shum-Tim D, Prakash S. Human serum albumin nanoparticles for use in cancer drug delivery: process optimization and in vitro characterization. Nanomaterials 2016;6(6):116.

[154] Kim TH, Jiang HH, Youn YS, Park CW, Tak KK, Lee S, et al. Preparation and characterization of water-soluble albumin-bound curcumin nanoparticles with improved antitumor activity. International Journal of Pharmaceutics 2011;403(1−2):285−91.

[155] Dal Pra I, Freddi G, Minic J, Chiarini A, Armato U. De novo engineering of reticular connective tissue in vivo by silk fibroin nonwoven materials. Biomaterials 2005;26(14):1987−99.

[156] Vepari C, Kaplan DL. Silk as a biomaterial. Progress in Polymer Science 2007;32(8−9):991−1007.

[157] Gidwani B, Vyas A. A comprehensive review on cyclodextrin-based carriers for delivery of chemotherapeutic cytotoxic anticancer drugs. BioMed Research International 2015;2015.

[158] Yallapu MM, Jaggi M, Chauhan SC. β-Cyclodextrin-curcumin self-assembly enhances curcumin delivery in prostate cancer cells. Colloids and Surfaces B: Biointerfaces 2010;79(1):113−25.

[159] Rocks N, Bekaert S, Coia I, Paulissen G, Guéders M, Evrard B, et al. Curcumin—cyclodextrin complexes potentiate gemcitabine effects in an orthotopic mouse model of lung cancer. British Journal of Cancer 2012;107(7):1083—92.

[160] Tang XZ, Kumar P, Alavi S, Sandeep KP. Recent advances in biopolymers and biopolymer-based nanocomposites for food packaging materials. Critical Reviews in Food Science and Nutrition 2012;52(5):426—42.

[161] Nitta SK, Numata K. Biopolymer-based nanoparticles for drug/gene delivery and tissue engineering. International Journal of Molecular Sciences 2013;14(1):1629—54.

[162] Samrot AV, Burman U, Philip SA, Shobana N, Chandrasekaran K. Synthesis of curcumin loaded polymeric nanoparticles from crab shell derived chitosan for drug delivery. Informatics in Medicine Unlocked 2018;10:159—82.

[163] Umerska A, Gaucher C, Oyarzun-Ampuero F, Fries-Raeth I, Colin F, Villamizar-Sarmiento MG, et al. Polymeric nanoparticles for increasing oral bioavailability of curcumin. Antioxidants 2018;7(4):46.

[164] Medel S, Syrova Z, Kovacik L, Hrdy J, Hornacek M, Jager E, et al. Curcumin-bortezomib loaded polymeric nanoparticles for synergistic cancer therapy. European Polymer Journal 2017;93:116—31.

[165] García-Pinel B, Porras-Alcalá C, Ortega-Rodríguez A, Sarabia F, Prados J, Melguizo C, et al. Lipid-based nanoparticles: application and recent advances in cancer treatment. Nanomaterials 2019;9(4):638.

[166] Duse L, Agel MR, Pinnapireddy SR, Schäfer J, Selo MA, Ehrhardt C, et al. Photodynamic therapy of ovarian carcinoma cells with curcumin-loaded biodegradable polymeric nanoparticles. Pharmaceutics 2019;11(6):282.

[167] Arya G, Das M, Sahoo SK. Evaluation of curcumin loaded chitosan/PEG blended PLGA nanoparticles for effective treatment of pancreatic cancer. Biomedicine & Pharmacotherapy 2018;102:555—66.

[168] Datta S, Jutková A, Šrámková P, Lenkavská L, Huntošová V, Chorvát D, et al. Unravelling the excellent chemical stability and bioavailability of solvent responsive curcumin-loaded 2-ethyl-2-oxazoline-grad-2-(4-dodecyloxyphenyl)-2-oxazoline copolymer nanoparticles for drug delivery. Biomacromolecules 2018;19(7):2459—71.

[169] Guo H, Xu YM, Ye ZQ, Yu JH, Hu XY. Curcumin induces cell cycle arrest and apoptosis of prostate cancer cells by regulating the expression of IκBα, c-Jun and androgen receptor. Die Pharmazie-An International Journal of Pharmaceutical Sciences 2013;68(6):431—4.

[170] Lv ZD, Liu XP, Zhao WJ, Dong Q, Li FN, Wang HB, et al. Curcumin induces apoptosis in breast cancer cells and inhibits tumor growth in vitro and in vivo. International Journal of Clinical and Experimental Pathology 2014;7(6):2818.

[171] Ma J, Fang B, Zeng F, Pang H, Zhang J, Shi Y, et al. Curcumin inhibits cell growth and invasion through up-regulation of miR-7 in pancreatic cancer cells. Toxicology Letters 2014;231(1):82—91.

[172] Salehi M, Movahedpour A, Tayarani A, Shabaninejad Z, Pourhanifeh MH, Mortezapour E, et al. Therapeutic potentials of curcumin in the treatment of non-small-cell lung carcinoma. Phytotherapy Research 2020;34(10):2557—76.

[173] Shehzad A, Lee J, Huh TL, Lee YS. Curcumin induces apoptosis in human colorectal carcinoma (HCT-15) cells by regulating expression of Prp4 and p53. Molecules and Cells 2013;35(6):526—32.

[174] Zhen L, Fan D, Yi X, Cao X, Chen D, Wang L. Curcumin inhibits oral squamous cell carcinoma proliferation and invasion via EGFR signaling pathways. International Journal of Clinical and Experimental Pathology 2014;7(10):6438.

[175] Kunnumakkara AB, Bordoloi D, Harsha C, Banik K, Gupta SC, Aggarwal BB. Curcumin mediates anticancer effects by modulating multiple cell signaling pathways. Clinical Science 2017;131(15):1781—99.

[176] Zhou H, S Beevers C, Huang S. The targets of curcumin. Current Drug Targets 2011;12(3):332—47.

[177] Chen A, Xu J, Johnson AC. Curcumin inhibits human colon cancer cell growth by suppressing gene expression of epidermal growth factor receptor through reducing the activity of the transcription factor Egr-1. Oncogene 2006;25(2):278—87.

[178] Sa G, Das T. Anti cancer effects of curcumin: cycle of life and death. Cell Division 2008;3(1):1−14.

[179] Anand P, Kunnumakkara AB, Newman RA, Aggarwal BB. Bioavailability of curcumin: problems and promises. Molecular Pharmaceutics 2007;4(6):807−18.

[180] Wong KE, Ngai SC, Chan KG, Lee LH, Goh BH, Chuah LH. Curcumin nanoformulations for colorectal cancer: a review. Frontiers in Pharmacology 2019;10:152.

[181] Yallapu MM, Jaggi M, Chauhan SC. Curcumin nanoformulations: a future nanomedicine for cancer. Drug Discovery Today 2012;17(1−2):71−80.

[182] Noh J, Kwon B, Han E, Park M, Yang W, Cho W, et al. Amplification of oxidative stress by a dual stimuli-responsive hybrid drug enhances cancer cell death. Nature Communications 2015;6(1):1−9.

[183] Batra H, Pawar S, Bahl D. Curcumin in combination with anti-cancer drugs: A nanomedicine review. Pharmacological Research 2019;139:91−105.

[184] Setyawati MI, Tay CY, Docter D, Stauber RH, Leong DT. Understanding and exploiting nanoparticles' intimacy with the blood vessel and blood. Chemical Society Reviews 2015;44(22):8174−99.

[185] Shi J, Votruba AR, Farokhzad OC, Langer R. Nanotechnology in drug delivery and tissue engineering: from discovery to applications. Nano Letters 2010;10(9):3223−30.

15

Nanohybrid drug delivery approach as a novel opportunity for curcumin delivery in cancer

Mehdi Sanati[1,2], Amir R. Afshari[3], Luis E. Simental-Mendía[4], Amirhossein Sahebkar[5,6]

[1]DEPARTMENT OF PHARMACOLOGY AND TOXICOLOGY, FACULTY OF PHARMACY, BIRJAND UNIVERSITY OF MEDICAL SCIENCES, BIRJAND, IRAN [2]EXPERIMENTAL AND ANIMAL STUDY CENTER, BIRJAND UNIVERSITY OF MEDICAL SCIENCES, BIRJAND, IRAN [3]DEPARTMENT OF PHYSIOLOGY AND PHARMACOLOGY, FACULTY OF MEDICINE, NORTH KHORASAN UNIVERSITY OF MEDICAL SCIENCES, BOJNURD, IRAN [4]BIOMEDICAL RESEARCH UNIT, MEXICAN SOCIAL SECURITY INSTITUTE, DURANGO, MEXICO [5]BIOTECHNOLOGY RESEARCH CENTER, PHARMACEUTICAL TECHNOLOGY INSTITUTE, MASHHAD UNIVERSITY OF MEDICAL SCIENCES, MASHHAD, IRAN [6]APPLIED BIOMEDICAL RESEARCH CENTER, MASHHAD UNIVERSITY OF MEDICAL SCIENCES, MASHHAD, IRAN

15.1 Introduction

Cancer treatment is a challenging area of research due to the complex pathology of malignancies. Despite significant advancements in preclinical cancer studies, current clinical chemotherapeutics often failed to improve patient survival and even caused noticeable adverse effects due to insufficient delivery to the tumor site as well as nonselective toxicity [1]. In this regard, originating novel drug delivery systems (DDS) is a beneficial approach to improving the pharmacokinetics and clinical efficacy of available drugs [2]. Curcumin (Cur), a promising phytochemical from *Curcuma longa*, has shown multiple biological and pharmacological effects [3–14]. Curcumin can exert numerous anticancer mechanisms, notably suppressing survival signal transducer and activator of transcription 3 (STAT3) and nuclear factor kappa B (NF-κB) signaling pathways and promoting programmed apoptotic death in preclinical studies [15–17]; nevertheless, the relative water insolubility and limited bioavailability are potential factors challenging the clinical application of these effects [18]. With this in mind, various DDS based on nanostructures bring back the hope of Cur effectiveness in cancer patients. Nano-DDS is a relatively new but quickly emerging field in which materials in the nanoscale range (e.g., nanoparticles [NPs], nanoliposomes, micelles, nanogels, and nanodisks) are exploited to administer therapeutic drugs to particular targeted locations in a controlled manner [19]. Incorporating Cur into these nanospecies results in the emergence of nanohybrids, increases Cur delivery to the site of action, and improves its clinical effectiveness while reducing off-target adverse effects [20]. Notably, attaching targeting ligands to the developed Cur-loaded nanocarriers further increases the Cur uptake by the tumor cells [21]. During the last decade, tremendous efforts have been conducted to originate novel, safe, and effective Cur nanohybrids; nevertheless, extensive research along with large-scale clinical trials is required to guarantee their clinical implication. This chapter highlighted the research progress in developing efficient nanohybrid Cur delivery systems as cancer therapeutics.

15.2 Nanohybrids as promising tools for curcumin delivery

DDS has revolutionized the therapeutic outcomes of medication due to the increased drug access to the site of action and reduced the undesired adverse or toxic effects. DDS-mediated drug accumulation at the site of action also reduces the required doses of medicines [22, 23]. Optimized and biocompatible nanocarriers are readily taken up by cells compared to larger molecules. In this regard, diverse nanostructures like NPs have shown significant promise in developing DDS for available bioactive compounds [24]. This is especially true in the case of Cur, which, despite excellent anticancer properties, has dismal pharmacokinetics, limiting its clinical implications. Nano-DDS increases Cur delivery to the site of action across various barriers and improves its cellular uptake [25]. In the following multiple nanostructures recruited for producing Cur nanohybrids are discussed.

15.2.1 Nanoparticle-based curcumin nanohybrids

15.2.1.1 Gold nanoparticles

Regarding their biocompatibility, unique proportions, modifiable functionalities on the surface, and controllable drug release, gold NPs (AuNPs) are among the best nanocarriers for a wide range of biomolecules [26]. Notably, incorporating Cur into AuNPs causes a remarkable increase in Cur bioavailability and apoptotic anticancer effects [27]. For example, Cur-capped AuNPs-conjugated reduced graphene oxide (CAG) nanocomposites showed significant and selective toxicity against colon cancer cells [28]. Similarly, Cur-coated AuNPs were recently shown to induce apoptosis in colorectal adenocarcinoma cells as indicated by upregulated apoptotic (e.g., Bax, P53, and P21) and downregulated antiapoptotic (e.g., bcl-2) proteins [29]. Furthermore, loading Cur into gelatin-coated AuNPs was shown to produce controlled released nanohybrids that preferentially release Cur at acidic tumor conditions [30]. Recruiting Cur as a capping and reducing agent in gold quantum cluster synthesis also yielded a selective anticancer nanohybrid with minimal effect on noncancerous cells. In vivo examinations confirmed the nanohybrid efficacy and selective toxicity [31]. More interestingly, Cur stabilized AuNPs were exhibited to be stable at room temperature for at least 6 months while releasing Cur at body temperature for 6 hours. Examinations on glioma cells showed remarkable cellular uptake and apoptotic effect of the nanohybrids [32]. These data, along with other numerous preclinical reports, show the potential of AuNPs in developing Cur nanohybrids with remarkable stability and bioavailability, selective delivery, significant efficacy, and controlled release behavior [27]. However, the physicochemical characteristics of Cur-loaded AuNPs, like particle size and surface charge, have a noticeable impact on the cellular uptake as well as the cytotoxicity of nanohybrids due to the surface interaction with various proteins in the biological medium [33]. Accordingly, further preclinical and even clinical trials are necessary to move AuNPs-based Cur nanohybrids toward the clinic. A comprehensive discussion on the role of nanogold species in advancing Cur delivery has recently been published [27].

15.2.1.2 Iron oxide nanoparticles

Ultrasmall magnetic NPs have great potential as novel nanocarriers for Cur delivery to the site of action [34]. Iron oxide NPs (IONPs), due to their good magnetic properties, favorable biocompatibility, and inexpensive synthesis, have been frequently recruited in biomedical applications such as designing targeted DDS [35]. However, based on size, surface trait, and zeta potential, IONPs may produce adverse effects; hence, optimizing their characteristics is critical [36, 37]. With this in mind, negatively charged ultrasmall nanohybrids constructed from Cur conjugation to IONPs (IONs@Cur) were shown to improve the Cur bioavailability and cellular uptake and caused greater cytotoxicity to HepG2 hepatocellular carcinoma cells. Interestingly, the nanohybrid formulation not only increased Cur delivery to the cancerous cells but also enhanced IONPs' safety toward normal cells [38]. In another attempt, ultrasmall superparamagnetic IONPs (SPIONs) were coated with poly (lactic-co-glycolic acid)-poly (ethylene glycol) (PLGA-PEG) diblock copolymer, loaded with Cur, and conjugated with glycine-arginine-glycine-aspartic acid-serine (GRGDS) peptide. The polymeric coating layer has Food and Drug Administration (FDA) approval for slowing SPIONs' degradation rate, improving targeted delivery, and enhancing blood–brain barrier (BBB) penetration. The developed DDS showed significant cytotoxicity against T98 glioma cells and needs further in vivo examination [39]. Colloidally stabilized ultrasmall SPIONs coated by water-soluble Cur-conjugated sodium alginate are also synthesized, benefiting from the delivery of stable and soluble Cur and the magnetic hyperthermia properties of the nanohybrid, and have a high anticancer potential. Notably, the nanoconjugate showed no toxic effect in fibroblast cells [40]. Recently, an intriguing experiment loaded Cur into a magneto-thermal nanocarrier consisting of SPIONs coated by three-block copolymer Pluronic F127 and F68 on the oleic acid. The concurrent impact of the nanohybrids and magnetic field was evaluated on MG-63 osteosarcoma cells. Results demonstrated that at 41°C under magnetic field and acidic conditions, the Cur release from nanocarriers and its apoptotic effects are optimum. Notably, the synergistic effect of the nanohybrids and hyperthermia on killing cancerous cells was demonstrated [41]. Accordingly, engineered IONPs with certain surface traits are valuable and relatively safe nanocarriers for Cur delivery and further add value to the treatment due to their magnetic properties.

15.2.1.3 Albumin nanoparticles

Albumin is a biocompatible, stable, and nonimmunogenic protein with multiple binding sites transporting drug molecules in the bloodstream [42]. Interestingly, the albumin-binding proteins are overexpressed on the surface of tumor vascular endothelial cells, facilitating the accumulation of albumin in the tumor site [43]. In this regard, Cur-loaded bovine serum albumin NPs (BSA@CUR NPs) have been developed as a nanohybrid DDS for Cur delivery. The BSA@CUR NPs showed a controlled release pattern for Cur and improved its water solubility as well as therapeutic efficacy. The nanohybrids were hemocompatible and nontoxic to HFF2 fibroblast cells while producing cytotoxic effects in MCF-7 cancer cells [42]. Consistently, Cur-loaded human serum albumin NPs (HSA@CUR NPs) showed more significant anticancer impacts in a xenografted HCT116 animal model than free Cur without producing significant adverse effects. Interestingly, the water-soluble HSA@CUR NPs showed superior vascular endothelial cell transport and accumulated 14 times higher than free Cur at the tumor site 1 hour after injection [44]. Another research originated Cur-loaded PEGylated albumin NPs and obtained interesting in vitro and in vivo results. The nanohybrid increased Cur water solubility and showed a favorable release profile with a small initial burst followed by a controlled release pattern. Notably, in vivo assessments showed that the presence of the PEG coating layer reduced NPs uptake by liver and Kupffer cells, increasing Cur bioavailability. The antiproliferative impact of nanohybrids on MD-MB-231 breast cancer cells was significantly higher than native Cur [45]. These findings demonstrated the promising potential of optimized albumin NPs in designing DDS for Cur-targeted delivery.

15.2.1.4 Solid lipid nanoparticles

Solid lipid NPs (SLNPs) are nanospecies manufacturing via dispersing synthetic or natural lipids in water or aqueous surfactants. These NPs are extensively engaged in designing DDS due to their high drug payload, long stability, promising biocompatibility, and easy production process. Interestingly, SLNPs provide an increased drug-to-lipid ratio expanding the water solubility and bioactivity of insoluble molecules [46]. In this regard, Cu-loaded SLNPs (Cur-SLNPs) favor better water solubility, bioavailability, stability, cellular uptake, as well as a controlled release nature compared to free Cur [47, 48]. For example, Cur-SLNPs exhibited an increased cellular uptake and strong apoptotic effect in SKBR3 breast cancer cells indicated by upregulated Bax/bcl-2 ratio and reduced cyclin D1 and cyclin-dependent kinase 4 (CDK4) [49]. In a Hodgkin's lymphoma xenografted mice model, Cur-SLNPs produced higher plasma concentration than nonformulated Cur and significantly suppressed tumor growth by reducing the expression of antiapoptotic proteins such as x-linked inhibitor of apoptosis (XIAP) and myeloid leukemia 1 (Mcl-1) [50]. Consistently, using a phase-inversion temperature method, Cur-SLNPs were shown to be the suitable carriers for Cur in aqueous media. In vitro analysis by confocal microscopy demonstrated that Cur-SLNPs are readily taken up by murine CT26 colon adenocarcinoma cells and produce more cytotoxicity than native Cur [51]. Furthermore, optimized SLNPs containing a Cur derivative, compared to free Cur, showed better cellular uptake, apoptosis induction, and suppression of MHCC-97H liver cancer cell proliferation, migration, and invasion. As proof of concept, the expression levels of NF-κB, cyclooxygenase-2 (COX-2), matrix metalloproteinases (MMPs), and urokinase plasminogen activator (uPA) were deceased. In vivo pharmacokinetic examinations also demonstrated increased Cur bioavailability and prolonged retention time with no remarkable liver toxicity [52]. In a nutshell, SLNPs showed advanced potential for improving Cur-targeted delivery and clinical efficacy. Of note, certain surface modifications of SLNPs by various bioactive agents have improved the targeting efficacy of Cur-SLNPs nanohybrids [53, 54]. For example, functionalizing Cur-loaded SLNPs with pectin and skimmed milk has been shown to augment the efficiency of SLNPs to enhance the oral bioavailability of Cur on colon-targeted release [53]. Accordingly, further investigations on SLNPs may provide unique opportunities for designing DDS for Cur delivery as cancer therapeutics.

15.2.1.5 Polymeric nanoparticles

Polymeric NPs have emerged as crucial tools for increasing medications' bioavailability or delivering them to the site of action. The versatility of polymers makes them potentially suitable for meeting the needs of any individual DDS [55]. Various polymers (e.g., PLGA, PEG, polyvinyl alcohol (PVA), polyvinyl pyrrolidone (PVP), hydrophobic starch, Eudragit E 100, and silk fibroin) have been recruited for generating Cur nanohybrids [56]. The Cur-loaded water-soluble PLGA NPs, for example, were shown remarkable efficacy in killing oral and gastric cancer cells. The nanohybrids, compared to Cur, demonstrated improved in vivo bioavailability and in vitro activity. In cancerous cells, the NPs caused noticeable Cur internalization, repressed the expression of multiple drug resistance protein 1 (MDR1), and induced reactive oxygen species (ROS) production as well as caspase-3 and -9 activation provoking mitochondrial apoptotic cell death while exhibiting no toxic effects against normal human gingival fibroblasts and normal human oral keratinocytes [57, 58]. Furthermore, Cur-loaded PLGA-PEG NPs showed more significant cytotoxic effects on MCF-7 breast cancer cells than unformulated Cur. Interestingly, conjugating with epidermal growth factor receptor (EGFR)-targeting GE11 peptides improved the PLGA-PEG NPs' capability in reducing MCF-7 cells' survival in vitro and tumor burden in vivo compared to Cur and even Cur-loaded PLGA-PEG NPs. The novel nanohybrids also showed a prolonged plasma retention time [21, 59]. In addition, incorporating Cur into chitosan/PEG-blended PLGA NPs results in polymeric NPs-based Cur DDS inducing apoptosis and hindering migration and invasion in metastatic pancreatic cancer cells better than its native counterpart [60]. Cur-loaded chitosan NPs also developed against Vero cancer cells. The nanohybrids showed better solubility, stability, and anticancer effects [61].

In addition, the cationic copolymer Eudragit E 100 was shown to improve the Cur bioavailability. By recruiting the emulsification-diffusion-evaporation method, Cur-loaded Eudragit E 100 NPs (CENPs) were synthesized and tested for anticancer effects. In vitro and in vivo pharmacokinetic evaluations revealed 19-fold reduced inhibitory concentration 50 (IC50), 91-fold increased Cmax, and 95-fold raised area under the curve (AUC), illustrating significant increased CENPs' cytotoxicity and bioavailability compared to native Cur. Pharmacodynamic evaluations in mice bearing tumors also revealed a more significant lowering of tumor volume and expanding survival rate [62]. Cur-loaded starch NPs also showed the potential for Cur delivery as osteosarcoma therapeutics. The designed nanohybrids exhibited a sustained Cur release and cytotoxic effect on MG-63 cancer cells while were nontoxic to human adipose mesenchymal stem cells. Although encapsulation of Cur increased its cytotoxic effects on cancerous cells, the sustained release nature of the designed DDS was argued to be more critical than the encapsulation efficacy for anticancer impacts [63]. Furthermore, loading Cur into starch-PVA NPs resulted in originating DDS in which the pH of the medium and storage conditions greatly affects the release of Cur from the polymer matrices. The nanohybrids showed greater in vitro anticancer impacts than Cur and were nontoxic to normal cells [64]. Moreover, encapsulating Cur into silk fibroin NPs showed continuous delivery and potent cytotoxicity to HCT116 colon cancer cells. Controlled release of Cur from the DDS caused better Cur uptake by cancerous cells and reduced its toxicity for normal cells [65]. Overall, polymeric NPs possess significant promise in designing Cur DDS with improved bioavailability, potent and selective toxicity, and targeted delivery to the site of action, making them a hot research topic in cancer drug delivery.

15.2.2 Nanostructures-based curcumin nanohybrids

15.2.2.1 Liposomes

Spherical vesicles composed of phospholipid bilayers called liposomes are established nanocarriers for various bioactive agents. Liposome-based nanohybrids are biocompatible and biodegradable DDS favoring characteristics such as easy penetration to biological barriers, controlled release pattern, precise targeting, steadiness, and safeness [66]. Accordingly, incorporating Cur into nanoliposomes is a rational strategy to improve its bioavailability, targeted delivery, and clinical efficacy. Numerous studies have shown the greater growth inhibitory and apoptotic effects of Cur in nanoliposomal formulations in various preclinical models of cancers [67]. Moreover, the surface modification of nanoliposomes attracted lots of interest to potentiate their targeting and delivery properties as well as loading efficiency. For example, in vivo examinations in U251MG-implanted mice revealed that brain-targeting peptide RDP labeled Cur-loaded nanoliposomes cross the BBB, access the tumor region, enter tumor cells through acetylcholine receptor—mediated endocytosis, and induce cell cycle arrest and apoptosis. The nanohybrid DDS also prolonged the survival of glioma animal models [68]. Another nanoliposomal formulation of Cur showed promising impacts in prostate cancer in vitro and in vivo. Cur-loaded nanoliposomes modified by A15 aptamer targeting C1D33 glycoprotein on the surface of prostate cancer cells have developed with a controlled release pattern and remarkable stability. The nanoliposome nanohybrid system showed successful cell internalization and growth inhibitory function in prostate cancer cells. Similarly, in mice bearing DU145 prostate carcinoma, the nanoliposomes reduced tumor growth more significantly compared to native Cur [69]. Furthermore, encapsulating Cur into natural lecithin-derived nanoliposomes significantly increased its cytotoxic effects on MCF-7 cancer cells. Of note, coating nanoliposomes with chitosan improved Cur loading amounts, augmenting the nanohybrid system's anticancer impacts [70]. Undoubtedly, nanoliposomes-based Cur nanohybrids are among the most promising delivery systems and further investigation will shed light on their hidden potential in cancer therapy.

15.2.2.2 Exosomes

Exosomes are nanosized bilayer membrane extracellular vesicles released by various cells and have a crucial function in cell–cell communication. Recruiting natural or surface-modified exosomes as efficient DDS has improved the delivery of bioactive molecules to the target cells. Characteristics such as prolonged circulation time, deep tissue penetration, crossing the BBB, preventing content degradation, and low immunogenicity make exosomes an attractive candidate for designing nano-DDS [71–74]. Loading Cur into bovine milk exosomes has been reported to enhance oral bioavailability by shielding Cur against the digestive system and intestinal epithelium metabolism. Furthermore, the nanohybrid system improved Cur solubility, stability, and absorption through the intestine barriers, increasing its bioavailability [75]. Notably, treating MDA-MB-231 breast cancer cells with Cur-loaded bovine milk–derived exosomes showed sixfold increased cytotoxicity and twofold increased intracellular accumulation rather than free Cur [76]. Furthermore, exciting research indicated the more significant antiproliferative effect of Cur-enriched exosomes on breast, lung, and cervical cancer cells than native Cur. In the xenografted mice model of cervical cancer, the nanohybrids showed improved targeting of tumor tissue and growth inhibitory impact [77]. Cur-primed exosomes have been consistently indicated to repress the proliferation, immigration, and invasion of lung cancer cells through downregulating methyltransferase (DNMT1) and upregulating transcription factor 21 (TCF21) expression, involved in cancer cell multiplication and aggressiveness. In H1299 cell-implanted mice, compared to free Cur, the nanohybrids caused a more potent upregulation of TCF21 [78]. Interestingly, a clinical trial is recruiting on the ability of plant exosomes in Cur delivery to colon cancer tissue (NCT01294072).

15.2.2.3 Micelles

Micelles are nanosized self-aggregates of amphiphilic surfactant molecules in an aqueous medium generating spherical vesicles as nanocarriers for water-insoluble drugs like Cur [79]. Due to the inherent stability and ease of formulation, micelles are promising DDS [80]. Cur-encapsulated micelles have originated for preclinical gastric cancer therapy. The outcomes showed the significant impact of the nanohybrid system in suppressing gastric cancer cell proliferation and colony formation through impairing mitochondrial membrane potential, promoting ROS generation, and inducing apoptosis. Examinations in xenografted nude mice also demonstrated the potent anticancer effects of Cur-encapsulated micelles [81]. Another experiment developed polymeric micelles using the nanoprecipitation method to improve Cur pharmacokinetics. Cur-loaded polymeric micelles were internalized by various cancer cells and provoked apoptotic cell death. In vivo pharmacokinetic evaluations also showed prolonged circulation time compared to nonformulated Cur [82]. A similar in vitro cytotoxicity assay revealed the more prominent cellular uptake and apoptotic efficiency of Cur micelles in eradicating multiple cancer cells. Intriguingly, compared to native Cur, intraperitoneal administration of Cur micelles exhibited superior tumor growth suppression in animal models through promoting apoptosis and suppressing angiogenesis [83]. It is worth mentioning that the size and loading efficiency of Cur micelles is critically involved in their biological activity. Cur-loaded micelles experience greater cellular uptake rather than unloaded micelles. Furthermore, larger micelles are more rapidly internalized and exocytosed. In this regard, smaller Cur micelles showed more toxic effects on human colon cancer cells than bigger micelles [84]. The application of nanomicelles of Cur in cancer therapy has recently been discussed thoroughly [80].

15.2.2.4 Nanospheres

Nanospheres are solid matrix NPs in which the active constituent (i.e., drug) is mixed. These nanocarriers are capable of increasing Cur's bioavailability without affecting its anticancer properties [85]. For example, Cur-encapsulated PEG-poly (lactic acid) (PEG-PLA) nanospheres have been synthesized to improve Cur stability and solubility. These nanospheres were taken up rapidly by HeLa and MDA-MB-231 cancer cells [86]. Consistently, an in vitro assay using Cur-loaded chitosan alginate nanospheres showed active targeting and apoptotic killing of breast tumor spheroids, emphasizing the capability of nanospheres in delivering Cur to the tumor site [87]. Furthermore, incorporating Cur into PLGA nanospheres has been shown to increase Cur uptake by prostate cancer cell and, in comparison to free Cur, caused a more profound killing effect [88]. More interestingly, loading Cur into mesopores and macropores of chitosan hollow nanospheres originated a nanohybrid system with controlled release behavior [89]. The nanohybrids composed by loading Cur into PLGA nanospheres also showed a sustained payload release pattern as well as the remarkable suppression of MDA-MB-231 breast cancer cells' survival, migration, and invasion [90]. These findings uncover the potential of engineered nanospheres in amplifying the Cur's clinical effectiveness through promoting its pharmacokinetic properties.

15.2.2.5 Nanogels and nanodisks

Nanogels are NPs containing hydrogels constructed via polymer cross-linking under certain conditions providing unique conditions for drug storage and release. Indeed, drug-loaded nanogels restrict the free diffusion and distribution of drug molecules and promote drug uptake by tumor cells [91]. With this in mind, Cur-loaded nanogels showed good stability, a low polydispersity index, and a PH-dependent release pattern. The nanohybrids induced prominent cytotoxicity toward HepG2 and HeLa cancer cells and strongly suppressed tumor growth and proliferation in HepG2 tumor-bearing mice by promoting apoptosis and necrosis [92]. A Cur-encapsulated colloidal nanogel carrier system has also been developed and tested for increasing Cur solubility and cytotoxicity. Compared to free Cur, the nanogel formulation showed more significant toxicity against tumor cells [93]. In another attempt, Cur was loaded into gum arabic aldehyde-gelatin nanogels. In vitro assessments revealed the controlled drug release pattern, good cellular uptake, and significant toxicity of nanohybrids toward MCF-7 breast cancer cells [94]. Furthermore, a thermoresponsive polymeric nanogel containing grafted hyaluronic acid was designed as a biocompatible Cur delivery system. The nanohybrid platform showed prominent cytotoxicity toward multiple cell lines while it was nontoxic to NIH-3T3 cells [95].

Nanodisks are nanosize disk-shaped phospholipid bilayers stabilized by apolipoproteins (apos) [96]. Notably, recruiting apoE as the scaffold protein of Cur nanodisks is critical for the nanohybrids' biological function. It has been demonstrated that apoE-mediated interaction of Cur nanodisks with glioma cells significantly improves Cur cellular uptake and cancer cell death [97]. Cur-nanodisk delivery systems were also shown to increase Cur solubility and, compared to free Cur, remarkably induced ROS generation, apoptosis, and cell cycle arrest in mantle cell lymphoma (MCL) [96,98]. It has been demonstrated that MCL cells express apoA1 receptors on their surface; hence, Cur nanodisks stabilized by apoA1 are suitable nanocarriers for Cur delivery, inducing apoptosis and cell cycle arrest in these cells [99]. Accordingly, apos-stabilized Cur nanodisks are potential DDS facilitating Cur clinical efficacy in certain cancers.

15.3 Conclusion

As noted, despite a considerable body of evidence underscoring the Cur multimechanistic anticancer impact, dismal pharmacokinetic properties impeded its clinical applications. Recent progress in nanotechnology has revolutionized cancer medication due to the excellent capacity of nanomedicines in delivering chemotherapeutics to the tumor site. Intriguingly, developing nano-DDS bring significant promise in terms of Cur effectiveness and safety in treating human cancers (Fig. 15–1). However, progress in this procedure is restrained due to the lack of clinical trials. Overall, further in-depth preclinical examinations along with clinical trials govern the development of safe and efficient Cur nanohybrid delivery systems as cancer therapeutics.

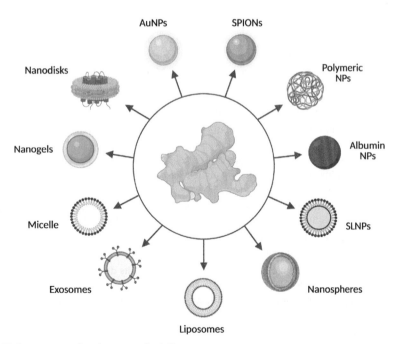

FIGURE 15–1 Various nanocarriers for curcumin delivery.

References

[1] Sapio L, Naviglio S. Innovation through tradition: the current challenges in cancer treatment. MDPI 2022;5296.

[2] Dang Y, Guan J. Nanoparticle-based drug delivery systems for cancer therapy. Smart Materials in Medicine 2020;1:10−19.

[3] Ganji A, Farahani I, Saeedifar AM, Mosayebi G, Ghazavi A, Majeed M, et al. Protective effects of curcumin against lipopolysaccharide-induced toxicity. Current Medicinal Chemistry 2021;28(33):6915−30.

[4] Hassanzadeh S, Read MI, Bland AR, Majeed M, Jamialahmadi T, Sahebkar A. Curcumin: an inflammasome silencer. Pharmacological Research 2020;159.

[5] Panahi Y, Fazlolahzadeh O, Atkin SL, Majeed M, Butler AE, Johnston TP, et al. Evidence of curcumin and curcumin analogue effects in skin diseases: a narrative review. Journal of Cellular Physiology 2019;234(2):1165−78. Available from: https://doi.org/10.1002/jcp.27096.

[6] Hosseini SA, Zahedipour F, Sathyapalan T, Jamialahmadi T, Sahebkar A. Pulmonary fibrosis: therapeutic and mechanistic insights into the role of phytochemicals. Biofactors (Oxford, England) 2021;47 (3):250−69.

[7] Keihanian F, Saeidinia A, Bagheri RK, Johnston TP, Sahebkar A. Curcumin, hemostasis, thrombosis, and coagulation. Journal of Cellular Physiology 2018;233(6):4497−511.

[8] Khayatan D, Razavi SM, Arab ZN, Niknejad AH, Nouri K, Momtaz S, et al. Protective effects of curcumin against traumatic brain injury. Biomedicine and Pharmacotherapy 2022;154.

[9] Mokhtari-Zaer A, Marefati N, Atkin SL, Butler AE, Sahebkar A. The protective role of curcumin in myocardial ischemia−reperfusion injury. Journal of Cellular Physiology 2018;234(1):214−22.

[10] Marjaneh RM, Rahmani F, Hassanian SM, Rezaei N, Hashemzehi M, Bahrami A, et al. Phytosomal curcumin inhibits tumor growth in colitis-associated colorectal cancer. Journal of Cellular Physiology 2018;233(10):6785−98. Available from: https://doi.org/10.1002/jcp.26538.

[11] Rahimi K, Hassanzadeh K, Khanbabaei H, Haftcheshmeh SM, Ahmadi A, Izadpanah E, et al. Curcumin: a dietary phytochemical for targeting the phenotype and function of dendritic cells. Current Medicinal Chemistry 2021;28(8):1549−64.

[12] Cicero AFG, Sahebkar A, Fogacci F, Bove M, Giovannini M, Borghi C. Effects of phytosomal curcumin on anthropometric parameters, insulin resistance, cortisolemia and non-alcoholic fatty liver disease indices: a double-blind, placebo-controlled clinical trial. European Journal of Nutrition 2020;59 (2):477−83. Available from: https://doi.org/10.1007/s00394-019-01916-7.

[13] Sahebkar A. Molecular mechanisms for curcumin benefits against ischemic injury. Fertility and Sterility 2010;94(5):e75−6.

[14] Soltani S, Boozari M, Cicero AFG, Jamialahmadi T, Sahebkar A. Effects of phytochemicals on macrophage cholesterol efflux capacity: impact on atherosclerosis. Phytotherapy Research 2021;35 (6):2854−78.

[15] Mohajeri M, Sahebkar A. Protective effects of curcumin against doxorubicin-induced toxicity and resistance: a review. Critical Reviews in Oncology/Hematology 2018;122:30−51.

[16] Momtazi AA, Sahebkar A. Difluorinated curcumin: a promising curcumin analogue with improved antitumor activity and pharmacokinetic profile. Current Pharmaceutical Design 2016;22(28):4386−97.

[17] Tomeh MA, Hadianamrei R, Zhao X. A review of curcumin and its derivatives as anticancer agents. International Journal of Molecular Sciences 2019;20(5).

[18] Zoi V, Galani V, Lianos GD, Voulgaris S, Kyritsis AP, Alexiou GA. The role of curcumin in cancer treatment. Biomedicines. 2021;9(9):1086.

[19] Patra JK, Das G, Fraceto LF, Campos EVR, Rodriguez-Torres MdP, Acosta-Torres LS, et al. Nano based drug delivery systems: recent developments and future prospects. Journal of Nanobiotechnology 2018;16 (1):1−33.

[20] Kabir MT, Rahman MH, Akter R, Behl T, Kaushik D, Mittal V, et al. Potential role of curcumin and its nanoformulations to treat various types of cancers. Biomolecules. 2021;11(3):392.

[21] Jin H, Pi J, Zhao Y, Jiang J, Li T, Zeng X, et al. EGFR-targeting PLGA-PEG nanoparticles as a curcumin delivery system for breast cancer therapy. Nanoscale. 2017;9(42):16365−74.

[22] Wilczewska AZ, Niemirowicz K, Markiewicz KH, Car H. Nanoparticles as drug delivery systems. Pharmacological Reports 2012;64(5):1020−37.

[23] Goradel NH, Mohammadi N, Haghi-Aminjan H, Farhood B, Negahdari B, Sahebkar A. Regulation of tumor angiogenesis by microRNAs: state of the art. Journal of Cellular Physiology 2019;234(2):1099−110.

[24] Suri SS, Fenniri H, Singh B. Nanotechnology-based drug delivery systems. Journal of Occupational Medicine and Toxicology 2007;2(1):1−6.

[25] Moballegh Nasery M, Abadi B, Poormoghadam D, Zarrabi A, Keyhanvar P, Khanbabaei H, et al. Curcumin delivery mediated by bio-based nanoparticles: a review. Molecules (Basel, Switzerland) 2020;25(3):689.

[26] Han G, Ghosh P, Rotello VM. Functionalized gold nanoparticles for drug delivery. Nanomedicine 2007;2 (1):113−23.

[27] Mahmoudi A, Kesharwani P, Majeed M, Teng Y, Sahebkar A. Recent advances in nanogold as a promising nanocarrier for curcumin delivery. Colloids and Surfaces B: Biointerfaces 2022;112481.

[28] Al-Ani LA, Yehye WA, Kadir FA, Hashim NM, AlSaadi MA, Julkapli NM, et al. Hybrid nanocomposite curcumin-capped gold nanoparticle-reduced graphene oxide: Anti-oxidant potency and selective cancer cytotoxicity. PLoS One 2019;14(5):e0216725.

[29] Akbari A, Shokati Eshkiki Z, Mayahi S, Amini SM. In-vitro investigation of curcumin coated gold nanoparticles effect on human colorectal adenocarcinoma cell line. Nanomedicine Research Journal 2022;7(1):66−72.

[30] Khodashenas B, Ardjmand M, Baei MS, Rad AS, Khiyavi AA. Gelatin−gold nanoparticles as an ideal candidate for curcumin drug delivery: experimental and DFT studies. Journal of Inorganic and Organometallic Polymers and Materials 2019;29(6):2186−96.

[31] Khandelwal P, Alam A, Choksi A, Chattopadhyay S, Poddar P. Retention of anticancer activity of curcumin after conjugation with fluorescent gold quantum clusters: an in vitro and in vivo xenograft study. ACS Omega 2018;3(5):4776−85.

[32] Paul W, Kumar KP, Sharma CP. Synthesis of curcumin stabilized thermo-sensitive gold nanoparticles and its uptake in C6 glioma cells. Trends in Biomaterials & Artificial Organs 2018;32(2):10−16.

[33] Nambiar S, Osei E, Fleck A, Darko J, Mutsaers AJ, Wettig S. Synthesis of curcumin-functionalized gold nanoparticles and cytotoxicity studies in human prostate cancer cell line. Applied Nanoscience 2018;8 (3):347−57.

[34] Yallapu MM, Othman SF, Curtis ET, Bauer NA, Chauhan N, Kumar D, et al. Curcumin-loaded magnetic nanoparticles for breast cancer therapeutics and imaging applications. International Journal of Nanomedicine 2012;7:1761.

[35] Tran H-V, Ngo NM, Medhi R, Srinoi P, Liu T, Rittikulsittichai S, et al. Multifunctional iron oxide magnetic nanoparticles for biomedical applications: a review. Materials. 2022;15(2):503.

[36] Sanati M, Aminyavari S, Khodagholi F, Hajipour MJ, Sadeghi P, Noruzi M, et al. PEGylated superparamagnetic iron oxide nanoparticles (SPIONs) ameliorate learning and memory deficit in a rat model of Alzheimer's disease: potential participation of STIMs. Neurotoxicology 2021;85:145−59.

[37] Vakili-Ghartavol R, Momtazi-Borojeni AA, Vakili-Ghartavol Z, Aiyelabegan HT, Jaafari MR, Rezayat SM, et al. Toxicity assessment of superparamagnetic iron oxide nanoparticles in different tissues. Artificial Cells, Nanomedicine, and Biotechnology 2020;48(1):443−51.

[38] Darwesh R, Elbialy NS. Iron oxide nanoparticles conjugated curcumin to promote high therapeutic efficacy of curcumin against hepatocellular carcinoma. Inorganic Chemistry Communications 2021;126:108482.

[39] Senturk F, Cakmak S, Kocum IC, Gumusderelioglu M, Ozturk GG. GRGDS-conjugated and curcumin-loaded magnetic polymeric nanoparticles for the hyperthermia treatment of glioblastoma cells. Colloids and Surfaces A: Physicochemical and Engineering Aspects 2021;622:126648.

[40] Lachowicz D, Kaczyńska A, Wirecka R, Kmita A, Szczerba W, Bodzoń-Kułakowska A, et al. A hybrid system for magnetic hyperthermia and drug delivery: SPION functionalized by curcumin conjugate. Materials. 2018;11(12):2388.

[41] Khodaei A, Jahanmard F, Hosseini HM, Bagheri R, Dabbagh A, Weinans H, et al. Controlled temperature-mediated curcumin release from magneto-thermal nanocarriers to kill bone tumors. Bioactive Materials 2022;11:107−17.

[42] Salehiabar M, Nosrati H, Javani E, Aliakbarzadeh F, Manjili HK, Davaran S, et al. Production of biological nanoparticles from bovine serum albumin as controlled release carrier for curcumin delivery. International Journal of Biological Macromolecules 2018;115:83−9.

[43] Elsadek B, Kratz F. Impact of albumin on drug delivery—new applications on the horizon. Journal of Controlled Release 2012;157(1):4−28.

[44] Kim TH, Jiang HH, Youn YS, Park CW, Tak KK, Lee S, et al. Preparation and characterization of water-soluble albumin-bound curcumin nanoparticles with improved antitumor activity. International Journal of Pharmaceutics 2011;403(1−2):285−91.

[45] Thadakapally R, Aafreen A, Aukunuru J, Habibuddin M, Jogala S. Preparation and characterization of PEG-albumin-curcumin nanoparticles intended to treat breast cancer. Indian Journal of Pharmaceutical Sciences 2016;78(1):65.

[46] Bhatt H, Rompicharla SV, Komanduri N, Aashma S, Paradkar S, Ghosh B, et al. Development of curcumin-loaded solid lipid nanoparticles utilizing glyceryl monostearate as single lipid using QbD approach: characterization and evaluation of anticancer activity against human breast cancer cell line. Current Drug Delivery 2018;15(9):1271−83.

[47] Nahar PP, Slitt AL, Seeram NP. Anti-inflammatory effects of novel standardized solid lipid curcumin formulations. Journal of Medicinal Food 2015;18(7):786−92.

[48] Gupta T, Singh J, Kaur S, Sandhu S, Singh G, Kaur IP. Enhancing bioavailability and stability of curcumin using solid lipid nanoparticles (CLEN): a covenant for its effectiveness. Frontiers in Bioengineering and Biotechnology 2020;8:879.

[49] Wang W, Chen T, Xu H, Ren B, Cheng X, Qi R, et al. Curcumin-loaded solid lipid nanoparticles enhanced anticancer efficiency in breast cancer. Molecules (Basel, Switzerland) 2018;23(7):1578.

[50] Guorgui J, Wang R, Mattheolabakis G, Mackenzie GG. Curcumin formulated in solid lipid nanoparticles has enhanced efficacy in Hodgkin's lymphoma in mice. Archives of Biochemistry and Biophysics 2018;648:12−19.

[51] Ganassin R, Da Silva VCM, Araujo VHS, Tavares GR, Da Silva PB, Cáceres-Vélez PR, et al. Solid lipid nanoparticles loaded with curcumin: development and in vitro toxicity against CT26 cells. Nanomedicine Nanotechnology, Biology, and Medicine 2022;17(3):167−79.

[52] Wei Y, Li K, Zhao W, He Y, Shen H, Yuan J, et al. The effects of a novel curcumin derivative loaded long-circulating solid lipid nanoparticle on the MHCC-97H liver cancer cells and pharmacokinetic behavior. International Journal of Nanomedicine 2022;17:2225.

[53] Mohamed JM, Alqahtani A, Ahmad F, Krishnaraju V, Kalpana K. Pectin co-functionalized dual layered solid lipid nanoparticle made by soluble curcumin for the targeted potential treatment of colorectal cancer. Carbohydrate Polymers 2021;252:117180.

[54] Santonocito D, Sarpietro MG, Carbone C, Panico A, Campisi A, Siciliano EA, et al. Curcumin containing PEGylated solid lipid nanoparticles for systemic administration: a preliminary study. Molecules (Basel, Switzerland) 2020;25(13):2991.

[55] Begines B, Ortiz T, Pérez-Aranda M, Martínez G, Merinero M, Argüelles-Arias F, et al. Polymeric nanoparticles for drug delivery: recent developments and future prospects. Nanomaterials. 2020;10(7):1403.

[56] Shome S, Talukdar AD, Choudhury MD, Bhattacharya MK, Upadhyaya H. Curcumin as potential therapeutic natural product: a nanobiotechnological perspective. Journal of Pharmacy and Pharmacology 2016;68(12):1481−500.

[57] Chang P-Y, Peng S-F, Lee C-Y, Lu C-C, Tsai S-C, Shieh T-M, et al. Curcumin-loaded nanoparticles induce apoptotic cell death through regulation of the function of MDR1 and reactive oxygen species in cisplatin-resistant CAR human oral cancer cells. International Journal of Oncology 2013;43(4):1141−50.

[58] Alam J, Dilnawaz F, Sahoo SK, Singh DV, Mukhopadhyay AK, Hussain T, et al. Curcumin encapsulated into biocompatible co-polymer PLGA nanoparticle enhanced anti-gastric cancer and anti-*Helicobacter pylori* effect. Asian Pacific Journal of Cancer Prevention 2022;23(1):61−70.

[59] Tabatabaei Mirakabad FS, Akbarzadeh A, Milani M, Zarghami N, Taheri-Anganeh M, Zeighamian V, et al. A comparison between the cytotoxic effects of pure curcumin and curcumin-loaded PLGA-PEG nanoparticles on the MCF-7 human breast cancer cell line. Artificial Cells, Nanomedicine, and Biotechnology 2016;44(1):423−30.

[60] Arya G, Das M, Sahoo SK. Evaluation of curcumin loaded chitosan/PEG blended PLGA nanoparticles for effective treatment of pancreatic cancer. Biomedicine & Pharmacotherapy 2018;102:555−66.

[61] Prasad M, Salar A, Salar RK. In vitro anticancer activity of curcumin loaded chitosan nanoparticles (CLCNPs) against Vero cells. Pharmacological Research-Modern Chinese Medicine 2022;3:100116.

[62] Chaurasia S, Chaubey P, Patel RR, Kumar N, Mishra B. Curcumin-polymeric nanoparticles against colon-26 tumor-bearing mice: cytotoxicity, pharmacokinetic and anticancer efficacy studies. Drug Development and Industrial Pharmacy 2016;42(5):694−700.

[63] Dehghan-Baniani D, Zahedifar P, Bagheri R, Solouk A. Curcumin-loaded starch micro/nano particles for biomedical application: the effects of preparation parameters on release profile. Starch-Stärke 2019;71 (5−6):1800305.

[64] Athira GK, Jyothi AN. Cassava starch-poly (vinyl alcohol) nanocomposites for the controlled delivery of curcumin in cancer prevention and treatment. Starch-Stärke 2015;67(5−6):549−58.

[65] Xie M, Fan D, Li Y, He X, Chen X, Chen Y, et al. Supercritical carbon dioxide-developed silk fibroin nanoplatform for smart colon cancer therapy. International Journal of Nanomedicine 2017;12:7751.

[66] Magar KT, Boafo GF, Li X, Chen Z, He W. Liposome-based delivery of biological drugs. Chinese Chemical Letters 2021;.

[67] Feng T, Wei Y, Lee RJ, Zhao L. Liposomal curcumin and its application in cancer. International Journal of Nanomedicine 2017;12:6027.

[68] Zhao M, Zhao M, Fu C, Yu Y, Fu A. Targeted therapy of intracranial glioma model mice with curcumin nanoliposomes. International Journal of Nanomedicine 2018;13:1601.

[69] Ma Q, Qian W, Tao W, Zhou Y, Xue B. Delivery of curcumin nanoliposomes using surface modified with CD133 aptamers for prostate cancer. Drug Design, Development and Therapy 2019;13:4021.

[70] Hasan M, Elkhoury K, Belhaj N, Kahn C, Tamayol A, Barberi-Heyob M, et al. Growth-inhibitory effect of chitosan-coated liposomes encapsulating curcumin on MCF-7 breast cancer cells. Marine Drugs 2020;18 (4):217.

[71] Tang X-J, Sun X-Y, Huang K-M, Zhang L, Yang Z-S, Zou D-D, et al. Therapeutic potential of CAR-T cell-derived exosomes: a cell-free modality for targeted cancer therapy. Oncotarget. 2015;6(42):44179.

[72] Vader P, Mol EA, Pasterkamp G, Schiffelers RM. Extracellular vesicles for drug delivery. Advanced Drug Delivery Reviews 2016;106:148−56.

[73] Malhotra H, Sheokand N, Kumar S, Chauhan AS, Kumar M, Jakhar P, et al. Exosomes: tunable nano vehicles for macromolecular delivery of transferrin and lactoferrin to specific intracellular compartment. Journal of Biomedical Nanotechnology 2016;12(5):1101−14.

[74] Hood JL. Post isolation modification of exosomes for nanomedicine applications. Nanomedicine Nanotechnology, Biology, and Medicine 2016;11(13):1745−56.

[75] Vashisht M, Rani P, Onteru SK, Singh D. Curcumin encapsulated in milk exosomes resists human digestion and possesses enhanced intestinal permeability in vitro. Applied Biochemistry and Biotechnology 2017;183(3):993−1007.

[76] Singh A, Sreenu B, Alvi S, Patnam S, Rajeswari K, Kutala V. Bovine milk derived exosomal-curcumin exhibiting enhanced stability, solubility, and cellular bioavailability. Clinical Oncology 2021;6:1769.

[77] Aqil F, Munagala R, Jeyabalan J, Agrawal AK, Gupta R. Exosomes for the enhanced tissue bioavailability and efficacy of curcumin. The AAPS Journal 2017;19(6):1691−702.

[78] Wu H, Zhou J, Zeng C, Wu D, Mu Z, Chen B, et al. Curcumin increases exosomal TCF21 thus suppressing exosome-induced lung cancer. Oncotarget. 2016;7(52):87081.

[79] Biswas S. Polymeric micelles as drug-delivery systems in cancer: challenges and opportunities. Nanomedicine Nanotechnology, Biology, and Medicine 2021;16(18):1541−4.

[80] Farhoudi L, Kesharwani P, Majeed M, Johnston TP, Sahebkar A. Polymeric nanomicelles of curcumin: potential applications in cancer. International Journal of Pharmaceutics 2022;121622.

[81] Lin X, Wang L, Zhao L, Zhu Z, Chen T, Chen S, et al. Curcumin micelles suppress gastric tumor cell growth by upregulating ROS generation, disrupting redox equilibrium and affecting mitochondrial bioenergetics. Food & Function 2020;11(5):4146−59.

[82] Bagheri M, Fens MH, Kleijn TG, Capomaccio RB, Mehn D, Krawczyk PM, et al. In vitro and in vivo studies on HPMA-based polymeric micelles loaded with curcumin. Molecular Pharmaceutics 2021;18 (3):1247−63.

[83] Li X, Chen T, Xu L, Zhang Z, Li L, Chen H. Preparation of curcumin micelles and the in vitro and in vivo evaluation for cancer therapy. Journal of Biomedical Nanotechnology 2014;10(8):1458−68.

[84] Chang T, Trench D, Putnam J, Stenzel MH, Lord MS. Curcumin-loading-dependent stability of PEGMEMA-based micelles affects endocytosis and exocytosis in colon carcinoma cells. Molecular Pharmaceutics 2016;13(3):924−32.

[85] Arunraj T, Rejinold NS, Mangalathillam S, Saroj S, Biswas R, Jayakumar R. Synthesis, characterization and biological activities of curcumin nanospheres. Journal of Biomedical Nanotechnology 2014;10 (2):238−50.

[86] Liang H, Friedman JM, Nacharaju P. Fabrication of biodegradable PEG−PLA nanospheres for solubility, stabilization, and delivery of curcumin. Artificial Cells, Nanomedicine, and Biotechnology 2017;45 (2):297−304.

[87] Afzali E, Eslaminejad T, Rouholamini SEY, Shahrokhi-Farjah M, Ansari M. Cytotoxicity effects of curcumin loaded on chitosan alginate nanospheres on the KMBC-10 spheroids cell line. International Journal of Nanomedicine 2021;16:579.

[88] Mukerjee A, Vishwanatha JK. Formulation, characterization and evaluation of curcumin-loaded PLGA nanospheres for cancer therapy. Anticancer Research 2009;29(10):3867−75.

[89] Liu M, Yang J, Ao P, Zhou C. Preparation and characterization of chitosan hollow nanospheres for anticancer drug curcumin delivery. Materials Letters 2015;150:114−17.

[90] Sharma A, Hawthorne S, Jha SK, Jha NK, Kumar D, Girgis S, et al. Effects of curcumin-loaded poly (lactic-co-glycolic acid) nanoparticles in MDA-MB231 human breast cancer cells. Nanomedicine Nanotechnology, Biology, and Medicine 2021;16(20):1763−73.

[91] Wang S, Ha Y, Huang X, Chin B, Sim W, Chen R. A new strategy for intestinal drug delivery via pH-responsive and membrane-active Nanogels. ACS Applied Materials & Interfaces 2018;10(43):36622−7.

[92] Peng Y, Yu S, Wang Z, Huang P, Wang W, Xing J. Nanogels loading curcumin in situ through microe-mulsion photopolymerization for enhancement of antitumor effects. Journal of Materials Chemistry B. 2022;10(17):3293−302.

[93] Reeves A, Vinogradov SV, Morrissey P, Chernin M, Ahmed MM. Curcumin-encapsulating nanogels as an effective anticancer formulation for intracellular uptake. Molecular and Cellular Pharmacology 2015;7(3):25.

[94] Sarika P, Nirmala RJ. Curcumin loaded gum arabic aldehyde-gelatin nanogels for breast cancer therapy. Materials Science and Engineering: C. 2016;65:331−7.

[95] Luckanagul JA, Ratnatilaka Na Bhuket P, Muangnoi C, Rojsitthisak P, Wang Q, Rojsitthisak P. Self-assembled thermoresponsive nanogel from grafted hyaluronic acid as a biocompatible delivery platform for curcumin with enhanced drug loading and biological activities. Polymers. 2021;13(2):194.

[96] Ghosh M, Singh AT, Xu W, Sulchek T, Gordon LI, Ryan RO. Curcumin nanodisks: formulation and char-acterization. Nanomedicine: Nanotechnology, Biology and Medicine 2011;7(2):162−7.

[97] Ghosh M, Ryan RO. ApoE enhances nanodisk-mediated curcumin delivery to glioblastoma multiforme cells. Nanomedicine Nanotechnology, Biology, and Medicine 2014;9(6):763−71.

[98] Singh AT, Ghosh M, Forte TM, Ryan RO, Gordon LI. Curcumin nanodisk-induced apoptosis in mantle cell lymphoma. Leukemia & Lymphoma 2011;52(8):1537−43.

[99] Singh AT, Ghosh M, Thaxton CS, Forte TM, Ryan RO, Gordon LI. The bioactive polyphenol curcumin (diferuloylmethane) in human apolipoprotein A-1 nanodisks enhances apoptosis and G1 cell cycle arrest in mantle cell lymphoma compared with free curcumin. Blood 2010;116(21):3934.

16

Codelivery of curcumin and siRNA as anticancer therapeutics

Milan Paul, Sanjay Ch, Sri Ganga Padaga, Balaram Ghosh, Swati Biswas

NANOMEDICINE RESEARCH LABORATORY, DEPARTMENT OF PHARMACY, BIRLA INSTITUTE OF TECHNOLOGY & SCIENCE-PILANI, HYDERABAD CAMPUS, HYDERABAD, TELANGANA, INDIA

16.1 Introduction

Cancer has become one of the leading causes of death globally, accounting for nearly 10 million deaths in 2020 (according to the World Health Organization report) [1]. Furthermore, it is estimated that by 2030, cancer will be the leading cause of death. Finding affordable, efficient, and relatively inexpensive cancer therapies is crucial because the disease is rising and the treatments are expensive. Medicinal plants' usage and efficacy in treating various diseases have drawn much attention recently. Due to their structural and chemical diversities, natural compounds have created new avenues for cancer treatment.

The effectiveness of natural products in cancer treatment has been examined in several studies. Natural substances can harm cancer cells' proliferation, viability, and metastasis due to their capacity for many targets. Among the wide range of medicinal herbs, curcumin has become one of the effective ingredients of the turmeric plant. It has a unique chemical structure with special biological and therapeutic properties. Because of its multiple functions, including its anticancer, antiangiogenic, antioxidant, antiinflammatory, antidiabetic, and antibacterial properties, curcumin has come more under the limelight in recent years [2]. It is also known as the "next-generation multipurpose medication." Due to its ability to suppress carcinogenesis, curcumin has been proposed as a medication supplement for cancer patients. Antimetastatic protein expression is increased by curcumin. In previous studies, it was discovered that curcumin improved patient survival and reduced the concentration of tumor markers. It has been demonstrated that curcumin helps prevent the growth and spread of malignant cells.

The induction of apoptotic cell death is the most frequent way natural products take part in anticancer therapy. Endoplasmic reticulum (ER)- and mitochondria-mediated apoptosis are induced by the administration of natural products. The formation of reactive oxygen species (ROS), which promote mitochondrial dysfunction and ER stress, is increased by natural

Curcumin-Based Nanomedicines as Cancer Therapeutics. DOI: https://doi.org/10.1016/B978-0-443-15412-6.00010-6

products [3]. An increase in ROS production compromises the mitochondrial membrane's integrity. The expression of the proapoptotic protein Bax is upregulated during this process, whereas Bcl-2, an inhibitor of apoptosis, is downregulated [4]. This occurs in the mitochondrial release of cytochrome C (Cyt C) and the caspase cascade activation, leading to apoptosis. Increased ROS production and natural product supplements could result in high ER stress, influencing apoptosis and leading to the overexpression of the C/EBP homologous protein, which kills apoptotic cells (CHOP) [5]. Natural products can target the molecular pathways involved in the proliferation of cancer cells in addition to causing apoptotic cell death. A critical pathway for the cancer cells' growth and proliferative ability is the PI3K/Akt signaling pathway. PTEN (phosphatase and TENsin) is an onco-suppressor factor that can block this pathway [6].

According to studies, curcumin can activate PTEN, inhibiting the PI3K/Akt signaling pathway and reducing cancer cells' capacity to proliferate and survive. Several natural compounds can target the molecular pathways used by cancer cells to invade and spread. Epithelial-to-mesenchymal transition (EMT) is a process that results in the malignant differentiation of epithelial cells into mesenchymal cells, which promotes the spread of cancer cells [7]. Natural remedies can reduce EMT, reduce cancer cell migration, and enhance prognosis. Natural compounds may also be directed to targeting the upstream EMT modulators. Wnt and STAT3 (signal transducer and activator of transcription 3) are believed to be the upstream modulators of EMT in cancer. Natural product administration inhibits STAT3 and Wnt to prevent EMT. In addition, natural products also inhibit zinc finger E-box-binding homeobox (ZEB) proteins that cause EMT during cancer spread [8].

16.2 Curcumin and its role in cancer prevention

By decreasing the alteration of the cell surface adhesion molecules nuclear factor kappa B (NF-κB), AP-1, and matrix metalloproteases (MMPs), curcumin prevents tumor invasion and metastasis [9]. Growth factors (human epidermal growth factor 2 receptor [HER2] and epidermal growth factor receptors [EGFR]), chemokines, tumor necrosis factor-α (TNF-α), tyrosine kinase protein, and N-terminal activity are all also inhibited. According to reports, curcumin inhibits the synthesis of inflammatory mediators, including COX-2, lipoxygenase 2, and associated cytokines, preventing the progression of numerous cancer types [10]. Some of the curcumin's anticancer activities result from how it affects the control of several immune modulators. In the early phases of cancer growth, free radicals and harmful by-products of oxidative stress play a significant role. As a result, substances with antioxidant activities may be beneficial in preventing the development of cancer. Since curcumin can capture free radicals, it can effectively prevent cancer development.

In addition, curcumin prevents free radicals and active oxygen species from damaging DNA in ways that counteract oxidative stress. The expression of several proteins, including cytokines and interferon (IFN), is regulated and controlled by the NF-κ factor. These proteins have a strong linkage to the development of cancer and inflammation. Due to curcumin's inhibition of the NF-κB-dependent pathway, tumors are suppressed and apoptosis is induced. It also has been noted that curcumin is beneficial to liver enzymes and inhibits NF-κ, which prevents cancer development. Recent studies have examined the effects of cytokines on murine cancer models, including interleukin (IL) IL-12, IL-15, and IFN-a. The effect of curcumin on the interaction of nuclear proteins with ILs or IFNs has been found to downregulate the production of pro-inflammatory cytokines [11,12].

Numerous immune system cell types, including B and T lymphocytes, macrophages, and natural killer cells, have shown that curcumin can influence their biological responses. Immune cytokines' expression and functionality are both affected by curcumin. TNF-α is a pleiotropic cytokine that stimulates growth and is essential for the immune system. This factor's expression can be altered by curcumin, which can also prevent TNF-α from being expressed as a result of lipopolysaccharide (LPS). Curcumin also targets dendritic cells, which are recognized for their immunostimulatory function. Curcumin has been demonstrated to specifically limit the maturation of myeloid dendritic cells (DCs), mostly through suppressing the expression of CD80 and CD86. Curcumin inhibits and activates Phase I enzymes, which are involved in the production of carcinogens and toxic metabolites, as well as Phase II enzymes, which are essential in the detoxification of toxic metabolites, to prevent the development and growth of tumors [13].

Numerous cellular adhesive molecules that are involved in tumor development and metastasis are impacted by curcumin. ICAM-1, VCAM, and MMPs, critical in cellular adhesion and metastasis, were less expressed inside the cells due to curcumin treatment. These molecules are essential for cellular adhesion and metastasis. The antimetastatic proteins, such as tissue inhibitor metalloproteinase (TIMP 2), NM23, and E-cadherin, are those whose expression is increased by curcumin [14].

Cancer therapy is a problem that necessitates novel approaches. Because of their exceptional therapeutic effectiveness and multitargeting capacity, natural compounds like curcumin are important in chemotherapy for cancer treatment. But the efficacy of natural compounds in cancer treatment has been constrained by their poor solubility and bioavailability. The substances', as mentioned earlier, ICAM-1, VCAM, and MMPs, anticancer efficacy have been enhanced using nanocarriers. It is generally established that gene therapy combined with natural remedies has advantages over monotherapy. Numerous therapeutic drugs or small interfering RNA (siRNA) can be delivered as a powerful gene-editing tool in cancer therapy to optimize the synergistic effects on tumor cells.

16.3 Combination therapy of siRNA-curcumin

Despite significant advancements in cancer treatment, there are still numerous obstacles to overcome. The off-targeting property of traditional cancer treatments, which considerably reduces their therapeutic effectiveness, is one of the difficulties. Targeted delivery techniques can stop tumor growth and lessen the tumor burden.

Natural products have the potential to affect a variety of targets, including cancer cell proliferation and migration, as well as other biochemical pathways, making them exciting candidates for anticancer treatment. The therapeutic efficacy of these beneficial compounds against cancer is adversely affected by their low bioavailability. By breaking through the blood−tumor barrier, nanocarriers can significantly improve the anticancer potential of natural products, shield them from degradation before they reach the tumor sites, and increase their concentration in cancer cells. These characteristics enable the use of nanoparticles for the delivery of natural products in cancer treatment [2].

The earlier reported studies found that curcumin has shown its efficacy in suppressing cancer cell proliferation, viability, and migration via targeting various molecular mechanisms and pathways such as apoptosis and autophagy. Therefore, it has been noted that loading curcumin into nanoparticles significantly increases its anticancer efficacy. Because curcumin has a low bioavailability, research has been focused on developing nanosized encapsulants for curcumin and siRNA codelivery (Fig. 16−1). Many nanotechnology-based therapeutic systems, including nanoparticles, liposomes, and nanoemulsions, have been developed to increase curcumin's low water solubility [15]. Data revealed that these formulations have enhanced treatment effectiveness while concurrently lowering harmful side effects. This is most likely due to the nano-formulated curcumin's specific localization and cellular uptake in the cancer cells [16].

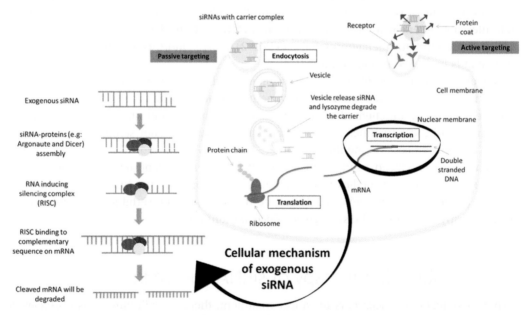

FIGURE 16–1 Schematic diagram of the mechanism of small interfering RNA (siRNA) in targeting messenger RNA (mRNA) for gene silencing (left) and exogenous siRNA duplex delivery into the cytoplasmic region via passive and active targeted delivery (right) [17]. *Adapted with permission from N. I. Kamaruzman, N. A. Aziz, C. L. Poh, and E. H. Chowdhury, Oncogenic signaling in tumorigenesis and applications of siRNA nanotherapeutics in breast cancer, Cancers (Basel), 11, 5, 2019, https://doi.org/10.3390/cancers11050632. Copyright (2021) Elsevier.*

It is possible to increase siRNA's effectiveness in gene silencing by developing new nanoscale delivery systems. The promise of targeted delivery systems appears to have been constrained by cancer cells' resistance to chemotherapy. SiRNA is an effective technique for reversing cancer cells' chemoresistance to chemotherapy by inhibiting oncogene factors, including Survivin, Bcl-xl, and Mcl-1 [18]. Understanding the characteristics of drug resistance can thereby improve the effectiveness of anticancer treatment.

Various extracellular and intracellular barriers hamper the effectiveness of siRNAs in anticancer therapy. The most significant of these siRNA limitations include off-targeting, instability in blood circulation, unintentional activation of the host immune system, and inability to enter cells (cell uptake). One-tenth of siRNAs are said to influence undesired genes in terms of off-targeting. In addition, siRNAs cause immunotoxicity by increasing cytokine levels and generating inflammation. By interfering with the microRNAs (miRNAs) function and promoting the overexpression of particular proteins, synthetic siRNAs have the potential to damage the RNA interference (RNAi) machinery. The main problem with siRNAs is that they cannot cross hydrophobic cellular membranes because of their hydrophilic and anionic properties [19].

Different siRNA delivery methods have been developed to overcome this problem. To deliver siRNAs, many types of nanoparticles have been designed to date. A subset of polymeric nanoparticles is dendrimers. Dendrimers have remarkable potential for anticancer drug delivery. Dendrimers can be loaded with siRNA to treat cancer. Dendrimers markedly improve the cellular absorption of siRNAs and their release from endosomes. As a result, their targets may be up- or downregulated more effectively, reducing cancer incidence. Polyamidoamine (PAMAM) dendrimers are now considered attractive options for medication and gene delivery because of their high surface group density (Fig. 16–2). Curcumin can be delivered with other nanocarriers such as carbon nanotubes, micelles, and liposomes. Curcumin and siRNA-STAT3-loaded cationic liposomes can inhibit the growth and aggressiveness of skin cancer in both in vitro and in vivo tests [20].

Because of their spherical form, low polydispersity, high surface group density, prolonged cargo release ability, and water solubility, PAMAM dendrimers have become a promising candidate for drug and gene delivery. PAMAM dendrimers' hydrophilic exterior provides locations for siRNA attachment, while their hydrophobic interior is suitable for encapsulating hydrophobic substances. PAMAM dendrimers are capable of delivering siRNA and curcumin into cancer cells. Combining curcumin's antitumor activity with siRNA's synergistic decrease of Bcl-2 expression resulted in an anticancer effect. An oncogene that promotes cancer cell invasion and proliferation is the STAT3 signaling pathway. Skin cancer cells experience apoptosis and are prevented from migrating and growing when STAT3 is downregulated. Codelivery of curcumin and STAT3 targeting siRNA can have synergetic benefits since curcumin aims to the STAT3 signaling pathway in anticancer treatment. Through the downregulation of STAT3 and disruption of cancer development, in vitro and in vivo researches show that curcumin and siRNA-STAT3-loaded cationic liposomes can inhibit the growth and malignancy of skin cancer. Another study investigated the efficacy of cationic liposomes for simultaneous curcumin delivery and siRNA-STAT3 in treating skin cancer.

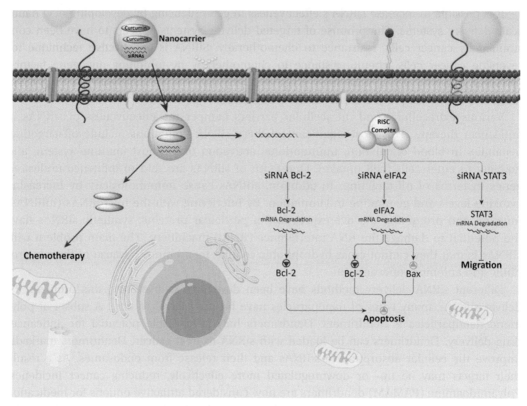

FIGURE 16-2 Codelivery of curcumin and siRNA in cancer therapy with a focus on molecular signaling pathways. Downregulation of Bcl-2, eIF5A2, and STAT3 by siRNA increases the antitumor activity of curcumin against cancer cells. Nanoparticles promote the cellular accumulation of siRNA and curcumin to enhance their antitumor potential. siRNA, small interfering RNA [21]. *Reprinted with permission from M. Ashra et al., Progress in natural compounds/siRNA co-delivery employing nanovehicles for cancer therapy, ACS Combinatorial Science, 2020, https://doi.org/10.1021/acscombsci.0c00099. Copyright (2013) Elsevier.*

The delivery of curcumin also strengthens STAT3's ability to prevent melanoma cell growth. Silica nanoparticles, carbon nanotubes, and other nonviral vehicles are not biodegradable. When biodegradable polymers, such as poly (lactic-co-glycolic acid) nanoparticles, degrade, acidic oligomers are produced and a low pH environment is created, both of which are harmful to cells. The problems mentioned earlier are not evident in zinc-curcumin nanoparticles. Curcumin is more soluble in zinc ions, making it more cellularly absorbable. Drug release at tumor locations is pH-dependent for zinc nanoparticles. SiRNA-elF5A2 is highly cellularly absorbed and rapidly penetrates cancer cells. In vitro and in vivo bladder cancer cell proliferation and malignancy are inhibited by the codelivery of curcumin with siRNA-elF5A2 [22].

By upregulating Bax and downregulating Bcl-2, the combination causes apoptosis in bladder cancer cells. Curcumin is one of the most popular phytochemicals used in cancer treatment. Numerous cell culture and animal studies have been conducted to assess its anticancer efficacy against various cancer types. Curcumin's low bioavailability may be improved by coadministering piperine, produced from black pepper, or by using nanoparticles, which markedly encourage curcumin deposition in cancer cells. By combining curcumin with siRNA, antitumor activity may be increased. For instance, siRNAs can inhibit the expression of Bcl-2, STAT3, and elF5A2 to prevent the progression of cancer cells. This opens the door for increased curcumin anticancer action against cancer cells. Effective anticancer treatment can be achieved by combining curcumin and siRNA and codelivering them utilizing nanoparticles. Few investigations have examined the effectiveness of this combination to this point. In the context of anticancer treatment, the capacity of curcumin and siRNA to inhibit the activity of other signaling networks, including Nrf2, Wnt, c-Myc, and SOX, could be the subject of future research. Curcumin can be delivered with other nanocarriers such as carbon nanotubes, micelles, and liposomes [23].

Because of their remarkable anticancer efficacy and capacity to target several molecular pathways, natural products are used in chemotherapy. Investigating the anticancer activity of natural compounds may be done in two ways. The first approach should concentrate on improving the intracellular accumulation of chemotherapeutic drugs and targeted delivery of those medicines using nanoparticles. Nanoparticles may be used to enhance several phytochemicals' low bioavailability. Other obstacles also restrict curcumin's ability to fight tumors. SiRNA and curcumin have been engineered to be carried by nanosized encapsulants made from polymer and lipid organic nanomaterials and inorganic-based nanometals. Nanotechnology may help siRNA overcome its off-targeting restriction. In addition, siRNA and curcumin are shielded by nano vehicles from deterioration during blood circulation. Consequently, combining nanocarriers, siRNA, and curcumin may help treat cancer.

16.4 RNA-induced silencing complex

RNAi is extensively found in eukaryotes and animals and is triggered by the presence of long double-stranded RNA, then cleaved into fragments called siRNA. siRNA is 21−23 nucleotides long and fragmented with the endonuclease dicer's help. The basis of RNAi forms from the strands of siRNA and messenger RNA (mRNA). RNA-induced silencing complex (RISC) loads the siRNA, and the RISC can cleave and remove strands of siRNA duplex due to the presence of Argonaute protein (Ago-2). The specificity of the target mRNA through complementary base pairing is promoted with the association of single-stranded RNA and RISC protein [24]. The Ago-2 protein achieves gene silencing by degrading the mRNA complementary to the antisense strand. In between 10 and 11 bases relative to the 50 ends of the antisense siRNA, endonucleocytic cleavage occurs, resulting in gene silencing. Gene silencing mainly occurs in these two stages: transcriptional gene silencing (TGS) and posttranscriptional gene silencing (PTGS) [25,26].

In PTGS, the sequence-specific cleavage is directed by RISC in which siRNA and target mRNA are perfectly complementary. The miRNA mediates the RNA degradation leading to translational repression, and despite limited complementarity to target mRNA, RNA degradation occurs. Triggering the PTGS mechanism can be achieved by transfecting the siRNA into the cells in which siRNA binds to the RISC. It stimulates the PTGS mechanism and can be utilized to target the genes and silence them specifically. The siRNA serves as a guide for RISC to recognize the specific gene sequence. Synthetic siRNAs came into the limelight in cancer research due to their specificity and ability to rapidly identify the key molecules in cancer cellular pathways (Fig. 16–2). Synthetic siRNAs comprise 22 nucleotides with dinucleotide hanging groups, which mimic the dicer cleavage products and facilitate binding to RISC. The gene silencing efficacy and the stability of siRNA make them significantly advantageous over other therapeutic agents. Furthermore, synthetic siRNA can be chemically modified to prevent unwanted immunostimulatory effects and block unintended target sequence mismatches, thus having low side effects. The tuning of refined RNAi technology to target essential molecular pathways in cancer therapy led to the increased exploration of siRNA therapy in vitro cellular antiproliferative studies and preclinical animal models [27,28].

16.5 Targeting cancer with siRNA

RNA interference (RNAi) approaches can target the cancer targets that control uncontrolled cell proliferation. These targets include cyclin-dependent kinases (CDKs), insulin growth factors (IGF), vascular endothelial growth factors (VEGF), and antiapoptotic factors, as examples. Cyclins and CDKs tightly control cell cycle checkpoints. The overexpression of cyclins disrupts the cell cycle, which can lead to cancer development. The application of siRNA to silence the cyclin B1 expressions for prostate and lung cancer is explored by Resnier et al. in 2013 [27]. Growth factors, such as IGF, are responsible for developing proliferative signals in cancer cells. These are generated by activating intracellular cascades accountable for cell proliferation, survival, and division; these provide cancer cells with a suitable growth environment.

Cell death pathway disruption is a crucial step in cancer development; in cancers such as leukemia and myeloma, the cancer cells exhibit cell death resistance mechanisms by overexpressing an apoptotic regulator, such as Bcl-2 proteins, that determines the cancer progression. VEGFs promote angiogenesis in the cancer progression through an angiogenic mechanism. Inhibiting the angiogenic mechanism could obstruct nutrients through rich vascular supply to the cancer cells and thus limit tumor diameter [28]. Besides these targets, siRNAs can be used in targeting the genetic lesions of cancer, where small molecules find it difficult to reach the targets. For instance, oncoproteins such as c-Myc or KRAS present in a mutated form in most human cancer types due to their ability to chemically interact with the small molecules, but no drugs targeting these proteins have been approved. In these scenarios, siRNA therapeutics against these genes could be a potential target. Targeting the immune system against the tumors and restricting the vasculature that facilitates tumor growth is also a potential strategy that can be achieved through siRNA therapy by modifying siRNA to the specific immune cell type and can be used for targeting multiple targets.

Immunotherapies mainly target the programmed cell death of protein 1 (PD1), ligand 1 (PDL1), and cytotoxic T lymphocyte antigen 4 (CTLA4) and act by blocking the inhibitory signals of the immune system and thereby achieving the increased immune response against cancer. This strategy has been successful in many cancer types, such as melanoma, bladder cancer, lung cancer, and Hodgkin lymphoma. Much reported literature on siRNA-antitumor immunosuppressive therapies against immunosuppressive factor saves has shown significant therapeutic efficacy in dendritic cells, monocytes, and macrophages in cancer [29]. RNAi targets in different cancer types are briefed and discussed below.

16.5.1 Lung cancer

RNAi therapeutics are targeted and delivered through cellular proliferation, migration, and apoptosis pathways. Many potential targeted pathways and genes are identified in small-cell lung carcinoma (SCLC) and nonsmall-cell lung carcinoma (NSCLC), and some of them include KRAS, EGFR, ALK, ROS1, HER2, BRAF, RET, and P53 [30]. By tuning the amount of siRNA used, the downregulation of the target gene could be easily adjusted. It is simple to work with siRNAs, and they may be utilized to target many genes in several cellular pathways simultaneously. To overcome the limitations of conventional chemotherapy, nanocarrier-mediated siRNA has emerged as a potential strategy for silencing the oncogenes and multidrug resistance (MDR)-related genes in lung cancer. To improve the therapeutic effectiveness of siRNA therapy, physicochemical characteristics and in-depth knowledge of lung cancer have been enhanced by understanding the underlying mechanisms to overcome the barriers of siRNA transmission to carry out gene therapy for lung cancer [31,32].

16.5.2 Pancreatic cancer

Pancreatic ductal adenocarcinoma (PDAC) is an invasive and lethal malignant tumor accounting for 90% of pancreatic cancer cases. Recent studies have shown that RNAi has great therapeutic potential in target gene silencing therapy and emerged as a new strategy in pancreatic cancer therapy. Combinational therapy of RNAi with chemotherapeutics has reduced the resistance of pancreatic cancer cells. The focus of using RNAi in pancreatic cancer has been finding the possible molecular targets in the pancreatic cancer signaling pathway and applying nano-gene silencing drugs to target MDR patients with PDAC. Recently, some potential targets were also studied extensively, including the silencing of KRAS oncogene, the most common mutated oncogene in human cancers, and some abnormally expressed molecules such as EphA2, CEACAM6, and thrombin [33,34].

16.5.3 Breast cancer

Breast cancer is the most common cancer and constitutes a majority of deaths in women. Breast cancer subtypes and their progressions are affected by the different genetic changes and gene expression patterns. The possible gene therapy strategy for breast cancer is repairing defective genes and regulating gene expressions. Targeting the HER2 + receptor for

RNAi-based therapy in breast cancer has been explored by Ngamcherdtrakul et al.; in their study, polyethylene glycol (PEG)-polylactic acid (PLA)-based nanoparticles were used for transporting siRNA to the target site HER2 + and results have shown successful targeted injection [35].

16.5.4 Colorectal cancer

Colorectal cancer is the most common digestive system tumor. With the current therapies (radiotherapy, immunotherapy, chemotherapy, and surgery), the patient's survival rate was not able to achieve more than 50%. RNAi therapy has emerged as a new strategy to counter the colonic epithelial neoplastic transformation resulting from genetic and epigenetic changes. Molecular pathways such as overexpression of different EGFR influence tumorigenesis in colon cancer. Cell proliferation and resistance to apoptosis are induced through myotic signals transmitted by the dimerized EGFR to tumor cells when binded to specific ligands. This approach has been considered as a potential strategy in colon cancer therapy [36]. High PANDAR expression may serve as a novel prognostic marker for colorectal cancer patients. According to earlier research, the overexpression of PANDAR in colorectal cancer, breast cancer, and other tissues is related to the decreased oxygen saturation, suggesting the possibility that it may be used as a biomarker for a poor prognosis [37].

16.6 Strategies of siRNA cancer therapy

The main strategy in siRNA cancer therapy is altering the cancer cell proliferation by limiting/preventing the target cellular protein expressions. siRNA therapy doesn't modify the cell genome permanently as siRNA is not integrated into the DNA [27]. The main challenges in activating the RNAi pathway reside in the siRNA to access the cytosol of target cells. siRNA has a large molecular weight and hydrophilic nature; this prevents siRNA from diffusing across the cellular membrane. So, strategies such as modifications to nucleic acids and other delivery approaches are important for siRNA therapy. Some strategies include chemical changes, bioconjugated siRNAs, siRNA-based polymeric nanoparticles, siRNA-lipid-based delivery, and a combination approach strategy.

16.6.1 Chemical modifications of siRNA

Exposing the naked siRNA to the bloodstream triggers the immune response system, and serum nucleases degrade the siRNA. By imparting chemical modifications on the RNA-backbone of siRNA, the stability in the serum and gene silencing potency can be enhanced. Modifying the 2' position on the ribose backbone such as 2-O-methyl, 2-O-methoxyethyl, 2-deoxy-2-fluorouridine, and locked nucleic acid (LNA) is the most common modification of RNA. Upon these chemical modifications, the stability of nucleases and thermal stability increases. The overmodification of the 2-O-methyl RNA, a natural variant of RNA, has shown reduced potency or siRNA inactivation in the RNAi pathway.

The 2'-fluoro alteration adds stability in the presence of nucleases and is consistent with siRNA function. Highly stable RNA duplexes in serum are produced by combining 2'-fluoro pyrimidine and 2'-O-methyl purine modification; these modifications also improve the in vivo activity [38]. The 2-O-methoxyethyl RNA alteration has also demonstrated significant nuclease resistance and improved thermal stability. It is rarely applied as frequently as the 2-O-methyl and 2-fluoro RNA modifications. The methylene bridge in LNA connects the ribose backbone's 2-O and 4-C locations, which results in higher thermal stability. Although LNA integration reduces siRNA's activity, limited alteration maintains functionality [39]. Chemical changes are often done to other siRNA components and the backbone to aid delivery to the target site. Because siRNA has a significant molecular weight and weak negative charge, that prone to degrade in the serum and be captured by the reticuloendothelial system (RES). Polymerized siRNA can form stable delivery complexes, which increases electrostatic interactions and makes it easier to incorporate into nanoparticles. SiRNA can also undergo chemical modifications such as base modification, changes to the overhangs and termini of RNA duplexes, and changes to its tertiary structure. Different chemical alterations are being looked at to enhance properties, including serum stability, siRNA potency, minimal immunostimulation, off-target effects, and target organ/cell delivery to develop siRNA for use in clinical trials as pharmaceuticals [40].

16.6.2 Bioconjugated siRNAs

To overcome the efficacy of siRNA in vivo, conjugating biological agents such as cholesterol, various peptides, antibodies, aptamers, and biopolymers of different physicochemical profiles can be conjugated covalently. Upon systemically injecting cholesterol-conjugated siRNA, the intracellular activity of siRNA and cellular import activity is improved. In circulation, cholesterol gets transported by serum and absorbed through low-density lipoprotein (LDL)-mediated endocytosis by hepatocytes. When targeted against the apolipoprotein B (apoB), cholesterol-conjugated siRNA showed improved serum stability and significant suppression of apoB mRNA level in the liver [41]. Currently, in siRNA therapy, siRNA is targeted for specific cells/tissues for achieving targeted delivery, and directly conjugating antibodies or aptamers achieve this to siRNA.

Nucleic acid−based aptamers are synthetic single-stranded RNA or DNA short-length ligands with high selectivity and affinity for target binding, thereby becoming an alternative target agent that can be conjugated to siRNA. A lot of attention has been paid to aptamers as active targeting moieties for cancer therapeutic agents like siRNA ever since they were developed to target the extracellular domains of transmembrane receptors that are overexpressed in cancer cells. Despite aptamers' excellent specificity and binding affinity, aptamer-siRNA conjugation is hampered by stability concerns caused by unprotected negative charge. siRNA-containing nanoparticles can be utilized to target both antibodies and aptamers as a surface-targeting moiety. Tumor site-specific nanoparticle delivery can be achieved by using different aptamers [29].

16.6.3 Polymeric nanoparticles

To overcome the limitations of nucleic acid formulations, encapsulation of siRNA into nano-particles is extensively used due to their stability in serum, the scope of alternating the sur-face of the nanoparticles for targeted delivery, biodegradability, and controlled delivery. Polymeric nanoparticles used for siRNA loading can be broadly divided into two categories: natural and synthetic polymers. Natural polymers such as gelatin, albumin, chitosan, colla-gen, and cyclodextrin can be used for siRNA delivery in cancer. In contrast, polymers such as PEG, polyethyleneimine (PEI), and poly (d,l-lactide-co-glycolic acid) (PLGA) belong to synthetic polymers and are extensively used as siRNA delivery agents [29].

16.6.4 Peptide-based delivery systems

Peptides have emerged as favorable candidates for siRNA mainly due to their cell specificity in delivery, pH membrane, efficient packaging, and membrane transport. Peptides are low-molecular-weight compounds and can be easily synthesized. Functionalization of peptide synthesis can be controlled easily, and the stability of the peptide oligonucleotide complex makes them superior over lipoplexes as siRNA delivery vehicles. Cell-penetrating peptides (CPPs) for siRNA delivery systems are the most widely studied. CPPs are protein transduc-tion domains and can be classified into naturally derived, synthetic, and chimeric peptides. Membrane perturbing peptides (MPPs) are used for DNA release and are considered peptide delivery systems. Based on their DNA release behavior, these are classified as endo-osmolytic, which act by endosomal lysis, and fusogenic peptides, which act by mediating the DNA release at endosomal pH release [42].

16.6.5 Lipid-based delivery

Lipid-based nanoparticles are biocompatible, low toxic, and potentially be used as an siRNA delivery agent compared to various inorganic and synthetic polymers among these lipids. Cationic-based lipids are advantageous over other lipids due to their ability to interact with nucleic acids electrostatically, high transfection efficiency through cells, and enhanced phar-macokinetic profile; cationic lipids emerged as potential delivery vehicles for siRNA. Several challenges had to be investigated with the lipid-based delivery in terms of toxicity and their evoked immediate immune responses [43].

16.6.6 Combination therapy

A wide variety of approaches to using siRNA are possible in cancer therapies, and the combina-tion therapy achieves the simultaneous action of multiple therapeutic agents to enhance thera-peutic efficacy. Besides enhancing the therapeutic efficacy, combination therapy also lowers the risk of individual drug cytotoxicity. The tumor heterogeneity and chemoresistant tumors can be targeted by applying combination therapy with siRNA and other cancer therapeutics in a syner-getic fashion. Some of the combined approaches of siRNA, such as chemotherapy, immuno-therapy, radiation therapy, or photodynamic therapy, have been developed. The primary strategy of this approach is to reduce MDR. Cancers being heterogenous create resistance to therapies, and the MDR resistance to cancers may even develop in different types of therapies such as chemotherapy, radiation therapy, and photodynamic therapy. In cancer cells, enhanced drug efflux and elevated antiapoptotic and resistance-related gene expressions lead to the MDR protein expression. Although chemotherapeutics are used as front-line treatment in cancers but due to MDR with chemotherapeutics, reduced therapeutic efficacy of many cancerous drugs is reported. Nucleic acid therapeutics, combined with chemotherapeutics, restores the tumor suppressors and apoptotic genes by specific gene silencing and antiapoptosis mechanisms [44]. The combination therapy of RNAi with chemotherapeutics can be achieved either by cotreatment of individual therapeutics or by codelivery of siRNA and chemotherapeutics through a single carrier. Nanoparticles can carry multiple agents and deliver in a controlled manner at the specific target site. Different nanocarriers such as polymeric-based nanoparticles, liposomes, and other inorganic nanoparticles have been explored in the codelivery of chemotherapeutics and siRNA to achieve the synergetic effect and target gene silencing [45].

16.7 Barriers to siRNA delivery

Although siRNA is a potential candidate for therapeutic gene silencing, there are still a number of obstacles to overcome before we can achieve efficiency and control in vivo. Systemic circulation poses a significant challenge for siRNA formulations in vivo to reach the cytoplasm of the target cell. Upon postinjection, the siRNA complex must overcome kidney filtration, phagocyte uptake, aggregation with serum protein, and enzymatic degradation of endogenous nucleases [45]. After administration, nuclease activity in plasma and tissue is the first barrier encountered with the siRNA. In plasma, nuclease comprises 30 exonucleases in the majority, and some cleavages of internucleotide bonds can also exist. Unmodified siRNA has a half-life in serum, which ranges from minutes to 1 h.

In addition, siRNA clearance is majorly affected by the kidney, where the kidney has the highest uptake of siRNA and high biodistribution. Besides nuclease degradation and renal clearance, siRNA uptake by the RES is a major barrier. The presence of phagocytic cells, tissue macrophages, and circulating monocytes detects siRNAs as foreign pathogens and then removes them. High concentrations of siRNA are accumulated in liver and spleen tissues after systemic circulation due to the high blood flow and perforated vasculature in these tissues. siRNA is not readily absorbed by the cells due to the hydrophilicity and negative charges of the RNA strands. These characteristics of siRNA prevent them from crossing the biological membranes and entering the cells. The siRNA needs to be packed in vesicles. After entering through the delivery system and reaching the target cell, early endosomes engulf the siRNA for transportation and then fuse with the late endosomes. Due to the ATPase proton pump, the late endosomal pH becomes acidic and the late endosome again fuses with the lysosomes and transfers the contents. Hence, the presence of low pH and nucleases degrade the RNA molecules [46]. Potential "off-target" effects are a significant challenge that needs to be overcome. Accidental knocking down by a gene that is similar to the target gene may lead to serious unwanted side effects.

Many unwanted transcripts with partial identity to sequence are silenced off-target by siRNA, like miRNA, posing unpredictable cellular consequences and phenotypic toxic effects. Innate immune response to siRNA is another challenge, in which the availability of huge concentrations of siRNA triggers the innate immune response mechanism. The factors that may activate through innate immune responses include dsRNA sensors, protein kinases, cytokines, and IFNs. These factors trigger the activation of NF-κB, toll-lie receptors (TLR), TLR-7,8, and 9 that recognize the siRNA [45]. Research on the pharmacokinetics and pharmacodynamics of siRNA-based therapeutics in vivo is still in its early stages. The ideal dosage, timing, and duration vary with the treatment strategy, delivery strategy, selectivity of gene targeting, and disease. As a result, our knowledge of medicines based on siRNA is still developing.

16.8 Nano drug delivery systems for codelivery of curcumin-siRNA

Chemotherapy is the most prominent and successful method for treating cancer in clinical practice [47]. Distinct treatment strategies with chemotherapeutic drugs are currently utilized efficiently for the treatment of cancer by targeting specific pathways. Furthermore, prolonged use of single chemotherapeutic drug leads to the emergence of MDR [48]. Conventional monotherapy is considered to be ineffective for cancer treatment, which works by targeting a single pathway and has no tumor selectivity leading to the requirement of high-dose results in cytotoxicity and serious side effects [49].

Gene therapy is the potential approach to treat many cancers. siRNA has considered being an effective method for suppressing particular targets inside tumor cells. For efficient gene delivery, both viral and nonviral vectors have recently been utilized as gene carriers. Although the viral vectors are beneficial because of high gene transfection, due to the adverse effects, their use is limited. Nonviral vectors have thus gained greater attention due to their benefits, including safety, low immunogenic detection, safety, high gene-carrying capacity, and stability [50].

The limitations of using siRNA alone in cancer therapy are the development of acquired resistance and siRNA alone cannot ensure the reduction of tumor volume [51]. In the codelivery of chemotherapeutic drug and siRNA, the drug targets tumor-related characteristics such as cell proliferation, and the siRNA works by targeting a particular mutation in the tumor.

Combination therapy involves utilizing various chemotherapeutic agents or combining chemotherapeutics with different treatment strategies. Combination therapy typically refers to the codelivery of two or more drugs or a combination of different therapies, including chemotherapy, radiotherapy, and hormone therapy [52]. Concurrent delivery of combining two or more anticancer therapeutic approaches with distinct signaling pathways can be used to overcome the drug resistance associated with conventional monotherapy and is found to be very effective in treating many cancers. To achieve more effective chemotherapy than traditional monotherapy, a variety of siRNA and natural chemical codelivery vehicles have been designed. Nanocarrier-based codelivery systems are crucial for enhancing the synergistic effects of antitumor activity because the anticancer agents used in the combination therapy work by different mechanisms and are targeted to specific sites [21]. Consequently, functionalized nano vehicles targeted to specific sites have gained significant interest for accurately delivering several drugs/RNA for enhanced synergistic effects.

The benefits of utilizing polymeric nanocarriers in cancer treatment include increased drug solubility and bioavailability. In addition, nanocarriers improve the biological activity of the encapsulated anticancer agents, lessen drug toxicity, and increase the localization of drug at the tumor sites. The nanocarriers can release the chemotherapeutics in a controlled or sustained manner at the tumor site [53]. The ideal codelivery system should have the ability to encapsulate both hydrophilic and hydrophobic drugs [54].

The polymer-based drug delivery devices include components that are responsive to changes in pH, temperature, the presence of glutathione, ROS, and enzymes that were developed to improve the efficacy of codeliver in anticancer treatment. Effective therapeutic activity can be provided by designing the tumor microenvironment-activated nanoformulations by conjugating the surface of the nanocarriers with tumor-activated ligands. Numerous studies investigating the combined delivery of anticancer agents by polymeric nanoparticles have been reported. In recent, stimuli-responsive polymers have been widely used to achieve target specificity. Amphiphilic copolymers can self-assemble into micelles and can accommodate both hydrophilic and hydrophobic drugs [54]. The pH variations between healthy and tumor tissues enable the development of pH-sensitive polymeric drug delivery systems with improved targeting and fewer adverse effects. Temperature sensitivity is considered as a significant factor for stimulating the release of drugs in a controlled manner after reaching the tumor. In general, the thermoresponsive nanocarriers hold the drug at body temperature (37°C) and release the drug by quick response to the elevated temperature of the tumor (40°C−42°C) [55].

Hydrophobicity, low absorption and penetration, and low bioavailability of curcumin limit its clinical use [56]. The anticancer potential of curcumin could be increased by incorporating it into nanocarriers. siRNA is a promising anticancer agent that can downregulate the expression of Bcl-2 and STAT3 and interfere with the proliferation of cancer cells [57]. But siRNA faces some challenges in imparting effective anticancer effects, including cancer heterogeneity and adaptive resistance [58]. An effective nucleic acid therapy could be achieved by combining nucleic acids with anticancer agents or other treatment strategies.

Due to the concurrent cytotoxicity and suppression, the gene expression produced by the combined delivery of chemotherapeutic agent and siRNA utilizing a single nano delivery vehicle could exhibit a synergistic effect [59,60]. Although utilizing a single nanocarrier system for combined delivery of curcumin and siRNA improves the therapeutic effect, combined delivery of drug-nucleic acid is challenging because of the significant differences in the physicochemical properties, including molecular weight, stability, and hydrophobicity of the two agents caused a greater difference in their biodistribution. A more effective, controlled, and nontoxic method of treating cancer cells will be accomplished by designing nanovesicles that can deliver both the drug and nucleic acid, and the sequence of delivery of specific agents can be controlled in an independent manner. A combination of anticancer drugs with gene silencing ability to suppress the expression of efflux transporters is the extensively investigated strategy [58].

Functional nano drug delivery vehicles such as liposomes, micelles, dendrimers, and nanoparticles have been prepared to achieve the codelivery of siRNA and curcumin. Furthermore, these nanocarriers protect the siRNA from rapid degradation by serum nucleic acid degrading enzymes in the blood circulation and prevent the premature release of the drug and siRNA before reaching the tumor site.

16.8.1 Liposomes

The liposomes are commonly used to facilitate the transfer of nucleic acids into mammalian cells [61]. The liposomal encapsulation of poorly water-soluble therapeutic agents like curcumin and biomolecules, including siRNA, enhances the bioavailability and therapeutic efficacy. The significant features of liposomes include prolonged circulation, and high tumor specificity can be achieved by PEGylation of liposome membrane through chemical conjugation [62]. Lipid-based nanocarriers are effective in delivering siRNA for the treatment of cancer. Numerous liposome formulations, including siRNA-conjugated liposomes, enter the cancer cells by interacting with the receptor-mediated serum lipoproteins by endocytosis [41].

The STAT3 can regulate critical aspects, including proliferation and apoptosis in melanoma. Many cancers, including skin cancer, have elevated levels of STAT3. The stratum corneum, the outer layer of skin, serves the barrier function, which limits the entry of therapeutic agents [63]. A study by Anup et al. demonstrated noninvasive anodal iontophoretic codelivery of liposomal formulation of curcumin and siRNA for the treatment of skin cancer to improve the penetration efficiency of the formulation. The curcumin was loaded into the liposomes by using 1,2-dioleoyl-3-trimethylammonium propane (DOTAP) and 1,2-dioleoyl-sn-glycero-3-phospho-ethanolamine (DOPE) lipids. Due to the increased uptake of the nanoformulation by the A431 cancer cells, significant suppression of STAT3 was observed [64]. Another study by Jose et al. developed a nano complex to compare the efficacy of topical cationic-liposome-mediated codelivery of curcumin and anti-STAT3, siRNA, and intratumoral injection of the same for the treatment of skin cancer. After the application of anodal iontophoresis, enhanced permeation of the liposomes was observed. The in vivo studies concluded that the combination therapy exhibited the significant inhibition of growth and tumor progression of B16F10 cancer cells than the curcumin and anti-STAT siRNA liposomal formulations alone. In contrast, intertumoral injection exhibited similar therapeutic efficacy with the iontophoretic administration [65].

16.8.2 Nanoparticles

Polymeric nanoparticles are colloidal particles widely used for the delivery of several drugs. These polymeric nanoparticles can recognize the binding sites that are overexpressed on the target cancer cells after modifying their surface with certain ligands [66].

Higher progression in the tumor's clinical stage was significantly linked with the overexpression of the EIF5A2 [67]. In a study by [68] Zhou-Hao Xing et al. developed Zn(II)-curcumin complex to deliver the siRNA into the human bladder cancer cells, which works by downregulating the expression of EIF5A2 and inhibits the growth of the cancer cells. After complexing with zinc, the solubility, bioavailability, and cellular uptake of curcumin were improved. The in vitro and in vivo studies showed that the coadministration of curcumin and EIF5A2 siRNA exhibited a synergistic anticancer effect, delivered in response to the acidic pH of the tumor microenvironment, and significantly inhibited tumor growth in the murine xenograft models. Kavya et al. developed a nanocarrier, poly (methacryloyl beta-alanine) (PMBA), by using radical polymerization in supercritical CO_2. In this work, the curcumin and Bcl-2-siRNA were incorporated into the prepared polymer by the emulsification technique. The anticancer potential of the formulation was evaluated on cervical cancer (HeLa) cells. The nanocomplex of curcumin and Bcl-2-siRNA significantly inhibited the growth of the cancer cells by inducing apoptosis and affecting the various signaling pathways responsible for the development of cancer [69].

To enable the targeted transport of siRNA in macrophages, Fischer et al. prepared a nanostructured cylindrical drug carrier made of mesoporous silica nanoparticles (mSNPs) to reduce the release of TNF-α. The formulation was added with curcumin as an antiinflammatory agent and loaded into the pores of the mSNPs. The formulation was evaluated on cell lines A549 and dTHP-1. The results showed that the particles significantly decreased TNF release, demonstrating enhanced codelivery of both drugs for the targeted suppression of TNF in the lungs than the individual drugs [70].

A study by Leila Mohammad Gholinia Sarpoli et al. developed PLGA nanoparticles for the codelivery of curcumin and Bcl-2-siRNA [71]. Curcumin was incorporated into the PLGA nanoparticles, and the surface was coated with PEI and complexed with Bcl-2-siRNA for the treatment of breast cancer. In vitro cytotoxicity studies were performed on the T47D cell line. The results showed that the nanoformulation was localized into the cancer cells and exhibited the highest toxicity with the decreased Bcl-2 expression (90.7%) by the siRNA.

16.8.3 Dendrimers

Due to the presence of several reactive end groups than the linear polymers, dendrimers are considered as effective drug carriers with higher loading capacity [72]. Nucleic acids and drugs interact with the dendrimers through electrostatic interaction and covalent conjugation [73]. The cellular uptake of siRNAs and their release from endosomes are markedly improved by dendrimers [21]. The enhanced permeation and retention (EPR) effect of the drug will be observed after loading into the PEGylated dendrimers (Fig. 16–3).

Amine-terminated PAMAM dendrimers offer a hydrophobic core to encapsulate the hydrophobic agents and hydrophilic surface for the attachment of siRNA [75]. A study by Gha et al. utilized this approach to improve the solubility and bioavailability of curcumin by encapsulating it in the hydrophobic core of the PAMAM, and the Bcl-2-siRNA was complexed via electrostatic interaction to exhibit the synergistic anticancer activity of curcumin and Bcl-2-siRNA.

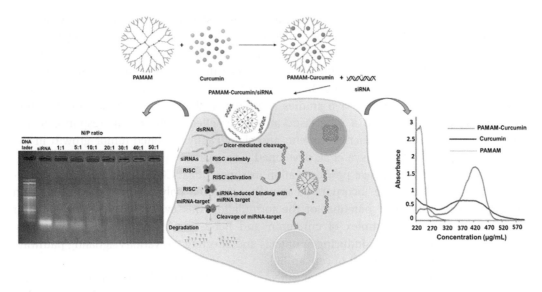

FIGURE 16–3 A PAMAM dendrimer encapsulated curcumin and a polyplex with siRNA against BCL-2 [74]. *PAMAM,* polyamidoamine. *Adapted permission from M. Gha et al., Co-delivery of curcumin and Bcl-2 siRNA by PAMAM dendrimers for enhancement of the therapeutic efficacy in HeLa cancer cells, Colloids and Surfaces B: Biointerfaces, 188, 110762, 2020, https://doi.org/10.1016/j.colsurfb.2019.110762. Copyright (2019), Elsevier.*

The in vitro cytotoxicity studies performed on the human cervical carcinoma (HeLa) cells revealed that, due to the combined anticancer effect, the PAMAM-Cur/siRNA nano complex exhibited more excellent antiproliferative activity compared with the PAMAM-Cur [74].

16.8.4 Micelles

Di- or triblock copolymers are the widely used polymers to deliver the siRNA along with the chemotherapeutic agent because the copolymers offer a hydrophobic core to encapsulate the drug and hydrophilic surface. To form the complex with anionic siRNA, the hydrophilic surfaces of the micelles are always replaced with cationic groups [76] such as poly(dimethyl aminoethyl methacrylate) (PEI), and the most frequently used hydrophobic polymers are polylactide (PLA) and poly (lactic-co-glycolic acid) (PLGA). Some micelle formulations exhibited EPR effects through receptor-mediated endocytosis leading to increased drug accumulation in the tumor sites [77].

A study by Muddineti et al. utilized low-molecular-weight chitosan to prepare cholesterol-conjugated chitosan micelles for the codelivery of siRNA and poorly water-soluble chemotherapeutic agent, curcumin, for the combined therapeutic effect. The nanoparticles were in the size range of 165 $\pm$ 2.6 nm and exhibited a zeta potential of $+24.8$ $\pm$ 2.2 mV. Cellular uptake studies performed on lung cancer (A549) cells demonstrated that the developed nano formulation delivered both curcumin and siRNA via a clathrin-dependent endocytosis mechanism in a time-dependent manner [78] (Table 16–1).

Table 16–1 Curcumin-siRNA codelivery in anticancer therapy.

Sl. No	Nanocarrier	Cancer type	Cell lines	Target gene	Size (nm)	Zeta potential (mV)	Encapsulation efficiency (EE) (%)	Therapeutic outcomes (%)	References
1	PAMAM dendrimer	Cervical cancer	HeLa cells	Bcl-2	180	48	82	High cellular uptake, synergistic impact, downregulation of Bcl-2 and stimulation of apoptosis	[79]
2	Cationic liposome	Skin cancer	Mouse melanoma cells (B16F10)	STAT3	276.9	42.8	86.8	Downregulation of STAT3 and effective inhibition of tumor growth and viability	[63]
3	Cationic liposome	Skin cancer	Human epidermoid carcinoma cells (A431)	STAT3	195	58.8	87.5	Significant reduction in STAT3 expression, resulting in inhibition of cancer growth and invasion	[63]
4	Zn nanoparticle	Bladder cancer	Human bladder cancer cell line	eIF5A2	80 – 500	+22.3		Effective knock down of eIF5A2, induction and apoptosis and reducing proliferation and growth of cancer cells	[80]

PAMAM, polyamidoamine; siRNA, small interfering RNA.

16.9 Conclusion

Although chemotherapy has been a common choice for treating cancer patients, multidrug resistance has become an obstacle to overcome. Out of many other strategies to increase the chemotherapeutic effectiveness, inducing different apoptosis and overcoming MDR, codelivery of siRNA with chemotherapeutic agents emerged as a promising treatment strategy in cancer therapy. Apart from the other chemotherapeutic agents, curcumin is a natural substance with enhanced anticancer and antiproliferative properties. Curcumin-siRNA codelivery through various polymeric nanocarriers significantly increases their in vivo tumor accumulation and enhances the therapeutic activity by showing a synergistic effect. The gene silencing mechanisms of siRNA downregulate the genes responsible for MDR and chemotherapeutic effectiveness. Despite many advantages, the codelivery of curcumin with siRNA as a cancer therapy requires further research to understand the drug-to-siRNA ratio and the pathways and mechanisms to avoid immune stimulation with simultaneous administration of siRNA and curcumin.

References

[1] Sadat N, *et al.*, (SLGHPLRORJLFFDO 3DWWHUQ RI % UHDVW & DQFHU LQ, UDQLDQ : RPHQ Is there an Ethnic Disparity?, pp. 4517−4520, 2012.

[2] Weng W, Goel A. Curcumin and colorectal cancer: an update and current perspective on this natural medicine. Seminars in Cancer Biology 2022;80:73−86. Available from: https://doi.org/10.1016/j.semcancer.2020.02.011 no. December 2019.

[3] Lai KC, et al. Gefitinib and curcumin-loaded nanoparticles enhance cell apoptosis in human oral cancer SAS cells in vitro and inhibit SAS cell xenografted tumor in vivo. Toxicology and Applied Pharmacology 2019;382:114734. Available from: https://doi.org/10.1016/j.taap.2019.114734 no. August.

[4] Mansourizadeh F, et al. Efficient synergistic combination effect of quercetin with curcumin on breast cancer cell apoptosis through their loading into Apo ferritin cavity. Colloids Surfaces B Biointerfaces 2020;191:110982. Available from: https://doi.org/10.1016/j.colsurfb.2020.110982 no. March.

[5] Rajamanickam V, et al. Allylated curcumin analog CA6 inhibits TrxR1 and leads to ROS-dependent apoptotic cell death in gastric cancer through Akt-FoxO3a. Cancer Management and Research 2020;12:247−63. Available from: https://doi.org/10.2147/CMAR.S227415 vol.

[6] Zhou M, Li G, Zhu L, Zhou H, Lu L. Arctiin attenuates high glucose-induced human retinal capillary endothelial cell proliferation by regulating ROCK1/PTEN/PI3K/Akt/VEGF pathway in vitro. Journal of Cellular and Molecular Medicine 2020;24(10):5695−706. Available from: https://doi.org/10.1111/jcmm.15232.

[7] Wang S, et al. miR-874 directly targets AQP3 to inhibit cell proliferation, mobility and EMT in non-small cell lung cancer. Thoracic Cancer 2020;11(6):1550−8. Available from: https://doi.org/10.1111/1759-7714.13428.

[8] Mazzucchelli S, et al. H-Ferritin-nanocaged olaparib: a promising choice for both BRCA-mutated and sporadic triple negative breast cancer. Scientific Reports 2017;7(1):1−15. Available from: https://doi.org/10.1038/s41598-017-07617-7.

[9] Mohamed SIA, Jantan I, Haque MA. Naturally occurring immunomodulators with antitumor activity: an insight on their mechanisms of action. International Immunopharmacology 2017;50:291−304. Available from: https://doi.org/10.1016/j.intimp.2017.07.010 no. June.

[10] Sethi G, Tergaonkar V. Potential pharmacological control of the NF-κB pathway. Trends in Pharmacological Sciences 2009;30(6):313−21. Available from: https://doi.org/10.1016/j.tips.2009.03.004.

[11] Lee S, Margolin K. Cytokines in cancer immunotherapy. Cancers (Basel) 2011;3(4):3856−93. Available from: https://doi.org/10.3390/cancers3043856.

[12] Bessard A, Solé V, Bouchaud G, Quéméner A, Jacques Y. High antitumor activity of RLI, an interleukin-15 (IL-15)-IL-15 receptor α fusion protein, in metastatic melanoma and colorectal cancer. Molecular Cancer Therapeutics 2009;8(9):2736−45. Available from: https://doi.org/10.1158/1535-7163.MCT-09-0275.

[13] Mapks C, *et al.*, Potential Targets 1, 2005.

[14] Mansouri K, et al. Clinical effects of curcumin in enhancing cancer therapy: a systematic review. BMC Cancer 2020;20(1):1−11. Available from: https://doi.org/10.1186/s12885-020-07256-8.

[15] Cai T, et al. A novel pectin from Akebia trifoliata var. australis fruit peel and its use as a wall-material to coat curcumin-loaded zein nanoparticle. International Journal of Biological Macromolecules 2020;152:40−9. Available from: https://doi.org/10.1016/j.ijbiomac.2020.02.234 vol.

[16] Cheng Y, Zhang Y, Deng W, Hu J. Antibacterial and anticancer activities of asymmetric lollipop-like mesoporous silica nanoparticles loaded with curcumin and gentamicin sulfate. Colloids Surfaces B Biointerfaces 2020;186:110744. Available from: https://doi.org/10.1016/j.colsurfb.2019.110744 vol.

[17] Kamaruzman NI, Aziz NA, Poh CL, Chowdhury EH. Oncogenic signaling in tumorigenesis and applications of siRNA nanotherapeutics in breast cancer. Cancers (Basel) 2019;11(5). Available from: https://doi.org/10.3390/cancers11050632.

[18] Kumar K, Rani V, Mishra M, Chawla R. New paradigm in combination therapy of siRNA with chemotherapeutic drugs for effective cancer therapy. Current Research in Pharmacology and Drug Discovery 2022;3:100103. Available from: https://doi.org/10.1016/j.crphar.2022.100103 no. September 2021.

[19] Charbe NB, et al. Small interfering RNA for cancer treatment: overcoming hurdles in delivery. Acta Pharmaceutica Sinica B 2020;10(11):2075−109. Available from: https://doi.org/10.1016/j.apsb.2020.10.005.

[20] Abedi-gaballu F, et al. HHS public access 2019;177−90. Available from: https://doi.org/10.1016/j.apmt.2018.05.002.PAMAM.

[21] Ashra M, et al. Progress in natural compounds/siRNA co-delivery employing nanovehicles for cancer therapy. ACS Combinatorial Science 2020;. Available from: 10.1021/acscombsci.0c00099.

[22] Bradley KT, Westlund NK. 乳鼠心肌提取 HHS public access. Journal of Neuroscience Research 2017;95 (6):1336−56. Available from: https://doi.org/10.1038/nmat2444.Intravaginal.

[23] Cai M, et al. An investigation of IRMOF-16 as a pH-responsive drug delivery carrier of curcumin. Journal of Science: Advanced Materials and Devices 2022;7(4):100507. Available from: https://doi.org/10.1016/j.jsamd.2022.100507.

[24] Singh A, Trivedi P, Jain NK. Advances in siRNA delivery in cancer therapy. Artificial Cells, Nanomedicine, and Biotechnology 2018;46(2):274−83. Available from: https://doi.org/10.1080/21691401.2017.1307210.

[25] Dogini DB, *et al.*, The new world of RNAs, 2014. [Online]. Available from: http://www.mirbase.org/.

[26] Castanotto D, Rossi JJ. The promises and pitfalls of RNA-interference-based therapeutics. Nature 2009;457(7228):426−33. Available from: https://doi.org/10.1038/nature07758.

[27] Resnier P, Montier T, Mathieu V, Benoit J-P, Passirani C. A review of the current status of siRNA nanomedicines in the treatment of cancer. Biomaterials 2013;34(27):6429−43. Available from: https://doi.org/10.1016/j.biomaterials.2013.04.060.

[28] Young SWS, Stenzel M, Jia-Lin Y. Nanoparticle-siRNA: a potential cancer therapy? Critical Reviews in Oncology/Hematology 2016;98:159−69. Available from: https://doi.org/10.1016/j.critrevonc.2015.10.015.

[29] Lee SJ, Kim MJ, Kwon IC, Roberts TM. Delivery strategies and potential targets for siRNA in major cancer types. Advanced Drug Delivery Reviews 2016;104:2−15. Available from: https://doi.org/10.1016/j.addr.2016.05.010.

[30] Rothschild SI. Targeted therapies in non-small cell lung cancer—beyond EGFR and ALK. Cancers 2015;7 (2):930−49. Available from: https://doi.org/10.3390/cancers7020816 MDPI AG.

[31] Tian Z, et al. Insight into the prospects for RNAi therapy of cancer. Frontiers in Pharmacology 2021;12. Available from: https://doi.org/10.3389/fphar.2021.644718.

[32] Zarredar H, Ansarin K, Baradaran B, Ahdi Khosroshahi S, Farajnia S. Potential molecular targets in the treatment of lung cancer using siRNA technology. Cancer Investigation 2018;36(1):37−58. Available from: https://doi.org/10.1080/07357907.2017.1416393.

[33] Chang H. RNAi-mediated knockdown of target genes: a promising strategy for pancreatic cancer research. Cancer Gene Therapy 2007;14(8):677−85. Available from: https://doi.org/10.1038/sj.cgt.7701063.

[34] Wu J, et al. Vertically integrated translational studies of PDX1 as a therapeutic target for pancreatic cancer via a novel bifunctional RNAi platform. Cancer Gene Therapy 2014;21(2):48−53. Available from: https://doi.org/10.1038/cgt.2013.84.

[35] Ngamcherdtrakul W, et al. Current development of targeted oligonucleotide-based cancer therapies: perspective on HER2-positive breast cancer treatment. Cancer Treatment Reviews 2016;45:19−29. Available from: https://doi.org/10.1016/j.ctrv.2016.02.005 vol.

[36] Binkhathlan Z, Alshamsan A. Emerging nanodelivery strategies of RNAi molecules for colon cancer therapy: preclinical developments. Therapeutic Delivery Aug. 2012;3(9):1117−30. Available from: https://doi.org/10.4155/tde.12.89.

[37] Rivandi M, et al. The prognostic and therapeutic values of long noncoding RNA PANDAR in colorectal cancer. Journal of Cellular Physiology 2019;234(2):1230−6. Available from: https://doi.org/10.1002/jcp.27136.

[38] Kawasaki AM, et al. Uniformly modified 2'-deoxy-2'-fluoro-phosphorothioate oligonucleotides as nuclease-resistant antisense compounds with high affinity and specificity for RNA targets. Journal of Medicinal Chemistry 1993;36(7):831−41. Available from: https://doi.org/10.1021/jm00059a007.

[39] Braasch DA, et al. RNA interference in mammalian cells by chemically-modified RNA. Biochemistry 2003;42(26):7967−75. Available from: https://doi.org/10.1021/bi0343774.

[40] Watts JK, Deleavey GF, Damha MJ. Chemically modified siRNA: tools and applications. Drug Discovery Today 2008;13(19):842−55. Available from: https://doi.org/10.1016/j.drudis.2008.05.007.

[41] Wolfrum C, et al. Mechanisms and optimization of in vivo delivery of lipophilic siRNAs. Nature Biotechnology 2007;25(10):1149−57. Available from: https://doi.org/10.1038/nbt1339.

[42] Dana H, et al., Molecular mechanisms and biological functions of siRNA, 2017. [Online]. Available from: http://www.ijbs.org.

[43] Schroeder A, Levins CG, Cortez C, Langer R, Anderson DG. Lipid-based nanotherapeutics for siRNA delivery. Journal of Internal Medicine 2010;267(1):9−21. Available from: https://doi.org/10.1111/j.1365-2796.2009.02189.x.

[44] Gillet J-P, Gottesman MM. Mechanisms of multidrug resistance in cancer. In: Zhou J, editor. Multi-Drug Resistance in Cancer. Totowa, NJ: Humana Press; 2010. p. 47−76.

[45] Wang S, et al. A review of the current status of siRNA nanomedicines in the treatment of cancer. Cancer Gene Therapy 2020;20(1):1−13. Available from: https://doi.org/10.1016/j.critrevonc.2015.10.015.

[46] Liu JF, et al. Combination cediranib and olaparib versus olaparib alone for women with recurrent platinum-sensitive ovarian cancer: a randomised phase 2 study. The Lancet Oncology 2014;15 (11):1207−14. Available from: https://doi.org/10.1016/S1470-2045(14)70391-2.

[47] Kakde D, Jain D, Shrivastava V, Kakde R, Patil AT. Cancer therapeutics- opportunities, challenges and advances in drug delivery. Journal of Applied Pharmaceutical Science 2011;01(09):1−10.

[48] Persidis A. Cancer multidrug resistance. Nature Biotechnology 1999;17:94−5.

[49] Longacre M, Snyder N, Sarkar S. Drug resistance in cancer: an overview. Cancers 2014;6:1769−92. Available from: https://doi.org/10.3390/cancers6031769.

[50] Patil S, Gao Y, Lin X, Li Y, Dang K. The development of functional non-viral vectors for gene delivery. International Journal of Molecular Sciences 2019;20:1−23.

[51] Oh Y, Gwan T. siRNA delivery systems for cancer treatment. Advanced Drug Delivery Reviews 2009;61 (10):850−62. Available from: https://doi.org/10.1016/j.addr.2009.04.018.

[52] Parhi P, Mohanty C, Sahoo SK. Nanotechnology-based combinational drug delivery: an emerging approach for cancer therapy. Drug Discovery Today 2012;17(17−18):1044−52. Available from: https://doi.org/10.1016/j.drudis.2012.05.010.

[53] Mahira S, Kommineni N, Mohammed G, Khan W. Cabazitaxel and silibinin co-encapsulated cationic liposomes for CD44 targeted delivery: a new insight into nanomedicine based combinational chemotherapy for prostate cancer. Biomedicine and Pharmacotherapy 2019;110:803−17. Available from: https://doi.org/10.1016/j.biopha.2018.11.145 no. November 2018.

[54] Pan J, Rostamizadeh K, Filipczak N, Torchilin VP. Polymeric co-delivery systems in cancer treatment: an overview on component drugs' dosage ratio effect. Molecules 2019;1035. Available from: https://doi.org/10.3390/molecules24061035.

[55] Mura S, Nicolas J, Couvreur P. Stimuli-responsive nanocarriers for drug delivery. Nature Materials 2013;12(11):991−1003. Available from: https://doi.org/10.1038/nmat3776.

[56] Sarkar N, Bose S. Liposome-encapsulated curcumin-loaded 3D printed scaffold for bone tissue engineering. ACS Applied Materials & Interfaces 2019;11:17184−92. Available from: https://doi.org/10.1021/acsami.9b01218.

[57] Rahman MA, et al. Systemic delivery of Bc12-targeting siRNA by DNA nanoparticles suppresses cancer cell growth. Angewandte Chemie 2017;56:16023−7. Available from: https://doi.org/10.1002/anie.201709485.

[58] Li J, Wang Y, Zhu Y, Oupický D. Recent advances in delivery of drug − nucleic acid combinations for cancer treatment. Journal of Controlled Release: Official Journal of the Controlled Release Society 2013;172:589−600. Available from: https://doi.org/10.1016/j.jconrel.2013.04.010.

[59] Sun W, et al. Co-delivery of doxorubicin and anti-BCL - 2 siRNA by pH-responsive polymeric vector to overcome drug resistance in in vitro and in vivo HepG2 hepatoma model. Biomacromolecules 2018;19:2248−56. Available from: https://doi.org/10.1021/acs.biomac.8b00272.

[60] Suo A, Qian J, Xu M, Xu W, Zhang Y, Yao Y. Folate-decorated PEGylated triblock copolymer as a pH / reduction dual-responsive nanovehicle for targeted intracellular codelivery of doxorubicin and Bcl-2 siRNA. Materials Science and Engineering C 2017;76:659−72. Available from: https://doi.org/10.1016/j.msec.2017.03.124.

[61] Engelhardt KH, Pinnapireddy SR, Baghdan E, Jedelská J, Bakowsky U. Transfection studies with colloidal systems containing highly purified bipolar tetraether lipids from *Sulfolobus acidocaldarius*. Archaea 2017;2017.

[62] Suk JS, Xu Q, Kim N, Hanes J, En LM. PEGylation as a strategy for improving nanoparticle-based drug and gene delivery. Advanced Drug Delivery Reviews 2015;. Available from: https://doi.org/10.1016/j.addr.2015.09.012.

[63] Naik A, Kalia YN, Guy RH, Guy RH. Transdermal drug delivery: overcoming the skin' s barrier function. Pharmaceutical Science & Technology Today 2000;3(9).

[64] Anup J, Suman L, Venkata V, Krishna V. Co-delivery of curcumin and STAT3 siRNA using deformable cationic liposomes to treat skin cancer. Journal of Drug Targeting 2016;25:1−37.

[65] Jose A, Labala S, Ninave KM, Gade SK, Vamsi V, Venuganti K. Effective skin cancer treatment by topical co-delivery of curcumin and STAT3 siRNA using cationic liposomes. AAPS PharmSciTech 2018;19 (1):166−75. Available from: https://doi.org/10.1208/s12249-017-0833-y.

[66] Zeinali M, et al. Nanovehicles for codelivery of anticancer agents. Drug Discovery Today 2020;25 (8):1416−30. Available from: https://doi.org/10.1016/j.drudis.2020.06.027.

[67] Wei J, et al. EIF5A2 predicts outcome in localised invasive bladder cancer and promotes bladder cancer cell aggressiveness in vitro and in vivo. British Journal of Cancer 2014;110:1767−77. Available from: https://doi.org/10.1038/bjc.2014.52.

[68] Xing ZH, et al. Bifunctional pH-sensitive Zn (II)−curcumin nanoparticles/siRNA effectively inhibit growth of human bladder cancer cells in vitro and in vivo. Journal of Materials Chemistry B 2014;2 (18):2714−24. Available from: https://doi.org/10.1039/c3tb21625j.

[69] Kavya KV, et al. A cationic amino acid polymer nanocarrier synthesized in supercritical CO_2 for codelivery of drug and gene to cervical cancer cells. Colloids Surfaces B Biointerfaces 2022;216:112584. Available from: https://doi.org/10.1016/j.colsurfb.2022.112584.

[70] Fischer T, Winter I, Drumm R, Schneider M. Cylindrical microparticles composed of mesoporous silica nanoparticles for the targeted delivery of a small molecule and a macromolecular drug to the lungs: exemplified with curcumin and siRNA. Pharmaceutics 2021;13:844.

[71] Mohammad Gholinia Sarpoli L. et al.,. Co-delivery of curcumin and Bcl-2 siRNA to enhance therapeutic effect against breast cancer cells using PEI-functionalized PLGA nanoparticles. Pharmaceutical Development and Technology 2022;27(7):785−93.

[72] Yang H, Lopina ÆST. Stealth dendrimers for antiarrhythmic quinidine delivery. Journal of Materials Science 2007;18:2061−5. Available from: https://doi.org/10.1007/s10856-007-3144-0.

[73] Esfand R, Tomalia DA, Arbor A, Arbor A. Poly (amidoamine) (PAMAM) dendrimers: from biomimicry to drug delivery and biomedical applications. Drug Discovery Today 2001;6(8):427−36.

[74] Gha M, et al. Co-delivery of curcumin and Bcl-2 siRNA by PAMAM dendrimers for enhancement of the therapeutic efficacy in HeLa cancer cells. Colloids and Surfaces B: Biointerfaces 2020;188:110762. Available from: https://doi.org/10.1016/j.colsurfb.2019.110762.

[75] Li J, Liang H, Liu J, Wang Z. Poly (amidoamine) (PAMAM) dendrimer mediated delivery of drug and pDNA / siRNA for cancer therapy. International Journal of Pharmaceutics 2018;546(1−2):215−25. Available from: https://doi.org/10.1016/j.ijpharm.2018.05.045.

[76] Zhao J, Feng S. Nanocarriers for delivery of siRNA and codelivery of siRNA and other therapeutic agents. Nanomedicine 2015;10:2199−228.

[77] Bae YH, Yin H. Stability issues of polymeric micelles. Journal of Controlled Release 2008;131:2−4. Available from: https://doi.org/10.1016/j.jconrel.2008.06.015.

[78] Muddineti OS, Shah A, Vishnu S, Rompicharla K, Ghosh B, Biswas S. Cholesterol-grafted chitosan micelles as a nanocarrier system for drug-siRNA codelivery to the lung cancer cells. International Journal of Biological Macromolecules 2018;118:857−63. Available from: https://doi.org/10.1016/j.ijbiomac.2018.06.114.

[79] Ghaffari M, et al. Co-delivery of curcumin and Bcl-2 siRNA by PAMAM dendrimers for enhancement of the therapeutic efficacy in HeLa cancer cells. Colloids Surfaces B Biointerfaces 2020;188:110762. Available from: https://doi.org/10.1016/j.colsurfb.2019.110762.

[80] Xing ZH, et al. Bifunctional pH-sensitive Zn(ii)-curcumin nanoparticles/siRNA effectively inhibit growth of human bladder cancer cells in vitro and in vivo. Journal of Materials Chemistry B 2014;2 (18):2714−24. Available from: https://doi.org/10.1039/c3tb21625j.

Challenges and future perspectives of nano-curcumin drug delivery

17

Challenges associated with nanocurcumin anticancer drug delivery systems

Debanik Deb[1,*], Shibam Chakraborty[1,*], Sumit Ghosh[2], Parames C. Sil[2]

1DEPARTMENT OF ZOOLOGY, RAMAKRISHNA MISSION VIDYAMANDIRA, BELUR MATH, HOWRAH, WEST BENGAL, INDIA 2DIVISION OF MOLECULAR MEDICINE, BOSE INSTITUTE, KOLKATA, INDIA

Abbreviations

Akt	serine/threonine protein kinase
AP-1	activator protein-1
APTES	(3-aminopropyl)triethoxysilane
BBB	blood−brain barrier
CDGA	curcumin diglutaric acid
CH	carboxy-methyl-hexanoyl chitosan
COX-2	cyclooxygenase 2
CSC	cancer stem cells
CTAB	cetyltrimethylammonium bromide
CUR	curcumin
DEX-CUR	enzymatically conjugated curcumin and dextran
Dox	doxorubicin
EBV	Epstein−Barr virus
FA	folic acid
Fmoc	fluorenyl-methoxy-carbonyl
GAP	glycidyl azide polymer
GI-GPx	gastrointestinal glutathione peroxidase
HA	hyaluronic acid
HBV	hepatitis B virus
HCV	hepatitis C virus
HES	hydroxyethyl starch
HHV-4	human gammaherpesvirus-4
HPH	high-pressure homogenization
HPV	human papillomavirus
HTLV-1	human T-cell leukemia virus type-1

* Authors contributed equally.

Curcumin-Based Nanomedicines as Cancer Therapeutics. DOI: https://doi.org/10.1016/B978-0-443-15412-6.00003-9

MACNP	magnetic alginate/chitosan layer-by-later nanoparticle
MAPK	mitogen-activated protein kinase
MCV	Merkel cell polyomavirus
MDR	multi-drug resistance
MNP	magnetic nanoparticles
MPEG	monomethoxy polyethylene glycol
MSN	mesoporous silica nanoparticle
MTX	methotrexate
NF-κB	nuclear factor-kappa B
NIPAAM	N-isopropylacrylamide
Nrf2/Keap1	nuclear factor erythroid 2−related factor 2/ Kelch-like ECH-associated protein 1
PAMAM	nanoscale G4 polyamidoamine
PCL	poly(3-caprolactone)
PDT	photodynamic therapy
PEG	polyethylene glycol
PEI	polyethyleneimine
PKA	protein kinase A
PLGA	poly D,L-lactide-co-glycolic acid
PS	photosensitizer
PVA	polyvinyl alcohol
PVP	Polyvinyl pyrrolidone
p53	tumor protein 53
RES	reticuloendothelial system
TfR	transferrin receptor
TPP	tripolyphosphate
YSN	Yolk-shell structured nanoparticles

17.1 Introduction

Cancer is a global disease of concern affecting a huge number of people worldwide annually [1]. Various natural compounds have been investigated regarding their anticancer properties [2,3]. The therapeutic role of curcumin (CUR) as an important natural bioactive molecule is well established [4]. Nanoformulations can help in overcoming the low bioavailability of the compound and ensure targeted delivery, controlled release, and greater retention of CUR at the site of tumor formation. To impart all such properties associated with the above-mentioned aspects, the nanosystem requires several surface modifications [5,6]. Formulation of such nanofabrications is a challenging work since a proper surface modification can ensure enhanced therapeutic effects of CUR. The mechanism of attachment or loading of CUR within the nanosystem is also an important challenging aspect because it ensures the retention of the drug in the nanosystem until it reaches the targeted site [7−9]. Study of the molecular mechanisms associated with the ameliorative effects of the nanocurcumins can help us in designing future approaches in investigating the anticancer effects of novel formulations [10]. A proper assessment of the latest developments in nanocurcumin formulations can help in overcoming the already mentioned challenges and pave the way for the generation of novel nanosystems with enhanced efficacy.

17.2 Curcumin

17.2.1 Curcumin as a therapeutic agent

Turmeric exerts therapeutic effects against pain, sprain, ache, wounds, liver dysfunction, and pulmonary, gastrointestinal, and skin diseases. CUR is an important active ingredient of turmeric (Fig. 17−1). It decomposes to ferulic acid at slightly alkaline pH [11−14]. It is reported to regulate the transcription factor activator protein-1 (AP-1), nuclear factor-kappa B (NF-κB), mitogen-activated protein kinase (MAPK), nuclear β-catenin, serine/threonine protein kinase (Akt), and the tumor protein 53 (p53) associated signaling pathways [15−17]. It regulates the cancer-associated estrogen receptors, epidermal growth receptors and gastrointestinal glutathione peroxidase (GI-GPx) via the nuclear factor erythroid 2−related factor 2/ Kelch-like ECH-associated protein 1 (Nrf2/Keap1) pathway [16]. It takes part in the intermolecular Diels−Alder reaction and neutralizes lipid radicals [18,19]. CUR activity has been found to be associated with xanthine oxidase, serum albumin, lipooxygenase, cyclooxygenase 2 (COX-2), thioredoxin reductase, protein kinase A (PKA), inositol 1,4,5 triphosphate receptor, Ca^{2+}-ATPase of sarcoplasmic reticulum, cytochrome p450 of rat liver, aryl hydrocarbon receptor, topoisomerase II, and so on [20,21]. It exhibits antineoplastic effects against myeloma, myelodysplastic syndrome, pancreatic, colon and breast cancers [14,22−25].

17.2.2 Significance of nanocurcumin delivery systems

The low oral bioavailability of CUR in mice, rats, and humans is a major drawback in the quest for understanding its medicinal effects [26]. Solubility of CUR in water is nearly 0.0004 mg/mL at a pH of 7.3 and this value is insignificant [27,28]. Oral administration of about 10−12 g/mL of CUR leads to the detection of only 50 ng/mL of the drug in serum [15]. Therefore, alongside other processes, use of nanoparticles as drug delivery systems is used to improve the bioavailability and therapeutic effects of CUR and its structural analogs [29,30].

FIGURE 17−1 Chemical structure of curcumin (drawn using ChemDraw Ultra 12.0).

17.3 Types of anticancer nanocurcumin drug delivery systems

17.3.1 Mesoporous silica nanoparticles

Silica-CUR conjugate has been reported to exhibit antineoplastic activity [14,28,31,32]. The interaction of CUR to mesoporous silica nanoparticle (MSN) is induced by the abundant silanol groups of the latter (Fig. 17−2) [33]. Targeted delivery of CUR can be achieved by

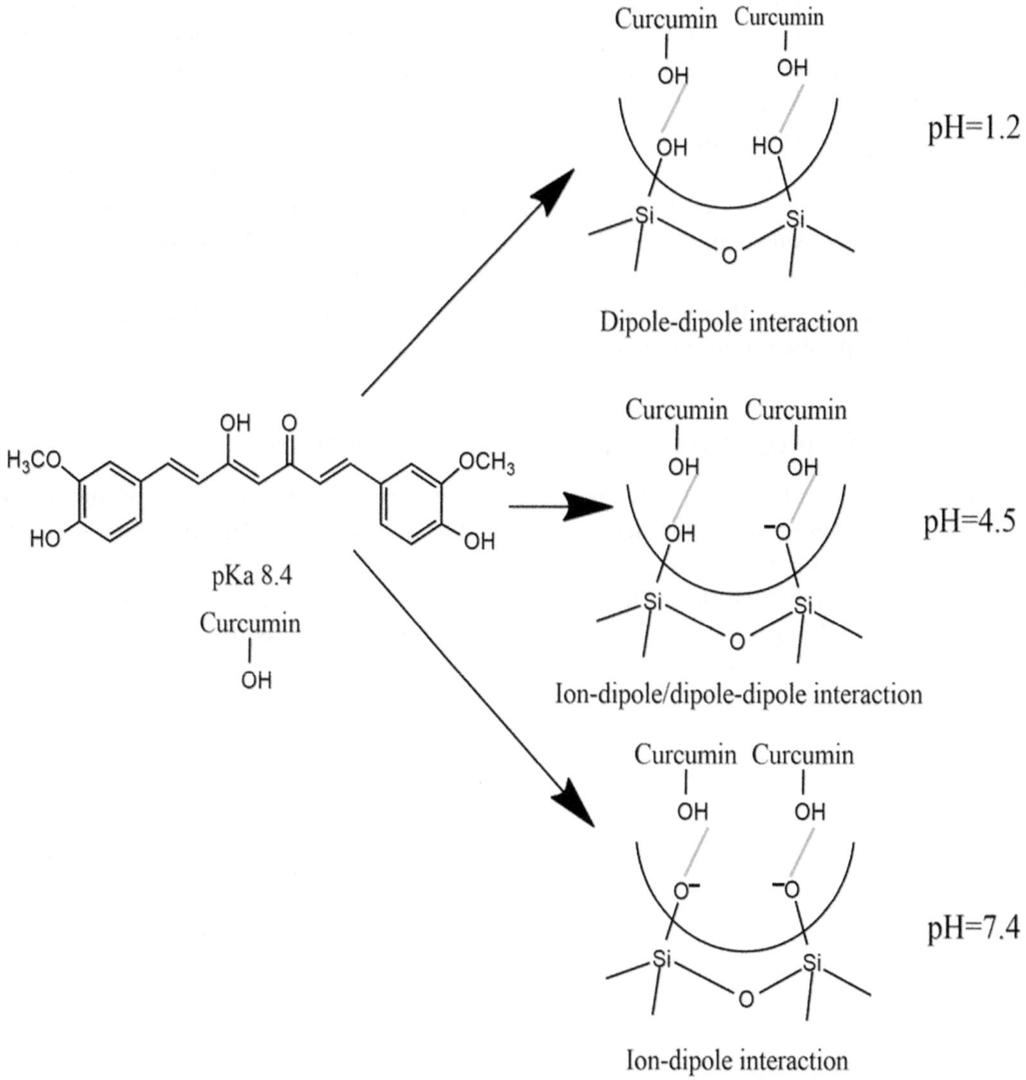

FIGURE 17–2 Interaction of silanol on silica surface and curcumin at various pH (light brown line indicates possible interactions) [33].

linking hyaluronic acid (HA) to MSN since numerous cancer cells overexpress CD44, which are HA receptors, on their surfaces [34]. HA conjugation also facilitates cell entry via HA receptor—mediated endocytosis. MSN-HA complex is formed by the interaction of amine groups of amine-functionalized MSN with the carboxyl groups of HA (Fig. 17–3) [35]. MSN-HA-CUR shows pH-dependent drug release behavior. Reports have shown that MSN-HA-CUR can induce apoptosis and retard cancer cell migration (Fig. 17–4) [36,37]. On the other hand, folate (FA) receptors are also overexpressed on the surface of cancerous cells [38–40]. The cationic polymer, polyethyleneimine (PEI), aids in the release of the nanoformulation from endosomes via the proton sponge effect [41]. Its toxicity is reduced when it is conjugated with MSN [41,42]. CUR-loaded MSN, surface customized with HA or polyethyleneimine-folic acid (PEI-FA) through disulfide bonds, covalent linkages, and electrostatic interactions, have been reported to exhibit cytotoxicity in MDA-MB-231 cells and augmented cellular uptake through endocytosis in comparison to the nontargeted nanoparticles [40,42–45].

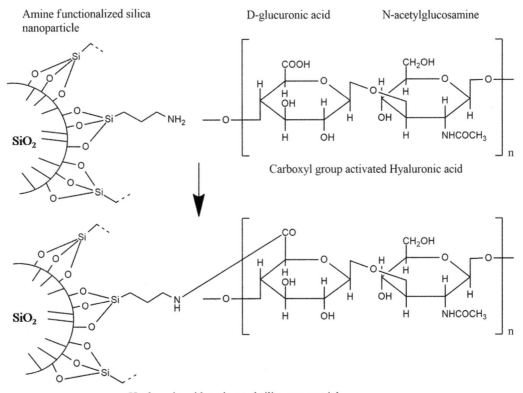

FIGURE 17–3 Chemistry of hyaluronic acid—conjugated silica nanoparticle preparation [35].

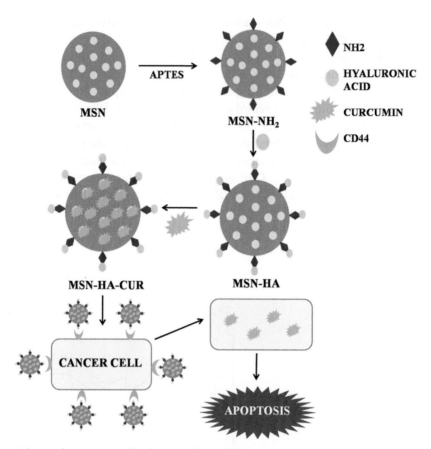

FIGURE 17–4 Scheme of preparation of hyaluronic acid–modified mesoporous silica nanoparticle and the targeted delivery of curcumin in breast cancer cells via such nanosystems [36].

17.3.2 Liposomes

Liposomes are globular vesicles bearing phospholipid bilayers mimicking cell membranes [46]. According to some reports, liposomal CUR suppressed tumor angiogenesis to a greater extent than free CUR in murine xenograft models and induced apoptosis in pancreatic cells of humans [14,30,47]. Studies on the anticancer activity of liposome nanoparticles covalently bound with CUR in B16BL6 melanoma cells have shown that the nanoformulation enhances intracellular drug entry and inhibition of PI3K/Akt pathway [48–50]. Nanoliposome CUR complex generated by the Mozafari process exhibited pH-dependent drug release [51,52]. Murine xenograft models have shown that liposomal CUR can reduce tumorigenesis and CD31 generation, thereby effectively preventing angiogenesis and pancreatic cancer [18,53].

17.3.3 Micelles

A micelle is a vesicle, usually spherical in shape, made from surfactant molecules, and exhibits amphiphilic property [46,54,55]. They are usually used for the delivery of water-insoluble drugs. Breast cancer is usually associated with the augmented expression of cyclin D1, which in turn activates cellular proliferation pathways and induces tumorigenesis via ErbB2 and Ras. It also induces metastasis through the inhibition of RhoGTPase, upregulation of Rock2, and enhances tumor invasion via phosphorylation of paxillin [56–59]. SinaCurcumin is a nanomicelle CUR delivery system, which is reported to increase the bioavailability of the drug when administered orally. Treatment of MCF-7 cells (breast cancer cell line) with this nanoformulation reduced its viability and rate of proliferation greater than the effects of adriamycin, cyclophosphamide, and 5-fluorouracil. The nanoformulation was also able to significantly lower the level of expression of cyclin D1 [60]. Hence, the nanoformulation can be considered as an effective drug for the treatment of breast cancer.

The monomethoxy polyethylene glycol (mPEG)-glycidyl azide polymer (GAP)-CUR micellar complex can be formed by the conjugation of carbonyl group of CUR with the amine-containing polymeric vehicles through imine linkage in the presence of acetic acid as catalyst (Fig. 17–5) [61]. This imine linkage dissociates in acidic tumor microenvironment and induces drug release [62]. Multistage drug delivery systems can enhance the anticancer effects of CUR. It is prepared using pH-sensitive and amphiphilic methoxy-poly(ethylene glycol)-poly(lactide)-poly(β-amino ester) copolymers and subsequent encapsulation of CUR [63,64]. The shrinkage of the micelles at the acidic tumor microenvironment induces cellular uptake of CUR in MCF-7 cells. The micellar product Genexol-PM is presently under phase II clinical trial [64,65]. CUR can be conjugated to hydroxyethyl starch (HES) through an acid-labile ester linker. The self-assembling HES-CUR micellar nanoparticles are reported to exhibit antioxidant, antiinflammatory, and anticancer properties [66,67]. Sodium dodecyl sulfate, cetyltrimethylammonium bromide (CTAB), Tween 80, and TritonX-100 are some of the detergents that arrange micelles and help in stabilizing CUR molecules. Cationic micelles are preferable because of their ability to impart stability to CUR at higher pH [12,14,68,69]. CUR loaded in monomethoxy-poly(ethylene glycol)-poly(ε-caprolactone) (mPEG-PCL) micelles have been reported to exhibit antiproliferative effects on colon carcinoma [48,70].

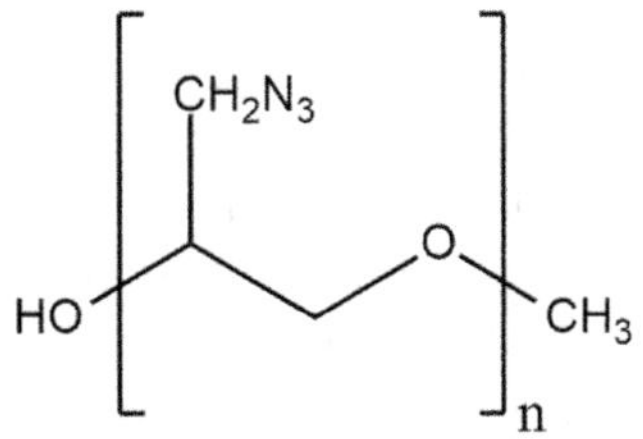

FIGURE 17–5 Chemical structure of glycidyl azide polymer (drawn using ChemDraw Ultra 12.0) [61].

17.3.4 Cyclodextrins

Cyclodextrins are macrocycle-producing oligosaccharides made up of six (α-), seven (β-), or eight (γ-) D-glucopyranose components linked by 1,4-glycosidic bond [46,71,72]. Self-assembled cyclodextrin−CUR conjugates have been reported to regulate death receptors in KBM-5 cells (leukemia cell line) and TNF-induced NF-κB pathway [14,32].

17.3.5 Chitosan/alginate nanoparticles

Alginate nanoparticles are prepared by cross-linkage and pH alteration [73]. Alginate-CUR conjugate is developed via the interaction of C-6 carboxyl group of alginate polymeric units and the phenolic hydroxyl group of CUR [74]. Chitosan nanoparticles are prepared using polyanion of tripolyphosphate (TPP) [75]. Electrostatic interaction among negatively charged CUR and positively charged chitosan chains helps in effective drug loading [76]. Magnetic nanoparticles (MNPs) are related to drug accumulation at the tumor site through magnetic forces. Heating of MNPs in a magnetic field promotes the release of the drug [77]. Layer-by-layer functionalized nanoparticles can be prepared by varnishing MNPs with the positively charged poly-L-lysine and negatively charged dextran [78]. Such layer-by-layer functionalization has been reported to enhance the loading of CUR while the nanocore promoted drug uptake by SKOV-3 cells. In another study, alginate and chitosan deposited as alternate layers on Fe_3O_4 MNPs based on electrostatic properties exhibited sustained release of CUR. The drug uptake and cytotoxic effect were higher in MDA-MB-231 cells treated with the nanoformulation compared to free CUR (Fig. 17−6) [67,79].

Single-walled carbon nanotubes are insoluble in water with limited dispersibility. Oxidative modification of such nanotubes by treatment with concentrated sulfuric and nitric acids helps in imparting water solubility. Their encapsulation by polysaccharides like chitosan and alginate impart biocompatibility. The anionic alginate and cationic chitosan get attached to the nanotubes through electrostatic and π-π stacking interactions. The characteristic high drug loading efficiency and slow drug release property of alginate-coated nanoformulations and the opposite features of the chitosan-coated ones are overcome by dual coating with both polysaccharides [80−82]. The electrostatic interactions between the positively charged modified nanotubes and CUR augment drug encapsulation. CUR is adsorbed onto the sidewalls of nanotubes through π-π stacking interactions. Time- and pH-dependent studies have shown that the nanosystem exhibits sustained drug release for several hours at pH 5.5 and 7.4. The nanoformulation has been shown to exhibit more cytotoxicity than free CUR at the same dose in A549 cells. Staining of nanocurcumin-treated A549 cells with fluorescent DNA intercalating dyes like acridine orange and ethidium bromide has shown that the nanodrug exhibits dose-dependent induction of apoptosis [45,83].

CUR diglutaric acid (CDGA), a prodrug of CUR, exhibits more solubility in comparison to CUR (Fig. 17−7) [84]. To increase its effects, CDGA was loaded onto alginate/chitosan nanoparticles owing to the latter's easy biodegradability, biocompatibility, and high-quality film formation. The nanocarrier was prepared via emulsification and ionotropic gelification

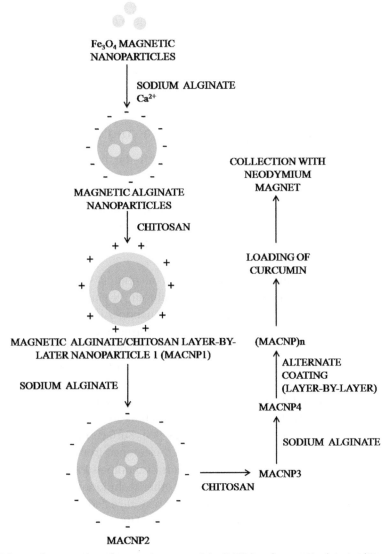

FIGURE 17–6 Scheme of preparation of magnetic nanoparticles (MNPs) and magnetic alginate/chitosan nanoparticles (MACNP) via alternate deposition of sodium alginate and chitosan. The alternative coating generates MACNPs 1, 2, 3, 4, … n bearing 1, 2, 3, 4, … n layers of the biopolymers coated on MNPs, respectively [79].

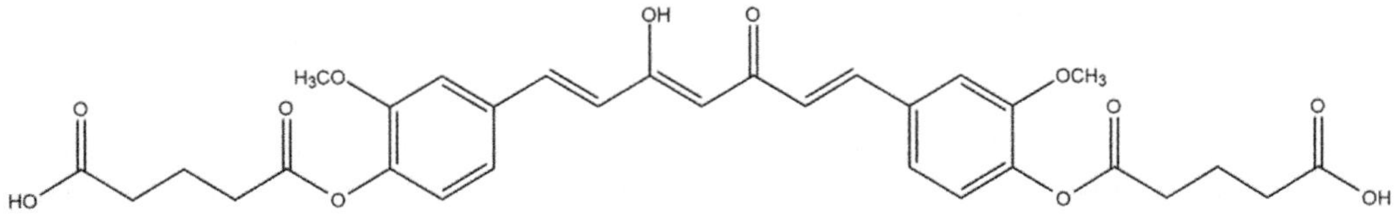

FIGURE 17–7 Chemical structure of curcumin diglutaric acid (drawn using ChemDraw Ultra 12.0) [84].

techniques. The Weibull model of best fit proposed that the pattern of drug release from the nanosystem was attributable to Fickian diffusion. The nanoformulation showed greater uptake in Caco-2 and enhanced antineoplastic activity against Caco-2, MDA-MB-231, and HepG2 cells [67,85]. In a similar study, nanoformulation of alginate, chitosan, and pluronic, prepared via ionotropic pregelation technique and subsequent polycationic cross-linkage, was used to encapsulate CUR. Pluronic F127 enhanced the solubility of CUR [67,86].

17.3.6 The poly(lactic acid) and poly(lactide-co-glycolide) family

Poly(lactic acid) nanocapsules can be generated with the help of the surfactant pectin, obtained from the extract of *Momordica charantia* fruit, via the emulsification-solvent evaporation method. CUR can be loaded onto the nanocapsules via intra- or intermolecular hydrogen bonding between the hydroxyl groups of the nanocapsule and CUR. The drug-nanocarrier exhibits sustained release of the drug and antibacterial activity, possibly imparted by pectin [87]. The PLA-CUR nanoformulation exhibits enhanced cytotoxicity in HeLa cells [67,88].

Poly D,L-lactide-co-glycolide (PLGA), polyvinyl alcohol (PVA), N-isopropylacrylamide (NIPAAM), polyethylene glycol monoacrylate silk fibroin, N-vinyl-2-pyrrolidone, and other natural polymeric materials are used to prepare CUR nanoparticles. CUR-encumbered PLGA nanoparticles increase reactive oxygen species (ROS) formation in cisplatin-resistant CAL27 cancer cells [46,89−95]. CUR-loaded PLGA nanoparticles have also been found to enhance lysosomal activity, apoptosis, inhibition of nuclear β-catenin activity, and androgen receptor in prostate cancer cells [48,96]. CUR-loaded PLGA nanoparticles, surface coated with hydrophilic polymers like polyethylene glycol (PEG) through nanoprecipitation, have been reported to exhibit cytotoxicity and apoptotic induction in metastatic pancreatic cancer [97,98]. CUR is attached to PLGA via ester linkages [99]. Surface modification with PEG and chitosan helps in preventing phagocytosis-mediated clearance from blood through the reticuloendothelial system (RES) [45,98,100−106]. Chitosan-modified PLGA nanoparticles can be prepared by the physical adsorption method and other techniques (Fig. 17−8) [45,98]. In a particular study, electrophoretic gel shift mobility assay revealed that CUR encapsulated in PLGA and PEG exhibited greater potency than free CUR in suppressing NF-κB, MMP-9, VEGF, cyclin D1, and TNF [14,15,22].

Various bacteria and viruses are intricately linked with tumor development. For example, *Helicobacter pylori* are associated with gastric cancers, *Chlamydia trachomatis* with cervical cancer, *Fusobacterium nucleatum* with colorectal cancer, and *Mycoplasma* sp. with prostate cancer [46]. On the other hand, human T-cell leukemia virus type-1 (HTLV-1), hepatitis B virus (HBV), hepatitis C virus (HCV), human papillomavirus (HPV), Epstein−Barr virus (EBV), human gammaherpesvirus-4 (HHV-4), and Merkel cell polyomavirus (MCV) are linked to cancer [107]. CUR exhibits antibacterial effects against antibiotic-resistant strains of Gram-negative and Gram-positive bacteria [108,109]. CUR-loaded PLGA nanoparticles effectively prevent gastric cancer greater than the free CUR [110]. CUR has been reported to

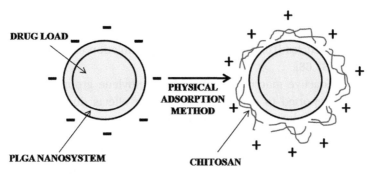

FIGURE 17–8 Preparation of chitosan-modified PLGA nanoparticles by physical adsorption method [98]. *PLGA*, poly D,L-lactide-co-glycolide.

function against Zika, human immunodeficiency virus (HIV), influenza, chikungunya, hepatitis, dengue, papillomavirus, and so on [111,112]. Thus, future studies on CUR nanoformulations should focus on their antiviral effects [46,113].

17.3.7 Other types of nanocurcumin

Nanoscale G4 polyamidoamine (PAMAM) dendrimers can bind with derivatives of CUR via hydrogen bonding. Addition of galactosamine to PAMAM via succinic acid linker helps in binding to asialoglycoprotein receptors that are overexpressed on HepG2 cells and decreases the surface positive charge of PAMAM dendrimer, thereby inhibiting PAMAM cytotoxicity. The nanoformulation has been reported to increase the solubility of the CUR derivative. The galactosamine provides steric hindrance thereby minimizing drug escape from the hydrophobic cavity of PAMAM. On reaching the targeted site, the acidic tumor microenvironment breaks the hydrogen bonds and induces drug release [114].

The bis(FLIVI)-K-K4 and bis(FLIVIGSII)-K-K4 are amphiphilic branched cationic peptides that undergo self-assembly to form nanocapsules like PepV-1 and PepV-2, which are capable of storing different proteins, dyes, and so on. Arginyl-glycyl-aspartic acid, fabricated on the surface of the nanoparticles, is used to target overexpressed integrins on the cancer cell surface [115,116]. Anticancer drugs like doxorubicin (Dox), CUR, and camptothecin can be loaded into the nanocapsules of bis(FLIVI)-K-K4 and bis(FLIVIGSII)-K-K4. The phenylalanine group of the two segments of PepV-1 and 2 is responsible for binding with the anticancer drugs. The histidine group of PepV-2 helps in targeted drug delivery and pH-dependent drug release. The side chain imidazole residue of histidine on coming in contact with acidic pH gets protonated, which results in electrostatic repulsion, disruption of the nanocapsular bilayer, and subsequent drug release in cancer cells like HeLa and DU145 [117]. CUR showed an increase in its activity when administered through PepV-1 and PepV-2 [118].

Pearl milling and high-pressure homogenization (HPH) techniques are used for producing CUR nanocrystals to overcome the low solubility of the free drug [69]. CUR crystals dissolve in water and alcohol in a time-dependent manner. Polyvinylpyrrolidone (PVP) helps in effective stabilization of these CUR nanoparticles [12]. HPH procedure helps in organizing bulk CUR into nanoparticles [16,119,120]. The nanoformulation exhibits greater stability and bioavailability [14,28,32,68].

Conjugation of bioactive macromolecules with methylene groups and phenolic rings of CUR has also been reported to exhibit the anticancer effects due to nanoscale properties [121,122]. Synthesis of the bioconjugate of luteinizing hormone-releasing hormone and CUR, by fluorenyl-methoxy-carbonyl (Fmoc) solid phase, has been instrumental in eliciting protective effects against xenograft model of pancreatic cancer [14,123].

Intravenous administration of human serum albumin nanoparticle-loaded CUR inhibited tumor growth in the HCT116 xenograft model owing to albumin-induced elevated solubility of CUR [14,23,124,125]. CUR-loaded self-organized capsules of carboxymethyl cellulose and casein nanogels effectively function against MEL-39 [46,126].

Dendrosomes increase the water solubility of CUR. CUR gets trapped in the hydrophobic core or membranous part of the dendrosomes, the latter formed by the self-assembly of concerned monomeric units in aqueous media [127−129]. It has been observed that synergistic effects of dendrosomal nanocurcumin and exogenous p53 exert antineoplastic effects on triple-negative breast cancer cells [48,130].

CUR microemulsions can be used for the treatment of skin cancer as they enhance the delivery of CUR through the transdermal route [14,131,132]. CUR nanodispersions of 2−40 nm particle size and of up to 3 mg/mL aqueous solubility were found to exhibit antiproliferative activity in A549, HepG2, and A431 cells [48,133].

CUR-loaded solid lipid nanoparticles have also been reported to exhibit anticancer activity [51,134−136]. CUR nanodisks act as adjuvants for the treatment of mantle cell lymphoma, glioblastoma, and other types of cancers [46,137,138].

Zinc oxide nanoparticles conjugated with CUR have been found to exert anticancer activity against various cancer cell lines of cervix, breast, myeloma, and osteosarcoma [51,139]. Administration of glucose nanogold particles loaded with CUR has been reported to increase the ROS level in MCF-7 and MDA-MB-231 cells [51,140]. Failure in the acquisition of desired results with CUR-capped copper nanoparticles has inspired the creation of silver nanoparticles for CUR delivery [46,141]. Studies on FM-55, MM-138, and MCF-7 cells have shown that the nanoformulation exhibits anticancer activity [46,142]. In the chicken chorioallantoic membrane model, CUR-loaded polymeric nanostructure fabricated with phenylboronic acid increased the antiangiogenic and anticancer effects of CUR [46,143]. Palladium (II) complexes linked with CUR exert anticancer effects on MCF-7, HeLa, and A549 cells [46,144].

Administration of Gemini surfactant nanostructures loaded with CUR inhibited metastasis in 3D spheroid HT-29 cells [46,145]. According to a particular study, in comparison to pure CUR, Gemini CUR increased the cellular uptake of the drug and suppressed OVCAR-3 cell proliferation through apoptotic induction [46,146].

17.4 Photodynamic therapy

Photodynamic therapy (PDT) is a therapeutic technique that involves photosensitizer (PS)-induced abnormal cellular sensitivity to light and phototoxicity-mediated generation of ROS. It is currently used for the treatment of cancer. However, long-term photosensitization can annoy patients but holistically reduces the necessity for painful operative procedures [51,147,148]. The PS usually bears chromophores [149,150]. The potent PSs accumulate in physiologically abnormal cells and in the presence of light produce toxic species against the target cancerous moiety. CUR is one such potent natural PS. Nanosystems can enhance this property of CUR.

According to recent studies, CUR-loaded liposomes in combination with PDT, that is, blue light can exhibit anticancer activity [151–153]. CUR nanoemulsions act as PSs in PDT application on MCF-7 breast cancer cells, CasKi and SiHa cervical carcinoma cells, and HaCa human keratinocyte cells [154,155]. CUR-loaded nanostructured lipid carriers produced from glyceryl dibehenate, glyceryl monooleate, glyceryl distearate, and olive oil in conjunction with PDT exert antineoplastic effects in MCF-7 cells [156]. On the other hand, CUR nanodrugs, in association with PDT, have been also reported to increase the expression levels of p-JNK, Bax, and cleaved caspase-3 in 4T-1 cells [157]. Administration of dendrosomal nanocurcumin on mouse embryonic fibroblasts (MEF) cells induced excessive generation of ROS when combined with PDT [158]. Furthermore, PLGA nanoparticles conjugated with anti-EGFRvIII monoclonal antibody have been found to enhance the photodynamic action of CUR on glioblastoma tumors [51,159].

17.5 Combinatorial therapies

Synergism of a drug is important for its clinical application as it can reduce the side effects of the other drug, decrease the amount of drug required, and show better effect than when it works alone. Amphiphilic poly B-amino ester copolymers can be used for the codelivery of the proapoptotic drug Dox and an antiangiogenesis drug CUR for the treatment of cancerous cells (Fig. 17–9). The nanoparticles have been reported to accumulate in human liver cancer SMMC 7221 cells and human umbilical vein endothelial tissue. The nanoparticle-administered cancer cells showed a decrease in mitochondrial membrane potential, which prompted toward a surge in the rate of apoptosis. The nanoformulation inhibited cell migration, proliferation, invasion, and tube formation via VEGF pathway in cancer cells both in vitro and in vivo [160]. On the other hand, the combinatorial therapy involving Dox and CUR on the self-assembled hexakis (m-PE) nanocarrier can improve therapeutic outcomes [161–165]. Codelivery of Dox and CUR through peptide hydrogel can help in the treatment of head and neck cancer [166]. Similar drug combinations in association with yolk-shell-structured nanoparticles (YSNs) exhibit anticancer activity [161,167]. CUR augments the interaction of Dox with the surface of the nanocarriers.

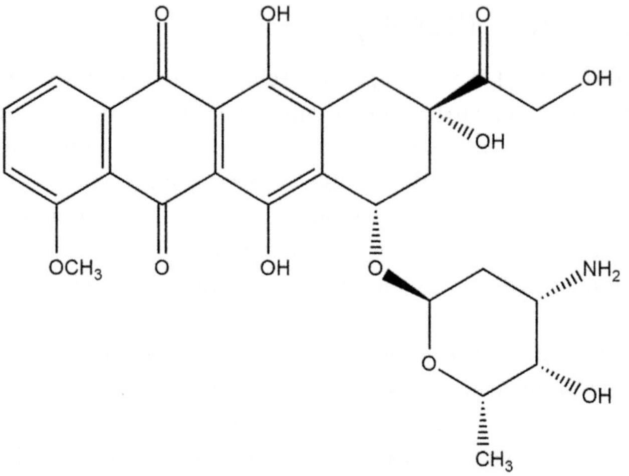

FIGURE 17–9 Chemical structure of doxorubicin (drawn using ChemDraw Ultra 12.0).

In another study, PLGA polymers loaded with anticancer drugs CUR and GANT61 have been reported to reduce cancer cell proliferation and augment apoptotic induction. In aqueous solution, GANT61 is hydrolyzed into the more active product GANT61-D. The two major pathways in breast cancer cells, which are needed for their proliferation, are the hedgehog pathway and epidermal growth factor receptor (EGFR) pathway. The hedgehog pathway alters the epithelial mesenchymal transition and interferes with the EGFR pathway. GANT61 targets GLI1 protein that is necessary for hedgehog signaling and CUR targets the EGFR pathway by inhibiting its phosphorylation. CUR is loaded onto PLGA polymers by ester linkages and GANT61 is used for fabrication of the PLGA polymers by van der Waals interactions. The breast cancer cells uptake the nanoparticles by endocytosis and pinocytosis. Furthermore, the nanoconjugate has been found to exhibit pH-dependent drug release [168].

Carboxy-methyl-hexanoyl chitosan (CHC), a biopolymer composed of N-acetylglucosamine units, loaded with the potent anticancer drug cisplatin and demethoxycurcumin and functionalized with CD133 antibody for augmented uptake by lung cancer stem cells (CSC) exhibited enhanced synergistic effects of the two drugs in multidrug resistant (MDR) A549-ON cells [169,170]. A549-ON is a stable cell line representing stem cell–like characteristics and the overexpression of CD133. It is prepared by transfecting human A549 lung adenocarcinoma cells with vectors encoding Nanog and Oct4 cDNA using a lentiviral infection system [171]. Chitosan transiently opens the tight junctions between cells. The hydrophobic domains of the CHC nanoparticles can provide an effective loading space for hydrophobic moieties such as demethoxycurcumin while the hydrophilic surface allows for suspension of aqueous solutions of cisplatin (Fig. 17–10). The resistance of cancerous cells against cisplatin is commonly attributable to cysteine-rich protein blocking and NF-κB-upregulated CD133 signaling pathway, which is highly active in CSC [172]. pH-dependent controlled release is observed. CHC is disassembled by lysozyme [173]. The intracellular release of the drugs is triggered to some extent by the enzymatic degradation in endolysosomes [174].

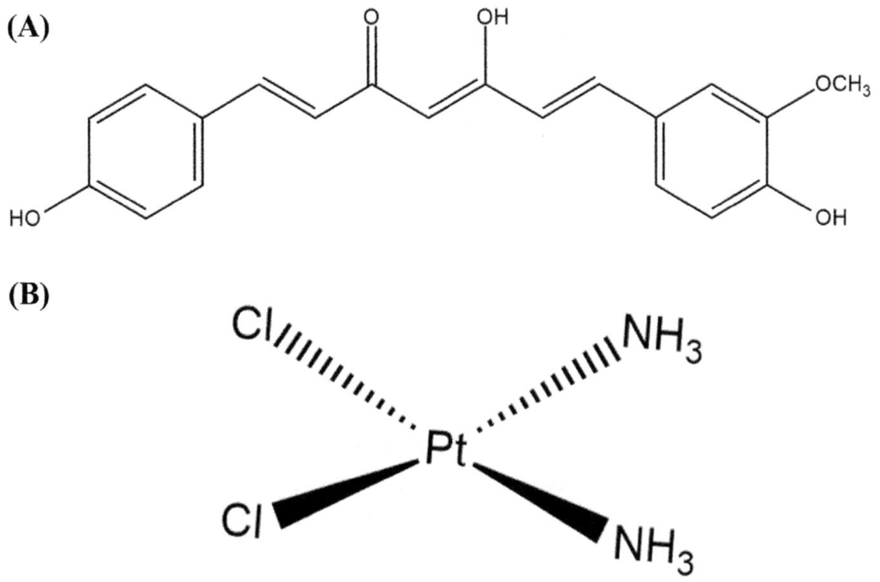

FIGURE 17–10 Chemical structure of (A) demethoxycurcumin and (B) cisplatin (drawn using ChemDraw Ultra 12.0).

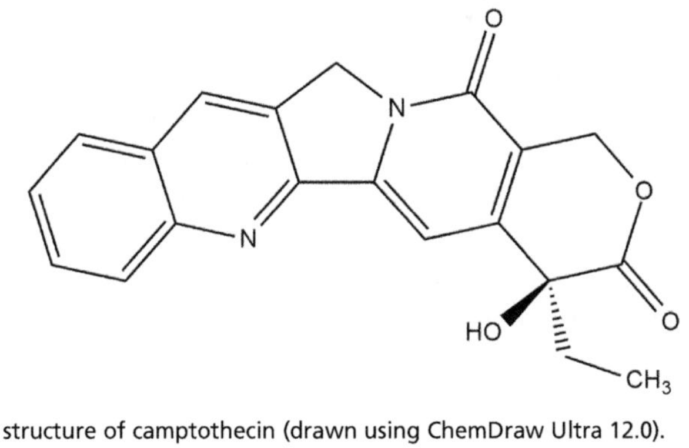

FIGURE 17–11 Chemical structure of camptothecin (drawn using ChemDraw Ultra 12.0).

Camptothecin, an anticancer drug, is used in glioma therapy (Fig. 17–11). The instances of hindrance to its therapeutic effects include the immunosuppressive milieu of tumor and the blood–brain barrier (BBB). Synthesis of the neurotransmitter analog modified liposomes by the technique of doping lipidized tryptamine with CUR and camptothecin has helped in overcoming such hindrances. The combinatorial therapy involving camptothecin and CUR helps in influencing the immunosuppressive environment in glioma [46,175].

Enzymatically conjugated CUR and dextran (DEX-CUR), a glucose homopolysaccharide, have been reported to encapsulate and control the release of methotrexate (MTX). DEX-CUR is prepared by means of an oxidative coupling reaction. Following its self-assembly, MTX is encapsulated within the nanocarrier to impart synergistic therapeutic effects. Studies in MCF-7 cells have shown enhancement in cytotoxicity [67,176].

Carboxymethyl chitosan−based T7 peptide-modified nanomaterials can selectively attach to transferrin receptor (TfR), which are expressed on the surface of lung cancer cells. The nanosystem exhibits pH-dependent drug release. Combinatorial therapy involving docetaxel and CUR through this nanoformulation exhibited potent protective effects against lung cancer [46,177].

17.6 Clinical trials and patents

Various recipes related to nanocurcumin have faced success in clinical trials [48]. For example, nanocurcumin formulation for prostate cancer patients can be detected by the Clinical Trial Identification No. NCT02724618 [48]. Patent No. WO2016167730A1 describes the effectivity of CUR nanoparticles against various types of cancers [178]. The European patent EP2649623B involves CUR-loaded MNPs, which function against various modes of cancer [179].

17.7 Addressing the research gap

A vast array of CUR nanoformulations have been only employed in preclinical experiments. Proper clinical trials are wanting, for understanding the risks of their usage in humans. Nanotoxicity is an important challenge in targeted drug delivery techniques. It can elicit DNA damage, allergic onsets, excitotoxicity, and neuroinflammation. Conjugate nanoformulations fabricated for targeted delivery have the risk of exhibiting side effects. Due to very limited clinical studies, confirmation of the lack of toxicity of nanocurcumins is still wanting. For the industrial production of nanocurcumins, adoption of cost-effective techniques is essential [48]. Therefore, a more concerted effort to investigate and address the loopholes of existing research on nanocurcumins and scheduled trials is important for the effective utilization of CUR for the benefit of mankind.

17.8 Conclusion

The antineoplastic therapeutic properties of CUR can be enhanced through nanoparticle-mediated targeted drug delivery systems. A thorough study of the challenges associated with the preparation of these nanocurcumins for the purpose of targeted delivery and controlled release of CUR at the site of tumorigenesis can help in the formulation of novel and effective strategies in the field of nanocurcumin therapeutics.

Declaration of interest

The authors share no conflict of interest.

References

[1] Chhikara BS, Parang K. Global Cancer Statistics 2022: the trends projection analysis, (2022).

[2] Morozkina SN, Nhung TH, Generalova Vu, YE, Snetkov PP, Uspenskaya MV. Mangiferin as new potential anti-cancer agent and mangiferin-integrated polymer systems—a novel research direction. Biomolecules 2021;11(1):79.

[3] Gao J, Yu H, Guo W, Kong Y, Li Q, Yang S, et al. The anticancer effects of ferulic acid is associated with induction of cell cycle arrest and autophagy in cervical cancer cells. Cancer Cell International 2018;18 (1):1−9.

[4] Ghosh S, Banerjee S, Sil PC. The beneficial role of curcumin on inflammation, diabetes and neurodegenerative disease: a recent update. Food and Chemical Toxicology: An International Journal Published for the British Industrial Biological Research Association 2015;83:111−24.

[5] Sheikh E, Bhatt M, Tripathi M. Role of nano-curcumin: a treatment for cancer. Journal of Medicinal Plants 2017;5:394−7.

[6] Prakash S, Karacor M, Banerjee S. Surface modification in microsystems and nanosystems. Surface Science Reports. 2009;64(7):233−54.

[7] Singh R, Lillard Jr JW. Nanoparticle-based targeted drug delivery. Experimental and Molecular Pathology 2009;86(3):215−23.

[8] Flora G, Gupta D, Tiwari A. Nanocurcumin: a promising therapeutic advancement over native curcumin. Critical Reviews in Therapeutic Drug Carrier Systems. 2013;30(4).

[9] Goncalves A, Macedo A, Souto E. Therapeutic nanosystems for oncology nanomedicine. Clinical & Translational Oncology: Official Publication of the Federation of Spanish Oncology Societies and of the National Cancer Institute of Mexico 2012;14(12):883−90.

[10] Janjua KA, Shehzad A, Shahzad R, Islam SU, Islam MU. Nanocurcumin: a double-edged sword for microcancers. Current Pharmaceutical Design 2020;26(45):5783−92.

[11] Kim DS, Park S-Y, Kim J-Y. Curcuminoids from *Curcuma longa* L.(Zingiberaceae) that protect PC12 rat pheochromocytoma and normal human umbilical vein endothelial cells from βA (1−42) insult. Neuroscience Letters 2001;303(1):57−61.

[12] Rachmawati H, Al Shaal L, Müller RH, Keck CM. Development of curcumin nanocrystal: physical aspects. Journal of Pharmaceutical Sciences 2013;102(1):204−14.

[13] Tønnesen HH, Másson M, Loftsson T. Studies of curcumin and curcuminoids. XXVII. Cyclodextrin complexation: solubility, chemical and photochemical stability. International Journal of Pharmaceutics. 244 (1−2) 2002;127−35.

[14] Rahimi HR, Nedaeinia R, Shamloo AS, Nikdoust S, Oskuee RK. Novel delivery system for natural products: nano-curcumin formulations. Avicenna Journal of Phytomedicine 2016;6(4):383.

[15] Garodia P, Ichikawa H, Malani N, Sethi G, Aggarwal BB. From ancient medicine to modern medicine: ayurvedic concepts of health and their role in inflammation and cancer. Journal of the Society for Integrative Oncology 2007;5(1):25−37.

[16] Hatcher H, Planalp R, Cho J, Torti F, Torti S. Curcumin: from ancient medicine to current clinical trials. Cellular and Molecular Life Sciences 2008;65(11):1631−52.

[17] Venkatesha SH, Berman BM, Moudgil KD. Herbal medicinal products target defined biochemical and molecular mediators of inflammatory autoimmune arthritis. Bioorganic & Medicinal Chemistry 2011;19 (1):21−9.

[18] Tagde P, Tagde P, Islam F, Tagde S, Shah M, Hussain ZD, et al. The multifaceted role of curcumin in advanced nanocurcumin form in the treatment and management of chronic disorders. Molecules 2021;26(23):7109.

[19] Enumo Jr A, Pereira CID, Parize AL. Temperature evaluation of curcumin keto−enolic kinetics and its interaction with two pluronic copolymers. The Journal of Physical Chemistry B 2019;123(26):5641−50.

[20] Shishodia S, Sethi G, Aggarwal BB. Curcumin: getting back to the roots. Annals of the New York Academy of Sciences. 2005;1056(1):206−17.

[21] Wang R, Xu Y, Wu H-L, Li Y-B, Li Y-H, Guo J-B, et al. The antidepressant effects of curcumin in the forced swimming test involve 5-HT1 and 5-HT2 receptors. European Journal of Pharmacology 2008;578(1):43−50.

[22] Goel A, Jhurani S, Aggarwal BB. Multi-targeted therapy by curcumin: how spicy is it? Molecular Nutrition & Food Research 2008;52(9):1010−30.

[23] Liu J, Chen S, Lv L, Song L, Guo S, Huang S. Recent progress in studying curcumin and its nano-preparations for cancer therapy. Current Pharmaceutical Design 2013;19(11):1974−93.

[24] Balogun E, Hoque M, Gong P, Killeen E, Green CJ, Foresti R, et al. Curcumin activates the haem oxygenase-1 gene via regulation of Nrf2 and the antioxidant-responsive element. The Biochemical Journal 2003;371(3):887−95.

[25] Pandey MK, Kumar S, Thimmulappa RK, Parmar VS, Biswal S, Watterson AC. Design, synthesis and evaluation of novel PEGylated curcumin analogs as potent Nrf2 activators in human bronchial epithelial cells. European Journal of Pharmaceutical Sciences 2011;43(1−2):16−24.

[26] Shaikh J, Ankola D, Beniwal V, Singh D, Kumar MR. Nanoparticle encapsulation improves oral bioavailability of curcumin by at least ninefold when compared to curcumin administered with piperine as absorption enhancer. European Journal of Pharmaceutical Sciences 2009;37(3−4):223−30.

[27] Mulik RS, Mönkkönen J, Juvonen RO, Mahadik KR, Paradkar AR. Transferrin mediated solid lipid nano-particles containing curcumin: enhanced in vitro anticancer activity by induction of apoptosis. International Journal of Pharmaceutics 2010;398(1−2):190−203.

[28] Yallapu MM, Jaggi M, Chauhan SC. Curcumin nanoformulations: a future nanomedicine for cancer. Drug Discovery Today 2012;17(1−2):71−80.

[29] Yang K-Y, Lin L-C, Tseng T-Y, Wang S-C, Tsai T-H. Oral bioavailability of curcumin in rat and the herbal analysis from Curcuma longa by LC−MS/MS. Journal of Chromatography B 2007;853(1−2):183−9.

[30] Anand P, Kunnumakkara AB, Newman RA, Aggarwal BB. Bioavailability of curcumin: problems and pro-mises. Molecular Pharmaceutics 2007;4(6):807−18.

[31] Gao Y, Li Z, Sun M, Li H, Guo C, Cui J, et al. Preparation, characterization, pharmacokinetics, and tissue distribution of curcumin nanosuspension with TPGS as stabilizer. Drug Development and Industrial Pharmacy 2010;36(10):1225−34.

[32] Tsai Y-M, Chien C-F, Lin L-C, Tsai T-H. Curcumin and its nano-formulation: the kinetics of tissue distri-bution and blood−brain barrier penetration. International Journal of Pharmaceutics 2011;416(1):331−8.

[33] Kim S, Stébé M-J, Blin J-L, Pasc A. pH-controlled delivery of curcumin from a compartmentalized solid lipid nanoparticle@mesostructured silica matrix. Journal of Materials Chemistry B 2014;2.

[34] Serafino A, Zonfrillo M, Andreola F, Psaila R, Mercuri L, Moroni N, et al. CD44-targeting for antitumor drug delivery: a new SN-38-hyaluronan bioconjugate for locoregional treatment of peritoneal carcino-matosis. Current Cancer Drug Targets 2011;11(5):572−85.

[35] Huo Z-J, Liu K, Wang Z-q, Wang S-j, Liu P, Qin Y-h, et al. Hyaluronic acid-tagged silica nanoparticles in colon cancer therapy: therapeutic efficacy evaluation. International Journal of Nanomedicine 2015;10:6445.

[36] Ghosh S, Dutta S, Sarkar A, Kundu M, Sil PC. Targeted delivery of curcumin in breast cancer cells via hyaluronic acid modified mesoporous silica nanoparticle to enhance anticancer efficiency. Colloids Surfaces B: Biointerfaces 2021;197:111404.

[37] Chou C-C, Yang J-S, Lu H-F, Ip S-W, Lo C, Wu C-C, et al. Quercetin-mediated cell cycle arrest and apoptosis involving activation of a caspase cascade through the mitochondrial pathway in human breast cancer MCF-7 cells. Archives of Pharmacal Research 2010;33(8):1181−91.

[38] Mattheolabakis G, Milane L, Singh A, Amiji MM. Hyaluronic acid targeting of CD44 for cancer therapy: from receptor biology to nanomedicine. Journal of Drug Targeting 2015;23(7−8):605−18.

[39] Porta F, Lamers GE, Morrhayim J, Chatzopoulou A, Schaaf M, den Dulk H, et al. Folic acid-modified mesoporous silica nanoparticles for cellular and nuclear targeted drug delivery. Advanced Healthcare Materials 2013;2(2):281−6.

[40] Li N, Wang Z, Zhang Y, Zhang K, Xie J, Liu Y, et al. Curcumin-loaded redox-responsive mesoporous silica nanoparticles for targeted breast cancer therapy. Artificial Cells, Nanomedicine, and Biotechnology 2018;46(Suppl. 2):921−35.

[41] Hom C, Lu J, Liong M, Luo H, Li Z, Zink JI, et al. Mesoporous silica nanoparticles facilitate delivery of siRNA to shutdown signaling pathways in mammalian cells. Small (Weinheim an der Bergstrasse, Germany) 2010;6(11):1185.

[42] Park IY, Kim IY, Yoo MK, Choi YJ, Cho M-H, Cho CS. Mannosylated polyethylenimine coupled mesoporous silica nanoparticles for receptor-mediated gene delivery. International Journal of Pharmaceutics 2008;359(1−2):280−7.

[43] Chen L, Zhou X, Nie W, Zhang Q, Wang W, Zhang Y, et al. Multifunctional redox-responsive mesoporous silica nanoparticles for efficient targeting drug delivery and magnetic resonance imaging. ACS Applied Materials & Interfaces 2016;8(49):33829−41.

[44] Lin J-T, Du J-K, Yang Y-Q, Li L, Zhang D-W, Liang C-L, et al. pH and redox dual stimulate-responsive nanocarriers based on hyaluronic acid coated mesoporous silica for targeted drug delivery. Materials Science and Engineering C 2017;81:478−84.

[45] Navya PN, Kaphle A, Srinivas SP, Bhargava SK, Rotello VM, Daima HK. Current trends and challenges in cancer management and therapy using designer nanomaterials. Nano Convergence 2019;6(1):23.

[46] Hafez Ghoran S, Calcaterra A, Abbasi M, Taktaz F, Nieselt K, Babaei E. Curcumin-based nanoformulations: a promising adjuvant towards cancer treatment. Molecules 2022;27(16):5236.

[47] Li L, Braiteh FS, Kurzrock R. Liposome-encapsulated curcumin: in vitro and in vivo effects on proliferation, apoptosis, signaling, and angiogenesis. Cancer 2005;104(6):1322−31.

[48] Karthikeyan A, Senthil N, Min T. Nanocurcumin: a promising candidate for therapeutic applications. Frontiers in Pharmacology 2020;11:487.

[49] Chen Y, Wu Q, Zhang Z, Yuan L, Liu X, Zhou L. Preparation of curcumin-loaded liposomes and evaluation of their skin permeation and pharmacodynamics. Molecules 2012;17(5):5972−87.

[50] Ghalandarlaki N, Alizadeh AM, Ashkani-Esfahani S. Nanotechnology-applied curcumin for different diseases therapy. BioMed Research International 2014;(2014).

[51] Ailioaie LM, Ailioaie C, Litscher G. Latest innovations and nanotechnologies with curcumin as a nature-inspired photosensitizer applied in the photodynamic therapy of cancer. Pharmaceutics 2021;13(10):1562.

[52] Zarrabi A, Zarepour A, Khosravi A, Alimohammadi Z, Thakur VK. Synthesis of curcumin loaded smart pH-responsive stealth liposome as a novel nanocarrier for cancer treatment. Fibers 2021;9(3):19.

[53] Amin SA, Adhikari N, Jha T. Design of aminopeptidase N inhibitors as anti-cancer agents. Journal of Medicinal Chemistry 2018;61(15):6468−90.

[54] Hanafy NA, El-Kemary M, Leporatti S. Micelles structure development as a strategy to improve smart cancer therapy. Cancers 2018;10(7):238.

[55] Smit B. Molecular-dynamics simulations of amphiphilic molecules at a liquid-liquid interface. Physical Review A 1988;37(9):3431−3.

[56] Welschinger R, Bendall LJ. Temporal tracking of cell cycle progression using flow cytometry without the need for synchronization. Journal of Visualized Experiments: JoVE 2015;102:e52840.

[57] Musgrove EA, Caldon CE, Barraclough J, Stone A, Sutherland RL. Cyclin D as a therapeutic target in cancer. Nature Reviews Cancer 2011;11(8):558−72.

[58] Casimiro MC, Velasco-Velázquez M, Aguirre-Alvarado C, Pestell RG. Overview of cyclins D1 function in cancer and the CDK inhibitor landscape: past and present. Expert Opinion on Investigational Drugs 2014;23(3):295−304.

[59] Fusté NP, Ferrezuelo F, Garí E. Cyclin D1 promotes tumor cell invasion and metastasis by cytoplasmic mechanisms. Molecular & Cellular Oncology 2016;3(5):e1203471.

[60] Hosseini S, Chamani J, Hadipanah MR, Ebadpour N, Hojjati AS, Mohammadzadeh MH, et al. Nano-curcumin's suppression of breast cancer cells (MCF7) through the inhibition of cyclinD1 expression. Breast Cancer (Dove Medical Press) 2019;11:137−42.

[61] Huang T, Jin B, Peng RF, Chen CD, Zheng RZ, He Y, et al. Synthesis and characterization of [60]fullerene-glycidyl azide polymer and its thermal decomposition. Polymers 2015;896−908.

[62] Rashidzadeh H, Rezaei SJT, Zamani S, Sarijloo E, Ramazani A. pH-sensitive curcumin conjugated micelles for tumor triggered drug delivery. Journal of Biomaterials Science Polymer Edition 2021;32 (3):320−36.

[63] Mohanty C, Acharya S, Mohanty AK, Dilnawaz F, Sahoo SK. Curcumin-encapsulated MePEG/PCL diblock copolymeric micelles: a novel controlled delivery vehicle for cancer therapy. Nanomedicine: Nanotechnology, Biology, and Medicine 2010;5(3):433−49.

[64] Yu Y, Zhang X, Qiu L. The anti-tumor efficacy of curcumin when delivered by size/charge-changing multistage polymeric micelles based on amphiphilic poly(β-amino ester) derivates. Biomaterials 2014;35 (10):3467−79.

[65] Lee KS, Chung HC, Im SA, Park YH, Kim CS, Kim S-B, et al. Multicenter phase II trial of Genexol-PM, a Cremophor-free, polymeric micelle formulation of paclitaxel, in patients with metastatic breast cancer. Breast Cancer Research and Treatment 2008;108(2):241−50.

[66] Chen S, Wu J, Tang Q, Xu C, Huang Y, Huang D, et al. Nano-micelles based on hydroxyethyl starch-curcumin conjugates for improved stability, antioxidant and anticancer activity of curcumin. Carbohydrate Polymers 2020;228:115398.

[67] Alqosaibi AI. Nanocarriers for anticancer drugs: challenges and perspectives. Saudi Journal of Biological Sciences 2022;103298.

[68] Ravichandran R. Development of an oral curcumin nanocrystal formulation. Journal of Nanotechnology in Engineering and Medicine 2013;3(4).

[69] Jantarat C. Bioavailability enhancement techniques of herbal medicine: a case example of curcumin. International Journal of Pharmacy and Pharmaceutical Sciences 2013;5:493−500.

[70] Gou M, Men K, Shi H, Xiang M, Zhang J, Song J, et al. Curcumin-loaded biodegradable polymeric micelles for colon cancer therapy in vitro and in vivo. Nanoscale 2011;3(4):1558−67.

[71] Ndong Ntoutoume GMA, Granet R, Mbakidi JP, Brégier F, Léger DY, Fidanzi-Dugas C, et al. Development of curcumin−cyclodextrin/cellulose nanocrystals complexes: new anticancer drug delivery systems. Bioorganic and Medicinal Chemistry Letters 2016;26(3):941−5.

[72] Guo S. Encapsulation of curcumin into β-cyclodextrins inclusion: a review. E3S Web of Conferences 2019;131.

[73] Ching SH, Bansal N, Bhandari B. Alginate gel particles−a review of production techniques and physical properties. Critical Reviews in Food Science and Nutrition 2017;57(6):1133−52.

[74] Dey S, Sreenivasan K. Conjugation of curcumin onto alginate enhances aqueous solubility and stability of curcumin. Carbohydrate Polymers 2014;99:499−507.

[75] Rampino A, Borgogna M, Blasi P, Bellich B, Cesàro A. Chitosan nanoparticles: preparation, size evolution and stability. International Journal of Pharmaceutics 2013;455(1):219−28.

[76] Bernkop-Schnürch A, Dünnhaupt S. Chitosan-based drug delivery systems. European Journal of Pharmaceutics and Biopharmaceutics 2012;81(3):463−9.

[77] Arruebo M, Fernández-Pacheco R, Ibarra MR, Santamaría J. Magnetic nanoparticles for drug delivery. Nano Today 2007;2(3):22−32.

[78] Mancarella S, Greco V, Baldassarre F, Vergara D, Maffia M, Leporatti S. Polymer-coated magnetic nanoparticles for curcumin delivery to cancer cells. Macromolecular Bioscience 2015;15(10):1365−74.

[79] Song W, Su X, Gregory DA, Li W, Cai Z, Zhao X. Magnetic alginate/chitosan nanoparticles for targeted delivery of curcumin into human breast cancer cells. Nanomaterials (Basel, Switzerland) 2018;8(11).

[80] Zhang X, Meng L, Lu Q, Fei Z, Dyson PJ. Targeted delivery and controlled release of doxorubicin to cancer cells using modified single wall carbon nanotubes. Biomaterials 2009;30(30):6041−7.

[81] Liu Z, Sun X, Nakayama-Ratchford N, Dai H. Supramolecular chemistry on water-soluble carbon nanotubes for drug loading and delivery. ACS Nano 2007;1(1):50−6.

[82] Vasconcelos T, Sarmento B, Costa P. Solid dispersions as strategy to improve oral bioavailability of poor water soluble drugs. Drug Discovery Today 2007;12(23):1068−75.

[83] Singh N, Sachdev A, Gopinath P. Polysaccharide functionalized single walled carbon nanotubes as nanocarriers for delivery of curcumin in lung cancer cells. Journal of Nanoscience and Nanotechnology 2018;18(3):1534−41.

[84] Muangnoi C, Jithavech P, Ratnatilaka Na Bhuket P, Supasena W, Wichitnithad W, Towiwat P, et al. A curcumin-diglutaric acid conjugated prodrug with improved water solubility and antinociceptive properties compared to curcumin. Bioscience, Biotechnology, and Biochemistry 2018;82:1−8.

[85] Sorasitthiyanukarn FN, Muangnoi C, Bhuket PRN, Rojsitthisak P, Rojsitthisak P. Chitosan/alginate nanoparticles as a promising approach for oral delivery of curcumin diglutaric acid for cancer treatment. Materials Science and Engineering C 2018;93:178−90.

[86] Das RK, Kasoju N, Bora U. Encapsulation of curcumin in alginate-chitosan-pluronic composite nanoparticles for delivery to cancer cells. Nanomedicine: Nanotechnology, Biology and Medicine 2010;6(1):153−60.

[87] Kumar V, Kumari A, Guleria P, Yadav SK. Evaluating the toxicity of selected types of nanochemicals. In: Whitacre DM, editor. Reviews of environmental contamination and toxicology. New York: Springer; 2012. p. 39−121.

[88] Alippilakkotte S, Sreejith L. Pectin mediated synthesis of curcumin loaded poly(lactic acid) nanocapsules for cancer treatment. Journal of Drug Delivery Science and Technology 2018;48:66−74.

[89] Shome S, Talukdar AD, Choudhury MD, Bhattacharya MK, Upadhyaya H. Curcumin as potential therapeutic natural product: a nanobiotechnological perspective. The Journal of Pharmacy and Pharmacology 2016;68(12):1481−500.

[90] Ferrari R, Sponchioni M, Morbidelli M, Moscatelli D. Polymer nanoparticles for the intravenous delivery of anticancer drugs: the checkpoints on the road from the synthesis to clinical translation. Nanoscale 2018;10(48):22701−19.

[91] Chang P-Y, Peng S-F, Lee C-Y, Lu C-C, Tsai S-C, Shieh T-M, et al. Curcumin-loaded nanoparticles induce apoptotic cell death through regulation of the function of MDR1 and reactive oxygen species in cisplatin-resistant CAR human oral cancer cells. International Journal of Oncology 2013;43(4):1141−50.

[92] Yallapu MM, Gupta BK, Jaggi M, Chauhan SC. Fabrication of curcumin encapsulated PLGA nanoparticles for improved therapeutic effects in metastatic cancer cells. Journal of Colloid and Interface Science 2010;351(1):19−29.

[93] Xie M, Fan D, Li Y, He X, Chen X, Chen Y, et al. Supercritical carbon dioxide-developed silk fibroin nanoplatform for smart colon cancer therapy. International Journal of Nanomedicine 2017;12:7751−61.

[94] Chaurasia S, Chaubey P, Patel RR, Kumar N, Mishra B. Curcumin-polymeric nanoparticles against colon-26 tumor-bearing mice: cytotoxicity, pharmacokinetic and anticancer efficacy studies. Drug Development and Industrial Pharmacy 2016;42(5):694–700.

[95] Montalbán MG, Coburn JM, Lozano-Pérez AA, Cenis JL, Víllora G, Kaplan DL. Production of curcumin-loaded silk fibroin nanoparticles for cancer therapy. Nanomaterials 2018;8(2):126.

[96] Yallapu MM, Nagesh PKB, Jaggi M, Chauhan SC. Therapeutic applications of curcumin nanoformulations. The AAPS Journal 2015;17(6):1341–56.

[97] Almoustafa HA, Alshawsh MA, Chik Z. Technical aspects of preparing PEG-PLGA nanoparticles as carrier for chemotherapeutic agents by nanoprecipitation method. International Journal of Pharmaceutics 2017;533(1):275–84.

[98] Wang Y, Li P, Kong L. Chitosan-modified PLGA nanoparticles with versatile surface for improved drug delivery. AAPS PharmSciTech 2013;14(2):585–92.

[99] Waghela B, Sharma A, Dhumale S, Pandey S, Pathak C. Curcumin conjugated with PLGA potentiates sustainability, anti-proliferative activity and apoptosis in human colon carcinoma cells. PLoS ONE 2015;10:e0117526.

[100] Arya G, Das M, Sahoo SK. Evaluation of curcumin loaded chitosan/PEG blended PLGA nanoparticles for effective treatment of pancreatic cancer. Biomedicine and Pharmacotherapy 2018;102:555–66.

[101] Parveen S, Misra R, Sahoo SK. Nanoparticles: a boon to drug delivery, therapeutics, diagnostics and imaging. Nanomedicine: Nanotechnology, Biology and Medicine 2012;8(2):147–66.

[102] Hu F-Q, Meng P, Dai Y-Q, Du Y-Z, You J, Wei X-H, et al. PEGylated chitosan-based polymer micelle as an intracellular delivery carrier for anti-tumor targeting therapy. European Journal of Pharmaceutics and Biopharmaceutics 2008;70(3):749–57.

[103] Illum L. Chitosan and its use as a pharmaceutical excipient. Pharmaceutical Research 1998;15 (9):1326–31.

[104] Otsuka H, Nagasaki Y, Kataoka K. PEGylated nanoparticles for biological and pharmaceutical applications. Advanced Drug Delivery Reviews 2003;55(3):403–19.

[105] El-Sherbiny IM, Smyth HDC. Controlled release pulmonary administration of curcumin using swellable biocompatible microparticles. Molecular Pharmaceutics 2012;9(2):269–80.

[106] Selvam P, El-Sherbiny IM, Smyth HDC. Swellable hydrogel particles for controlled release pulmonary administration using propellant-driven metered dose inhalers. Journal of Aerosol Medicine and Pulmonary Drug Delivery 2010;24(1):25–34.

[107] Zella D, Gallo RC. Viruses and bacteria associated with cancer: an overview. Viruses 2021;13(6):1039.

[108] Zheng D, Huang C, Huang H, Zhao Y, Khan MRU, Zhao H, et al. Antibacterial mechanism of curcumin: a review. Chemistry & Biodiversity 2020;17(8):e2000171.

[109] Dai C, Lin J, Li H, Shen Z, Wang Y, Velkov T, et al. The natural product curcumin as an antibacterial agent: current achievements and problems. Antioxidants (Basel, Switzerland) 2022;11(3).

[110] Alam J, Dilnawaz F, Sahoo SK, Singh DV, Mukhopadhyay AK, Hussain T, et al. Curcumin encapsulated into biocompatible co-polymer PLGA nanoparticle enhanced anti-gastric cancer and anti-*Helicobacter pylori* effect. Asian Pacific Journal of Cancer Prevention: APJCP 2022;23(1):61–70.

[111] Jennings MR, Parks RJ. Curcumin as an antiviral agent. Viruses 2020;12(11):1242.

[112] Mathew D, Hsu W-L. Antiviral potential of curcumin. Journal of Functional Foods 2018;40:692–9.

[113] Maher DM, Bell MC, O'Donnell EA, Gupta BK, Jaggi M, Chauhan SC. Curcumin suppresses human papillomavirus oncoproteins, restores p53, Rb, and PTPN13 proteins and inhibits benzo[a]pyrene-induced upregulation of HPV E7. Molecular Carcinogenesis 2011;50(1):47–57.

[114] Yousef S, Alsaab HO, Sau S, Iyer AK. Development of asialoglycoprotein receptor directed nanoparticles for selective delivery of curcumin derivative to hepatocellular carcinoma. Heliyon 2018;4(12): e01071.

[115] Wang F, Chen L, Zhang R, Chen Z, Zhu L. RGD peptide conjugated liposomal drug delivery system for enhance therapeutic efficacy in treating bone metastasis from prostate cancer. Journal of Controlled Release 2014;196:222−33.

[116] Shahin M, Ahmed S, Kaur K, Lavasanifar A. Decoration of polymeric micelles with cancer-specific peptide ligands for active targeting of paclitaxel. Biomaterials 2011;32(22):5123−33.

[117] Chen L, Tu Z, Voloshchuk N, Liang JF. Lytic peptides with improved stability and selectivity designed for cancer treatment. Journal of Pharmaceutical Sciences 2012;101(4):1508−17.

[118] Chen J, Wang W, Wang Y, Yuan X, He C, Pei P, et al. Self-assembling branched amphiphilic peptides for targeted delivery of small molecule anticancer drugs. European Journal of Pharmaceutics and Biopharmaceutics 2022;179:137−46.

[119] Mukerjee A, Vishwanatha JK. Formulation, characterization and evaluation of curcumin-loaded PLGA nanospheres for cancer therapy. Anticancer Research 2009;29(10):3867.

[120] Safavy A, Raisch KP, Mantena S, Sanford LL, Sham SW, Krishna NR, et al. Design and development of water-soluble curcumin conjugates as potential anticancer agents. Journal of Medicinal Chemistry 2007;50(24):6284−8.

[121] Gangwar RK, Tomar GB, Dhumale VA, Zinjarde S, Sharma RB, Datar S. Curcumin conjugated silica nanoparticles for improving bioavailability and its anticancer applications. Journal of Agricultural and Food Chemistry 2013;61(40):9632−7.

[122] Kumar S, Dubey KK, Tripathi S, Fujii M, Misra K. Design and synthesis of curcumin-bioconjugates to improve systemic delivery. Nucleic Acids Symposium Series 2000;44(1):75−6.

[123] Vareed SK, Kakarala M, Ruffin MT, Crowell JA, Normolle DP, Djuric Z, et al. Pharmacokinetics of curcumin conjugate metabolites in healthy human subjects. Cancer Epidemiology, Biomarkers and Prevention 2008;17(6):1411−17.

[124] Manju S, Sreenivasan K. Conjugation of curcumin onto hyaluronic acid enhances its aqueous solubility and stability. Journal of Colloid and Interface Science 2011;359(1):318−25.

[125] Simoni E, Bergamini C, Fato R, Tarozzi A, Bains S, Motterlini R, et al. Polyamine conjugation of curcumin analogues toward the discovery of mitochondria-directed neuroprotective agents. Journal of Medicinal Chemistry 2010;53(19):7264−8.

[126] Priya P, Mohan Raj R, Vasanthakumar V, Raj V. Curcumin-loaded layer-by-layer folic acid and casein coated carboxymethyl cellulose/casein nanogels for treatment of skin cancer. Arabian Journal of Chemistry 2020;13(1):694−708.

[127] Tahmasebi Birgani M, Erfani V, Babaei E, Najafi F, Zamani M, Shariati M, et al. Dendrosomal nanocurcumin; The novel formulation to improve the anticancer properties of curcumin. Progress in Biological Sciences 2015;5:143−58.

[128] Babaei E, Sadeghizadeh M, Hassan ZM, Feizi MAH, Najafi F, Hashemi SM. Dendrosomal curcumin significantly suppresses cancer cell proliferation in vitro and in vivo. International Immunopharmacology 2012;12(1):226−34.

[129] Tahmasebi Mirgani M, Sadeghizadeh M, Najafi F, Mowla SJ. Dendrosomal curcumin induced apoptosis by suppression of pluripotency genes in 5637 bladder cancer cells. Journal of Pathobiology Research 2013;16(1):23−39.

[130] Baghi N, Bakhshinejad B, Keshavarz R, Babashah S, Sadeghizadeh M. Dendrosomal nanocurcumin and exogenous p53 can act synergistically to elicit anticancer effects on breast cancer cells. Gene 2018;670:55−62.

[131] Liu C-H, Chang F-Y. Development and characterization of eucalyptol microemulsions for topic delivery of curcumin. Chemical and Pharmaceutical Bulletin 2011;59(2):172−8.

[132] Liu C-H, Chang F-Y, Hung D-K. Terpene microemulsions for transdermal curcumin delivery: effects of terpenes and cosurfactants. Colloids and Surfaces B, Biointerfaces 2011;82(1):63−70.

[133] Basniwal RK, Khosla R, Jain N. Improving the anticancer activity of curcumin using nanocurcumin dispersion in water. Nutrition and Cancer 2014;66(6):1015−22.

[134] Wang W, Chen T, Xu H, Ren B, Cheng X, Qi R, et al. Curcumin-loaded solid lipid nanoparticles enhanced anticancer efficiency in breast cancer. Molecules 2018;23(7):1578.

[135] Jourghanian P, Ghaffari S, Ardjmand M, Haghighat S, Mohammadnejad M. Sustained release curcumin loaded solid lipid nanoparticles. Advanced Pharmaceutical Bulletin 2016;6(1):17−21.

[136] Sun J, Bi C, Chan HM, Sun S, Zhang Q, Zheng Y. Curcumin-loaded solid lipid nanoparticles have prolonged in vitro antitumour activity, cellular uptake and improved in vivo bioavailability. Colloids and Surfaces. B, Biointerfaces 2013;111:367−75.

[137] Singh ATK, Ghosh M, Forte TM, Ryan RO, Gordon LI. Curcumin nanodisk-induced apoptosis in mantle cell lymphoma. Leukemia and Lymphoma 2011;52(8):1537−43.

[138] Ghosh M, Ryan RO. ApoE enhances nanodisk-mediated curcumin delivery to glioblastoma multiforme cells. Nanomedicine: Nanotechnology, Biology, and Medicine 2013;9(6):763−71.

[139] Somu P, Paul S. A biomolecule-assisted one-pot synthesis of zinc oxide nanoparticles and its bioconjugate with curcumin for potential multifaceted therapeutic applications. New Journal of Chemistry 2019;43(30):11934−48.

[140] Yang K, Liao Z, Wu Y, Li M, Guo T, Lin J, et al. Curcumin and Glu-GNPs induce radiosensitivity against breast cancer stem-like cells. BioMed Research International 2020;2020:3189217.

[141] Kamble S, Utage B, Mogle P, Kamble R, Hese S, Dawane B, et al. Evaluation of curcumin capped copper nanoparticles as possible inhibitors of human breast cancer cells and angiogenesis: a comparative study with native curcumin. AAPS PharmSciTech 2016;17(5):1030−41.

[142] Ali I, Ahmed SBM, Elhaj BM, Ali HS, Alsubaie A, Almalki ASA. Enhanced anticancer activities of curcumin-loaded green gum acacia-based silver nanoparticles against melanoma and breast cancer cells. Applied Nanoscience 2021;11(11):2679−87.

[143] van der Vlies AJ, Morisaki M, Neng HI, Hansen EM, Hasegawa U. Framboidal nanoparticles containing a curcumin−phenylboronic acid complex with antiangiogenic and anticancer activities. Bioconjugate Chemistry 2019;30(3):861−70.

[144] Li Y, Gu Z, Zhang C, Li S, Zhang L, Zhou G, et al. Synthesis, characterization and ROS-mediated antitumor effects of palladium(II) complexes of curcuminoids. European Journal of Medicinal Chemistry 2018;144:662−71.

[145] Zibaei Z, Babaei E, Rezaie Nezhad Zamani A, Rahbarghazi R, Azeez HJ. Curcumin-enriched Gemini surfactant nanoparticles exhibited tumoricidal effects on human 3D spheroid HT-29 cells in vitro. Cancer Nanotechnology 2021;12(1):3.

[146] Ghaderi S, Babaei E, Hussen BM, Mahdavi M, Azeez HJ. Gemini curcumin suppresses proliferation of ovarian cancer OVCAR-3 cells via induction of apoptosis. Anti-Cancer Agents in Medicinal Chemistry 2021;21(6):775−81.

[147] Kwiatkowski S, Knap B, Przystupski D, Saczko J, Kędzierska E, Knap-Czop K, et al. Photodynamic therapy - mechanisms, photosensitizers and combinations. Biomedicine and Pharmacotherapy 2018;106:1098−107.

[148] Sivasubramanian M, Chuang YC, Lo L-W. Evolution of nanoparticle-mediated photodynamic therapy: from superficial to deep-seated cancers. Molecules 2019;24(3):520.

[149] Abrahamse H, Hamblin MR. New photosensitizers for photodynamic therapy,. The Biochemical Journal 2016;473(4):347−64.

[150] Josefsen LB, Boyle RW. Photodynamic therapy and the development of metal-based photosensitisers. Metal-Based Drugs 2008;2008:276109.

[151] Ambreen G, Duse L, Tariq I, Ali U, Ali S, Pinnapireddy SR, et al. Sensitivity of papilloma virus-associated cell lines to photodynamic therapy with curcumin-loaded liposomes. Cancers (Basel) 2020;12(11):3278.

[152] Moballegh Nasery M, Abadi B, Poormoghadam D, Zarrabi A, Keyhanvar P, Khanbabaei H, et al. Curcumin delivery mediated by bio-based nanoparticles: a review. Molecules 2020;25(3):689.

[153] Lehmann J, Agel MR, Engelhardt KH, Pinnapireddy SR, Agel S, Duse L, et al. Improvement of pulmonary photodynamic therapy: nebulisation of curcumin-loaded tetraether liposomes. Pharmaceutics 2021;13(8):1243.

[154] Machado FC, Adum de Matos RP, Primo FL, Tedesco AC, Rahal P, Calmon MF. Effect of curcumin-nanoemulsion associated with photodynamic therapy in breast adenocarcinoma cell line. Bioorganic & Medicinal Chemistry 2019;27(9):1882−90.

[155] de Matos RPA, Calmon MF, Amantino CF, Villa LL, Primo FL, Tedesco AC, et al. Effect of curcumin-nanoemulsion associated with photodynamic therapy in cervical carcinoma cell lines. BioMed Research International 2018;2018:4057959.

[156] Kamel A, Fadel M, Louis D. Curcumin-loaded nanostructured lipid carriers prepared using Peceol™ and olive oil in photodynamic therapy: development and application in breast cancer cell line. International Journal of Nanomedicine 2019;14:5073−85.

[157] Sun M, Zhang Y, He Y, Xiong M, Huang H, Pei S, et al. Green synthesis of carrier-free curcumin nano-drugs for light-activated breast cancer photodynamic therapy. Colloids and Surfaces B, Biointerfaces 2019;180:313−18.

[158] Ebrahiminaseri A, Sadeghizadeh M, Moshaii A, Asgaritarghi G, Safari Z. Combination treatment of dendrosomal nanocurcumin and low-level laser therapy develops proliferation and migration of mouse embryonic fibroblasts and alter TGF-β, VEGF, TNF-α and IL-6 expressions involved in wound healing process. PLoS ONE 2021;16:e0247098.

[159] Jamali Z, Khoobi M, Hejazi SM, Eivazi N, Abdolahpour S, Imanparast F, et al. Evaluation of targeted curcumin (CUR) loaded PLGA nanoparticles for in vitro photodynamic therapy on human glioblastoma cell line. Photodiagnosis and Photodynamic Therapy 2018;23:190−201.

[160] Zhang J, Li J, Shi Z, Yang Y, Xie X, Lee SM, et al. pH-sensitive polymeric nanoparticles for co-delivery of doxorubicin and curcumin to treat cancer via enhanced pro-apoptotic and anti-angiogenic activities. Acta Biomaterialia 2017;58:349−64.

[161] Pasban S, Raissi H. New insights into Hexakis macrocycles as a novel nano-carrier for highly potent anti-cancer treatment: a new challenge in drug delivery. Colloids and Surfaces B, Biointerfaces 2021;197:111402.

[162] Lin S, Xie P, Luo M, Li Q, Li L, Zhang J, et al. Efficiency against multidrug resistance by co-delivery of doxorubicin and curcumin with a legumain-sensitive nanocarrier. Nano Research 2018;11(7):3619−35.

[163] Gupta PK, Pappuru S, Gupta S, Patra B, Chakraborty D, Verma RS. Self-assembled dual-drug loaded core-shell nanoparticles based on metal-free fully alternating polyester for cancer theranostics. Materials Science and Engineering C 2019;101:448−63.

[164] Limtrakul P. Curcumin as chemosensitizer. In: Aggarwal BB, Surh Y-J, Shishodia S, editors. The molecular targets and therapeutic uses of curcumin in health and disease. Boston, MA: Springer; 2007. p. 269−300.

[165] Zhang Y, Yang C, Wang W, Liu J, Liu Q, Huang F, et al. Co-delivery of doxorubicin and curcumin by pH-sensitive prodrug nanoparticle for combination therapy of cancer. Scientific Reports 2016;6(1):21225.

[166] Karavasili C, Andreadis DA, Katsamenis OL, Panteris E, Anastasiadou P, Kakazanis Z, et al. Synergistic antitumor potency of a self-assembling peptide hydrogel for the local co-delivery of doxorubicin and curcumin in the treatment of head and neck cancer. Molecular Pharmaceutics 2019;16(6):2326−41.

[167] Niu D, Jiang Y, He J, Jia X, Qin L, Hao J, et al. Extraction-induced fabrication of yolk—shell-structured nanoparticles with deformable micellar cores and mesoporous silica shells for multidrug delivery. ACS Applied Bio Materials 2019;2(12):5707—16.

[168] Borah A, Pillai SC, Rochani A, Palaninathan V, Nakajima Y, Maekawa T, et al. GANT61 and curcumin-loaded PLGA nanoparticles for GLI1 and PI3K/Akt-mediated inhibition in breast adenocarcinoma. Nanotechnology 2020;31:185102.

[169] Larsson M, Huang W-C, Hsiao M-H, Wang Y-J, Nydén M, Chiou S-H, et al. Biomedical applications and colloidal properties of amphiphilically modified chitosan hybrids. Progress in Polymer Science 2013;38(9):1307—28.

[170] Lee D, Lim H, Chong H, Shim W. Advances in chitosan material and its hybrid derivatives: a review. The Open Biomaterials Journal 2009;1:10—20.

[171] Chiou S-H, Wang M-L, Chou Y-T, Chen C-J, Hong C-F, Hsieh W-J, et al. Coexpression of Oct4 and Nanog enhances malignancy in lung adenocarcinoma by inducing cancer stem cell—like properties and epithelial—mesenchymal transdifferentiation. Cancer Research 2010;70(24):10433—44.

[172] Cojoc M, Mäbert K, Muders MH, Dubrovska A. A role for cancer stem cells in therapy resistance: cellular and molecular mechanisms. Seminars in Cancer Biology 2015;31:16—27.

[173] Chou H-S, Larsson M, Hsiao M-H, Chen Y-C, Röding M, Nydén M, et al. Injectable insulin-lysozyme-loaded nanogels with enzymatically-controlled degradation and release for basal insulin treatment: in vitro characterization and in vivo observation. Journal of Controlled Release 2016;224:33—42.

[174] Huang W-T, Larsson M, Lee Y-C, Liu D-M, Chiou G-Y. Dual drug-loaded biofunctionalized amphiphilic chitosan nanoparticles: enhanced synergy between cisplatin and demethoxycurcumin against multidrug-resistant stem-like lung cancer cells. European Journal of Pharmaceutics and Biopharmaceutics 2016;109:165—73.

[175] Wang Z, Wang X, Yu H, Chen M. Glioma-targeted multifunctional nanoparticles to co-deliver camptothecin and curcumin for enhanced chemo-immunotherapy. Biomaterials Science 2022;10(5):1292—303.

[176] Curcio M, Cirillo G, Tucci P, Farfalla A, Bevacqua E, Vittorio O, et al. Dextran-curcumin nanoparticles as a methotrexate delivery vehicle: a step forward in breast cancer combination therapy. Pharmaceuticals 2019;13(1):2.

[177] Zhu X, Yu Z, Feng L, Deng L, Fang Z, Liu Z, et al. Chitosan-based nanoparticle co-delivery of docetaxel and curcumin ameliorates anti-tumor chemoimmunotherapy in lung cancer. Carbohydrate Polymers 2021;268:118237.

[178] Oguz OA, Ozgul M, Aydin M. Nanomicelles for the treatment of cancer, (2016) WO Patent No 2016167730A1.

[179] Chauhan S, Jaggi M, Yallapu MM. Magnetic nanoparticle formulations, methods for making such formulations, and methods for their use, (2015) European Patent Number EP2649623B.

18

Curcumin-loaded nanoparticles used for in vivo cancer models: an approach about their physicochemical properties and mechanism of action

Douglas Dourado[1,2], Éverton do Nascimento Alencar[1,3],
Matheus Cardoso de Oliveira[1], Daniel Torres Pereira[1],
Talita Azevedo Amorim[1], Danielle Teixeira Freire[1],
Eryvaldo Sócrates Tabosa do Egito[1]

[1]DISPERSED SYSTEMS LABORATORY (LASID), FEDERAL UNIVERSITY OF RIO GRANDE DO NORTE (UFRN), RUA GEN. GUSTAVO CORDEIRO DE FARIA, SN, NATAL, RN, BRAZIL
[2]DEPARTMENT OF IMMUNOLOGY, AGGEU MAGALHÃES INSTITUTE (IAM), OSWALDO CRUZ FOUNDATION (FIOCRUZ), AV PROFESSOR MORAES REGO, SN, RECIFE, PE, BRAZIL
[3]COLLEGE OF PHARMACEUTICAL SCIENCES, FOOD AND NUTRITION (FACFAN), FEDERAL UNIVERSITY OF MATO GROSSO DO SUL (UFMS), AV. COSTA E SILVA, SN, CAMPO GRANDE, MS, BRAZIL

18.1 Introduction

Cancer is a large group of diseases that have in common the uncontrolled growth of cells that invade tissues and organs. It can spread across the body, which characterizes metastasis [1]. These disorders have been the leading cause of death and an important barrier to the increasing life expectancy around the world [1]. Chemotherapy is the most widely practiced cancer treatment. Several Food and Drug Administration (FDA)-approved drugs are used specifically for certain types of cancers and patients. However, drug resistance is a major issue in the success of cancer chemotherapy [2]. To overcome the limitations of current treatments, many efforts have been made to increase drug efficacy, decrease drug dosage, and reduce side effects [2]. In this scenario, natural products—derived drugs, such as curcumin (CUR), have been of great interest to cancer treatment. CUR, a natural bioactive compound obtained from the rhizome of *Curcuma longa L*, has been widely explored as a therapeutic agent due to its nontoxic profile, at high concentrations (12 g/day) [3].

Curcumin-Based Nanomedicines as Cancer Therapeutics. DOI: https://doi.org/10.1016/B978-0-443-15412-6.00007-6

CUR has several pharmacological properties, such as anticancer, antioxidant, antidepressant, immunomodulatory, antimicrobial, and antiviral activities. Among these, its anticancer activity has been extensively investigated, suggesting a potential role for both the prevention and the treatment of a wide variety of cancers, such as colorectal, breast, pancreatic, colon, and others [4]. However, its clinical application has been compromised due to its low bioavailability resulting from factors such as low aqueous solubility, low oral absorption, intense metabolism, and rapid elimination [5]. In this perspective, nanosystems, such as nanoparticles, have been used to overcome free CUR's limitations [5]. In this context, this chapter summarizes the advances from the association of CUR and organic nanoparticles, as promising nanomedicines for anticancer treatment, highlighting their physicochemical aspects and their biological impacts in different in vivo cancer models.

18.2 Curcumin

CUR, (1E-6E)-1,7-bis(4-hydroxy-3-methoxyphenyl)-1,6-heptadiene-3,5-dione), is a polyphenol obtained from the rhizome of *Curcuma longa* L, popularly known as turmeric [6]. The rhizome displays 3%–5% of curcuminoids, among which CUR (77%), demethoxycurcumin (17%) (curcumin II), bisdemethoxycurcumin (3%) (curcumin III), and the recently identified cyclocurcumin are the most relevant [7,8].

This molecule has the molecular formula of $C_{21}H_2O_6$ and has a molar mass of 368.385 g/mol. Furthermore, its structure is symmetrical (Fig. 18–1), displaying two aromatic rings with methoxyl and hydroxyl groups in the ortho position, connected by a seven-carbon chain consisting of an α, β-unsaturated β-diketone fraction [9].

The chemical structure of CUR is subjected to changes depending on parameters such as temperature, polarity, and solvent properties [10]. Its tautomeric forms (Fig. 18–2), keto and enol,

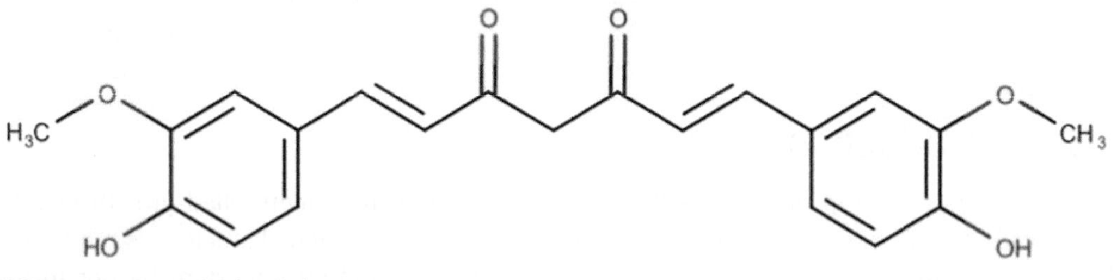

FIGURE 18–1 Curcumin chemical structure.

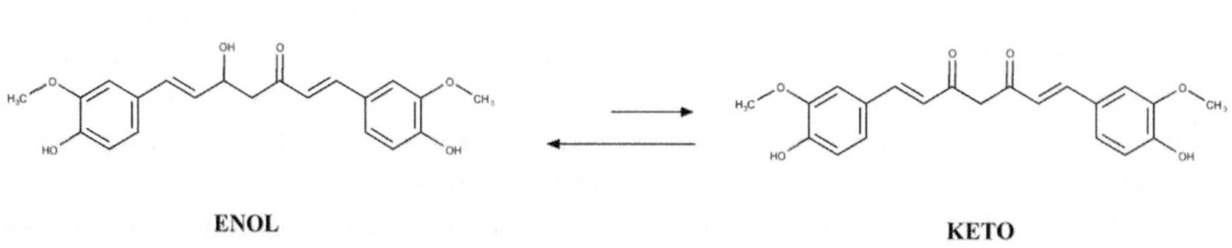

ENOL   KETO

FIGURE 18–2 Curcumin enol and keto tautomerism.

change according to the intramolecular transfer of hydrogen atoms in the β-diketone chain [11], the main pharmacophoric group, and the main site of hydrogen abstraction at physiological pH [12].

In aqueous media, this molecule is found in the enolic form, while the keto form prevails in organic solvents [13]. This tautomerism can be easily controlled by pH, exhibiting great influence upon the photophysical properties of CUR, in which the keto form generates a highly fluorescent yellow color, while the enol form is bright red and slowly becomes nonfluorescent with increasing pH [14]. In addition, its solubility changes with the keto-enol equilibrium, and even though CUR is a relatively hydrophobic molecule (logP 3.29) and practically insoluble in water (pH < 7) [10], an increase in solubility may occur in alkaline conditions due to the deprotonation of the hydroxyl groups in its chemical structure [15]. In addition to enol (-OH), phenolic −OH groups prove to be more resistant to oxidation but are susceptible to this reaction by electron transfer and abstraction of hydrogen atoms with more alkaline pH [6].

Excellent pharmacological benefits of CUR have been reported [16]. Among these, its anticancer properties have been extensively studied, due to chemopreventive and direct therapeutic action (Fig. 18−3). The anticancer properties of CUR have been proven in vitro,

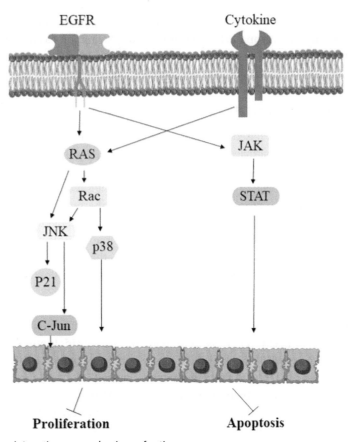

FIGURE 18–3 Curcumin's anticancer mechanisms of action.

in vivo, and by clinical studies, involving the (1) inhibition of cell proliferation, (2) induction of apoptosis, and (3) decrease of tumor burden.

Despite its promising anticancer potential, CUR has numerous limitations, among them low aqueous solubility, rapid clearance, inadequate tissue absorption, and degradation at neutral and alkaline pH values [17], which makes its bioavailability extremely low [18] and, hinder its therapeutic use. Given this issue, galenic strategies, such as the association of CUR with nanoparticles, have been used to overcome such drawbacks.

18.3 Nanoparticles

Nanoparticles (NPs) are promising drug carriers because of their ability to deliver hydrophobic and/or hydrophilic drug molecules, peptides, extracts, natural oils, or antibodies to the tumor site with minimum toxicity to surrounding tissues [19]. There are several different types of solid nanostructures with the potential to deliver anticancer chemotherapeutic agents; however, organic structures, mainly based on (1) polymers and (2) lipids, are most often produced for CUR research due to their ease of production, biocompatibility, and wide applications in therapeutics. Therefore, this chapter focuses on such systems, despite several other nanostructures (carbon nanotubes, metallic nanoparticles, and others) displaying increasing relevance in therapeutics. For further discussion of their in vivo performance, Sections 18.3.1 and 18.3.2 describe the production and characterization of the nanoparticles included in this chapter.

18.3.1 Lipid-based nanoparticles

Several nanostructured systems based on lipid molecules have been developed and investigated. Among these, solid lipid nanoparticles (SLNs) are crystalline lipid-core nanostructures stabilized by surfactants at their interface. These nanoparticles are considered promising carriers for drug administration, due to their ability to store and release molecules, which can be modulated from the nature of the lipids and surfactants [20]. Due to the biopharmaceutical limitations of CUR, SLNs have been used as drug carriers, once they can trap the molecule into a solid lipid matrix protecting it against physical/biochemical stressors, such as free radicals, pH, high ionic strength media, and metabolizing enzymes [21]. Current studies show that CUR carried by orally administered SLNs showed improved absorption [22]. Thanks to the optimization of CUR's biopharmaceutical properties, SLNs have been explored for cancer treatment [23,24]. However, in vivo studies focusing exclusively on CUR encapsulation in SLNs are still limited. Wang and collaborators [25] developed two SLNs by a sol-gel method. Formulations differed in proportions between SLNs:CUR (2:1 and 4:1, respectively). SLNs were made of stearic acid, lecithin, chloroform, polyoxyethylene 50 stearate (Myrj53), and distilled water. Among a variety of lipids, stearic acid (melting point of $55°C-70°C$) is solid at the body temperature ($37°C$) and the reduced size of its chain, when compared to larger chain lipids such as glyceryl behenate and tripalmitin, reflects in small particle sizes and low polydispersity indexes (PdI), optimized drug encapsulation and release properties [26]. The nanoparticles obtained by Wang and collaborators [25] were characterized for particle size, morphology (transmission electronic microscopy [TEM]), and encapsulation efficiency (EE). Nanoparticles in the 2:1 and 4:1 ratio displayed particle sizes of 20 and 80 nm and EE of 62% and 75%, respectively, and were both spherical. It is inferred that the higher the lipid-to-drug proportion (4:1), the greater the encapsulation capacity obtained by the lipid matrix. Greater zeta potential was also observed for the 4:1 SLN-CUR formulation, providing greater electrostatic stability to the system. Finally, to measure how well SLNs can protect CUR, the stability of free and encapsulated CUR at pH 7.4 (physiological) was evaluated, wherein 50% of free CUR degraded over 6 hours against only 20% of CUR degradation when encapsulated in SLNs, at the same time frame. Thus, the nanoencapsulated CUR underwent hydrolysis to a lower degree than free CUR [25].

Jung and colleagues [27] developed CUR-loaded epidermal growth factor (EGF)-conjugated phospholipid nanoparticle-based DSPE-PEG (polyethylene glycol) micelles. PEG-lipid micelles have been extensively investigated as vehicles to increase the solubility and the bioavailability of poorly water-soluble drugs owing to their high stability, controlled drug release potential, and low toxicity [28,29]. Li and collaborators [30] claim that phospholipids have characteristics of great interest for biomedical applications, with adequate biocompatibility as they are the main components of the cell membrane, and amphiphilicity, which allows their application as emulsifying, wetting, and self-assembling compounds. In this study, the authors prepared micelles (EGF-conjugated and unconjugated DSPE-PEG) and, then, added CUR using the thin-film hydration method [31]. The nanoparticles were characterized in terms of particle size distribution, zeta potential (in pH 74), drug loading (DL), and morphology (TEM). The particle morphology evaluated by TEM showed Cur-NP and EGF-Cur-NP uniformity and the absence of clusters. The average particle size of the Cur-DSPE-PEG and Cur-EGF-DSPE-PEG nanoparticles was 200 nm, with no significant changes after functionalization with EGF. The nanoparticles displayed monomodal distribution, PdI $\geq$ 0.2, and zeta potential < 5 mV, with a negative charge for both particles. Phospholipid NPs formed micellar structures with a CUR DL of 63.3% [27].

18.3.2 Polymeric nanoparticles

Polymer nanoparticles are part of the arsenal of nanostructures that are developed to improve the efficacy and the targeting of drugs in cancer therapy [32]. From the physico-chemical properties of polymers, delivery can be adjusted across the multiple biological barriers present in the human body [33]. Naksuriya and collaborators [34] have reviewed multiple studies and observed that when CUR is encapsulated in polymeric nanoparticles, there is greater internalization of this drug compared to the free one, resulting in cytotoxicity and apoptosis in cancer cells.

Among different studies, the development of CUR-loaded mPEG-PCL nanoparticles [35] was performed on the claim that mPEG-PCL is a synthetic, amphiphilic, biodegradable, biocompatible, and semicrystalline group of copolymers with a very low glass transition temperature. Due to their slow degradation, mPEG-PCLs are ideal for extended release. In this study, mPEG-PCL nanoparticles were produced by the cosolvent method and characterized by particle size distribution (dynamic light scattering [DLS]) and morphology (TEM).

The formation of this nanoparticle has been proposed as a self-assembly process, wherein CUR and copolymers made a core-shell micelle with CUR encapsulated in the core [35]. The nanoparticles revealed a particle size (DLS) of 139 nm in suspension, whereas the dry nanoparticles, from the morphology evaluation (TEM), presented a spherical shape with 110 nm. The particle size reduction in the dry form was justified by the amphiphilic nature of the copolymers, as they are found to be less cohesive in the presence of water. The encapsulation of CUR in the nanoparticles was determined by absorbance and fluorescence. Besides displaying larger sizes, the CUR loading in the nanoparticles was confirmed by the absorbance at 425 nm and the fluorescence intensity shift from 570 nm to 520−480 nm. Such displacement suggests an interaction between the polymers of this nanoparticle and CUR [35]. Other authors have also observed the same displacement phenomenon when comparing an ethanol solution of CUR and polymeric nanoparticles, associating such behavior to a polymer-CUR interaction [36].

Yin and collaborators also developed CUR-loaded mPEG-PCL nanoparticles [37,38]. The authors used the nanoprecipitation method, in which the copolymer and the CUR were dissolved in acetone. The organic solution was dripped into the aqueous phase under slight stirring. The final solution was dialyzed and filtered to remove the organic solvent, drug particles, and polymer aggregates. The nanoparticles were developed and studied in vitro in a second study from the group [38]. Subsequently, the particles with a diameter of 140.3 ± 14.2, PdI of 0.16 ± 0.04, zeta potential of -7.8 ± 1.4, DL% of $12.3\% \pm 1.5\%$, and EE% superior to 80% [38] were reproduced for the in vivo assessment [37].

Jin and colleagues developed PEGylated nanoparticles based on PLGA (polylactic-co-glycolic acid) [39]. PLGA is a highly biocompatible FDA-approved polymer of great interest in the production of therapeutic systems due to its wide clinical applications, favorable degradation characteristics, and possibilities for sustained drug delivery [40]. PEGylation of PLGA nanoparticles may increase drug encapsulation, half-life time, and stability, and, on the other hand, decrease the system uptake by the reticuloendothelial system [41].

The authors produced the PEG-PLGA nanoparticles by ultrasonic emulsification and evaporation method, with subsequent freeze-drying. The PEG-PLGA nanoparticles were functionalized with the GE11 peptide, for vectorization to the epidermal growth factor receptor (EGRF) presented in breast cancer cells [39]. PEG-PLGA nanoparticles, Curc-loaded PEG-PLGA nanoparticles, and GE11-Curc-loaded-PEG-PLGA nanoparticles were characterized for particle size distribution, zeta potential, morphology, by scanning electron microscopy (SEM), and EE, by HPLC. PEG-PLGA nanoparticles, CUR-loaded PEG-PLGA nanoparticles, and GE11-CUR-loaded-PEG-PLGA nanoparticles presented sizes of 133 ± 22 nm, 168 ± 38 nm, and 210 ± 54 nm, respectively. All particles displayed PdI below 0.2, with a higher value for the GE11-Curc-loaded-PEG-PLGA nanoparticles (0.112 ± 0.019). All particles were negatively charged, with higher values for CUR-loaded nanoparticles $(-17$ mV$)$ and peptide-functionalized nanoparticles $(-22 \pm 3.6$ mV$)$, when compared to empty nanoparticles $(-10 \pm 3.5$ mV$)$. CUR encapsulation was not affected by the peptide functionalization (PEG-PLGA nanoparticles: $91 \pm 3.8\%$ and GE11-CUR-loaded PEG-PLGA nanoparticles: $92.3 \pm 2.7\%$).

Orunoglu et al. also used PLGA in the development of CUR-loaded nanoparticles to be used against a mouse glioma-2 (RG2) tumor model [42]. The nanoparticles were functionalized with PEG containing 1,2-distearoyl-sn-glycero-3-phosphoethanolamine-N- [amino (PEG)-2000] (ammonium salt) (DSPE-PEG). DSPE-PEG is a phospholipid-polymer conjugate widely used in drug delivery applications. It is a biocompatible, biodegradable, and functionalizable amphiphilic material [43]. The method for production of the nanoparticles in this study was the emulsification by sonication method. After produced, the nanoparticles were filtered, washed with phosphate-buffered saline (PBS, pH 7.4), and freeze-dried [42]. The nanoparticles were characterized in terms of particle size distribution (169 ± 4.8 nm and PdI 0.22) and DL (35 ± 1.2% by HPLC).

Chen and collaborators, on the other hand, developed CUR-loaded PLGA nanoparticles functionalized with D-α-tocopheryl polyethylene glycol 1000 succinate (TPGS) for the treatment of liver cancer [44]. The use of TPGS allows the system to improve permeability and reduce multiple drug resistance (MDR) mediated by the glycoprotein P in cancer cells [44]. Unlike the one proposed by Orunoglu et al. [42], the technique used to prepare the nanoparticles was the emulsification-solvent evaporation method, also used by Braden and collaborators [45] for the development of PLGA nanoparticles with active molecules for the treatment of cancer. Chen's nanoparticles showed an average size of 110.6 ± 2.3 nm and a zeta potential of −23.6 mV, providing adequate electrostatic repulsion between the particles. They presented an EE of 83.2 ± 2.7% and a DL of 10.1 ± 1.5%. TEM images showed that the particles were spherical in shape and uniform in size, as corroborated by the PdI < 0.1.

Different studies have been conducted toward the development of chitosan-based delivery systems [46]. Chitosan is a copolymer obtained from the alkaline deacetylation of chitin, formed by d-glucosamine and N-acetyl-d-glucosamine units, linked by -1,4 glycosidic linkages [47]. This copolymer has numerous advantages when it comes to pharmaceutical applications because of its biocompatibility and controlled biodegradability, which results in nontoxic and noninflammatory degradation products. Chitosan can also act as a penetration enhancer by opening the tight junctions of the epithelium, facilitating both paracellular and transcellular transport of drugs. In addition, chitosan interacts with mucus (negatively charged) due to its cationic nature, forming complexes through ionic bonds, hydrogen bonds, and hydrophobic interactions. Due to these properties, chitosan has been widely used in the development of CUR-containing nanoparticles intended for anticancer activity [48].

Some studies have functionalized nanoparticles with chitosan due to its mucoadhesive properties. Examples of this application can be found from the studies of Duan et al. and Loch-Neckel et al. who refer to chitosan as a coating agent in CUR-loaded polymeric nanoparticles [49,50].

Duan et al. developed chitosan-coated poly (butyl) cyanoacrylate (PBCA) nanoparticles [49]. PBCA is biocompatible, biodegradable, and derived from the polymerization of butyl cyanoacrylate (BCA). In recent years, PBCA nanoparticles have been used as an effective drug delivery system to (1) reach tumor tissues, (2) cross the blood−brain barrier, and (3) protect proteins and peptides against the chemically hostile environment of the stomach [51]. Duan's PBCA nanoparticles were prepared by the emulsion polymerization method [49].

Chitosan (0.1%, w/v) was, then, dissolved in the polymerization medium containing HCl. BCA and chitosan concentrations were variables in the experimental design. The resulting nanoparticles were characterized by particle size distribution, zeta potential, morphology, and EE. CUR-loaded PBCA nanoparticles were also assayed by fluorescence spectroscopy.

The mean particle size for the selected CUR-loaded chitosan-coated PBCA nanoparticles (100 uL BCA/10 mg chitosan) was 200 nm, confirmed by TEM, in which smaller spherical particles were observed at around 250 nm. Is it important to highlight that particles smaller than 400 nm can accumulate in the interstitial space of tumor tissues, thus delivering anticancer molecules to the tumor interstitium or cytoplasm [52]. In addition, the nanoparticles presented EE of 90.4% (0.1%, w/w) and a zeta potential of 29.11 ± 1.69 mV. It is known that cationic nanoparticles may be favorable for drug delivery due to their interaction with negatively charged biological membranes and site-specific targeting in vivo [49].

Loch-Neckel et al. produced CUR-loaded chitosan-coated polycaprolactone (PCL) nanoparticles [50]. Initially, CUR-loaded PCL nanoparticles were developed by the nanoprecipitation method. Then, a chitosan solution (0.1%–0.75%) was added to the previously obtained nanoparticles. To understand the composition and structure of this polymeric nanoparticle, one must understand the nature of each polymer participating in the production of the nanoparticle. PCL is a polyester obtained by the ring-opening polymerization of ε-caprolactone monomers, which can proceed via anionic, cationic, coordination, or radical polymerization mechanism [53]. This polymer is biocompatible, biodegradable, and has been widely used in drug delivery systems. The formation of the PCL-chitosan block allows the production of mucoadhesive nanoparticles with extended residence time in the organism, thus, promoting great CUR bioavailability and, consequently, greater activity against cancer cells when compared to pure CUR. Loch-Neckel's nanoparticles were characterized for particle size distribution, zeta potential, and EE [50]. The empty nanoparticles exhibited a size of 216 ± 5.9 nm, while CUR-loaded nanoparticles were slightly smaller (189.3 ± 1.4 nm), a behavior that can be explained by the cohesive interactions between the drug and the polymer (PCL-CUR), which is also corroborated by the high rate of encapsulation ($96.8\% \pm 2.8\%$). All systems displayed PdI below 0.2. The zeta potential of the nanoparticles was around 32 mV, thanks to the positive nature of the adsorbed chitosan.

Another study worth mentioning regarding CUR delivery for cancer studies is the one conducted by Yang and partners, who developed poly-L-lysine (PLL) nanoparticles with pH-sensitive release of CUR intended for theranostics in liver cancer in vitro and in vivo [54]. PLL has in its structure amine groups that allow the conjugation of hydrophobic substances (carboxyl groups), which enables the encapsulation of lipophilic drugs and the binding of substances, such as ligands and contrast agents [55]. In addition, this group can convert into a positively charged hydrophilic amino group in an acidic medium, which interacts to the negative charge of the cancer cell membranes.

The nanoparticles produced by Yang and partners had a matrix core of PLL conjugated with deoxycholic acid (DOCA), which increased the encapsulation of CUR. The particles were functionalized with methoxy polyethylene glycol (MPEG) for stealthiness and with cyanine 5.5 (cy5.5) for fluorescence [54] via the condensation reaction.

The nanoparticles were characterized by nuclear magnetic resonance (NMR H^1), transmission electron microscopy (TEM), and DLS. The values of particle size distribution and zeta potential were evaluated at pH values of 5.5, 6.8, and 7.4. The EE and DL of CUR were evaluated by ultraviolet-visible spectroscopy. NMR H^1 confirmed the conjugation of DOCA, MPEG-COOH, and Cy5.5 to PLL and demonstrated that conjugated PLL is organized in micelles when in contact with water, due to the self-assembly of DOCA [54]. All nanoparticles showed an average size of 246 ± 5.8 nm, with an increase in particle size as the pH decreased. Produced nanoparticles were spherical, with positive zeta potential, due to the presence of the amine group of the PLL chain. Finally, the EE was determined to be $78.53 \pm 2.31\%$ and DL was $13.12 \pm 1.29\%$.

Polymers based on methacrylate groups were also used for the development of CUR nanoparticles. Chaurasia and colleagues [56] developed Eudragit E100 (EE100) nanoparticles aiming the enhancement of the oral bioavailability and the anticancer efficacy of CUR in the treatment of colorectal cancer (CRC). EE100is a cationic copolymer formed by methyl methacrylate, N, N-dimethylaminoethyl methacrylate, and butyl methacrylate monomers (1:2:1). It is widely used because it has nontoxic, nonirritating, and essentially safe characteristics in humans [57]. EE100 can ionize in gastric fluids and enhance dissolution in the gastric environment, which makes it an ideal excipient for dissolution improvement [56].

The CUR-loaded EE100 nanoparticles produced by the emulsification-diffusion evaporation method were 248.40 ± 3.89 nm in hydrodynamic size. They showed a PdI of 0.212 ± 0.013, a zeta potential of 28.9 ± 0.47 mV, and an EE of $65.77 \pm 3.17\%$. After 3 months of storage, average size values were 249.80 ± 3.90 nm, PdI was 0.224 ± 0.002, zeta potential was 20.42 ± 0.62 mV, and EE was $63.99 \pm 2.12\%$, which indicated that the formulation was stable in this preformulation stage. The nanoparticles were also spherical, as determined by atomic force microscopy (AFM) [56]. Regardless of the drug, EE100 nanoparticles are fairly reproducible, as Kalimuthu and colleagues [58] also obtained EE100 nanoparticles by the same method as Chaurasia et al. [56]. However, their system contained carvedilol and still, it displayed similar particle size, PdI, zeta potential, morphology, and EE.

18.4 Cancer in vivo studies

As previously introduced, CUR is a polyphenol with anticancer properties against different types of cancer [4]. However, biopharmaceutical limitations have compromised its clinical use [17]. The previous section presented a multitude of polymeric nanoparticles developed from different polymers and strategies for the desired end. Despite the use of different polymers, all studies overviewed in this chapter evaluated the antitumor activity of CUR nanoparticles. The previously described physicochemical characteristics were dictated by the behavior of the polymer and/or the copolymer used in the synthesis of the nanoparticles (Table 18–1).

Thus, CUR's association with nanoparticles has been investigated for the improvement of its biological performance. Table 18–2 reveals several in vivo studies that have evidenced

Table 18–1 Summary of curcumin-loaded nanoparticle formulations and their characteristics.

Nanoparticles	Composition	Production	Physicochemical characteristics	References
Lipidic	Stearic acid, lecithin, chloroform, polyoxyethylene 50 stearate	Sol-Gel	Size: 20–80 nm and EE 60%–75%	Wang et al. (2013) [25]
Lipidic	EGF-phospholipid, DSPE-PEG	Thin-film hydration	Size: 200 nm, Pdl: ≥ 0.2, Zeta potential: −1.73 mV, and EE: 63%	Jung et al. (2018) [27]
Polymeric	mPEG-PCL	Cosolvent	Size ~ 100 nm	Wang et al. (2018) [35]
Polymeric	mPEG-PCL	Nanoprecipitation	Size ~ 140 nm, Pdl: < 0.2, Zeta potential: −7.8 mV, DL ~ 12% and EE: > 80%	Yin et al. (2013) and Yin et al. (2013) [37,38]
Polymeric	PEG-PLGA	Emulsification-solvent evaporation	Size: 100–200 nm, Pdl: < 0.2, Zeta potential: −17 to −22 mV, and EE: > 90%	Jin et al. (2017) [39]
Polymeric	DSPE-PEG-PLGA	Emulsification	Size: 170 nm, Pdl: 0.2, and DL: 35%	Orunoglu et al. (2017) [42]
Polymeric	PLGA-TPGS	Emulsification-solvent evaporation	Size: 110 nm, Pdl: < 0.1, Zeta potential: -23.6 mV, EE: 83%, and DL: 10%	Chen et al. (2019) [44]
Polymeric	Chitosan-PCL	Nanoprecipitation	Size: 190 nm, Pdl: 0.2, Zeta potential: >30 mV, and EE: 97%	Loch-Neckel et al. (2015) [50]
Polymeric	Chitosan-PBCA	Emulsion polymerization	Size: 200 nm, Zeta potential: 29 mV, and EE: 90%	Duan et al. (2010) [49]
Polymeric	mPEG-DOCA-PLL	Condensation reaction and dialysis	Size: 240, DL: 13%, and EE: 78%	Yang et al. (2018) [54]
Polymeric	Eudragit E100	Emulsification-diffusion evaporation	Size ~ 250 nm, Pdl: ~ 0.2, Zeta potential: 28 mV, and EE: 65%	Chaurasia et al. (2016) [56]

DL, drug loading, EE, encapsulation efficiency; Pdl, polydispersity index.

Table 18–2 Summary of in vivo experimental conditions and anticancer effect of curcumin-loaded nanoparticles.

Nanoparticles	Cancer	Administration	in vivo model	in vivo performance	References
mPEG-PLC	Breast	Subcutaneous (1×10^{-3} M)	MDAMB-231 cells subcutaneously administered in mice	• Tumor growth was inhibited • Caspase cleavage expression—increased apoptosis induction mechanism	Wang et al. (2018) [35]
GE11(Peptide)-modified PLGA-PEG	Breast	5 mg/kg was administered intravenously every 24 h for 20 days	MCF-7 cells were subcutaneously administered to female BALB/c nude mice at day 0 and day 7	• Reduction in TNFα and IFNγ • Tumor weight and volume reduction	Jin et al. (2017) [39]
EGRF-DSPE-PEG phospholipid	Breast	Intraperitoneal (10 mg/kg) at three times per week	5×10^6 MDA-MB-468 cells injected subcutaneously in BALB/c nude mice	• Tumor growth retardation	Jung et al. (2018) [27]
EE100	Colorectal	Oral (50 mg/kg/day) for 30 days	C26-bearing mice	• Higher reduction of tumor volume	Chaurasia et al. (2016) [56]
PLGA	Glioblastoma	25 μM intratumoral and intravenous route	RG2 rat glioma model	• Decrease in tumor size treated intravenously	Orunoglu et al. (2017) [42]
SLNs	Lung	Intraperitoneal (200 mg/kg) for 5 days/week (total of 19 days)	A549 cells were implanted subcutaneously in old female nude mice	• Tumor inhibition effects	Wang et al. (2013) [25]
mPEG-PCL	Lung	Intravenous (15 mg/kg) for 15 days	Xenograft model of A549 cells into nude mice	• Smaller tumor volume and increased delay time compared to free curcumin	Yin et al. (2013) [37]
PLL-DOCA-MPEG-cy5.5	Hepatocellular	Intravenous tail vein (2.66 mg/kg) in 100 μL of water for 27 days	Hep3B cell tumors implanted in mice	• Necrosis was observed throughout the tumor area • Mechanism mediated by EPR effect	Yang et al. (2018) [54]
PLGA-TPGS	Hepatocellular	Intravenous tail vein treatment (10 mg / kg) once daily for 7 days	HCFa-F cells were administered subcutaneously into the underarm of mice	• Greater cellular internalization, biocompatibility, and greater tumor volume reduction	Chen et al. (2019) [44]

(Continued)

Table 18–2 (Continued)

Nanoparticles	Cancer	Administration	in vivo model	in vivo performance	References
Chitosan-PBCA	Hepatocellular	(190 mg/kg) were administered over a 4-week period with intravenous injection three times weekly	HepG2 cells were administered subcutaneously in mice and followed up to 10 days	• Inhibition of tumor growth of HepG2 cells • Reduction of VEGF and COX-2, in tumor levels.	Duan et al. (2010) [49]
Chitosan-PCL	Melanoma	Orally treated 3 or 6 mg/kg once a day for 14 consecutive days	C57Bl/6 mice and melanoma metastatic model was achieved through intravenous injection of 1×10^5 B16F10 melanoma cells on mice tail vein	• Reduction of metastatic potential	Loch-Neckel et al. (2015) [50]

EPR, enhanced permeability retention.

the in vivo anticancer activity of CUR nanoparticles. Furthermore, this section describes the summary of their findings regarding the in vivo preclinical anticancer activity of the previously mentioned nanoparticles according to different cancer types.

18.4.1 Breast cancer

Breast carcinoma is known as one of the most common and lethal malignant tumors in female patients [59]. It is classified according to marker expression as (1) luminal (often differentiated in two or three subgroups based on estrogen receptor (ER), ER regulatory genes, and the expression of genes expressed in normal luminal epithelial cells); (2) human epidermal growth factor 2 receptor (HER-2) positive (based on erbB2 protein/HER-2 amplification and overexpression); and (3) basal (based on ER progesterone receptor [PR] and HER-2 negative, and the expression of genes expressed in normal breast basal and/or myoepithelial cells) [60]. Numerous studies have shown that CUR inhibits cancer cell proliferation and metastasis by inducing cell cycle arrest and apoptosis. In fact, CUR has shown potent inhibitory effects against breast cancer by downregulating receptors (HER-2, IR, ER-a, and Fas receptor) and growth factors (PDGF, TGF, FGF, and EGF) [61,62].

Current studies have been developing nanoparticles as CUR carriers to promote their antitumor activity against breast cancer [63]. However, robust in vivo studies are still scarce. In fact, we found only six studies that idealized CUR-loaded nanoparticles for breast anticancer activity on in vivo models.

Wang et al. developed CUR MPEG-PCL polymeric nanoparticles. Initially, in vitro assays were conducted regarding cell viability analysis, cell apoptosis analysis, mitochondrial membrane potential, and reactive oxygen species production, which directed the research to the in vivo studies [35]. The authors investigated the inhibition of tumor growth in vivo in nude mice with tumors after 2 months of subcutaneous administration of 1.5×10^6 MDAMB-231 cells. Mice were treated with saline, blank nanoparticles (without CUR), free-form CUR $(1 \times 10^{-3} \, M)$, and CUR-loaded nanoparticles $(1 \times 10^{-3} \, M)$. The expression of the caspase-3 protein was also evaluated in the study of the mechanism of action of CUR-loaded nanoparticles. The study revealed that tumor growth was inhibited by CUR MPEG-PLC nanoparticles. The animals treated with this system exhibited tumors with smaller volumes when compared to the other test groups, indicating that nanoparticles can increase CUR activity and inhibit MDAMB-231 breast cancer in vivo. In addition, caspase cleavage expression increased for CUR MPEG-PLC nanoparticles compared to free CUR. These data suggest an apoptosis induction mechanism against breast cancer cells in vivo, corroborating the in vitro mechanism investigation conducted before studies in animals.

Jung and collaborators, on the other hand, developed epidermal growth factor-N-hydroxysuccinimide-polyethylene glycol-1,2-distearoyl-sn-glycero-3-phosphoethanolamine (EGRF-DSPE-PEG phospholipid) nanoparticles for triple-negative MDA-MB-468 breast cancer [27]. In this study, the antitumor activity was evaluated in vivo by measuring the tumor size/volume during treatment. Tumor cells were administered subcutaneously in BALB/c nude mice at 5×10^6 MDA-MB-468 of cells. When tumors reached a volume of 50 mm^3, treatment with empty nanoparticles (DSPE-PEG phospholipid nanoparticles), nonfunctiona-lized nanoparticles (CUR-loaded-DSPE-PEG phospholipid nanoparticles), and EGF receptor (EGRF) nanoparticles (EGF-CUR-loaded-DSPE-PEG phospholipid nanoparticles) at the dose of 10 mg/kg was initiated. The control group was treated with saline. The nanoparticles were administered intraperitoneally three times per week in a total of eight administrations. The volume of the tumors was calculated from the measured diameters. In vivo images from F-fluorodeoxyglucose (F-FDG) uptake by the tumor were micrographed. The authors evaluated the metabolic response of MDA-MB-468 tumors. After the eight administrations, a tumor growth rate of 59% slower was found in the animals treated with EGF-CUR-loaded-DSPE-PEG phospholipid nanoparticles when compared to the blank and the nonfunctionalized nanoparticles. As a metabolic response, from the F-FDG uptake, a 48% reduction in tumor uptake was observed after only one administration of EGF-CUR-loaded-DSPE-PEG phospho-lipid nanoparticles. The results revealed that the EGF functionalization allows selective tar-geting of cancer cells, amplifying antitumor action, when compared to other systems without any specific recognition receptor.

18.4.2 Lung cancer

Lung cancer is among the leading causes of death by cancer worldwide, accounting for a quarter of all cancer deaths [64]. Lung cancer was responsible for 2 million new cases and 1,796,144 deaths worldwide each year [65]. As an alternative to treat this pathology, studies have shown that CUR can inhibit NSCLC by mTOR/PI3K/AKT signaling suppression mechanisms, thereby, inducing lung cancer cell apoptosis and autophagy [66].

Despite the high mortality, only a few studies have been conducted to test CUR against this type of cancer in in vivo models. Nevertheless, different natures of nanoparticles have been explored for this type of cancer.

Wang and partners evaluated SLNs in nonsmall cell lung cancer [25]. They previously performed in vitro assays with NCL-H460 and A549 cells to determine cell death events, evidencing the occurrence of apoptosis of these cells when exposed to the formulations. For the in vivo assays, A549 cells were implanted subcutaneously in old female nude mice. Mice with A549 xenografts were treated for 5 days/week (total of 19 days), intraperitoneally, with control (PBS), free CUR, and CUR lipid nanoparticles, at a dose of 200 mg/kg. The monitored parameter was tumor size. Free CUR did not significantly inhibit tumor growth in this xeno-graft in vivo model. However, the CUR-loaded solid lipid nanoparticle showed a remarkable tumor inhibition effect from the first days of treatment, between 1 and 4 days, and an expres-sive effect between days 7 and 10. At the end of the 19 days, the nanoparticle remained effi-cient in tumor inhibition activity, promoting a low and stable tumor growth scenario. When compared to the control group, free CUR showed a decrease in tumor size of 19.5%, whereas CUR-loaded SLNs promoted a decrease of 65.3%.

Using a similar overall experimental model, Yin et al. evaluated the in vivo anticancer effect of mPEG-PCL nanoparticles in a xenograft model of A549 cells [37]. Initially, A549 cells were injected into nude mice. After 7 days, mice with a tumor size of 100 mm^3 were selected. Treatment groups were divided into four: saline solution, blank nanoparticles, free CUR, and CUR-loaded mPEG-PCL nanoparticles. About 15 mg/kg of samples were administered intravenously for 15 days. The evaluated parameter was the tumor volume. Free and nanoencapsulated CUR showed antitumor activity from the fourth day of administration. However, the most pronounced antitumor effect was observed in animals treated with CUR-loaded mPEG-PCL nanoparticles, which greatly reduced tumor volumes and growth rates compared to free CUR.

18.4.3 Hepatocellular cancer

Hepatocellular carcinoma (HCC), the most common primary liver malignancy, is a leading cause of cancer-related death worldwide and is considered a medical challenge. The development of HCC is a complex multistep process that involves sustained inflammatory damage, including hepatocyte necrosis and regeneration, associated to fibrotic deposition [67]. Surgery is still an option to remove the tumor as first-line therapy, followed by systematic chemotherapy to eliminate residual cancer and prevent cancer recurrence [68]. A possible alternative to avoid surgical procedures would be the administration of potent chemotherapeutic drugs, such as CUR, a promising new drug for liver cancer treatment. This molecule still has a poorly understood mechanism of action when it comes to inhibiting liver cancer. Activation of the nuclear factor κB (NF-κB) signaling pathway has been associated to liver cancer progression. The "heat-shock" protein 70 (HSP70) can activate the NF-κB by binding to the TLR4 receptor. In this context, CUR is reported to inhibit HSP70 and TLR4 signaling, therefore, it could display an anticancer potential [69]. Indeed, some authors have evaluated the antitumor activity of CUR nanoparticles against liver cancer and their possible mechanisms of action [44,54].

Yang and collaborators produced CUR-loaded poly-L-lysine nanoparticles functionalized with DOCA, MPEG, and cyanine 5.5 (cy5.5) (PLL-DOCA-MPEG-cy5.5/CUR NPs) for modulated release by specific pH. Before the in vivo assessment, the authors evaluated the in vitro effect of the formulation in Hep3B cells, conducting antiproliferation and uptake assays. Given the prominent effect of the formulations, they were assayed in vivo against lung cancer (antitumor effect) [54]. Free and nanoparticulate CUR were administered to the tail of mice with Hep3B cell tumors every 3 days for 27 days, with continuous monitoring of tumor volume (30 days of study). Histological and ex vivo distribution evaluations were performed over the initial 5 days of the study. Histological images of PLL-DOCA-MPEG-cy5.5/CUR NPs revealed cup-wide distribution; however, concentrated in the tumor region over the 5 days. This accumulation of nanoparticles in liver tumor cells may be indicative of the enhanced permeability retention (EPR) effect, which refers to a vectorized passive delivery to tumors, based on the physiological and anatomical nature of tumor tissues. These present high permeability and defective lymphatic clearance, which causes the progressive accumulation of the nanotechnological structures in the target tumors [70,71]. This theoretical basis was proven by the performed *ex vivo* kinetic model, wherein an increase in fluorescence of these nanoparticles occurred over the monitored period.

As for the tumor progression, the authors observed that over the 30 days of treatment, the nanoparticles remarkably controlled the tumor volume. At the histological level, a wide range of necrosis was observed throughout the tumor area, while free CUR caused partial necrosis. Thus it can be stated that the mechanism of action of PLL-DOCA-MPEG-cy5.5/CUR NPs occurs due to the EPR effect (Fig. 18–4), since the accumulation of the nanoparticles in the region, offered a higher concentration of CUR, triggering anticancer activity in the targeted cells.

Chen and colleagues prepared CUR-loaded PLGA nanoparticles decorated with TPGS (CUR-loaded PLGA-TPGS NPs). The in vitro cytotoxicity in HepG2 cells and intracellular uptake were previously assessed, which directed the in vivo antitumor activity in HCa-F cells [44]. The HCFa-F cells were administered subcutaneously into the underarm of the mice. After the tumor was found at the expected volume, intravenous tail vein treatment (10 mg/kg once daily for 7 days) was started with saline, free CUR, CUR-loaded PLGA, and CUR-loaded PLGA-TPGS nanoparticles. The parameter evaluated for antitumor activity in vivo was tumor volume. Compared to the control group (saline), both free and encapsulated CUR in the two nanoparticles showed antitumor activity. However, a reduction in the body mass of the mice treated with free CUR was observed, which is indicative of toxicity. The authors highlighted the occurrence of a transient increase in liver enzymes and anticoagulant properties mediated by the suppression of the platelet aggregation. However, the researchers claimed, from clinical studies, that CUR presents minimal risks and adverse events occur in isolated cases, once human studies have shown no CUR toxicity, from 8 to 12 g daily for up to 3 months [8]. Thus only the evidence of loss of body mass in mice as an indication of CUR toxicity is a fragile parameter in facing several opposing clinical evidence.

For the nanoparticles, on the other hand, the pronounced antitumor activity of the CUR-loaded PLGA-TPGS nanoparticle was highlighted by the remarkable cellular internalization, biocompatibility, and greater tumor volume reduction. TGPS is a nonionic surfactant capable

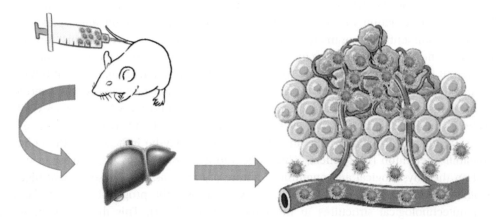

FIGURE 18–4 Enhanced permeability and retention (EPR) effect of nanoparticles targeted to liver tumor cells.

of stabilizing nanoparticulate systems at low amounts. Functionalization of the PLGA nanoparticles with this excipient may increase the oral bioavailability of drugs such as CUR and especially reduce P-glycoprotein (P-gp)-mediated multidrug resistance in cancer cells, which justifies its use in this study to initially assure its safety in vivo and to allow its future applications in studies with oral administration [72].

A different study produced CUR-loaded PBCA nanoparticles coated with chitosan [49]. In vitro (cell viability and uptake cells) and in vivo assays were performed to elucidate the system's antitumor activity against liver cancer cells. Initially, HepG2 cells were administered subcutaneously in mice for 10 days, when tumor formation was observed. Thus, saline, PBCA nanoparticles (290 mg/kg), and CUR-loaded PBCA nanoparticles (190 mg/kg) were administered over 4 weeks with intravenous injections three times/week. Tumor volume was the parameter used to assess the antitumor activity. In addition, immunohistochemical studies evaluated the expression of vascular endothelial growth factor (VEGF) and cyclooxygenase-2 (COX-2) in the tumor tissue. CUR-loaded PBCA nanoparticles showed inhibition of tumor growth of HepG2 cells, significantly reducing the tumor volume. Such activity may be due to a HepG2 apoptosis mechanism, according to the in vitro assays. Regarding the expression of VEGF and COX-2, there was a reduction in tumor levels. VEGF is known to be an essential proangiogenic factor whose production is mediated by growth factors, cytokines, and other extracellular molecules produced in response to the various metabolic and mechanical conditions presented in the cell environment, thus playing a key role in tumor angiogenesis [73,74]. COX-2 is also induced by cytokines, growth factors, and tumor promoters. Studies indicate that COX-2 promotes cell proliferation and inhibits apoptosis by mediating the activation of oncogenic pathways [75]. Thus, a decrease in the COX-2 levels in the tumor tissue points out the antiangiogenic and antiproliferative effects of the CUR-loaded PBCA nanoparticles.

18.4.4 Melanoma

Melanoma is the most dangerous form of cutaneous cancer due to its evasiveness, high metastasis rate, quick progression, and poor prognosis [76]. It represented nearly 8% of the new cancer cases in 2020. Although nonmelanoma represents most of the skin cancer cases and shows 99% survival rates, melanoma deserves attention once it presents multifactorial development, high mortality, usual poor diagnosis, and high resistance to treatment. Accordingly, CUR becomes a potential molecule for its treatment due to its wide range of activities, including antioxidant, antiinflammatory, and antiproliferative effects [77]. CUR has shown its effectiveness against melanoma cell death, for example, B16F10 and A375, over signaling pathways (e.g., MST1, Mcl-1, BCl-2, Bax, and JAK-2/STAT-3). Considering this information, we present henceforward two experimental cases wherein researchers evaluated CUR-loaded nanoparticles against a metastatic melanoma model.

Loch-Neckel et al. developed chitosan-coated PCL nanoparticles (CCNP) and conducted in vitro assays to evaluate CUR's mechanism in preventing B16F10 (melanoma) cell line metastasis [50]. These authors reported that under in vitro conditions at the IC_{50}, CUR and

Cur-CCNP triggered apoptosis, membrane potential disruption, colony forming, and reduced expression of matrix metalloproteinases (MMP), which are associated to metastasis. In vivo experiments were conducted on C57BL/6 mice and a melanoma metastatic model was achieved through intravenous injection of 1×10^5 B16F10 melanoma cells in mice tail. The animals were divided into six groups of eight animals each. The groups were orally treated with 0.9% NaCl, free CUR (3 or 6 mg/kg), Cur-CCNP (3 or 6 mg/kg), or unloaded CCNP once a day for 14 consecutive days. Then, on day 15, they were euthanized and the *in situ* lung evaluation was performed. The number of lung tumor nodules formed was an indication of lung metastasis. Herein, Cur-CCNP 3 mg/kg and 6 mg/kg caused a much greater decrease in nodule formation (56% and 64%, respectively), when compared to free CUR ($\sim$20%), whereas unloaded CCNP had no effect upon the decrease of metastatic nodules. Altogether, the in vitro and the in vivo results showed that CUR was able to reduce the metastatic potential of melanoma and its encapsulation in CCNP enhanced its effectiveness improving CUR bioavailability.

18.4.5 Colorectal cancer

CRC is the third most incident cancer in men and the second most incident in women [78]. It may progress slowly from adenomatous polyps and adenomas [78]. CRC has multifactor development, which may be inherited and/or acquired. Moreover, its metastatic potential is related to the expression of cell adhesion molecules, such as catenins [78]. Therefore, CUR has shown a remarkable response against CRC, while downregulating β-catenin and decreasing Bcl-2/Bax expression ratio, factors involved in cell adhesion and apoptosis, respectively [79,80].

In this perspective, Chaurasia et al. formulated CUR-loaded EE100 Nanoparticles (CENPs) for oral administration [56]. Attempting to overcome CUR's low bioavailability by the oral route, the authors assessed the pharmacokinetics of free CUR, equimolar physical mixture of CUR (1:1:1; CUR, poloxamer 188, and EE100, respectively; PM[CUR]) and CENPs. The in vitro cytotoxicity in the C26 cell line was also tested. Finally, the in vivo anticancer activity was evaluated in C26-bearing mice with $\sim$8 mm^3 tumor size. Groups were orally treated with a 50 mg/kg dose of CUR, PM [CUR], or CENPs daily for 30 days. As a result, CENPs showed a higher decrease in tumor volume compared to free CUR and PM [CUR], which showed slight decreases in tumor volume compared to the control. Altogether, the in vivo pharmacokinetics and in vivo antitumor activity data are unarguable when stating that there is a direct correlation between the greater bioavailability of CENPs (870 ng/mL) and their enhanced activity. Associated with the known physiopathology of cancer, the nanoparticles had a longer circulation time on blood vessels and, due to the EPR effect, they easily accumulated in the tumor site, releasing CUR to act against cancer cells.

18.4.6 Glioblastoma

Glioblastoma (GBM) is the most common primary malignant brain tumor. Despite standard multimodality treatment, the highly aggressive nature of GBM makes it one of the deadliest human malignancies [81]. Among the possible new therapeutic candidates, CUR should be further explored, once it can inhibit proliferation and induce apoptosis of GBM cell line, based on the mechanisms of p53 and caspase-3 activation or decreasing antiapoptotic genes, including AP-1, NF-κB, and Bcl-2 [82,83]. In addition, the more effective and safe treatment of GBM requires crossing the blood−brain barrier and targeting tumors, which may be accomplished by a drug delivery system [84].

In this perspective, Orunoglu and colleagues [42] developed CUR-loaded PLGA nanoparticles and evaluated the in vivo performance in RG2 rat glioma model. Initially, the tumor was induced in Wistar rats. The administration of blank nanoparticles, CUR-loaded nanoparticles (25 μM), and free CUR (25 μM) was performed by intratumoral and intravenous routes. An untreated group was established as a control. The tumor volume was used as an evaluation parameter from magnetic resonance and histopathology (before and 5 days after administrations). The authors observed a decrease in tumor size treated intravenously with CUR-loaded PLGA nanoparticles. Untreated tumors increased significantly, and the other groups did not show significant changes. Such behavior may be discussed in terms of poor local bioavailability once intravenous administration of free CUR implicates in a short half-life and limited tissue distribution [85]. On the other hand, the intraperitoneal administration directed to the tumor could provide adequate bioavailability of free CUR and even higher bioavailability of CUR-loaded PLGA nanoparticles, due to their increased permeability across biological barriers [42].

18.5 Conclusion

CUR is a potential anticancer therapeutic agent that has been widely investigated. However, its biopharmaceutical limitations may compromise its clinical use. As a result, the association of this molecule with nanoparticles has been a promising strategy for its more efficient delivery. This work summarized the literature information on the concepts, development, and characterization parameters of lipid-based and polymer-based nanoparticles containing CUR intended for cancer treatment.

In addition to promoting an improvement in the physicochemical properties of this molecule, the association with nanotechnology has been performed to promote an increase in bioavailability, selectivity, permeability, and anticancer effect in different types of cancer cells in the in vivo models exemplified in this chapter. In addition, it was possible to demonstrate that regardless of the carefully designed nanostructures, in vivo model, or cancer type used in the studies herein summarized, CUR demonstrated a limited anticancer effect, which was significantly increased when incorporated into nanostructures. This chapter also demonstrated that the use of functionalizing agents was a viable strategy in the development of nanoparticles as anticancer therapy. Finally, although promising, the anticancer nanosystems based on CUR still have a long way to become nanomedicines. More robust studies must be carried out to delineate the mechanisms of action involved in the in vivo models and to assure CUR's efficacy as a human anticancer agent. In addition, the drug itself still needs to be approved for clinical studies by regulatory agencies before research can move on to the nanotechnology aspects of CUR delivery.

References

[1] WHO. Cancer. 2022; Available from: <https://www.who.int/health-topics/cancer>.

[2] Nedeljkovic M, Damjanovic A. Mechanisms of chemotherapy resistance in triple-negative breast cancer-how we can rise to the challenge. Cells 2019;8(9):1–32.

[3] Dourado D, Oliveira MC, Araujo GRS, et al. Low-surfactant microemulsion, a smart strategy intended for curcumin oral delivery. Colloids and Surfaces. A, Physicochemical and Engineering Aspects 2022;652.

[4] Mansouri K, Rasoulpoor S, Daneshkhah A, et al. Clinical effects of curcumin in enhancing cancer therapy: a systematic review. BMC Cancer 2020;20(1):791.

[5] Sandhiutami NMD, Arozal W, Louisa M, et al. Curcumin nanoparticle enhances the anticancer effect of cisplatin by inhibiting PI3K/AKT and JAK/STAT3 pathway in rat ovarian carcinoma induced by DMBA. Frontiers in Pharmacology 2020;11:603235.

[6] Sun J, Chen F, Braun C, et al. Role of curcumin in the management of pathological pain. Phytomedicine: International Journal of Phytotherapy and Phytopharmacology 2018;48(9):129–40.

[7] Araiza-Calahorra A, Akhtar M, Sarkar A. Recent advances in emulsion-based delivery approaches for curcumin: from encapsulation to bioaccessibility. Trends in Food Science and Technology 2018;71 (1):155–69.

[8] Goel A, Kunnumakkara AB, Aggarwal BB. Curcumin as "curecumin": from kitchen to clinic. Biochemical Pharmacology 2008;75(4):787–809.

[9] Sahne F, Mohammadi M, Najafpour GD, et al. Enzyme-assisted ionic liquid extraction of bioactive compound from turmeric (Curcuma longa L.): isolation, purification and analysis of curcumin. Industrial Crops and Products 2017;95(1):686–94.

[10] Souza F, Bruschi M. Improving the bioavailability of curcumin: is micro/nanoencapsulation the key? Therapeutic Delivery 2019;10(2):83–6.

[11] Naksuriya O, Steenbergen M, Torano J, et al. A kinetic degradation study of curcumin in its free form and loaded in polymeric micelles. The AAPS Journal 2016;18(3):777–87.

[12] Priyadarsini K. The chemistry of curcumin: from extraction to therapeutic agent. Molecules (Basel, Switzerland) 2014;19(12):20091–112.

[13] Santin L, Toledo E, Carvalho-Silva V, et al. Methanol solvation effect on the proton rearrangement of curcumin's enol forms: an ab initio molecular dynamics and electronic structure viewpoint. The Journal of Physical Chemistry C 2016;120(36):19923–31.

[14] Kaur R, Khullar P, Mahal A, et al. Keto-enol tautomerism of temperature and pH sensitive hydrated curcumin nanoparticles: their role as nanoreactors and compatibility with blood cells. Journal of Agricultural and Food Chemistry 2018;66(45):11974–80.

[15] Aboudiaba B, Tehrani-Baghaa AR, Patra D. Curcumin degradation kinetics in micellar solutions: enhanced stability in the presence of cationic surfactants. Colloids and Surfaces. A, Physicochemical and Engineering Aspects 2020;592(5):1–8.

[16] Boroumand N, Samarghandian S, Hashemy S. Immunomodulatory, anti-inflammatory, and antioxidant effects of curcumin. Journal of Herbmed Pharmacology 2018;7(4):211–19.

[17] Paolino D, Vero A, Cosco D, et al. Improvement of oral bioavailability of curcumin upon microencapsulation with methacrylic copolymers. Frontiers in Pharmacology 2016;7:485.

[18] Shekhawat P, Pokharkar V. Understanding peroral absorption: regulatory aspects and contemporary approaches to tackling solubility and permeability hurdles. Acta Pharmaceutica Sinica B 2017;7(3):260–80.

[19] Jadia R, Scandore C, Rai P. Nanoparticles for effective combination therapy of cancer. International Journal of Nanotechnology and Nanomedicine 2016;1:1.

[20] Pink DL, Loruthai O, Ziolek RM, et al. On the structure of solid lipid nanoparticles. Small (Weinheim an der Bergstrasse, Germany) 2019;15(45):1903156.

[21] Ban C, Jo M, Park YH, et al. Enhancing the oral bioavailability of curcumin using solid lipid nanoparticles. Food Chemistry 2020;302:1−10.

[22] Ji H, Tang J, Li M, et al. Curcumin-loaded solid lipid nanoparticles with Brij78 and TPGS improved in vivo oral bioavailability and in situ intestinal absorption of curcumin. Drug Delivery 2016;23(2):459−70.

[23] Moideen MMJ, Karuppaiyan K, Kandhasamy R, et al. Skimmed milk powder and pectin decorated solid lipid nanoparticle containing soluble curcumin used for the treatment of colorectal cancer. Journal of Food Process Engineering 2019;1−15.

[24] Rompicharla SVK, Bhatt H, Shah A, et al. Formulation optimization, characterization, and evaluation of in vitro cytotoxic potential of curcumin loaded solid lipid nanoparticles for improved anticancer activity. Chemistry and Physics of Lipids 2017;208:10−18.

[25] Wang P, Zhang L, Peng H, et al. The formulation and delivery of curcumin with solid lipid nanoparticles for the treatment of on non-small cell lung cancer both in vitro and in vivo. Materials Science & Engineering C-Materials for Biological Applications 2013;33(8):4802−8.

[26] Öztürk AA, Aygül A, Şenel B. Influence of glyceryl behenate, tripalmitin and stearic acid on the properties of clarithromycin incorporated solid lipid nanoparticles (SLNs): formulation, characterization, antibacterial activity and cytotoxicity. Journal of Drug Delivery Science and Technology 2019;54.

[27] Jung KH, Lee JH, Park JW, et al. Targeted therapy of triple negative MDA-MB-468 breast cancer with curcumin delivered by epidermal growth factor-conjugated phospholipid nanoparticles. Oncology Letter 2018;15(6):9093−100.

[28] Wang T, Petrenko VA, Torchilin VP. Paclitaxel-loaded polymeric micelles modified with MCF-7 cell-specific phage protein: enhanced binding to target cancer cells and increased cytotoxicity. Molecular Pharmaceutics 2010;7(4):1007−14.

[29] Ren H, Gao C, Zhou L, et al. EGFR-targeted poly(ethylene glycol)-distearoylphosphatidylethanolamine micelle loaded with paclitaxel for laryngeal cancer: preparation, characterization and in vitro evaluation. Drug Delivery 2015;22(6):785−94.

[30] Li J, Wang X, Zhang T, et al. A review on phospholipids and their main applications in drug delivery systems. Asian Journal of Pharmaceutical Sciences 2015;10(2):81−98.

[31] Zhao BJ, Ke XY, Huang Y, et al. The antiangiogenic efficacy of NGR-modified PEG-DSPE micelles containing paclitaxel (NGR-M-PTX) for the treatment of glioma in rats. Journal of Drug Targeting 2011;19(5):382−90.

[32] Vauthier C, Ponchel G. Polymers nanoparticles for nanomedicine. Vol. 1. Cham: Springer; 2016.

[33] Karlsson J, Vaughan HJ, Green JJ. Biodegradable polymeric nanoparticles for therapeutic cancer treatments. Annual Review of Chemical and Biomolecular Engineering 2018;9:105−27.

[34] Naksuriya O, Okonogi S, Schiffelers RM, et al. Curcumin nanoformulations: a review of pharmaceutical properties and preclinical studies and clinical data related to cancer treatment. Biomaterials 2014;35(10):3365−83.

[35] Wang Y, Luo Z, Wang Z, et al. Effect of curcumin-loaded nanoparticles on mitochondrial dysfunctions of breast cancer cells. Journal of Nanoparticle Research 2018;20(10).

[36] Liu M, Teng CP, Win KY, et al. Polymeric encapsulation of turmeric extract for bioimaging and antimicrobial applications. Macromolecular Rapid Communications 2019;40(5):1800216.

[37] Yin H, Zhang H, Liu B. Superior anticancer efficacy of curcumin-loaded nanoparticles against lung cancer. Acta Biochimica et Biophysica Sinica 2013;45(8):634−40.

[38] Yin HT, Zhang DG, Wu XL, et al. In vivo evaluation of curcumin-loaded nanoparticles in a A549 xenograft mice model. Asian Pacific Journal of Cancer Prevention 2013;14(1):409−12.

[39] Jin H, Pi J, Zhao Y, et al. EGFR-targeting PLGA-PEG nanoparticles as a curcumin delivery system for breast cancer therapy. Nanoscale 2017;9(42):16365−74.

[40] Makadia HK, Siegel SJ. Poly lactic-co-glycolic acid (plga) as biodegradable controlled drug delivery carrier. Polymers (Basel) 2011;3(3):1377−97.

[41] D'Souza A A, Shegokar R. Polyethylene glycol (PEG): a versatile polymer for pharmaceutical applications. Expert Opinion on Drug Delivery 2016;13(9):1257−75.

[42] Orunoglu M, Kaffashi A, Pehlivan SB, et al. Effects of curcumin-loaded PLGA nanoparticles on the RG2 rat glioma model. Materials Science & Engineering C-Materials for Biological Applications 2017;78:32−8.

[43] Che J, Okeke CI, Hu ZB, et al. DSPE-PEG: a distinctive component in drug delivery system. Current Pharmaceutical Design 2015;21(12):1598−605.

[44] Chen X-p, Yi L, Yu Z, et al. Formulation, characterization and evaluation of curcumin- loaded PLGA-TPGS nanoparticles for liver cancer treatment. Drug Design, Development and Therapy 2019;Volume 13:3569−78.

[45] A.R. C. Braden, J.K. Vishwanatha, E. Kafta, Formulation of active agent loaded activated PLGA nanoparticles for targeted cancer nano-therapeutics, in US 2008/0253961 A1. (2008): EUA.

[46] Kamalabadi-Farahani M, Vasei M, Ahmadbeigi N, et al. Anti-tumour effects of TRAIL-expressing human placental derived mesenchymal stem cells with curcumin-loaded chitosan nanoparticles in a mice model of triple negative breast cancer. Artificial Cells, Nanomedicine, and Biotechnology 2018;46 (sup3):1011−21.

[47] Muxika A, Etxabide A, Uranga J, et al. Chitosan as a bioactive polymer: Processing, properties and applications. International Journal of Biological Macromolecules 2017;105(Pt 2):1358−68.

[48] Vunain E, Mishra AK, Mamba BB. Fundamentals of chitosan for biomedical applications. Chitosan Based Biomaterials, Volume 1. 2017. p. 3−30.

[49] Duan J, Zhang Y, Han S, et al. Synthesis and in vitro/in vivo anti-cancer evaluation of curcumin-loaded chitosan/poly(butyl cyanoacrylate) nanoparticles. International Journal of Pharmaceutics 2010;400 (1−2):211−20.

[50] Loch-Neckel G, Santos-Bubniak L, Mazzarino L, et al. Orally administered chitosan-coated polycaprolactone nanoparticles containing curcumin attenuate metastatic melanoma in the lungs. Journal of Pharmaceutical Sciences 2015;104(10):3524−34.

[51] Zhou Y, Peng Z, Seven ES, et al. Crossing the blood-brain barrier with nanoparticles. Journal of Controlled Release: Official Journal of the Controlled Release Society 2018;270:290−303.

[52] Morales-Cruz M, Delgado Y, Castillo B, et al. Smart targeting to improve cancer therapeutics. Drug Design, Development and Therapy 2019;13:3753−72.

[53] Espinoza SM, Patil HI, San Martin Martinez E, et al. Poly-ε-caprolactone (PCL), a promising polymer for pharmaceutical and biomedical applications: focus on nanomedicine in cancer. International Journal of Polymeric Materials and Polymeric Biomaterials 2019;69(2):85−126.

[54] Yang DH, Kim HJ, Park K, et al. Preparation of poly-l-lysine-based nanoparticles with pH-sensitive release of curcumin for targeted imaging and therapy of liver cancer in vitro and in vivo. Drug Delivery 2018;25(1):950−60.

[55] Zhou Z, Tang J, Sun Q, et al. A multifunctional PEG−PLL drug conjugate forming redox-responsive nanoparticles for intracellular drug delivery. Journal of Materials Chemistry B 2015;3(38):7594−603.

[56] Chaurasia S, Chaubey P, Patel RR, et al. Curcumin-polymeric nanoparticles against colon-26 tumor-bearing mice: cytotoxicity, pharmacokinetic and anticancer efficacy studies. Drug Development and Industrial Pharmacy 2016;42(5):694−700.

[57] Guzman ML, Manzo RH, Olivera ME. Eudragit E100 as a drug carrier: the remarkable affinity of phosphate ester for dimethylamine. Molecular Pharmaceutics 2012;9(9):2424−33.

[58] Kalimuthu S, Yadav AV. Formulation and evaluation of carvedilol loaded Eudragit E 100 nanoparticles. International Journal of Pharmtech Research 2009;1(2).

[59] Xiong H, Wang C, Wang Z, et al. Intracellular cascade activated nanosystem for improving ER + breast cancer therapy through attacking GSH-mediated metabolic vulnerability. Journal of Controlled Release: Official Journal of the Controlled Release Society 2019;309:145−57.

[60] Eliyatkin N, Yalcin E, Zengel B, et al. Molecular classification of breast carcinoma: from traditional, old-fashioned way to a new age, and a new way. Journal of Breast Health 2015;11(2):59−66.

[61] Liu H-T, Ho Y-S. Anticancer effect of curcumin on breast cancer and stem cells. Food Science and Human Wellness 2018;7(2):134−7.

[62] Talib WH, Al-Hadid SA, Ali MBW, et al. Role of curcumin in regulating p53 in breast cancer: an overview of the mechanism of action. Breast Cancer (Dove Med Press) 2018;10:207−17.

[63] Minafra L, Porcino N, Bravata V, et al. Radiosensitizing effect of curcumin-loaded lipid nanoparticles in breast cancer cells. Scientific Reports 2019;9(1):11134.

[64] Siegel RL, Miller KD, Jemal A. Cancer statistics, 2019. CA: a Cancer Journal for Clinicians 2019;69 (1):7−34.

[65] Sung H, Ferlay J, Siegel RL, et al. Global Cancer Statistics 2020: GLOBOCAN estimates of incidence and mortality worldwide for 36 cancers in 185 countries. CA: a Cancer Journal for Clinicians 2021;71 (3):209−49.

[66] Wang A, Wang J, Zhang S, et al. Curcumin inhibits the development of non-small cell lung cancer by inhibiting autophagy and apoptosis. Experimental and Therapeutic Medicine 2017;14(5):5075−80.

[67] Forner A, Reig M, Bruix J. Hepatocellular carcinoma. The Lancet 2018;391(10127):1301−14.

[68] Hu J, Dong Y, Ding L, et al. Local delivery of arsenic trioxide nanoparticles for hepatocellular carcinoma treatment. Signal Transduction and Targeted Therapy 2019;4:1−7.

[69] Ren B, Luo S, Tian X, et al. Curcumin inhibits liver cancer by inhibiting DAMP molecule HSP70 and TLR4 signaling. Oncology Reports 2018;40(2):895−901.

[70] Matsumura YM, Maeda H. A new concept for macromolecular therapeutics in cancer chemotherapy: mechanism of tumoritropic accumulation of proteins and the antitumor agent smancs. Cancer Research 1986;46:6387−92.

[71] Fang J, Islam R, Islam W, et al. Augmentation of EPR effect and efficacy of anticancer nanomedicine by carbon monoxide generating agents. Pharmaceutics 2019;11(7):1−13.

[72] Guo Y, Luo J, Tan S, et al. The applications of vitamin E TPGS in drug delivery. European Journal of Pharmaceutical Sciences: Official Journal of the European Federation for Pharmaceutical Sciences 2013;49(2):175−86.

[73] Groothuis A, Duda GN, Wilson CJ, et al. Mechanical stimulation of the pro-angiogenic capacity of human fracture haematoma: involvement of VEGF mechano-regulation. Bone 2010;47(2):438−44.

[74] Gardner V, Madu CO, Lu Y. Anti-VEGF therapy in cancer: a double-edged sword, in physiologic and pathologic angiogenesis - signaling mechanisms and targeted therapy. Intechopen 2017;385−410.

[75] Chen H, Cai W, Chu ESH, et al. Hepatic cyclooxygenase-2 overexpression induced spontaneous hepato-cellular carcinoma formation in mice. Oncogene 2017;36(31):4415−26.

[76] Oliveira WN, Alencar EN, Rocha HAO, et al. Nanostructured systems increase the in vitro cytotoxic effect of bullfrog oil in human melanoma cells (A2058). Biomedicine & Pharmacotherapy 2022;145:112438.

[77] Mirzaei H, Naseri G, Rezaee R, et al. Curcumin: a new candidate for melanoma therapy? International Journal of Cancer. Journal International du Cancer 2016;139(8):1683−95.

[78] Aran V, Victorino AP, Thuler LC, et al. Colorectal cancer: epidemiology, disease mechanisms and interventions to reduce onset and mortality. Clinical Colorectal Cancer 2016;15(3):195−203.

[79] Dou H, Shen R, Tao J, et al. Curcumin suppresses the colon cancer proliferation by inhibiting Wnt/β-catenin pathways via miR-130a. Front Pharmacol 2017;8(877):1−9.

[80] Rana C, Piplani H, Vaish V, et al. Downregulation of PI3-K/Akt/PTEN pathway and activation of mitochondrial intrinsic apoptosis by diclofenac and curcumin in colon cancer. Molecular and Cellular Biochemistry 2015;402(1−2):225−41.

[81] Shahcheraghi SH, Zangui M, Marzieh M. Lotfi, et al., Therapeutic potential of curcumin in the treatment of glioblastoma multiforme. Current Pharmaceutical Design 2019;25:3.

[82] Ambegaokar SS, Wu L, Alamshahi K, et al. Curcumin inhibits dose-dependently and time-dependently neuroglial cell proliferation and growth. Neuro Endocrinology Letters 2003;24:469 -469.

[83] Shabaninejad Z, Pourhanifeh MH, Movahedpour A, et al. Therapeutic potentials of curcumin in the treatment of glioblstoma. European Journal of Medicinal Chemistry 2020;188:112040.

[84] Kim SS, Harford JB, Pirollo KF, et al. Effective treatment of glioblastoma requires crossing the blood-brain barrier and targeting tumors including cancer stem cells: the promise of nanomedicine. Biochemical and Biophysical Research Communications 2015;468(3):485−9.

[85] Bangphumi K, Kittiviriyakul C, Towiwat P, et al. Pharmacokinetics of curcumin diethyl disuccinate, a prodrug of curcumin, in wistar rats. European Journal of Drug Metabolism and Pharmacokinetics 2016;41(6):777−85.

19

Clinical trials, patents, and marketed products of nanocurcumin-based anticancer drug delivery systems

Shirin Hassanizadeh[1], Gholamreza Askari[1,2], Prashant Kesharwani[3], Mohammad Bagherniya[1,2], Amirhossein Sahebkar[4,5]

[1]NUTRITION AND FOOD SECURITY RESEARCH CENTER AND DEPARTMENT OF COMMUNITY NUTRITION, SCHOOL OF NUTRITION AND FOOD SCIENCE, ISFAHAN UNIVERSITY OF MEDICAL SCIENCES, ISFAHAN, IRAN [2]ANESTHESIA AND CRITICAL CARE RESEARCH CENTER, ISFAHAN UNIVERSITY OF MEDICAL SCIENCES, ISFAHAN, IRAN [3]DEPARTMENT OF PHARMACEUTICS, SCHOOL OF PHARMACEUTICAL EDUCATION AND RESEARCH, JAMIA HAMDARD, NEW DELHI, INDIA [4]APPLIED BIOMEDICAL RESEARCH CENTER, MASHHAD UNIVERSITY OF MEDICAL SCIENCES, MASHHAD, IRAN [5]BIOTECHNOLOGY RESEARCH CENTER, PHARMACEUTICAL TECHNOLOGY INSTITUTE, MASHHAD UNIVERSITY OF MEDICAL SCIENCES, MASHHAD, IRAN

19.1 Introduction

Repetitive genetic mutations cause abnormal cell proliferation and cell cycle progression in cancer [1]. In other words, cancer develops when oncogenes and tumor suppressor genes are mutated sequentially, resulting in mismatched DNA base pairings and abnormal chromosome segregation [2]. This disease still remained one of the world's most serious and major health concerns [3]. Approximately 19,292,789 cancer cases and 9,958,133 cancer deaths were reported by the Global Cancer Observatory in 2020 [4]. In recent years, as early diagnosis and more therapeutic options have become available, death rates have declined [5]. Despite this, the rise of drug-resistant cancers calls for new, more effective drugs and delivery systems [6]. A variety of treatments are currently available, including chemotherapy, radiotherapy, and drugs derived from chemicals. While chemotherapy has its benefits, it can also have side effects and cause a great deal of stress for the patient. The use of alternative therapies and treatments against cancer has become increasingly popular. Compared to the

Curcumin-Based Nanomedicines as Cancer Therapeutics. DOI: https://doi.org/10.1016/B978-0-443-15412-6.00004-0

current treatments such as chemotherapy, naturally derived compounds have fewer toxic side effects, which is what has drawn research and scientific attention to this area [7]. A variety of plant sources are known to contain anticancer compounds, such as ginger (*Zingiber officinale*) [8], ginseng [9], resveratrol [10], *Silybum marianum* [11], *Nigella sativa* [12], *Curcuma longa* L., and other species [13]. Curcumin is one of these compounds, which has been identified as one of the most abundant compounds in *Curcuma longa* (turmeric) [14]. Curcumin is a polyphenol compound, its chemical formula is $C_{21}H_{20}O_6$ and its molecular weight is 368.38 [5]. Over the last two decades, curcumin and its derivatives have garnered a lot of attention due to their biofunctional properties such as antitumor, antioxidant, and anti-inflammatory properties [15]. These properties have been attributed to the curcumin structure [16]. While curcumin has many pharmacological benefits [17−28], it is relatively poorly absorbed from the gastrointestinal tract due to its low solubility in water, rapid metabolism, and systemic elimination after oral administration. All of these factors may restrict its maximal efficacy [29−31]. In recent years, there have been many advances in technologies for nanomedicines, most importantly, nanoparticles that are used to control the release of compounds to enhance the anticancer activity of plant-derived drugs [7]. It is easy for nanoparticles to penetrate blood vessel walls or even enter most body cells, which makes them ideal for delivering tailored amounts of drugs to specific locations. Nanoparticles can affect cancerous cells, preventing unnecessary exposure or damage to healthy tissues [32−34]. As a result, nanoparticles have been synthesized to replace conventional curcumin forms to enhance absorption and bioavailability [35]. The bioavailability of curcumin is increased by more than five times using curcumin nanoparticles. Recent studies have demonstrated that curcumin nanoparticles can enhance the therapeutic efficacy of curcumin, despite the fact that both curcumin and nanocurcumin have the same chemical structure [36−40]. It has been demonstrated that curcumin nanoparticles have an antiproliferative effect similar to or stronger than conventional curcumin in aqueous conditions [41]. Due to the prevalence of cancer as one of the leading causes of death and the continual search for less toxic and more effective anticancer drugs, this study examines the clinical trials evaluating nanocurcumin anticancer activity. It also highlights recent advances in nanocurcumin anticancer drug delivery systems, patents, and marketed products.

19.2 Results and discussion

19.2.1 Anticancer drug delivery systems

In chemotherapy and radiation, which are traditional cancer treatments, cancer cells can be killed but they can harm healthy tissues as well as produce different results from patient to patient [42,43]. Furthermore, drug delivery systems can alter the pharmacokinetics and biodistribution of traditional chemotherapeutics, improving their pharmacological properties [44,45]. The ideal carrier for a target drug delivery system should possess three properties: (1) effects on specific targets, (2) strong absorption properties so that drugs are delivered to the relevant sites, and (3) release of drugs at the relevant sites [46]. Several types of nanodrug delivery vehicles are currently used for nanocurcumin in cancer treatment. Among them, chitosan (CS), magnetic nanocomposites, polymer nanocomposites, and montmorillonite (MMT) have gained the most attention in recent years.

19.2.2 Chitosan-based nanocomposites

CS is an economic and biocompatible nanocarrier that can be administered orally to susceptible populations [47]. Due to its mucoadhesive properties, CS is better than other types of nanocarriers for chemoprevention [48,49]. The polysaccharide CS is formed by the deacetylation of chitin that is found in crustaceans [50,51]. Chemically, the compound dissolves in dilute acids and ionic liquids. CS is biocompatible, highly biologically active, biodegradable, nonallergenic, and low in toxicity [52,53]. CS molecules dissolve more efficiently when their NH_2 functional groups are protonated to NH_3^+ and interact with negatively charged surfaces. [54]. Drug molecules such as curcumin can be kept in CS-based composites through electrostatic interactions between positively charged chains of CS and negatively charged drug molecules, resulting in prolonged drug release [55]. Due to its properties as nanocarriers, CS and its chemical modifications, such as carboxymethyl CS, have received much attention [50,56]. Researchers have discovered that encapsulating curcumin in nanoparticles of CS reduces the risk of lung cancer caused by benzo[a]pyrene. The use of CS nanocurcumin enhanced the cellular uptake of curcumin and extended its tissue retention. The curcumin-loaded CS nanoparticles were between 170 and 200 nanometers in size. Furthermore, this formulation was found to be safe from a toxicological standpoint. This formulation, even at one-fourth dose of free curcumin, reduced tumor incidence and multiplicity more effectively in mice with lung adenocarcinomas [47]. In another study, nanocurcumin formulated with low-viscosity CS was found to have substantial potential as an anticancer agent. This study emphasizes that this complex had reasonable stability in artificial intestinal fluid and could penetrate into the cytosol of cells. In addition, it was nontoxic to normal cell lines [57].

19.2.3 Magnetic nanoparticles

Nanoparticles made from magnetite have been used for cancer diagnosis, cancer treatment, and chemotherapy monitoring [58]. The superparamagnetism, biocompatibility, and biodegradability of iron oxide−based nanoparticles make them ideal for use in medical applications [58]. A study demonstrated that curcumin possessed anticancer properties in CS−polyethylene glycol−polyvinylpyrrolidone nanocomposites. The study concluded that this compound was well encapsulated, released slowly, and did not interact with cancer cells [59]. The efficacy of magnetic nanoparticles loaded with curcumin for treating breast cancer was assessed in an experiment. As an anticancer therapy, this formulation showed greater uptake in cancer cells, a greater loss of mitochondrial potential, and a greater amount of reactive oxygen species (ROS). Moreover, it enhanced the delivery of curcumin to cancer cells. Consequently, this formulation can be utilized for the delivery of cancer therapeutics [60].

19.2.4 Polymer nanocomposites

The physicochemical properties of polymer nanocomposites make them increasingly popular. In recent years, nanocomposites have attracted intensive research interest due to their potential applications in a wide range of medical fields [61]. Curcumin release can be controlled by both synthetic and natural polymers [62]. As synthetic materials, polyolefins, fluorinated polymers, polyesters, silicones, and many other materials can be mentioned. Increasing use of polysaccharides (CS, hyaluronic acid, starch, cellulose, and alginates), as well as proteins, has also occurred [61]. In a study, alginate, CS, and pluronic were used as a composite for delivering curcumin to cancer cells. ALG-CS nanoparticles were formulated with pluronic F127 to enhance curcumin's solubility. In comparison to ALG-CS nanoparticles without pluronic, this composite nanoparticle encapsulated curcumin more effectively. Injection of composite nanoparticles at a concentration of 500 mcg/mL did not harm cervical carcinoma (HeLa) cells. Therefore, these composites could be used in cancer therapy and to deliver hydrophobic drugs [62]. A study showed that curcumin encapsulated in biocompatible poly (lactic-co-glycolic acid) nanoparticles significantly increased antigastric cancer effects. Nanocurcumin treatment increased the apoptotic cell population in comparison to native curcumin treatment after 72 hours. As a result, nanocurcumin may offer potential therapeutic benefits against gastric cancer [63]. Curcumin nanoemulsions were woven into zein polymer at three percentages (5%, 10%, and 15%) (V/V) in another study. Zein/nanocurcumin (15%) nanofibers were found to release more in vitro than other zein/nanocurcumin composites. Based on the results of viability and antioxidant tests, zein/nanocurcumin (10%) nanofibers provide optimal conditions for cell proliferation. Finally, this study indicated that nanocurcumin can be successfully woven into zein nanofibers while maintaining their biological properties [64].

19.2.5 Montmorillonite nanoparticles

MMT is a type of phyllosilicate mineral that has a low price, a large surface area, good absorption capacity, effective drug-carrying ability, and high cation exchangeability [65]. The MMT can be used as a drug delivery agent for transcatheter arterial embolization. This technique involves blocking the arterial vessels around tumors with microsized MMT particles, which block oxygen and nutrients from the blood flow and release drugs into the tumor. When oxygen and nutrition are cut off around the tumor, it is possible to reduce the tumor size through devascularization and drug release [66]. A rough and porous surface contributed to the excellent absorption properties of these composites [67]. A montmorillonite/chitosan (MMT/CS) nanocomposites exhibit good mechanical, thermal, and water uptake properties and have been developed as a novel drug delivery system [68]. The loading efficiency of curcumin in a hydrogel nanocomposite of CS-agarose (AG)-MMT improved from 49% to 62%. The nanocomposite particles had an average diameter of 30 nm and showed good stability. As a result, these composites may enhance the anticancer activity of curcumin [69].

19.2.6 Clinical trials of nanocurcumin and anticancer effects

Nanocurcumin exerts its specific anticancer activity by activating apoptosis as well as blocking a variety of cell signaling pathways. There have been several in vitro and in vivo studies demonstrating nanocurcumin ability to target multiple cancerous cells, including gastric, lung, breast, and prostate cancers. Nevertheless, only limited clinical trials have been carried out on the anticancer effects of nanocurcumin. Table 19−1 summarizes the clinical studies that were conducted on humans. Radiation therapy triggers different cellular signaling pathways that lead to the activation of proinflammatory cytokines and thus the development of inflammatory responses [70]. One study found that the administration of 160 mg/d of nanocurcumin to patients with differentiated thyroid cancer (DTC) could prevent genetic damage in peripheral blood lymphocytes by radiation. In this study, the administration of nanocurcumin from 3 days before up to 7 days after radiation therapy prevented the increase of peripheral lymphocyte micronuclei that cause significant genotoxic damage [71]. Cellular and molecular mechanisms by which nanocurcumin exerts its radioprotective effects may be due to its antiinflammatory and antioxidant properties. Nanocurcumin inhibits nuclear factor-κB signaling, scavenging free radicals, and enhancing antioxidant enzyme expression [72]. It also reduces inflammatory factors and DNA damage [73]. However, the administration of 120 mg/d of nanocurcumin to patients receiving radiation therapy for prostate cancer showed no radioprotective effect [74]. In addition, 180 mg/d of nanocurcumin administered

Table 19–1 A summary of clinical studies on nanocurcumin and cancer.

Author, year	Region of study	Dose of nanocurcumin	Treatment duration	Study population	Number of participants	Mean age	Main findings
Maryam Farhadi et al. (2018)	Iran	160 mg/d	10 days	Patients with differentiated thyroid carcinoma	11/10	43.45	Reduction in the frequency of micronuclei after I-131 therapy Prevented the genetic damage in human lymphocyte.
Afshin Saadipoor et al. (2018)	Iran	120 mg/d	<1 week	Prostate cancer patients	33/31	69/71.5	No significant reduction in the rate of proctitis
Saleh Sandoughdaran et al. (2021)	Iran	180 mg/d	4 weeks	Bladder cancer patients	12/14	68.2/64.7	Nanocurcumin was superior to placebo with respect to complete clinical response rates as the primary endpoint but this association was not significant. No significant difference was found between the two groups with regard to grade 3/4 renal and hematologic toxicities as well as hematologic nadirs.

to patients undergoing induction chemotherapy with localized muscle-invasive bladder cancer was not significantly associated with clinical response rates, renal and hematologic toxicity, and hematological nadirs [75]. The cause of nanocurcumin failure can be attributed to the short duration of treatment before and after radiotherapy and chemotherapy as well as the small size of these studies. Lastly, more clinical trials are necessary to determine the effects of nanocurcumin on cancer.

19.2.7 Patents

An overview of some patents published concerning nanocurcumin bioavailability and cancer treatment is provided in Table 19−2.

19.2.8 Marketed products

The use of nanocurcumin in improving human health is on the rise. There are many forms of nanocurcumin on the market, including capsules, tablets, powder, and liquid. In addition, there are various doses of nanocurcumin in these supplements, and sometimes they are also combined with other ingredients. A list of the most common conventional supplements (registered and unregistered trademarks) is shown in Table 19−3.

Table 19–2   Patents related to nanocurcumin.

Patent	Title	Inventor
US2014065061A1	Curcumin-ER, a liposomal-PLGA sustained release nanocurcumin for minimizing QT prolongation for cancer therapy	Ranjan et al. (2014)
AU2021103073A4	Phyto-mediated curcumin decorated gold and silver nanoparticles for biomedical applications	Harikrishnan et al. (2020)
US2013330412A1	Smart polymeric nanoparticles that overcome multidrug resistance to cancer chemotherapeutics and treatment-related systemic toxicity	Maitra et al. (2013)
CN111213880A	Soybean protein-based nanocurcumin suitable for researching and developing functional health-care food for preventing intestinal cancer and production method of soybean protein-based nanocurcumin	Chuanhe et al. (2020)
WO2011101859A1	A novel water-soluble curcumin-loaded nanoparticulate system for cancer therapy	Sahoo et al. (2011)
US10076552B2	Multifunctional formulation composed of natural ingredients and method of preparation/manufacturing thereof	Rajan et al. (2018)
CN110075316A	Delivery system for specifically targeting cancer cells and method of use thereof	James (2019)
WO2011063178A2	Intravenous infusion of curcumin and a calcium channel blocker	Helson (2011)
US20110190399A1	Curcumin nanoparticles and methods of producing the same	Santosh et al. (2011)
US9555011B2	Formulation of active agent loaded activated PLGA nanoparticles for targeted cancer nanotherapeutics	Braden et al. (2017)

ER, Endoplasmic reticulum; *PLGA*, poly lactic-co-glycolic acid.

Table 19–3 Some conventional supplements contain nanocurcumin on the market.

Product	Description	Form
Dharma Nutriherbs Nano Curcumin Longa	Nanocurcumin 500 mg *Curcumin longa* (10%)	Capsule
Quote Nutriherbs Nano Curcumin Longa	Nanocurcumin 500 mg *Curcumin longa* (10%)	Capsule
Nutriherbs Nano Curcumin	Nanocurcumin 500 mg	Capsule
OIC Nano Curcumin Dietary Supplements	Nanocurcumin 330 mg Direct absorption into blood up to 99%. Bioavailability increased hundreds of times compared with normal curcumin.	Capsule
SCurma Fizzy Nano Turmeric Curcumin	Nanocurcumin 12,000 mg Increased bioavailability by 40 times Increased absorption by 7500 times	Effervescent tablets
Ramini Bio Nutrition Nano Curcumin with Boswellia	Nanocurcumin (25%) 350 mg Boswelic acid (65%) 150 mg	Capsule
Nano Autumn Turmeric Extract Granules	Its included autumn turmeric extract (Made in Okinawa), dextrin, soybean lecithin, trihalose, calcium phosphate	Powder packet (2 g)
Ramini Bio Nutrition Nano Curcumin with Astaxanthin	Nanocurcumin (25%) 400 mg Astaxanthin (1%) 4 mg Co Enzyme Q_{10} 50 mg	Capsule
Nanoceutical Solutions Nano Turmeric Curcumin	Turmeric curcumin (standardized to 95% tetrahydrocurcuminoids) 400 mg	Liquid
Ramini Bio Nutrition Nano Curcumin 500 mg	Nanocurcumin (25%) 500 mg	Capsule
BioEnergyTech Nano Curcumin	Nanocurcumin 500 mg black pepper	Capsule
One Planet Nutrition Nano Curcumin	Nanocurcumin 500 mg Increased absorption by 40 times	Capsule
Nano Curcumin Plus Tam That Xa Den Plus	Nanocurcumin 300 mg *Panax pseudoginseng* 50 mg *Celastrus hindsii* 50 mg Noni fruit extract 40 mg Brown algae extract 20 mg Collagen peptide 20 mg Vitamin E 60 IU Bioperine 0.5 mg	Capsule
Nano Curcumin Double Plus	Nanocurcumin 250 mg Piperine 0.5 mg	Capsule

19.3 Conclusions

Studies conducted in vitro and in vivo have shown that nanocurcumin is capable of improving several cancer types, including prostate, breast, and gastric cancers. A number of studies have demonstrated its safety for cancer cells. Nanocurcumin anticancer properties can be enhanced using a variety of approaches, including drug delivery systems. It has been demonstrated that some carriers can deliver curcumin to cancer cells more effectively, thus improving its anticancer activity. However, there are still several concerns regarding nano-curcumin's specificity, bioavailability, and potency for target tissues. Clinical trials evaluating the effectiveness and ability of these formulations to enhance curcumin absorption and cellular uptake have not been conducted. It is imperative to conduct further studies, especially clinical studies, to verify the results.

References

[1] Shehzad A, Lee J, Lee YS. Curcumin in various cancers. Biofactors (Oxford, England) 2013;39(1):56−68.

[2] Salk JJ, Fox EJ, Loeb LA. Mutational heterogeneity in human cancers: origin and consequences. Annual Review of Pathology 2010;5:51.

[3] Su J, Jing P, Jiang K, Du J. Recent advances in porous MOFs and their hybrids for photothermal cancer therapy. Dalton Transactions 2022;51(23):8938−44.

[4] Xia C, Dong X, Li H, Cao M, Sun D, He S, et al. Cancer statistics in China and United States, 2022: profiles, trends, and determinants. Chinese Medical Journal 2022;135(5):584−90.

[5] Giordano A, Tommonaro G. Curcumin and cancer. Nutrients. 2019;11(10):2376.

[6] Barone D, Cito L, Tommonaro G, Abate AA, Penon D, De Prisco R, et al. Antitumoral potential, antioxidant activity and carotenoid content of two Southern Italy tomato cultivars extracts: San Marzano and Corbarino. Journal of Cellular Physiology 2018;233(2):1266−77.

[7] Greenwell M, Rahman PK. Medicinal plants: their use in anticancer treatment. International Journal of Pharmaceutical Sciences and Research 2015;6(10):4103−12.

[8] Prasad S, Tyagi AK. Ginger and its constituents: role in prevention and treatment of gastrointestinal cancer. Gastroenterology Research and Practice 2015;2015:142979.

[9] Li X, Chu S, Lin M, Gao Y, Liu Y, Yang S, et al. Anticancer property of ginsenoside Rh2 from ginseng. European Journal of Medicinal Chemistry 2020;203:112627.

[10] Lee Y, Shin H, Kim J. In vivo anti-cancer effects of resveratrol mediated by NK cell activation. Journal of Innate Immunity 2021;13(2):94−106.

[11] Fallah M, Davoodvandi A, Nikmanzar S, Aghili S, Mirazimi SMA, Aschner M, et al. Silymarin (milk thistle extract) as a therapeutic agent in gastrointestinal cancer. Biomedicine & Pharmacotherapy 2021;142:112024.

[12] Almatroudi A, Khadri H, Azam M, Rahmani AH, Al Khaleefah FK, Khateef R, et al. Antibacterial, antibiofilm and anticancer activity of biologically synthesized silver nanoparticles using seed extract of Nigella sativa. Processes 2020;8(4):388.

[13] Asadi-Samani M, Kooti W, Aslani E, Shirzad H. A systematic review of Iran's medicinal plants with anti-cancer effects. Journal of Evidence-Based Complementary & Alternative Medicine 2016;21(2):143−53.

[14] Alibeiki F, Jafari N, Karimi M, Peeri, Dogaheh H. Potent anti-cancer effects of less polar curcumin analogues on gastric adenocarcinoma and esophageal squamous cell carcinoma cells. Scientific Reports 2017;7(1):1−9.

[15] Nagahama K, Utsumi T, Kumano T, Maekawa S, Oyama N, Kawakami J. Discovery of a new function of curcumin which enhances its anticancer therapeutic potency. Scientific Reports 2016;6(1):1−14.

[16] Aggarwal BB, Deb L, Prasad S. Curcumin differs from tetrahydrocurcumin for molecular targets, signaling pathways and cellular responses. Molecules (Basel, Switzerland) 2014;20(1):185−205.

[17] Hewlings SJ, Kalman DS. Curcumin: a review of its effects on human health. Foods. 2017;6(10):92.

[18] Mohammadi A, Blesso CN, Barreto GE, Banach M, Majeed M, Sahebkar A. Macrophage plasticity, polarization and function in response to curcumin, a diet-derived polyphenol, as an immunomodulatory agent. Journal of Nutritional Biochemistry 2019;66:1−16. Available from: https://doi.org/10.1016/j.jnutbio.2018.12.005.

[19] Cicero AFG, Sahebkar A, Fogacci F, Bove M, Giovannini M, Borghi C. Effects of phytosomal curcumin on anthropometric parameters, insulin resistance, cortisolemia and non-alcoholic fatty liver disease indices: a double-blind, placebo-controlled clinical trial. European Journal of Nutrition 2020;59 (2):477−83. Available from: https://doi.org/10.1007/s00394-019-01916-7.

[20] Keihanian F, Saeidinia A, Bagheri RK, Johnston TP, Sahebkar A. Curcumin, hemostasis, thrombosis, and coagulation. Journal of Cellular Physiology 2018;233(6):4497−511.

[21] Marjaneh RM, Rahmani F, Hassanian SM, Rezaei N, Hashemzehi M, Bahrami A, et al. Phytosomal curcumin inhibits tumor growth in colitis-associated colorectal cancer. Journal of Cellular Physiology 2018;233(10):6785−98.

[22] Mohajeri M, Sahebkar A. Protective effects of curcumin against doxorubicin-induced toxicity and resistance: a review. Critical Reviews in Oncology/Hematology 2018;122:30−51.

[23] Mokhtari-Zaer A, Marefati N, Atkin SL, Butler AE, Sahebkar A. The protective role of curcumin in myocardial ischemia−reperfusion injury. Journal of Cellular Physiology 2018;234(1):214−22.

[24] Panahi Y, Sahebkar A, Amiri M, Davoudi SM, Beiraghdar F, Hoseininejad SL, et al. Improvement of sulphur mustard-induced chronic pruritus, quality of life and antioxidant status by curcumin: results of a randomised, double-blind, placebo-controlled trial. British Journal of Nutrition 2012;108(7):1272−9. Available from: https://doi.org/10.1017/S0007114511006544.

[25] Panahi Y, Fazlolahzadeh O, Atkin SL, Majeed M, Butler AE, Johnston TP, et al. Evidence of curcumin and curcumin analogue effects in skin diseases: a narrative review. Journal of Cellular Physiology 2019;234(2):1165−78. Available from: https://doi.org/10.1002/jcp.27096.

[26] Hassanzadeh S, Read MI, Bland AR, Majeed M, Jamialahmadi T, Sahebkar A. Curcumin: an inflammasome silencer. Pharmacological Research 2020;159.

[27] Khayatan D, Razavi SM, Arab ZN, Niknejad AH, Nouri K, Momtaz S, et al. Protective effects of curcumin against traumatic brain injury. Biomedicine and Pharmacotherapy 2022;154.

[28] Momtazi-Borojeni AA, Haftcheshmeh SM, Esmaeili SA, Johnston TP, Abdollahi E, Sahebkar A. Curcumin: a natural modulator of immune cells in systemic lupus erythematosus. Autoimmunity Reviews 2018;17(2):125−35.

[29] Anand P, Kunnumakkara AB, Newman RA, Aggarwal BB. Bioavailability of curcumin: problems and promises. Molecular Pharmaceutics 2007;4(6):807−18.

[30] Sasaki H, Sunagawa Y, Takahashi K, Imaizumi A, Fukuda H, Hashimoto T, et al. Innovative preparation of curcumin for improved oral bioavailability. Biological and Pharmaceutical Bulletin 2011;34(5):660−5.

[31] Islam A, Rebello L, Chepyala S. Review on nanoformulations of curcumin (*Curcuma longa* Linn.): Special emphasis on Nanocurcumin®. International Journal of Nature and Life Sciences 2019;3(1):1−12.

[32] Bansal SS, Goel M, Aqil F, Vadhanam MV, Gupta RC. Advanced drug delivery systems of curcumin for cancer chemoprevention. Cancer Prevention Research 2011;4(8):1158−71.

[33] Pandey MK, Kumar S, Thimmulappa RK, Parmar VS, Biswal S, Watterson AC. Design, synthesis and evaluation of novel PEGylated curcumin analogs as potent Nrf2 activators in human bronchial epithelial cells. European Journal of Pharmaceutical Sciences 2011;43(1−2):16−24.

[34] Setthacheewakul S, Mahattanadul S, Phadoongsombut N, Pichayakorn W, Wiwattanapatapee R. Development and evaluation of self-microemulsifying liquid and pellet formulations of curcumin, and absorption studies in rats. European Journal of Pharmaceutics and Biopharmaceutics 2010;76(3):475−85.

[35] Stohs SJ, Chen O, Ray SD, Ji J, Bucci LR, Preuss HG. Highly bioavailable forms of curcumin and promising avenues for curcumin-based research and application: a review. Molecules (Basel, Switzerland) 2020;25(6):1397.

[36] Liu Q, Jing Y, Han C, Zhang H, Tian Y. Encapsulation of curcumin in zein/ caseinate/sodium alginate nanoparticles with improved physicochemical and controlled release properties. Food Hydrocolloids 2019;93:432−42.

[37] Moballegh Nasery M, Abadi B, Poormoghadam D, Zarrabi A, Keyhanvar P, Khanbabaei H, et al. Curcumin delivery mediated by bio-based nanoparticles: a review. Molecules (Basel, Switzerland) 2020;25(3):689.

[38] Khosropanah MH, Dinarvand A, Nezhadhosseini A, Haghighi A, Hashemi S, Nirouzad F, et al. Analysis of the antiproliferative effects of curcumin and nanocurcumin in MDA-MB231 as a breast cancer cell line. Iranian Journal of Pharmaceutical Research: IJPR 2016;15(1):231.

[39] Dende C, Meena J, Nagarajan P, Nagaraj VA, Panda AK, Padmanaban G. Nanocurcumin is superior to native curcumin in preventing degenerative changes in experimental cerebral malaria. Scientific Reports 2017;7(1):1−12.

[40] Mohammed ES, El-Beih NM, El-Hussieny EA, El-Ahwany E, Hassan M, Zoheiry M. Effects of free and nanoparticulate curcumin on chemically induced liver carcinoma in an animal model. Archives of Medical Science 2021;17(1):218−27.

[41] Basniwal RK, Khosla R, Jain N. Improving the anticancer activity of curcumin using nanocurcumin dispersion in water. Nutrition and Cancer 2014;66(6):1015−22.

[42] Phan JH, Moffitt RA, Stokes TH, Liu J, Young AN, Nie S, et al. Convergence of biomarkers, bioinformatics and nanotechnology for individualized cancer treatment. Trends in Biotechnology 2009;27(6):350−8.

[43] Wong K, Liu X. Nanomedicine: a primer for surgeons. Pediatric Surgery International 2012;28 (10):943−51.

[44] Allen TM, Cullis PR. Drug delivery systems: entering the mainstream. Science (New York, N.Y.) 2004;303 (5665):1818−22.

[45] Torchilin VP. Micellar nanocarriers: pharmaceutical perspectives. Pharmaceutical Research 2007;24(1):1−16.

[46] Mathur M, Sundaramoorthy S. Anticancer herbal drugs and their improvement through novel drug delivery approaches. Applied Biological Research 2013;15(1):1−20.

[47] Retnakumari AP, Nandan CD, Somaraj J, Antony J, Alex VV, Vinod BS, et al. Chitosan encapsulation enhances the bioavailability and tissue retention of curcumin and improves its efficacy in preventing B [a] P-induced lung carcinogenesis.

[48] Sogias IA, Williams AC, Khutoryanskiy VV. Why is chitosan mucoadhesive? Biomacromolecules 2008;9 (7):1837−42.

[49] Ramalingam P, Ko YT. Enhanced oral delivery of curcumin from N-trimethyl chitosan surface-modified solid lipid nanoparticles: pharmacokinetic and brain distribution evaluations. Pharmaceutical Research 2015;32(2):389−402.

[50] Ma Z, Garrido-Maestu A, Jeong KC. Application, mode of action, and in vivo activity of chitosan and its micro-and nanoparticles as antimicrobial agents: a review. Carbohydrate Polymers 2017;176:257−65.

[51] Zhong S, Zhang H, Liu Y, Wang G, Shi C, Li Z, et al. Folic acid functionalized reduction-responsive magnetic chitosan nanocapsules for targeted delivery and triggered release of drugs. Carbohydrate Polymers 2017;168:282−9.

[52] Honarkar H, Barikani M. Applications of biopolymers I: chitosan. Monatshefte für Chemie-Chemical Monthly 2009;140(12):1403−20.

[53] Rinaudo M. Chitin and chitosan: properties and applications. Progress in Polymer Science 2006;31 (7):603−32.

[54] Van de Velde F, Ruiter GA. Carrageenan. In: Steinbuchel A, DeBaets S, VanDamme EJ, editors. Biopolymers. Polysaccharides II: Polysaccharides from Eukaryotes, Vol. 6. Weinheim: Wiley-VCH; 2002. p. 245−74. Available from: https://doi.org/10.1002/3527600035.bpol6009.

[55] Barua S, Chattopadhyay P, Phukan M, Konwar B, Islam J, Karak N. Biocompatible hyperbranched epoxy/silver-reduced graphene oxide−curcumin nanocomposite as an advanced antimicrobial material. RSC Advances 2014;4:47797−805.

[56] Jin Z, Li D, Dai C, Cheng G, Wang X, Zhao K. Response of live Newcastle disease virus encapsulated in N-2-hydroxypropyl dimethylethyl ammonium chloride chitosan nanoparticles. Carbohydrate Polymers 2017;171:267−80.

[57] Chabib L, Martien R, Ismail H. Formulation of nanocurcumin using low viscosity chitosan polymer and its cellular uptake study into T47D cells. Indonesian Journal of Pharmacy 2012;23(1):27−35.

[58] Revia RA, Zhang M. Magnetite nanoparticles for cancer diagnosis, treatment, and treatment monitoring: recent advances. Materials Today 2016;19(3):157−68.

[59] Prabha G, Raj V. Preparation and characterization of polymer nanocomposites coated magnetic nanoparticles for drug delivery applications. Journal of Magnetism and Magnetic Materials 2016;408:26−34.

[60] Yallapu MM, Othman SF, Curtis ET, Bauer NA, Chauhan N, Kumar D, et al. Curcumin-loaded magnetic nanoparticles for breast cancer therapeutics and imaging applications. International Journal of Nanomedicine 2012;7:1761−79.

[61] Feldman D. Polymers and polymer nanocomposites for cancer therapy. Applied Sciences 2019;9(18):3899.

[62] Das RK, Kasoju N, Bora U. Encapsulation of curcumin in alginate-chitosan-pluronic composite nanoparticles for delivery to cancer cells. Nanomedicine: Nanotechnology, Biology and Medicine 2010;6(1):153−60.

[63] Alam J, Dilnawaz F, Sahoo SK, Singh DV, Mukhopadhyay AK, Hussain T, et al. Curcumin encapsulated into biocompatible co-polymer PLGA nanoparticle enhanced anti-gastric cancer and anti-*Helicobacter pylori* effect. Asian Pacific Journal of Cancer Prevention 2022;23(1):61−70.

[64] Fereydouni N, Movaffagh J, Amiri N, Darroudi S, Gholoobi A, Goodarzi A, et al. Synthesis of nano-fibers containing nano-curcumin in zein corn protein and its physicochemical and biological characteristics. Scientific Reports 2021;11(1):1902.

[65] Azeez AA, Rhee KY, Park SJ, Hui D. Epoxy clay nanocomposites−processing, properties and applications: a review. Composites Part B: Engineering 2013;45(1):308−20.

[66] Bekaroğlu MG, Nurili F, İşçi S. Montmorillonite as imaging and drug delivery agent for cancer therapy. Applied Clay Science 2018;162:469−77.

[67] Jahanizadeh S, Yazdian F, Marjani A, Omidi M, Rashedi H. Curcumin-loaded chitosan/carboxymethyl starch/montmorillonite bio-nanocomposite for reduction of dental bacterial biofilm formation. International Journal of Biological Macromolecules 2017;105:757−63.

[68] Salcedo I, Aguzzi C, Sandri G, Bonferoni MC, Mori M, Cerezo P, et al. In vitro biocompatibility and mucoadhesion of montmorillonite chitosan nanocomposite: a new drug delivery. Applied Clay Science 2012;55:131−7.

[69] Samadi A, Haseli S, Pourmadadi M, Rashedi H, Yazdian F, Navaei-Nigjeh M, editors. Curcumin-loaded chitosan-agarose-montmorillonite hydrogel nanocomposite for the treatment of breast cancer. 2020 27th National and 5th International Iranian Conference on Biomedical Engineering (ICBME); 2020 26−27 Nov. 2020.

[70] Farhood B, Goradel NH, Mortezaee K, Khanlarkhani N, Salehi E, Nashtaei MS, et al. Intercellular communications-redox interactions in radiation toxicity; potential targets for radiation mitigation. Journal of Cell Communication and Signaling 2019;13(1):3−16.

[71] Farhadi M, Bakhshandeh M, Shafiei B, Mahmoudzadeh A, Hosseinimehr SJ. The radioprotective effects of nano-curcumin against genotoxicity induced by iodine-131 in patients with differentiated thyroid carcinoma (DTC) by micronucleus assay.

[72] Shi H-s, Gao X, Li D, Zhang Q-w, Wang Y-s, Zheng Y, et al. A systemic administration of liposomal curcumin inhibits radiation pneumonitis and sensitizes lung carcinoma to radiation. International Journal of Nanomedicine 2012;7:2601.

[73] Ak T, Gülçin İ. Antioxidant and radical scavenging properties of curcumin. Chemico-Biological Interactions 2008;174(1):27−37.

[74] Saadipoor A, Razzaghdoust A, Simforoosh N, Mahdavi A, Bakhshandeh M, Moghadam M, et al. Randomized, double-blind, placebo-controlled phase II trial of nanocurcumin in prostate cancer patients undergoing radiotherapy.

[75] Sandoughdaran S, Razzaghdoust A, Tabibi A, Basiri A, Simforoosh N, Mofid B. Randomized, double-blind pilot study of nanocurcumin in bladder cancer patients receiving induction chemotherapy. Urology Journal 2020;18(3):295−300.

Index

Note: Page numbers followed by "*f*" and "*t*" refer to figures and tables, respectively.

Printed and bound by CPI Group (UK) Ltd, Croydon, CR0 4YY

03/10/2024

01040325-0009